Lecture Notes in Computer Science

Edited by G. Goos, J. Hartmanis, and J. van L

Springer
Berlin
Heidelberg
New York
Barcelona
Hong Kong
London
Milan
Paris
Tokyo

Sihan Qing   Tatsuaki Okamoto
Jianying Zhou (Eds.)

Information and Communications Security

Third International Conference, ICICS 2001
Xian, China, November 13-16, 2001
Proceedings

 Springer

Series Editors

Gerhard Goos, Karlsruhe University, Germany
Juris Hartmanis, Cornell University, NY, USA
Jan van Leeuwen, Utrecht University, The Netherlands

Volume Editors

Sihan Qing
Chinese Academy of Sciences
Engineering Research Center for Information Security Technology (ERCIST)
P.O. Box 8718, Beijing 100080, China
E-mail: qsihan@yahoo.com

Tatsuaki Okamoto
NTT Labs
1-1 Hikarinooka, Yokosuka-shi 239-0847, Japan
E-mail: okamoto@isl.ntt.co.jp

Jianying Zhou
Oracle Corporation
500 Oracle Parkway, Redwood Shores, CA 94065, USA
E-mail: Jianying.Zhou@oracle.com

Cataloging-in-Publication Data applied for

Die Deutsche Bibliothek - CIP-Einheitsaufnahme

Information and communications security : third international conference ; proceedings / ICICS 2001, Xian, Chinas, November 13 - 16, 2001. Sihan Qing .. (ed.). - Berlin ; Heidelberg ; New York ; Barcelona ; Hong Kong ; London ; Milan ; Paris ; Tokyo : Springer, 2001 (Lecture notes in computer science ; Vol. 2229) ISBN 3-540-42880-1

CR Subject Classification (1998): E.3, G.2.1, D.4.6, K.6.5, F.2.1, C.2, J.1

ISSN 0302-9743
ISBN 3-540-42880-1 Springer-Verlag Berlin Heidelberg New York

Springer-Verlag Berlin Heidelberg New York
a member of BertelsmannSpringer Science+Business Media GmbH

http://www.springer.de

© Springer-Verlag Berlin Heidelberg 2001
Printed in Germany

Typesetting: Camera-ready by author, data conversion by PTP-Berlin, Stefan Sossna
Printed on acid-free paper   SPIN: 10841000   06/3142   5 4 3 2 1 0

Preface

ICICS 2001, the Third International Conference on Information and Communications Security, was held in Xi'an, China, 13-16 November 2001. Among the preceding conferences, ICICS'97 was held in Beijing, China, 11-14 November 1997 and ICICS'99 in Sydney, Australia, 9-11 November 1999. The ICICS'97 and ICICS'99 proceedings were released as volumes 1334 and 1726 of Springer-Verlag's Lecture Notes in Computer Science series.

ICICS 2001 was sponsored by the Chinese Academy of Sciences (CAS), the National Natural Science Foundation of China, and the China Computer Federation. The conference was organized by the Engineering Research Center for Information Security Technology of the Chinese Academy of Sciences (ERCIST, CAS) in co-operation with the International Association for Cryptologic Research (IACR), the International Communications and Information Security Association (ICISA), and the Asiacrypt Steering Committee.

The format of ICICS 2001 was selected to cover the complete spectrum of information and communications security, and to promote participant interaction. The sessions were designed to promote interaction between the major topics of the conference: theoretical foundations of security, secret sharing, network security, authentication and identification, boolean functions and stream ciphers, security evaluation, signatures, block ciphers and public-key systems, information hiding, protocols and their analysis, and cryptanalysis.

The 29-member Program Committee considered 134 submissions from 23 different countries and regions, among them 56 papers were accepted for presentation. Each paper was carefully reviewed blindly by a minimum of three referees from the respective field. The accepted papers came from 17 different countries and areas, including some 17 papers from China, 7 from Korea, 5 each from Australia and the USA, 3 each from Germany, Japan, Singapore, and Taiwan, 2 each from the UK, and 1 each from Finland, France, India, Israel, Italy, Portugal, Spain, and Thailand. We would like to take this opportunity to thank all who submitted papers to ICICS 2001 and the authors of accepted papers for their excellent work in preparing the camera-ready manuscripts.

We wish to thank the members of the program committee and reviewers for their effort in reviewing the papers in a short time and their great contribution to the conference in variety of ways. We are also pleased to thank Prof. Xizhen Ni, Dr. Yeping He, and the other members of the organizing committee for helping with many local details. Special thanks to Dr. Jianying Zhou of Oracle who took care of most of the tough work related to the publishing affairs. Finally, we would like to thank all the ICICS 2001 participants, organizers, and contributors for their work in making the conference a successful one.

August 2001

Sihan Qing
Tatsuaki Okamoto

ICICS 2001

Third International Conference
on Information and Communications Security

Xi'an, China
November 13-16, 2001

Sponsored by

Chinese Academy of Sciences (CAS)
National Natural Science Foundation of China
China Computer Federation

Organized by

Engineering Research Center for Information Security Technology (ERCIST)
Chinese Academy of Sciences

In co-operation with

International Association for Cryptologic Research (IACR)
International Communications and Information Security Association (ICISA)
Asiacrypt Steering Committee

Conference Chairs

Qiheng Hu, general chair (Vice President, China Association
  for Science and Technology)
Yongfei Han, vice chair (MIAN, China)
Sihan Qing, program chair (ERCIST, CAS, China)
Tatsuaki Okamoto, program chair (NTT, Japan)

Program Committee

Tuomas Aura (HUT, Finland)
Thomas Berson (Anagram, USA)
Chin-Chen Chang (MOE, Taiwan)
Lily Chen (Motorola, USA)
Welland Chu (THALES, Hong Kong, China)
Edward Dawson (QUT, Australia)
Jan Eloff (RAU, South Africa)
Dengguo Feng (CAS, China)
Dieter Gollmann (MicroSoft Lab in Cambridge, UK)
Kwangjo Kim (ICU, Korea)
Xuejia Lai (Entrust, Switzerland)

Chi-Sung Laih	(NCKU, Taiwan)
Wenbo Mao	(Hewlett-Packard Labs, Bristol, UK)
David Naccache	(Gemplus, France)
Eiji Okamoto	(Toho Univ., Japan)
David Pointcheval	(ENS, France)
Jean-Jacques Quisquater	(UCL, Belgium)
Bimal Roy	(ISICAL, India)
Pierangela Samarati	(UNIMI, Italy)
Vijay Varadharajan	(UWS, Australia)
Yumin Wang	(Xidian Univ., China)
Susanne Gudrun Wetzel	(Bell Lab, USA)
Tara Whalen	(CRC, Canada)
Guozhen Xiao	(Xidian Univ., China)
Lisa Yiqun Yin	(NTT, USA)
Moti Yung	(Columbia, USA)
Jianying Zhou	(Oracle, USA)

Organizing Committee

Xizhen Ni, chair	(ERCIST, CAS, China)
Yeping He, vice chair	(ERCIST, CAS, China)

Contents

X   Contents

Security of Blind Discrete Log Signatures against Interactive Attacks

Claus Peter Schnorr

Fachbereiche Mathematik/Informatik, Universität Frankfurt, PSF 111932,
D-60054 Frankfurt am Main, Germany. schnorr@cs.uni-frankfurt.de

Abstract. We present a novel parallel one-more signature forgery against blind Okamoto-Schnorr and blind Schnorr signatures in which an attacker interacts some l times with a legitimate signer and produces from these interactions $l + 1$ signatures. Security against the new attack requires that the following ROS-problem is intractable: find an overdetermined, solvable system of linear equations modulo q with random inhomogenities (right sides).

There is an inherent weakness in the security result of POINTCHEVAL AND STERN. Theorem 26 [PS00] does not cover attacks with 4 parallel interactions for elliptic curves of order 2^{200}. That would require the intractability of the ROS-problem, a plausible but novel complexity assumption. Conversely, assuming the intractability of the ROS-problem, we show that Schnorr signatures are secure in the random oracle and generic group model against the one-more signature forgery.

1 Introduction and Summary

We study the security of blind Schnorr signatures and blind Okamoto-Schnorr signatures against the one-more signature forgery in which an attacker interacts some l times with the legitimate signer and produces from these l interactions $l + 1$ signatures. Let these signatures be based on the discrete logarithm of an arbitrary group G of prime order q, e.g. an elliptic or hyperelliptic curve or a subgroup of units in $\mathbf{Z}_n^*$ for a composite or prime module n. We introduce the novel parallel attack that succeeds in a one-more signature forgery against blind Schnorr signatures and blind Okamoto-Schnorr signatures with the same efficiency. The attack is in the Random Oracle and Generic Group Model (ROM + GM) explained in Section 3. The new attack merely requires a solution of the ROS-problem, a possibly intractable problem: find an overdetermined, solvable system of linear equations modulo q with random inhomogenities (right sides). Specifically, given a system of $t \gg l$ linear equations modulo q in l unknowns with random inhomogenities (right sides) find a solvable subsystem of $l + 1$ equations — a solvable subsystem corresponds to a $(l + 1) \times l$-submatrix of rank l.

The new parallel attack has the interesting feature not to depend on the public key. Traditional security proofs do not seem to work in the presence of such an attack. Usually, traditional security proofs use the attacker to solve a DL-problem or a decisional Diffie-Hellman-problem associated with the public

S. Qing, T. Okamoto, and J. Zhou (Eds.): ICICS 2001, LNCS 2229, pp. 1–12, 2001.
© Springer-Verlag Berlin Heidelberg 2001

key. However, the generic parallel attack uses a solution of the ROS-problem that is not related to the public key and thus the attacker cannot be used to solve a DL- or a DDH-problem. How could [PS00,PS96b] prove security ? Theorem 26 of [PS00] only covers cases where solutions of the ROS-problem exist with negligible probability. While Theorem 26 [PS00] is optimal in the traditional security model, the new attack points to an inherent weakness of this result.

Theorem 26 of [PS00] shows that an attacker mounting a one-more signature forgery with a probability of success $\varepsilon > 4Q^{l+1}/q$ can be used to compute a discrete logarithm.[1] Here Q is the number of hash queries, l is the number interactions with the signer and q is the prime order of the group G. For an elliptic curve G of order $q \approx 2^{200}$ and $Q = 2^{50}$ we must have $l \leq 3$ as $\varepsilon \leq 1$. For a subgroup G of units of order $\leq 2^{1000}$ we must have $l \leq 20$. The security for larger values of l is an open problem [PS00]. Our generic parallel attack shows that the security of blind DL-signatures against one-more signature forgeries requires the intractability of the ROS-problem. The ROS-problem is related to a NP-complete problem [H97].

Conversely, assuming the intractability of the ROS-problem Theorem 2 gives a practical security guarantee for blind Schnorr signatures in the ROM + GM. A generic attacker performing t generic steps, including some l interactions with the signer, cannot produce $l+1$ signatures with a better probability than $\binom{t}{2}/q$. For elliptic curves G of order $q \approx 2^{200}$ this guarantee covers up to $t = 2^{100}$ generic steps including up to 2^{100} parallel signer interactions that can be interleaved in an arbitrary way. Blind Schnorr signatures have the same security level in the ROM + GM as the double-keyed blind Okamoto-Schnorr signatures, thus reducing a considerable overhead.

Our result suggests to use blind Schnorr signatures in connection with strong elliptic/hyperelliptic curves rather than double-keyed blind Okamoto-Schnorr signatures with subgroups of units. We prove security of the most practical schemes under reasonable assumptions. The less practical schemes of [P98], [AO 00] are provably secure for a polynomial number of interactions, but some restrictions apply. [2] The security proofs of [P98], [AO 00] do not use the GM. The new attack does not apply to the less simple signatures of [A01].

Is the GM-assumption to strong ? Contrary to claims of previous anonymous referees we are not aware of a practical cryptographic scheme that is secure in the

---

[1] In terms of asymptotic bounds the security results of POINTCHEVAL, STERN [PS96b,PS00] show that blind Okamoto-Schnorr signatures are secure against parallel interactive attacks provided that the number of interactions with the signer is poly-logarithmic — $polylog(|q|)$ for the binary length $|q|$ of q. The polylog bound on the number of signer interactions has not been explicitly mentioned in [P00] but it is required as the proof is based on the results of [PS00].

[2] In [P98] a third party — the *checker* — has been introduced, and it is shown that the resulting three-party signature protocol is secure for a polynomial number of *synchronized* signer interactions, where the synchronization forces the completion of each step for all the different protocol invocations before the next step of any other invocation is started. The [AO 00] scheme uses the [P98] scheme, thus the same restrictions apply.

ROM + GM but is insecure in reality. [CGH98] give a very intricate example of a secure scheme in ROM (only) that does not have a secure implementation. Of course the random hash function must be independent of the generic group [F00]. Moreover, FISCHLIN [F00] shows that generic verifier zeroknowledge is provably weaker than black-box TM verifier zeroknowledge. There are two reasons [Sc01b]: firstly, generic verifiers are more restricted than TM-verifiers, secondly black-box simulators are less powerful than generic verifier simulators that control the generic group steps. Fischlin's result does not amount to a security break as we do not know that generic verifier zeroknowledge is weaker than "general" TM-verifier zeroknowledge. The restriction via the black-box mode may be to rigid.

The paper is organized as follows. We present in Section 2 blind Schnorr signatures and the novel parallel attack against blind Schnorr and against blind Okamoto-Schnorr signatures. We determine in Theorem 1 the probability for the existence of a solution for the ROS-problem. In Section 3 we describe the ROM + GM as introduced in [SJ00]. Assuming the intractability of the ROS-problem we give in Section 4, Theorem 2 a practical security guarantee for blind Schnorr signatures in the ROM + GM.

2   Blind Schnorr Signatures and the Parallel Attack

We are interested in blind signatures as required for anomymous digital cash. Blind signatures are generated by an interaction with the signer who controls the secret signature key.

Schnorr signatures refer to an arbitrary group G of prime order q and an arbitrary message space M. We describe signer interactions, an interactive protocol that enables a user to generate Schnorr signatures of messages of its choice. We first describe the setting and the structure of the signatures, after which we review the protocol for generation of signatures. We also show how to generate blind signatures of the same type. Signatures will be based on an ideal hash function $H : G \times M \to \mathbf{Z}_q$, where M is the set of messages.

Private/public key pairs. The *private key* x of the signer is random in $\mathbf{Z}_q$. The corresponding *public key* is $h = g^x \in G$, a random group element. We have $x = \log_g h$.

Signatures. A Schnorr signature on a message m is a triple $(m, c, z) \in M \times \mathbf{Z}_q^2$ such that $H(g^z h^{-c}, m) = c$. For this paper, we let signatures (m, c, z) comprise the message.

Signing a message $m \in M$: Pick a random $r \in_R \mathbf{Z}_q$, compute g^r, $c := H(g^r, m)$ and $z := r + cx$. Output the signature: (m, c, z). The result is a valid signature since we have $g^z h^{-c} = g^{r+cx} h^{-c} = g^r$, and thus $H(g^z h^{-c}, m) = c$. We call a signature (m, c, z) constructed by this protocol a *standard signature*.

A *signer interaction* is a three round interactive protocol between the signer and a user. The signer picks a random $r \in_R \mathbf{Z}_q$ and sends the commitment g^r to the user. The user selects a challenge $c \in \mathbf{Z}_q$ and sends c. The signer responses by sending $z := r + cx \in \mathbf{Z}_q$. We let $(r, c, z) \in \mathbf{Z}_q^3$ denote the signer interaction consisting of the signer's random coin r, the user's *challenge* c and the signer's *response* z. A signer interaction (r, c, z) can be used to generate the *standard signature* (m, c, z), where $c := H(g^r, m)$ or a transformation (m, c', z') of this signature.

Blind Signature Protocol. We call the signature protocol *blind* if it generates a signature (m, c', z') that is statistically independent of the interaction (r, c, z) that provides the view of the signer. Lateron, blind signatures cannot be identified and related to the signer interaction. The blindness concept is from [CP92].

To generate a blind signature (m, c', z') the user picks random numbers $\alpha, \beta \in_R \mathbf{Z}_q$, and responses to the commitment g^r by sending the challenge $c = H(g^{r+\alpha} h^\beta, m) + \beta \in \mathbf{Z}_q$. After receiving $z = r + cx \in \mathbf{Z}_q$ he computes $z' = z + \alpha, c' = c - \beta$.

Validity. For the output of the interaction $(m, c', z') = (m, c - \beta, z + \alpha)$ we have $g^{z'} h^{-c'} = g^{r+cx+\alpha} h^{-c+\beta} = g^{r+\alpha} h^\beta$. Hence $H(g^{z'} h^{-c'}, m) = c - \beta = c'$, and thus (m, c', z') is a valid signature.

Blindness Property. The generated signature $(m, c - \beta, z + \alpha)$ is — for a constant interaction (r, c, z) — uniformly distributed over all signatures on message m due to the random $\alpha, \beta \in_R \mathbf{Z}_q$. Each signature (m, c', z') is produced for a unique pair (α, β) : $\alpha = z' - z, \ \beta = c - c'$.

2.1   A New Parallel Attack against Blind Schnorr Signatures

We present a variant of the attack that does not even use the generator g and the public key h. We first present the attack for Schnorr signatures. Thereafter, we extend it to Okamoto-Schnorr signatures. We show that Okamoto-Schnorr signatures do not protect better against the attack than plain Schnorr signatures. The new attack uses a solution of the following

ROS-problem: Find an overdetermined, solvable system of linear equations modulo q with random inhomogenities. Specifically, given an oracle random function $F : \mathbf{Z}_q^l \to \mathbf{Z}_q$, find coefficients $a_{k,l} \in \mathbf{Z}_q$ and a solvable system of $l+1$ distinct equations (1) in the unknowns $c_1, ..., c_l$ over $\mathbf{Z}_q$:

$$a_{k,1} c_1 + ... + a_{k,l} c_l = F(a_{k,1}, ..., a_{k,l}) \quad \text{for } k = 1, ..., t. \tag{1}$$

We evaluate the expected number of solvable subsystems consisting of $l + 1$ out of t equations (1).

Theorem 1. *For arbitrary coefficients $a_{k,\ell} \in \mathbf{Z}_q$, the average number of solvable subsystems of $l+1$ out of the t equations (1) is at most $\binom{t}{l+1}/q$. For statistically independent coefficients $a_{k,\ell} \in_R \mathbf{Z}_q$ the average number of solvable subsystems is $\binom{t}{l+1} q^{-1} (1 - q^{-1} + O(q^{-2}))$.*

Proof. Consider a constant selection of $l + 1$ out of the t equations (1) with arbitrary coefficients $a_{k,\ell}$. Let the subsystem have s linearly independent vectors

$(a_{k,1}, ..., a_{k,l}) \in \mathbf{Z}_q^l$. The subsystem is solvable if and only if the rank of the submatrix of the corresponding vectors $(a_{k,1}, ..., a_{k,l}, F(a_{k,1}, ..., a_{k,l}))$ is s. The probability that the subsystem is solvable has a maximum q^{-1} for $s = l$. For $s = l$ the l linearly independent equations have a unique solution and that solution satisfies the remaining equation with probability q^{-1}. As there are $\binom{t}{l+1}$ selections out of t, the average number of solvable subsystems is at most $\binom{t}{l+1}/q$.

Next, consider random coefficients $a_{k,\ell} \in_R \mathbf{Z}_q$. Then l vectors $(a_{k,1}, ..., a_{k,l})$ are linearly independent with probability $(1 - q^{-1})(1 - q^{-2}) \cdot ... \cdot (1 - q^{-l+1})$. Hence, a constant selection of $l + 1$ equations (1) is solvable with probability $q^{-1}(1 - q^{-1} + O(q^{-2}))$.

Consider two distinct selections of $l + 1$ equations. The solvability of two systems of $l + 1$ equations is (nearly) statistically independent as the systems differ in at least one random value $F(a_{k,1}, ..., a_{k,l})$. The law of large numbers holds for a sequence of pairwise independent, identically distributed random variables. Therefore, the expected number of solvable subsystems with $l + 1$ equations is $\binom{t}{l+1} q^{-1}(1 - q^{-1} + O(q^{-2}))$. □

The attack against Schnorr signatures. The signer sends commitments $g_1 = g^{r_1}, ..., g_l = g^{r_l}$. The attacker $\mathcal{A}$ selects $a_{k,1}, ..., a_{k,l} \in \mathbf{Z}_q$ and messages $m_1, ..., m_t$, and computes $f_k = g_1^{a_{k,1}} \cdot ... \cdot g_l^{a_{k,l}}$ and $H(f_k, m_k)$ for $k = 1, ..., t$. Then $\mathcal{A}$ solves $l + 1$ of the t equations (2) in the unknowns $c_1, .., c_l$ over $\mathbf{Z}_q$:

$$H(f_k, m_k) = \sum_{\ell=1}^{l} a_{k,\ell} c_\ell \quad \text{for } k = 1, ..., t. \tag{2}$$

$\mathcal{A}$ sends the solutions $c_1, ..., c_l$ as challenges to the signer. The signer sends back $z_\ell := r_\ell + c_\ell x \in \mathbf{Z}_q$ for $\ell = 1, .., l$. For each solved equation (2), the attacker gets a valid signature (m_k, c'_k, z'_k) by setting

$$c'_k := \sum_{\ell=1}^{l} a_{k,\ell} c_\ell = H(f_k, m_k) \quad \text{and} \quad z'_k := \sum_{\ell=1}^{l} a_{k,\ell} z_\ell.$$

Correctness. The equations (2) imply that

$$g^{z'_k} h^{-c'_k} = g_1^{a_{k,1}} \cdot ... \cdot g_l^{a_{k,l}} = f_k \quad \text{and} \quad H(g^{z'_k} h^{-c'_k}, m_k) = c'_k.$$

In the ROM the values $H(f_k, m_k)$ are random. The coefficients $a_{k,\ell}$ selected by the attacker are arbitrary values. The solution $(c_1, ..., c_l)$ of $l + 1$ of the t equations (2) does not depend on g, h. As $\mathcal{A}$ does not use g, h, $\mathcal{A}$ cannot help in black-box mode to compute $\log_g h$ or to solve a Diffie-Hellman or a decisional Diffie-Hellman problem related to h.

The new attack is generic, it works for arbitrary groups with an efficient multiplication. We call it the *generic, parallel attack*. The attack is intrinsic parallel. Theorem 1 shows that the number l of parallel interactions with the signer must be at least logarithmic in q. Otherwise, the probability $\binom{t}{l+1}/q$ for the existence of a solvable subsystem of $l + 1$ equations (2) is negligible.

The attack against Okamoto-Schnorr signatures. We follow the notation of [PS00]. There are two public keys h and $y = g^{-r} h^{-s}$ for random secret keys $r, s \in_R \mathbf{Z}_q$ while $\log_g h$ is unknown. A signature of message m is a tuple $(m, \varepsilon, \sigma, \rho) \in M \times \mathbf{Z}_q^3$ satisfying $H(g^\rho h^\sigma y^\varepsilon, m) = \varepsilon$.

The signer picks random $t_\ell, u_\ell \in_R \mathbf{Z}_q$ and sends commitments $g_\ell = g^{t_\ell} h^{u_\ell}$ for $\ell = 1, .., l$. The attacker $\mathcal{A}$ selects coefficients $a_{k,\ell} \in \mathbf{Z}_q$ and messages $m_1, ..., m_t$, and computes $f_k = g_1^{a_{k,1}} \cdot ... \cdot g_l^{a_{k,l}}$ and $H(f_k, m_k)$ for $k = 1, ..., t$. $\mathcal{A}$ solves $l + 1$ of the t linear equations (2) modulo q in the unknowns $c_1, ..., c_l$. $\mathcal{A}$ sends the solutions $c_1, ..., c_l$ as challenges to the signer. The signer sends back $R_\ell := t_\ell + c_\ell r$, $S_\ell := u_\ell + c_\ell s \in \mathbf{Z}_q$ for $\ell = 1, .., l$. For each solved equation (2) $\mathcal{A}$ gets a valid signature $(m_k, \varepsilon_k, \rho_k, \sigma_k)$ by setting

$$\varepsilon_k = H(f_k, m_k) = \sum_{\ell=1}^{l} a_{k,\ell}\, c_\ell, \quad \rho_k = \sum_{\ell=1}^{l} a_{k,\ell}\, R_\ell, \quad \sigma_k = \sum_{\ell=1}^{l} a_{k,\ell}\, S_\ell.$$

Correctness. From the equations (2) we get that

$$g^{\rho_k} h^{\sigma_k} y^{\varepsilon_k} = \prod_{\ell=1}^{l} g_\ell^{a_{k,\ell}} = f_k \quad \text{and} \quad H(g^{\rho_k} h^{\sigma_k} y^{\varepsilon_k}, m_k) = \varepsilon_k.$$

Conclusion. The generic parallel attack $\mathcal{A}$ does not use the public g, h, y. Thus, it is impossible to use a successful attacker to solve a DL- DH- or DDH-problem. The generic, parallel attack has been excluded in Theorem 26 [PS00] by assuming that the attacker has a probability of success $4t^{(l+1)}/q$ which is greater than the probability $\binom{t}{l+1}/q$ for the existence of a solvable subsystem of $l + 1$ equations (2). The second part of Theorem 1 shows that solutions to the ROS-problem are very likely to exist for $l = 4, t = 2^{50}$ and $q \approx 2^{200}$. The generic parallel attack is possible for $l = 4$ parallel interactions, $t = 2^{50}$ hash queries for elliptic curves of order $q \approx 2^{200}$. A meaningful security guarantee for elliptic curves of order $\approx 2^{200}$ requires that solvable subsystems of $l + 1$ equations (2) are hard to find.

3   The Random Oracle and the Generic Group Model

The Random Oracle Model (ROM). Let G be a group of prime order q with generator g, a range M of messages, and let $\mathbf{Z}_q$ denote the field of integers modulo q. Let H be an *ideal* hash function with range $\mathbf{Z}_q$, modelled as an oracle that given an input (query) in $G \times M$, outputs a random number in $\mathbf{Z}_q$. Formally, H is a random function $H : G \times M \to \mathbf{Z}_q$ chosen at random over all functions of that type with uniform probability distribution.

The Generic Group Model (GM). Generic algorithms for G do not use the binary encodings of the group elements, as they access group elements only for group operations and equality tests. NECHAEV [Ne94] proves that the discrete logarithm problem is hard in such a model, see [Sc01a] for a stronger result. The generic model of algorithms was further elaborated on by SHOUP [Sh97]. We present the Shoup model in a slightly different setup[3] and we extend it

---

[3] We count the same generic steps as in [Sh97]; however, we allow arbitrary multivariate exponentiations while Shoup merely uses multiplication and division. The technical setup in [Sh97] looks different as groups G are *additive* and associated with a random injective encoding $\sigma : G \to S$ of the group G into a set S of bit strings — the generic algorithm performs arbitrary computations on these bit strings. Addition/subtraction is done by an oracle that computes $\sigma(f_i \pm f_j)$ when given $\sigma(f_i), \sigma(f_j)$ and the specified sign bit. As the encoding σ is random it contains only the information about which group elements coincide — this is what we call the set of *collisions*.

to algorithms that interact with a decryption oracle. Encryptions are for the private/public key pair (x, h), where x is random in $\mathbf{Z}_q$ and $h = g^x$. We describe the extended generic model in detail, first focusing on non-interactive algorithms and thereafter on algorithms interacting with oracles for hashing and signing.

The *data of a generic algorithm* is partitioned into group elements in G and non-group data. The *generic steps* for group elements are multivariate exponentiations:

- mex: $\mathbf{Z}_q^d \times G^d \to G$, $(a_1, ..., a_d, g_1, ..., g_d) \mapsto \prod_i g_i^{a_i}$ with $d \geq 0$.

The cases $d = 2, a_1 = 1, a_2 = \pm 1$ present multiplication/division. The case $d = 0$ presents *inputs* in G — e.g., g, h are inputs for the DL-computation.

Def. A (non-interactive) *generic algorithm* is a sequence of t generic steps[4]

- $f_1, \ldots, f_{t'} \in G$ (inputs) $1 \leq t' < t$,
- $f_i = \prod_{j=1}^{i-1} f_j^{a_j}$ for $i = t' + 1, \ldots, t$, where $(a_1, \ldots, a_{i-1}) \in \mathbf{Z}_q^{i-1}$ depends arbitrarily on i, the non-group input and the set $\mathcal{CO}_{i-1} := \{(j, \ell) \mid f_j = f_\ell, 1 \leq j < \ell \leq i - 1\}$ of previous *collisions* of group elements.

Typical non-group inputs are various integers in $\mathbf{Z}_q$ contained in given ciphertexts or signatures. $\mathcal{CO}_t$ is the set of all collisions of the algorithm.

Some group inputs f_i depend on random coin flips, e.g., the random public key $h = g^x$ depends on the random secret key $x \in_R \mathbf{Z}_q$. The *probability space* consists of the random group elements of the input. The logarithms $\log_g f_i$ of the random inputs f_i play the role of *secret parameters*. Information about the secret parameters can only be revealed by collisions. E.g., $g^a = f_i^b$ implies $\log_g f_i = a/b$. We let the non-group input and the generator g not depend on random bits.

The *output* of a generic algorithm consists of

- non-group data that depend arbitrarily on the non-group input and on the set $\mathcal{CO}_t$ of all collisions,

- group elements $f_{\sigma_1}, \ldots, f_{\sigma_d}$ where the integers $\sigma_1, \ldots, \sigma_d \in \{1, \ldots, t\}$ depend arbitrarily on the non-group input and on $\mathcal{CO}_t$.

Next, we elaborate on *interactive, generic algorithms*. We count the following generic steps :

- group operations,   mex : $\mathbf{Z}_q^d \times G^d \to G$, $(a_1, ..., a_d, g_1, ..., g_d) \mapsto \prod_i g_i^{a_i}$,

- queries to the hash oracle H,

- interactions with a signature oracle (*signer* for short).

A *generic adversary* $\mathcal{A}$ — mounting a one-more signature forgery — is an interactive algorithm that interacts with a signer. It performs some t generic steps resulting in $t' \leq t$ group elements $f_1, ..., f_{t'}$. $\mathcal{A}$ iteratively selects the next generic step — a group operation, a query to H, an interaction with the signer

---

Shoup's random encoding allows for an efficient sorting of group elements. We do not need such efficient sorting as equality tests are for free.

[4] We can allow that the number t of generic steps varies with the input. We can let the algorithm decide after each step whether to terminate depending arbitrarily on the given non-group data.

— depending arbitrarily on the non-group input and on previous collisions of group elements.

The *input* consists of the generator g, the public key $h \in G$, the group order q, a collection of messages and ciphertexts and so on, all of which can be broken down into group elements and non-group data.

The computed *group elements* $f_1, ..., f_{t'} \in G$ are the group elements contained in the input, such as g, h. When counting the number of group operations, we count each input as one operation. As a signer interaction is counted as a generic step the number t' of group elements is bounded by the number t of generic steps, $t' \le t$. We have $t = t'$ for a non-interactive $\mathcal{A}$.

The given *non-group data* consists of the non-group data contained in the input, the previous hash replies $H(Q)$ of queries Q, and the set of previous collisions of group elements. *Signer interactions* are described in Section 2.

$\mathcal{A}$'s *output* and *transmission* to the signer consists of non-group data NG and previously computed group elements f_σ, where NG and σ, $1 \le \sigma \le t'$, depend arbitrarily on given non-group data.

$\mathcal{A}$'s *transmission* to the hash oracle H depends arbitrarily on given group elements and given non-group data. The *probability space* consists of the random H, the random input group elements and the random coin flips of the signer.

The *restriction of the generic model* is that $\mathcal{A}$ can use group elements only for generic group operations, equality tests and for queries to the hash oracle, whereas non-group data can be arbitrarily used without charge. The computed group elements $f_1, ..., f_{t'}$ are given as explicit multiplicative combinations of given group elements. Let $g_\ell = g^{r_\ell}$ for $\ell = 1, ..., l$ be the group elements that $\mathcal{A}$ gets from the signer. A computed $f_j \in G$ is of the form $f_j = g^{a_{j,-1}} h^{a_{j,0}} g_1^{a_{j,1}} \cdot ... \cdot g_l^{a_{j,l}}$, where the exponents $a_{j,-1}, ..., a_{j,l} \in \mathbf{Z}_q$ depend arbitrarily on given non-group data. $\mathcal{A}$ can arbitrarily use the coefficients $a_{j,-1}, ..., a_{j,l}$ from this explicit representation of f_j. A generic adversary does not use internal coin flips, this is not a restriction as internal coin flips would be useless.[5]

Trivial collisions. We call a collision $(i, j) \in \mathcal{CO}_t$ *trivial* if $f_i = f_j$ holds with probability 1, i.e., if it holds for all choices of the secret data such as the secret key x and the random bits r of the encipherer. We write $f_i \equiv f_j$ for a trivial collision. Trivial collisions do not release any information about the secret data while non-trivial collisions can completely release some secret data. Trivial collisions can be excluded from $\mathcal{CO}_t$. Therefore, we ignore trivial collisions.

---

[5] $\mathcal{A}$ could select interior coin flips that maximize the probability of success — there is always a choice for the internal coin flips that does not decrease $\mathcal{A}$'s probability of success. Moreover, it would be useless for $\mathcal{A}$ to generate random group elements — in particular ones with unknown DL. Using one generic step, $\mathcal{A}$ could replace random elements in G by some deterministic g^a where $a \in \mathbf{Z}_q$ is chosen as to maximize the probability of success.

4   Security of Signatures against Interactive Attacks

Assuming the intractability of the ROS-problem and the ROM + GM we give in Theorem 2 a practical security guarantee for blind Schnorr signatures against one-more signature forgeries.

This section refers to a generic adversary $\mathcal{A}$ performing some t generic steps — including some l interactions $(r_1, c_1, z_1), ..., (r_l, c_l, z_l)$ with the signer — producing some t' group elements and some t'' queries to the hash oracle. We let $\mathbf{r} = (r_1, ..., r_l)$ denote the signers random coins. Let $f_1 = g$, $f_2 = h = g^x$, $f_3, ... f_{t'} \in G$ denote the group elements of $\mathcal{A}$'s computation. The generic $\mathcal{A}$ computes $f_j = g^{a_{j,-1}} h^{a_{j,0}} g_1^{a_{j,1}} \cdot ... \cdot g_l^{a_{j,l}}$, where $g_1 = g^{r_1}, ..., g_l = g^{r_l}$ are the signer's commitments and the exponents $a_{j,\ell} \in \mathbf{Z}_q$ depend arbitrarily on the previously computed non-group data. As each signer interaction yields one group element g^{r_ℓ} we have that $t'' = t - t' \geq 0$ is the number of interactions with the hash oracle. We first present the basic Lemma 1 and 2 that extend results of [SJ00] from a non-interactive attacker to an adversary using a hash oracle and a signature oracle.

Lemma 1. *Collisions among $f_1, ..., f_{t'}$ occur at most with probability $\binom{t'}{2}/q$. The probability refers to the random h, H and the random coins $\mathbf{r}$ of the signer.*

Proof. We show for $i < j$ that $\Pr_{x, \mathbf{r}, H}[f_i = f_j] \leq \frac{1}{q}$ under the condition that there is no prior collision of group elements. So let us assume that there is no such prior collision. The main point is to show that f_i, f_j are either statistically independent or f_i/f_j is constant with $f_i \neq f_j$. Considering x and $r_1, ..., r_l$ as indeterminates over $\mathbf{Z}_q$, $\log_g f_j = a_{j,-1} + a_{j,0} x + \sum_{\ell=1}^l a_{j,\ell} r_\ell$ is a linear polynomial in $\mathbf{Z}_q[x, r_1, ..., r_l]$.

For a *non-interactive* $\mathcal{A}$, where $l = 0$ and $\mathbf{r} = (r_1, ..., r_l)$ is empty we have $f_i = f_j$ iff $a_{i,-1} - a_{j,-1} + (a_{i,0} - a_{j,0}) x = 0$. Therefore, x is statistically independent of the $a_{i,\ell}, a_{j,\ell}$, and thus $\Pr_{x,H}[f_i = f_j] \leq \frac{1}{q}$.[6]

Next, consider an *interactive* $\mathcal{A}$. We call r_ℓ, g^{r_ℓ} *prior* to f_j if the value $a_{j,\ell}$ depends on the signer's response $z_\ell = r_\ell + c_\ell x$, otherwise r_ℓ is *subsequent* to f_j. When given $f_j = g^{a_{j,-1}} h^{a_{j,0}} g_1^{a_{j,1}} \cdot ... \cdot g_l^{a_{j,l}}$ the probability space — from $\mathcal{A}$'s point of view — consists of x, H and the r_ℓ subsequent to f_j. The $r_\ell = z_\ell - c_\ell x$ prior to f_j are linear functions in x, with given coefficients z_ℓ, c_ℓ. Consider $\log_g f_j = a_{j,-1} + a_{j,0} x + \sum_{\ell=1}^l a_{j,\ell} r_\ell$ as a linear function in x and the r_ℓ subsequent to f_j. The coefficients $a_{j,\ell}, c_\ell, z_\ell \in \mathbf{Z}_q$ depend on $x, H, \mathbf{r}$ only via prior r_ℓ and prior hash values. Thus x is statistically independent of the given coefficients. Therefore, the values of the function $\log_g f_i - \log_g f_j$ are either constant or uniformly distributed over $\mathbf{Z}_q$. The case that $\log_g f_i - \log_g f_j = 0$ for all x and all r_ℓ subsequent to f_j has been excluded as $f_i \not\equiv f_j$. This shows that $\Pr_{x,\mathbf{r},H}[f_i = f_j] \leq \frac{1}{q}$, which implies the claim of Lemma 1 as there are $\binom{t'}{2}$ pairs $i < j$.   □

Lemma 2. *If there are no collisions among $f_1, ..., f_{t'}$ the random x is statistically independent of the computed non-group data except that the random coins $(\mathbf{r}, x)$ leading to collisions are excluded.*

---

[6] The equality $f_i = f_j$ holds with zero probability if $a_{i,-1} \neq a_{j,-1}$ and $a_{i,0} = a_{j,0}$. As $f_j \not\equiv f_i$ we cannot have that $(a_{i,-1}, a_{i,0}) = (a_{j,-1}, a_{j,0})$.

Proof. The random x enters into the generic computation only via the the random values $z_\ell = r_\ell + c_\ell x$, random hash values and $h = g^x$. In a signer interaction $\mathcal{A}$ gets the pair (g^{r_ℓ}, z_ℓ). Due to the random r_ℓ the distribution of z_ℓ does not depend on $h = g^x$. The probability distribution of the non-group data generated from hash values and signer responses does not depend on x. Therefore, x is statistically independent of all non-group data ($h = g^x$ is NOT statistically independent of (g^{r_ℓ}, z_ℓ), however g^{r_ℓ} enters into the computation of non-group data only by collisions of group elements and via random hash values).   □

Theorem 2 shows that Schnorr signatures are secure against the one-more signature forgery in the ROM + GM. Theorem 2 covers blind signatures as required for anonymous electronic cash. This is the first sharp security result for simple DL-signatures in the interactive setting.

Theorem 2. *Let a generic adversary $\mathcal{A}$ be given the generator g, the public key h, an oracle for H. Let $\mathcal{A}$ interact with the signer some l times and perform t generic steps including l signer interactions. If $\mathcal{A}$ succeeds in a parallel attack to produce $l+1$ signatures with a better probability of success than $\binom{t}{2}/q$ then $\mathcal{A}$ must solve the ROS-problem : solve $l+1$ distinct equations (2) in the unknowns $c_1, ..., c_l \in \mathbf{Z}_q$. The probability space consists of h, H and the random coins of the signer.*

Proof. In the interaction (r_ℓ, c_ℓ, z_ℓ) the signer correctly transmits $g_\ell := g^{r_\ell}$ and responds to $\mathcal{A}$'s challenge c_ℓ by $z_\ell = r_\ell + c_\ell x$. It is assumed that $\mathcal{A}$ outputs distinct triples $(m_i, c_i', z_i') \in M \times \mathbf{Z}_q^2$ for $i = 1, ..., l+1$. We study the probability that the $l+1$ outputs are all signatures. Let there be t'' (distinct) queries to the hash oracle resulting in independent hash values $H(f_{\sigma_k}, m_k) \in \mathbf{Z}_q$ for $k = 1, ..., t''$ for an arbitrary function $k \mapsto \sigma_k$ that selects f_{σ_k} from the computed group elements f_j. Lemma 3 shows that the group element $g^{z_i'} h^{-c_i'}$ corresponding to a signature (m_i, c_i', z_i') must be among $f_{\sigma_1}, ..., f_{\sigma_{t''}}$. We let $f_{\sigma_i} = g^{z_i'} h^{-c_i'}$.

Lemma 3. *Let the output (m_i, c_i', z_i') be a signature with a better probability than $\frac{1}{q}$. Then we have that $c_i' = H(f_{\sigma_i}, m_i)$ for some hash query satisfying $f_{\sigma_i} = g^{z_i'} h^{-c_i'}$. Moreover, c_i', z_i', σ_i satisfy the equations $z_i' = a_{\sigma_i, -1} + \sum_{\ell=1}^l a_{\sigma_i, \ell} z_\ell$ and*

$$H(f_{\sigma_i}, m_i) = -a_{\sigma_i, 0} + \sum_{\ell=1}^l a_{\sigma_i, \ell} c_\ell. \tag{3}$$

Conversely, given a solution $(c_1, ..., c_l)$ of equation (3) one easily gets a signature (m_i, c_i', z_i') for each solved equation.

Proof. The first claim follows from the equation $c_i' = H(g^{z_i'} h^{-c_i'}, m_i)$ required for signatures (m_i, c_i', z_i'). In the ROM this equation necessitates that $\mathcal{A}$ selects c_i' from given hash values $H(f_{\sigma_k}, m_k)$ — otherwise the equality only holds with probability $\frac{1}{q}$ as the hash value is random. W.l.o.g. let $c_i' = H(f_{\sigma_i}, m_i)$ where $f_{\sigma_i} = g^{z_i'} h^{-c_i'}$ holds for the output (m_i, c_i', z_i') which determines σ_i. [7] The equations $g^{z_i'} h^{-c_i'} = f_{\sigma_i} = g^{a_{\sigma_i, -1} + a_{\sigma_i, 0} x + \sum_{\ell=1}^l a_{\sigma_i, \ell} r_\ell}$ and $r_\ell = z_\ell - c_\ell x$ imply

---

[7] For simplicity we abbreviate $f_{\sigma_i} = g^{z_i'} h^{-c_i'}$ even though that equation only holds a posteriori. The output (m_i, c_i', z_i') defines σ_i except that there is a collision $H(f_{\sigma_i}, m_i) = H(f_{\sigma_j}, m_j)$ with $m_i = m_j$.

$$z_i' = \log_g g^{z_i} h^{-c_i} + c_i' x$$
$$z_i' = a_{\sigma_i,-1} + \sum_{\ell=1}^{l} a_{\sigma_i,\ell} z_\ell + (a_{\sigma_i,0} - \sum_{\ell=1}^{l} a_{\sigma_i,\ell} c_\ell + c_i')x, \tag{4}$$

If $c_i' = -a_{\sigma_i,0} + \sum_{\ell=1}^{l} a_{\sigma_i,\ell} c_\ell$ then $\mathcal{A}$ can easily compute the correct z_i' . In this case, the equation (4) does not depend on the secret key x and we have $z_i' = a_{\sigma_i,-1} + \sum_{\ell=1}^{l} a_{\sigma_i,\ell} z_\ell$, where the signers responses $z_1, ..., z_l$ and the coefficients $a_{\sigma_i,-1}, \dots , a_{\sigma_i,l}$ are known to $\mathcal{A}$.

Conversely, $\mathcal{A}$ must select $c_1, ..., c_l$ as to zero the coefficient of the secret key x in (4). Otherwise, Equation (4) holds with probability $\frac{1}{q}$ as x is by Lemma 2 statistically independent of the non-group data $z_i', a_{\sigma_i-,1}, ..., a_{\sigma_i,l}, c_1, ..., c_l$, and thus $\mathcal{A}$'s probability of success is not better than $\frac{1}{q}$. This proves that $\mathcal{A}$ must solve the equation $\qquad\square$

We see that the parallel attacker $\mathcal{A}$ can only succeed in either of four cases:

- $\mathcal{A}$ solves $l + 1$ out of t'' distinct equations
$$H(f_{\sigma_i}, m_i) = -a_{\sigma_i,0} + \sum_{\ell=1}^{l} a_{\sigma_i,\ell} c_\ell. \tag{3}$$
Each solved equation (3) yields a corresponding signature (m_i, c_i', z_i') by setting $z_i' = a_{\sigma_i,-1} + \sum_{\ell=1}^{l} a_{\sigma_i,\ell} z_\ell$. This is the *generic, parallel attack*.

- For some i, $1 \le i \le l+1$ equation (3) does not hold but equation (4) holds. This event has probability $\frac{1}{q}$.

- There is a collision of group elements. This event has probability $\le \binom{t'}{2}/q$.

- There is a collision of hash values $H(f_{\sigma_i}, m_i) = H(f_{\sigma_j}, m_j)$, where $m_i = m_j$, $f_{\sigma_i} \ne f_{\sigma_j}$ and $a_{\sigma_i,0} = a_{\sigma_j,0}, ..., a_{\sigma_i,l} = a_{\sigma_j,l}$. In this case the equations (3) with indices i and j coincide. This event has probability $\le \binom{t''}{2}/q$.

W.l.o.g. we can assume that $t', t'' \ge 1$, and thus $\binom{t'}{2} + \binom{t''}{2} + 1 \le \binom{t}{2}$. We see that $\mathcal{A}$ succeeds in the last three cases with no better probability than $\binom{t}{2}/q$. This proves Theorem 2 as $\mathcal{A}$ does not succeed with a better probability than $\binom{t}{2}/q$, except that $\mathcal{A}$ solves $l + 1$ out of t'' distinct equations (3). $\qquad\square$

Security against sequential attacks. It can be seen from the above proof that a sequential attack cannot succeed in the GM + ROM with a better probability than $\binom{t}{2}/q$. Here, the intractability of the ROS-problem is not needed. This characterizes the different power of sequential and of parallel attacks.

For a sequence of l sequential attacks, each with a single signer interaction, $\mathcal{A}$ selects the coefficients $a_{i,\ell}$ in (3) such that there is for each k at most one non-zero coefficient $a_{k,\ell}$ with $\ell \ge 1$.

References

[A01]   M. Abe: A Secure Three-move Blind Signature Scheme for Polynomially Many Signatures. Proc. Eurocrypt'01, LNCS 2045, pp. 136–151, 2001.

[AO00]   M. Abe and T. Okamoto: Provably Secure Partially Blind Signatures. Proc. Crypto'00, LNCS 1880, pp. 271–286, 2000.

[CP92]   D. Chaum and T.P. Pedersen Wallet Databases with Observers. Proc.
           Crypto'92, LNCS 740, pp. 89–105, 1992.
[BL96]   D. Boneh and R.J. Lipton : Algorithms for black-box fields and their appli-
           cation in cryptography. Proc. Crypto'96, LNCS 1109, pp. 283–297, 1996.
[BR93]   M. Bellare and P. Rogaway : Random Oracles are Practical: a Paradigms
           for Designing Efficient Protocols. Proc. 1st ACM Conference on Computer
           Communication Security, pp. 62–73, 1993.
[CGH98]   R. Canetti, O. Goldreich and S. Halevi : The Random Oracle Methodology,
           Revisited. Proc. STOC'98, ACM Press, pp. 209–218, 1998.
[F00]   M. Fischlin : A Note on Security Proofs in the Generic Model. Proc. Asi-
           acrypt'00, LNCS 1976, Springer-Verlag, pp. 458–469, 2000.
[FFS88]   U. Feige, A. Fiat and A. Shamir : Zero-knowledge proofs of identity. Jour-
           nal of Cryptology, 1 , pp. 77–94, 1988.
[FS87]   A. Fiat and A. Shamir : How to Prove Yourself: Practical Solutions of
           Identification and Signature Problems. Proc. Crypto'86, LNCS 263, pp.
           186–194, 1987.
[H97]   J. Håstad: Some Optimal Inapproximability Results. Proc. ACM Sympo-
           sium on Theory of Computing 1997, ACM Press, pp. 1–10, 1997.
[Ne94]   V.I. Nechaev: Complexity of a Determinate Algorithm for the Discrete
           Logarithm. Mathematical Notes 55, pp. 165-172, 1994.
[O92]   T. Okamoto : Provably Secure Identification Schemes and Corresponding
           Signature Schemes. Proc. Crypto'92, LNCS 740, Springer-Verlag, pp. 31–
           53, 1992.
[P98]   D. Pointcheval : Strengthened Security for Blind Signatures. Proc. Euro-
           crypt'98 LNCS 1403, Springer Verlag, pp. 391–405, 1998.
[P00]   D. Pointcheval : The Composite Discrete Logarithm and Secure Authenti-
           cation. Proc. PKC'2000, LNCS 1751, Springer-Verlag, pp. 113–128, 2000.
[PS96a]   D. Pointcheval and J. Stern : Security Proofs for Signature Schemes. Proc.
           Eurocrypt'96, LNCS 1070, Springer-Verlag, pp. 387–398, 1996.
[PS96b]   D. Pointcheval and J. Stern : Provably Secure Blind Signature Schemes.
           Proc. Asiacrypt'96, LNCS 1163, Springer Verlag, pp. 387–393, 1996.
[PS00]   D. Pointcheval and J. Stern : Security Arguments for Digital Signatures
           and Blind Signatures. Journal of Ctyptology, 13, 3, pp. 361–396, 2000.
[Sc91]   C.P. Schnorr : Efficient Signature Generation for Smart Cards. Journal of
           Cryptology 4, pp. 161–174, 1991.
[SJ00]   C.P. Schnorr and M. Jakobsson : Security of Signed ElGamal Encryption.
           Proc. Asiacrypt'00, LNCS, Springer-Verlag, 2000.
[Sc01a]   C.P. Schnorr : Small Generic Hardcore Subsets for the Discrete Logarithm:
           Short Secret DL-Keys. Information and Processing Letters, 79, pp. 93–98,
           2001.
[Sc01b]   C.P. Schnorr : Security of DL-Encryption and Signatures Against Generic
           Attacks, a Survey. Proc. of Public-Key Cryptography and Computational
           Number Theory Conference, Warsaw Sept. 2000, Eds. K. Alster, H.C.
           Williams, J. Urbanowicz. De Gruyter GMBH, July, 2001.
[Sh97]   V. Shoup : Lower Bounds for Discrete Logarithms and Related Problems.
           Proc. Eurocrypt'97, LNCS 1233, Springer-Verlag, pp. 256-266, 1997.

An Intelligent Intruder Model for Security Protocol Analysis

Dongxi Liu, Xiaoyong Li, and Yingcai Bai

Shanghai Jiaotong University, Shanghai 200030, China,
dxliu924@mail1.sjtu.edu.cn

Abstract. An intelligent intruder model is proposed in this paper. Except for the algebraic abilities to process messages like the Dolev-Yao intruder, it can decide when to generate what terms and whether or not to launch a new session, which principal to choose, and what roles the principal will play based on some strand-added rules. By this heuristic method, we can get a finite state space without the explicit configuration needed by most model checking tools.

1 Introduction

Security protocols are used to achieve secure communication over public network by exploiting cryptography in protocol message, and with the rapid growth of Internet, it plays a more and more important role in some security-critical sessions, such as electronic commerce. They may involve 2-5 message to exchange, but their design and analysis are notoriously complex and error-prone [1], and some of them are found to have flaws after many years they have been published [2].

Because of the subtlety to reason about the correctness of security protocols, a lot of researchers have turned to formal methods to analysis security protocols. Three main approaches exist. The first one is logic method that use belief logic to express and deduce security properties, such as BAN [3] and Theory Generator [4] that is a tool to automate deduction process. The second kind of approach is based on model checking or state spaces exploration [5,6,7], and they are automatic completely and can give counterexamples when flaw is found. The third approach depends on theorem proof [8,9] which are difficult to use but can prove the correctness of the protocol.

In order to make the analysis procedure tractable, all above methods rely on an ideal model called Dolev-Yao model [10]. This model make two assumptions: one is perfect encryption, that is, one can get plain text from cipher only if using corresponding key, and the other is the set of actions probably taken by intruder which can be applied nondeterministically during the protocol execution. The intruder is generally called Dolev-Yao intruder which can intercept any messages from network, decompose a message into parts and remember them, generate fresh data as needed, compose a new messages from known information, send a new message. At each step of protocol execution, the intruder can choose

S. Qing, T. Okamoto, and J. Zhou (Eds.): ICICS 2001, LNCS 2229, pp. 13–22, 2001.

one from those actions nondeterministically. In [11], Cervesato gives a standard presentation of Dolve-Yao model by using multiset rewriting with existential quantification. Another intruder model is called Machiavelli [12] which is proved to be equivalent with Dolve-Yao Intruder.

Dolev-Yao intruders take full control of the network and are very powerful, but Dolve-Yao intruder model just specify how to process a message for an intruder, such as to compose or to decompose a message. However, it does not tell what message to process and when to process a particular kind of message. So we call Dolve-Yao intruder model as algebraic intruder model. In this paper, we propose an intelligent intruder model used by state space exploration method based on dynamic strand spaces.

The remainder of this paper is organized as follows. In section 2, we will model the security protocol execution by using the state space exploration method based on dynamic strand spaces; In section 3, we will formulate and discuss the intelligent intruder model. At last, we conclude all paper in section 4.

2   Model the Security Protocol

In this section, we will first give the basic notions needed in this paper and extend strand space model [9] into a dynamic one. Strand space model is a new way used to analysis protocol in which the exact causal relations between events are considered so the proof procedure of a protocol's property is much simpler than that based on trace based model. In addition, strand space model has also been used as the basis of model checking tool, such as Athena [13]. And then we describe the state structure based dynamic strand space model.

2.1   Basic Notions

Here, we use term to represent the message exchanged by protocol participants, and the smallest term is atomic term that can not be divided any more. The formal definition is as the following.

Definition 1. *Let S_{name} be the set of protocol principal, S_{ks} the key set for symmetric cryptography, S_{kp} the key set for public key cryptography, and S_{nonce} be the set of nonces. A is the atomic terms term set, $A=S_{name} \cup S_{ks} \cup S_{kp} \cup S_{nonce}$.*

For brevity, we limit our discussion to just these three kinds of atomic messages, and other atomic term can be appended the above definition easily without affecting our analysis substantially.

Definition 2. *Let M be the set of all possible terms, then it can be defined inductively over atomic terms A as follows:*

1. *If $a \in A$, then $a \in M$.*
2. *If $m_1 \in M$ and $m_2 \in M$, then $m_1 \cdot m_2 \in M$.*
3. *If $m \in M$ and $k \in S_{ks} \cup S_{kp}$, then $m_k \in M$.*

And each atomic term in m, $m \in M$, is called an element of m.

Definition 3. *Let $m \in M$, checkpart(m) indicate the set of elements that is checked by protocol participant to determine whether m is acceptable; infopart(m) is the set of elements that make protocol participants learn more information.*

We distinguish between these two parts of a term so as to know what parts in a term must be kept and what can be changed when intruder generates new terms. For example, the principal checks the nonce field to justify whether it is a valid term, and then get an account number from this term, thus he can debit some money from this account.

Definition 4. *The space of term m, denoted as space(m), is the set of terms in which every element has the same check part with m, that is, for $\forall t \in$ space(m), checkpart$(m) =$ checkpart(t) is satisfied. And the dimension of space(m) is the ordinal of infopart(m), and bigger dimension means a big term set.*

Definition 5. *Let $m_1 \in M$ and $m_2 \in M$, m_1 is equivalent with m_2, denoted as $m_1 \cong m_2$, if $m_1 \in$ space(m_2) and $m_2 \in$ space(m_1). So if m_1 can be accepted by a principal, m_2 can be accepted by the same principal too, thus these two messages are equivalent with each other.*

Based on the term equivalence, we can model all possible terms constructed by intruder that can be accepted by an honest principal. This is useful for state space exploration tool that is based on forward search.

2.2 Dynamic Strand Space Model

In [9], strand is static and can not characterize the features of protocol execution since strand space is a proof based method at beginning. In this subsection, we will enhance the strand space model with dynamic features by introducing the notions of active node.

Definition 6. *A protocol role is defined by protocol specification and its behavior is determined by a sequence of events composed of $< +a >$ or $< -a >$ for $a \in M$, that is, term a is sent or received. All atomic terms in the event trace are parameters that need be instantiated when protocol executing.*

Definition 7. *A strand s is an instance of protocol role. Its corresponding event trace is denoted as tr(s). A strand can be treated as a chained graph, and every signed term is a node of the graph, that is a node is a pair of $< s, i >$, $1 \leq i \leq$ length$(tr(s))$.*

Definition 8. *An active node is a node n in strand s and it indicates that s prepare to execute this node. If $n = < s, i >$ is an active node of s, then next active node will be $< s, i + 1 >$, with $1 \leq i \leq$ length$(tr(s))$. If term$(n) = -a$, then this active node n is waiting to receive a term a; If term$(n) = +a$, then this active node n will send a term a.*

Definition 9. *A dynamic strand space consists of a set of strand $\sum$.*

1. *For nodes $< s, i >$ and $< s, i+1 >$, there exists $< s, i > \Longrightarrow < s, i+1 >$. N denotes the set of nodes.*
2. *Let $s_1 \in \sum$ and $s_2 \in \sum$, if $term(< s_1, i >) = +a$ and $term(< s_2, j >) = -a$, then there exists $< s_1, i > \longrightarrow < s_2, j >$.*
3. *For $s \in \sum$, there must be a node that is active on s, and if the active node is the last one of s, then s is a complete strand, or s is still in the progress of execution. A strand with active node is called dynamic strand.*

So dynamic strand space is a dynamic graph $(N, Active, (\Longrightarrow \cup \longrightarrow))$ where $Active$ is the set of active nodes in the strand space.

Definition 10. *A bundle is subgraph of strand space, denoted by $C = (N_c, (\Longrightarrow \cup \longrightarrow))$, and the following properties hold :*

1. *If $< s, i > \in C$, then $\forall n \in s, n \in C$.*
2. *If $< s_1, i > \in C$ and $< s_1, i > \longrightarrow < s_2, j >$ hold, then $< s_2, j > \in C$.*

This definition is different from the one in [9], and it is more suitable to construct bundles automatically.

2.3   Computation Model of Security Protocol

In this subsection, we describe a computation model of security protocol used in this paper that is based on dynamic strand space model and exploited by forward state space exploration. The state structure of this model define as follows :

Definition 11. *A state is a tuple $< C, Active, I, \longrightarrow >$, where*

1. *C is a bundle, and it become complete until the final state is reached, or it is an illegal bundle. An incomplete bundle means that there are some negative nodes in strand but no edge $\longrightarrow$ incident with it. An illegal bundle is an incomplete one that can not become complete from the current state. At the first state, C just contains an intruder strand that is empty.*
2. *$Active$ is the set of active nodes in bundle C, and each strand in C can has an active node. At final state, $Active$ is empty. The active node is mainly used to determine the accepted term of each strand in C.*
3. *I is an intruder model that will be described in the next section.*
4. *$\longrightarrow$ is a binary relation. For $n_1 \in C$ and $n_2 \in C$, if $n_1 \longrightarrow n_2$, then $(n_1, n_2) \in C$, so $\longrightarrow$ help us to keep track of the evolution of the bundle C, thus when the final state is reached, we can complete the bundle and get an attack to this protocol if it exists. At the initial state, $\longrightarrow$ is empty.*

Proposition 1. *If $Active$ is empty in a state $< C, Active, I, \longrightarrow >$, then this state is a final state and by substituting $\longrightarrow$ of this state for $\longrightarrow$ in C, we can get a complete bundle. If C contains the intruder strand, then it is an attack, or it is a regular bundle.*

3   Formulate the Intruder Model

In this section, we will give the intruder model that is more intelligent than the algebraic intruder model in the literatures. This intruder model still take full control over the communication network, and it can do everything Dolev-Yao intruder is allowed to do, so it is al least as powerful as Dolev-Yao intruder model. Moreover, it has the ability to decide when to generate what terms and decide whether or not to initiate a new session with a principal and how to choose the principal as well as what roles the principal will play.

3.1   The Structure of the Intruder Model

The structure of intelligent intruder model consists of three parts, that is terms processor, rule bases and knowledge bases. Fig.1 gives its structure. There are

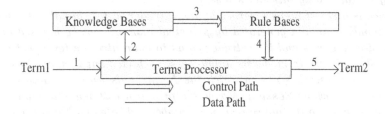

Fig. 1. The Structure of Intelligent Intruder Model

five direct edges in the structure, and the direct edge can indicate the direction of information flow. The edge 1 represent that terms in network are intercepted by intruder, and by terms processor, the intruder can decompose these terms and put these terms' elements into its knowledge bases by the edge 2. According to the state of knowledge bases by edge 3, rule bases decide what action the intruder will take, and this is done by edge 4. If the intruder need to generate new terms, then terms generator get the terms element needed from knowledge bases by edge 2, that is edge 2 is bidirection. At last, the new term is sent to network by edge 5, so the term1 and term2 in figure 2 maybe are different, but also can be same, and in this case the intruder does nothing to the term.

In addition, the edges can be divided into two classes, control path and data path. In figure 1, edge 1, 2, and 5 are data paths in which real terms are transmitted; edge 3, 4 are control paths which can transmit control information such as the information used to decide what term is generated by Intruder.

3.2   Knowledge Bases

Knowledge bases in the intelligent model contain the information known up to now by the intruder during the execution procedure of the protocol. Below we will introduce the structure of knowledge bases.

Definition 12. *Knowledge bases is a tuple* $< PS, Key, Nonce, Msg >$, *where*

1. *PS contains the state information related to the corresponding participants, and it is a set and each element in which is $< Name, Role, Session >$, where the Name is the principal's identifier, $Name \in S_{name}$. And Role indicates what role the principal will play which decides a strand for this principal, such as initiator strand or responder strand. Session can distinguish the different instances the same principal takes part in because the same principal maybe appear many times in the same bundle. At initial state, PS is empty.*
2. *Key is the set of keys known by the intruder which includes all principals' public keys, and the keys owned by the intruder, such as his private hey or shared keys with other honest principals. Each element in Key is a predicate, that is, $k := pubKA|privKA|shKAB$ where A and B are the principal variable that can be instantiated by any principal in PS and three predicate represent public key, private key or shared key respectively. At initial state, Key contains only intruder's keys.*
3. *Nonce is a set of nonces learned by the intruder in this bundle. An nonce is the number random generated by principal and can not be guessed by non-intended receivers and the intruder so as to guarantee the term just received is fresh. In order to model its uniqueness, each element is defined as a tuple $< Name, Session, No >$ in which the Name tells which principal produce the nonce in which Session. Maybe the principal will generate many nonces in one strand, so the nonce sequence number indicated by No can model this case. At last, the Name must belong to PS or be the intruder itself. At initial state, Nonce contains nothing.*
4. *Msg is the set of compound terms that can not be divided into atomic terms by intruder according to its knowledge for example the intruder lacks of the suitable decryption key for a encrypted term. At initial state, Msg is empty.*

Knowledge bases are dynamic during the protocol execution that need to be updated when the intruder intercepts new terms or the intruder initiates a new session. And the update rules will be describe in the following two sections.

3.3   Terms Processor

Terms processor is composed of two parts, and one is terms decomposer, the other terms composer. Terms decomposer can divide the terms intercepted from network into the smallest terms, and it may not be the atomic terms. Terms composer is used to generate the new terms from the knowledge the intruder has known up to now. Moreover, the first part is a decidable procedure, that is, given a term, it can be divided into subterms in a unique way, and the latter is undecidable because the intruder can generate infinite new terms from the current knowledge bases by using encryption and composition operations infinite times.

Four rules are used to decompose the intercepted terms by terms decomposer, called decomposition rules. Let m be the intercepted terms, $k \in S_{ks} \cup S_{kp}$, and

Key the key set in knowledge bases. The $Decomposition(m)$ function based on these rules looks as following:

procedure $Decomposition(m)$

{

    if $m \in A$, then $Add(m)$;

    If $m = m_1 \cdot m_2$, then $Add(m_1)$ and $Add(m_2)$;

    If $m = m\prime_k$ and $k^{-1} \notin Key$, then $Add(m\prime)$;

    If $m = m\prime_k$ and $k^{-1} \in Key$, then $Add(m)$;

}

The function $Add(m)$ adds a term m to the knowledge bases that can be defined as the following:

procedure Add(m)

{

    if $m \in S_{name}$, then

        add nothing; //the PS is update when protocol instances is created.

    if $m \in S_{nonce}$, then

        add m to set $Nonce$ by the proper form;

    if $m \in S_{ks} \cup S_{kp}$, then

        add m to set Key by the proper form;

        for each $t \in Msg$,

            $decomposition(t)$;

    otherwise,

        add m to set Msg.

}

The process of generating a new term is very complex, and it needs a term template to decide what kind of terms to produce. The term space can be used as the template, so it is critical to get a finite $space(m)$. The basic composition rules are defined as follows:

Definition 13. *Let I indicate the union of all sets in knowledge bases, then*

1. *If $I \vdash m$, $m \in I$; (extend meaning)*
2. *If $I \vdash m_1$ and $I \vdash m_2$, then $I \vdash m_1 \cdot m_2$;*
3. *If $I \vdash m$ and $I \vdash k$, then $I \vdash m_k$;*

In fact, we can decompose each element in $space(m)$ according to the knowledge bases of the intruder, and if all subterms can be found in the corresponding set of the knowledge bases, then this element can be generated by intruder using its known knowledge.

If term m can be derived from the knowledge bases of the intruder, there exist a unique normal derivation only if every decomposition rule occurs before every composition rule [5], so term decomposer should be used before term composer in order to get a unique derivation.

3.4   Rule Bases

Rule bases are the just part related to the intelligence of the intruder. Some researcher have presented some principles for security protocol design [14] that can be used to enhance the intruder's intelligence. In this subsection, we will describe the rules used by intruder to decide when to generate what terms and decide whether or not to initiate a new session with a principal and how to choose the principal as well as what role the principal will play.

The temporal feature of the protocol execution in the state exploration method introduced in this paper is characterized by the set of active node in a state each element in which can decide the term accepted by the involved participant, so for each term t decided by an active node, $space(t)$ indicates the set of terms acceptable to the corresponding participant with the different attack effects.

In our model, the protocol execution must be launched by the intruder. At each time, the intruder initiates a new session, it will update the principal state PS in knowledge bases, that is, the principal name, its role and the session it is taking part in as well as the set Key by adding its public key. If it launch a new session with the principal as a responder, then it will impersonate the initiator and if as an initiator, it will play the responder role.

Moreover, the following rules are used to initiate a new session, called *strand-added rules*, that is, adding a strand to the set C in a state which are drawn from [14,15,16].

- Man-in-middle attack.If the intruder intercepts the first term from initiator, then it will produce the next states by adding the responder strand with its owner other than initiator principal; Moreover, $space(t)$ where t is the term described in parametric responder strand is used to characterize the terms for the different responder strand instances and each results in a different successive state. For examples, naming attack in [14] and attack on case c in [16] belong to this case.
- No responder attack. If the intruder intercepts the first term from initiator, then it will produce the successive states by adding the responder strands with its owner same to initiator principal; Similarly, $space(t)$ is used to characterize the terms for the different responder strand instances. The attacks for this case include parallel session attacks in [15].
- No initiator attack. In this case, the intruder impersonates the initiator without invoving the initiator in protocol execution such as attack on B in [16] and freshness attacks in [15]. And, $space(t)$ is still used to produce the different responder strand instances.

Certainly, the above rules can not cover all attack patterns, but the new pattern can be afforded easily. In the first case, the intruder has to generate appropriate terms for initiator and responder at the same time that is man-in-middle attack. In the second case, the intruder disguises as a responder talking to initiator and no real responder is present. At last case, the intruder impersonates the initiator to talk with responder.

3.5 Discussions about the Intelligent Intruder

The intelligent intruder takes the full control over the network like Dolev-Yao intruder, and also have the algebraic ability to intercept, remember and generate new messages, so it is as powerful as Dolev-Yao intruder. In present protocol analysis methods based on model checking, some protocol parameters, such as the numbers of principal, have to be configured previously in order to get a finite state space. As a result, if no attacks are found, it just prove the protocol is correct under this small configuration, that is, it can not guarantee the correctness of general protocol execution. Depending on the term space, the intelligent intruder can help to limit the numbers of the terms to generate at a protocol execution step, that is to bind the numbers of types of bundle for the security protocols. And using strand added rules, the intelligent intruder can limit the bundle size by just adding a new strand with different attack effect, that is, with different attack patterns. Thus, it can help to get a finite state space by limiting the bundle types and bundle size without an explicit configuration, so it is more flexible to protocol analysis methods based on state space exploration. Moreover, the rules used by intruder to add strand can be extended easily when some new attack patterns are found in the future.

4 Conclusion

In this paper, we propose an intruder model that is more intelligent compared to the algebraic Dolev-Yao intruder model. The intruder model is introduced under the state space exploration method based on dynamic strand space model. Original strand space model is static, that is, it can not model the dynamic procedure of protocol execution. Here, we introduce active node to make it dynamic. The state includes the bundle, during the protocol execution, the strand was added to this bundle gradually and at final state, it will indicate a protocol execution. The intelligent intruder is composed of knowledge bases, rule bases and terms processor, and controls the evolution of bundle. It can decide when to generate what terms according to the term space of active node set in a state and decide whether or not to initiate a new session with a principal and what roles the principal will play based on some rules. By this heuristic method, we can get a finite state space without the explicit configuration needed by many model checking tools.

References

1. Anderson, R., Needham, R.: Programming Satan's computer. In J. van Leeuwen, editor, Computer Science Today: Recent Trends and Developments, LNCS 1000, Springer. (1995) 426–440
2. Lowe, G.: An attack on the Needham-Schroeder public key authentication protocol. Information Processing Letter. **56(3)** (1995) 131–136
3. Burrows, M., Abadi, M., Needham, R.: A logic of authentication. Proceedings of the Royal Society of London. (1989) 233-271

4. Kindred, D., Wing, J.: Fast, automatic checking of security protocols. In USENIX 2nd Workshop on Electronic Commerce. (1996)
5. Clarke, E., Jha, S., Marrero, W.: Using state space exploration and a natural style message derivation engine to verify security protocols. In Proceedings of the IFIP Working Conference on Programming Concepts and Methods. (1998)
6. Lowe, G.: Breaking and fixing the Needham-Schroeder public-key protocol using CSP and FDR. In T. Margaria, and B. Steffen, editors, Tools and Algorithms for the Constructions and Analysis of Systems. Second International Workshop, TACAS'96, LNCS 1055. (1996) 147–166
7. Mitchell, C., Mitchell, M., Stern, U.: Automated analysis of cryptographic protocols using murϕ. In Proceedings the 1997 IEEE Symposium on Security and Privacy. IEEE Computer Society Press. (1997)
8. Pauson, L.: Proving properties of security protocols by induction. In proceedings of the 1997 IEEE Computer Society Symposium on Research in Security and Privacy. (1997) 70–83
9. Thayer, F., Herzog, J., Guttman J.: Strand spaces: Why is a security protocol correct? In Proceedings of 1998 IEEE Symposium on Security and Privacy. (1998)
10. Dolev, D., Yao, A.: On the security of public-key protocols. IEEE Transactions on Information Theory.**29** (1983) 198–208
11. Cervesato, I., Durgin, N., Lincoln, P., Mitchell, J., Scedrov, A.: A meta-notation for protocol analysis. In P. Syverson, editor, Proceedings of the 12th IEEE Computer Security Foundations Workshop, IEEE Computer Society Press, Mordano, Italy. (1999) 55–69
12. Syverson, P., Meadows, C.: Dolev-Yao is no better than Machiavelli. First Workshop on Issues in the Theory of Security — WITS'00, Geneva, Switzerland. (2000) 87–92
13. Song, D.: Athena: a new efficient automatic checker for security protocol analysis. In P. Syverson, editor, Proceedings of the 12th IEEE Computer Security Foundations Workshop, Mordano, Italy, IEEE Computer Society Press. (1999) 192–202
14. Abadi, M., Needham, R.: Prudent engineering practice for cryptographic protocols. IEEE Transactions on Software Engineering. **22(1)** (1996) 6–15
15. Clark, J., Jacob, J.: A survey of authentication protocol literature. Available at http://www.cs.york.ac.uk/ jac.
16. Mitchell, J., Shmatikov, V., Stern, V.: Finite-state analysis of SSL 3.0. In Seventh USENIX Security Symposium. (1998) 201–216

Primitive Polynomials over GF(2) – A Cryptologic Approach

Kishan Chand Gupta[1] and Subhamoy Maitra[2]

[1] Applied Statistics Unit, Indian Statistical Institute,
203, B T Road, Calcutta 700 035, INDIA
kishan_t@isical.ac.in

[2] Computer and Statistical Service Center, Indian Statistical Institute,
203, B T Road, Calcutta 700 035, INDIA
subho@isical.ac.in

Abstract. Linear Feedback Shift Registers (LFSR) are important building blocks in stream cipher systems. The connection polynomials of the LFSRs need to be primitive over GF(2). Also the polynomial should have high weight and it should not have sparse multiples of moderate degree. Here we provide results which have immediate application in synthesis of connection polynomials for stream cipher systems. We show that, given any primitive polynomial $f(x)$ of degree d there exists $2^{d-1} - 1$ many distinct trinomial multiples of degree less than $2^d - 1$. Among these trinomial multiples, it is known that a trinomial of the form $x^{\frac{2}{3}(2^d-1)} + x^{\frac{1}{3}(2^d-1)} + 1$ contains all the degree d (d even) primitive polynomials as its factors. We extend this result by showing that, if d_1 (even) divides d (even) and $\frac{2^d-1}{3} \not\equiv 0 \bmod (2^{d_1} - 1)$, then the trinomial $x^{\frac{2}{3}(2^d-1)} + x^{\frac{1}{3}(2^d-1)} + 1$ contains all the primitive polynomials of degree d_1 as its factor. We also discuss algorithmic issues in getting trinomial multiples of low degree. Next we present some results on t-nomial multiples of primitive polynomials which help us in choosing primitive polynomials that do not have sparse multiples.

Keywords: *Primitive Polynomials, Cyclotomic Cosets, Galois field, Stream Cipher.*

1 Introduction

A standard model of stream cipher [14,15,1] combines the outputs of several independent Linear Feedback Shift Register (LFSR) sequences using a nonlinear Boolean function to produce the keystream. This keystream is bitwise XORed with the message bitstream to produce the cipher. The decryption machinery is identical to the encryption machinery. The properties of the nonlinear combining Boolean function received a lot of attention in literature for the last two decades and it is now possible to get good Boolean functions which are cryptographically strong (see [13] and the references in this paper). However, here we will be looking into the other building block of such a system, the LFSRs. We concentrate on

S. Qing, T. Okamoto, and J. Zhou (Eds.): ICICS 2001, LNCS 2229, pp. 23–34, 2001.
© Springer-Verlag Berlin Heidelberg 2001

the problems evolved from the design criteria of the LFSRs in stream cipher system.

The connection polynomial of the LFSRs are the polynomials over GF(2). The relationship between this polynomial and the connection pattern of the LFSR is explained in [2,1,12]. It is important to note that towards resisting cryptanalytic attacks, the LFSRs should be designed keeping the following points in mind [11,5].

1. The connection polynomial must be primitive over GF(2).
2. The weight of the connection polynomial must be high.
3. There should not be any sparse multiple of moderate degree for the connection polynomial.

It is also important to point out that if we use such polynomials with these properties, then it is also not possible to cryptanalyse the standard model [14, 15,1] even with the currently known techniques (see [7] and the references in this paper).

Our motivation in this effort is to find out polynomials with these properties. In a recent work [5], similar problem was posed and it has been shown that for a primitive polynomial $f(x)$ of degree d, it may have a trinomial multiple or not, i.e., it was not clearly mentioned whether such trinomials will exist or not for any primitive polynomial $f(x)$ of degree d. We here completely settle the issue by showing that given any primitive polynomial $f(x)$ of degree d there exists $(2^{d-1} - 1)$ many distinct trinomial multiples. It is known [3] that a trinomial of the form $x^{\frac{2}{3}(2^d-1)} + x^{\frac{1}{3}(2^d-1)} + 1$ contains all the degree d (d even) primitive polynomials as its factors. We generalize the result by proving that, if d_1 (even) divides d (even) and $\frac{2^d-1}{3} \not\equiv 0 \bmod (2^{d_1} - 1)$, then the trinomial $x^{\frac{2}{3}(2^d-1)} + x^{\frac{1}{3}(2^d-1)} + 1$ contains all the primitive polynomials of degree d_1 as its factor. We also provide some results on finding trinomial multiples of low degree.

Apart from these results, we identify a large class of primitive polynomials of high weight which have sparse multiples at a very low degree. If $f(x)$ is a primitive t-nomial of degree d, then there exists a t-nomial multiple of degree sd where $\gcd(s, 2^d - 1) = 1$. As example, we show that there are trinomial multiples of degree $3d$ for a large class of primitive polynomials of degree d. This helps in providing a specific design strategy for the primitive polynomials to be used in stream cipher systems.

At this point we also like to mention the problem of finding Zech's logarithm. Given a primitive element $\alpha \in GF(2^d)$, we can write $1 + \alpha^n = \alpha^{Z(n)}$. Given n, calculation of $Z(n)$ is called the problem of finding Zech's logarithm [10, Page 91, Volume 1]. This problem [6,4,3] is related to the problem of getting trinomial multiples of a primitive polynomial.

2   Preliminaries

In this section we make precise certain terms and also present some basic results. Most of these concepts are taken from [9,10]. We will denote the field of p elements (p is prime) by $GF(p)$ and by $GF(p^d)$ we will denote the extention field of dimension d over $GF(p)$. In this paper base field is $GF(2)$ if not otherwise stated.

Definition 1. *For every prime p and positive integer d there is exactly one finite field (up to isomorphism) of order p^d. This field $GF(p^d)$ is usually referred to as the Galois Field of order p^d, and p is called the characteristics of $GF(p^d)$. The non zero elements of $GF(p^d)$ forms a cyclic group under multiplication. So it will have a generator α which will generate all the elements of $GF(p^d)$ except zero and $\alpha^{p^d-1} = 1$. For example if $p = 2$ and $d = 4$, $GF(2^4) = \{0, \alpha^0, \alpha^1, \alpha^2, \ldots, \alpha^{14}\}$.*

Definition 2. *A polynomial is irreducible over a field if it is not the product of two polynomials of lower degree in the field. For example $x^4 + x + 1$ is irreducible polynomial of degree four over $GF(2)$ but $x^4 + x^2 + 1$ is not irreducible because $x^4 + x^2 + 1 = (x^2 + x + 1)^2$.*

Definition 3. *An irreducible polynomial of degree d is called primitive polynomial if its roots are the generator of the field $GF(p^d)$. It can be proved that there are $\frac{\phi(p^d-1)}{d}$ number of primitive polynomials, where ϕ is Euler phi-function. For example if $p = 2$ and $d = 4$, $\frac{\phi(2^4-1)}{4} = 2$, i.e., there exists exactly two primitive polynomials of degree 4 over $GF(2)$.*

Euler phi-function is defined for positive integer m by $\phi(m) = s$, where s is the number of positive integer less than or equal to m that are relatively prime to m. For example if $m = 15$ then 1, 2, 4, 7, 8, 11, 13, 14 are relatively prime to 15 and so $\phi(15) = 8$. A well known result [10, Chapter 4, Page 98] from number theory is $\phi(m) = m \prod_{i=1}^{N}(1 - \frac{1}{p_i})$, where $m = p_1^{\alpha_1} p_2^{\alpha_2} \ldots p_N^{\alpha_N}$.

Definition 4. *Let $f(x)$ be a polynomial of degree $d \geq 1$. with $f(0) \neq 0$ then there exists a least positive integer $e \leq p^d - 1$ such that $f(x)$ divides $x^e - 1$. i.e. $x^e \equiv 1 \bmod f(x)$. This e is called exponent/order of the polynomial and we say the polynomial $f(x)$ belongs to exponent e.*

It can be proved that if $f(x)$ is primitive polynomial of degree d then $e = 2^d - 1$. Thus for a primitive polynomial $x^4 + x + 1$, we have $e = 15$. However, the result is not similar for irreducible polynomials. As example, the irreducible polynomial $x^4 + x^3 + x^2 + x + 1$ belongs to exponent 5, since $x^5 \equiv 1 \bmod (x^4 + x^3 + x^2 + x + 1)$.

Definition 5. *The operation of multiplying by p divides the integers $\bmod (p^d - 1)$ into different sets called cyclotomic cosets $\bmod (p^d - 1)$. The cyclotomic coset containing s consists of $\{s, ps, p^2s, \ldots, p^{d_s-1}s\}$ where d_s is the smallest positive integer such that $p^{d_s} \cdot s \equiv s \bmod (p^d - 1)$. Note that d_s is called the length of the cyclotomic coset $\bmod (p^d - 1)$.*

The set of all cyclotomic cosets $\bmod (2^6 - 1)$, where $p = 2$ are as follows.

$C_0 = \{0\}$ $C_1 = \{1, 2, 4, 8, 16, 32\}$ $C_3 = \{3, 6, 12, 24, 48, 33\}$
$C_5 = \{5, 10, 20, 40, 17, 34\}$ $C_7 = \{7, 14, 28, 56, 49, 35\}$ $C_9 = \{9, 18, 36\}$
$C_{11} = \{11, 22, 44, 25, 50, 37\}$ $C_{13} = \{13, 26, 52, 41, 19, 38\}$ $C_{15} = \{15, 30, 60, 57, 51, 39\}$
$C_{21} = \{21, 42\}$ $C_{23} = \{23, 46, 29, 58, 53, 43\}$ $C_{27} = \{27, 54, 45\}$
$C_{31} = \{31, 62, 61, 59, 55, 47\}$

Definition 6. *Let $\beta \in GF(p^d)$. The minimal polynomial over $GF(p)$ of β is the lowest degree monic (has leading coefficient 1) polynomial $M(x)$ with coefficient from $GF(p)$ s.t. $M(\beta) = 0$.*

Some properties of minimal polynomial are as follows. (1) $M(x)$ is irreducible over $GF(p)$. (2) If $f(x)$ be a polynomial with coefficient in $GF(p)$ and $f(\beta) = 0$ then $M(x) \mid f(x)$. (3) $M(x) \mid x^{p^d} - x$. (4) deg $M(x) \leq d$. (5) The minimal polynomial of a primitive element of $GF(p^d)$ has degree d. Such a polynomial is called a primitive polynomial.

Definition 7. *A polynomial with t non zero terms, one of them being the constant term is called t-nomial, or in other words a polynomial of weight t.*

As example, $x^s + x^t + 1$ is 3-nomial (trinomial), and $x^s + x^t + x^r + 1$ is a 4-nomial or a polynomial of weight 4. Note that, in literature, by a polynomial with *sparse* weight generally means $t \leq 10$ [11, Page 160].

As we have already discussed, a primitive polynomial can be written in the form $x^d + \sum_{i=0}^{d-1} a_i x^i$, where $a_i \in \{0, 1\}$. Let this polynomial is of weight t. When we use this polynomial as a connection polynomial of an LFSR, the implementation will have $(t - 1)$ taps in the circuit.

3   Trinomial Results

In this section we provide results related to trinomial multiples of primitive polynomials.

Theorem 1. *Let $f(x)$ be a primitive polynomial of degree d. Then there exists a trinomial $x^i + x^j + 1$ which is divisible by $f(x)$.*

Proof. Let $f(x)$ be a primitive polynomial over GF(2) of degree d. Let α be a root of it. So α is a primitive element of $GF(2^d)$. As $f(x)$ is primitive its exponent $e = 2^d - 1$. Now $\alpha^i \in GF(2^d)$, for any $i, 1 \leq i < e$. So $1 + \alpha^i \in GF(2^d)$, which gives, $1 + \alpha^i = \alpha^j$ for some $j \neq i, 1 \leq j < e$. Hence, $1 + \alpha^i + \alpha^j = 0$. Thus, α is the root of the trinomial $1 + x^i + x^j$. As $f(x)$ is the minimal polynomial of α, it must divide $x^i + x^j + 1$.   □

Corollary 1. *Given a primitive polynomial $f(x)$ of degree d, there will be $(2^{d-1} - 1)$ distinct trinomial (of degree $< 2^d - 1$) multiples of $f(x)$.*

Proof. We consider the trinomials of the form $1 + x^i + x^j$. We need to choose the value of i. Now, $1 \leq i < e = 2^d - 1$. So there are $2^d - 2$ options for i. Now for each i, we will get some $j \neq i, 1 \leq j < e$ such that $1 + \alpha^i = \alpha^j$. Also we can interchange the role of i, j. Thus, there are $\frac{2^d - 2}{2}$ such trinomials.   □

Note that the way we have found the trinomials here is dependent on the primitive polynomial. Thus given the value of i, such that $1 + \alpha^i = \alpha^j$, the value of j will be fixed depending on the primitive element α, which in turn depends on the specific primitive polynomial. However, it is possible that one trinomial may have more than one primitive polynomials of same degree as its factors. In fact, we know [3] that for even d, it is possible to get a trinomial which has all the primitive polynomials of degree d as its factors.

First let us discuss a few technical points. We take the prime factorization $d = p_1^{a_1} p_2^{a_2} \dots p_N^{a_N}$. The cyclotomic coset of length l containing s consists of $\{s, 2s, 2^2 s, \dots, 2^{l-1} s\}$ where l is the smallest positive integer such that $2^l \cdot s \equiv s \bmod (2^d - 1)$. So, $s \cdot (2^l - 1) \equiv 0 \bmod (2^d - 1)$. Now we provide a proof for the following folklore result for clarity.

Proposition 1. *Cyclotomic cosets of length l exists iff l divides d.*

Proof. First we prove that if l divides d, then cyclotomic cosets of length l exists. Suppose l divides d but a cyclotomic coset of length l does not exist, i.e., there does not exist an integer $s, 0 < s < 2^d - 1$, satisfying $s \cdot (2^l - 1) \equiv 0 \bmod (2^d - 1)$ (see Definition 5). This is false as we can get an integer $s = \frac{2^d - 1}{2^l - 1}$ satisfying $s \cdot (2^l - 1) \equiv 0 \bmod (2^d - 1)$. Hence we land into a contradiction. Note that, as l divides d, we get, $2^l - 1$ divides $2^d - 1$ [10, Volume 1, Chapter 4, Page 103], which gives s is an integer.

Now we prove the other direction, i.e. if a cyclotomic coset $\bmod (2^d - 1)$ of length l exists then l must divide d. Let $\gcd(l, d) = r \le l$. Then $\gcd(2^l - 1, 2^d - 1) = 2^r - 1$ [10, Volume 1, Chapter 4, Page 103]. For cyclotomic cosets of length l we know $s \cdot (2^l - 1) \equiv 0 \bmod (2^d - 1)$, where $0 < s < 2^d - 1$. Therefore, $s \cdot \frac{(2^l - 1)}{(2^r - 1)} \equiv 0 \bmod \frac{(2^d - 1)}{(2^r - 1)}$. Now, as $\gcd(\frac{(2^l - 1)}{(2^r - 1)}, \frac{(2^d - 1)}{(2^r - 1)}) = 1$, $s \equiv 0 \bmod \frac{(2^d - 1)}{(2^r - 1)}$, i.e. $s \cdot (2^r - 1) \equiv 0 \bmod (2^d - 1)$. Again, l is the smallest positive integer satisfying $s \cdot (2^l - 1) \equiv 0 \bmod (2^d - 1)$, so $r = l$. Thus, l divides d. $\qquad\square$

In particular, we can easily find out the number of cyclotomic cosets of prime length. The number of cyclotomic cosets of prime length p_k is $\frac{2^{p_k} - 2}{p_k}$. This is proved as follows. As $p_k \mid d$, $2^{p_k} - 1 \mid 2^d - 1$. Let $y = \frac{2^d - 1}{2^{p_k} - 1}$. Now, $s \cdot 2^{p_k} \equiv s \bmod (2^d - 1)$. Thus, $s \cdot (2^{p_k} - 1) \equiv 0 \bmod (2^d - 1)$ which gives, $s \equiv 0 \bmod y$. As $\gcd(2^{p_k} - 1, 2^d - 1) = 2^{p_k} - 1$, s will have $2^{p_k} - 1$ solutions $\bmod (2^d - 1)$ [8, page 32]. One solution of s is 0, so number of nonzero solutions are $2^{p_k} - 2$. Cyclotomic cosets of length p_k has p_k elements and hence the number of cyclotomic cosets of length p_k is $\frac{2^{p_k} - 2}{p_k}$.

Next we present the following known result [3]. We also provide a detailed proof for clarity.

Theorem 2. *Let $f(x)$ be a primitive polynomial over GF(2) of even degree d. Then the trinomial $x^{\frac{2}{3}(2^d - 1)} + x^{\frac{1}{3}(2^d - 1)} + 1$ is divisible by $f(x)$.*

Proof. Let $x^i + x^j + 1$ be a trinomial multiple of $f(x)$. We know that [3] (see also [5, Theorem 3]) the values i, j belong to same length cyclotomic coset ($\bmod (2^d - 1)$). Now we consider the cyclotomic coset of length 2. From the above discussion, the number of cyclotomic coset of length 2 is $\frac{2^2 - 2}{2} = 1$ and the cyclotomic coset is $\{\frac{1}{3}(2^d - 1), \frac{2}{3}(2^d - 1)\}$.

Let $f(x)$ be a primitive polynomial over GF(2) of degree d. Let α be a root of it. So α is a primitive element of $GF(2^d)$. As $f(x)$ is a primitive polynomial its exponent $e = 2^d - 1$. Now $\alpha^i \in GF(2^d)$, for any $i, 1 \le i < e$. Here we choose

$i = \frac{1}{3}(2^d - 1)$. So, $1 + \alpha^i \in GF(2^d)$ which gives $1 + \alpha^i = \alpha^j$ for some $j, 1 \leq j < e$ and $j \neq i$. So α is the root of the trinomial $1 + x^i + x^j$. Since $f(x)$ is the minimal polynomial of α, $f(x) \mid x^i + x^j + 1$. Now as the values i, j must belong to [5, Theorem 3] same length cyclotomic coset mod $(2^d - 1)$ and $i = \frac{1}{3}(2^d - 1)$, j must be $\frac{2}{3}(2^d - 1)$. Thus $f(x)$ divides $x^{\frac{2}{3}(2^d - 1)} + x^{\frac{1}{3}(2^d - 1)} + 1$.   □

Note that, this trinomial is not dependent on any specific primitive polynomial of degree d. So all the primitive polynomials of degree d will divide this trinomial.

Corollary 2. *For d even, the trinomial $x^{\frac{2}{3}(2^d - 1)} + x^{\frac{1}{3}(2^d - 1)} + 1$ contains all the primitive polynomials of degree d as its factors.*

For any d, we are aware about the polynomial $x^{2^d - 1} + 1$ which contains all the primitive polynomials of degree d as its factors [9]. Note that for even d, the polynomial $x^{\frac{2}{3}(2^d - 1)} + x^{\frac{1}{3}(2^d - 1)} + 1$ also has all the primitive polynomials as its factors and it is of lower degree than $x^{2^d - 1} + 1$. The multiplication of $\frac{\phi(2^d - 1)}{d}$ many different primitive polynomials of degree d gives total multiplication degree $\phi(2^d - 1)$. So there will be some other polynomials whose multiple will contribute the degree $\frac{2}{3}(2^d - 1) - \phi(2^d - 1)$.

Example 1. The trinomial $x^{\frac{2}{3}(2^d - 1)} + x^{\frac{1}{3}(2^d - 1)} + 1$ for $d = 8$, is $x^{170} + x^{85} + 1$. When we factorize $x^{170} + x^{85} + 1$, we get the following factors of which the first 16 give the complete list of primitive polynomials of degree 8.
$(1 + x^2 + x^3 + x^4 + x^8)$, $(1 + x + x^3 + x^5 + x^8)$, $(1 + x^2 + x^3 + x^5 + x^8)$, $(1 + x^2 + x^3 + x^6 + x^8)$, $(1 + x + x^2 + x^3 + x^4 + x^6 + x^8)$, $(1 + x + x^5 + x^6 + x^8)$, $(1 + x^2 + x^5 + x^6 + x^8)$, $(1 + x^3 + x^5 + x^6 + x^8)$, $(1 + x^4 + x^5 + x^6 + x^8)$, $(1 + x + x^2 + x^7 + x^8)$, $(1 + x^2 + x^3 + x^7 + x^8)$, $(1 + x^3 + x^5 + x^7 + x^8)$, $(1 + x + x^6 + x^7 + x^8)$, $(1 + x + x^2 + x^3 + x^6 + x^7 + x^8)$, $(1 + x + x^2 + x^5 + x^6 + x^7 + x^8)$, $(1 + x^2 + x^4 + x^5 + x^6 + x^7 + x^8)$, $(1 + x + x^2)$, $(1 + x + x^4)$, $(1 + x^3 + x^4)$, $(1 + x^4 + x^5 + x^7 + x^8)$, $(1 + x + x^3 + x^4 + x^8)$, $(1 + x + x^2 + x^3 + x^4 + x^7 + x^8)$, $(1 + x + x^4 + x^5 + x^6 + x^7 + x^8)$.

In the above example we also have an interesting observation. We find that apart from the primitive polynomials of degree 8, we also have the exhaustive list of primitive polynomials of degree 4 and 2. In this direction we provide the following extension of Theorem 2.

Theorem 3. *If d_1 (even) divides d (even) and $\frac{2^d - 1}{3} \not\equiv 0 \mod (2^{d_1} - 1)$, then the trinomial $x^{\frac{2}{3}(2^d - 1)} + x^{\frac{1}{3}(2^d - 1)} + 1$ contains all the primitive polynomials of degree d_1 as its factor.*

Proof. We have d_1 divides d. Hence $2^{d_1} - 1$ divides $2^d - 1$. Also both d_1, d are even and hence 3 divides both $2^{d_1} - 1$ and $2^d - 1$. Thus, we get $\frac{2^{d_1} - 1}{3}$ divides $\frac{2^d - 1}{3}$. Also we have $2^{d_1} - 1$ does not divide $\frac{2^d - 1}{3}$. Hence, $\frac{2^d - 1}{3} \mod (2^{d_1} - 1)$ is either $\frac{1}{3}(2^{d_1} - 1)$ or $\frac{2}{3}(2^{d_1} - 1)$.

Now consider any primitive polynomial $f_1(x)$ of degree d_1. Here, $x^{\frac{2}{3}(2^d - 1)} + x^{\frac{1}{3}(2^d - 1)} + 1 \mod f_1(x)$ is equal to $x^{\frac{2}{3}(2^d - 1) \mod (2^{d_1} - 1)} + x^{\frac{1}{3}(2^d - 1) \mod (2^{d_1} - 1)} +$

1 mod $f_1(x)$, as exponent of $f_1(x)$ is $2^{d_1} - 1$ [9]. Since, $\frac{2^d - 1}{3}$ mod $(2^{d_1} - 1)$ is either $\frac{1}{3}(2^{d_1} - 1)$ or $\frac{2}{3}(2^{d_1} - 1)$, we get $x^{\frac{2}{3}(2^d - 1)} \bmod (2^{d_1} - 1) + x^{\frac{1}{3}(2^d - 1)} \bmod (2^{d_1} - 1) + 1$ mod $f_1(x)$ equals to $x^{\frac{2}{3}(2^{d_1} - 1)} + x^{\frac{1}{3}(2^{d_1} - 1)} + 1$ mod $f_1(x)$ which is zero by Theorem 2. Thus, we get that any primitive polynomial $f_1(x)$ of degree d_1 divides $x^{\frac{2}{3}(2^d - 1)} + x^{\frac{1}{3}(2^d - 1)} + 1$. Hence, all primitive polynomials of degree d_1 divide $x^{\frac{2}{3}(2^d - 1)} + x^{\frac{1}{3}(2^d - 1)} + 1$. □

Corollary 3. *Let* $d = 2^k$. *Then any primitive polynomial of degree* $d_1 = 2^j$, $0 \le j \le k$ *will divide* $x^{\frac{2}{3}(2^d - 1)} + x^{\frac{1}{3}(2^d - 1)} + 1$.

Proof. The proof follows from the above theorem noting that $\frac{2^d - 1}{3} \not\equiv 0$ mod $(2^{d_1} - 1)$. □

Theorem 2, Theorem 3 and Corollary 2 have been considered only even d only. Thus, in this case, given any primitive polynomial we have a specific construction of its trinomial multiple. The more general case is when d is either even or odd. Consider a prime p_k which divides d. Let $f(x)$ be any primitive polynomial over GF(2) of degree d. Then there exists a trinomial $x^i + x^j + 1$ which is divisible by $f(x)$, where i, j must be selected properly from the cyclotomic cosets of length p_k [5]. If p_k is small then to get a trinomial multiple of any primitive polynomial of degree d we can exhaustively search cyclotomic cosets of length p_k only for a specific construction.

3.1   Algorithms to Find Trinomial Multiples

Next we provide a randomized algorithm to find out trinomial multiples of a primitive polynomial. This will work for any primitive polynomial of degree d both even or odd. We once again concentrate on Corollary 1. We know that given a primitive polynomial $f(x)$ of degree d, there will be $(2^{d-1} - 1)$ distinct trinomial (of degree $< 2^d - 1$) multiples of $f(x)$. Now the trinomial multiples will have degree from $d + 1$ to $2^d - 2$. Also it should be noted that given a specific degree d_1, $d + 1 \le d_1 \le 2^d - 2$, there will either be no trinomial multiple of degree d_1 or there will be only a single trinomial multiple of degree d_1. Thus, out of $(2^d - 2 - d)$ different degree positions from $d + 1$ to $2^d - 2$, we have $2^{d-1} - 1$ degree positions where we have trinomial multiples. Now let us provide the following randomized algorithm.

Algorithm 1.

1. Choose an integer d_r in the range $d + 1$ to $2^d - 2$ uniformly at random.
2. For $i = 1$ to $i = d_r - 1$, consider the trinomials $x^{d_r} + x^i + 1$ and check whether any one of them is divisible by $f(x)$. If we get a trinomial multiple of $f(x)$, then terminate else go to the Step 1.

End Algorithm

We have experimentally checked that given a d-degree primitive polynomial $f(x)$, it is expected that there will be a lot of trinomial multiples of $f(x)$ close to degree $2^d - 2$ (from less than side of $2^d - 2$) and there are very few trinomial multiples of $f(x)$ close to degree $d + 1$ (from greater than side of $d + 1$). Even then, if we consider that the degrees of the trinomial multiples are distributed uniformly in the range $d + 1$ to $2^d - 2$, we can say that the probability that there exists a trinomial multiple at a (uniformly randomly chosen) degree d_r is $\frac{2^{d-1}}{2^d - d - 2} > \frac{1}{2}$. Thus, it is expected that Algorithm 1 will have very few iterations before termination.

At this point, it is important to refer a result on 4-nomial multiples of a primitive polynomial [11, Page 174]. Given a primitive polynomial $f(x)$ of degree d, it is possible to get a 4-nomial multiple $f_4(x)$ of $f(x)$ of degree less than $2^{\frac{d}{4}}$ having time complexity $O(2^{\frac{d}{2}})$ with high probability. The technique uses probabilistic results related to birthday attack. The above randomized algorithm, we propose here, provides trinomial multiple in small time with high probability. The only drawback is that, the degree of the trinomial multiple may be high. However, it is important to mention at this point that it may not be possible to get trinomial multiples with low degree. As example, consider two primitive polynomials $x^{24} + x^7 + x^2 + x + 1$ and $x^{24} + x^{16} + x^{13} + x^{11} + x^{10} + x^9 + x^8 + x^6 + 1$ of degree 24. We have checked that they do not have any trinomial multiple upto degree $2^{\frac{d}{3}} = 2^{\frac{24}{3}} = 2^8$.

The idea we have so far discussed provides trinomial multiples. However, the degree of these trinomial multiples may be very high. We know from [11] that if the connection polynomial of a primitive polynomial is of low weight, then it is possible to exploit cryptanalytic attacks. In the same direction, it is also clear that if there is a primitive polynomial $f(x)$ of degree d with high weight which has a moderate degree ($> d$) trinomial multiple $f_t(x)$, then the recurrence relation satisfied by $f(x)$ will also be satisfied by $f_t(x)$. It is then important to find out trinomial multiples of low degree for fast cryptanalytic attacks [11]. Hence it is a very important question that given a primitive polynomial $f(x)$ of degree d, how can we find the trinomial multiple $f_t(x)$ of $f(x)$ with minimum possible degree. We next provide a simple algorithm to find the minimum degree trinomial of a primitive polynomial.

Algorithm 2.

1. for $i = d + 1$ to $2^d - 2$, for $j = 1$ to $i - 1$,
   a) Consider the trinomials $x^i + x^j + 1$.
   b) If $f(x)$ divides $x^i + x^j + 1$ then report this trinomial and terminate.

End Algorithm

It is important to note that this is an output sensitive algorithm in the sense that it will always provide the correct result and the complexity depends on the degree of the minimum degree trinomial multiple of $f(x)$. Let us consider that for a degree d primitive polynomial $f(x)$, the degree of the minimum degree trinomial multiple $f_t(x)$ is d_f. Then the complexity of Algorithm 2 is $\sum_{i=d+1}^{d_f} (i - 1) Div(i, d)$ where $Div(i, d)$ is the complexity of dividing a degree i trinomial by a degree d polynomial. It will be of interest to find an algorithm for this problem which has the time complexity polynomial in d. Also note that in [5, Theorem 1], it has been said that if a degree d primitive polynomial $f(x)$ has any trinomial multiple, then $f(x)$ must have a trinomial multiple with degree $\leq \frac{2^d+2}{3}$. Since we have already proved that each primitive polynomial must have a trinomial multiple, it is clear that each primitive polynomial must have a trinomial multiple with degree $\leq \frac{2^d+2}{3}$. However, this degree is also very high and we have experimentally checked that there are trinomial multiples with degree much less that $\frac{2^d+2}{3}$. Hence the bound provided in [5] is not tight. It will be an interesting question to get a better bound at lower degree.

Now we conclude this issue discussing the relationship of our problem to the discrete log problem [12]. The discrete log problem can be seen as follows in terms of finite fields. Let β_1 be a nonzero element of GF(2^d) and β_2 be a primitive element of this field. Then $\beta_1 = \beta_2^k$ for some k. The discrete log problem is to find out this k, given β_1, β_2.

Now we come back to our problem of finding a trinomial multiple of a primitive polynomial. Let us consider a primitive polynomial $f(x)$ of degree d. Let α be a root of $f(x)$. Note that α is a primitive element. Now we need to find out some $i, j, 1 \leq i \neq j \leq 2^d - 2$ such that $1+\alpha^i = \alpha^j$. Now it is very easy to find out $\beta = 1+\alpha^i$ in polynomial time in d. Hence, if we can use the discrete log algorithm as a subroutine, we can find out the value of j, where $\beta = \alpha^j$. Since we know that the discrete log problem has subexponential time algorithm [12], we can solve the problem of finding out a trinomial multiple of a primitive polynomial in subexponential time in d.

The next interesting issue is to decide whether this trimomial multiple problem is as hard as discrete log problem. To show this one needs to show that the discrete log problem is polynomial time reducible to this trinomial multiple problem. This is not yet solved, though we can provide some partial result. Consider the following version of the discrete log problem, which we call as $\mathcal{P}_1$. Given an element $\beta_1 \in GF(2^d)$, it is hard to find the value of k, where $\beta_1 = (\beta_1 + 1)^k$, if at all exists. Note that here β_1 may not be a primitive element. Now consider the following problem $\mathcal{P}_2$. Given any element $\gamma \in GF(2^d)$, how to find out j, if at all exists, such that $1+\gamma = \gamma^j$. We show that $\mathcal{P}_1$ is polynomial time reducible to $\mathcal{P}_2$. Let $\beta_1 = 1 + \beta_1 + 1 = 1 + \beta_2$, where $\beta_2 = \beta_1 + 1$ and this step can be done in constant time. Now we use the algorithm for problem $\mathcal{P}_2$ to find out the value of j, if at all exists, where, $1 + \beta_2 = \beta_2^j$. This means we can find out j, where $\beta_1 = (\beta_1 + 1)^j$. This j of problem $\mathcal{P}_2$ gives the value of k in $\mathcal{P}_1$. Hence the problem $\mathcal{P}_2$ is at least as hard as $\mathcal{P}_1$.

Note that in problem $\mathcal{P}_2$, we have taken γ as any element of GF(2^d). For the cases where γ is a primitive element, solution of this problem provides a trinomial multiple of the form $1 + x + x^j$ to a primitive polynomial $f(x)$. Hence, it is also not very clear whether finding out a trinomial multiple of $f(x)$ of the form $1 + x + x^j$ is as hard as discrete log problem.

4 On t-Nomial Multiples

Given a primitive polynomial we have considered the issues related to trinomial multiples ($t = 3$) of it. It is also important to discuss the issues on t-nomial multiples when t is low, as example, $t = 5, 7, \ldots$ etc. If one can find a t-nomial multiple of a primitive polynomial (may be of high weight), where t is low, then the system may get succeptible to cryptanalytic attacks. In this direction we provide the following result which is a generalization of [5, Theorem 7].

Theorem 4. *Let there exists a primitive t-nomial $f(x)$ of degree d. Then there exists a degree d primitive polynomial $g(x)$ which divides some t-nomial of degree sd (s odd) when $gcd(s, 2^d - 1) = 1$.*

Proof. Let $f(x)$ be a primitive t-nomial of degree d and α be a root of it. Let s be an odd integer such that $gcd(s, 2^d - 1) = 1$. Let β be the s-th root of α, i.e., $\beta^s = \alpha$ and β is a primitive element of $GF(2^d)$. Note that, minimal polynomial $g(x)$ of β is primitive polynomial and its degree is d. Now, $f(\beta^s) = f(\alpha) = 0$, i.e., β is a root of $f(x^s)$. On the other hand $g(x)$ is the minimal polynomial of β. Hence $g(x)$ divides $f(x^s)$. It is clear to see that $f(x^s)$ is t-nomial and its degree is sd. Hence we can produce a primitive polynomial $g(x)$ of degree d which divides a t-nomial of degree sd. □

Note that in the above theorem we have taken s odd as we are working over $GF(2)$. If s is even, then we can write $s = 2^r s_1$, where s_1 is odd and replace s by s_1 in Theorem 4.

The importance of Theorem 4 is that there exists a lot of primitive polynomials of degree d which have sparse multiple at a low degree making them susceptible to cryptanaytic attacks. As example, consider a primitive trinomial of $x^7 + x + 1$. Also we have $gcd(3, 2^7 - 1) = 1$. Now consider the trinomial $x^{21} + x^3 + 1$. Theorem 4 guarantees that there exists a primitive polynomial of degree 7, which divides the trinomial $x^{21} + x^3 + 1$. In fact, the primitive polynomial is $x^7 + x^6 + x^4 + x + 1$, which is also of high weight. Hence when we are choosing a primitive polynomial of some degree d, even if we go for a high weight, it is no way guaranteed that it will not have a sparse multiple of low degree sd.

We now provide the motivation of using the weight distribution of the primitive polynomials over GF(2). Let us consider the case for primitive polynomials with degree $d = 23$. Note that $gcd(3, 2^{23} - 1) = 1$. Now look into the weight distribution of degree 23 polynomials [16]. There are 4 primitive trinomials. Hence there must be 4 primitive polynomials of degree 23 which divides trinomials of degree $3 * 23 = 69$. Similarly, there are 292 primitive 5-nomials of degree 23. Thus, there are 292 primitive polynomials of degree 23 which divides 5-nomials of degree $3 * 23 = 69$. Once again, there are 4552 primitive 7-nomials of degree 23. This gives that, there are 4552 primitive polynomials of degree 23 which divides 7-nomials of degree $3 * 23 = 69$.

This has different implications to the attackers and designers. For the existing systems, the attackers may try to find out t-nomial (small t) moderate degree multiples of the primitive polynomials which may even be of high weight. On the other hand, the designers should check whether the primitive polynomials they are using possess any sparse multiple or not. That is, given a degree d, the designer should find out the primitive polynomials $p(x)$ of low weight. Then if $gcd(s, 2^d - 1) = 1$, for some small s, then $p(x^s)$ need to be factorized. Clearly from Theorem 4, one of the factors of $p(x^s)$, will be a primitive polynomial $g(x)$ of degree d, which is different from $p(x)$. Now, even if $g(x)$ may be of high weight, this should not be used in the system. Thus using this idea, one can identify a large class of primitive polynomials of high weight which have sparse multiples at a moderate degree. These should not be recommended for use in cryptographic scheme. The weight distribution table [16] helps a lot in such an analysis. Next we discuss an interesting observation towards generation of primitive polynomials. We will consider the degree 7 and 8.

We start with the case for degree 7. Note that $gcd(3, 2^7 - 1) = 1$. Now we start from the primitive polynomial $f_1(x) = x^7 + x + 1$. Now we consider the polynomial $f_1(x^3) = x^{21} + x^3 + 1$. From Theorem 4, $f_1(x^3)$ must have another primitive polynomial of degree 7 as its factor. We have factorized $f_1(x^3)$ and found primitive polynomial $f_2(x) = x^7 + x^6 + x^4 + x + 1$ as a factor of $f_1(x^3)$. Similarly $f_2(x^3)$ has a primitive polynomial factor $f_3(x) = x^7 + x^5 + x^4 + x^3 + x^2 + x + 1$. If we continue this process, we can exhaust all the 18 primitive polynomials of degree 7. This provides a fast technique to exhaust the list of all the primitive polynomials of degree 7.

For degree 8, the scenario is little different. Here we have $gcd(7, 2^8 - 1) = 1$. If we start from $g_1(x) = x^8 + x^4 + x^3 + x^2 + 1$ and factorize $g_1(x^7)$, we will get the primitive polynomial $x^8 + x^6 + x^4 + x^3 + x^2 + x + 1$. In this way we will get a cycle which exhausts 8 primitive polynomials. On the other hand if we start with $h_1(x) = x^8 + x^5 + x^3 + x + 1$ and factorize $h_1(x^7)$, this will provide $x^8 + x^6 + x^5 + x + 1$. This will again move in a cycle to exhaust the remaining 8 primitive polynomials of degree 8.

Hence, one may choose a primitive polynomial $f(x)$ of certain degree d and find out the smallest s satisfying $gcd(s, 2^d - 1) = 1$. Then factorization of $f(x^s)$ will provide another primitive polynomial of degree d. Now we can generate the complete list of polynomials over GF(2) of low weight t (say 3 or 5) and then check for primitivity of each of these. This will take $\binom{d-1}{t-2}$ primitivity testing. Hence it is easy to find the initial primitive polynomial and then we can use the above method for finding out primitive polynomial of high weight with the constraint that its multiple at degree sd will also have high weight. This kind of technique will help in providing cryptographically strong primitive polynomials.

We have already discussed that given a primitive polynomial $f(x)$ of degree d, we can construct $f(x^s)$ and then factorizing this, we will get another primitive polynomial $g(x)$ of same degree d, where $gcd(s, 2^d - 1) = 1$. In the other direction, given $g(x)$ we can generate $g(x^{s'})$, where $ss' \equiv 1 \bmod (2^d - 1)$ and $g(x^{s'})$ will generate $f(x)$ as its factor.

This has an important implication in choosing a proper connection polynomial. This will at least help in discarding some possibilities of getting a sparse multiple at low degree. Suppose we have chosen a primitive polynomial $g(x)$ with high weight. We choose some small values of s, such that $gcd(s, 2^d - 1) = 1$. Then it is possible to calculate s' where $ss' \equiv 1 \bmod (2^d - 1)$. Next we factorize $g(x^{s'})$, which will generate some primitive polynomial $f(x)$ as its factor. If $f(x)$ is of low weight, then $f(x^s)$ is also of the same low weight, which is a sparse multiple of $g(x)$. Thus, the designer should use this technique to discard some possibility of existence of a sparse multiple in this way.

Acknowledgement. We acknowledge Prof. Bimal Roy, Prof. Rana Barua, Dr. Palash Sarkar and Mr. Sandeepan Chowdhury of Indian Statistical Institute for carefully reading this paper and providing valuable suggestions.

References

1. C. Ding, G. Xiao, and W. Shan. *The Stability Theory of Stream Ciphers.* Number 561 in Lecture Notes in Computer Science. Springer-Verlag, 1991.
2. S. W. Golomb. *Shift Register Sequences.* Aegean Park Press, 1982.
3. K. Huber. Some comments on Zech's logarithms. *IEEE Transactions on Information Theory*, IT-36(4):946–950, July 1990.
4. K. Imamura. A method for computing addition tables in $GF(p^n)$. *IEEE Transactions on Information Theory*, IT-26(3):367–369, May 1980.
5. K. Jambunathan. On choice of connection polynomials for LFSR based stream ciphers. In *Progress in Cryptology - INDOCRYPT 2000*, number 1977 in Lecture Notes in Computer Science, pages 9–18. Springer Verlag, 2000.
6. F. M. Assis and C. E. Pedreira. An architecture for computing Zech's logarithms in $GF(2^n)$. *IEEE Transactions on Computers*, volume 49(5):519–524, May 2000.
7. T. Johansson and F. Jonsson. Fast correlation attacks through reconstruction of linear polynomials. In *Advances in Cryptology - CRYPTO 2000*, number 1880 in Lecture Notes in Computer Science, pages 300–315. Springer Verlag, 2000.
8. W. J. Leveque. *Topics in Number Theory*, volume 1. Addison Wesley Publishing Company, Inc, 1955.
9. R. Lidl and H. Niederreiter. *Encyclopedia of Mathematics.* Addison Wesley, 1983.
10. F. J. MacWilliams and N. J. A. Sloane. *The Theory of Error Correcting Codes.* North Holland, 1977.
11. W. Meier and O. Stafflebach. Fast correlation attacks on certain stream ciphers. *Journal of Cryptology*, 1:159–176, 1989.
12. A. J. Menezes, P. C. van Oorschot, and S. A. Vanstone. *Handbook of Applied Cryptography.* CRC Press, 1997.
13. P. Sarkar and S. Maitra. Nonlinearity bounds and constructions of resilient boolean functions. In *Advances in Cryptology - CRYPTO 2000*, number 1880 in Lecture Notes in Computer Science, pages 515–532. Springer Verlag, 2000.
14. T. Siegenthaler. Correlation-immunity of nonlinear combining functions for cryptographic applications. *IEEE Transactions on Information Theory*, IT-30(5):776–780, September 1984.
15. T. Siegenthaler. Decrypting a class of stream ciphers using ciphertext only. *IEEE Transactions on Computers*, C-34(1):81–85, January 1985.
16. http://www.theory.csc.uvic.ca/~ cos/inf/neck/den_prim.html.

Unconditionally-Secure Oblivious Transfer*

Bo Yang[1], Shixiong Zhu[2], and Yumin Wang[1]

[1] National Key Laboratory on ISN, Xidian University, Xi'an,
Shaanxi Province 710071, P.R. China
[2] Southwest Communications Institute of China, Cheng'du,
Sichuan Province 610041, P.R. China

Abstract. This paper investigates oblivious transfer protocol based on privacy amplification that uses Rényi entropy of order α for any $1 < \alpha < 2$, the conditions under which the protocol is secure are given. In protocol it makes no assumptions about receiver's computing power, so under the given conditions the protocol is unconditionally-secure.

Keywords: Oblivious transfer, Rényi entropy, Privacy amplification, Unconditionally-secure.

1 Introduction

Oblivious transfer is an important primitive in modern cryptography, and has become the basis for realizing a broad class of cryptographic protocols, such as bit commitment, zero-knowledge proofs, and general secure multiparty computation.

Oblivious transfer can be divided into five classes:

OT: Alice sends a bit b and Bob receives either nothing or b, both with probability 1/2, but Alice does not learn which one [1].

$\binom{2}{1} - OT$: It is chosen one-out-of-two OT, where Alice has two input b_0 and b_1, Bob chooses c and obtains b_c, but Alice does not learn c [2].

$\binom{2}{1} - OT^k$: It is string OT, where Alice has two k-bit input strings w_0 and w_1, Bob chooses c and obtains b_c, but Alice does not learn c [2].

GOT: It is generalized OT, where Alice has input bits b_0 and b_1, Bob chooses any function $f : \{0, 1\}^2 \to \{0, 1\}$ and obtains $f(b_0, b_1)$, but Alice does not learn f [3].

UOT: It is universal OT, where Alice sends a random variable X with alphabet $\mathcal{X}$ and Bob obtains a random variable Y. Bob can secretly specify the distributions $P_{Y|X=x}$ for all $x \in \mathcal{X}$ such that Y does not give Bob complete information about X (If not stated otherwise, random variables are always denoted by capital letters and the alphabet of a random variable is denoted by the corresponding script letter) [4].

* This research was supported by the China National Science Foundation, grant no. 69972034, Foundation of National Laboratory For Secure Communications, grant no. 99JS06.3.1.DZ0112

S. Qing, T. Okamoto, and J. Zhou (Eds.): ICICS 2001, LNCS 2229, pp. 35–41, 2001.

In [2], $\binom{2}{1} - OT^k$ was reduced to $\binom{2}{1} - OT$ by using particular types

of error-correcting codes called self-intersecting codes. In [5], $\binom{2}{1} - OT^k$ and

GOT were reduced to $\binom{2}{1} - OT$ based on privacy amplification with Rényi

entropy of order two. In [4], $\binom{2}{1} - OT^k$ was reduced to UOT based on privacy
amplification with min-entropy, and its security was proven by using the side-
information called spoiling knowledge, this type of side-information will increase
Bob's Rényi entropy of Alice's input. However, to obtain more knowledge about
what was sent by Alice, it is desired for Bob to decrease the Rényi entropy of
Alice's input.

In this paper, we utilize the protocol same as the one in [4,5] to reduce $\binom{2}{1} -$

OT^k to UOT, but we use privacy amplification with Rényi entropy of order α for
any α between 1 and 2. Privacy amplification, for short, is a process that allows
two parties to distill a secret key from common information about which an
adversary has partial knowledge. The two parties do not know anything about
the adversary's knowledge except that it satisfies a general bound. By using
a publicly chosen compression function, they are nevertheless able to extract
a short key from their common information such that the total knowledge of
adversary about the key is arbitrarily small.

In [7,8], it was shown that the privacy amplification with Rényi entropy of
order α for $1 < \alpha < 2$ is better than those with Rényi entropy of order 2 and
min-entropy, and in our oblivious transfer protocol, we prove its security not
using side-information of spoiling knowledge .

2   Preliminaries

Definition 1 [7, 8, 9]. Let X be a random variable with alphabet $\mathcal{X}$ and distri-
bution P_X, the Rényi entropy of order α of X is $H_\alpha(X) = \frac{1}{1-\alpha} \log \sum_{x \in \mathcal{X}} P_X(x)^\alpha$,
for $\alpha \geq 0$ and $\alpha \neq 1$.

When $\alpha = 2$, $H_2(X) = -\log \sum_{x \in \mathcal{X}} P_X(x)^2$. Because the limiting case of Rényi
entropy for $\alpha \to 1$ is Shannon entropy, we can extend the definition to

$$H_1(X) = H(X) = -\sum_{x \in \mathcal{X}} P_X(x) \log P_X(x).$$

Definition2 [7, 8, 9].   The relative entropy between two probability distri-
butions P_X, P_Y with the same alphabet $\mathcal{X}$ is defined as $D(P_X \| P_Y) = \sum_{x \in \mathcal{X}} P_X(x) \log \frac{P_X(x)}{P_Y(x)}$.

If P_Y is uniform distribution over $\mathcal{X}$, $D(P_X \| P_Y) = \log |\mathcal{X}| - H(X)$.

Definition 3 [7, 8, 9]. Let M be a nonuniformity measure and let $\Delta : \mathcal{R} \to \mathcal{R}$ be a decreasing non-negative function. A random X with alphabet $\mathcal{X}$ has smooth entropy $\Psi(X)$ within $\Delta(s)$ [in terms of M] with probability $1 - \varepsilon$ if $\Psi(X)$ is the maximum of all ψ such that for any security parameter $s \geq 0$, there exist a random variable T and a function $f : \mathcal{X} \times \mathcal{T} \to \mathcal{Y}$ with $|\mathcal{Y}| = \lfloor 2^{\psi - s} \rfloor$ such that there is a failure event $\mathcal{E}$ that has probability at most ε and the expected value over T of the nonuniformity M of $Y = f(X, T)$, given T and $\overline{\mathcal{E}}$, is at most $\Delta(s)$. Formally,

$$\Psi(X) = \max_{\psi} \{\psi \,|\, \forall s \geq 0 : \exists T, f : \mathcal{X} \times \mathcal{T} \to \mathcal{Y}, |\mathcal{Y}| = \lfloor 2^{\psi - s} \rfloor :$$

$$Y = f(X, T), \exists\, \mathcal{E} : P[\,\mathcal{E}\,] \leq \varepsilon, M(Y | T\,\overline{\mathcal{E}}\,) \leq \Delta(s)\}.$$

Theorem 1 [7, 8, 9]. Fix $\lambda, t > 0$, let m be an integer such that $m - \log(m + 1) > \log|\mathcal{X}| + t$, and s be the security parameter for smooth entropy. For any $1 < \alpha < 2$, the smooth entropy of a random variable X within $\frac{2^{-s}}{\ln 2}$ in terms of relative entropy with probability $1 - 2^{-\lambda} - 2^{-t}$ is lower bounded by Rényi entropy of order α in the sense that

$$\Psi(X) \geq H_\alpha(X) - \log(m + 1) - \frac{r}{\alpha - 1} - t - 2.$$

Definition 4 [10]. A class $\mathcal{F}$ of functions: $\mathcal{A} \to \mathcal{B}$ is called Universal$_2$ (or simply *Universal*) if, for $\forall x_1, x_2 \in \mathcal{A}$ with $x_1 \neq x_2$, the probability that $f(x_1) = f(x_2)$ is at most $1/|\mathcal{B}|$, when f is chosen from $\mathcal{F}$ according to the uniform distribution.

Theorem 2 [7, 8]. Let α, r, t, m, s are the same as Theorem1, V summarizes Eve's total knowledge about W and v be a particular value of V observed by Eve; Alice and Bob select $K = G(W)$ as their secret key, where G is chosen at random from a universal class of hash functions $\mathcal{W} \to \{0, 1\}^k$, then

$$k \leq H_\alpha(W | V = v) - \log(m + 1) - \frac{r}{\alpha - 1} - t - 2 - s$$

with probability $1 - 2^{-r} - 2^{-t}$, and Eve's information about $K \leq \frac{2^{-s}}{\ln 2}$.
Proof. It is easy to see that $|\mathcal{K}| = \lfloor 2^{\psi(W|V=v) - s} \rfloor \leq 2^{\psi(W|V=v) - s}$, $k = \log|\mathcal{K}| \leq \psi(W | V = v) - s$ by the definition of smooth entropy .
    Take $k \leq H_\alpha(W | V = v) - \log(m + 1) - \frac{r}{\alpha - 1} - t - 2 - s$, which will meet the definition of smooth entropy (with the probability $1 - 2^{-r} - 2^{-t}$).
    Applying theorem1 and the definition of relative entropy shows that

$$H(X) = \log|\mathcal{X}| - D(P_X \| P_U) \geq \log|\mathcal{X}| - \frac{2^{-s}}{\ln 2}$$

Thus, $H(K | G, V = v) \geq \log|\mathcal{K}| - \frac{2^{-s}}{\ln 2} = k - \frac{2^{-s}}{\ln 2}$, which is equivalent to the inequality that Eve's information about $K \leq \frac{2^{-s}}{\ln 2}$.

3 The Oblivious Transfer Protocol

In the section, we implement a reduction of $\binom{2}{1} - OT^k(w_0, w_1)(c)$ to $UOT(X, Y)$, such that $\mathcal{X} = \{0, 1\}^{2n}$, where w_0 and w_1 are two k-bit strings chosen by Alice, c is chosen by Bob such that it is not known by Alice.

Step1: Let $X = X_0 X_1$, where X_0 and X_1 both are random binary strings of length n and chosen by Alice according to the uniform distribution, X is the concatenation of X_0 and X_1.

Step2: Alice and Bob run $UOT(X, Y)$, where Bob secretly chosen $P_{Y|X=x}$ for $x \in \mathcal{X}$ to obtain $Y = X_c$.

Step3: Alice chooses independently two members G_0, G_1 from a class universal hash functions mapping n-bit strings to k-bit strings and announces them to Bob.

Step4: Alice computes $M_0 = G_0(X_0), M_1 = G_1(X_1)$. She encodes w_0 and w_1 as $Z_0 = M_0 \oplus w_0$ and $Z_1 = M_1 \oplus w_1$ and sends Z_0 and Z_1 to Bob.

Step5: Bob computes w_c as $w_c = G_c(Y) \oplus Z_c$.

It can be obtained by the definition of the $UOT(X, Y)$ in step2, the protocol is perfectly private for Bob (Alice learns nothing about Bob's choice). That the protocol is private for Alice means Bob can not learn information on both w_0 and w_1 except perhaps with negligible probability, in addition, Bob must not be able to obtain joint information on w_0 and w_1 except for what follows from his a priori knowledge and his learning one of the two strings. From step4, Alice encrypts w_0 and w_1 using M_0 and M_1 as one-time pads, so the security of Alice depends on M_0 and M_1, further depends on X. Because the length k of w_0 and w_1 is constant, if both the length of X is too short and X's Rényi entropy of order α conditioned Y is too small, the information leaked by Alice to Bob in step4 will be very large, therefore it can not assure Alice the system safe.

Below, we will deduce the length of X and the minimum of X's Rényi entropy of order α conditioned Y.

To compare $H_\alpha(X_0 | Y = y)$ and $H_\alpha(X_1 | Y = y, X_0 = x_0)$, we need the lemma below:

Lemma 1. For any N_1-tuple $(i_1, i_2, \cdots, i_{N_1})$, where $1 \le i_1 < i_2 < \cdots < i_{N_1} \le N$, let S be R's sub-string $(R_{i_1}, R_{i_2}, \cdots, R_{i_{N_1}})$, then we get

$$H_\alpha(S) \ge H_\alpha(R) - (N - N_1)$$

Proof. For fixed string $s = (r_{i_1}, r_{i_2}, \cdots, r_{i_{N_1}})$, R have exactly 2^{N-N_1} strings $(r_1, r_2, \cdots, r_N)$ corresponding to it. Let $p_1, p_2, \cdots, p_{2^{N-N_1}}$ are the probabilities of these strings, and $p_0 = P_S(s) = \sum_{i=1}^{2^{N-N_1}} p_i$.

Then we have

$$\sum_{i=1}^{2^{N-N_1}} p_i^{\alpha} = p_0^{\alpha-1} \sum_{i=1}^{2^{N-N_1}} \left(\frac{p_i}{p_0}\right)^{\alpha-1} p_i \geq p_0^{\alpha-1} \left(\frac{1}{2^{N-N_1}}\right)^{\alpha-1} \sum_{i=1}^{2^{N-N_1}} p_i$$

$$= \frac{p_0^{\alpha}}{2^{(N-N_1)(\alpha-1)}},$$

$$p_0^{\alpha} \leq 2^{(N-N_1)(\alpha-1)} \sum_{i=1}^{2^{N-N_1}} p_i^{\alpha}$$

Thus,

$$\sum_{s\in\{0,1\}^{N_1}} P_S(s)^{\alpha} = \sum_{s\in\{0,1\}^{N_1}} p_0^{\alpha} \leq 2^{(N-N_1)(\alpha-1)} \sum_{s\in\{0,1\}^{N_1}} \sum_{i=1}^{2^{N-N_1}} p_i^{\alpha}$$

$$= 2^{(N-N_1)(\alpha-1)} 2^{N_1} \sum_{i=1}^{2^{N-N_1}} p_i^{\alpha}$$

$$= 2^{(N-N_1)(\alpha-1)} \sum_{r\in\{0,1\}^N} P_R(r)^{\alpha},$$

$$\log \sum_{s\in\{0,1\}^{N_1}} P_S(s)^{\alpha} \leq (N-N_1)(\alpha-1) + \log \sum_{r\in\{0,1\}^N} P_R(r)^{\alpha}$$

Divided by $1-\alpha$ we obtain: $H_\alpha(S) \geq H_\alpha(R) - (N-N_1)$.

Corollary. Let $X = X_0 X_1$, where X_0 and X_1 be two n-bit binary strings, then

$$H_\alpha(X_0 | Y = y) \geq H_\alpha(X | Y = y) - n.$$

Lemma 2 [9]. Let $1 < \alpha < 2$ and let $r, t > 0$. For arbitrary random variable X and Y, the probability that Y takes y for which

$$H_\alpha(X | Y = y) \geq H_\alpha(XY) - \log|\mathcal{Y}| - \frac{r}{\alpha-1} - t$$

is at least $1 - 2^{-r} - 2^{-t}$.

By lemma2, we have $H_\alpha(X_1 | Y = y, X_0 = x) \geq H_\alpha(X_0 X_1 | Y = y) - \log|\mathcal{X}_0| - \frac{r}{\alpha-1} - t = H_\alpha(X | Y = y) - n - \frac{r}{\alpha-1} - t$, take $H_\alpha(X_1 | Y = y, X_0 = x_0)$ as minimum, that is

$$H_\alpha(X_1 | Y = y, X_0 = x) = H_\alpha(X | Y = y) - n - \frac{r}{\alpha-1} - t,$$

the inequality $H_\alpha(X_0 | Y = y) \geq H_\alpha(X_1 | Y = y, X_0 = x_0)$ holds with probability at least $1 - 2^{-r} - 2^{-t}$. So, for the protocol safe, among twice privacy amplification, it is only need to consider the second privacy amplification, that is, utilizing $H_\alpha(X_1 | Y = y, X_0 = x_0)$ to universal hash function G_1.

Theorem 3. Let $1 < \alpha < 2$, $r > 1$, $t > 1$, m is an integer such that $m - \log(m+1) > n+t$, and $s \geq 0$ is the security parameter for smooth entropy. Let $X = X_0 X_1$ be the concatenation of two n-bit binary strings X_0 and X_1. Then when

$$n \geq k + \log(m+1) + \frac{2r}{\alpha - 1} + 2t + 2 + s$$

$$H_\alpha(X \mid Y = y) \geq 2\left[k + \log(m+1) + \frac{2r}{\alpha - 1} + 2t + 2 + s\right]$$

the protocol $\binom{2}{1} - OT^k(w_0, w_1)(c)$ can safely be reduced to a single execution of $UOT(X,Y)$ with the probability at least $1 - 2^{-r+1} - 2^{-t+1}$.

Proof. By theorem2, $k \leq H_\alpha(X_1 \mid Y = y, X_0 = x_0) - \log(m+1) - \frac{r}{\alpha-1} - t - 2 - s$, therefore

$$H_\alpha(X_1 \mid Y = y, X_0 = x_0) \geq k + \log(m+1) + \frac{r}{\alpha - 1} + t + 2 + s \qquad (1)$$

that is

$$H_\alpha(X \mid Y = y) - n - \frac{r}{\alpha - 1} - t \geq k + \log(m+1) + \frac{r}{\alpha - 1} + t + 2 + s \qquad (2)$$

so

$$H_\alpha(X \mid Y = y) \geq n + k + \log(m+1) + \frac{2r}{\alpha - 1} + 2t + 2 + s \qquad (3)$$

Again because $2n \geq H_\alpha(X \mid Y = y)$, therefore $2n \geq n + k + \log(m+1) + \frac{2r}{\alpha-1} + 2t + 2 + s$, that is

$$n \geq k + \log(m+1) + \frac{2r}{\alpha - 1} + 2t + 2 + s \qquad (4)$$

so

$$H_\alpha(X \mid Y = y) \geq 2\left[k + \log(m+1) + \frac{2r}{\alpha - 1} + 2t + 2 + s\right].$$

From theorem2 and inequality (1), after obtaining X_0 (further w_0), the information about X_1 (further about w_1) obtained by Bob is

$$I(X_1, X_0 Y) \leq \frac{2^{-s}}{\ln 2} \qquad (5)$$

with the probability at least $1 - 2^{-r} - 2^{-t}$.

Because both inequalities (1) and (2) hold with probability at least $1 - 2^{-r} - 2^{-t}$, the process above does not hold with probability at most $1 - (1 - 2^{-r} - 2^{-t}) \cdot (1 - 2^{-r} - 2^{-t}) < 2^{-r+1} + 2^{-t+1}$.

4   Conclusion

For oblivious transfer protocol of two k-bit binary strings based on privacy amplification with Rényi entropy of order α for any α between 1 and 2, so long as the length and conditional Rényi entropy (conditioned information about the sender's input obtained by the receiver) of the sender's input to privacy amplification are respectively larger than two constant depended on k , the receiver obtains one of two k-bit strings, he will obtain arbitrary small information about another k-bit string with some probability. In protocol it makes no assumptions about receiver's computing power, so under the given conditions the protocol is unconditionally-secure.

References

1. M. O. Rabin. How to exchange secrets by oblivious transfer, Tech. Report TR-81, Harvard, 1981.
2. Shimon Even, Oded Goldreich, and A. Lempel. A randomized protocol for signing contracts, CRYPTO'82, Plenum Press, 1983, 205-210.
3. Gilles Brassard, Claude Crépeau, and Jean-Marc Robert, Information theoretic reductions among disclosure problems, Proc. 27th IEEE Symposium on Foundations of Computer Science, 1986,168-173.
4. Christian Cachin. On the foundations of oblivious transfer, EUROCRYPT'98, Lecture Notes in Computer Science, Springer-Verlag, 1998, 361-374.
5. Gilles Brassard, Claude Crépeau. Oblivious transfer and privacy amplification, EUROCRYPT'97, Lecture Notes in Computer Science, Springer-Verlag, 1997, 334-347.
6. Charles H. Bennett, Gilles Brassard, Claude Crépeau, and Ueli M. Maurer. Generalized Privacy amplification, IEEE Trans. Inform. Theory, 1995, 41 (6): 1915-1923.
7. Bo Yang, Tong Zhang and Yumin Wang. Distillation of Unconditionally-Secure Secret-Key Based on Smooth Entropy. Acta Electronica Sinica, 2001, 29(7).
8. Bo Yang, Tong Zhang and Yumin Wang. Distillation of Unconditionally-Secure Secret-Key against Active Adversaries Based on Smooth Entropy. Acta Electronica Sinica, accepted to publish.
9. Christian Cachin. Smooth entropy and Rényi entropy, EUROCRYPT'97, Lecture Notes in Computer Science, Springer-Verlag, 1997, 193-208.
10. J. L. Carter and M. N. Wegman. Universal classes of hash functions, J.Comput.Syst.Sci., 1979, 18 (2): 143-154.

Cryptanalysis of the Improved User Efficient Blind Signatures

Chin-Chen Chang and Iuon-Chang Lin

Department of Computer Science and Information Engineering,
National Chung Cheng University, Chaiyi, Taiwan 62107
{ccc, iclin}@cs.ccu.edu.tw

Abstract. Fan and Lei proposed an user efficient blind signature scheme based on quadratic residues. The main merit of this scheme is that only a few number of arithmetic modular operations are required for a user to get a legal signature. Therefore, it is very suitable for commerce applications. However, Shao pointed out that this scheme did not achieve the unlinkability property. Furthermore, he also proposed an improved blind signature scheme to remedy this weakness and reduce the computations for requests. In this article, we presents a linking strategy to show that this improved version is also not a true blind signature scheme.

Keywords: Blind signature, cryptography

1 Introduction

Some public key cryptosystems, such as RSA, Rabin[3] and so on, can be used to sign digital signatures. Without the private key, no one can forge a legal signature. Therefore, digital signatures are widely used to prove the integrity of data and the identity of signee. However, in some applications, such as electronic cash systems or anonymous electronic voting systems, in order to protect the privacy of users, the anonymity property is necessary. Hence, in 1982, David Chaum invented a blind signature scheme [1], which not only achieves the unforgeability property but also achieves the unlinkability property. The protocol is briefly described as below. When a requester sends a blind message to request his signature from the signee, the signee signs the blind message and sends the result to the requester. Then, the requester can obtain the signature of the chosen message from performing the unblinding function. The signature can be verified, but the signee can not link the relationship between the blind message and the signature of the chosen message. A secure blind signature scheme must satisfy the unforgeability property and the unlinkability property.

Generally, users have less computation capacities than the signee in most applications of blind signatures. For example, in an electronic cash system, the bank always acts as the signee and the customers always act as the requesters. Therefore, in 1998, Fan and Lei proposed a blind signature scheme for user efficiency [2], and its security is completely based on quadratic residues (QR). The characteristic of this scheme is low computations for users. User only requires

S. Qing, T. Okamoto, and J. Zhou (Eds.): ICICS 2001, LNCS 2229, pp. 42–46, 2001.

a few number of arithmetic modular computations to obtain a legal signature. Therefore, it is more suitable for many commerce applications, such as mobil communications or smart card implementations.

However, Shao [4] showed that Fan and Lei's blind signature scheme is not really "blind". Signee can trace the identity of the user while the user reveals the signature in transactions. Therefore, the scheme can not protect the user's privacy. Moreover, Shao proposed an improved scheme to remedy the weakness and reduce the computation overheads for users or requesters. In this paper, we show that Shao's method is also not a true blind signature scheme. Signee can derive some secret parameters and then link the relationship between the signature and the requester's identity.

The rest of this paper is organized as follows. In Section 2, we shall briefly review Shao's scheme. Then we shall show that it is not really blind in Section 3. Finally, some conclusions are made in the last section.

2 Overview of Shao's Improved User Efficient Blind Signature Scheme

Shao proposed an improved version of Fan and Lei's user efficient blind signature scheme [2]. The improved scheme is more efficient than Fan and Lei's, it performs 12 modular multiplications, selects two random integers, and requests two data transmissions between the signee and the requester, while the corresponding numbers are 14, 3, and 4 in Fan and Lei's scheme. We briefly introduce Shao's scheme [4] as below.

In Shao's scheme, there are two kinds of participants, a signee and a group of requesters. Requesters request the blind signatures from the signee, and the signee issues the blind signatures to the requesters. In addition, the scheme can be divided into four phases: (1) the initialization phase, (2) the requesting phase, (3) the signing phase, and (4) the extraction phase. In the initialization phase, the signee sets up and publishes some necessary information. In the requesting phase, the requester delivers some encrypted message to request a blind signature from the signee. The signee computes the blind signature and sends it back to the requester. From the received message, the requester can extract the signature in the extraction phase. The processes of the four phases are itemized as follows.

The Initialization Phase
The signee computes $n = pq$, where p, q are two large primes, and $p \equiv q \equiv 3$ (*mod* 4). Furthermore, let H be a one-way hash function. The signee keeps p and q secret, and publishes n and H.

The Requesting Phase
To obtain a signature of the message m, the requester randomly chooses two integers u and b, such that

$$\alpha = b^2 H(m)(u^2 + 1) \bmod n. \tag{1}$$

Then the requester delivers α to the signee.

The Signing Phase
While receiving α, the signee randomly chooses an integer x. Because the signee knows the factors p and q of n, and $\alpha(x^2+1) \bmod n$ is a QR in Z_n*, therefore, the signee has the ability to derive t from

$$t^{-2} = \alpha(x^2+1) \bmod n. \tag{2}$$

Then, the signee delivers the pair (t, x) to the requester.

The Extraction Phase
After receiving (t, x), the requester computes

$$c = (ux-1)(x+u)^{-1} \bmod n, \ and \tag{3}$$
$$s = bt(x+u) \bmod n. \tag{4}$$

The pair (c, s) is a signature of m. To verify the validity of (c, s) of m, the verifier checks whether or not the following equation holds,

$$H(m)s^2(c^2+1) = 1 \bmod p. \tag{5}$$

In the following, we prove that Equation (5) always holds while the signature (c, s) is correct.

According to Equation (2), we get

$$t^2\alpha(x^2+1) = t^2 t^{-2} = 1 \bmod n. \tag{6}$$

Hence, we have

$$H(m)s^2(c^2+1)$$
$$= (\frac{\alpha}{b^2(u^2+1)})(bt(x+u))^2((\frac{ux-1}{x+u})^2+1)$$
$$= (\frac{\alpha}{b^2(u^2+1)})(bt)^2((ux-1)^2+(x+u)^2)$$
$$= (\frac{\alpha}{b^2(u^2+1)})(bt)^2(x^2+1)(u^2+1)$$
$$= t^2\alpha(x^2+1) = 1 \ (\bmod \ n).$$

3   The Weakness of Shao's Improved User Efficient Blind Signature Scheme

In this section, we show that the signatures can be traced by the signee in Shao's scheme. Therefore, this scheme does not really achieve unlinkability property. We consider the follow scenario.

1. Let RI_i be the requester i's identity. The signee keeps a set of records $S = \{(RI_i, \alpha_i, t_i, x_i)|i = 1, 2, \cdots, z\}$ for z instances of the blind signed messages. Furthermore, the signee obtains the signature $(H(m), c, s)$ of the message m when it is revealed by a requester.

2. With c and s, the signee computes

$$cs = (ux - 1)bt \mod n. \tag{7}$$

Then, the signee takes out t from some tuples in the set S and computes

$$cst^{-1} = (ux - 1)b \mod n, \ and \tag{8}$$

$$
\begin{aligned}
(cst^{-1})^2 &= (ux - 1)^2 b^2 \\
&= (u^2 x^2 - 2ux + 1)b^2 \\
&= u^2 b^2 x^2 + b^2 - 2uxb^2 \pmod{n}.
\end{aligned}
\tag{9}
$$

3. Since

$$\alpha = b^2 H(m)(u^2 + 1) \mod n,$$

the signee can compute

$$\alpha H^{-1}(m) = b^2(u^2 + 1) = b^2 u^2 + b^2 \pmod{n}. \tag{10}$$

4. Now, in the signing phase, if the signee chooses $x = 1$ for some requesters on purpose, then Equation (9) can be rewritten as

$$(cst^{-1})^2 = u^2 b^2 + b^2 - 2ub^2 \mod n. \tag{11}$$

From Equations (10) and (11), the signee can derive

$$(cst^{-1})^2 = \alpha H^{-1}(m) - 2ub^2 \mod n.$$

Therefore,

$$2ub^2 = \alpha H^{-1}(m) - (cst^{-1})^2 \mod n.$$

That is,

$$ub^2 = 2^{-1}(\alpha H^{-1}(m) - (cst^{-1})^2) \mod n. \tag{12}$$

5. From Equation (4), since $s = tb + tub \mod n$, we have

$$sb = tb^2 + tub^2 \mod n. \tag{13}$$

To replace ub^2 with $2^{-1}(\alpha H^{-1}(m) - (cst^{-1})^2)$ from Equation (12), Equation (13) becomes

$$sb = tb^2 + t(2^{-1}(\alpha H^{-1}(m) - (cst^{-1})^2)) \mod n. \tag{14}$$

Since $tb^2 - sb = -t(2^{-1}(\alpha H^{-1}(m)) - (cst^{-1})^2) \mod n$, we have
$b^2 - st^{-1}b = -(2^{-1}(\alpha H^{-1}(m)) - (cst^{-1})^2) \mod n$.
Therefore, the signee can derive

$$b(b - st^{-1}) = (cst^{-1})^2 - 2^{-1}\alpha H^{-1}(m) \mod n. \tag{15}$$

6. The improved blind signature scheme is based on the theory of quadratic residues. The security of this scheme is based on the difficulty of finding the square roots modulo a composite number. According to Rabin's public key cryptosystem[3], to encrypt the message M, the encryption function is

$$E(M) = C = M(M + a) \bmod n, \tag{16}$$

where C is the corresponding ciphertext and a and n are made public. The decryption function is

$$D(C) = M = \frac{-a}{2} \pm \sqrt{(a/2)^2 + C} \mod p \tag{17}$$

$$or \quad \frac{-a}{2} \pm \sqrt{(a/2)^2 + C} \mod q. \tag{18}$$

Without knowing the factors p and q of the modulus n, it is infeasible to compute the square root M from the given messages a and C. Recall the computation of the square root b from Equation (15). Since the signee knows the factors p and q of n, $st^{-1} \bmod n$, and $(cst^{-1})^2 - 2^{-1}\alpha H^{-1}(m) \bmod n$, the parameter b in Equation (15) can be easily computed from the decryption function of Rabin's public key cryptosystem.

7. Since b can be obtained, therefore the signee can compute u from Equation (12). Further, the signee can compute c' and s' from Equations (3) and (4). If (c', s') is equal to the received signature (c, s), then the signee can get the identity of the requester from some record in the set S.

Obviously, by the blind signature $(H(M), c, s)$, the signee can make a linkage between it and the identity of the requester. Therefore, the scheme does not achieve the unlinkability property.

4   Conclusions

Shao's scheme is designed to be more efficient for users. Therefore, the scheme is suitable for many applications that users have low computation capabilities. However, Shao's scheme is not a true blind signature. In this article, we have presented a link strategy to show that Shao's blind signature scheme is not really "blind".

References

1. D. Chaum, "Blind signature for untraceable payments," *Advances in Cryptology: Crypto'82*, pp. 199–203, 1982.
2. C. I. Fan and C. L. Lei, "User efficient blind signatures," *Electronics Letters*, vol. 34, no. 6, pp. 544–546, 1998.
3. M. O. Rabin, "Digitalized signatures and public-key functions as intractable as factorization," *Technical Report, MIT/LCS/TR212*, MIT Lab., Computer Science, Cambridge, Mass., January 1979.
4. Z. Shao, "Improved user efficient blind signatures," *Electronics Letters*, vol. 36, no. 16, pp. 1372–1374, 2000.

Towards the Forgery of a Group Signature without Knowing the Group Center's Secret

Chin-Chen Chang and Kuo-Feng Hwang

Department of Computer Science and Information Engineering
National Chung Cheng University, Chia-Yi, Taiwan 621
{ccc,luda}@cs.ccu.edu.tw

Abstract. A group signature scheme allows the group member to sign messages on behalf of a group. In 1996, Kim et al. proposed a new type of group signature, called "convertible group signature". Recently, Saeednia pointed out that there are weaknesses in a convertible group signature scheme proposed by Kim et al. Furthermore, Saeednia proposed a modified scheme to eliminate these weaknesses. In this paper, we show that there is a way to forge a group signature even if adopting Saeednia's modified scheme.

Keywords: Cryptography, convertible group signature, cryptanalysis

1 Introduction

In 1991, Chaum and Heyst [1] proposed the notion of group signature, which allows a group member to make a digital signature on behalf of the group. A group signature scheme has the following three characteristics:

1. Only the group member can make signatures.
2. Everybody can be a verifier to certify the validity of a group signature, but cannot discover who made it.
3. If necessary, all the group members together or the group center can find out who signed a specific message.

Kim et al. [2] proposed a new type of group signature, called "convertible group signature". In addition to the above characteristics, a convertible group signature can be verified without the help of group members or a trusted authority. In Kim et al.'s scheme, the group member's secret key consists of two integers, one is chosen by the member himself and the other is calculated by the group center. The integer chosen by the group member keeps secret from the group center, because it is protected by adopting a one-way function. The group center uses his secret key to compute another secret key for the group member. According to the above mechanism, Kim et al. argued that the group member can sign messages on behalf of the group and the signatures can be verified without the cooperation of the group member or the group center. Kim et al.'s scheme is secure if it is difficult to construct a valid secret key without knowing the group center's secret.

In 2000, Saeednia [3] pointed out that Kim et al.'s scheme allows an adversary to forge a signature on behalf of the group if some conditions are met. In other words, without

S. Qing, T. Okamoto, and J. Zhou (Eds.): ICICS 2001, LNCS 2229, pp. 47–51, 2001.
© Springer-Verlag Berlin Heidelberg 2001

losing the group center's secret, an adversary has the capability to forge a signature if the group's public key satisfies a particular condition. Moreover, Saeednia also proposed a modified scheme to eliminate these weaknesses. Briefly, Saeednia uses a mechanism to make sure that the group's public key does not satisfy this particular condition.

In this paper, we show that even if Saeednia's modified scheme is adopted, a group member still has the capability to forge a signature on behalf of the group. In Section 2, we review Kim et al.'s scheme, Saeednia's attacks as well as his modified scheme. In Section 3, we propose an approach to forge a signature without knowing the group center's secret. Finally, Section 4 states the conclusions of our work.

2   Previous Work

2.1   Kim et al.'s Group Signature Scheme

There are four stages in Kim et al.'s [2] convertible group signature scheme: Initialization, key generation, signature generation, and signature verification. We review these stages as follows:

Initialization. The group center is referred to below as GC. First, GC chooses three prime numbers p', q', and f. Here another two prime numbers p and q have to be formed, such that $p = 2fp' + 1$ and $q = 2fq' + 1$. An integer n is defined as the product of p and q. Next, GC chooses an integer g of order f modulo n, i.e., $g^f = 1 \pmod{n}$. Furthermore, GC chooses an integer γ, such that $(\gamma, p - 1) = 1$ and $(\gamma, q - 1) = 1$. Afterward GC computes its secret key d, such that $\gamma \cdot d = 1 \pmod{\phi(n)}$. Finally, n, f, g, and γ are made public, and then p and q are discarded.

Key generation. In this stage, a group member A registers his secret key to GC. Afterward, A has capability to sign a message M on behalf of the group $\mathrm{ID_G}$. Here $\mathrm{ID_G}$ denotes the group identity and represents the public key of the group.

A chooses a random integer $s_A \in \mathbb{Z}_f$ as a part of his secret key and sends $(\mathrm{ID_G}, g^{s_A} \bmod n)$ to GC. Then GC computes

$$x_A = (\mathrm{ID_G} \cdot g^{s_A})^{-d} \pmod{n},$$

and sends x_A to A secretly. Finally, A's secret key is the pair (s_A, x_A). Although GC does not know s_A, he can identify the signer by x_A and g^{s_A}.

Signature generation. For a message M, a group member A computes the triple (e, z_1, z_2) as $\mathrm{ID_G}$'s signature. First, A chooses two random integers $r_1, r_2 \in \mathbb{Z}_f$, and the signature is computed as follows:

$$e = h(V, M), \text{ where}$$
$$V = g^{r_1} r_2^{\gamma} \pmod{n},$$
$$z_1 = r_1 + s_A \cdot e \pmod{f},$$
$$\text{and } z_2 = r_2 \cdot x_A^e \pmod{n}.$$

Here $h()$ denotes a publicly known one-way hash function.

Signature verification. To make sure (e, z_1, z_2) is the group $\mathrm{ID_G}$'s signature for M, the verifier computes

$$\overline{V} = (\mathrm{ID_G})^e g^{z_1} z_2^{\gamma} \pmod{n}.$$

If the equation $e = h(\overline{V}, M)$ is satisfied, the verifier concludes that (e, z_1, z_2) is a valid signature for M.

2.2 Saeednia's Attacks and His Solutions

Saeednia [3] pointed out that there are two possible ways to forge a signature in Kim et al.'s scheme. Furthermore, Saeednia proposed some solutions for these weaknesses. In this paper, we only focus on Saeednia's first attack and its solution, because his second attack is relatively negligible if his first solution still has weaknesses. Saeednia's first attack is successful if $\mathrm{ID_G} \in \mathcal{F}$. Here $\mathcal{F}$ denotes the set of the integers that their order is 2, f, or $2f$ modulo n. That is to say, $\mathrm{ID_G}^{2f} = 1 \pmod{n}$.

If $\mathrm{ID_G} \in \mathcal{F}$, one can obtain another usable GC's secret key d', such that $\gamma \cdot d' = 1$ $\pmod{2f}$. Because $(\gamma, p - 1) = 1$ and $(\gamma, q - 1) = 1$, γ is also relatively prime to $2f$. Thus, for any $k \in \mathcal{F}$, $k^{\gamma d'} = k \pmod{n}$ is true. Obviously, if $\mathrm{ID_G} \in \mathcal{F}$, one can obtain a valid secret key (s_j, x_j), such that $x_j = (\mathrm{ID_G} \cdot g^{s_j})^{-d'} \pmod{n}$. Here $s_j \in \mathbb{Z}_f$ is an arbitrarily chosen integer. Afterward, an adversary can forge a signature for any message M on behalf of the group $\mathrm{ID_G}$ by introducing the secret key (s_j, x_j).

To eliminate the above mentioned weakness, Saeednia suggested to reform the group identity $\mathrm{ID_G}$ as $\mathrm{I}_G = h(J \| \mathrm{ID_G})$ such as $\mathrm{I}_G \notin \mathcal{F}$. Here J represents an arbitrary k-bit integer. And the group member's secret key is computed by $x_i = (\mathrm{I}_G \cdot g^{s_i})^{-d} \pmod{n}$. In the verification stage, the verifier first checks whether $h(J \| \mathrm{ID_G})^{2f} \neq 1 \pmod{n}$. If so, the verifier believes that the signer is authenticated by GC. The rest of the verification procedure remains unchanged, except that the verifier uses I_G rather than $\mathrm{ID_G}$.

3 To Forge a Group Signature

In this section, we present a way which allows a group member to forge a valid secret key without knowing GC's secret as well as $ID_G \notin \mathcal{F}$.

We describe the way to generate a valid secret key by a group member A as follows:

Step 1. A selects a random number $s_1 \in \mathbb{Z}_f$, and then sends $(\mathrm{ID_G}, g^{s_1} \bmod n)$ to GC. Afterward, A obtains a secret key x_{A_1} from GC, where x_{A_1} is computed by

$$x_{A_1} = (\mathrm{ID_G} \cdot g^{s_1})^{-d} \pmod{n}. \tag{1}$$

Step 2. A selects another random number $s_2 \in \mathbb{Z}_f$, such that $s_2 = -s_1 \pmod{f}$, and then sends $(\mathrm{ID_G}, g^{s_2} \bmod n)$ to GC. Similarly, A obtains the second secret key x_{A_2} from GC, where x_{A_2} is computed by

$$x_{A_2} = (\mathrm{ID_G} \cdot g^{s_2})^{-d} \pmod{n}. \tag{2}$$

Step 3. Again, A selects a random number $s_3 \in \mathbb{Z}_f$, such that $s_3 \neq s_1$ and $s_3 \neq s_2$, and then sends $(\mathrm{ID_G}, g^{s_3} \bmod n)$ to GC. Afterward, A obtains the third secret key x_{A_3} from GC such as

$$x_{A_3} = (\mathrm{ID_G} \cdot g^{s_3})^{-d} \quad (\bmod \; n). \tag{3}$$

Finally, A obtains a valid secret key (s_A', x_A'), where $x_A' = x_{A_2}^{-1} \cdot x_{A_3}^2$ $(\bmod \; n)$ and $s_A' = s_1 + 2s_3 \; (\bmod \; f)$, i.e., $x_{A_2}^{-1} \cdot x_{A_3}^2 = (\mathrm{ID_G} \cdot g^{s_1+2s_3})^{-d}$ $(\bmod \; n)$.

Proposition 1. *If* $s_2 = -s_1 \; (\bmod \; f)$ *and* s_3 *does not equal to* s_1 *nor* s_2, *then*

$$x_{A_2}^{-1} \cdot x_{A_3}^2 = (\mathrm{ID_G} \cdot g^{s_1+2s_3})^{-d} \quad (\bmod \; n)$$

holds. Here $x_{A_i} = (\mathrm{ID_G} \cdot g^{s_i})^{-d} \; (\bmod \; n)$ *and* $s_i \in \mathbb{Z}_f$.

Proof. Compute the product of Equations (1) and (2) as follows:

$$
\begin{aligned}
x_{A_1} \cdot x_{A_2} &= (\mathrm{ID_G} \cdot g^{s_1})^{-d} \cdot (\mathrm{ID_G} \cdot g^{s_2})^{-d} \quad (\bmod \; n) \\
&= (\mathrm{ID_G}^2 \cdot g^{s_1+s_2})^{-d} \quad (\bmod \; n) \\
&= (\mathrm{ID_G}^2 \cdot g^0)^{-d} \quad (\bmod \; n) \\
&= (\mathrm{ID_G}^2)^{-d} \quad (\bmod \; n). \tag{4}
\end{aligned}
$$

Next, compute $((\mathrm{ID_G}^2)^{-1})^{-d} \cdot (x_{A_1} \cdot x_{A_2}) \; (\bmod \; n)$ as follows:

$$((\mathrm{ID_G}^2)^{-1})^{-d} \cdot (x_{A_1} \cdot x_{A_2}) = ((\mathrm{ID_G}^2)^{-1})^{-d} \cdot (\mathrm{ID_G}^2)^{-d} \quad (\bmod \; n),$$

$$((\mathrm{ID_G}^2)^{-1})^{-d} \cdot (x_{A_1} \cdot x_{A_2}) = 1 \quad (\bmod \; n).$$

Thus, we have the following equation:

$$((\mathrm{ID_G}^2)^{-1})^{-d} = (x_{A_1} \cdot x_{A_2})^{-1} \quad (\bmod \; n). \tag{5}$$

The result of Equation (1) multiplied by the square of Equation (3) is

$$x_{A_1} \cdot x_{A_3} \cdot x_{A_3} = (\mathrm{ID_G} \cdot g^{s_1})^{-d} \cdot (\mathrm{ID_G} \cdot g^{s_3})^{-d} \cdot (\mathrm{ID_G} \cdot g^{s_3})^{-d} \quad (\bmod \; n),$$

$$x_{A_1} \cdot x_{A_3}^2 = (\mathrm{ID_G}^3 \cdot g^{s_1+2s_3})^{-d} \quad (\bmod \; n). \tag{6}$$

Finally, compute the product of Equations (5) and (6), and then we have Equation (7) as follows:

$$(x_{A_1} \cdot x_{A_3}^2)(x_{A_1} \cdot x_{A_2})^{-1} = (\mathrm{ID_G}^3 \cdot g^{s_1+2s_3})^{-d} ((\mathrm{ID_G}^2)^{-1})^{-d} \quad (\bmod \; n).$$

That is, $x_{A_2}^{-1} \cdot x_{A_3}^2 = (\mathrm{ID_G} \cdot g^{s_1+2s_3})^{-d} \quad (\bmod \; n). \tag{7}$

□

According to Proposition 1, Kim et al.'s scheme allows a group member A to obtain a valid secret key (s'_A, x'_A), such that $x'_A = x_{A_2}^{-1} \cdot x_{A_3}^2 \pmod{n}$ and $s'_A = s_1 + 2s_3$ (mod f). Note that x'_A is not generated by GC, so GC cannot exactly identify who has signed the messages from the signatures that were generated using (s'_A, x'_A). Therefore, A has the capability to forge a group signature for any message M on behalf of the group ID_G and he has no responsibility for this signature. In particular, no matter $ID_G \notin \mathcal{F}$, the above mechanism is still workable. Therefore, in spite of Saeednia's scheme reformed the identity ID_G into $I_G \notin \mathcal{F}$, Saeednia's scheme is still allowing a group member to forge a group signature.

Furthermore, we consider that if GC allows a group member to register his secret key only once, a valid secret key is still can be counterfeited by collusion. In other words, any three members in the same group can conspire to construct a valid secret key by choosing the integers $s_1, s_2,$ and s_3 to be their part of secret keys such as in Steps 1, 2, and 3, respectively.

4   Conclusions

In this paper, we have presented that Saeednia's modified group signature scheme still has a serious weakness. In other words, not only Kim et al.'s scheme but also Saeednia's modified scheme enables a group member to forge a signature for any message M without the knowledge of GC's secret as well as $ID_G \notin \mathcal{F}$.

References

1. D. Chaum and E. van Heyst, "Group signatures," in *Advances in Cryptology (Proceedings of EuroCrypt'91)*, pp. 47–53, Lecture Notes in Computer Science, Springer-Verlag, Berlin, 1992.
2. S. J. Kim, S. J. Park, and D. H. Won, "Convertible group signatures," in *Advances in Cryptology (Proceedings of AsiaCrypt'96)*, pp. 311–321, Lecture Notes in Computer Science, Springer-Verlag, Berlin, 1996.
3. S. Saeednia, "On the security of a convertible group signature scheme," *Information Processing Letters*, vol. 73, pp. 93–96, Feb. 2000.

Evaluation of the Image Degradation for a Typical Watermarking Algorithm in the Block-DCT Domain

Xiaochen Bo, Lincheng Shen, and Wensen Chang

Institute of Automation, National University of Defense Technology,
Changsha 410073, P.R.CHINA
boxiaoc@163.com

Abstract. Digital watermarking is a key technique for protecting intellectual property of digital media. As a number of methods have been proposed in recent years to embed watermarks in images for various applications, evaluation of watermarking algorithms becomes more and more important. The degradation of watermarked images, which can be measured by signal to noise ratio (SNR) or peak signal to noise ratio (PSNR), is one of the major performance indexes of watermarking algorithms. In this paper, based on the Laplacian distribution model of DCT coefficients, we deduce a theoretical relationship between the scaling parameter in a typical watermarking algorithm and the degradation of watermarked images. Experimental results show that the estimation error of SNR and PSNR is less than 1 dB. Using this relationship, we design an adaptive insertion strategy that can be employed to embed watermarks in natural images with assigned SNR or PSNR.

1 Introduction

Digital watermarking, which has been proposed as a solution to the problem of copyright protection of multimedia data in the networked environment, is a process of embedding information (or signature) directly into the media data by making small modifications to them. With the detection/extraction of the signature from the watermarked media data, it has been claimed that digital watermarks can be used to identify the rightful owner, the intended recipients, as well as the authenticity of media data.

As a number of watermarking methods have been proposed in recent years, evaluation of watermarking algorithms becomes more and more important. Among the major performance indexes, the degradation of watermarked images, which can be measured by signal to noise ratio (SNR) or peak signal to noise ratio (PSNR), is cared about by most of the users. In this paper, based on the Laplacian distribution model of AC DCT coefficients, we deduce a theoretical relationship between the scaling parameter in a typical watermarking algorithm and the degradation of watermarked images. Experimental results show that the estimation error of SNR and PSNR is less than 1 dB. Based on this work, not only can we estimate how degraded the images will be after embedding watermarks, but also realize an adaptive watermark embedding algorithm in the DCT domain for natural images with assigned SNR or PSNR.

S. Qing, T. Okamoto, and J. Zhou (Eds.): ICICS 2001, LNCS 2229, pp. 52-61, 2001.

The rest of the paper is organized as follows: Section 2 reviews watermarking schemes proposed by Cox [2, 3] and Barni [11]. In section 3, after briefly describing statistical models that have been proposed to better characterize the DCT coefficients of common images, we introduce mathematical analysis of the DCT coefficient distributions which has been reported by Lam and Goodman [1]. In section 4, we deduce the theoretical relationship between the scaling parameter in watermarking algorithms and SNR or PSNR of watermarked images. Based on this work, a new watermark insertion strategy that can be used to embed watermarks with assigned quality grade in images is obtained. Section 5 illustrates experimental results. Section 6 draws some conclusions.

2 Embedding Image Watermark in the Block-DCT Coefficients

Since Cox et al. [2, 3] proposed a global DCT-based spread spectrum approach to hide watermarks, more and more watermarking schemes in the DCT domain have been presented. As a private watermarking method, the constraint of accessing the original image limits the use of Cox's algorithm, since if there are too many images to be authenticated, it must be difficult to find the original image according to a watermarked image. As a matter of fact, it becomes a special case of content based image retrieval. More serious, Craver [8, 9] reported a counterfeit attack to private watermarking system, which is called "IBM attack". Most of current private watermarking systems could not resist this attack. We notice that more and more blind watermarking schemes have been proposed recently. Barni [11] improved Cox's algorithm, and made it a blind watermarking scheme by embedding the signature in the fixed position. To achieve both perceptual invisibility and robustness against JPEG compression, the watermarking algorithms always select host coefficients in the low-middle frequency band. In this paper, the watermark embedding algorithm to be evaluated is just like Barni's. What changes here is that we use the 8×8 block-wise DCT coefficients to embed watermark, not the full frame DCT coefficients, so that the algorithm can adapt to JPEG standard.

Like [2, 3, 11], watermark $W = \{w_1, w_2, \cdots, w_n\}$ consists of a pseudo-random sequence of length n, each value w_i, $i = 1, 2, \ldots, n$, is a random real number with a normal distribution having zero mean and unity variance. Given an Image I, the 8×8 block-wise DCT transform $D = DCT(I)$ is computed. Some low-frequency coefficients of each block are then extracted and reordered into zig-zag order. Thus we obtain the host sequence $H = \{h_1, h_2, \cdots, h_n\}$. The watermarked sequence $H' = \{h'_1, h'_2, \cdots, h'_n\}$ is obtained according to

$$h'_i = h_i \cdot (1 + \alpha w_i), i = 1, 2, \cdots, n \tag{1}$$

where α is the scaling parameter. Finally, H' is reinserted in the zig-zag scan and the inverse 8×8 block-wise DCT is performed, thus we obtain the watermarked image $I' = DCT^{-1}(D')$.

3 Statistical Modeling of the DCT Coefficients

The discrete cosine transform (DCT) is widely used in transform image coding systems because of its nearly optimal energy compaction properties. Since efficient quantizer design and noise mitigation for image enhancement are based on source models, there have been various studies on the distributions of the DCT coefficients for images over the past two decades. Most of these studies concentrated on fitting the empirical data from some standard images with a variety of well-known statistical distributions, and then comparing their goodness-of-fit [1].

Early on, Pratt [7] conjectured that the AC coefficients follow a zero-mean Gaussian distribution, defined as

$$f_G(x) = (1/\sqrt{2\pi}\sigma) \cdot e^{-x^2/2\sigma^2} \tag{2}$$

By using the Kolmogorov-Smirnov test, Reininger and Gibson verified that the AC coefficients had a Laplacian distribution [4] , defined as

$$f_L(x) = (1/\sqrt{2}\sigma) \cdot e^{-\sqrt{2}|x|/\sigma} \tag{3}$$

Joshi and Fischer modeled the AC coefficients with a general Gaussian density function [5], defined as

$$f_{GGD}(x) = \frac{\gamma\alpha(\gamma)}{2\sigma\,\Gamma(1/\gamma)} \exp\left\{-[\alpha(\gamma)|x/\sigma|]^{\gamma}\right\} \tag{4}$$

where $\alpha(\gamma) = \sqrt{\dfrac{\Gamma(3/\gamma)}{\Gamma(1/\gamma)}}$, $\Gamma(\cdot)$ denotes the usual gamma function, γ is the shape parameter of the p.d.f., which describes the exponential rate of decay, and σ is the standard deviation. The General Gaussian distribution model contains the Laplacian and Gaussian distribution as special cases, using $\gamma = 1$ and $\gamma = 2$, respectively. The shape of $f_{GGD}(x)$ for some shape parameters is depicted in figure 1.

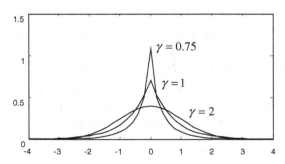

Fig. 1. Shape of the $f_{GGD}(x)$ for some shape parameters. The Laplacian and Gaussian distribution as special cases, using $\gamma = 1$ and $\gamma = 2$, respectively.

According to the maximum likelihood criterion, Barni [6] evaluated the shape parameter using 170 natural images. The experimental results demonstrated that ac coefficients could be effectively modeled by Laplacian density function. In [5], Joshi and Fischer concluded that the probability density of the AC coefficients is much closer to Laplacian or Gaussian with block classification based on ac energy.

Although the Laplacian distribution remains a popular choice balancing simplicity of the model and fidelity to the empirical data, few of the authors provides analytic justification for the choice of this model. In [1], Lam and Goodman offered a comprehensive mathematical analysis of the DCT coefficient distributions of natural images. They demonstrated that using a doubly stochastic model could derive Laplacian distribution of the coefficients. Our work in this paper is based on their demonstration.

For simplicity, assume that the size of image I is $8m \times 8n$. After dividing I into nonoverlapping blocks of size 8×8, the set of sub-images $\{I_1, I_2, \cdots, I_{m \times n}\}$ is obtained. Each block is then subjected to the discrete cosine transform, thus we get the block set $\{V_1, V_2, \cdots, V_{m \times n}\}$, where $V_i = DCT(I_i)$, $i = 1, 2, \cdots, m \times n$. Since DCT is a quasi-optimal transform, we can assume AC coefficients in V_i to be statistically independent. Therefore, by the central limit theorem, the AC coefficients within a block should be approximately distributed as Gaussian with zero mean, while the variance is proportional to the variance of pixels in the block. The probability density function is

$$f\left(V_i(x,y)/\sigma_i^2\right) = \frac{1}{\sqrt{2\pi}\sigma_i} e^{-V_i(x,y)/2\sigma_i^2}, \quad x, y = 1, 2, \cdots 7 \tag{5}$$

After some observation, Lam assumed that the histogram of the variance of natural images could be reasonably approximated by exponential distribution, i.e.,

$$f(\sigma^2) = \lambda \cdot e^{-\lambda\sigma^2} \tag{6}$$

The density function of AC block-DCT coefficients can be obtained using conditional probability

$$f(V(x,y)) = \int_0^\infty f\left(V(x,y)/\sigma^2\right) \cdot f(\sigma^2) \cdot d(\sigma^2) \tag{7}$$

Substituting (5) and (6) into (7), we get

$$f(V(x,y)) = \frac{1}{\sqrt{2}\sigma_V} e^{-\sqrt{2}|V(x,y)|/\sigma_V} \tag{8}$$

where the standard deviation is

$$\sigma_V = \frac{1}{\sqrt{\lambda}} \tag{9}$$

4 Evaluating the Degradation of Watermarked Images

4.1 Relationship between σ_I^2 and σ_V^2

Notice that the watermark is very weak compared with the AC coefficients, we can assume that the Laplacian statistical model of DCT AC coefficients will not change after watermark embedded, and only the variance will be different. To analyze the relationship between the scaling parameter and the degradation of watermarked images, we must first of all deduce the relationship between variance of image luminance and variance of the AC coefficients.

Among the set of sub-images $\{I_1, I_2, \cdots, I_{m\times n}\}$, let μ_i be the mean luminance of I_i, i.e. $\mu_i = E(I_i)$, then the mean luminance of the whole image I is

$$\mu_I = E(I) = E(\mu_i) , i = 1, 2, \cdots, m \times n \tag{10}$$

Its variance is

$$\sigma_I^2 = E(I^2) - [E(I)]^2 = E[E(I_i^2)] - \mu_I^2 \tag{11}$$

For each sub-image, $\sigma_i^2 = E(I_i^2) - \mu_i^2$, then (11) can be rewritten as

$$\sigma_I^2 = E(\sigma_i^2 + \mu_i^2) - \mu_I^2 = E(\sigma_i^2) + E(\mu_i^2) - \mu_I^2 \tag{12}$$

From the previous section, we know that σ_i^2 follows an exponential distribution, so it is easy to know that

$$E(\sigma_i^2) = \frac{1}{\lambda} \tag{13}$$

Substituting (9), (13) into (10), we obtain the follow result

$$\sigma_I^2 = \sigma_V^2 + E(\mu_i^2) - \mu_I^2 \tag{14}$$

Let $\sigma_\mu^2 = E(\mu_i^2) - \mu_I^2 = E(\mu_i^2) - E^2(\mu_i)$ to be the variance of the mean for luminance of sub-images, (14) can be simplified as

$$\sigma_I^2 = \sigma_V^2 + \sigma_\mu^2 \tag{15}$$

As the watermark is embedded in the AC coefficients, according to the definition of inverse DCT (IDCT), the direct components μ_i will be constant during the watermark embedding procedure. Thus σ_μ^2 is merely depended on the original image I, and the change of σ_I^2 relies on the alteration of σ_V^2 only.

4.2 Evaluation of SNR and PSNR

Just like noise interference, watermark embedding degrade the image's quality. In spatial domain, the watermarked image can be modeled as $I' = I + n$. To measure the degradation of watermarked image I', two objective criteria that have been used in image compression research are introduced. They are signal to noise ratio (SNR) and peak signal to noise ratio (PSNR), defined as

$$SNR(dB) = 10\lg(\sigma_I^2/\sigma_n^2) \tag{16}$$

$$PSNR(dB) = 10\lg(255^2/\sigma_n^2) \tag{17}$$

Since the watermarking algorithm leaves the DC component unchanged, it can be derived from (15) that

$$\sigma_n^2 = \sigma_{I'}^2 - \sigma_I^2 = \sigma_{V'}^2 - \sigma_V^2 \tag{18}$$

Substituting (18) into (16) and (17), we obtain the definitions of SNR and PSNR of image I in the DCT domain

$$SNR = 10\lg\{\sigma_I^2/(\sigma_{V'}^2 - \sigma_V^2)\} \tag{19}$$

$$PSNR = 10\lg\{255^2/(\sigma_{V'}^2 - \sigma_V^2)\} \tag{20}$$

Assume that the watermark is embedded in DCT AC coefficients according to (1), based on the Laplacian model of V, the variance of AC coefficients of watermarked images can be determined as

$$\sigma_{V'}^2 = (1 + \alpha^2)\sigma_V^2 \tag{21}$$

Substituting (15) and (21) into (19) and (20), we obtain the relationship

$$SNR = 10\lg\sigma_I^2 - 10\lg(\sigma_I^2 - \sigma_\mu^2) - 20\lg\alpha \tag{22}$$

$$PSNR = 20\lg 255 - 10\lg(\sigma_I^2 - \sigma_\mu^2) - 20\lg\alpha \tag{23}$$

From the expression (22) and (23), we can conclude that SNR and PSNR will decrease following the native log law as the scaling parameter α increases. As for different images, the watermarked image quality is also depended on the "energy" of original image σ_I^2, and the variance of the mean for luminance of sub-images σ_μ^2. The higher the image energy is, the less is the degradation. On the other hand, the higher σ_μ^2 is, that is to say, the more complex the image content is (the less uniform the luminance distribution is), the less is the image degradation. Apparently, these conclusion accords with our subjective sensation very well.

4.3 Adjusting α According to Assigned Quality Grade and Image

Until now, a lot of algorithms have been proposed to make the scaling parameter adaptive to local images or local areas in image. But from the commercial point of view, since the value of digital images are closely associated with the their quality, there will be obvious benefits if the insertion strategy can embeds watermark with assigned quality grade for different images. Based on our evaluation formula (22) and formula (23), we can design such a strategy.

Given a quality parameter SNR or PSNR, it is easy to obtain the estimation of scaling parameter $\hat{\alpha}$ according to specified image I from (22) or (23). If the estimation have enough precision, the strategy will also perform well.

5   Experimental Results

Selecting the first nine AC DCT coefficients in zig-zag order in every blocks as the host sequence, we sign the standard image "cameraman" with some scaling parameters range from 0.01 to 0.1. The theoretical estimation of image degradation (SNR, PSNR) and corresponding experimental results are shown in Table1, Table 2 and Figure 2. Both the SNR (left) and PSNR (right) agree quite well with their theoretical calculations. The estimation error is less than 1 dB.

Table 1. Theoretical estimation and experimental results of signal to noise ratio (SNR)

α	0.01	0.02	0.03	0.04	0.05
SNR (Theoretical)	48.15	42.13	38.60	36.10	34.17
SNR (Empirical)	47.26	41.24	37.72	35.22	33.28
α	0.06	0.07	0.08	0.09	0.10
SNR (Theoretical)	32.58	31.24	30.08	29.06	28.15
SNR (Empirical)	31.70	30.36	29.20	28.18	27.26

Table 2. Theoretical estimation and experimental results of peak signal to noise ratio (PSNR)

α	0.01	0.02	0.03	0.04	0.05
PSNR (Theoretical)	60.38	54.36	50.84	48.34	46.40
PSNR (Empirical)	59.50	53.48	49.95	47.46	45.52
α	0.06	0.07	0.08	0.09	0.10
PSNR (Theoretical)	44.82	43.48	42.32	41.30	40.38
PSNR (Empirical)	43.93	42.59	41.43	40.41	39.50

To test our watermark insertion strategy, we embed watermarks with specified SNR and PSNR (indicated by dashed in figure 4) in eight images shown in figure 3. Computing results of SNR(above) and PSNR(below) are illustrated in fig 4.

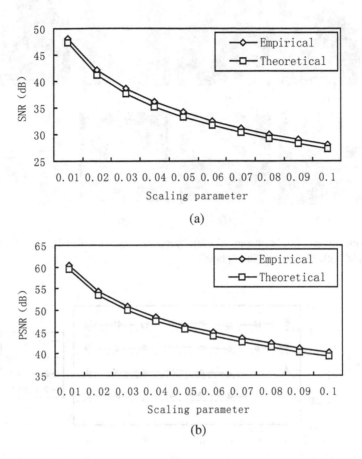

Fig. 2. The relationship between scaling parameter and image quality. (a) shows the relationship between scaling parameter and SNR, (b) shows the relationship between scaling parameter and PSNR.

6   Conclusion

In this paper, a theoretical relationship between the scaling parameter in a typical watermarking algorithm and the degradation of watermarked images has been explored. We began our analysis by extending Lam's mathematical justification for Laplacian distribution model of DCT coefficients of natural image [1]. A relationship between variance of image luminance and variance of the block-DCT coefficients has been deduced. Then the estimation formulas of SNR and PSNR have been obtained according to their definition. These evaluation formulas not only accord with subjective sensation very well, but also have very high estimated accuracy demonstrated in our experiments.

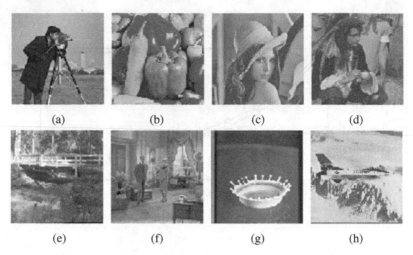

Fig. 3. Test Images. (a): "cameraman". (b): "peppers". (c): "Lena". (d): "man". (e): "bridge". (f): "couple". (g): "milkdrop". (h): "plane".

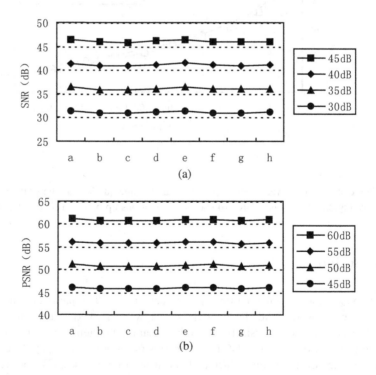

Fig. 4. Assigned and computed image quality. (a) shows the assigned and computed SNR, (b) shows the assigned and computed PSNR.

References

1. Lam, E.Y., Goodman, J.W.: A Mathematical Analysis of the DCT Coefficient Distributions for Images. IEEE Trans. on Image Processing. 10 (200) 1661-1666
2. Cox, I.J., Kilian. J., Leighton T., Shamoon T.: Secure Spread Spectrum Watermarking for Multimedia. IEEE Trans. on Image Processing. 6 (1997) 1673-1687
3. Cox, I.J., Kilian, J., Leighton, T., Shamoon, T.: Secure Spread Spectrum Watermarking for Multimedia. NEC Research Institute Tech. Report 10 (1995)
4. Reininger R.C., Gibson, J.D.: Distributions of the two-dimensional DCT Coefficients for Images. IEEE Trans. on Communications. 6 (1983) 835-839
5. Joshi, R.J., Fischer, T.R.: Comparison of Generalized Gaussian and Laplacian Modeling in DCT Image Coding. IEEE Signal Processing Letters. 5 (1995) 81-82
6. Barni, M., Bartolini, F., Cappellini, V., Piva, A.: Statistical Modeling of Full Frame DCT Coefficients. Proceedings of EUSIPCO'98, Rhodes, Greece (1998) 1513-1516
7. Pratt, W.K., Digital Image Processing. New York Wiley (1978)
8. Craver, S., Memon, N., Yeo, B., Yeung, M.: Can Invisible Watermarks Resolve Rightful Ownerships?. SPIE Electronic Imaging: Storage and Retrieval of Image and Video Databases. 3022 (1997) 310-321
9. Craver, S., Memon, N., Yeo, B., Yeung, M.: Resolving Rightful Ownerships with Invisible Watermarking Techniques: Limitations, Attacks, and Implication. IEEE Journal on Selected Areas in Comm. 4 (1998) 573-586
10. Zeng, W.J., Liu, B.: A Statistical Watermark Detection Technique Without Using Original Images for Resolving Rightful Ownership of Digital Images. IEEE Trans. on Image Processing. 11 (1999) 1534-1548
11. Barni, M., Bartolini, F., Cappellini, V., Piva. A.: A DCT-Domain System for Robust Image Watermarking. Signal Processing. 3 (1998) 357-372

A Cyclic Window Algorithm for ECC Defined over Extension Fields

Kazumaro Aoki[1]*, Fumitaka Hoshino[2], and Tetsutaro Kobayashi[2]

[1] NTT Communications
[2] NTT Information Sharing Platform Laboratories, NTT Corporation
{maro,fhoshino,kotetsu}@isl.ntt.co.jp

Abstract. This paper presents a new sliding window algorithm that is well-suited to an elliptic curve defined over an extension field for which the Frobenius map can be computed quickly, e.g., optimal extension field. The algorithm reduces elliptic curve group operations by approximately 15% for scalar multiplications for a practically used curve in comparison with Lim-Hwang's results presented at PKC2000, the fastest previously reported. The algorithm was implemented on computers. As a result, scalar multiplication can be accomplished in $573\mu s$, $595\mu s$, and $254\mu s$ on Pentium II (450 MHz), 21164A (500 MHz), and 21264 (500 MHz) computers, respectively.

1 Introduction

Many studies have been conducted on fast exponentiation algorithms, since many public key cryptosystems require exponentiation g^e [1, Sect. 8]. If the base or exponent cannot be fixed, the sliding window exponentiation [1, 14.85 Algorithm in p. 616] is one of the most efficient algorithms for computing exponentiations.

Recently, elliptic curve cryptosystems have been the focus of much attention, since there are many advantages, for example, a short key length and fast computation speed. In particular, the use of an optimal extension field (OEF) [2] for software implementation has determined that an elliptic curve cryptosystem is faster than a public key cryptosystem based on modular exponentiations.

The algorithms for an exponentiation can be used for scalar multiplications in group operations defined over an elliptic curve. Moreover, if an extension field is used for an elliptic curve, another technique called the base-ϕ expansion [3] can be employed. Until now, several studies on base-ϕ expansion have been conducted including application to OEF [4], but these studies focused on expanding a scalar representation to a base-ϕ representation and the results of the expansion are only analogous to modular exponentiation algorithms.

Solinas presented base-ϕ expansion with a window algorithm for an elliptic curve [5]. His algorithm was considered only for a field with characteristic two, and he used a (sliding) window algorithm. While, Lim and Hwang presented the

---

* This work was done while the author was in NTT Information Sharing Platform Laboratories.

S. Qing, T. Okamoto, and J. Zhou (Eds.): ICICS 2001, LNCS 2229, pp. 62–73, 2001.
© Springer-Verlag Berlin Heidelberg 2001

Lim-Lee algorithm [6] application to an elliptic curve defined over OEF [7,8]. They used a more sophisticated algorithm to compute a scalar multiplication using base-ϕ representation, but they did not use any special property derived from elliptic curve properties. Moreover, Tsuruoka and Koyama used optimal addition sequences for this scenario [9]. After finishing constructing the addition sequence, their algorithm performs fast, but computing the addition sequence requires long time for small extension fields.

This paper focuses on a mixture of the sliding window and base-ϕ expansion. Computing Frobenius map ϕ is very fast in a suitably-represented extension field. This property ensures that we can smoothly "slide" in the other direction for computing a scalar multiplication.

2 Preliminaries

2.1 Elliptic Curve

An elliptic curve cryptosystem consists of group arithmetics defined in an elliptic curve over a finite field. The number of field operations follows the representation of a point on an elliptic curve. We can roughly classify the representation into two groups: one is the projective system which does not require field inversion, and the other is the affine system which requires field inversions. For more details, Cohen et al. [10] presents a discussion on the advantages and disadvantages of these systems.

Below is an example of Jacobian coordinates, one of the projective systems. Using a and b as a parameters, a non-supersingular elliptic curve with a characteristic greater than 3 is defined as

$$Y^2 = X^3 + aXZ^4 + bZ^6 \quad (4a^3 + 27b^2 \neq 0) \ . \tag{1}$$

We can define the group operations for the rational points on the curve.

2.2 Previous Studies on OEF

This section provides a brief overview of the history of the implementations of scalar multiplication on an elliptic curve over OEF.

Bailey and Paar proposed OEFs [2]. An OEF can be represented as $\mathrm{GF}(p)[x]$ $/(f(x))$, where $p = 2^n - c$ ($\log_2 c \leq \frac{1}{2}n$) and $f(x) = x^m - \omega$. (Note that n is the size of p and m is the extension degree.) An OEF is very well suited to software implementation because the conditions,

$$2^n \equiv c \pmod{p}$$
$$x^m \equiv \omega \pmod{f(x)} \ ,$$

can be used to reduce the complexity of field multiplications. They showed that their implementations are significantly faster than the implementations previously reported.

Kobayashi et al. applied the base-ϕ expansion technique [3] to scalar multiplication in $E(\mathrm{GF}(p^m))/\mathrm{GF}(p)$ [4]. Similar to an elliptic curve over $\mathrm{GF}(2^m)$, which we call a binary field hereafter, the computational cost of Frobenius endomorphism ϕ, is very low. This condition made their implementations about twice as fast as that reported by Bailey and Paar.

Lim and Hwang presented implementations that do not use any epoch-making techniques; however, their accumulation of minor techniques increased the speed of their implementation by approximately two-fold [7,8].

2.3   Window Algorithms

The window algorithm is an algorithm that computes kP using online precomputation. A brief description of the algorithm is given below.

Step 1: Compute $Q_i \leftarrow iP$ for $(2 \leq i < 2^w)$, and let $Q_0 = \mathcal{O}$ and $Q_1 = P$.

Step 2: Using c_i that satisfies $k = \displaystyle\sum_{i=0}^{\lfloor (\log_2 k)/w \rfloor} 2^{wi} c_i \quad (0 \leq c_i < 2^w)$, compute

$$kP = \sum_{i=0}^{\lfloor (\log_2 k)/w \rfloor} 2^{wi} Q_{c_i}.$$

It accelerates scalar multiplication in comparison to the binary algorithm [1, 14.76 and 14.79 Algorithms in pp. 614–615].

Moreover, the sliding window algorithm [1, 14.85 Algorithm in p. 616] was proposed to improve the window algorithm. By using c_i and w_i satisfying $k = \displaystyle\sum_{i=0}^{\lfloor (\log_2 k)/w \rfloor} 2^{w_i} c_i$, compute $kP = \displaystyle\sum_{i=0}^{\lfloor (\log_2 k)/w \rfloor} 2^{w_i} Q_{c_i}$, where $w_i \geq w_{i-1} + w$.

This paper applies this approach to the base-ϕ expansion algorithm, and proposes an improved version of the sliding window algorithm called the *cyclic window algorithm* to compute $\displaystyle\sum_{i=0}^{m-1} c_i \phi^i P$.

3   Cyclic Window Algorithm

This section proposes the *cyclic window algorithm* and analyzes the algorithm. The cyclic window algorithm computes scalar multiplication kP.

3.1   Notations

This section defines the notations used in the following sections that have not appeared in the previous sections.

Definition 1. *Let $\overline{x}$ be the complementation of all elements in binary vector x. That is*

$$\overline{[x_0, x_1, \ldots, x_{m-1}]} := [\overline{x_0}, \overline{x_1}, \ldots, \overline{x_{m-1}}] . \tag{2}$$

Definition 2. ϕ *mapping for vector* $[x_0, x_1, \ldots, x_{m-1}]$ *is defined as*

$$\phi[x_0, x_1, \ldots, x_{m-2}, x_{m-1}] := [x_{m-1}, x_0, x_1, \ldots, x_{m-2}] \ .$$

Definition 3. *"$a \sqsupseteq b$" is* true *if binary vector a includes binary vector b. More precisely,*

$$[x_0, x_1, \ldots, x_{m-1}] \sqsupseteq [y_0, y_1, \ldots, y_{m-1}]$$
$$:= \begin{cases} \text{true} & \text{if } x_j \vee \overline{y_j} = 1 \ (i.e., \ x_j \geq y_j) \text{ for } \forall j \ (0 \leq j < m) \\ \text{false} & \text{otherwise} \end{cases}$$

Definition 4. $w_H(x)$: *Hamming weight of x, i.e., number of non-zero elements in vector x.*

Definition 5. $v_i := [1, e_{i,0}, e_{i,1}, \ldots, e_{i,m-2}]$, *where* $\{e_{i,j}\}_{j=0}^{m-2}$ *is the binary representation of i $(0 \leq i < 2^{m-1})$ in the little endian fashion, i.e., $e_{i,j}$ satisfies the following equation.*

$$i = \sum_{j=0}^{m-2} e_{i,j} 2^j, \quad \text{where } e_{i,j} \in \{0, 1\} \ . \tag{3}$$

For example, we have $v_1 = [1, 1, 0, 0, 0, 0, 0]$ *and* $v_{13} = [1, 1, 0, 1, 1, 0, 0]$ *for* $m = 7$.

3.2 Our Approach

This section describes the key idea of the cyclic window algorithm using an example.

We assume that k is already expanded to base-ϕ representation, for example,

$$k = 4 + 11\phi + 7\phi^2 + 2\phi^3 + 3\phi^4 + 1\phi^5 + 0\phi^6 \ ,$$

and $m = 7$. The expansion can be done using [4, Step 1 in Base-ϕ Scalar Multiplication Procedure], for example. Let n' be the size of the coefficients of the expansion.

We use the online precomputation table as follows.

$$Q_1 = (v_1 \bullet [1, \phi, \ldots, \phi^{m-1}]^T) P = (1 + \phi) P$$
$$Q_2 = (v_2 \bullet [1, \phi, \ldots, \phi^{m-1}]^T) P = (1 + \phi^2) P$$
$$Q_3 = (v_3 \bullet [1, \phi, \ldots, \phi^{m-1}]^T) P = (1 + \phi + \phi^2) P$$

Let L be the number of points in the table.

First, we denote the base-ϕ representation as binary representations (see Fig. 1). Second, we reduce 1s using signed-binary forms applying the condition $2^j(1 + \phi + \cdots + \phi^{m-1})P = \mathcal{O}$ [4][1] (see Fig. 2).

---

[1] Take care of choosing P. There may be a point that the equation does not hold, because $\mathbb{Z}[\phi]$ is not always an integral domain.

Coeff.		Bin. Rep.			
4	ϕ^0	0	1	0	0
11	ϕ^1	1	0	1	1
7	ϕ^2	0	1	1	1
2	ϕ^3	0	0	1	0
3	ϕ^4	0	0	1	1
1	ϕ^5	0	0	0	1
0	ϕ^6	0	0	0	0

Fig. 1. Binary Representation of the Coefficients in Base-ϕ Expansion

Coeff.		Bin. Rep.					Precomp.
4	ϕ^0	0	[1]	[-1]	[-1]		[1][1][1]
11	ϕ^1	[1]	[0]	0	0		[1][0][1]
7	ϕ^2	0	[1]	0	0		[1][1]
2	ϕ^3	0	0	0	[-1]	$\cdots - \phi^3 P$	$Q_1 Q_2 Q_3$
3	ϕ^4	0	0	0	0		
1	ϕ^5	0	0	[-1]	0		
0	ϕ^6	0	0	[-1]	[-1]	$\cdots - \phi^6 Q_1$	

Fig. 2. How to Use the Precomputation Table

Since we can compute $\phi^i Q_l$ from precomputed point Q_l with a low level of complexity, we can use not only Q_l but also $\phi^i Q_l$ $(0 \le i \le m-1)$ referring to a precomputed point. Fig. 2 shows that $-\phi^6 Q_1$ can be used in the least significant bit. If we use the basic sliding window algorithm, the scalar multiplication for the least significant bits is computed by

$$-P - \phi^3 P - \phi^6 P \ ,$$

but we can "wrap" precomputed point Q_1 from ϕ^6 to ϕ^0, since $\phi^7 P = P$ holds. Thus, we can cyclically use the precomputed points as follows.

$$-\phi^3 P - \phi^6 Q_1$$

Following the above observations, we can compute kP using (4) with the precomputed points Q_1, Q_2, and Q_3 similar to the left-to-right binary algorithm for multiple bases [1, Algorithm 14.88 in p. 618]. It requires only four elliptic curve additions and three elliptic curve doublings after three elliptic curve additions and subtractions in the online precomputation stage.

$$kP = 2(2(2(\phi P) + Q_2) - \phi^5 Q_3) - \phi^3 P - \phi^6 Q_1 \tag{4}$$

3.3 Procedure

Using the notations defined above, we propose the cyclic window algorithm in Fig. 3[2]. The algorithm computes scalar multiplication, kP, but we assume that scalar k is already expanded to base-ϕ representation using [4, Steps 1 and 2 in Base-ϕ Scalar Multiplication Procedure] to hold

$$k = \sum_{i=0}^{m-1} c_i \phi^i \quad (c_i \ge 0) \ .$$

---

[2] It is trivial that we can omit the first elliptic curve doubling and addition in the main computation stage, but we do not describe this in the figure, since we describe the algorithm as simple as possible for easy understanding.

By using [8, the explanation for (14)], we assume $\log_2 c_i \leq n \ (= n')$, where n is the size of p and n' is the maximum size of coefficient c_i. The algorithm inputs the structure of the online precomputation table, $\{u_0, u_1, \ldots, u_L\}$. The structure is defined in Sect. 4.1.

Note that the algorithm is a generalization of Solinas' algorithm [5].

Input: c_i $(0 \leq c_i < 2^{n'})$, P, m, $\{u_0, u_1, \ldots, u_L\}$ $(\subseteq \{v_0, v_1, \ldots v_{2^{m-1}-1}\})$

Output: $\displaystyle\sum_{i=0}^{m-1} c_i \phi^i P$

Step 1: [Coefficient adjustment stage]

Let $c_{i,j}$ be the j-th bit of c_i and d_j be a vector which is a collection of $c_{i,j}$s, i.e.,

$$c_i = \sum_{j=0}^{n'-1} c_{i,j} 2^j, \text{ where } c_{i,j} \in \{0,1\}$$

and

$d_j \leftarrow [c_{0,j}, c_{1,j}, \ldots, c_{m-1,j}].$

If $w_{\mathrm{H}}(d_j) \geq (m+1)/2$ then

$\qquad s_j \leftarrow -1$ and $d_j \leftarrow \overline{d_j}$,

else

$\qquad s_j \leftarrow 1.$

Step 2: [Online precomputation stage]

Compute $Q_l \leftarrow u_l \bullet [P, \phi P, \phi^2 P, \ldots, \phi^{m-1} P]^{\mathrm{T}}$, for $0 \leq l \leq L$.

Step 3: [Main computation stage]

$R \leftarrow \mathcal{O}$

for $j = n' - 1$ downto 0 do

$\qquad R \leftarrow 2R$

$\qquad$ for $l \leftarrow L$ downto 0 do

$\qquad\qquad$ for $i \leftarrow 0$ to $m - 1$ do

$\qquad\qquad\qquad$ if $d_j \sqsupseteq \phi^i u_l$ then

$\qquad\qquad\qquad\qquad d_j \leftarrow d_j \oplus \phi^i u_l, \ R \leftarrow R + s_j \phi^i Q_l$

$\qquad\qquad\qquad$ end if

$\qquad\qquad$ end for i

$\qquad$ end for l

end for j

Output R.

Fig. 3. Cyclic Window Algorithm Procedure

4   Evaluation of Cyclic Window Algorithm

In this section, we evaluate the performance of the cyclic window algorithm applied to OEF for practically used parameters: the size of the maximum prime order subgroup is at least 160 bits and at most 256 bits.

4.1   Table Structure

Deciding on the structure of the online precomputation table is difficult. We propose the following heuristic strategy.

Let $T = \{u_0, u_1, \ldots, u_L\}$ be the subset of $\{v_0, v_1, \ldots, v_{2^{m-1}-1}\}$ that satisfies the following conditions:

- $u_0 = v_0$
- $\forall u_l [T \cap \{\phi^1(u_l), \ldots, \phi^{m-1}(u_l), \phi^0(\overline{u_l}), \phi^1(\overline{u_l}), \ldots, \phi^{m-1}(\overline{u_l})\} = \emptyset]$
- $w_{\mathrm{H}}(u_l) \le w_{\mathrm{H}}(u_{l+1})$
- $\sigma(l) < \sigma(l+1)$ if $w_{\mathrm{H}}(u_l) = w_{\mathrm{H}}(u_{l+1})$, where $\sigma(\cdot)$ is a permutation of the set $\{0, 1, \ldots, 2^{m-1} - 1\}$ and satisfies $u_l = v_{\sigma(l)}$.
- $\sigma(L)$ is as small as possible.

4.2   Table Size

In this section, we evaluate the bound of the online precomputation table size, L. Since the extension degree is m and the table does not need to contain $\mathcal{O}$ and P, the table size is at most $2^m - 2$. However, we need only one point in

$$\left\{ uP \mid u \in \{\phi^0(v_l), \phi^1(v_l), \ldots, \phi^{m-1}(v_l), \phi^0(\overline{v_l}), \phi^1(\overline{v_l}), \ldots, \phi^{m-1}(\overline{v_l})\} \right\}, \quad (5)$$

because the other points can be easily computed in the main computation stage. Since m is odd prime, the size of Set (5) is exactly $2m$. Thus, it is sufficient to choose

$$L = \frac{2^{m-1} - 1}{m} - 1 \quad (6)$$

at most.

Table 1 gives the values derived from (6).

Table 1. Table Size Bound

Extension degree m	3	5	7	11	13	17	19
Bound of table size L	0	2	8	92	314	3854	13796

4.3   Small Extension Degree

In this section, we consider the preparation of a table which is at maximum. This case only needs at most 1 elliptic curve addition in the main loop in the main computation stage. However, of course, large m requires a higher degree of complexity of the online precomputation stage. Referring to Table 1, we study the case of a small m, that is, $m \leq 7$. In this case, we do not need a large table according to Table 1. The size of the table is at most 8. Because of the coupon collector's paradox, the probability that there exists a point in the table which is not referred in Step 3 in Fig. 3 is very low, if the size of the coefficients of the base-ϕ expansion n' is greater than $8 \log 8$ that is approximately equal to 17. On the other hand, n, which equals the size of p, is large because the prime order subgroup must be sufficiently large. Since n' is larger than $160/(m - 1)$ which is approximately equal to 27, it overwhelms 17. Thus, maximizing L makes the cyclic window algorithm perform the fastest.

To summarize the above discussion, the cyclic window algorithm requires $\dfrac{2^{m-1} - 1}{m} - 1$ elliptic curve additions for the online precomputation, $n' - 1$ elliptic curve doublings and $(n' - 1)(1 - \dfrac{2}{2^m})$ elliptic curve additions for the main computation on average.

4.4   Large Extension Degree

In this section, we consider a large m value, say $m \geq 11$. As we consider the previous sections, to maximize the table size is not effective because the maximum table size is very large. It seems very difficult to analyze the precise complexity. Therefore, we computed the average elliptic curve additions in j-loop of Step 3 in Fig. 3 for all d_j, which is not applied to the "if" clause in Step 1 by a computer. Table 2 shows the computed results for m and L. Let $t_{m,L}$ be a value in Table 2. The cyclic window algorithm requires L elliptic curve additions for the online precomputation, $n' - 1$ elliptic curve doublings and $(n' - 1)t_{m,L}$ elliptic curve additions for the main computation on average.

Table 2 shows that the table construction described in Sect. 4.1 is not the best. There are some numbers greater than one that use less of the precomputation table. However, the tendency of the values in Table 2 shows that the greater the table size, the fewer matches.

4.5   Comparison with the Best Previous Result

To the best of the author's knowledge, Lim and Hwang's results [7,8] are the fastest previously reported. Their computational complexity is evaluated in [8, Sect. 5]. They tried to evaluate their algorithm for general cases, but precise numbers were not clear, since their evaluation contains parameters. However, they could derive precise numbers when m and n' were fixed. They showed numbers for $(m, n') = (7, 28)$, $(11, 16)$, and $(13, 14)$. We derive the optimal table

Table 2. Average Matches for Each Bit in the Coefficients of the Base-ϕ Expansion

		m					m					m		
L	11	13	17	19	L	11	13	17	19	L	11	13	17	19
0	4.15	5.03	6.83	7.74	8	1.97	2.39	3.17	3.57	16	1.82	2.03	2.79	3.09
1	3.09	3.70	4.94	5.57	9	1.96	2.33	3.12	3.51	17	1.80	2.05	2.78	3.09
2	2.67	3.20	4.30	4.85	10	1.93	2.26	3.04	3.42	18	1.79	2.04	2.75	3.07
3	2.45	2.93	3.89	4.37	11	1.90	2.20	2.97	3.33	19	1.78	2.03	2.72	3.05
4	2.31	2.78	3.69	4.16	12	1.90	2.16	2.94	3.28	20	1.77	2.01	2.69	3.01
5	2.17	2.64	3.51	3.95	13	1.87	2.11	2.88	3.22	21	1.76	1.98	2.66	2.98
6	2.08	2.53	3.36	3.79	14	1.84	2.07	2.83	3.16	22	1.75	1.97	2.63	2.95
7	2.02	2.45	3.23	3.63	15	1.83	2.06	2.80	3.11	23	1.74	1.96	2.60	2.92

size for the above parameters in order to draw a comparison to their results. However, we only compare the number of elliptic curve additions, since the cyclic window algorithm and Lim and Hwang algorithm require the same number of elliptic curve doublings.

When m equals 7, $L = 8$ is optimal choice according to Sect. 4.3[3]. Thus, the scalar multiplication requires

$$8 + (28 - 1)(1 - \frac{2}{2^7}) = 34.6$$

elliptic curve additions on average.

When m equals 11 or 13, we need to find the smallest

$$L + (n' - 1)t_{m,L} \tag{7}$$

using Table 2. We tried all combinations of (7). We found that $L = 6$ for $m = 11$ and $L = 7$ for $m = 13$ are the optimal choices[4]. These cases require

$$6 + (16 - 1)2.08 = 37.2 \quad \text{and} \quad 7 + (14 - 1)2.45 = 38.9$$

elliptic curve additions, respectively. We summarize the above numbers and compare with Lim and Hwang results in Table 3.

5   Implementation Examples

5.1   Parameters

We use the following parameters which are constructed [4] by the Weil conjecture, and the field parameters are shown in the upper columns in Table 4. Note that α is a root of $f(x)$ used by $GF(p)[x]/(f(x))$, and we choose the base as a generator of the maximum prime order subgroup.

---

[3] This case requires 448 bytes for storing the online precomputation table, when using the parameter shown in Table 4.

[4] These cases require 264 and 364 bytes for storing the online precomputation table, respectively, when using the parameters shown in Table 4.

Table 3. Comparison with Lim and Hwang's Results

	Online precomp.		Main comp.		Total	
(m, n')	Ours	[8]	Ours	[8]	Ours	[8]
(7, 28)	8Ae	15Ae	34.6Ae+27De	41.2Ae+27De	42.6Ae+27De	56.2Ae+27De
(11, 16)	6Ae	13Ae	37.2Ae+15De	41.7Ae+15De	43.2Ae+15De	54.7Ae+15De
(13, 14)	7Ae	14Ae	38.9Ae+13De	44.1Ae+13De	45.9Ae+13De	58.1Ae+13De

"Ae" and "De" denote the computational cost of an elliptic curve addition and an elliptic curve doubling, respectively.

Word length: 16 bits $\qquad y^2 = x^3 - 3x - 172$

Maximum prime order in subgroups 3 7735447064 0784663733 8580162818 7749646114 9221530761 (exceeding 168 bits)

Base point $(10869\alpha^{12}+3898\alpha^{11}+15358\alpha^{10}+3782\alpha^9+4242\alpha^8+7589\alpha^7+5310\alpha^6+$ $12599\alpha^5+10370\alpha^4+9316\alpha^3+8340\alpha^2+184\alpha+9573, 8924\alpha^{12}+9141\alpha^{11}+9472\alpha^{10}+$ $8964\alpha^9+14633\alpha^8+4204\alpha^7+5379\alpha^6+13644\alpha^5+11470\alpha^4+15042\alpha^3+6518\alpha^2+$ $15906\alpha+7391)$

Word length: 32 bits $\qquad y^2 = x^3 - 3x - 85$

Maximum prime order in subgroups 239 4696831448 0862150279 8948628438 5174133848 4034750169 (exceeding 174 bits)

Base point $(200472906\alpha^6+172723217\alpha^5+174386879\alpha^4+403718784\alpha^3$ $+23043362\alpha^2+525400877\alpha+17252111, 523133120\alpha^6+178522781\alpha^5$ $+357710308\alpha^4+10611891\alpha^3+423928020\alpha^2+2135201\alpha+535095305)$

5.2 Timings

Based on the above discussion, we implemented scalar multiplication in the elliptic curves. The timing is summarized in Table 4. In the table, "$\frac{1}{2}$" means that we adopted the parallel multiplication technique described in [11]. For example, we can compute two OEF multiplications in 604 cycles on a Pentium II. Table 4 also shows Lim and Hwang's results [7,8] as a reference. We refer to the detailed timings shown in [7]. However, we refer to the timings of the scalar multiplication shown in [8], since the timings of a scalar multiplication shown in [8] are faster than those in [7]. The results are scaled to 450 MHz for Pentium II and 500 MHz for 21164.

Our implementations on the Pentium II, 21164A, and 21264 use the Jacobian coordinate, the affine coordinate, and the coordinate proposed in [7, Sect. 2.2], respectively. We selected a 160-bit random integer as a scalar. Even if we select a number close to the order of subgroup generated by the base point as a scalar, the time for main computation stage hardly increases, but the time for converting a scalar to the base-ϕ representation will slightly increase. Note that $a = -3$ is always used in (1) for fast implementation purposes.

Table 4. Elliptic Curve Scalar Multiplication (cycles)

	Current study			[7]		
CPU	Pentium II	21164A	21264	Pentium II		21164
p	$2^{14}-3$	$2^{29}-3$	$2^{29}-3$	$2^{14}-3$	$2^{28}-57$	$2^{28}-57$
$f(x)$	$x^{13}-2$	x^7-2	x^7-2	$x^{13}-2$	x^7-2	x^7-2
Subgroup order	168	174	174	168	168	168
scalar mult (μs)	573	595	254	791	687	672
scalar mult (10^3)	258	298	127	356	309	336
EC add (A)	NA	3412	1544	6091	4628	4866
EC dbl (A)	NA	3830	1621	6863	5107	5543
EC add (P)	(M)3692	4152	1524	6171	4256	4696
EC dbl (P)	2528	3128	1164	4442	3086	3518
OEF inv	$\frac{1}{2}$4824	2120	1010	4200	3259	3292
OEF mult	$\frac{1}{2}$604	323	117	543	379	383
OEF sqr	$\frac{1}{2}$525	309	99	404	301	359
OEF ϕ	111	116	70			
OEF add	26	58	28	91	42	59
OEF sub	21	58	28			
GF(p) inv	1	266	219	19	457	376

- (A): affine, (P): projective
- (M): the addend is represented by affine coordinate
- NA: Not Available
- Pentium II (450 MHz), Other CPU (500 MHz)

6   Conclusion

This paper presented the cyclic window algorithm, a new scalar multiplication algorithm for elliptic curves defined over OEF. The algorithm first makes an online precomputation table and then computes a scalar multiplication using the precomputation table with the Frobenius map. The condition of the Frobenius map $\phi^m = 1$ allows us to use the precomputation table cyclically. This highly used Frobenius map makes scalar multiplication about 15% faster than the previously reported best results [7,8]. We also implemented our algorithm by software. A scalar multiplication can be computed in $573\mu s$, $595\mu s$, and $254\mu s$ on Pentium II (450 MHz), 21164A (500 MHz), and 21264 (500 MHz) computers, respectively.

Finally, how to decide the structure of the online precomputation table is left for future study.

References

1. Menezes, A.J., van Oorschot, P.C., Vanstone, S.A.: Handbook of applied cryptography. CRC Press (1997)
2. Bailey, D.V., Paar, C.: Optimal extension fields for fast arithmetic in public-key algorithms. In Krawczyk, H., ed.: Advances in Cryptology — CRYPTO'98. Volume 1462 of Lecture Notes in Computer Science. Springer-Verlag, Berlin, Heidelberg, New York (1998) 472–485
3. Koblitz, N.: CM-curves with good cryptographic properties. In Feigenbaum, J., ed.: Advances in Cryptology — CRYPTO'91. Volume 576 of Lecture Notes in Computer Science. Springer-Verlag, Berlin, Heidelberg, New York (1992) 279–287
4. Kobayashi, T., Morita, H., Kobayashi, K., Hoshino, F.: Fast elliptic curve algorithm combining frobenius map and table reference to adapt to higher characteristic. In Stern, J., ed.: Advances in Cryptology — EUROCRYPT'99. Volume 1592 of Lecture Notes in Computer Science. Springer-Verlag, Berlin, Heidelberg, New York (1999) 176–189 (A preliminary version was written in Japanese and presented at SCIS'99-W4-1.4).
5. Solinas, J.A.: An improved algorithm for arithmetic on a family of elliptic curves. In Kaliski Jr., B.S., ed.: Advances in Cryptology — CRYPTO'97. Volume 1294 of Lecture Notes in Computer Science. Springer-Verlag, Berlin, Heidelberg, New York (1997) 357–371
6. Lim, C.H., Lee, P.J.: More flexible exponentiation with precomputation. In Desmedt, Y.G., ed.: Advances in Cryptology — CRYPTO'94. Volume 839 of Lecture Notes in Computer Science. Springer-Verlag, Berlin, Heidelberg, New York (1994) 95–107
7. Lim, C.H., Hwang, H.S.: Fast implementation of elliptic curve arithmetic in $GF(p^n)$. In Imai, H., Zheng, Y., eds.: Public Key Cryptography — Third International Workshop on Practice and Theory in Public Key Cryptosystems, PKC 2000. Volume 1751 of Lecture Notes in Computer Science. Springer-Verlag, Berlin, Heidelberg, New York (2000) 405–421
8. Lim, C.H., Hwang, H.S.: Speeding up elliptic scalar multiplication with precomputation. In Song, J.S., ed.: Information Security and Cryptology — ICISC'99. Volume 1787 of Lecture Notes in Computer Science. Springer-Verlag, Berlin, Heidelberg, New York (2000) 102–119
9. Tsuruoka, Y., Koyama, K.: Fast computation over elliptic curves $E(\mathbf{F}_{q^n})$ based on optimal addition sequences. IEICE Transactions Fundamentals of Electronics, Communications and Computer Sciences (Japan) **E84-A** (2001) 114–119
10. Cohen, H., Miyaji, A., Ono, T.: Efficient elliptic curve exponentiation using mixed coordinates. In Ohta, K., Pei, D., eds.: Advances in Cryptology — ASIACRYPT'98. Volume 1514 of Lecture Notes in Computer Science. Springer-Verlag, Berlin, Heidelberg, New York (1998) 51–65
11. Aoki, K., Hoshino, F., Kobayashi, T., Oguro, H.: Elliptic curve arithmetic using SIMD. In Davida, G., Frankel, Y., eds.: Information Security Conference — ISC'01. Lecture Notes in Computer Science. Springer-Verlag, Berlin, Heidelberg, New York (2001) to appear. (Preliminary version written in Japanese was appeared in SCIS2000-B05 and ISEC2000-161.).

Fast Scalar Multiplication on the Jacobian of a Family of Hyperelliptic Curves*

Fangguo Zhang, Futai Zhang, and Yumin Wang

National Key Laboratory on ISN, Xidian University
Xi'an, 710071, People's Republic of China
fgzh@hotmail.com; ymwang@xidian.edu.cn

Abstract. Hyperelliptic curve cryptosystems (HCC for short) is a generalization of ECC. It has been drawing the attention of more and more researchers in recent years. The problem of how to decrease the amount of addition and scalar multiplication on the Jacobians of hyperelliptic curves so that the implementation speed can be improved is very important for the practical use of HCC. In this paper, Using Frobenius endomorphism as a tool, we discuss the problem of faster scalar multiplication. A faster algorithm on Jacobian's scalar multiplication of a family of specific hyperelliptic curves is proposed with its computational cost analyzed. Analysis reveals that our algorithms's computational cost is less than that of Signed Binary Method.

1   Introduction

The security of many public key cryptosystems is based on the complexity of computing the discrete logarithm in finite abelian groups. The major issue arising in this context is the choice of a suitable group. For example, the multiplicative group of a finite field, which was proposed by the inventors of public key cryptography, turned out to be inappropriate, since it allows a subexponential algorithm for solving the discrete logarithm problem: The index calculus method.

Elliptic curves have been shown to be a good choice for building public key cryptosystems which was proposed independently by Neal Koblitz[6] and Victor Miller[9] in 1985, because the corresponding discrete logarithm problem seems to be very hard. In particular, methods like index calculus are not applicable to them. Since they offer high level of security even for shorter keys, elliptic curve cryptosystems are the optimal choice for smart cards and a number of other environments, which provide only limited storage space. Therefore, they are widely used today. As an natural extension, Neal Koblitz[8] proposed the hyperelliptic curve cryptosystems (HCC) in 1989, which is based on the discrete logarithm problem on the Jacobian of hyperelliptic curves over finite fields. The Jacobian of hyperelliptic curves turned out to be a rich source of finite abelian groups for defining one-way functions. Cantor's algorithm [2] provided an efficient method to implement the group operation on the Jacobian of a hyperelliptic curves. At

---

* This work was supported by the project 973 of China under the reference number G1999035804.

S. Qing, T. Okamoto, and J. Zhou (Eds.): ICICS 2001, LNCS 2229, pp. 74–83, 2001.

the same level of security, the basis field of hyperelliptic curve cryptosystems is smaller than that of ECC, and almost all protocols based on the standard DLP such as DSA and ElGamal can be planted to HCC. HCC may be faster than elliptic curve cryptosystems, as the usage of multiprecision integer arithmetic can be avoided for appropriate parameters.

There are many theoretical results on elliptic curves, however, up to now, the results on hyperelliptic curves are still not enough for the construction of efficient cryptosystems. As hyperelliptic curves promise to be the foundation of cryptosystems for the next decades.

Current research on HCC concentrates on finding construction methods for secure hyperelliptic curves and speeding up the arithmetics needed in HCC. At present, the common method used to compute the order of Jacobian is Weil conjecture method. Although the Weil conjecture method can find a few curves, it is simple and fast. About the scalar multiplication in Jacobian, most methods are similar to the addition group of elliptic curves. In [5], C.Gunther etc. extended the Frobenius expansion [10] of elliptic curves scalar multiplication over $GF(2)$, and used it in the scalar multiplication of Jacobian of hyperelliptic curves over $GF(2)$, thus speeded up the computation. The available implementations of HCC show that they are slower than the implementations of ECC[12][13][14]. Hence, how to decrease the amount of point addition and scalar multiplication on the Jacobians of hyperelliptic curves so as to improve the implementation speed of HCC is a very important problem for the practical use of HCC.

In this paper, the Jacobian of a kind of hyperelliptic curves is discussed. Using Frobenius endomorphism as a tool we study the faster scalar multiplication, and present a faster algorithm on Jacobian's scalar multiplication of a family of specific curves. We also analyze computational cost of the algorithm. The analysis shows that the computational cost of our algorithm is less than that of Signed Binary Method.

The paper is organized as follows. In Section 2, we introduce Hyperelliptic curves and its operation. While in Section 3, we introduce the Frobenius Automorphism of Jacobian of hyperelliptic curves and its properties. Section 4 studies a family of hyperelliptic curves with genius g=2 over $GF(q)$. In Section 5 we propose a faster algorithm on Jacobian's scalar multiplication of a family of specific curves and analyze its computational cost. Section 6 contains some concluding remarks.

2 Hyperelliptic Curves and Its Operations

2.1 Hyperelliptic Curves and Their Jacobian

We first introduce the definition and properties of hyperelliptic curves over finite field, more details can be found in reference [1][2][7][8]. Let F_q be a finite field and $\bar{F}_q$ be its algebraic closure. A hyperelliptic curve over F_q with genus g is defined by the following equation:

$$C: \ y^2 + h(x)y = f(x) \tag{1}$$

where $f(x)$, $h(x)$ in $F_q[x]$, $f(x)$ is a monic polynomial with degree $2g+1$ and $h(x)$ is a polynomial with degree at most g, and also there are no points $(x, y) \in \bar{F}_q \times \bar{F}_q$ which simultaneously satisfy the equation $y^2 + h(x)y = f(x)$ and the partial derivative equations $2y + h(x) = 0$ and $h'(x)y - f'(x) = 0$(A point satisfies the above conditions is called a singular point, and there is no singular point on HC). Let F_{q^n} be an extended field of F_q, the set of F_{q^n}-rational points on C, denoted $C(F_{q^n})$, is the set of all points $P = (x, y) \in F_{q^n} \times F_{q^n}$ which satisfy the equation (1) together with a special point at infinity denoted ∞ . Let $P = (x, y)$ is a finite point on hyperelliptic curve C, the opposite of P denoted $\tilde{P}$, defined as $\tilde{P} = (x, -y-h(x))$, $\tilde{\infty} = \infty$. A divisor on C is a finite formal sum $D = \Sigma_P m_P P$, where m_P are integers that are 0 for almost all P. The degree of D is defined by $deg D = \Sigma_P m_P$. If $D = \sigma(D)$, $\sigma \in Gal(\bar{F}_{q^n}/F_{q^n})$ (The Galois group of $\bar{F}_{q^n}$), then D is said to be defined over F_{q^n} . The set of all the divisors $D_C(F_{q^n})$ defined over F_{q^n} forms an abelian group with the set of divisors of degree 0 as its subgroup, that is $D_C^0(F_{q^n}) \subset D_C(F_{q^n})$. The divisor of a polynomial $G(x, y) \in \bar{F}_q[x, y]$ is defined by

$$div(G(x, y)) = \Sigma_P ord_P(G)P - \Sigma_P ord_P(G)\infty$$

where $ord_P(G)$ is the order of zero or pole of $G(x, y)$ at P . Now the divisor of a rational function $G(x, y)/H(x, y)$ is defined by $div(G(x, y)/H(x, y)) = div(G(x, y)) - div(H(x, y))$ and is called a principal divisor. We denote the group of principal divisors as $P_C(F_{q^n})$. Since every principal divisor has degree 0, $P_C(F_{q^n})$ is a subgroup of $D_C^0(F_{q^n})$. Finally, the Jacobian of C defined over F_{q^n} is given by $J(C; F_{q^n}) = D_C^0(F_{q^n})/P_C(F_{q^n})$.

2.2   The Group Operation and Discrete Logarithm over Jacobian

A hyperelliptic curve C with genus g is defined on a finite field F_q(let $q = p^r$), and its Jacobian over F_{q^n} is an abelian group. From the work of Neal Koblitz[8] and Cantor[2], we can know that the element $D = \Sigma m_i P_i - (\Sigma m_i)\infty$ (here $\Sigma m_i \leq g$, $P_i = (x_i, y_i)$) of $C's$ Jacobian can be only determined by two polynomials a and b in $F_{q^n}[x]$, where $a(x) = \Pi(x - x_i)^{m_i}$, and a, b satisfy: 1) $deg\, b < deg\, a \leq g$; 2) $b(x_i) = y_i$, for all the i that made $m_i \neq 0$; 3) $b^2 + hb - f \equiv 0 \pmod{a}$. $D = g.c.d.(div(a(x)), div(b(x) - y))$, in general we write it as $D = [a, b]$. The g.c.d. of two divisors $D_1 = \Sigma m_i P_i - (\Sigma m_i)\infty$ and $D_2 = \Sigma n_i P_i - (\Sigma n_i)\infty$ is defined as follows: $g.c.d.(D_1, D_2) = \Sigma min(m_i, n_i)P_i - (\Sigma min(m_i, n_i))\infty$.

Addition in the Jacobian is accomplished by two procedures: Composition and Reduction.

Algorithm 1: Addition in the Jacobian
Input: two divisors $D_1=[a_1, b_1]$ and $D_2 = [a_2, b_2]$ in the Jacobian
Output: $D_3 = [a_3, b_3] = D_1 + D_2$
Composition:
1) Compute $d = gcd(a_1, a_2, b_1 + b_2 + h) = s_1 a_1 + s_2 a_2 + s_3(b_1 + b_2 + h)$.
2) Let $a = a_1 a_2/d^2$,
3) Let $b = (s_1 a_1 b_2 + s_2 a_2 b_1 + s_3(b_1 b_2 + f))/d \pmod{a}$.
Reduction:
4) Let $a_3 = (f - bh - b^2)/a$, $b_3 = (-h - b) \pmod{a_3}$.

5) If $deg\ a_3 > g$, let $a = a_3$ and $b = b_3$, return to 4).

6) Let $a_3 = c^{-1}a_3$, where c is the first coefficient of a_3.

7) Output (a_3, b_3).

Algorithm 2: Double in the Jacobian

Input: a divisors $D_1 = [a_1, b_1]$ in the Jacobian,

Output: $D_2 = [a_2, b_2] = D_1 + D_1$.

Composition:

1) Compute $d = gcd(a_1, 2b_1+h) = s_1 a_1 + s_3(2b_1+h)$,

2) Compute $a = a_1^2/d^2$, $b = (2s_1a_1b_1 + b_1^2 + f)/d \pmod{a}$.

Reduction:

3) Let $a_2 = (f - bh - b^2)/a$, $b_2 = (-h - b) \pmod{a_2}$,

4) If $deg\ a_2 > g$, then let $a = a_2$, $b = b_2$ return to 2),

5) Let $a_2 = c^{-1}a_2$, where c is the first coefficient of a_2,

6) Output (a_2, b_2).

The generic operation need $17g^2 + O(g)$ operations in F_{q^n} whereas doubling needs $16g^2 + O(g)$ operation in F_{q^n}. So, we can assume that both operations have roughly the same complexity. It is important to note that inversion in the Jacobian is basically for free, since the opposite of $D = [a(x), b(x)]$ is given by $div[a(x), -h(x) - b(x)]$.

By the discussion of [3], for the divisor addition, it is not difficult to compute the average number of operations in $GF(2^n)$ for curves with $p = 2$, $g = 2$, $h = x$:

Composition needs $4g^2 + 5g + 2 = 28$ multiplications and 2 inversions; reduction needs $(7/6)g^3 + 3g^2 - (1/6)g = 21$ multiplications and $(1/2)g + 1 = 2$ inversions. The total number of operations is 49 multiplications and 2 inversions (or 89 multiplications under the assumption that one inversion is equivalent to 10 multiplications).

In this case, the composition of double divisor can be simplified as follows (let $a_1(x) = x^2 + \gamma x + \theta$):

1) If $\theta = 0$, then $d = x$, $s_1 = 0$, $s_3 = 1$; else, $d = 1$, $s_1 = \theta^{-1}$, $s_3 = \theta^{-1}(x+\gamma)$;

2) Compute $a = a_1^2/d^2$, $b = (b_1^2 + f)/d \pmod{a}$.

The probability of $\theta = 0$ is $1/2^n$, it is negligible. In characteristic 2, squaring a polynomial of degree l take $l+1$ squares in the underlying field. Assuming that the field arithmetic is implemented using normal bases, these squares are essentially for free, hence we do not count them. Therefore the average number of operations in $GF(2^n)$ for double divisor is 11 multiplications and 2 inversions in composition, $(7/6)g^3 + 3g^2 - (1/6)g = 21$ multiplications and $(1/2)g + 1 = 2$ inversions in reduction. The total is 32 multiplications and 4 inversions (about 72 multiplications).

The scalar multiplication on $J(C; F_{q^n})$ is to compute $mD = D + D + \cdots + D$ where D is a generator of $J(C; F_{q^n})$ (or a subgroup of $J(C; F_{q^n})$ with order n), m is a random integer with $m \mid \#J(C; F_{q^n})$ (or $m \mid n$).

The discrete algorithm problem in $J(C; F_{q^n})$ is: given two divisors D_1, D_2 defined on the $J(C; F_{q^n})$ over F_{q^n}, to determine the integer m such that $D_2 = mD_1$ (if such a m exists).

3   Frobenius Automorphism and Its Properties

Let F_q be a finite field and $\bar{F}_q$ its algebraic closure, $C : y^2 + h(x)y = f(x)$ be a hyperelliptic curve with genius g defined over F_q , F_{q^n} be a n-th extension field of F_q. The Frobenius automorphism $\phi : \bar{F}_q \to \bar{F}_q$, $x \to x^q$ induces an automorphism over Jacobian:

$$\phi : J(C; \bar{F}_q) \to J(C; \bar{F}_q)$$

$$D = \Sigma_P m_P P \bmod P_C(\bar{F}_q) \to \phi(D) = \Sigma_P m_P \phi(P) \bmod P_C(\bar{F}_q)$$

where $\phi(P) = (x^q, y^q)$, if $P = (x, y)$; $\phi(P) = \infty$, if $P = \infty$.

If D is an element in $J(C; F_{q^n})$, $D = [a(x), b(x)]$, $a(x) = \Sigma_{i=0}^k a_i x^i \in F_{q^n}[x]$, $b(x) = \Sigma_{i=0}^k b_i x^i \in F_{q^n}[x]$, then $\phi(D) = [\phi(a(x)), \phi(b(x))] = [\Sigma_{i=0}^k a_i^q x^i, \Sigma_{i=0}^k b_i^q x^i]$ It is not difficult to prove that the Frobenius automorphism of $J(C; F_{q^n})$ is a linear transformation, and it has a characteristic polynomial with order $2g$. In the case of $g=2$, the characteristic polynomial of the Frobenius automorphism in the Jacobian of hyperelliptive curve defined over F_q is [11]:

$$P(T) = T^4 - s_1 T^3 + s_2 T^2 - s_1 q T + q^2 \tag{2}$$

where $s_1 = q - (M_1 - 1)$, $s_2 = (M_2 - 1 - q^2 + s_1^2)/2$, and M_1, M_2 are the numbers of the rational points of the curves defined over F_q and F_{q^2}(including a infinity point). For any $D \in J(C; \bar{F}_q)$, we have $\phi^4(D) - s_1 \phi^3(D) + s_2 q \phi^2(D) + q^2(D) = \infty$.

4   A Family of Hyperelliptic Curves with Genius g=2 over $GF(q)$

In the sequel, we assume that $q = 2^m$.

Within the curves $y^2 + h(x)y = f(x)$ with $g=2$ defined over $GF(q)$, there is a family of curves which have such a property: the characteristic polynomial of their Jacobian's Frobenius automorphism have fewer terms (these characteristic polynomials are required to be irreducible at first). In this paper, through computation, we will find this kind of curves over $GF(2)$ and $GF(8)$. Such kind of hyperelliptic curves over larger finite field or over finite field with characteristic not equal to 2 also exists, but we will not discuss them here. Next, we give a description of such kind of curves over $GF(2)$ and $GF(8)$ and compute the orders of their Jacobians using Weil conjecture method.

For such kind of curves over $GF(2)$, we have:

Curve: $y^2 + (x^2 + x + 1)y = x^5 + x^4 + x^3$

Characteristic polynomial of Frobenius Automorphism: $T^4 + T^2 + 4$,

$\#Jac(C)(GF(2^{107}))$=26328072917139296674479506920917301414787852721508015252463986134

=6*6421*74994216391141*911249661956189334780398060108557963153473 6049

Curve: $y^2 + (x^2 + x)y = x^5 + x^4 + x$

Characteristic polynomial of Frobenius Automorphism: $T^4 - T^2 + 4$,

$\#Jac(C)(GF(2^{79}))$=365375409332725729550922292183917789809461213276

=4*913438523333181432387730573045979447452365303319

$\#Jac(C)(GF(2^{91}))$=61299821634635554334333881044271201546344654723 40027756

=4*2029*4159*8269*219621705701566583558242380977067437571706 21

$\#Jac(C)(GF(2^{97}))$=25108406941546723055343157693015513330857555182 110701284884

=4*14511*43138627828923653108623389617578711653593490451018 3171

Let $GF(2) = \{0, 1\}$, $GF(8) = GF(2)(\theta) = \{0, 1, \theta, \theta + 1, \theta^2, \theta^2 + 1, \theta^2 + \theta, \theta^2 + \theta + 1\} = \{0,1,2,3,4,5,6,7\}$, here θ is a root of equation $x^3 + x + 1 = 0$. Among the hyperelliptic curves of the form $y^2 + xy = f(x)$ with $g=2$ over $GF(8)$, there are only two sort of them whose characteristic polynomials of Frobenius Automorphism have fewer terms. The description of this two sort of curves is listed in the following table.

M_1, M_2	characteristic polynomial of Frobenius Automorphism	number of curves	Extending degree n for which secure is gotten	Number of curves subjected to WD attack
8,64	$T^4 - T^3 - 8T + 64$	2112	41,43,47	384
10,64	$T^4 + T^3 + 8T + 64$	2112	31,49	384

For $P(T) = T^4 - T^3 - 8T + 64$, there are 2112 such curves and only 384 of them can be attacked by Weil Descent. For the detailed discussion we refer the reader to reference [4]. There are still 1728 such curves defined on $GF(8)$ that can be used to construct cryptosystems. (10210), (14441), (41421), and (55621) are examples, where (f_0 f_1 f_2 f_3 f_4) represents the hyperelliptic curve $y^2 + xy = x^5 + f_4x^4 + f_3x^3 + f_2x^2 + f_1x + f_0$, for example, (10210) represents $y^2 + xy = x^5 + x^3 + 2x^2 + 1 = x^5 + x^3 + \theta x^2 + 1$;

$\#Jac(C)(GF(8^{41}))$=113078212145816597108204018598183329912387001 81 94334816820376532278683608 24

=56*83*5167*41616149*7119759061*158908513708137778441652402527 59 545846421631650901.

$\#Jac(C)(GF(8^{43}))$=463168356949264781745235535174725263173159053 24 0972337174219720620296817725224

=56*1033*5591*211540360267*676967470990293939970617979540455830 5 43764805226817767 4679.

$\#Jac(C)(GF(8^{47}))$=777067556890291628367244089375236340517224524 25 07718134518926224896252091723638270344

=56*659*417737*5837429329*863496847435731496322843927343164918 74 6122992851701334462435003 57.

For $P(T) = T^4 + T^3 + 8T + 64$, such as (03730), (12721),(22511),(55721), we have

$\#Jac(C)(GF(8^{31}))$=980797146154196225879243115247604657576488900 7 995525114

=74*49922801947*265490216327224596367433456743071541684519 63.

$\#Jac(C)(GF(8^{49}))$=31828687130226345097944466132589330488005475511
579693383345227425707234830532387720854599994

=74*701*84640781*72491873757741723605890549260086436890191556045227
50504238001716466988031460301.

With the hyperelliptic curve and its Jacobian , and the characteristic polynomial of Frobenius automorphism and its solutions, we can use the t-adic expansion (here t is a root of the characteristic polynomial of Frobenius automorphism) according to the discussion similar to [5], thus speed up the scalar multiplication of Jacobian. The detailed discussion is similar to the method in [5], here we don't discuss.

5   Fast Computation of a Special Kind of Curve Based on Subfield

The characteristic polynomial of Frobenius automorphism of hyperelliptic curve over $GF(q)$ is $P(T) = T^4 - s_1T^3 + s_2T^2 - s_1qT + q^2$. To compute mD, using the q^2-ary (or signed q^2-ary) expansion of m, we can replace q^2D with $(s_1q\phi - s_2\phi^2 + s_1\phi^3 - \phi^4)D$. If the amount of computation in computing $(s_1q\phi - s_2\phi^2 + s_1\phi^3 - \phi^4)D$ is smaller than that of in computing q^2D, our method will be faster than the ordinary method of computing mD. And the computation of $\phi(D)$ can then be reduced to at most $2g*2^{m-1}$ operations in F_{q^n} .

In the following, we take the curves with $P(T)=T^4-T^3-8T+64$ as an example to illustrate our algorithm. Let C be such a curve, we consider its Jacobian over $GF(8^{43})$. Suppose the domain parameters have been appropriately chosen.

Let

$\#Jac(C)(GF(8^{43}))$=56*1033*5591*211540360267*6769674709902939399706
17979540455830543764805226817767467967=56*1033*5591*211540360267*p.

Let D be an element in $J(C; GF(8^{43}))$, then D satisfies $\phi^4(D) - \phi^3(D) - 8\phi(D) + 64D = \infty$, and we have $64D = 8\phi(D) + \phi^3(D) - \phi^4(D)$. Let D be a p-order element in $J(C; GF(8^{43}))$ and $m < p$, in order to compute mD, we first precompute $-D, \pm 2D, \pm 3D, \cdots, \pm 63D$, then we represent m as 64-ary presentation: $m = \Sigma_{i=0}^l c_i 64^i$, $1 \le c_i \le 63$.

So $mD = \Sigma_{i=0}^l c_i 64^i D = \Sigma_{i=0}^l 64^i(c_iD) = \Sigma_{i=0}^l(8^i\phi^i(c_iD) + \phi^{3i}(c_iD) - \phi^{4i}(c_iD))$.

Next, we describe our faster algorithm on Jacobian's scalar multiplication.

Algorithm 4: Scalar multiplication of the divisor in Jacobian

Input: a p-order element $D = [a, \; b] = [x^2 + a_1x + a_0, \; b_1x + b_0]$ in $J(C; GF(8^{43}))$ and an integer $m < p$,

Output: mD

1) Pre-compute $-D, \pm 2D, \pm 3D, \cdots, \pm 63D$;

2) Initialize $H = \infty$, in fact we often let $H = [1, 0]$;

3) Convert m into signed 64-ary representation: $m = \Sigma_{i=0}^l c_i 64^i$, where $c_i \in \{-63, -62, \cdots, 0, \cdots, 62, 63\}$;

4) For i from l downto 0 do

(1)$H \leftarrow 8\phi(H) + \phi^3(H) - \phi^4(H)$,

(2) if $c_i \neq 0$, let$H \leftarrow H + c_iD$;

5) Output $H = mD$.

Computation Analysis and Comparison with Other Methods:

For $\phi(D) = [\phi(a(x)), \phi(b(x))] = [\Sigma_{i=0}^{1} a_i^q x^i, \Sigma_{i=0}^{1} b_i^q x^i]$, it only needs 12=2g*m multiplication in $GF(8^{43})$, and $\phi^4(D) = \phi^4([a, b]) = [\Sigma_{i=0}^{1} a_i^{q^4} x^i, \Sigma_{i=0}^{1} b_i^{q^4} x^i]$ needs 48 multiplication in $GF(8^{43})$. And these discussions are at the case that $GF(8^{43})$ is represented in polynomial basis. $64D = 8\phi(D) + \phi^3(D) - \phi^4(D)$ only needs 3 double divisor, 2 divisor addition, and 48 multiplication in $GF(8^{43})$. When the elements of $GF(8^{43})$ are represented in normal basis, $a(x)$ and $b(x)$ can be determined by simply shifting the normal basis representation of each coefficient a_i and b_i in order to compute $\phi(D)$. The complexity is therefore at most 12 cyclic shifts. These shift operations are basically "for free" when compared to the more expensive group operation in the Jacobian. $64D = 8\phi(D) + \phi^3(D) - \phi^4(D)$ only needs 3 double divisor, 2 divisor addition. Its total amount of computation is equal to 394 multiplications in finite field. Compared with simply using double divisor $64D$ needs 6 double divisor, it is equal to 432 multiplications in finite field), the amount of computation is decreased by 8.8% or 38 multiplications in $GF(8^{43})$. We give a comparison of our method of computing the scalar multiplication mD of divisor with the general binary method and 64-ary method in the following table.

Method	Number of Divisor addictions	Number of double Divisors	Number of Operations in $GF(8^{43})$
Binary method[1]	Max:$log_2 m$ Average:$\frac{1}{2}log_2 m$	$log_2 m$	Max: $89log_2 m + 72log_2 m$ Average:$\frac{1}{2}89log_2 m + 72log_2 m$
Signed binary method[1]	Max:$\frac{1}{3}log_2 m$ Average:$\frac{1}{6}log_2 m$	$log_2 m + 1$	Max: $\frac{1}{3}89log_2 m + 72(log_2 m + 1)$ Average:$\frac{1}{6}89log_2 m + 72(log_2 m + 1)$
64-ary method[1]	Max:$log_{64} m$ Average:$\frac{63}{64}log_{64} m$	$6log_{64} m$	Max: $89log_{64} m + 72 * 4log_{64} m$ Average:$\frac{63}{64}89log_{64} m + 72 * 4log_{64} m$
Signed 64-ary method[1]	Max:$\frac{63}{65}log_{64} m$ Average: $\frac{63^2}{64*65}log_{64} m$	$6log_{64} m$ $+6$	Max: $\frac{63}{65}89log_{64} m + 72 * 6(log_{64} m + 1)$ Average: $\frac{63^2}{64*65}89log_{64} m + 72 * 6(log_{64} m + 1)$
Our method	Max: $\frac{63}{65}log_{64} m + 2log_{64} m$ Average: $(\frac{63^2}{64*65} + 2)log_{64} m$	$3log_{64} m$ $+3$	Max: $89(\frac{63}{65}+2)log_{64} m)+72*3(log_{64} m + 1)$ Average: $89(\frac{63}{65}+2)log_{64} m+72*3(log_{64} m + 1)$

To the 64-ary representation of m, we select the signed 64-ary representation, then $c_i \in \{-63, -62, \cdots, 0, \cdots, 62, 63\}$, and the number of non-zero c_i's is smaller than that of 64-ary representation, so the amount of computation in the scalar multiplication will decrease, and computation will be speeded up. In algorithm 4, it needs pre-computing 125 elements. From the above table, we can see that our method needs less computation. So our method is better than the Signed Binary Method (or NAF) which is commonly considered as the best method at present. And the average ratio of the amount of computation of our method to that of the Signed Binary Method is

$(89(\frac{63^2}{64\times 65}\log_{64}m+2\log_{64}m)+ 72*3 \ (\log_{64}m+1))/ \ (89\frac{1}{6}\log_2 m+72(\log_2 m+1))$
≈ 0.928 .

Here $m \in [0, \ 2^{190}]$, and the average size of m is 189 bit.

This shows that the amount of computation of our method is decreased by 7.2% compared with Signed Binary Method. We also have

$(89(\frac{63^2}{64\times 65}\log_{64}m+2\log_{64}m)+ 72*3 \ (\log_{64}m+1))/(89\frac{63^2}{64\times 65}\log_{64}m+72*6*$
$(\log_{64}m+1))\approx 0.915$.

This shows that the amount of computation of our method is decreased by 8.5% compared with Signed 64-ary Method.

The analysis and examples above reveal that the bigger the ratio of the amount of divisor addition to that of double divisor is the better is our method.

6   Conclusion

Because ECC and HCC have no sub-exponent time attacks at present, and their key is small, they are especially suitable for constrained computation power and memory such as Smart card and other cryptosystems products. At the same level of security, the based field of HCC is smaller than that of ECC, but from the existed implementation [12][13][14], the implementation speed of HCC is slower than that of ECC. So how to decrease the computation of points addition and scalar multiplication in Jacobian of hyperelliptic curve is the key step to speed up the implementation of HCC and make it practical. It will be very significant in practice even if there is only a little decrease in computation and a little improvement in the implementation speed. In this paper, Using Frobenius endomorphism as a tool we have studied the faster scalar multiplication, and proposed a new faster algorithms on Jacobian's scalar multiplication of a class of specific curves. The analysis has shown that our algorithms's computation is less than that of Signed Binary Method. Hence our method will have practical application in the implementation of HCC.

References

1. Blake, I.F., Seroussi, G.: Smart, N.P., Elliptic Curves in Cryptography, London Mathematical Society Lecture Note Series.265. Cambridge University Press 1999
2. Cantor, D.G.: Computing in the Jacobian of a hyperelliptic curve, *Mathematics of Computation*, Vol. 48. (1987) 95-101
3. Enge, A.: The extended Euclidian algorithm on polynomials, and the computational efficiency of hyperelliptic cryptosystems. http://www.math.uni-augsburg.de/~enge/Publikationen.html
4. Galbraith, S.D.: Weil descent of Jacobians, http://www.cs.bris.ac.uk/~stenve
5. Gunther, C., Lange, T., Stein, A.: Speeding up the arithmetic on Koblitz curves of genus 2.Techn.Report CORR#2000-04,University of Waterlo. http://www.cacr.math.uwaterloo.ca
6. Koblitz, N.: Elliptic Curve Cryptosystems, Math. of Computation,Vol. 48. (1987) 203–209
7. Koblitz, N.: Algebraic Aspects of Cryptography, Algorithms and Computation in Math. Vol. 3. Springer-Verlag 1998.

8. Koblitz, N.: Hyperelliptic cryptography, J.of Crypto.,No.1.(1989) 139–150
9. Miller, U.S.: Use of Elliptic Curve in Cryptography, In Advances in Cryptology–CRYPTO'85(Santa Barbara,Calif.,1985),Spring-Verlag, LNCS 218 (1986) 417–426
10. Muller, U.: Fast Multiplication on Elliptic Curves over Small Fields of Characterristic Two. J. of Crypto.,No.11,(1998) 219–234
11. Pila, J.: Frobenius maps of abelian varieties and finding roots of unity in finite fields. *Math.Comp.*Vol. 55.(1996) 745–763
12. Sakai, Y., Sakurai, K., Ishizuka, H.: Secure hyperelliptic cryptosystems and their performance. In PKC,Imai, H.,Zheng, Y.,(eds.) Springer-Verlag, LNCS 1431. (1998) 164–181
13. Sakai, Y., Sakurai, K.: Design of hyperelliptic Cryptosystems in small characteristic and a software implementation over $F(2^n)$. In ASIACRYPT 98, Ohta, K., Pei, D.,(eds.) Springer-Verlag, LNCS 1514. (1998) 80–4
14. Smart,N.: On the performance of hyperelliptic cryptosystems. In EURO-CRYPT'99, Stern, J.(ed.), Springer-Verlag, LNCS 1592. (1999) 165–175

Attacks on Two Digital Signature Schemes Based on Error Correcting Codes*

Dingfeng Ye[1], Junhui Yang[2], Zongduo Dai[1], and Haiwen Ou[1,3]

[1]State Key Laboratory of Information Security
Graduate School, Academia Sinica
100039-08, Beijing, China
[2]Institute of Software, Academia Sinica
100080, Beijing, China, yangdai@mimi.cnc.ac.cn
[1,3] Beijing Institute of Electronic Science and Technology, Beijing, 100070

Abstract. Xinmei Wang [1] proposed a digital signature scheme based on error-correcting codes, and then a revised scheme was proposed in [6]. Some attacks on the operation of its basic form and some variations were given in [2,3,4,5], and then an attack on Xingmei'basic scheme and Xingmei's revised scheme based on a valid signature of a single message was given in [7]. In this paper, we give a totally trapdoor attack on Xinmei's constructions. Our attack can obtain the equivalent private key just by some simple matrix computations given only the public key. Another scheme [10] proposed by Weizhang Du and Xinmei Wang uses two maximum rank distance codes. We will show that this later scheme is insecure against a known-message attack.

Keywords: error-correcting code, digital signature, cryptanalysis

1   Introduction

It is well known that error-correcting codes can be used to construct public key encryption schemes[8,9]. The key idea is that the efficient decoding algorithm for some code (such as Goppa code) can be made a secret given only the generating or parity check matrix of the code. The encryption is just adding random errors to the code words corresponding to messages. Only the person knowing the decoding algorithm can identify the errors and recover the plain-texts. Note that the one way function implicitly used in such an encryption scheme is the function which maps an error vector (with weight $< t$) to its syndrome vector. If the code admits an efficient decoding algorithm, then the efficient decoding algorithm is a trapdoor for this one way function. It is not straightforward to exploit this trapdoor one way function to construct signature schemes. The difficulty lies in the fact that there are no obvious methods to use the set of the said syndrome vectors to encode messages without using the error vectors.

* Supported by 973-Foundation (No. G1999035804) and National Natural Science Foundation of China (No. 69773015).

S. Qing, T. Okamoto, and J. Zhou (Eds.): ICICS 2001, LNCS 2229, pp. 84–89, 2001.
© Springer-Verlag Berlin Heidelberg 2001

XinMei WANG [1] proposed a digital signature algorithm based on error-correcting codes not using the one-way function mentioned above. In this scheme, the signer uses some private matrices to act on a message plus an error vector in such a way that the message and the error satisfy some relation specified by the public matrices. The verifier use the public matrices to recover the error and then check if the expected relation holds. It would be quite mysterious that such matrices operations could produce onewayness. Previous attacks [2,3,4,5] exploited the weaknesses in operations of the scheme. For example, it is possible [2] to combine some valid signatures of messages into a valid signature of another message, or its private key can be obtained by a chosen-ciphertext attack [3] if the cryptanalyst can get $n+1$ signatures of the same message (see also [6]). These attacks exploited the linear correlations between messages and their signatures or some assumptions on operation mode of the scheme, so can be defended if M is properly protected by a hash function. In fact, these attacks are ineffective to the revised scheme in [6]. The recent attack proposed in [7] broke the basic scheme [1] and its variations [6] in the sense that any receiver of a signature can forge signatures of arbitrary messages: the receiver can make valid signatures of any other messages based on only one signature of any single message. The attack in [7] can only forge signatures related to a given error vector associated with the known valid signature. This denies Xinmei's construction as a signature scheme. It would be possible to use the algorithm in a challenge-response identification scheme where the error vector is used as the challenge of the verifier. In this paper, we show that such an application of the algorithm is still insecure. In fact,we can construct some matrices equivalent to the private key just from the public key, i.e., our attack is a totally trapdoor attack.

Another signature scheme [10] using error-correcting codes is proposed by Weizhang Du and Xinmei Wang. The scheme does use the one way function associated with an error-correcting code. To circumvent the difficulty of message encoding mentioned above, the scheme restrict the errors to be code words of another error-correcting code C, and the C is kept secret. This restriction makes the above one-way function vulnerable to known message attacks. If we know the syndromes of some errors which span C, then we can find the error corresponding to any syndrome in the specified range just by linear algebra.

2 Cryptanalysis of Xinmei's Schemes

2.1 Description of the Basic Xinmei Scheme

Public key and Private key: Each user of the the basic Xinmei scheme chooses an (n, k, d) binary Goppa code or other linear binary error-correcting code C_A, which has a $k \times n$ generator matrix G and the ability to correct t errors. The public key is the tuple (J, W, T, H, t), where

$$W = G^* S^{-1}, \ J = P^{-1} W, \ T = P^{-1} H',$$

here S and P are invertible matrices of order $k \times k$ and of order $n \times n$ respectively, H is a $(n - k) \times n$ parity check matrix of C_A and H' is its transpose of order

$n \times n - k$, and G^* is an $n \times k$ matrix satisfying $GG^* = I_k$, where I_k denotes the identity matrix of order k. The private key is the tuple (G, S, P).

Signature Algorithm: To sign a k-bit message M, the signer can compute the signature as follows:

1. Choose an n-bit error-vector, denoted by E, of Hamming weight less than t randomly,
2. Compute $C = (E + MSG)P$.

Then the signature for M will be C.

Verification Algorithm: After getting the tuple (M, C), to verify whether C is a valid signature for M, the verifier can compute as follows:

1. Compute $S = CT$, which turns out to be the syndrome of the error vector E, since $S = CT = (E + MSG)PP^{-1}H' = EH'$.
2. Recover E using a decoding algorithm (say, Berlekamp-Messay algorithm).
3. Check if $M = CJ - EW$.

The verifier accepts the signature C if $M = CJ - EW$, and rejects C otherwise.

2.2   Cryptanalysis of the Basic Xinmei Scheme

Matrix pair (P, A) regarded as the private key: Let $A = SGP$, then the signature for the message M is $C = EP + MA$, hence the matrix pair (P, A) can be regarded as the private key of the scheme. Let $B = (T, J)$, the private key (P, A) satisfies the following equations

$$PB = P(T, J) = P(P^{-1}H', P^{-1}W) = (H', W)$$

and

$$AB = A(T, J) = SGP(T, J) = SG(H', W) = (0, I_k).$$

We have the following proposition.

Proposition 1 (Matrix pair (P_1, A_1) equivalent to private key): Any matrix pair (P_1, A_1), where P_1 is an $n \times n$ matrix and A_1 is an $k \times n$ matrix, satisfying $P_1(T, J) = (H', W)$ and $A_1(T, J) = (0, I_k)$, is equivalent to the private key. To be more precise, one can forge a signature of any k-bit message M by using the pair (P_1, A_1) as follows:

1. Take an n-bit error-vector E of weight $w(E) < t$ randomly.
2. Compute $C = EP_1 + MA_1$.

Then C is a valid signature of M.
Proof: The verifier computes CT, which is exactly the syndrome of the error vector E since $CT = (EP_1 + MA_1)T = EH'$. Then the verifier recovers E using the Berlekamp-Messay algorithm. Finally, note that $CJ - EM = (EP_1 + MA_1)J - EM = EW + M - EW = M$, so C is a valid signature of M.

Computing a matrix pair (P_1, A_1) **equivalent to private key**: A matrix pair (P_1, A_1) which is equivalent to the private key can be computed using a generalized inverse of the matrix $B = (T, J)$ as follows. Choose two invertible matrices R and Q of both order n such that

$$RBQ = \begin{pmatrix} I_r & 0 \\ 0 & 0 \end{pmatrix},$$

and let

$$B^* = Q \begin{pmatrix} I_r & 0 \\ 0 & 0 \end{pmatrix} R,$$

then it is easy to check that B^* is a generalized inverse of B in the sense that $BB^*B = B$. Set $A_1 = (0, I_k)B^*$ and $P_1 = (H', W)B^*$. Then we have

$$A_1(T, J) = A_1 B = (0, I_k)B^* B = ABB^* B = AB = (0, I_k),$$
$$P_1(T, J) = P_1 B = (H', W)B^* B = PBB^* B = PB = (H', W),$$

so (A_1, P_1) is a matrix pair equivalent to the private key by Proposition 1.

2.3   Cryptanalysis of the Revised Xinmei Scheme

In the basic Xinmei scheme, messages and signatures (including the error vector) are linearly correlated. This makes it vulnerable to various attacks of operational type, such as the well-known broadcast-attack and homomorphism-attack. The standard technique to defend these attacks is to hash the messages before sign. A revised scheme [6] applies this idea to the basic Xinmei scheme, which just replace M with $h(E, M)$ in both the signature and verification algorithms, where $h(*, *)$ is a Hash function. It is easy to see that (P_1, A_1) constructed above can be used to sign any message in the revised scheme just as in the original scheme.

3   Cryptanalysis of Du and Wang's Scheme

Weizhang Du and XingMei Wang proposed a signature scheme based on maximum rank distance codes in [10]. In this section we show how to crack the scheme with a known-message attack.

3.1   Description of Du-Wang's Scheme

Public key and private key: User Alice chooses a linear $(n, n - r)$ code V with $r(V) > 2t_2$ over the finite field F_{q^N}, and chooses another linear (n', k') code C over F_{q^N} with $t_1 < r(c) < t_2 \forall c \in C$. Here $r(c)$, $c = (c_1, c_2, \cdots, c_{n'}), c_i \in F_{q^N}$, is defined as the dimension of the linear space spanned over F_q by all the components c_i, $1 \leq i \leq n'$, of c, and $r(C) = \min\{r(c) \mid c \in C\}$ which is called as the minimum rank distance of the code C, similarly for $r(V)$. Let H be a parity matrix of the code V, which is a $r \times n$ matrix over F_{q^N}, and let G be a generating matrix of the code C, which is a $k' \times n'$ matrix over F_{q^N}. Select a subset $J = \{j_i \; 1 \leq i \leq n'\}$ of n' elements in the set $\{1, 2, \cdots, n\}$, and assume $1 \leq j_1 < j_2 < \cdots < j_{n'} \leq n$. We denote by H_J the $r \times n'$ submatrix of H, which is consisting of the columns of index belonging to J, and let $F = H_J G'$. Let f be a hash function from $F_{q^N}^*$ to $F_{q^N}^{k'}$, where $F_{q^N}^{k'}$ is the set consisting of all k'-tuples over F_{q^N} (written in row), and $F_{q^N}^*$ is the union of all $F_{q^N}^i$, $i \geq 1$. The public key of Alice is (H, F), and her private key is (G, J).

Signature Algorithm: For any message $m \in F_{q^N}^*$, Alice's signature is $\underline{e} = (e_1, e_2, \cdots, e_n) \in F_{q^N}^n$, where $(e_{j_1}, e_{j_2}, \cdots, e_{j_{n'}}) = f(m)G$ and $e_j = 0 \forall j \notin J$.

Verification Algorithm: The verifier accepts $\underline{e}$ as a valid signature of m if and only if the two conditions $H\underline{e}^\tau = Ff(m)^\tau$ and $t_1 < r(\underline{e}) < t_2$ hold true.

3.2   Cryptanalysis on Du-Wang's Scheme

Proposition 2: The attacker can forge a signature for any message if he gets the signatures for approximately $O(k')$ messages as follows. Suppose he gets k' messages whose hash values $f(m_i) \in F_{q^N}^{k'}, 1 \leq i \leq k'$, are linearly independent over F_{q^N}, or equivalently, if the corresponding k' signatures $sig(m_i) = \underline{e}_i, 1 \leq i \leq k'$, linearly independent over F_{q^N}. Then for any message m, the tuple $\underline{e} = f(m)\Phi^{-1}E$ is the valid signature, where

$$
\Phi = \begin{pmatrix} f(m_1) \\ f(m_2) \\ \vdots \\ f(m_{k'}) \end{pmatrix}, \quad E = \begin{pmatrix} \underline{e}_1 \\ \underline{e}_2 \\ \vdots \\ \underline{e}_{k'} \end{pmatrix}.
$$

Proof: We have

$$
\begin{aligned}
H\underline{e}^\tau &= HE^\tau(\Phi^{-1})^\tau f(m)^\tau \\
&= H(\underline{e}_1^\tau, \underline{e}_2^\tau, \cdots, \underline{e}_{k'}^\tau)(\Phi^\tau)^{-1}f(m)^\tau \\
&= (H\underline{e}_1^\tau, H\underline{e}_2^\tau, \cdots, H\underline{e}_{k'}^\tau))(\Phi^\tau)^{-1}f(m)^\tau \\
&= (Ff(m_1)^\tau, Ff(m_2)^\tau, \cdots, Ff(m_{k'})^\tau)(\Phi^\tau)^{-1}f(m)^\tau \\
&= F\Phi^\tau(\Phi^\tau)^{-1}f(m)^\tau \\
&= Ff(m)^\tau.
\end{aligned}
$$

And it is clear that $\underline{e} = f(m)\Phi^{-1}E$ is in the subspace spanned by $\underline{e}_i = f(m_i)G \in C$, hence $\underline{e} \in C$, and then $t_1 < r(\underline{e}) < t_2$, which is the property assumed for the code C. The above two facts show $(m, \underline{e})$ passes the verification algorithm, hence $\underline{e}$ is the valid signature for m.

4   Conclusion

We conclude that Weizhang Du and Xinmei Wang's constructions for digital signature schemes based on error-correcting codes are not secure. It remains open to design secure and practical signature schemes using the one way function originated from the theory of error-correcting codes.

References

1. W.Xinmei Digital signature scheme based on error-correcting codes. IEE Electronics Letters,1990,26(13):898-899.
2. L.Harm, D.C. Wang, Cryptanalysis and modification of digital signature scheme based on error-correcting codes. IEE Electronics letters,1992,28(2):157-159.
3. M.Alabbadi,S.B.Wicker. Security of Xinmei digital signature scheme. IEE Electronics letters,1992,28(9):890-891.
4. Y.X. Li, An attack on Xinmei's digital signature scheme. IEEE ISIT'93,1993,236
5. M.Alabbadi,S.B.Wicker, Digital signature scheme based on error-correcting codes, IEEE ISIT'93,1993,199
6. X.M.Wang, Modification of the digital signature scheme based on error-correcting codes. ACTA ELECTRONICA SINICA,2000,28(2):110-112.
7. Z.D.Dai, J.H.Yang, D.F.Ye and G. Gong, Cryptanalysis of Wang's original and revised digital signatue schemes, Electronic-Letters, 15th Feb.2001 vol 37, No 4, p220.
8. R. J. McEliece, A public-key crypyosystem based on algebraic coding theorey, DSN progress report 42-44, Jet Propulsion Laboratory, Pasadena, 1978.
9. Niederreiter H., Knapsack-type cryptosystems and algebraic coding theory, Problems of control and information theory, Vol. 15, No. 2, 1986.
10. Weizhang Du and XinMei Wang, A digital signature scheme based on maximum rank-distance code, "Communication Privacy"(Chinese), No,3,2000, pp 39-40.

A Derivative of Digital Objects and Estimation of Default Risks in Electronic Commerce

Kanta Matsuura

Institute of Industrial Science, University of Tokyo,
Komaba 4-6-1, Meguro-ku, Tokyo 153-8505, Japan
kanta@iis.u-tokyo.ac.jp

Abstract. In electronic commerce, traded digital objects are likely associated with several numerical values as well as their prices. These values may change unpredictably over time and bring risks both to the providers and to the consumers of the application. One possible strategy for hedging the risks is to introduce derivatives regarding the uncertain values. This paper shows a theoretical pricing equation of the derivatives when the underlying digital objects have systematic default or revocation risks. We can make use of this pricing to estimate the risks.

1 Introduction

With the help of applied cryptography, we are going to trade more and more digital objects over an open network. Since digital objects can keep their original bit strings virtually forever, one may expect that there would be no risk of change. This is, unfortunately, not always the case. Digital objects can have not only prices but also other important numerical values. For example, digital certificates may have confidence values or trust metrics [1]. Access-grant tickets may have priority numbers or QoS (Quality-of-Service) values [2] reserved. Digitally-watermarked images [3] may have innocence values about their origins in terms of copyright protection. Any product may be associated with some insurance contracts [4]. Reward points may be attached. Those additional values and their effectiveness may change unpredictably over time and cause risks. At the worst case, the values get into defaults (*e.g.* the corresponding certificate is revoked) and the holder may have a large financial damage.

A popular way for hedging such stochastic risks is to introduce derivatives or options written on underlying assets, typically regarding their prices. In financial theory, encouraged by the seminal paper by Black and Scholes [5], option-pricing theories have been developed a lot. Most of them use assumptions including *divisibility* of the underlying assets, which is *not trivial* in the case of the digital objects. Thus we are motivated to study option pricing with models and assumptions suitable for digital objects. The rest of this paper consists of modeling (Sect. 2), pricing (Sect. 3), discussion including an application (Sect. 4), and conclusions (Sect. 5).

S. Qing, T. Okamoto, and J. Zhou (Eds.): ICICS 2001, LNCS 2229, pp. 90–94, 2001.

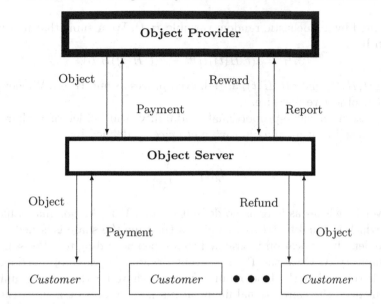

Fig. 1. A network commerce architecture where boxes with wider lines indicate that the entities inside are more trusted.

2   Objects with Default/Revocation Risks

Our model is based on an architecture illustrated in Fig. 1.

(Object Provider.)   Copyright management and related technical maintenance are difficult and non-trivial tasks. So are management and maintenance of network-security infrastructure (*e.g.* public-key infrastructure). These tasks may require sufficient trustworthiness and reliability. We need specialized entities. They would be happier if the objects they provide are distributed and circulated more frequently in larger amounts; it would improve their reputation and/or make attached advertisement more profitable.

(Object Server.)   Selling digital objects to untrusted customers through poor communication channels is difficult task, too. We need specialized entities.

(Customer.)   We do not trust individuals in terms of (i) their own behaviour, (ii) their financial situation, and (iii) resources (for communication and computation) available to them.

In a network life, we would want to pay for digital objects in electronic cash. Such digital payment systems could be more efficient if the monetary value of each coin is less granular [6]. Therefore, if we want to allow as wide variety of electronic cash systems as possible, highly discrete (*i.e.* very sparse) prices would be helpful. So we firstly assume an object whose price is fixed. For notational simplicity, we assign this fixed price as the unit of network currency. Also for simplicity, we assume each share of the object has a single value. This value is represented by a stochastic random variable $H(t)$. We assume that its dynamics is given by

$$dH = \mu(t, H(t))H dt + \sigma(t, H(t))H dW \tag{1}$$

where $\mu(t, H(t))$ and $\sigma(t, H(t))$ are adapted processes and W is a Wiener process under the objective measure.

We assume a value-proportional tradability; the holder of a share of the object can sell it at a *value-proportional price* S_p defined by

$$S_p(t) = \frac{\bar{V}}{H(t)} \tag{2}$$

whenever he wishes as long as no default occurs. $\bar{V}$ is the nominal value of the share, which is equal to $H(t_0)$ where t_0 is the time the share is issued.

The default/revocation is assumed to happen according to a Poisson process with intensity λ. Once the Poisson event occurs, the value-proportional tradability is ruined but the holder can refund his share for the original unit price. Different from the conventional financial market, we do **not** assume the divisibility of the object. We do **not** assume that we can go short for it, either. Also different from the conventional financial market, we assume that the Poisson process represents a systematic risk which can fully appear in the risk premium. As for other issues, we assume a typical liquid and arbitrage-free market [7].

The derivative we study here is a European call option written not on the price but on the value as follows. We assign the issuing time of the option as the time origin ($t=0$) for notational convenience.

Definition 1 (A European Call). *A European call option on the object is a derivative which provides a* right *to buy one share of the object with a reserved value K at a particular time T_m in the future for its fixed price, 1, regardless of the up-to-date value $H(T_m)$ at $t = T_m$. The reserved value K is called the* strike value, *and T_m is called the* maturity.

Let $C(t) = c(t, H(t))$ be the price process of the call option. As a continuous-time model, we place the following mathematical assumptions.

- The function $c(t, h)$ is a $C^{1,2}$-mapping in the domain $\boldsymbol{R}_+ \times \boldsymbol{R}_{++}$, and $c(t, 0) = 0$ for all $t \in \boldsymbol{R}_+$. $\boldsymbol{R}_{++}$ is the set of positive real numbers and $\boldsymbol{R}_+$ is the set of non-negative real numbers.
- The price process of the riskless asset is described by $dB(t) = r_f B(t) dt$, where the short rate r_f is a deterministic constant.

3   Pricing

By establishing a riskless portfolio composed of one share of the digital object and adjusted amount of options, we can reach the following pricing theorem. Due to the space limitation, the full proof [8] is not given here.

Theorem 1 (Boundary Value Problem for Pricing). *The only pricing function of the form* $C(t) = c(t, H(t))$ *is obtained when*

$$c(t,h) = \begin{cases} \hat{c}(t, 1/h) \text{ for } h > 0 \\ 0 \quad \text{ for } h = 0 \end{cases}$$

and $\hat{c}(t, g)$ *is the solution of the boundary value problem*

$$\frac{\sigma^2}{2} g^2 \hat{c}_{gg} + (r_f - \lambda)g\hat{c}_g - (r_f + \lambda)\hat{c} + \hat{c}_t = 0, \ \hat{c}(T_m, g) = \max\{0, Kg - 1\}$$

in the domain $[0, T_m] \times \boldsymbol{R}_{++}$.

4 Discussion

4.1 Jump Processes

We derived Theorem 1 by using a systematic risk assumption. This is different from the conventional finance [9]. The conventional nonsystematic-risk assumption is an extreme assumption and there have been a lot of arguments about it [11]. In fact, jumps observed in stock prices are reported to be systematic across the market portfolio [12]. Heuristically speaking, the more similarly network entities look at the default/revocation risk, the better model our choice would give. Our choice could go better with the recent trend in the public-key infrastructure toward a single-directory system [13], [14].

4.2 Application

According to Theorem 1, the option price depends on σ, T_m, r_f, h, K, and the risk of default/revocation λ. This suggests that the market data $(C, \sigma, T_m, r_f, h, K)$ may help us with an indirect measurement of the risk λ. This needs an inverse estimation, which may be too heavy. However, if what you want to do is just to see whether λ exceeds a certain value, say, λ_0, then you may be able to use a more practical strategy. That is, in the region where C is locally monotone-increasing/decreasing with respect to λ, the following procedure without repeat is worth a try.

1. By using recent market data, estimate the short rate r_f and the volatility σ.
2. Set $\lambda = \lambda_0$.
3. Solve the boundary value problem in Theorem 1.
4. Compare the result with the current option price data.
5. By using a tool for statistical test, examine whether you can say the computed price is higher(monotone-decreasing case)/lower(monotone-increasing case) than the observed price with sufficient probability.
6. If the answer is Yes, think of it as an alarm.

5 Concluding Remarks

We described an E-commerce architecture and a simple model of digital objects; each object has an abstracted value as well as a fixed price. The value can change stochastically and can be ruined at the worst case. The object is not divisible and we cannot go short for it. A European call option written not on the price but on the value was introduced. A PDE for pricing the option was derived. In the discussion, applications of the pricing were studied: to estimate the probability of revocation and to detect an alarm of high probability.

References

1. Reiter, M. K., Stubblebine, S. G.: Resilient Authentication Using Path Independence. IEEE Trans. Comput. **47** (1998) 1351–1362
2. Xiao, X., Ni, L. M.: Internet QoS: A Big Picture. IEEE Network. **13** (1999) 8–18
3. Katzenbeisser, S., Petitcolas, F. (eds.): Information Hiding Techniques for Steganography and Digital Watermarking. Artech House Publishers, Boston London (2000)
4. Reiter, M. K., Stubblebine, S. G.: Authentication Metric Analysis and Design. ACM Trans. Info. & Sys. Security **2** (1999) 138–158
5. Black, F., Scholes, M.: The Pricing of Options and Corporate Liabilities. J. Political Econ. **81** (1973) 637–654
6. Eng, T., Okamoto, T.: Single-Term Divisible Electronic Coins. In: De Santis, Alfredo (ed.): Advances in Cryptology — EUROCRYPT'94. Lecture Notes in Computer Science, Vol. 950. Springer-Verlag, Berlin Heidelberg New York (1995) 306–319
7. Björk, T.: Arbitrage Theory in Continuous Time. Oxford University Press, New York (1998)
8. Matsuura, K.: Security Tokens and Their Derivatives. Technical Reports, Centre for Communication Systems Research, University of Cambridge (2001)
   http://www.ccsr.cam.ac.uk/techreports/tr29/index.html
9. Merton, R. C.: Option Pricing When Underlying Stock Returns are Discontinuous. J. Financial Econ. **3** (1976) 125–144
10. Sharpe, W. F.: Capital Asset Prices: A Theory of Market Equilibrium under Conditions of Risk. J. Finance **19** (1964) 425–442
11. Colwell, D. B., Elliott, R. J.: Discontinuous Asset Prices and Non-Attainable Contingent Claims. Math. Finance **3** (1993) 295–308
12. Jarrow, R. A., Rosenfeld, E. R.: Jump Risks and the Intertemporal Capital Asset Pricing Model. J. Business **57** (1984) 337–351
13. Buldas, A., Laud, P., Lipmaa, H.: Accountable Certificate Management Using Undeniable Attestations. In: Proc. 7th ACM Conf. on Comp. & Comm. Security, Athens (2000) 9–18
14. Gassko, I., Gemmell, P. S., MacKenzie, P.: Efficient and Fresh Certification. In: Imai, H., Zheng, Y. (eds.): Public Key Cryptography — PKC 2000. Lecture Notes in Computer Science, Vol. 1751. Springer-Verlag, Berlin Heidelberg New York (2000) 342–353

A New Approach for Secure Multicast Routing in a Large Scale Network

Young-Chul Shim

Hong-Ik University Department of Computer Engineering
72-1 Sangsudong, Mapogu Seoul, 121-791 Korea
Shim@cs.hongik.ac.kr

Abstract. This paper presents an approach for providing security services for multicasting using PIM-SM and BGMP routing algorithms. Members and senders are authenticated and receive/use proper capabilities when they join a multicast group so that illegal hosts or routers may not be able to expand the multicast delivery tree. Messages are encrypted with either a group data key or sender specific key that is shared by all members and changed efficiently whenever a membership changes. So not only illegal hosts cannot read packets but also members cannot read packets exchanged before they join the group or after they leave the group. The authenticity of a packet is checked by the edge router of the sending host and then by the core routers to efficiently thwart an illegal host or corrupt router's attempt to inject a bogus packet or replay a packet. ...

1 Introduction

Multicasting has been used in many application areas and is becoming more important as an enabler for providing many new services in the Internet[1]. In multicasting data delivery trees are built by multicast routing algorithms and data packets are transmitted along the data delivery trees. Multicast routing algorithms are classified into intra-domain algorithms such as PIM-SM[2] and inter-domain routing algorithms such as BGMP[3].

The attacks to multicast delivery trees can be classified into edge attacks and internal attacks[4]. An edge attack originates from a host connected to a router at the leaves of a delivery tree. There are two types of edge attacks as follows.

- EA1 - Sender attacks: the delivery tree is attacked by the hosts sending bogus data packets to the group with the correct multicast address, thereby causing the packets to be sent to all receivers in the group. This attack consumes bandwidth, since the packet would be delivered to all host-members. Although such attacks are possible also within unicast, the impact is magnified in multicast due to the replication effect within the distribution tree. Such hosts may also send bogus control packets.
- EA2 - Receiver attacks: non-members simply join the group, causing the tree to expand and for multicast traffic to be forwarded to the non-member.

S. Qing, T. Okamoto, and J. Zhou (Eds.): ICICS 2001, LNCS 2229, pp. 95–106, 2001.

Even if the traffic content is encrypted from the source, the encrypted packets would still be forwarded regardless, thereby consuming bandwidth. The attackers then simply discard the encrypted message.

In internal attacks, the attacks originate from within the tree, either from a compromised router or from a tapped-line. Two types of internal attacks are as follows.

- IA1 - Data attacks: the attacker injects bogus data packets into the data stream. The attack can be aimed at the subtree of members downstream from the point of attack, or the attacker can perform a sender attack(EA1) with the result of the bogus data packets being received by all members of the group.
- IA2 - Control attacks: the attacker injects bogus control packets destined for other routers participating in the multicast distribution tree. The aim of this attack would be either to confuse and cripple the distribution or to influence the behavior of the distribution tree. Note that this kind of control attacks may also originate from the edge.

Now we explain the issues that we have to consider when we develop security mechanisms to guard against the attacks mentioned above.

- Dynamic environment: A multicasting group can be dynamic. It means that senders and receivers can join and leave the multicast group during the existence of the group. A newly joining member should not be able to capture the packets exchanged before its join and decipher them with the key that it receives when it joins the group. A leaving member should not be able to capture the packets exchanged after its leave and decipher them with the key that it possessed before it leaves the group. This means the message encryption key should be changed whenever a member joins or leaves a multicast group. And there are two cases how a member leaves a multicast group. It can leave the group voluntarily or be evicted due to its suspicious activity. Both cases should be considered.
- Member semantics: There are two types of participants in a multicast group. They are members and senders. Members can both send and receive multicast packets while senders can only send multicast packets. This means that each sender should have its own sender-specific key and this key should be distributed to all the group members.
- Scalability: The proposed security mechanism should be efficient so that it can be applied to a multicast group consisting of a large number of members. Moreover, the overhead incurred upon the routers on the delivery tree should be minimized. Especially the overhead on the border routers that connect two or more adjacent domains should be minimized because they have to handle tremendous amount of packets crossing domain boundaries.
- Required security services: The security services required for multicasting include authentication, access control, confidentiality, and integrity so that only legal hosts can join the multicast group and send/receive multicast packets.

There have been many related works on the multicast security. Ballardie has presented the scalable multicast key distribution scheme (SMKD) as part of the CBT multicasting architecture[5]. He proposes a scalable approach to authenticate a joining member and distribute a multicast key to that new member. But the key is static and the approach does not have any other security measures. There are many works on scalable approaches for distributing new multicast keys as the group membership changes. Mittra[6] proposes a key distribution approach based upon hierarchies of multicast domains while Wong et al[7] introduces a key distribution mechanism based upon hierarchies of multicast keys. All the works in this category just present the scalable key distribution method and provide no other multicast security services. Recently Shields and Garcia-Luna-Aceves proposed a scalable protocol for secure multicast routing[8]. The proposed mechanism provides security measures guarding against both edge attacks and internal attacks explained above assuming the hierarchical multicast routing algorithm called HIP. It changes the multicast key when membership changes. But it does not either consider the eviction of a member/sender or provide ways to generate/distribute sender-specific keys. Moreover all the message replay attempts are thwarted at the border routers and, therefore, the overhead on the border routers can become very heavy when there are many attempts to replay multicast packets.

In this paper we present a new approach for scalable secure multicast routing in a very large scale network. We assume the use of PIM-SM and BGMP. Our approach provides security measures to guard against both edge attacks and internal attacks and provides all the required 4 security services. It has a mechanism for efficiently changing the multicast key as the membership changes. The proposed approach can evict ill-behaving members and/or senders securely and also supports the distribution of sender-specific keys. It tries to eliminate the flooding attempts at the edge routers as much as possible so that the overhead on the border routers can be reduced. The rest of the paper is organized as follows. In Section 2, we explain the multicast routing algorithms on which our security protocols are designed. Section 3 describes what kinds of keys are used and how they are structured in our approach. Section 4 presents secure protocols for building and maintaining multicast trees, and sending packets, and Section 5 is the conclusion.

2   Multicast Delivery Trees

In this section we describe the multicast delivery trees that are built by the routing algorithms, PIM-SM and BGMP. A multicast tree can be considered as a hierarchy of domains. The domain that includes the center point, that is the root of the whole multicast tree, is designated as the root domain and other domains form a tree with this root domain as the tree root. The connections between domains are created by the BGMP. In a domain that wishes to join the multicast tree, there is one border router that has the shortest path to the existing multicast tree and that border router is the best exit router of that

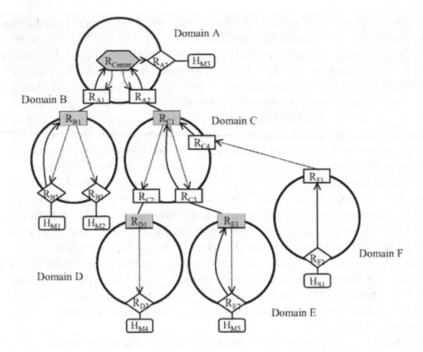

Fig. 1. Multicast Delivery Tree in a Hierarchy of Domains

domain. This best exit router communicates with the external peer border router in the neighboring domain, which is already on the multicast tree, toward the root domain. This neighboring domain is called the parent domain of the new domain and the neighboring router in this domain is called the parent router of that best exit router. A bi-directional path is formed between these two border routers using BGMP. The best exit router of the new domain becomes the core of that domain and all the group members and routers in that domain build an intra-domain multicast tree around this core using PIM-SM.

Figure 1 shows an example of a delivery tree. The network is divided into 6 domains from A to F. Square boxes, R_{A1}, R_{A2}, R_{B1}, R_{C1}, R_{C2}, R_{C3}, R_{C4}, R_{D1}, R_{E1}, and R_{F1} are border routers. Diamonds, R_{A3}, R_{B2}, R_{B3}, R_{D2}, R_{E2}, and R_{F2}, are edge routers. Rounded boxes, H_{M1}, H_{M2}, H_{M3}, H_{M4}, and H_{M5}, are member hosts while H_{S1} is a sender host. The router, R_{Center}, in the domain A is the center point of the whole delivery tree and is called the center router. The domain A becomes the center domain. The solid lines between two border routers in adjacent domains are the bi-directional delivery paths built by the BGMP. The delivery tree in each domain is built as a shared unidirectional tree by the PIM-SM algorithm. These intra-domain delivery trees are represented as dotted line trees in the domains A through E. And the routers, R_{Center}, R_{B1}, R_{C1}, R_{D1}, and R_{E1} are core routers in each domain. The edge routers are the leaf routers in the delivery tree and are connected to the member hosts. For a host to be able to send packets to the delivery tree, there should be a packet delivery path from the edge router of this sending host up to the center router. In the figure the member hosts H_{M1} and H_{M5} are also senders. The solid arrow lines in each domain from these hosts toward the center router are the sending paths. The host H_{S1} is a sender but not a member. Although there is no delivery path toward H_{S1}, there is a sending path from H_{S1} toward the center.

3   Key Management Structure

In addition to the public key and private key pair owned by each host or router, we use the kinds of keys for secure multicast routing as follows.

- Group Data Key(GDK) : This symmetric key is generated by the center and shared by all group members. All members and senders encrypt packets with this key. It is changed whenever a member joins or leaves so that a leaving member cannot read any packets exchanged after it leaves and a joining member cannot read any packets exchanged before it joins.
- Domain Control Key(DCK) : This symmetric key is generated by the center in the center domain and by the core router in all other domains. It is shared by all leaf nodes of a domain. The leaf nodes of a domain are the member hosts in that domain and the core routers of all the child domains of that domain. It is changed whenever there occurs a change in the set of the leaf

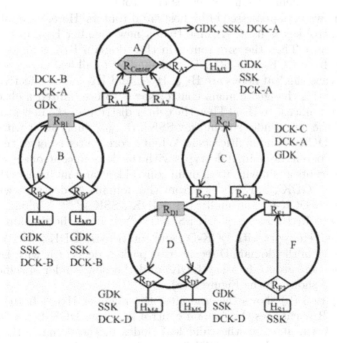

Fig. 2. Key Management Structure

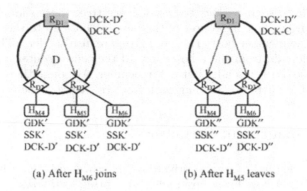

(a) After H_{M6} joins   (b) After H_{M5} leaves

Fig. 3. Usage of Domain Control Keys

nodes of a domain. Its purpose is to efficiently distribute a new group data key to all the leaf nodes.

- Sender Specific Key(SSK) : This symmetric key is generated by the center whenever a new non-member sender joins the group. It is shared by the non-member sender and all group members. Different non-member senders receive different sender-specific keys. The packet sent by a non-member sender is encrypted with the sender-specific key of that sender. This key is changed whenever a member joins or leaves the group.

Figure 2 shows keys possessed of by hosts and routers. Here, we explain how the domain control key is used. Assume that a new member H_{M6} in the domain D joins the group. Then the core router in that domain R_{D1} changes the domain control key from DCK-D to DCK-D' and sends it to all leaf nodes of the domain D. In this case the leaf nodes are H_{M4}, H_{M5}, and H_{M6}. One effective method of distributing this changed domain control key is to use limited multicast to H_{M4} and H_{M5} and unicast to H_{M6}. Then the center distributes the new group data key GDK' and the new sender specific key SSK'. R_{Center} encrypts it with its domain control key DCK-A and multicasts it. When a core router receives this encrypted key from its parent domain, it decrypts with the domain control key of the parent domain, encrypts again with its domain control key, and multicasts the result. So R_{C1} receives (GDK', SSK')$^{DCK-A}$ from the domain A, decrypts with DCK-A, encrypts with DCK-C, and multicasts (GDK', SSK')$^{DCK-C}$ along the delivery tree. Likewise R_D1 receives (GDK', SSK')$^{DCK-C}$ from the domain C, decrypts with DCK-C, encrypts with DCK-D', and multicasts (GDK', SSK')$^{DCK-D'}$. All the leaf nodes in the domain D receive this packet, decrypt it with DCK-D', and retrieve the new group data key GDK' and the new sender specific key SSK'. The result is shown in the Figure 3 (a).

The figure 3 (b) shows the case after the member H_{M5} left the group. The core router R_{D1} changes the domain control key from DCK-D' to DCK-D" and securely unicasts it to all the valid leaf nodes in the domain, H_{M4} and H_{M6}. Then the new group data key GDK" and the new sender-specific key SSK" are generated and distributed as in the previous case.

4   Protocols for Secure Multicast Routing

In this section we describe protocols to build and maintain multicast delivery trees and send packet over this tree securely. We use the following notations.

- PK-A : the public key of A
- SK-A : the private key of A
- M^K : a message M encrypted with a key K
- H(M) : the hash of a message M
- $\{M\}^{SK-A}$: a message M along with a signature generated with A's private key. So if we use the RSA algorithm for the signature, it becomes M, $(H(M))^{SK-A}$.

And we assume the existence of the following entities.

- AS : Authorization service. Its main job is to distribute capabilities on request. There are four types of capabilities : Initiator, Center, Member, and Sender. A capability for a host or router, E, in a multicast group with a multicast IP address, MA, has the following format
$$CAP_E = \{IP_E, PK\text{-}E, MA, Permit, TS, Life\}^{SK-AS}$$
where IP_E is the IP address of an entity E and the Permit is the permit allowed for E. The permit can be Initiator, Center, Member, or Sender. The TS(timestamp) shows when this capability was created and the Life(lifetime) specifies when this capability expires. We assume that all the hosts and routers know its public key
- I : Group initiator. It is the creator of a multicast group. It starts with an access control list for the group. An access control list is an ordered set of a tuple (name, permit). There are three types of permits : Center, Member, Sender.
- CP : Center point of the whole tree and this corresponds to the center router, R_{Center}.
- C: Core of a domain. It is the border router acting as the core for a PIM-SM shared tree within a domain.
- E : An edge router

4.1   Building a Multicast Tree

To start a secure multicast session, the initiator must first authenticate itself through AS and get the capability as an initiator, I-CAP (initiator capability), from AS. Then the initiator sends the access control list to AS. The access control list tells who is the center, who can be the members, and who can be the senders. Upon receiving the access control list, AS retrieves each tuple from the list and makes a capability using the information stored in the tuple. So receiving the following access control list for a multicast group with the IP address, MA,
$$((CP, CP\text{-}Permit), (A, M\text{-}Permit), (B, S\text{-}Permit))$$
AS generates the capabilities as follows and sends them securely to the initiator.
$$CP\text{-}CAP_{CP} = \{IP_{CP}, PK\text{-}CP, MA, CP\text{-}Permit, TS, Life\}^{SK-AS}$$
$$M\text{-}CAP_A = \{IP_A, PK\text{-}A, MA, M\text{-}Permit, TS, Life\}^{SK-AS}$$
$$S\text{-}CAP_B = \{IP_B, PK\text{-}B, MA, S\text{-}Permit, TS, Life\}^{SK-AS}$$

After receiving the capability list from AS, the initiator contacts the center point and authenticates it. Then the initiator sends a packet to the center point and asks it to start building a delivery tree. The center point checks validity of this message by checking the signature of this message and the initiator capability stored in the message. The following packet is sent from the initiator to the center point.

$$I \rightarrow CP : \{\text{Create a tree}, IP_I, MA, CP\text{-}CAP, I\text{-}CAP\}^{SK-I}$$

Note that the packet also includes the center point capability. The center point retrieves this capability and stores it. One of the major jobs of the center point is to generate and distribute new group data key and sender specific keys whenever a membership change occurs. The packet carrying these new keys should also include the center point capability and be signed with the private key of the center point. Any node that retrieves the keys from this packet can verify that the packet was generated from the center point by checking the center point's signature and capability.

Now we explain what happens when a member wants to join a multicast group as a receiver. First a member host M contacts the initiator, authenticates itself, and receives its capability as a member, $M\text{-}CAP_M$. We assume that there are mechanisms which enable a member to obtain the location of the initiator and the core of the domain in which it belongs. We also assume that the cores can be trusted. M sends a join request as a member to its core C as follows :

$$M \rightarrow C : \{\text{Join-Request}, IP_M, MA, M\text{-}CAP_M\}^{SK-M}$$

The core authenticates the received packet and checks the requesting host has a member host capability. The core changes its domain control key from DCK to DCK' and multicasts it to the leaf nodes in its domain. Then the core sends the following join acknowledgement message back to the member.

$$C \rightarrow M : \{\text{Join-ACK}, IP_M, MA, DCK'^{PK-M}\}^{SK-C}$$

As this join acknowledgement message travels from the core toward the member host, a multicast path toward the edge router of the member host is created. The member host receives the packet and retrieves/stores the new domain control key. After sending the join acknowledgement packet to the member host, the core contacts the center and requests a new group data key to be created. Upon receiving this request the center creates a new group data key and multicasts it to all the members using the mechanism explained in Section 3.

Now we explain what happens when a member host wants to send a packet to the group. We assume that this member has already joined the multicast group as a receiver. This member host sends a sender join request to its edge router E along with a random number which it will use as the initial value for the packet sequence number as follow.

$$M \rightarrow E : \{\text{Sender-Join-Req}, IP_M, MA, SEQ\#, M\text{-}CAP_M\}^{SK-M}$$

The purpose of this sequence number is to thwart any multicast packet replay attack by a host connected to this edge router. The edge router includes its identity in this request and sends the resulting message to the core as follow. The identity of the edge router enables the core to evict this member sender with the cooperation of the edge router if necessary.

$$E \rightarrow C : \{\{\text{Sender-Join-Req}, IP_M, MA, SEQ\#, M\text{-}CAP_M\}^{SK-M}, IP_E\}^{SK-E}$$

Upon receiving this request, the core checks the capability of the sending host and finds the requesting host is a member. The core stores the information, (MA, IP_M, $SEQ\#_M$, IP_E), in its sender information table. This means that the member sender IP_M has sent to the multicast group MA the packets with the sequence number up to $SEQ\#_M$ and its edge router has the IP address IP_E. So any packet sent later by this member sender should have a sequence number greater than $SEQ\#_M$. Then the core sends the following acknowledgement message back to the member host and a multicast packet sending path from the edge router of the requesting host to the core is established.

$$C \to M : \{Sender\text{-}Join\text{-}Ack, IP_M, MA, SEQ\#_M\}^{SK-C}$$

This packet is first caught by the edge router and then sent to the member host. The edge router stores in its sender information table the information,(MA, IP_M, $SEQ\#_M$) Now we explain how a non-member sender joins a multicast group. The procedure is the same as in the previous case except after the core receives the sender join request packet. Upon receiving the request, the core checks the capability of the sending host and finds that the requesting host is a non-member. The core notifies of the center point that a new sender S has joined the group as a sender. The center generates a new sender specific key, unicasts it to the sender, and securely multicasts it to all the members. Then the core stores the information, (MA, IP_S, $SEQ\#_S$, IP_E), in its sender information table. Then the core just sends the following acknowledgement message back to the non-member sender.

$$C \to S : \{Sender\text{-}Join\text{-}Ack, IP_S, MA, SEQ\#_S\}^{SK-C}$$

This packet is first caught by the edge router and then sent to the non-member host. The edge router stores in its sender information table the information, (MA, IP_S, $SEQ\#_S$), as in the case of the member sender.

4.2   Sending a Multicast Packet Securely

In this subsection we explain how a packet flows from a sender to group members securely. A member sender or non-member sender, S, which wants to send a message, D, to a group, multicasts the following packet.

$$\{D^K\}^{SK-S}, \{IP_S, SEQ\#_S, H(\{D^K\}^{SK-S})\}^{SK-S}$$

Here the symmetric key, K, is the group data key for the member sender or the sender specific key for the non-member sender depending upon if the sender is a member or not. The purpose of sending the signed message, $\{D^K\}^{SK-S}$, in the first part of the packet is to enable any receiving member to check the authenticity of the packet. This packet is received by the edge router first. The edge router checks the second part of the packet with the public key of the sender. It checks the authenticity of the packet by calculating the hash of the first part of the packet and comparing it with the hash in the second part. The IP address in the second part tells who signed this second part. It also checks the sequence number of the packet by comparing with the sender's sequence number that it stored in its sender information table whose entry has the form of (MA, IP_S, $SEQ\#_S$). If the number in the packet is not greater than that in the table, the packet is rejected as an attempt to replay a previously sent packet. This checking at the edge router prevents any host connected to the same edge router from replaying or injecting false packets. Otherwise the edge router updates the sequence number in the table with that in the packet and then sends the packet toward the core. The core again checks the authenticity and freshness of the packet using the same method as the edge router. If the packet does not pass either of these two tests, it is discarded. This additional checking at the core router tries to prevent any corrupt router's attempt to replay or inject bogus packets along the sending path in the domain. If the checking succeeds, the core replaces the address and the sequence number in the second part with its address and its sequence number and sends the following packet along the multicast delivery tree.

$$\{D^K\}^{SK-S}, \{IP_C, SEQ\#_C, H(\{D^K\}^{SK-S})\}^{SK-C}$$

After sending this packet, the core router updates the sequence number in its sender information table like the edge router. This packet is sent to all the members in the core's domain. It is also sent to the core routers in the neighboring domains that are participating in the delivery tree. These core routers again checks the authenticity and freshness of the packet, replaces the address and sequence number of its own, and forwards it along the tree.

Now we explain why the sequence number is changed at a core router. The purpose of this is to efficiently prevent any replayed or bogus packets from being transmitted to the neighboring domain. Any packet that is either generated in a domain or coming up from its child domain is given the sequence number of the core router in this domain and then sent to the parent domain. To check the freshness of this packet, the core of the parent domain just need remember the sequence number of the child core that sent the packet. Unless we substitute the sequence number at the core router, the core router should remember the identity and sequence number of all the senders in the whole multicast group. In our scheme, the core just need remember the identity and sequence number of the senders in its domain and the cores in the child domains. Likewise, to prevent replayed or compromised packets from being spread to the downstream domain, a core router should know the sequence number of the core router of its parent domain and change the sequence number of its parent core to its own before distributing the packet along the tree. In summary a core router should remember the sequence number of not only senders in its domain but also all the cores in the neighboring domain.

4.3   Members and Senders Leaving a Multicast Group

If a member which is not a sender wants to leave a multicast group, it sends such a request to its core. The core changes the domain control key and sends it to all the leaf nodes in the domain except the leaving member. Then the core informs the center point of the leaving member. The center point changes the group data key and all the sender specific keys and multicasts them to all the members in the group. Each new sender specific key is unicast to the corresponding non-member sender. If a member sender wishes to leave a group and sends such a request to its core, the core and the center point do the exactly same thing as in the above. But the core also deletes information about the leaving member from its sender information table and tells the member's edge router to do the same thing. If a non-member sender wants to leave a group and sends such a request to the core, the core and the edge router deletes information about that sender from their sender information table. The core also informs the center point of the leaving sender and the center multicasts to all the members a message to throw away the sender-specific key of the leaving sender.

4.4   Evicting Member Senders or Non-member Senders

If a suspicious activity is found in a member sender, the initiator can request the eviction of such a host. The initiator removes the capability of the suspicious host from the capability list and requests the center point to send out the packet requesting the eviction of that packet. The center point multicasts the packet containing the following content.

(Evict Member Sender, IP_M, MA, CP-CAP)

This packet is specially marked so that it should be processed by the core routers only. Upon receiving this packet, a core router checks its storage to find an entry (MA, IP_M, $SEQ\#_M$, IP_E) with the matching multicast address and member address. The core that finds such an entry removes the table entry and destroys the packet sending path from this corrupt member. The core also tells the edge router of the corrupt member to delete the similar table entry and destroy the packet receiving path to this member. Then the core changes the domain control key and requests the center point to distribute new group data key and sender specific keys. If a non-member sender is to be evicted, a similar procedure is executed. But there is no packet receiving path to be destroyed and no new keys need to be distributed. Instead, all the members are told to discard the sender specific key of the evicted non-member sender. If a member which does not send a packet is to be evicted, the core should remember its identity when it joins the group and use this information to delete the packet receiving path to this member. Therefore, the joining protocol in the section 4.1 should be slightly modified.

5   Conclusion

In this paper an approach for providing security services for multicasting has been presented. We assume the use of PIM-SM and BGMP for routing algorithms. The approach provides authentication, authorization, confidentiality, and integrity services for a multicast routing algorithm. Only member hosts which are authenticated and have a member capability can join the multicast group to receive and send packets while non-member senders with a sender capability can send packets. But as soon as they are found to be ill-behaving, their capabilities are invalidated and they are evicted from the multicast group. Multicast packets are encrypted with either a group data key or sender specific key so that only legitimate group members can decipher the packets. Multicast packets are signed properly and attached with a sequence number and they are checked at both the edge router and core routers and, therefore, the authenticity and freshness of packets can be verified. Our approach can guard against the four types of attacks on multicasting explained in the introduction. An illegal host cannot send a multicast packet because it cannot build a sending path without a proper capability and its attempt to replay is blocked by the edge router which checks the authenticity and sequence number of the packets. An illegal host cannot receive and decipher a multicast packet because it cannot join the multicast tree without a member capability and it cannot decipher the multicast packets that it overhear without a proper key. A corrupt router's attempt to inject a replayed or compromised packet into the multicast group is thwarted or at least its effect will be contained in one domain by the core router which checks the authenticity and freshness of the packets. A corrupt router cannot expand the multicast tree because it does not have the proper capability. Our approach changes the group data key and sender specific keys whenever a membership change occurs and is suitable for the dynamic environments where members can join and leave the group and only the legitimate hosts can receive and/or send multicast packets. We support the member and sender semantics of IETF documents by providing the member and sender capabilities and the protocols for members and senders to join, leave, and be evicted from the multicast group. Through the use of the domain control keys, we can efficiently distribute new keys to the changed group. The compromised or replayed packets from illegal hosts are blocked at edge routers while corrupt packets from malicious routers are handled by the core routers. These two features make the proposed scheme scalable in the large Internet.

References

1. C. Miller, C.K., Multicast Networking and Application. Addison Wesley (1999)
2. Estrin, D. et al, Protocol Independent Multicast - Sparse Mode (PIM-SM) : Protocol Specification. IETF RFC 2117 (1997)
3. S. Kumar, S. et al, The MASC/BGMP Architecture for Inter-Domain Multicast Routing. Proceedings of the ACM SIGCOMM Conference (1998)
4. Hardjono, T. Key Management Framework for IP Multicast Infrastructure Security. IS&N 99, Springer-Verlag LNCS 1597 (1999)
5. Ballardie, T., Scalable Multicast Key Distribution. RFC 1949, (1996)
6. Mittra, S., Iolus: A Framework for Scalable Secure Multicasting. Proceedings of the ACM SIGCOMM Conference (1997)
7. Wong, C., Gouda, M., and Lam, S., Secure Group Communications Using Key Graphs. Proceedings of the ACM SIGCOMM Conference (1998)
8. Shields, C. and Garcia-Luna-Aceves, J.J., KHIP - A Scalable Protocol for Secure Multicast Routing. Proceedings of the ACM SIGCOMM Conference (1999)

A Transaction Length-Sensitive Protocol Based on Altruistic Locking for Multilevel Secure Database Systems

Hee-Wan Kim[1], Hae-Kyung Rhee[2], Tai M. Chung[3], Young Ik Eom[3], and
Ung-Mo Kim[3]

[1] Dept of Computer Science, Shamyook University, Nowon-Gu, Seoul, Korea
hwkim@syu.ac.kr
[2] Dept of Multimedia Information Computing, Kyungin Women's College, Inchon,
Korea
rheehk@dove.kyungin-c.ac.kr
[3] School of Electrical & Computer Engineering, Sungkyunkwan University, Suwon,
Korea
{tmchung, yieom}@simsan.skku.ac.kr
umkim@yurim.skku.ac.kr

Abstract. We propose a transaction length-sensitive protocol based on altruistic locking to satisfy the security requirements and improve the degree of concurrency for multilevel secure database. This protocol expended the two-way donation locking protocol in multilevel secure database, and eliminated unauthorized information flows. Altruistic locking has attempted to reduce delay effect associated with lock release moment by use of the idea of donation. An improved form of altruism has also been deployed for extended altruistic locking. We adapted XAL to multilevel secure database and we investigated limitations inherent in both altruistic schemes from the perspective of alleviating starvation occasions for transactions in particular of short-lived nature for multilevel secure database. Our protocol ensures serializability, eliminates covert channels to have preference to a lower level transaction, and reduces the starvation of short-lived transaction. The efficiency of the proposed protocol was verified by experimental results.

1 Introduction

A Multilevel secure database is a secure system which is shared by users from more than one clearance levels and contains data of more than one sensitivity levels [2]. When the database scheduler use the scheduling protocol to multilevel secure database, it must satisfy both the concurrency and the security requirements at the same time.

A data item's correctness is guaranteed by standard transaction scheduling schemes like *two-phase locking* (2PL)[7] for the context of concurrent execution environments. Generally, when short-lived transactions are normally mixed with long-lived ones, degree of concurrency might be hampered by selfishness associated with lock retention. In 2PL, lazy release of lock could aggravate fate of misfortune for long-lived ones in that they are more vulnerable to get involved in deadlock situations. To

S. Qing, T. Okamoto, and J. Zhou (Eds.): ICICS 2001, LNCS 2229, pp. 107–118, 2001.
© Springer-Verlag Berlin Heidelberg 2001

reduce the degree of livelock, the idea of altruism has been suggested in the literature. *Altruistic locking* [5], *AL* for short, is basically an extension to 2PL in the sense that several transactions may hold locks on an object simultaneously under certain conditions. Such conditions are signaled by an operation *donate*. Like another primitive *unlock*, donate is used to inform the scheduler that further access to a no longer required by a transaction certain data item of that donation. *Extended altruistic locking* [5], *XAL* for short, attempted to expand the scope of donation in a way that data to be early disengaged is augmented by extra data originally not conceived to be rendered. Our protocol is based on extended altruistic locking (XAL) but a new method, namely two-way donation locking for multilevel secure database (2DL/MLS), is additionally used in order to improve the concurrency and satisfy security requirements in multilevel secure database.

2 Related Work

2.1 Multilevel Secure Database

Each data item in multilevel secure database is labeled with its security classification and each user is assigned a clearance level. In example, we will use the following hierarchical levels ordered as follows:

Top Secret ≥ Secret ≥ Confidential ≥ Unclassified

We applied the security models using Bell and LaPadula model [2] to multilevel secure database. Information is allowed to flow from an object(subject) with security classification level l_1 to a subject(object) with classification level level l_2 only if $l_2 \geq l_1$. The BLP model requires that the system satisfy the following properties. [3]

Simple Security Condition

A subject may have read access to an object only if the subject's classification level dominates the object's sensitivity level.

*-Property (Star Property)

A subject may have write access to an object only if the object's sensitivity level dominates the subject's classification level.

We must also consider information flow through covert channels. A covert channels allows information to be transferred in violation of the security policy(i.e., either from a high-level subject to a low-level subject or between two subjects with incomparable security levels)[1]. We would like to prevent covert channels by ensuring that transactions at lower security levels are never delayed by the actions of a transaction at a higher security level. We used ts, s, c and u to denote the hierarchical level for subject(transaction) and object(data item) orderly.

2.2 Altruistic Locking

A transaction consists of database accesses and concurrency control operation, such as Lock and Unlock. It is well known that schedules of well-formed two-phase transactions that observe this rule is correct[4]. 2PL ensure that when conditions are met, they produce serializable schedules. *AL* is a modification to *2PL* under certain conditions. *AL* provides a third concurrency control operation, called Donate, along with Lock and Unlock. Donate operation is used to inform the scheduler that access to an object is no longer required by the locking transaction. When Donate is used, the donating transaction is free to continue to acquire new locks. Several rules control the use of the Donate operation by well-formed transactions. Transactions can only donated objects which currently have locked. However, they may not access any object that they have donated. A well-organized transactions must unlock every object that it locks, regardless of whether it donated any of those objects. Transactions are never required to donate any objects. Donate operations are beneficial since they can permit other transactions to lock the donated object before it is unlocked.

2.3 Operations of XAL/MLS

While the donation of wake is rigid in *AL* in terms of fixedness of its size, a dynamic way of forming a wake could be devised given that serializability is never violated. This was realized in *XAL* by simply letting data originally not intended to bestow to be dynamically included in a wake predefined. The rule is that wake expansion comes true only after a short transaction has already accessed data in its predefined wake list. So, the presumption made for *XAL* is that a short transaction still restlessly wishes to access data of its wake-dependent long transaction even after it has done with data in its wake list. The assumption could be called wake-first/other-later access fashion. *XAL* therefore performs badly if others-first/wake-later access paradigm is in fact to be observed. Example 1 shows this.

Example 1(Delay Effect Caused by Donation Extension in Short-Lived Transactions): Suppose that the long-lived transaction $T_{L1}(R, ts)$ attempts to access data items, $A(ts)$, $B(s)$, $C(c)$ and $D(u)$, orderly in multilevel secure database. Note that data items, $E(ts)$, $F(s)$, $I(ts)$, and $J(s)$ shall not be accessed by $T_{L1}(R, ts)$ at all. Presume that $T_{L1}(R, ts)$ has already locked and successfully donated $A(ts)$, $B(s)$ and $C(c)$. $T_{L1}(R, ts)$ now is supposed in the stage of accessing D(u). Suppose also that there are three more short-lived transactions concurrently in execution along with $T_{L1}(R, ts)$: $T_{S1}(W, s)$ wishing for $B(s)$ and $E(ts)$, $T_{S2}(R, s)$ wishing for $E(ts)$ and $F(s)$, and $T_{S3}(W, c)$ wishing for $F(s)$ and $J(s)$ (Fig.1).

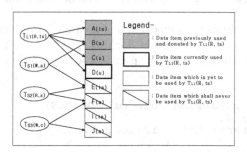

Fig. 1. Three Short-lived Transactions Competing for Same Data Donated

In case XAL/MLS, If $T_{S1}(W, s)$ initially requests $E(ts)$ first rather than $B(s)$, $T_{S1}(W, s)$ can certainly acquire $E(ts)$ but it fails for $B(s)$ because wake relationship cannot honor $E(ts)$ as a member of the wake list. Once this sort of wake dependency is detected, $T_{S1}(W, s)$ can be allowed to access $B(s)$ only after it is finally released by $T_{L1}(R, ts)$. $T_{S1}(W, s)$ in this case is therefore blocked. $T_{S2}(R, s)$ must then be blocked for $E(ts)$ to be released by $T_{S1}(W, s)$. $T_{S3}(W, c)$ as well must be blocked for $F(s)$ to be released by $T_{S2}(R, s)$, forging a chain of blockage. End of Example 1.

To resolve this sort of chained delay, others-first/wake-later approach could be made viable in a way of including others, not honored before, to a wake list. This enhancement is one of substances, made in our proposed protocol, which could be considered as *backward donation*, compared to *XAL's forward donation*. One other major substance of our proposed protocol is to let more than one long transaction donate while serializability is preserved in multilevel secure database. The notion of *two-way donation locking with multilevel secure database* is thus developed in our protocol. Our protocol allows more donation than one long transaction, but for the sake of presentation simplicity, degree of donation is limited to two in this paper.

3 Proposed Protocol

3.1 Assumptions

To describe wake expansion rule in detail, simplifications were made mainly with regard to transaction management principle.

① *(Transaction Operation)*: All transactions have either read or write operation to their data items.
② *(Security Policy)*: A transaction and its data items follow MAC policy by the Bell and LaPadula model.
③ *(Lower Level Transaction First)*: A lower level transaction holds a privilege on data item rather than a higher-level ones.
④ *(Donation Privilege)*: Only long-lived transactions are privileged to use donate operation.
⑤ *(Commit Policy)*: A long-lived transaction eventually commits.
⑥ *(Deadlock Handling)*: If a transaction happens to fall into deadlock situation, that transaction will be eliminated by using a certain deadlock timeout scheme.

In this paper, the multiplicity is rendered to the case of two to measure the effect of donation variety. Two- way donation locking protocol with Multilevel Secure Database, *2DL/MLS* for short, can be pseudo-coded as follows (Algorithm Wake Expansion).

```
Algorithm(Wake Expansion Rule of 2DL/MLS)
Input:LT1; LT2; ST
  /* ST:short trans; LT1, LT2:long trans */
BEGIN
 FOREACH LockRequest
    IF(LockRequest.ST.data = Lock)
    THEN
 /* Locks being requested by ST already granted to long
    trans other than LT1 and LT2 */
    Reply:=ScheduleWait(LockRequest);
    ELSE IF(LockRequest.ST.data = Donated) THEN
```

```
/* Locks being requested by ST donated by long trans other
   than LT1 and LT2 */
      FOREACH (ST.wake LT1 OR LT2)
       IF(ST.wake = LT1) THEN
/* Donation conducted by LT1? */
        IF(ST.data LT1.marking-set) THEN
/* Data requested by ST to be later accessed by LT1 ? */
         Reply:=ScheduleWait(LockRequest)
         ELSE
         Reply:=SecurityCheck(LockRequest)
         ENDIF
       ELSE
       IF(ST.data LT2.marking-set) THEN
/* Data requested by ST to be later accessed by LT2 ? */
         Reply := ScheduleWait(LockRequest)
         ELSE
         Reply := SecurityCheck(LockRequest)
       ENDIF
     ENDIF
     ENDFOR
ELSE
         Reply := SecurityCheck(LockRequest)
     ENDIF
      IF(Reply = Abort) THEN
/* Lock request of ST aborted */
      Abort Transaction(Transactionid);
      Send(Abort);
      Return();
       ENDIF
     ENDFOR
END
SecurityCheck(TRAN, DATA, GUBUN)
   /* TRAN:transaction : DATA:data item to be transferred */
BEGIN
  IF(TRAN.R = True) THEN /*Simple-property (Read Option) */
   IF( TRAN.level Data.level ) THEN
                            /* Transaction's level check */
     IF( GUBUN = Lock ) THEN
          Reply := ScheduleLock(LockRequest)
     ELSE
          Reply := ScheduleDonated(LockRequest)
     ENDIF
     ELSE                   /* No read up */
       Reply := DiscardData(LockRequest)
     ENDIF
ELSE                       /* *-property(Write Option) */
    IF( TRAN.level Data.level ) THEN
                            /* transaction level check */
     IF( GUBUN = Lock ) THEN
          Reply := ScheduleLock(LockRequest)
     ELSE
          Reply := ScheduleDonated(LockRequest)
     ENDIF
     ELSE                  /* No write down */
       Reply := DiscardData(LockRequest)
     ENDIF
ENDIF
END
```

3.2 Operations of 2DL/MLS

In case donated data items are used under *XAL/MLS*, it is allowed to request data items which are donated by only one transaction. Under *2DL/MLS*, short-lived transactions treat to be given more freedom in accessing donated objects by eliminating the single-donation constraint. Short-lived transactions can access objects donated by two different long-lived transactions in multilevel secure database.

   2DL/MLS permits short-lived transactions requesting data items which donated by two different long-lived transactions. A way to conduct a two-way donation is shown, in Example 2, with two separate long transactions and a single short transaction.

   Example 2(Allowing Proceeding of Short-lived Transaction with Two Concurrent Long-lived Ones in Multilevel Secure Database): Suppose that $T_{L1}(R, ts)$, a long-lived transaction with Read/Top-secret secure level, attempts to access data items, *A(ts)*, *B(s)*, *C(c)*, *D(u)* and *E(ts)*, orderly in multilevel secure database. Presume that $T_{L1}(R, ts)$ has already locked and successfully donated *A(ts)* and *B(s)*. $T_{L1}(R, ts)$ now is supposed in the stage of accessing *C(c)*. Suppose also that there are two more concurrent transactions in execution along with $T_{L1}(R, ts)$: $T_{L2}(W, s)$, a long-lived transaction, wishing for data items, *F(s)*, *G(c)*, *H(u)*, *I(ts)* and *J(s)*, in an orderly manner and $T_{S1}(R, c)$, a short-lived transaction with low level, wishing for *B(s)*, *G(c)* and *K(u)* similarly.

Presume that $T_{L2}(W, s)$ has already locked and successfully donated *F(s)* and skipped *G(c)* due to *-property in BLP model. $T_{L2}(W, s)$ now is supposed in the stage of accessing *H(u)* (Fig.2).

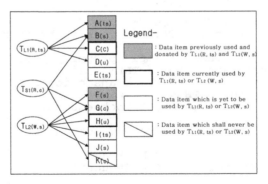

Fig. 2. Execution of $T_{S1}(R, c)$ with Two Concurrent Long-Lived Transactions

   If we apply *XAL/MLS* for these transactions, a lock request for *B(s)* by $T_{S1}(R, c)$ would be allowed to be granted but a lock request *G(c)* would not because *G(c)* has already been donated by another long-lived transaction. Only after $T_{L2}(W, s)$ commits, *G(c)* can be tossed to $T_{S1}(R, c)$.

   In case *2DL/MLS*, $T_{S1}(R, c)$ could fortunately be allowed to access without any delay. This is made possible by simply including the wake of $T_{L2}(W, s)$ into the wake of $T_{L1}(R, ts)$. At the same time, $T_{S1}(R, c)$ is not delayed by neither $T_{L1}(R, ts)$ or $T_{L2}(W, s)$ with higher security level transaction. So *2DL/MLS* prevents covert channels by ensuring that transactions at lower level transactions are never delayed by the actions of a transaction at a higher level ones. End of Example 2.

3.3 Correctness of 2DL/MLS

In this section, we will show that 2DL/MLS satisfy both serialization and security requirement. To do so, we will make use of the serializability theorem [4], the definition of Crest Before [5] and a lemma used in proving the correctness of AL [5]. The serializability theorem states that a history H is serializable iff its serialization graph is acyclic, and the definition of Crest Before state that for two transactions, say Ti uTj if Ti unloaks some data items before Tj locks some data items.

We use oi[x], pi[x] or qi[x] to denote the execution of either read or write operation issued by a transaction Ti, on a data item x. Reads and writes of data items are denoted by ri[x] and wi[x], respectively. Locking operation is also represented by oli[x], pli[x], qli[x], rli[x] or wli[x]. Unlock and donate operations are denoted by ui[x] and di[x], respectively. H represents a history which may be produced by *2DL/MLS* and O(H) is a history obtained by deleting all operations of aborted transactions from H. The characteristics of histories which may be produced by *2DL/MLS* are as follows.

Property 1(Two-Phase Property): If oli[x] and ui[y] are in O(H), oli[x] < ui[y].

Property 2(Lock Property): If oi[x] is in O(H), oli[x] < oi[x] < ui[x].

Property 3(Donate Property): If oli[x] and di[x] is in O(H), oi[x] < di[x].

Property 4(Unlock Property): If di[x] and ui[x] is in O(H), di[x] < ui[x].

Property 5(Security Property): If level(Ti)$\geq$level(ri[x]) in O(H), rli[x] < ui[x]. If level(Ti)$\leq$level(wi[x]) in O(H), wli[x] < ui[x].

Property 6(Lower Level Transaction First Property): If level(Ti) < level(Tj) in O(H), dj[x] < oli[x].

Transactions cannot simultaneously hold conflicting locks unless one has been altruistically donated. Next, we can formalize our notion of wakes.

Definition 1(Indebtedness): A transaction Tj is said to be *indebted* to Ti in H if oi[x], di[x], and oj[x] exist in H and di[x] < oj[x] < uj[x] and either

- oi[x] and oj[x] conflict, or
- some intervening operation ok[x] confilcts with both oi[x] and oj[x].

   (Operation ok[x] is intervening if di[x] < ok[x] < oj[x].)

Definition 2(In The Wake): An operation oj[x] is *in the wake* of transaction Tj if di[x] exists in H and di[x] < oj[x] < uj[x].

Definition 3(Completely In The Wake): A transaction Tj is in the wake of Ti if any of Tj's operations are in the wake of Ti. Tj is *completely* in the wake of Ti if all of its operations are in Ti's wake.

With these definitions out of the way, we can express the second altruistic locking rule.

Property 7(Indebtedness Property): If Tj is indebted to Ti for every oj[x] in O(H), either oj[x] is in the wake of Ti or there exists ui[y] in O(H) such that ui[y] < oj[x].

If a transaction is indebted to another, it must remain completely in the other's wake until it begins to unlock objects.

Lemma 1(Altruism): If pi[x] and qj[x] (i$\neq$j) are conflicting operations in O(H) and qi[x] < qj[x], then ui[x] < qlj[x] or di[x] < qlj[x].

Proof: A data item must be locked before and unlocked after it is accessed by Property 1. In Wake Expansion Rule of *2DL/MLS*, a conflict lock on the data item, say *a*, is allowed only when no transaction locks *a* or the transactions which hold locks on *a* has donated it. Thus, the history, O(H), satisfies Lemma 1. End of Lemma 1.

Lemma 2(Complexity-In-Wake): If T1→ T2 is in serialization graph, then either T1→uT2 or T1→dT2.

Proof: T1→T2 in serialization graph means that there exist conflicting operations, say p1[x] and q2[x], in H such that p1[x] < q2[x]. There are only two cases that may occur for this by Lemma 1. One is that there is p1[x] < d1[x] < ql2[x] < q2[x] in O(H), i.e., T2 accesses the data items donated by T1.

A transaction T2 has to access only wake of another transaction T1 , once T2 makes conflict locks on the data items donated by T1. T2 must be completely in the wake of T1 if T2 has accessed any of the wake of T1. This is ensured by the first else if condition in algorithm. Even if T2 has already accessed any data items which do not belong to the wake of T1 , such data items would be included into the wake of T1 as long as T1 does not access any of such data items at all for its execution. If the data items locked by T2 will be accessed by T1, the access of T2 to the data items donated by T1 is not allowed by the second foreach condition. Thus, T1→T2 corresponds to T1→dT2 in the case that p1[x] < d1[x] < ql2[x] < q2[x] in H, or in the case that p1[x] < u1[x] < ql2[x] < q2[x] in O(H) by Lemma 1. Thus, T1→T2 corresponds to T1→uT2 in the case. End of Lemma 2.

Lemma 3(Correctness of *AL*): Consider a path T1→···Tn-1→Tn in O(H). Either T1→uT2, or there exists some Ti on the path such that T1→uTi.

Proof: We will use induction on the path length n. By Lemma 2, the lemma is true for n=2. Assume the lemma is true for paths of length n-1, and consider a path of length n. By the inductive hypothesis, there are two cases:

① There is a TI between T1 and Tn-1 such that T1→uTk. The lemma is also true for paths of length n.

② T1→dTn-1→Tn and Tn-1 conflicts on at least one object, x. Since Tn-1 is completely in the wake of T1, we must have d1[x] < qln-1[x] in O(H). By Property 1, Tn must lock x. By Property 4, T1 must unlock x. Either u1[x] < oln[x] or oln[x] < u1[x]. In the first case, we have that T1→uTn, i.e., Tn is the Tk of the lemma. In the second case, Tn is indebted to T1. By Property 6, Tn is completely in the wake of T1(T1→dTn) or T1→uTn.

Theorem 1(Serializability of *2DL/MLS*): If O(H) is acyclic, O(H) is serializable.

Proof: Assume that there exists a cyclic T1→···Tn-1→Tn in serialization graph. By Lemma 3, T1→dT1, or T1→uTi. By Property 3, only T1→uTi is possible. Since Ti is prohibited to lock any more data items once T1 unlocks any one, Ti cannot be T1. Again, by applying Lemma 3 to the same cycle T1→Ti+1→···Ti , we get Ti→uTk.for the same reason and thus we get T1→uTi uTk in all. Since the relation u is transitive, T1→uTk is satisfied. Thus, Tk cannot be any of T1 and Ti. If we are allowed to continue to apply Lemma 3 to the given cycle n-3 times more in this manner, we will get a path T1→uTiu→Tk→u···→uTm containing all transactions, i.e., T1 through Tn. If we apply Lemma 3 to the given cycle starting from Tm one more time, we are enforced to get a cycle T1→uTi→uTk→u···→uTm→uT1 and we get a contradiction of violating Property 1 or Lemma 3. Thus serialization graph is acyclic and by the serializability theorem O(H) is serializable. End of Theorem 1.

Theorem 2(Security Satisfaction of *2DL/MLS*): If H is a history with Property 5 and 6, then H satisfies security requirements.

Proof : By Property 5, a transaction can read data items at its own or lower level, and write data items at its own or higher level. Let Ti and Tj be two transactions such that L(Ti) > L(Tj). If Ti and Tj are conflicting with each other, then we can see that Ti read down the data item x while Tj writes into x. Then, there are two possible cases: (i) Tj holds a lock on x before Ti requests a read lock on x, and (ii) Ti holds a read lock on x before Tj requests a lock. In the first case, Ti must wait for the data item x until Tj's donation of data x by Property 6. Therefore, the lower level transaction Tj is not delayed by the higher level one Ti. In the second case, in order to prevent covert channels, Tj can lock x without delaying by Property 6. Thus, Tj is neither delayed nor aborted by Ti. According to the above cases, the proposed protocol satisfies security requirements. End of Theorem 2.

4 Performance Evaluation

4.1 Simulation Model

4.1.1 Queuing System Model

The simulation model, in (Fig.3), consists of subcomponents in charge of fate of a transaction from time of inception to time of retreat: *transaction generator* (TG), *transaction manager*(TM), *scheduler* (SCH), *data manager*(DM), *database*(DB).

TG generates user transactions one after another and sends their operations to TM one at a time in a way of interleaving. TM receives transactions from terminals and passes them SCH queue.

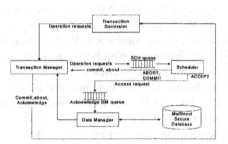

Fig. 3. Simulation Model

DM analyzes an operation from SCH to determine which data item the operation is intended to access, and then sends the operation to the disk where the requested data item is stored. Whenever an operation is completed at the server, it sends to TM the message informing that the requested operation has been completed successfully.

This simulation model has been implemented using *Scheme* [6] discrete-event simulation(DEVS) language. In DEVS formalism one must specify basic models from which larger ones are built, and describe how these models are connected together in hierarchical fashion [8].

4.1.2 Experimental Metodology

<Table 1> summarizes the model parameters and shows the range of parameter values used in our experiments.

Table 1. Simulation Parameters

Parameters	Values
db_size	100
num_cpus	2
num_disks	4
num_of_level	4
short_tran_size	2, 3, 4
long_tran_size	5, 7, 9, 11, 13, 15
tran_creation_time	2 units
sim_leng	100, 300, 500, 700, 900, 1100, 1300, 1500

To see performance tradeoff between *2PL/MLS* and *2DL/MLS*, average transaction length represented by number of operation in transaction were treated to vary. The shortest one is assumed to access 20 percent of the entire database, while it is 80 percent for the longest one. The number of CPUs and disks, *num_cpus* and *num_disks*, are set to 2 and 4, respectively. The idea behind this status of balance by 1-to-2 ratio has been consulted from[7].

4.2 Simulation Result and Interpretations

4.2.1 Effect of Security Requirement Level

This experiment has been revealed that 2DL/MLS satisfied the security requirement by Bell and LaPadula model. We have counted the processing ratio data item which satisfy the security requirement against total ones. Each transaction has Read/Write option, four clearance level and data items which they process. Each data items have four sensitivity levels. If the transaction satisfies the security requirements which it wish to process the data item, it processes the data item the next time slice. Otherwise, the transaction discards the data item, and it remains the current time slice of operating system. In this experimental, the entire processing ratio was 61.4 percent. So this model satisfies the security requirement by BLP model.

4.2.2 Effect of Long-Lived Transaction Size

This experiment shows that *2DL/MLS* generally appears to outperform *2PL/MLS* in terms of throughput. The best throughput performance is also exhibited by *2DL/MLS* and the worst average waiting time is portrayed by *2PL/MLS*.

Performance gain of *2DL/MLS* against *2PL/MLS* is from 112 to 125 percent increment in terms of throughput except long transaction size is 11. And *2DL/MLS* outperforms *2PL/MLS* from 94 to 72 percent decrease of performance at transaction waiting time at every case. This is because *2DL/MLS* has the 2PL/MLS plus the donation of data items of long transaction.

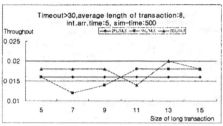

Fig. 4. Throughputs

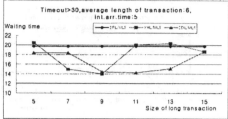

Fig. 5. Average Waiting Time

4.2.3 Effect of Timeout

At a higher range of *timeout*, *2DL/MLS* show a higher medium throughput and a lower transaction waiting time for three schemes. Throughputs of the three schemes show the same value at timeout size 35.

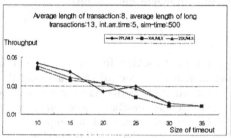

Fig. 6. Throughputs

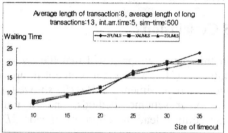

Fig. 7. Average Waiting Time

Throughput of *2DL/MLS* outperforms *XAL/MLS* and *2PL/MLS* when timeout size is 30. We can observe that average waiting time curve of *2PL/MLS* rapidly increase from 30 to 35 in Fig.7. *2DL/MLS* performs better than *2PL/MLS* between 100 percent and 123 percent of performance at transaction throughput. If the timeout size is far extended beyond a certain point, say 30, the average waiting time curve of *2PL/MLS* increase than other two schemes. *2DL/MLS* outperforms *2PL/MLS* with 87.9 percent of performance at transaction waiting time when the timeout size is 35.

4.2.4 Effect of Simulation Time with Long-Lived Transaction

As the simulation time is getting longer, short-lived transactions can get more chance to use donated objects. This experiment is used to investigate the effect of the simulation time on the performance of concurrency control schemes, as the degree of donations varies. *2DL/MLS* shows a higher throughput and a lower transaction waiting time for three schemes. Throughputs of the three schemes show the same value at simulation time 100. But as the simulation time is getting longer, throughput of *2DL/MLS* outperforms *XAL/MLS* and *2PL/MLS* when simulation time is greater than 500. We can observe that the throughput curves of *XAL/MLS* and *2DL/MLS* schemes tend to be flat as the simulation time is greater than 900. It has been observed that the throughput of *2DL/MLS* continually increased from beginning of simulation.

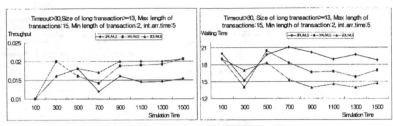

Fig. 8. Throughputs   **Fig. 9.** Average Waiting Time

2DL/MLS eventually performs best in terms of average waiting time at all simulation time. If the simulation time is far extended beyond 500, the average waiting time curve of *2DL/MLS* decrease than other two schemes. *2DL/MLS* outperforms *2PL/MLS* with 69 percent of performance at transaction waiting time when the simulation time is 900.

Overall behaviors have been revealed that as the simulation time increases, *2DL/MLS* generally outperforms in terms of throughput and waiting time.

5 Conclusions

In this paper we proposed that the two-way donation locking for multilevel secure database (2DL/MLS) is a protocol improving concurrency control and satisfying the security requirements. *2DL/MLS* showed a more satisfying performance compared to any other scheme methods, and in multilevel secure database when long-lived transactions lead to abort overhead, *2DL/MLS* is recommended to improve the concurrency degree for multilevel secure database systems. *2DL/MLS* is considered to be a practical solution to take where short-lived or lower level transactions quickly access database without any delay by long-lived or higher level ones for multilevel secure database.

References

1. T. F. Keefe, W. T. Tsai and J. Srivastava, "Database Concurrency Control in Multilevel Secure Database Management Systems," IEEE Transactions on Knowledge and Data Engineering, Vol.5, No.6, pp.1039-1055, December 1993.
2. T. F. Keefe, W. T. Tsai and J. Srivastava, "Multilevel Secure Database Concurrency Control," Data Engineering, Proceedings. Sixth International Conference on, 1990.
3. D. E. Bell, and L. J. LaPadula, "Secure Computer Systems: Unified Exposition and Multics Interpretations," Technical Report MTR-2997, Mitre Corp., March 1976
4. P. A. Bernstein, V. Hadzilacos and N. Goodman,, "Concurrency Control and Recovery in Database Systems," Addison- Wesley, Massachusetts, U.S.A., 1987.
5. K. Salem, H. Garcia-Molina and J. Shands, "Altruistic Locking," ACM Transactions on Database Systems, Vol.19, No.1, pp.117-169, March 1994.
6. H. Bartley, C. Jensen and W. Oxley, "Scheme User's Guide and Language Reference Manual," Texas Instruments, Texas, U.S.A., 1988.
7. R. Agrawal, M. J. Carey and M. Linvy, "Concurrency Control Performance Modeling: Alternative and Implications," ACM Transactions on Database Systems, Vol.12, No.4, pp. 609-654, December 1987.
8. Zeigler, B. P., "Object-Oriented Simulation with Hierarchical, Modular Models: Intelligent Agents and Endomorphic Systems," Academic press, San Diego, CA, 1990

Dealing with Uncertainties in Risk Analysis Using Belief Functions

Sungbaek Cho and Zbigniew Ciechanowicz

Information Security Group, Royal Holloway College,
University of London, Egham, Surrey, TW20 0EX, UK
{Sungbaek.Cho, Z.Ciechanowicz}@rhul.ac.uk

Abstract. The purpose of this paper is to introduce a way to deal with uncertainties in risk analysis. Risk analysis is a key process in security management in that its result provides a decision-basis for safeguard implementation. However, it must often rely on speculation, educated guesses, incomplete data, and many unproven assumptions. Users of risk analysis often provide their uncertain subjective opinions as input values to risk analysis. Therefore, the consideration of uncertainties in input data should be made when performing a risk analysis. As a tool for expressing and dealing with uncertainties in input data, we suggest the use of belief functions. We provide examples of how to use belief functions in qualitative risk analysis methods.

1 Introduction

Risk analysis is the process of identifying security risks, determining their magnitude and identifying areas that need safeguards [5]. Risk analysis is a key process in risk management as it identifies potential risks and provides a basis for investing in safeguards. Owing to the critical role of risk analysis in security management, a number of risk analysis methods have been developed since the early 1980s. Examples include annualized loss expectancy (ALE), Courtney, the Livermore risk analysis method (LRAM) and CRAMM [2]. Risk analysis methods are mainly classified into either a quantitative or qualitative methodology.

In quantitative risk analysis approaches such as ALE, risks are represented as a function of probabilistic variables. On the other hand, qualitative risk analysis approaches such as CRAMM attempt to express risk in terms of descriptive variables (e.g., high, medium and low). Although the quantitative approach provides sound logical justification for the analysis results, it relies heavily on the accuracy of parameter estimation. In addition, organizations may encounter a situation where they cannot provide any estimates. On the other hand, the qualitative methodology maintains a view that risk analysis variables cannot be expressed in exact probabilistic measures. Qualitative approaches are relatively easier than quantitative ones since they do not require probabilistic estimates. However, qualitative analysis lacks mathematical justification when compared with quantitative approaches and therefore the evaluation is likely to be more subjective than the quantitative approach.

S. Qing, T. Okamoto, and J. Zhou (Eds.): ICICS 2001, LNCS 2229, pp. 119–130, 2001.

Regardless of the methodology, the result of any risk analysis includes uncertainties. Uncertainties in risk analysis imply potential differences between risk analysis outcomes and the realities. Uncertainties are important issues in risk analysis since we may trust the result of an assessment even though the result is based on uncertain evaluations. This situation leads us to the implementation of inappropriate safeguards and a false sense of security. Although this problem should be properly addressed in risk analysis, little attention has been paid to uncertainties. Our approach to this problem is based on the theory of belief functions, which is a general tool for representing someone's degree of belief in an uncertain situation, where a degree of belief is understood as strength of opinion.

2   Uncertainties in Risk Analysis

Risk analysis must often rely on speculation, best guesses, incomplete data, and many unproven assumptions [7]. According to [7], there are two primary sources of uncertainty: (1) a lack of confidence or precision in the risk analysis model or methodology, and (2) a lack of sufficient information to determine the exact value of the elements of the risk model such as threat frequency, safeguard effectiveness and consequences. The first type of uncertainty comes from the assumptions and omissions imposed within the risk analysis model due to the inability of precise modelling of the real world. The second type of uncertainty usually resides in risk analysis input values. Risk analysis data normally come from two sources: statistical data and expert analysis. Although statistical data sounds authoritative, there are many potential problems with statistics such as invalid sampling and sample size. Expert analysis is usually based on subjective opinion, which also includes assumptions made (but not always explicitly articulated) by the expert.

Uncertainty is different from ambiguity; ambiguity is generally handled by fuzzy set theory in risk analysis (for example, fuzzy metrics). According to [11], imprecision (ambiguity) covers cases where the value of a variable is given but not with the required precision, whereas uncertainty covers cases where an agent can construct a personal subjective opinion (belief) in a proposition that is not definitively established. Consider the following example: 'how much financial loss is incurred from the disclosure of specific data?' Assume that the analyst is sure that it would be a medium loss (say, $\geq\$1000$ and $\leq\$5000$) although he cannot express the exact figure. In this case, fuzzy theory can be applied. On the other hand, assume that he thinks that it could be a medium loss but is not sure about this because the actual loss might be smaller or bigger than he expects. This situation represents the uncertainty in the analyst's opinion.

In this paper, our interest is limited to the second type of uncertainty, i.e. the uncertainty in input data. The first type of uncertainty is related to the validity of the risk analysis model itself. There is no definitive way of building a risk analysis model. The reason for this is that there are inevitable assumptions and omissions in any risk analysis due to impossibility of constructing a model that exactly reflects the real world. In addition, we consider only the qualitative approach, especially the scoring method, in this paper. The belief function approach is normally defined on finite and discrete variables and therefore it fits the qualitative approach. If we use an interval scale to estimate the probabilistic variables and assign the degree of our belief to each interval, the belief function approach could, to some extent, be applied to the quantitative approach. However, we do not consider quantitative approaches in this paper since in this case the belief function approach requires a meta-probability (the probability over the value of an unknown probability). In most quantitative approaches, point estimates are usually used to represent the amount of loss and/or probability of threat occurrence. The PERT (Project Evaluation Review Technique) approach could be used for a simple way of dealing with uncertainties in point estimates. For the estimation of the expected loss, [3] suggests the use of the PERT technique. In the PERT approach, there are three point estimates for each variable: pessimistic, most likely and optimistic cases. For example, assume that the expected loss may vary from a to c and is b in the most likely case. The expected loss in the PERT approach is then expressed as $(a+4b+c)/6$. Although there is still a possibility that the actual value does not lie in this range, it provides a cost-efficient way of dealing with uncertainties.

3   Basics of Belief Functions

The theory of belief functions (also called Dempster-Shafer theory of evidence) has been introduced by Shafer [9] as a new approach for representing uncertainties. The belief function approach is used in this paper to represent and deal with uncertainties in scoring method based risk analysis. There are a number of variations in the scoring method. However, the common feature of the scoring method is that scores are assigned to each possible answer to a question, according to an analyst's opinion. Examples of the scoring method and the belief function approaches will appear in the next section.

Belief functions start from constructing a finite set of worlds, denoted by Θ, called the *frame of discernment*. In the scoring method, it will represent the set of possible answers to a question. One of its elements, denoted by θ_0, corresponds the real world (i.e., the totally correct answer to the question). An analyst does not know which answer in Θ is θ_0. However, he has some opinion about which world might be θ_0. For every $A \subseteq \Theta$, he can express the strength of his opinion that the actual answer θ_0 belongs to A. This is done using basic probability assignment, which is a function m: $2^\Theta \rightarrow [0,1]$ that satisfies $\sum \{m(A)|\ A \subseteq \Theta\}=1$ and $m(\emptyset)=0$.

The quantity $m(A)$ is understood to be the measure of belief that is committed exactly to A. Suppose that the frame of discernment on variable X (Θ_X) is $\{x_1, x_2, x_3\}$. Therefore, there exist seven m-values such as $m_X(\{x_1\})$, $m_X(\{x_2\})$, $m_X(\{x_3\})$, $m_X(\{x_1,x_2\})$, $m_X(\{x_1,x_3\})$, $m_X(\{x_2,x_3\})$ and $m_X(\{x_1,x_2,x_3\})$. The m-value of any subset represents the partial belief that the actual answer belongs to it. The subscript represents the name of the variable to which evidence is applied. Each element of the frame (x_i) represents each possible answer to the question. For example, suppose that the question is 'how many security incidents have occurred last year?' and the possible answers are (1) x_1: equal to or less than twice, (2) x_2: more than twice, but less than five times, and (3) x_3: equal to or more than five times. Suppose that an analyst has identified that x_2 is likely to be the right answer based on an interview with appropriate staff. However, he is not totally sure since it is based on their memory and a written incident record is not available. He feels that this interview supports x_2 with a medium level of support (say 0.6). Therefore, he has assigned 0.6 to $m_X(\{x_2\})$. The remaining uncommitted amount $(1-m_X(\{x_2\})=0.4)$, which represents ignorance, is then committed to Θ_X (therefore, $m_X(\{x_1,x_2,x_3\})=0.4$).

As this example indicates, the way of assigning m-values is by using an analyst's subjective judgment. However, the uncertainty in the subjective judgement is considered by the concept of ignorance. The basic difference, when compared to probability theory, is that m-values are assigned to a subset of elements of a frame whereas probabilities are assigned to individual elements of the frame. Therefore, the situation where $m(B)>0$ and $m(A)=0$ for all $A \subset B$ can happen, which cannot be satisfied by probability theory.

The total belief in a subset B of a frame Θ is defined as $Bel(B)=\sum\{m(A)|$ $A \subseteq B\}$ for all $B \subseteq \Theta$, and the plausibility of B is defined as $Pl(B)=\sum\{m(A)|$ $B \cap A \neq \emptyset\}=1 - Bel(B^c)$. The value $Bel(B)$ summarizes all our reasons for believing B based on the given evidence, and the value $Pl(B)$ represents how much we should believe B if all currently unknown facts (i.e. underlying ignorance) were to support B. The difference is that $Bel(B)$ quantifies the total amount of justified supports given to B, while $Pl(B)$ quantifies the maximum amount of potential supports that could be given to B.

If $m_1(C)$ and $m_2(C)$ are two m-values for the same variable induced by two independent evidential sources, then the combined m-value is calculated according to Dempster's rule, which is $m_1 \oplus m_2(C)=k^{-1}\sum\{m_1(A)m_2(B)|\ A \cap B=C\}$, where $k=1-\sum\{m_1(A)m_2(B)|\ A \cap B=\emptyset\}$ is a normalization constant. Normalization is required to satisfy the axiom that the sum of m-values on a frame equals 1 where a conflict exists. A conflict exists whenever $\sum\{m_1(A)m_2(B)|\ A \cap B=\emptyset\}>0$. Dempster's rule cannot be used when $k=0$, in which case the two items are not combinable.

4   Scoring Method with Belief Functions

The scoring method manipulates scores gathered from a set of questions that have a predefined set of scores for each possible answer; the purpose of the question is to analyze the value of asset, severity of threat and/or magnitude of vulnerability. A typical example of the scoring method can be found in CRAMM [2]. In CRAMM, multiple-choice questions are used to gather information about threats and vulnerabilities. A major drawback of the scoring method is that full justification on the scoring system is not always possible. However, the scoring method provides an efficient form of analysis and may be the only available approach in many situations. For example, the quantitative approaches, which are based on probability measures, may not be applicable due to unavailability of these measures and production rule (IF-THEN rule) based systems may not permit detailed assessment as the number of rules increases dramatically when the granularity of analysis increases. Although the determination of the importance of each question is critical, we do not consider this here since there is no absolute answer to this problem, as mentioned earlier. Our concern is how to deal with an analyst's uncertain answers to questions. An analyst may often encounter the situation where he cannot provide the right answer due to lack of knowledge or information; irrespective of this, the scoring method still forces him to choose one answer.

4.1 Multiple-Choice Question

Figure 1 illustrates an example scoring system used in CRAMM. As shown in figure 1, each multiple-choice question may have a different number of possible answers and the score for each possible answer ranges according to the importance of the question (e.g. question 6 is much more important than question 1). Total score for a specific set of questions is used to determine the severity of threat or magnitude of vulnerability. Although several variations may be possible to deal with uncertainties in such questions, let us consider the following simple strategy. For illustration purposes, we use question 6 in figure 1.

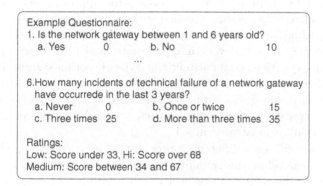

Fig. 1. Example Multiple-Choice Questionnaire

Suppose that the analyst feels that the currently available evidence provides a high degree of support (say 0.8) that the actual answer is 'b'. At the same time, he is certain that an incident has occurred and therefore 'a' cannot be the right answer. Therefore, $m(\{b\})=0.8$ and $m(\{b,c,d\})=0.2$. Since we are familiar with probabilities rather than the m-values, we shall transform these m-values to the corresponding probabilities (denoted by BetP). This transformation is defined by Smets [10] and is called the pignistic transformation.

$$\text{BetP}(x)=\sum\{m(A)/\ |A|\ |\ A \subseteq \Theta \text{ such that } x \in A\} \quad \text{for all } x \text{ in } \Theta$$

where $|A|$ represents the number of elements in A. With the above example, $BetP(a)=0$, $BetP(b)=m(\{b\})+m(\{b,c,d\})/3\approx0.87$, and $BetP(c)=BetP(d)$ $=m(\{b,c,d\})/3\approx0.07$. Once we have such pignistic probabilities, we can use them in various decision-making frameworks. The expected value of the score in this example is 15.25 ($=0\cdot0+15\cdot0.87+25\cdot0.07+35\cdot0.07$). The consideration of uncertainties has been reflected in this value since it is based on the pignistic probabilities, which have been induced by the analyst's beliefs.

If there are several analysts performing the same evaluation (i.e., same question) or there are several pieces of information regarding the same question, Dempster's rule can be used to combine m-values from different sources. In addition, we can assign a weight factor to each source (i.e., discounting m-values) if required. Suppose that there are n evidential sources and m_i represents m-values from the evidential source i. Discounting m-values by some weight w_i ($0\leq w_i\leq1$ and $\sum w_i=1$) is as follows. The discounted m-value is $(1-w_i)m_i(A)$ for all $A\subset\Theta$ and $(1-w_i)m_i(\Theta)+w_i$ if $A=\Theta$.

4.2   Direct Score Assignment

Assume that a questionnaire for threat valuation has n questions and the score to be assigned to each question ranges from 1 to 5 (integer). An analyst then assigns a score ranging from 1 to 5 as an answer to each question according to the result of his analysis. An example question is 'assess the appropriateness of the access privilege guidelines'. Depending on the result of evaluation of an organization's manuals regarding the granting of access privileges, an analyst will assign a score ranging 1 to 5 (1 for 'very inappropriate' and 5 for 'very appropriate'). Multiple-choice questions could also fit this type of scoring system. For example, if there are five possible answers in each question (say, a, b, c, d and e), each answer, a, b, c, d and e will stand for the score 1, 2, 3, 4 and 5, respectively. The pignistic transformation could be used to obtain an expected score value for each question, as illustrated in 4.1.

However, we will use a different approach that is based on [4], which assesses the value of a candidate under multiple criteria. The approach in [4] transfers the m-values for the score with respect to each criterion i (denoted by m_{Ci}), to the m-values for the overall 'goodness' score. The transformation is defined as follows. Let $f_i(x)$ be the value of the goodness score when the value of the score for criterion i is x and let $f_i(A)=\{f_i(x)|\ x\in A\}$. A represents a subset of the set of values of the score for the criterion i, ranging from 1 to 5 and therefore $A\subseteq\{1,2,3,4,5\}$. The m-values for the overall goodness score derived from the m-values for the score of criterion i, denoted by m_i, are $m_i(B)=\sum\{m_{Ci}(A)|\ f_i(A)=B\}$. B is a subset of the set of possible values for the goodness score, ranging from 1 to 5 ($B\subseteq\{1,2,3,4,5\}$). The values of $f_i(x)$ are provided in table 1. β represents the level of importance (weight factor) of criterion i. Combining the m-values derived from each criterion by Dempster's rule yields the m-values for the overall goodness score, which are $m(B)=(m_1\oplus m_2\oplus\ldots\oplus m_n)(B)$, where n is the number of criteria.

Table 1. Example Table for Goodness Score (Source: [4])

β	1	2	3	4	5
e	1	3	4	5	5
f	1	2	4	5	5
g	1	2	3	4	5

Let us consider the following example. Suppose that one question (Q_1) in the questionnaire that evaluates the threat of unauthorized access is 'what is the trend in unauthorized access incident rate'. The score for this question varies from 1 to 5 (1 for 'very low' and 5 for 'very high') and the overall threat score also varies from 1 to 5 (1 for 'very low' and 5 for 'very high'). An analyst feels that it is either medium or high with 0.7 degree of support and he has no opinions for other subsets of the score values. Therefore, $m_{Q_1}(\{3,4\})=0.7$ and $m_{Q_1}(\{1,2,3,4,5\})=0.3$. Assume that the level of importance of this question is g in table 1. Then, the m-values for overall threat valuation score, derived from the m-values for the score of this question, are $m_1(\{1\})=m_{Q_1}(\{1\})$, $m_1(\{1,2,3,4,5\})=m_{Q_1}(\{1,2,3,4,5\})$, and m-value for any other subset is 0. These m-values are to be combined with the m-values derived from other questions to obtain the m-values for the threat valuation score.

4.3   Risk Matrix

A risk matrix is a decision-basis for determining the level of risk based on the significance of an asset, the likelihood of a relevant threat's occurrence and the magnitude of the vulnerability for this asset and threat pair. For example, the risk score in CRAMM is '7' if the significance of the asset is '10', the likelihood of the threat is 'very high' and the magnitude of vulnerability is 'high'. A similar matrix approach (called threat evaluation) is used in RiskWatch [8] to evaluate the threat although the main approach within RiskWatch is quantitative. The threat rating in RiskWatch is 'A1' if the likelihood of threat occurrence is 'virtually certain' and the impact of this threat occurrence is 'fatal'.

The risk matrix is used within the risk management process to assist the selection of cost-effective safeguards. It also can be used at a high-level to provide an overview of the areas at high risk. Uncertainty issues should be properly addressed in determining the level of risk from the sets of scores for assets, threats and vulnerabilities. For simplicity, our example considers only two levels (high (H) and low (L)) of asset, threat and vulnerability valuation and three levels (high (H), medium (M) and low (L)) of risk valuation. This example risk matrix is shown in table 2. Thus, for example, if threat is 'high', vulnerability is 'high' and asset is 'high', then risk is 'high'.

Assume that we have m-values for asset (A), threat (T) and vulnerability (V) variables and, based on these m-values, we want to obtain m-values for risk variable (R). The frames for these variables are $\Theta_A=\{l_A,h_A\}$, $\Theta_T=\{l_T,h_T\}$, $\Theta_V=\{l_V,h_V\}$ and $\Theta_R=\{l_R,m_R,h_R\}$ respectively. Unlike the example in 4.2, we

Table 2. Example Risk Matrix

Threat	L	L	H	H
Vulnerability	L	H	L	H
Asset: L	L	L	M	M
Asset: H	M	M	H	H

cannot use the transformation of m-values. This is because, for example, a high asset value does not necessarily mean a high risk, as shown in table 2. Rather, the risk is determined by considering all the asset, threat and vulnerability values. The resulting m-values for the risk variable after considering the relationships in table2, denoted by $m^{\downarrow R}$, are as follows (proof is provided in the appendix). Here, we will omit the set symbol ({}) for simplicity (e.g., l_T instead of $\{l_T\}$).

$$
\begin{aligned}
m^{\downarrow R}(\{l_R\}) = {} & m_T(l_T)m_V(l_V)m_A(l_A) + m_T(l_T)m_V(h_V)m_A(l_A) \\
& + m_T(l_T)m_V(\Theta_V)m_A(l_A) \ .
\end{aligned}
\tag{1}
$$

$$
\begin{aligned}
m^{\downarrow R}(\{m_R\}) = {} & m_T(l_T)m_V(l_V)m_A(h_A) + m_T(l_T)m_V(h_V)m_A(h_A) \\
& + m_T(h_T)m_V(l_V)m_A(l_A) + m_T(h_T)m_V(h_V)m_A(l_A) \\
& + m_T(l_T)m_V(\Theta_V)m_A(h_A) + m_T(h_T)m_V(\Theta_V)m_A(l_A) \ .
\end{aligned}
\tag{2}
$$

$$
\begin{aligned}
m^{\downarrow R}(\{h_R\}) = {} & m_T(h_T)m_V(l_V)m_A(h_A) + m_T(h_T)m_V(h_V)m_A(h_A) \\
& + m_T(h_T)m_V(\Theta_V)m_A(h_A) \ .
\end{aligned}
\tag{3}
$$

$$
\begin{aligned}
m^{\downarrow R}(\{l_R, m_R\}) = {} & m_T(l_T)m_V(l_V)m_A(\Theta_A) + m_T(\Theta_T)m_V(l_V)m_A(l_A) \\
& + m_T(l_T)m_V(h_V)m_A(\Theta_A) + m_T(\Theta_T)m_V(h_V)m_A(l_A) \\
& + m_T(l_T)m_V(\Theta_V)m_A(\Theta_A) + m_T(\Theta_T)m_V(\Theta_V)m_A(l_A) \ .
\end{aligned}
\tag{4}
$$

$$
\begin{aligned}
m^{\downarrow R}(\{m_R, h_R\}) = {} & m_T(\Theta_T)m_V(l_V)m_A(h_A) + m_T(\Theta_T)m_V(h_V)m_A(h_A) \\
& + m_T(h_T)m_V(l_V)m_A(\Theta_A) + m_T(h_T)m_V(h_V)m_A(\Theta_A) \\
& + m_T(\Theta_T)m_V(\Theta_V)m_A(h_A) + m_T(h_T)m_V(\Theta_V)m_A(\Theta_A) \ .
\end{aligned}
\tag{5}
$$

$$
\begin{aligned}
m^{\downarrow R}(\Theta_R) = {} & m_T(\Theta_T)m_V(l_V)m_A(\Theta_A) + m_T(\Theta_T)m_V(h_V)m_A(\Theta_A) \\
& + m_T(\Theta_T)m_V(\Theta_V)m_A(\Theta_A) \ .
\end{aligned}
\tag{6}
$$

Suppose that we feel that the likelihood of threat occurrence is 'low' with 0.8 degree of support ($m_T(l_T)$=0.8), the magnitude of vulnerability is 'high' with 0.6 degree of support ($m_V(h_V)$=0.6), and the value of asset is 'high' with 0.7 degree of support ($m_A(h_A)$=0.7). Also, suppose that $m_T(h_T)=m_V(l_V)=m_A(l_A)=0$. From the equations above, we have $m^{\downarrow R}(\{m_R\})$=0.56, $m^{\downarrow R}(\{l_R, m_R\})$=0.24 and $m^{\downarrow R}(\{m_R, h_R\})$=0.14. These m-values can be used during decision-making processes such as safeguard selection if they are transformed to probabilities by the pignistic transformation.

4.4 Questions with Yes/No Answers

Now, let us look at risk analysis based on questions that require Yes/No answers. This kind of risk analysis often appears in checklist methods. Checklists are used to check if specific controls exist. One simple scoring system with the checklist method is to use a percentage of the number of controls in place when compared with the number of controls listed in the checklist; this highlights areas where many controls are missing. A typical question in the checklist method is 'ensure that the access privileges are managed properly'. Although the analyst has identified that well-defined access control lists exist, he cannot give a 'Yes' answer to this question if he has not examined whether they preserve the principle of least privilege. This imperfect information regarding the question gives him only a partial belief in 'Yes' rather than a definite 'Yes'.

Using belief function formulas for an AND-tree [12], we apply the belief function approach to the checklist method. AND-tree (figure 2) is a special type of evidential network that consists of '&' circles, rounded rectangles and proper rectangles. A rounded rectangle represents a variable and a proper rectangle represents evidence, which is connected to a variable that it directly supports. A '&' circle implies that the variable on the left of the '&' is true if and only if the variables on the right of the '&' are true. For example, suppose that a variable on the left-side of the '&' circle is an asset (A). Also suppose that there are n variables on the right-side of the '&' circle and these variables correspond to the baseline security controls (C_i). Each control variable C_i has two propositions ($\Theta_{C_i}=\{c_i,\neg c_i\}$): one proposition is that the control is in place (c_i), and the other proposition is that the control is not in place ($\neg c_i$). The propositions at the asset variable ($\Theta_A=\{a,\neg a\}$) are that the asset is secured (a) and that the asset is not secured ($\neg a$).

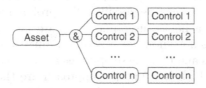

Fig. 2. Example AND-Tree for Checklist Method

In the baseline approach [6], we protect an asset by baseline protection, which means that the controls listed in the baseline protection manual should be placed whenever they are applicable. Therefore, if any of these controls are missing, we can say that the asset is not properly secured. This characteristic of baseline protection (and therefore the checklist method) suits the AND-tree in that the asset is properly secured if and only if all the relevant baseline controls are in place. The process for obtaining these marginal m-values is similar to 4.3 except that the frame of discernment on the '&' circle reflects the characteristic of AND trees. The proof for these equations is detailed in [13]. The marginal m-values for the asset variable in an AND-tree are as follow.

$$m_A(\{a\}) = \prod_{i=1}^{n} m_{Ci}(\{c_i\}) \ . \tag{7}$$

$$m_A(\{\neg a\}) = 1 - \prod_{i=1}^{n}[1 - m_{Ci}(\{\neg c_i\})] \ . \tag{8}$$

$$m_A(\{a, \neg a\}) = 1 - m_A(\{a\}) - m_A(\{\neg a\}) \ . \tag{9}$$

Suppose that an organization performs self-assessment of their compliance with BS7799-Part2 [1]. There are two controls ($n=2$) to prevent compromise of theft of information and IT facilities (control objective 5.3 in [1]). One is about the clear desk policy and the other is about the removal of property. Let us denote this control objective by O and the controls by C_1 and C_2 respectively. Assume that the organization feels that these controls have been implemented with 0.8 degree of belief for C_1 ($m_{C_1}(\{c_1\})=0.8$) and 0.3 for C_2 ($m_{C_2}(\{c_2\})=0.3$). Also, assume that $m_{C_1}(\{\neg c_1\})=m_{C_2}(\{\neg c_2\})=0$. From the equations (7)~(9) (but replacing A with O), we have $m_O(\{o\})=0.24$ and $m_O(\{o,\neg o\})=0.76$. Therefore, the degree of belief that this objective has been met is 0.24. The degree of plausibility that this objective has not been met is 0.76, which represents the maximum potential amount of support that the objective has not been met.

5   Conclusion

We have briefly overviewed some scoring methods that are used in qualitative risk analysis. The belief function approach can provide these risk analysis methods with the ability to express and manipulate uncertainties that exist in input data. The advantage of using the belief function approach is that the result of a risk analysis is more reliable in that the analyst's ignorance has been considered; by expressing the uncertainties (by degree of belief and degree of ignorance), more reliable risk analysis can be possible. The problem with computerized risk analysis tools is that a novice user may generate an impressive risk analysis report; even if he does not know the answers to questions, he must provide his opinions in many cases and then these opinions are treated as definitive answers.

Disadvantages of the belief function approach are that there is no detailed explanation about measurement of m-values, and this approach usually includes some level of computational complexity. The first disadvantage is not limited to m-values but is equally relevant in any decision-making problems that are based on subjective judgment (e.g., subjective probabilities). The solution for the second disadvantage is the use of automated facilities for dealing with belief functions. A major trend in risk analysis today is the use of automated risk analysis tools. Therefore, a module for belief functions can be embedded within automated tools. To date, there has been only limited consideration of uncertainties within risk analysis. Therefore, the belief function approach need to be further examined to obtain sounder risk analysis methods.

References

1. BS7799-Part2: Information security management part2-specification for information security management systems. British Standard Institution (1999)
2. CRAMM: CRAMM user guide (Issue 1.0). The Security Service, London (1996)

3. Cerullo, M.J., Cerullo V.: EDP risk analysis. Computer Audit J. **2** (1994) 9–30
4. Dubois, D., Grabisch, M., Prade, H., Smets, Ph.: Using the transferable belief model and a qualitative possibility theory approach on an illustrative example-the assessment of the value of a candidate. Intl. J. of Intelligent System (to appear)
5. ISO/IEC TR13335-1: Guideline for management of IT security Part1-Concepts and models for IT security (1996)
6. ISO/IEC TR 13335-2: Guideline for management of IT security Part2-Managing and planning of IT security (1997)
7. NIST Special Publication 800-12: The NIST Handbook-An introduction to computer security. National Institute of Standards and Technology (1995)
8. RiskWatch: Physical security training manual (Ver. 8.1). RiskWatch Inc. (1999)
9. Shafer, G.R.: A mathematical theory of evidence. Princeton Univ. Press, NJ (1976)
10. Smets, Ph., Kennes, R.: The transferable belief model. Artificial Intelligence **66** (1994) 191–234
11. Smets, Ph.: Varieties of ignorance and the need for well-founded theories. Information Sciences **57-58** (1991) 135–144
12. Srivastava, R.P., Shafer, G.R.: Belief-function formulas for audit risk. The Accounting Review **67** (1992) 249–283
13. Srivastava, R.P., Shenoy, P.P., Shafer, G.R.: Propagating belief functions in AND-trees. Intl. J. of Intelligent Systems **10** (1995) 647–664

Appendix

To obtain m-values for the risk variable from m-values of asset, threat and vulnerability variables, we use some basic techniques in evidence theory (called vacuous extension and marginalization). Vacuous extension deals with the addition of extra coordinates to the current frame whereas marginalization deals with the dropping of extra coordinates. According to table 2, there are only 8 possible combinations of risk, threat, vulnerability and asset values. Let this set of combinations be $\Theta = \{(l_R, l_T, l_V, l_A), (m_R, l_T, l_V, h_A), (l_R, l_T, h_V, l_A), (m_R, l_T, h_V, h_A), (m_R, h_T, l_V, l_A), (h_R, h_T, l_V, h_A), (m_R, h_T, h_V, l_A), (h_R, h_T, h_V, h_A)\}$.

This represents the frame of discernment on the joint node where all the variables are being put together[1]. The next step is to extend m-values for threat, vulnerability and asset variables vacuously onto Θ so that all the m-values for every variable are defined on the same frame (Θ). The vacuous extension of the m-values of the threat variable yields the following m-values (denoted by $m^{T\uparrow\{R,T,V,A\}}$):

$$m^{T\uparrow\{R,T,V,A\}}(\{(l_R,l_T,l_V,l_A),(m_R,l_T,l_V,h_A),(l_R,l_T,h_V,l_A),(m_R,l_T,h_V,h_A)\})=m_T(\{l_T\}),$$

$$m^{T\uparrow\{R,T,V,A\}}(\{(m_R,h_T,l_V,l_A),(h_R,h_T,l_V,h_A),(m_R,h_T,h_V,l_A),(h_R,h_T,h_V,h_A)\})=m_T(\{h_T\}),$$

$$m^{T\uparrow\{R,T,V,A\}}(\Theta)=m_T(\{\Theta_T\}), \text{ and } m\text{-values for all other subsets of } \Theta \text{ are } 0.$$

Similarly, the vacuous extensions of the m-values of the vulnerability variable are as follows:

$$m^{V\uparrow\{R,T,V,A\}}(\{(l_R,l_T,l_V,l_A),(m_R,l_T,l_V,h_A),(m_R,h_T,l_V,l_A),(h_R,h_T,l_V,h_A)\})=m_V(\{l_V\}),$$

---

[1] In general, the joint m-values are defined on the Cartesian product of the frames of variables, which has 24 elements for this example. Our approach is based on [13].

$m^{V\uparrow\{R,T,V,A\}}(\{(l_R,l_T,h_V,l_A),(m_R,l_T,h_V,h_A),(m_R,h_T,h_V,l_A),(h_R,h_T,h_V,h_A)\})=m_V(\{h_V\})$,

$m^{V\uparrow\{R,T,V,A\}}(\Theta)=m_V(\{\Theta_V\})$, and m-values for all other subsets of Θ are 0.

The vacuous extensions of the m-values of the asset variable are as follows:

$m^{A\uparrow\{R,T,V,A\}}(\{(l_R,l_T,l_V,l_A),(l_R,l_T,h_V,l_A),(m_R,h_T,l_V,l_A),(m_R,h_T,h_V,l_A)\})=m_A(\{l_A\})$,

$m^{A\uparrow\{R,T,V,A\}}(\{(m_R,l_T,l_V,h_A),(m_R,l_T,h_V,h_A),(h_R,h_T,l_V,h_A),(h_R,h_T,h_V,h_A)\})=m_A(\{h_A\})$,

$m^{A\uparrow\{R,T,V,A\}}(\Theta)=m_A(\{\Theta_A\})$, and m-values for all other subsets of Θ are 0.

Using Dempster's rule of combination, we now combine these m-values to obtain the joint m-values (denoted by m), which are shown in table 3 (1, 2, 3, 4, 5, 6, 7 and 8 stands for (l_R,l_T,l_V,l_A), (m_R,l_T,l_V,h_A), (l_R,l_T,h_V,l_A), (m_R,l_T,h_V,h_A), (m_R,h_T,l_V,l_A), (h_R,h_T,l_V,h_A), (m_R,h_T,h_V,l_A) and (h_R,h_T,h_V,h_A) respectively). From these m-values, we can obtain marginal m-values (denoted by $m^{\downarrow R}$) of the risk variable by marginalizing them onto the frame of the risk variable (i.e. $\Theta_R=\{l_R,m_R,h_R\}$). Marginalization, similar to marginalization of probabilities, sums all the m-values for a given set of elements of Θ_R, which yields the equations (1)~(6) in 4.3.

Table 3. The joint m-values for risk, threat, vulnerability and asset variables

$m(\{1\})=m_T(l_T)m_V(l_V)m_A(l_A)$	$m(\{2\})=m_T(l_T)m_V(l_V)m_A(h_A)$
$m(\{3\})=m_T(l_T)m_V(h_V)m_A(l_A)$	$m(\{4\})=m_T(l_T)m_V(h_V)m_A(h_A)$
$m(\{5\})=m_T(h_T)m_V(l_V)m_A(l_A)$	$m(\{6\})=m_T(h_T)m_V(l_V)m_A(h_A)$
$m(\{7\})=m_T(h_T)m_V(h_V)m_A(l_A)$	$m(\{8\})=m_T(h_T)m_V(h_V)m_A(h_A)$
$m(\{1,2\})=m_T(l_T)m_V(l_V)m_A(\Theta_A)$	$m(\{1,3\})=m_T(l_T)m_V(\Theta_V)m_A(l_A)$
$m(\{1,5\})=m_T(\Theta_T)m_V(l_V)m_A(l_A)$	$m(\{2,4\})=m_T(l_T)m_V(\Theta_V)m_A(h_A)$
$m(\{2,6\})=m_T(\Theta_T)m_V(l_V)m_A(h_A)$	$m(\{3,4\})=m_T(l_T)m_V(h_V)m_A(\Theta_A)$
$m(\{3,7\})=m_T(\Theta_T)m_V(h_V)m_A(l_A)$	$m(\{4,8\})=m_T(\Theta_T)m_V(h_V)m_A(h_A)$
$m(\{5,6\})=m_T(h_T)m_V(l_V)m_A(\Theta_A)$	$m(\{5,7\})=m_T(h_T)m_V(\Theta_V)m_A(l_A)$
$m(\{6,8\})=m_T(h_T)m_V(\Theta_V)m_A(h_A)$	$m(\{7,8\})=m_T(h_T)m_V(h_V)m_A(\Theta_A)$
$m(\{1,2,3,4\})=m_T(l_T)m_V(\Theta_V)m_A(\Theta_A)$	$m(\{1,2,5,6\})=m_T(\Theta_T)m_V(l_V)m_A(\Theta_A)$
$m(\{1,3,5,7\})=m_T(\Theta_T)m_V(\Theta_V)m_A(l_A)$	$m(\{2,4,6,8\})=m_T(\Theta_T)m_V(\Theta_V)m_A(h_A)$
$m(\{3,4,7,8\})=m_T(\Theta_T)m_V(h_V)m_A(\Theta_A)$	$m(\{5,6,7,8\})=m_T(h_T)m_V(\Theta_V)m_A(\Theta_A)$
$m(\Theta)=m_T(\Theta_T)m_V(\Theta_V)m_A(\Theta_A)$	m-value for any other subset is 0

RBAC for XML Document Stores

Michael Hitchens and Vijay Varadharajan

Distributed System and Network Security Research Group
Department of Computing
Macquarie University
{michaelh,vijay}@ics.mq.edu.au

Abstract. Web based services and applications have increased the availability and accessibility of information. XML (eXtensible Markup Language) has recently emerged as an important standard in the area of information representation. XML documents can represent information at different levels of sensitivity. Access control for XML document stores must recognise the fine-grained nature of the document structure. In this paper we present an approach to access control for XML document stores. This framework is based on RBAC and includes a syntax for specifying access control policies for the store.

1. Introduction

Web based services and applications have increased the availability and accessibility of information. It has also increased the need to share information between different applications running on different platforms. This in turn has necessitated the need to have suitable standards for information representation and transfer. XML (eXtensible Markup Language) [12] has recently emerged as an important standard in the area of information representation using markup languages. For technical writers, XML provides a syntax that allows them to capture the meaning of their documents. For the enterprise programmer, XML provides a syntax for moving data between objects. For the programmer building systems to provide e-commerce services between business partners, XML provides a syntax to capture the richness of the transactions, making the transactions more accurate and timely. XML is a simplified version of SGML. It is easier to learn and use than SGML while still providing many of the benefits of SGML. With XML elements have tags and one can define nested documents and document types that describe the structure of the documents.

Because XML documents can represent information at different levels of sensitivity, it is necessary to develop access control mechanisms that define which part of the document can be accessed by whom. Traditionally, the work on access control classifies security models into two broad categories, namely discretionary access control and mandatory access control. Typically in discretionary access control models leave the specification of access control policies to individual users and control the access of users to information on the basis of identity of users. In mandatory access control models, the standard approach is to have the access defined by a system administrator and employ attributes such as classifications and clearances. The need for access control for the web, and XML documents stores in particular, has been recognized [1,2,4]. Recently, there has been extensive interest in role based access control (RBAC) [5] even though the idea of the use

S. Qing, T. Okamoto, and J. Zhou (Eds.): ICICS 2001, LNCS 2229, pp. 131-143, 2001.
© Springer-Verlag Berlin Heidelberg 2001

of roles for controlling access to entities and objects is as old as the traditional access control models. In the RBAC models, the attributes used in access control are the roles associated with the principals and the privileges are associated with the roles.

In this paper, we consider a role based access control model for XML based information objects. Section 2 briefly discusses the characteristics of XML and defines the relevant components of the XML syntax. Section 3 describes the characteristics of the role based access control model. In section 4, we define the requirements of access control for XML based documents. In particular, we consider the various design aspects such as fine-grained policy control, propagation and control of policies and modelling of relationship between the document type definitions and documents. Section 5 proposes a role based access control model for XML and defines the authorisations on target objects, which can be documents and document type definitions or both. Section 6 considers the evolution of the access control system in terms of the operations that can be defined on roles and permission. Finally some conclusions and further work are outlined in Section 7.

2. XML

XML is a format for placing any form of structured data on the World Wide Web. The type of data covered includes, but is not limited to, graphics, spreadsheets, databases and other forms of structured information. For example, an XML document may contain, directly or by reference, the complete medical history of a patient. Another XML document may represent a database built from such patient records. XML provides a means of designing formats for data that are capable of being widely understood, can be generated and read by computer and are extensible. The full definition for XML is supplied by the W3C [12].

The basic component of an XML document is an *element*. An element is delimited by matching start and end tags. A tag of the form <tag-name> marks the start of an element and a tag of the form </tag-name> marks its end. An element may have content and attributes associated with it. Attributes may only appear within the start tag of an element. Their declaration gives their name, type and a default value. Attributes are used to provide additional information. One predefined attribute type, ID, may be used to uniquely name the element. Another, IDREF can be used to refer to named elements. Between the tags of an element is that element's content. This content may be either other elements or character data or both. Element nesting may be to any depth. It can be seen that XML documents may be regarded as directed graphs.

A special type of XML document is the *Document Type Definition* (DTD). A DTD provides the rules for the structure of XML documents. The DTD may be a separate file or included with the documents. The DTD provides rules for the element and attribute structure of the document. XML documents which conform to a DTD can be thought of as instances of the schema represented by that DTD.

XML documents may be *well-formed* or *valid*. A document is *well-formed* if it conforms to the syntax of XML. A document is *valid* if it conforms to a DTD. Note that a valid document is also well-formed. Examples of a DTD and corresponding document are given in figures 1 and 2. This example illustrates a situation where there may be multiple users of the information. For example, a receptionist may be allowed to consult the identification parts of the record (essentially everything other than the treatment records) while a doctor may have access to all the information. This is also an example of a requirement for different users (or classes of users) to have different levels of access to the information within a single document.

```
<!DOCTYPE patient-record [
<!ELEMENT patient (name, address, health-care-num, treatment-rec*)>
<!ELEMENT name (#PCDATA)>
<!ELEMENT address (street,city,postcode,state,telnum)>
<!ELEMENT street (#PCDATA)>
<!ELEMENT city (#PCDATA)>
<!ELEMENT postcode (#PCDATA)>
<!ELEMENT state (#PCDATA)>
<!ELEMENT telnum (#PCDATA)>
<!ELEMENT health-care-num (#PCDATA)>
<!ELEMENT treatment-rec (date,doctor,notes)
<!ELEMENT date (#PCDATA)>
<!ELEMENT doctor (#PCDATA)>
<!ELEMENT notes empty>
<ATTLIST patient id ID (#REQUIRED)>
<ATTLIST notes xml-link CDATA #FIXED "SIMPLE"
xml-attributes CDATA #FIXED "HREF URL"
URL CDATA #REQUIRED>
]>
```

Fig. 1. An Example DTD

```
<patient-record id = "PNUM123"
    <name> John Smith </name>
    <address>
        <street> 38, Some Street </street> <city> Somewhere </city>
        <postcode> 1234 </postcode> <state> NA </state>
        <telnum> 02 1234 5678 </telnum>
    </address>
    <health-care-num> 1234 56789 0 </health-care-num>
    <treatment-rec>
        <date> 5-5-00 </date> <doctor> J. S. Who </doctor>
        <notes xml-link = "simple" xml-attributes = "hred url"
        url = "http://www.medcentre.com/treatrecs/PNUM123-1.xml>
    </treatment-rec>
    <treatment-rec>
        <date> 12-8-00 </date> <doctor> J. S. Who </doctor>
        <notes xml-link = "simple" xml-attributes = "hred url"
        url = "http://www.medcentre.com/treatrecs/PNUM123-2.xml>
    </treatment-rec>
</patient-record>
```

Fig. 2. An Example XML Document

3. RBAC

The central idea of Role-Based Access Control (RBAC) is the *role*. A role models the functions of a particular job within an organisation (such as programmer, physician or shift manager). Permissions are assigned to roles based on the access required for a person in the corresponding position to carry out their job functions. Users are assigned to one or more roles on the basis of their actual job classifications. Roles therefore embody both the access allowed to users and the extent to which resources may be accessed. The mappings between users and roles and roles and permissions form a central part of any RBAC system. The exact form a permission takes will vary from system to system but can be thought of as an authorisation or approval to carry out a particular, specified, action. A permission can be as general or highly detailed as required (and the system allows).

The interaction between users and roles is more sophisticated than a simple mapping. Each user has a set of roles (one or more) to which they are assigned. These are generally termed the *authorised* roles for the user. When the user wishes to interact with the system they initiate a *session*. This could be as simple as creating a process. For each session of a user there is a set of *active* roles, which is a subset of the authorised roles for the corresponding user. Access for the session is limited to what is available through the active roles.

Roles themselves are usually related through two further concepts, *constraints* and *hierarchies*. Constraints are used to limit the roles that may be simultaneously occupied by a user. This may be either at the level of authorised or active roles. Constraints may be simple in nature, for example simple mutual exclusion (which enables separation of duty to be modelled) or more complicated, for example limiting the number of members of a role on insisting on membership of one role being a prerequisite for membership of a second. The form of constraint possible depends on the expressive power of the actual implementation, there is no theoretical limitation.

A role hierarchy is a partial order on the roles within a system. With in the hierarchy a role inherits from its ancestors all their permissions. The permissions of the role itself and the permissions of all its ancestors within the hierarchy determine the actual access conveyed by the role. For example, the role *specialist* may inherit all the permissions of *general-practitioner*.

4. Requirements for XML Access Control

XML documents can embody a wide range of semantic information. The information in a document can be presented in a complex structure. Access control policies for XML document stores must reflect the rich semantic and structural nature of the information. This results in a set of requirements for the design of the access control mechanism for an XML document store:

- Fine-grained policy control
- Propagation of policy through the document structure
- Control of propagation through restriction
- Modelling the relationship between DTDs and Documents
- Abstraction over sets of subjects

4.1. Fine Grained Policy Control

XML was designed to allow semantically rich documents, both in terms of content and structure. Documents can be viewed as having a hierarchical structure. Each element will be composed of a number of attributes and/or links as well as, possibly, other elements. Access control policies for such documents may distinguish between the different elements (or their components) of a document. For example, consider a document which lists groups, their individual members and contact details and contains links to technical documents produced by the groups. While the contact details may need to be widely available, access to the technical documents may be restricted. It follows that only some subjects should be given access to the elements which contain the links to these documents. Such distinctions must be supported by the access control mechanism. This can only be met by allowing access control policies to be expressed at a very fine-grained level, i.e. at the granularity of element.

It could be argued that the access could be specified at an even finer grain than the element level, i.e. at the attribute/link level. It should be remembered that the element is the semantic structuring unit for XML documents. Within an element there are only attributes, links and sub-elements. In the next sub-section restricting access granted to sub-elements will be discussed. If access to sub-elements is not allowed than only attributes and links remain. If the set of attributes and links in an element should have different access control then an argument could be made that the different groups should be placed in separate semantic units (i.e. elements) and the primary granularity remains that of the element. However, if such separations are not desired, the changes required to the following to refine the granularity to the level of individual attributes and links are minor, consisting mainly in some added complexity in the definition of the scope of a permission. For space reasons, amongst others, we limit ourselves to the element as the base granularity for access control.

4.2. Propagation

As argued in the previous sub-section the rich structure of XML documents results in a need for policy control which can allow for finer-grained control than document level policies would. However, requiring policies to specified on each element (or attribute, etc) would be tedious and confusing. Policy granularity must be flexible, reflecting the hierarchical structure of XML documents. It must be possible to specify policies at the document, element or intermediate levels. It must be possible for policies to propagate down the hierarchical structure. This propagation may be defined, for individual policies, to be fully down the hierarchy, or limited in some way (e.g., to a number of levels). Consider the document of figure 2. If access is to be granted to the address of the patient it should only be necessary to specify the policy at the level of the address element (or higher) and not individually for each sub-element of address (street, city, etc).

Such restriction should allow the policy managers to specify how far down the hierarchy the access propagates. If it does not propagate at all, than the access applies only to the attributes/links of an element, and not its sub-elements.

4.3. Restriction

Fine grained access control, which may propagate throughout a document, results in a flexible control mechanism. However, it cannot easily implement all possible policies. There need to be more limits on the propagation than the fairly coarse one of restricting the number of levels of propagation. It is too unwieldy a device to satisfy all requirements. For example, it does not easily allow restriction of access to some sub-branches of the document hierarchy

It must be possible to restrict access to certain parts of an XML documents. If authorisations are propagated down the tree structure of an XML document or DTD then there will be a need for negative authorisations to control the propagation. These negative authorisations may themselves be propagated down the document. As noted earlier, while a receptionist may be given access to most of the fields of the document in figure 2, the receptionist would not be given access to the treatment records. The sensible way to handle this would be to give the receptionist access to the document at the patient element level. This would then propagate through the document. The access would be restricted at the level of the treatment-rec level. The result is two policy expressions, not one per element.

4.4. Modelling the Relationship between DTDs and Documents

While propagation within a document is a useful tool for specifying policies, it is not the only form of propagation applicable to an XML document store. Many (if not most) XML documents will have a corresponding DTD specification. Often documents which share a DTD will also share access control policies. It would therefore be useful to be able to specify policies on a DTD which propagate to documents based on that DTD. This propagation is orthogonal to the propagation along the hierarchical structure of documents and DTDs

As a corollary of this there must be the ability to specify the precedence of policies at the DTD and documents levels. Normally those at the individual document level would take precedence (if they exist). It must be possible to specify other precedence orders. Taking our example from the previous sub-section further, it would probably be preferable if the policy outlined could be applied the DTD and then extend to all patient records, rather than have to state it for each record.

4.5. Subjects

Accesses to an XML document store will likely be from a variety of locations. Some will be local to the store, others remote. Given the potentially rich semantic content of such a store it is also likely that the users requesting access will form a diverse set. It is obviously unrealistic to require the store to maintain policies individually for each user. Instead, it should be possible to abstract over this diverse set of users.

Various techniques for such abstraction exist, including groups and roles. Roles offer more semantic power due to the ability to define relationships between the various roles via a hierarchy of inheritance. Groups tend to be distinct, unrelated, structures. For this reason, amongst others, we will use roles to abstract over the users accessing the document store. More details on this is given in the next section. For our (simplistic) medical example, it may be desirable to divide users into two classifications - receptionists and doctors.

5. RBAC for XML

As outlined in the previous section one of the requirements for an access control mechanism for an XML document store is the ability to abstract over subjects. A high proportion of the subjects seeking access to the store will not be from the same node or local network as the store itself. In such circumstances it is unwieldy for the store (or its access control) to record the subjects individually. The subjects will need to be classified, allowing single policies to apply to groups of subjects.

The most common methods for such classification are assigning users to groups or to roles. In many ways groups and roles are similar. Both allow subjects to be grouped together. Both allow single polices to apply to multiple subjects. However, roles have a significant advantage over groups for expressing access control policies for an XML document store available to a distributed user base. These advantages are

- Roles can be formed into hierarchies.
- Roles allow different sessions of the one subject to have different privileges.
- Privileges are stored with the role, not the object.

Most group-based access control treats groups as completely separate and unrelated collections of subjects. It has been said that roles are merely groups structured hierarchically, with one role (group) consisting of other roles (groups). While this is an oversimplification, the ability to structure roles hierarchically does yield enhanced expressiveness. Roles allow the classification of subjects to be structured. This allows for a more easily understood and managed view of subjects.

Given the anticipated widespread use of XML it has to be expected that access control policies for XML document stores will be managed by users who are domain specialists, not computing specialists. RBAC is known to have advantages in modelling real-world organisations [7] and should be suitable for describing access control policies for XML document stores.

It is possible that RBAC would be used both at the XML document store and at the home site of remote users. This would mean that subjects would be assigned to roles at their home system. The document store could accept the role assignments of remote users. Some suggestions for distributed RBAC have proposed that the system where access is requested simply accept the role assignment made at the subject's home or, implicitly, assume that both subject and document store employ the same role hierarchy [6,9,11]. Even where the later is correct the acceptance of remote role assignment is potentially dubious and does not reflect real world practice (one of the stated strengths of RBAC). For example, simply because a user is a programmer at their system does not automatically meant hey should be accorded all the privileges of a programmer at a remote system. It is also simplistic to assume the roles and the role hierarchy will be uniform across all home nodes and systems of users of a given document store.

The node on which the document store is held cannot simply accept the role assignments (or other access control decisions) made at a remote node. This means that the node at which access is requested will have to make some mapping between the remote roles for the subject and existing local roles. This becomes especially true when the role hierarchies at the local and remote nodes show little, if any, similarity.

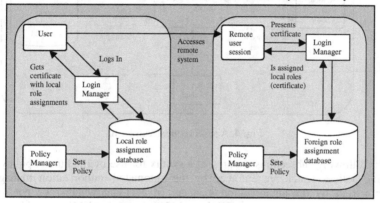

Fig. 3. Role Assignment for Remote Access

Normal practice in access control is to give a subject access to objects subject to policies laid down by the store (or system) administrator. This will require the administrator to create policies which specify the translation between remote and local role assignment. This will usually result in a lower level of access being granted than if the remote role assignments were used unchanged. This is not unreasonable – in the real world a visitor usually has much lower access than local staff. If no explicit policy exists on how to treat a particular remote role assignment than default policies assigning such subject to very low privilege local roles can be formulated. Where the remote role assignments are recognised (on the basis of remote system and assignment) more informed decisions can be made, on the basis of explicit policies. The architecture for role assignment is illustrated in figure 3. Note that the decisions about role assignment made by the policy managers in both systems will affect the access of the user in the remote system

When a subject presents a request for access the document store only needs to be concerned with the current role assignment of the subject. This will probably be presented within a certificate signed by an authority within the subject's home system. We assume that the access control system of the document store has trust (either directly or indirectly) in this authority. The access control system only needs to be concerned with the current active roles of the subject (the dynamic situation) not the long term static role authorisations. Groups tend to be much more static, concerned with the long term grouping of subjects. This again makes roles more suitable for an XML environment.

In an RBAC system privileges are stored (logically at least) with the roles, not the objects. The makes the determination of the access allowed via a particular role an easy matter. Storing privileges with objects makes the determination of a subject's total access a time-consuming and difficult question. Given that an XML store is to be available to remote subjects the question of the total access allowed such users is relevant. Again the RBAC approach appears suitable as it provides an easy way to determine the access available to a remote subject.

When after a user has established a remote session and been assigned local roles, as illustrated in figure 3, that session can be used to access XML documents in the local document store. This process is displayed in figure 4.

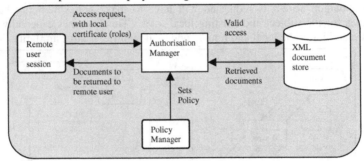

Fig. 4. Access request validation

In the following subsections we present a syntax for use by the human policy manager in setting polices which are enforced by the automated authorization manager. The algorithm used by the authorization manager in deciding whether or not to grant a requested access is given in section 5.7. It could be argued that XML should be used as the basis for the specification of policy. However, this may not be the best syntax for the policy manager to use. We present a more friendly, high-level syntax. However, there is nothing to prevent the actual storage representation of these policies being in XML. The possible translation between the syntax presented here and XML is not discussed and is left for future work.

5.1. Authorisations

The actual authorisations in an RBAC system are expressed in the permissions (policies), which are then grouped together within the roles themselves. The requirements outlined in section 4 give us the following broad structure for a permission for an XML document store

- Target identification - may be for one or more DTDs and/or documents
- Element identification – to which elements within the DTD (document) does the permission apply
- Propagation – does the permission propagate beyond the specified elements and if so, how
- Authorisation – does the permission convey positive or negative (denial) authorisation

- Priority – does the permission override the normal rule for propagation of authorisations between DTDs and documents.

This broad outline of a permission obviously applies to XML document stores in general and is not limited by the adoption of RBAC. It could be converted into an actual syntax in many ways. That which we give below is based on our language for object-oriented RBAC systems, called Tower [8].

We assume the following default precedence rules:

- authorisations specified for a DTD propagate to documents based on that DTD but are overriden by conflicting permissions expressed explicitly on the document.
- negative permissions override positive permissions

The basic syntax for a permission is:

```
permission_name := [priority] permission | negpermission
        target {target_oid, target_oid, ...}
        [path [not]{path_expression,path_expression,...}
        [propagation_rule ]]
        [condition_expression]
    end_permission
```

5.2. Priority and Access

The optional key word *priority* is used to specify whether or not the access granted by the permission overrides (has priority over) the normal precedence rule of DTD permissions being subordinate to document specific permissions. If the permission is given *priority* then the access it specifies on any target DTDs overrides any conflicting access specified for documents which conform to those DTDs. We provide no mechanism to override the priority negative permissions have over positive permissions. While this could have been provided we believe that this could lead to difficult to understand policy expressions. It also raises the question of whether it should be possible to override the override. DTD to documents is a single level transfer. Positive and negative permissions could, in theory, override each other indefinitely through the hierarchical document structure and this is undesirable

The second key word within the permission (*permission* or *negpermission*) specifies whether the permission grants (*permission*) or disallows (*negpermission*) access. While a permission can apply to targets (both in terms of documents and of elements/attributes within those documents) the form of access that it gives to its targets is the same, either positive or negative.

5.3. Target Documents and Elements

After the keyword *target* is a list of object identifiers which are the targets for the permission. These may be for documents, DTDs or both. The object identifiers are expressed in whatever syntax is applicable to the host system of the store.

After the keyword *path* is an optional set of path expressions. These specify the elements of the documents to which access is being granted or denied by the permission. We use Xpath [13], the XML path language for these expressions. An expression in Xpath is a sequence of names and identifies one or more elements in the target document. Note that, by default, we take the initial context for the resolution of the X-path expressions to be the target document. An access request will specify the parts of the document to which access is sought. Each path expression in a permission is evaluated to determine if it matches the path expression in the request. The optional keyword *not* simply allows a short hand for defining the scope of the permission. Then if the path in the access request matches **none** of the paths in the permission, the permission applies. If no path expression is included within the permission then the access defined in the permission is for all elements of the target objects.

5.4. Propagation and Conditions

The *propagation_rule* defines how the access granted by a permission propagates to the children of the explicitly named elements. By children we mean its descendants in the hierarchical structure of the XML document or DTD. The syntax for this clause is

```
propagation rule:  recursion {target_spec}
recursion: local I [n]recursive
target_spec: attributes I links
```

If the propagation is **local** then the permission only applies to the attributes, links and data of the specified elements (as defined by the target specification). The level of recursion, if any, is specified by the use of the keyword **recursive.** If used without a limiting integer than the permission applies to all attributes and links (as restricted by target specification) of the elements, their sub-elements and further sub-elements. Including an integer limits the recursion (e.g., a 1 limits the permission to the elements and their direct sub-elements only).

A permission automatically applies to any data of the governed elements. The *target_spec* specifies whether the permission also applies to attributes and/or links. If no target specification is given the permission applies only to the data of the elements given by the path expression, and possibly sub-elements, as specified by the propagation. It does not grant or deny access to links or attributes.

If the propagation rule is not specified, it is assumed to be **recursive** and apply to both attributes and links as well as data.

The *condition_expression* is a boolean expression which is checked before access is granted or denied. The permission only takes effect (negatively or positively) if the boolean expression evaluates to true. The expression may include checks on environment variables, such as time of day or physical location. For more detail see [8].

5.5. Roles and the Access Control Algorithm

A role is not simply a collection of permissions. Two other important components of the role concept are the role hierarchy and constraints [10]. The role hierarchy allows roles to be composed of other roles. For example, if role r1 has permission p1 and role r2 inherits from r1 then the access allowed by p1 is also available through r2. Constraints place restrictions on how users are assigned to roles. The syntax for a role is as follows:

```
role_name := role
    [constraint_expression]
    [roles {role,role,...}]
    [permissions{permission, permission,...}]
end_role
```

Constraints in a role may be used to impose restrictions upon whether a user may have this role added to his/her set of roles, or whether a user may add another role while possessing this one. Such a constraint is specified as a Boolean function which must evaluate to true if the role is to be added. A short hand is provided for the common case of exclusion, which is that possession of the current role is mutually exclusive with the roles in the role set.

```
exclude role_set
```

Requests for access in a XML document store will need to specify the following information:
- a session identifier, s_x which can be used to identify a user, u
- the identity of the XML document(s) being accessed, d
- the portions of the document(s) being accessed, identified by Xpath path expression(s), p

Conceptually an access request takes the form $access(s,d,p)$, where d and p may be singular or sets. If multiple documents are accessed they must adhere to the same DTD so that the path expressions in p can apply to all documents d.

The access control system will report whether the access is to be allowed or disallowed, according to the following algorithm:

> for each active role r_i for the session, s
> > for each permission p_i of r_i
> > > if d is a target of p_i and if the elements and/or attributes/links
> > > identified by p are covered by p_i and the condition expression of
> > > p_i evaluates to true
> > > > allow the access

6. System Evolution

The structure of roles defined in the previous section, essentially consisting of a set of roles (for inheritance) and a set of permissions. As the system evolves, any of these structures may need to have their values updated. Set operations may be applied to each of these structures, for example

```
R1 := R1 + {P1,P2}
```

Role *R1* now has permissions *P1* and *P2* added to its set of permissions. Although a role has two sets, the fact that values being added are permissions makes it clear that the update must be to the permission set of the role. Therefore we can simply use the role name without further qualification. The same applies to the sets of a permission (i.e. its targets and path expressions).

Further forms of alteration are possible, as in the following examples:

```
R := {P1,P2}
```

The permissions in R are now P1 and P2.

```
R1 := R1 + {R2,R3}
```

R1 has R2 and R3 added to its roles

```
R1 := R1 - {R4}
```

R4 is no longer one of R1's roles

The system can determine if the roles or permissions of a role are being updated by resolving the names on the right hand side of the assignment statements.

The other information held in a structure may also be updated within assignment statements. For example, the condition within a permission may be added to. For example,

```
P1 := P1 + condition_expression
```

The new condition expression for the privilege is formed by joining the previous expression and that in the assignment statement with the *and* conjunction.

7. Conclusions

Defining access control in web based services is becoming increasingly significant due to the growth in Internet and E-Commerce applications. XML is fast becoming a de-facto standard for representing documents and information in web based services and applications. Access control for an XML document store must reflect the potential for fine grained nature to the store and provide a flexible format for specifying policies over the document structures. While some work on using XML for RBAC [3] has been done, it focuses on intranets, not remote access via the web and does not consider whether XML is a suitable medium in which managers an express policy. Other uses of XML for access control do not apply an RBAC approach [1].

The access control proposal in this paper, centred on RBAC, meets the criteria identified for access control of XML document stores. It also easily allows for abstraction over subjects, which is necessary to easily allow remote access through the world wide web by large numbers of users. We have defined structures for specifying roles and the privileges available through them and have also described operations to allow for evolution of the access control structures themselves. The syntax is flexible and user-friendly. We believe that such a model can be used to specify access control in practical web based systems and can be easily integrated with existing applications. Further work in this area include the development of tools for access control policy management, and in the translation of our syntax into XML documents.

References

1. Bertino, E., Castano, S. & and Ferrari, E., *On specifying security policies for web documents with an XML-based language*, Sixth ACM Symposium on Access control models and technologies May 2001, Chantilly, USA, pp. 57-65.
2. Bonatti, P. & Samarati, P., *Regulating Service Access and Information Release on the Web*, In Proc. Of the 7th ACM Conference on Computer and Communication Security, Athens, Greece, November 2000.
3. Chandramouli, R., *Application of XML tools for enterprise-wide RBAC implementation tasks*, Proceedings of the fifth ACM workshop on Role-based access control July 2000, Berlin, pp. 11-18.
4. Damiani, E., De Capitani di Vimercati, Paraboschi, S & Samarati, P., *XML Access Control Systems: A Component Based Approach*, In Fourteenth Annual IFIP WG 11.3 Working Conference on Database Security, Schoorl, The Netherlands, August 2000.
5. Ferraiolo, D., and Kuhn, R.: *Role based access controls*, Proceedings of the 15th NIST-NCSC National Computer Security Conference, Baltimore MD, USA, 1992, pp. 554-563.

6. Giuri, L., *Role-based access control on the Web using Java*, Proceedings of the fourth ACM workshop on role-based access control on Role-based access control October 1999, Fairfax, USA, pp. 11-18.
7. Hilchenbach, B., *Observations on the real-world implementation of role-based access control*, Proceedings of the 20th National Information Systems Security Conference, Baltimore MD, USA, 1997, pp. 341-52.
8. Hitchens, M. & Varadharajan, V. *Design and specification of role based access control policies*, IEE Proc.-Softw., Vol. 147, No. 4 August 2000, pp. 117-129.
9. Park, J. & Sandhu, R., *RBAC on the Web by smart certificates*, Proceedings of the fourth ACM workshop on role-based access control on Role-based access control October 1999, Fairfax, USA, pp. 1-9.
10. Sandhu, R., Coyne, E.J., and Feinstein, H.L., *Role based access control models*, IEEE Computer, 1996, 29, (2), pp. 38-47.
11. Sandhu, R. & Park, J., *Decentralised User-role Assignment for Web-based Intranets*, 3rd ACM Workshop on RBAC, Fairfax, USA, October 1998.
12. World Wide Web Consortium (W3C), *Extensible Markup Language (XML)*, February 1998, http://www.w3.org/XML.
13. World Wide Web Consortium (W3C), *XML Path Language (XPath) Version 1.0*, November 1999, http://www.w3.org/TR/xpath.

Cheating Immune Secret Sharing

Xian-Mo Zhang[1] and Josef Pieprzyk[2]

[1] School of IT and CS, University of Wollongong
Wollongong, NSW 2522, AUSTRALIA, xianmo@cs.uow.edu.au
[2] Algorithms and Cryptography Centre, Department of Computing
Macquarie University, Sydney , NSW 2109, AUSTRALIA, josef@ics.mq.edu.au

Abstract. We consider secret sharing with binary shares. This model allows us to use the well developed theory of cryptographically strong boolean functions. We prove that for given secret sharing, the average cheating probability over all cheating and original vectors, i.e., $\bar{\rho} = \frac{1}{n} \cdot 2^{-n} \sum_{c=1}^{n} \sum_{\alpha \in V_n} \rho_{c,\alpha}$, satisfies $\bar{\rho} \geq \frac{1}{2}$, and the equality holds $\Longleftrightarrow \rho_{c,\alpha}$ satisfies $\rho_{c,\alpha} = \frac{1}{2}$ for every cheating vector δ_c and every original vector α. In this case the secret sharing is said to be cheating immune. We further establish a relationship between cheating-immune secret sharing and cryptographic criteria of boolean functions. This enables us to construct cheating-immune secret sharing.

1 Introduction and Background

Since its invention in 1978 by Blakley [2] and Shamir [9], secret sharing has evolved dramatically. Initially, it was designed to facilitate a distributed storage for a secret in an unreliable or insecure environment. Later, however, secret sharing has been incorporated into public key cryptography giving rise to the well-known concept of group or society oriented cryptography (see [5]). Now secret sharing is one of the basic cryptographic tools with variety of very interesting schemes based on algebraic or geometric structures. Tompa and Woll [11] observed that Shamir secret sharing can be subject to cheating by dishonest participants. The cheater is able to recover the valid secret from the invalid one passed by the combiner. As the result, the honest participants are left with invalid secret while the cheater holds the valid one. This observation is true for all linear secret sharing. The cheating attack can also be extended for geometrical secret sharing. Cheating prevention can be considered in the context of conditionally and unconditionally secure secret sharing. We focus our attention on unconditionally secure secret sharing. In this setting, cheating can be thwarted by (1) share verification by the combiner – all invalid shares are identified and discarded, where the key recovery goes ahead only if there are enough valid shares to recover the valid secret (see [3,4,6]), and (2) discouraging cheaters from sending invalid shares to the combiner – this argument works if the cheater gains no advantage over honest participants. In other words, sending invalid share will result with recovery of an invalid secret which gives no clues to the cheater as to the value of the valid secret. We intend to consider a class of secret sharing

S. Qing, T. Okamoto, and J. Zhou (Eds.): ICICS 2001, LNCS 2229, pp. 144–149, 2001.
© Springer-Verlag Berlin Heidelberg 2001

for which, a cheating participant is no better off than a participant who tries simply to guess a secret. Ideally, the probability of successful cheating should be equal to the probability of guessing the secret by a participant. To make our considerations explicit, we assume that secret and shares are binary. For this case we prove that there is a secret sharing, further in the work called *cheating immune*, that gives no advantage to a cheater making it, in a sense, immune against cheating.

Secret sharing allows a group of participants $\mathcal{P} = \{P_1, \ldots, P_n\}$ to collectively hold a secret $K \in \mathcal{K}$, where $\mathcal{K}$ is a set of elements from which the secret is drawn. Secret sharing is created by a trusted algorithm called a *dealer* who for a given secret, generates a collection of shares $s_i \in \mathcal{S}$, where $\mathcal{S}$ is a set of shares. Note that s_i is given to P_i, $i = 1, \ldots, n$. The collective ownership of the secret is defined by the access structure of secret sharing. The access structure Γ is a collection of subgroups of $\mathcal{P}$ that are authorized to recover the secret. An authorized group of participants $\mathcal{A} \in \Gamma$ is able to reconstruct the secret by invoking a trusted algorithm called *combiner*. The combiner always returns the valid secret if the group $\mathcal{A}$ submits their valid shares. If the group, however, is too small, i.e. $\mathcal{A} \notin \Gamma$, then the algorithm returns a value which is not the valid secret (with an overwhelming probability). In this work, we describe a secret sharing by a set of *distribution rules* [10], where a distribution rule is a function $f : \mathcal{P} \to \mathcal{S}$ that represents possible distribution of shares to the participants. In other words, secret sharing is a set $\mathcal{F} = \bigcup_{K \in \mathcal{K}} \mathcal{F}_K$ where $\mathcal{F}_K$ is a distribution rule corresponding to the secret K. Equivalently, $\mathcal{F}$ can be presented in the form of *distribution table* $\mathcal{T}$. The table has $(n + 1)$ columns – the first one includes secrets and the other n ones list shares assigned to participants $(P_1, \ldots, P_n)$, respectively. Each row of the distribution table specifies the secret for a collection of shares held by $\mathcal{P}$. Note that $\mathcal{F}_K$ can be seen as a part of the distribution table with rows whose first entry is K. This table is denoted by $\mathcal{T}_K$. Most of practical secret sharing schemes are linear and therefore subject to an attack observed by Tompa and Woll [11]. The attack permits a dishonest participant who at the pooling stage submits an invalid share, to recover the valid secret from an invalid one returned by the combiner.

2   Model of Cheating

We introduce the following notations. Set $\alpha = (s_1, \ldots, s_n)$, the sequence of shares held by $\mathcal{P}$ and the secret $K = f(\alpha)$, and $\alpha^* = (s_1, \ldots, s_{c-1}, 1 \oplus s_c, s_{c+1}, \ldots, s_n)$, the sequence of shares submitted to the combiner where P_c modified her share. Set $\delta_c = (0, \ldots, 0, 1, 0, \ldots, 0)$ where all zero except the c-th position. δ_c represents modification done by the cheater and $K^* = f(\alpha^*)$ is the invalid secret returned by combiner. Let $\Omega_\alpha^* = \{(x_1, \ldots, x_{c-1}, s_c, x_{c+1}, \ldots, x_n) \mid f(x_1, \ldots, x_{c-1}, 1 \oplus s_c, x_{c+1}, \ldots, x_n) = K^*\}$, the set of all shares taken from rows of $\mathcal{T}$ containing α and K which are consistent with the invalid secret returned by the combiner. The set Ω_α^* determines the view of the cheater after getting back K^* from the combiner. Let $\Omega_\alpha = \{(x_1, \ldots, x_{c-1}, s_c, x_{c+1}, \ldots, x_n) \mid f(x_1, \ldots, x_{c-1}, s_c, x_{c+1},$

$\ldots, x_n) = K\}$, the set of rows which contain the current share of P_c and the valid secret K. The function f is called *defining function*. The nonzero vector $\delta_c = (0, \ldots, 0, 1, 0, \ldots, 0)$, where only the c-th coordinate is nonzero, is called the *cheating vector*. $\alpha = (s_1, \ldots, s_n)$ is called the *original vector*. The value of $\rho_\alpha = \#(\Omega_\alpha^* \cap \Omega_\alpha)/\#\Omega_\alpha^*$, where $\#X$ denotes the the number of elements in the set X, expresses the probability of cheater success with respect to $\alpha = (s_1, \ldots, s_n)$. As the original vector $\alpha = (s_1, \ldots, s_n)$ is always in $\Omega_\alpha^* \cap \Omega_\alpha$, the probability of successful cheating is always nonzero or $\rho_{c,\alpha} > 0$. Given secret sharing with its defining function f on V_n. The value of $\rho_c = 2^{-n} \sum_{\alpha \in V_n} \rho_{c,\alpha}$ is the average cheating probability over all original vectors in V_n for a fixed cheating vector. The value of $\overline{\rho} = \frac{1}{n} \sum_{c=1}^n \rho_c = \frac{1}{n} \cdot 2^{-n} \sum_{c=1}^n \sum_{\alpha \in V_n} \rho_{c,\alpha}$ is the average cheating probability over all cheating vectors (with Hamming weight one) and all original vectors in V_n. Of course $\overline{\rho}$ depends on particular f.

Theorem 1. *Given secret sharing with its defining function f on V_n. Then for each fixed integer c with $1 \le c \le n$, we have $\rho_c \ge \frac{1}{2}$ where the equality holds $\Longleftrightarrow$ $\rho_{c,\alpha} = \frac{1}{2}$ for each $\alpha \in V_n$.*

Proof. Write $y = (x_1, \ldots, x_{c-1})$ and $z = (x_{c+1}, \ldots, x_n)$. Set $R_1 = \{(y, z) | f(y, 1, z) = 1, f(y, 0, z) = 1\}$, $R_2 = \{(y, z) | f(y, 1, z) = 1, f(y, 0, z) = 0\}$, $R_3 = \{(y, z) | f(y, 1, z) = 0, f(y, 0, z) = 1\}$, $R_4 = \{(y, z) | f(y, 1, z) = 0, f(y, 0, z) = 0\}$, and $\#R_i = r_i$, $i = 1, 2, 3, 4$. Obviously $r_1 + r_2 + r_3 + r_4 = 2^{n-1}$. Let $\beta_1 \in V_{c-1}$, $\beta_2 \in V_{n-c}$ and $\alpha = (\beta_1, 0, \beta_2)$ or $\alpha = (\beta_1, 1, \beta_2)$. By definition, $\rho_{c,\alpha}$ can be expressed as follows: (1) $\frac{r_1}{r_1+r_2}$ when $\alpha = (\beta_1, 0, \beta_2)$ with $(\beta_1, \beta_2) \in R_1$, (2) $\frac{r_2}{r_1+r_2}$ when $\alpha = (\beta_1, 0, \beta_2)$ with $(\beta_1, \beta_2) \in R_2$, (3) $\frac{r_3}{r_3+r_4}$ when $\alpha = (\beta_1, 0, \beta_2)$ with $(\beta_1, \beta_2) \in R_3$, (4) $\frac{r_4}{r_3+r_4}$ when $\alpha = (\beta_1, 0, \beta_2)$ with $(\beta_1, \beta_2) \in R_4$, (5) $\frac{r_1}{r_1+r_3}$ when $\alpha = (\beta_1, 1, \beta_2)$ with $(\beta_1, \beta_2) \in R_1$, (6) $\frac{r_3}{r_1+r_3}$ when $\alpha = (\beta_1, 1, \beta_2)$ with $(\beta_1, \beta_2) \in R_3$, (7) $\frac{r_2}{r_2+r_4}$ when $\alpha = (\beta_1, 1, \beta_2)$ with $(\beta_1, \beta_2) \in R_2$, (8) $\frac{r_4}{r_2+r_4}$ when $\alpha = (\beta_1, 1, \beta_2)$ with $(\beta_1, \beta_2) \in R_4$. There exist following two cases to be considered:

Case 1: $R_j \cup R_i \ne \emptyset$ for each $(j, i) \in \{(1, 2), (3, 4), (1, 3), (2, 4)\}$. In this case $r_j + r_i \ne 0$ for each $(j, i) \in \{(1, 2), (3, 4), (1, 3), (2, 4)\}$. Therefore $\rho_c = 2^{-n} \sum_{\alpha \in V_n} \rho_{c,\alpha} = 2^{-n}(\frac{r_1^2}{r_1+r_2} + \frac{r_2^2}{r_1+r_2} + \frac{r_3^2}{r_3+r_4} + \frac{r_4^2}{r_3+r_4} + \frac{r_1^2}{r_1+r_3} + \frac{r_3^2}{r_1+r_3} + \frac{r_2^2}{r_2+r_4} + \frac{r_4^2}{r_2+r_4})$. It is easy to see that $\frac{a^2+b^2}{a+b} \ge \frac{1}{2}(a + b)$ for any two real numbers $a, b \ge 0$ with $a + b > 0$ where the equality holds $\Longleftrightarrow a = b$. Therefore $\rho_c \ge 2^{-n}(\frac{1}{2}(r_1+r_2) + \frac{1}{2}(r_3+r_4) + \frac{1}{2}(r_1+r_3) + \frac{1}{2}(r_2+r_4)) = 2^{-n}(r_1+r_2+r_3+r_4) = \frac{1}{2}$ where the equality holds $\Longleftrightarrow r_1 = r_2 = r_3 = r_4 \Longleftrightarrow \rho_{c,\alpha} = \frac{1}{2}$ for each $\alpha \in V_n$.

Case 2: $R_{j_0} \cup R_{i_0} = \emptyset$ for some $(j_0, i_0) \in \{(1, 2), (3, 4), (1, 3), (2, 4)\}$. Without loss of generality let $R_1 \cup R_2 = \emptyset$. Thus $r_1 = r_2 = 0$ and thus $r_3 + r_4 = 2^{n-1}$. There exist following two cases to be considered:

Case 2.1: $R_j \cup R_i \ne \emptyset$ for each $(j, i) \in \{(3, 4), (1, 3), (2, 4)\}$. In this case $r_j + r_i \ne 0$ for each $(j, i) \in \{(3, 4), (1, 3), (2, 4)\}$. Thus $\rho_c = 2^{-n} \sum_{\alpha \in V_n} \rho_{c,\alpha} = 2^{-n}(\frac{r_3^2}{r_3+r_4} + \frac{r_4^2}{r_3+r_4} + \frac{r_3^2}{r_1+r_3} + \frac{r_4^2}{r_2+r_4})$. Since $r_1 = r_2 = 0$, we have $\rho_c = 2^{-n} \sum_{\alpha \in V_n} \rho_{c,\alpha} = 2^{-n}(\frac{r_3^2+r_4^2}{r_3+r_4} + r_3 + r_4) \ge 2^{-n}(\frac{1}{2}(r_3 + r_4) + r_3 + r_4) = \frac{3}{4}$.

Case 2.2: $R_{j_1} \cup R_{i_1} = \emptyset$ for some $(j_1, i_1) \in \{(3,4), (1,3), (2,4)\}$. Recall that $r_3 + r_4 = 2^{n-1}$. Thus $(j_1, i_1) \neq (3,4)$. Without loss of generality let $R_1 \cup R_3 = \emptyset$. Thus $r_3 = 0$ and $r_4 = 2^{n-1}$. Therefore $\rho_c = 2^{-n} \sum_{\alpha \in V_n} \rho_{c,\alpha} = 2^{-n}(\frac{r_4^2}{r_3 + r_4} + \frac{r_4^2}{r_2 + r_4})$. Since $r_2 = r_3 = 0$, we have $\rho_c = 2^{-n}(r_4 + r_4) = 1$.

Summarizing Cases 1 and 2, we have proved that $\rho_c \geq \frac{1}{2}$ where the equality holds $\Longleftrightarrow \rho_{c,\alpha} = \frac{1}{2}$ for each $\alpha \in V_n$.   □

Theorem 2. *Given secret sharing with its defining function f on V_n. Then $\overline{\rho} \geq \frac{1}{2}$ where the equality holds $\Longleftrightarrow \rho_{c,\alpha} = \frac{1}{2}$ for each integer c with $1 \leq c \leq n$ and each $\alpha \in V_n$.*

Proof. By using Theorem 1, we have $\overline{\rho} = \frac{1}{n} \sum_{c=1}^{n} \rho_c \geq \frac{1}{2}$. Assume $\overline{\rho} = \frac{1}{2}$. Since $\overline{\rho} = \frac{1}{2}$ and $\rho_c \geq \frac{1}{2}$, $c = 1, \ldots, n$, $\rho_c = \frac{1}{2}$, $c = 1, \ldots, n$. Due to Theorem 1, $\rho_{c,\alpha} = \frac{1}{2}$ for each integer c with $1 \leq c \leq n$ and each $\alpha \in V_n$. We have proved the necessity. The sufficiency is obvious.   □

3   Cheating Immune Secret Sharing and Its Construction

Due to Theorem 2, if $\min\{\rho_{c,\alpha} | \alpha \in V_n, \ 1 \leq c \leq n\} < \frac{1}{2}$ then $\max\{\rho_{c,\alpha} | \alpha \in V_n, \ 1 \leq c \leq n\} > \frac{1}{2}$. Naturally it is desirable that $\rho_{c,\alpha} = \frac{1}{2}$ for each integer c with $1 \leq c \leq n$ and each $\alpha \in V_n$. In this case the secret sharing is said to be *cheating immune*. Due to Theorems 1 and 2, we conclude

Corollary 1. *Given secret sharing with its defining function f on V_n. Then the following statements are equivalent: (i) $\overline{\rho} = \frac{1}{2}$, (ii) $\rho_c = \frac{1}{2}$ for each integer c with $1 \leq c \leq n$, (iii) $\rho_{c,\alpha} = \frac{1}{2}$ for each integer c with $1 \leq c \leq n$ and each $\alpha \in V_n$.*

Cheating immunity of secret sharing can be investigated in the context of well-known characteristics of the defining function f such as resiliency (see [14]) and the SAC (see [12,13]).

Theorem 3. *Given secret sharing with its defining function f on V_n. Then the secret sharing is cheating immune $\Longleftrightarrow f$ is 1-resilient and satisfies the SAC.*

Proof. We keep using the notations in the proof of Theorem 1. It is easy to verify that $f(x_1, \ldots, x_n)|_{x_c=1}$ is balanced (1-resiliency) $\Longleftrightarrow r_1 + r_2 = r_3 + r_4$, while $f(x_1, \ldots, x_n)|_{x_c=0}$ is balanced (1-resiliency) $\Longleftrightarrow r_1 + r_3 = r_2 + r_4$. From the proof of Theorem 1, $f(x) \oplus f(x \oplus \delta_c) = \begin{cases} 0 \text{ if } (y,z) \in R_1 \cup R_4 \\ 1 \text{ if } (y,z) \in R_2 \cup R_3 \end{cases}$. Thus $f(x) \oplus f(x \oplus \delta_c)$ is balanced (SAC) $\Longleftrightarrow r_1 + r_4 = r_2 + r_3$. Note that $r_1 + r_2 = r_3 + r_4$, $r_1 + r_3 = r_2 + r_4$ and $r_1 + r_4 = r_2 + r_3$ together $\Longleftrightarrow r_1 = r_2 = r_3 = r_4$. From the proof of Theorem 1, $r_1 = r_2 = r_3 = r_4 \Longleftrightarrow \rho_{c,\alpha} = \frac{1}{2}$ for each $\alpha \in V_n$. Due to the arbitrariness of the integer c with $1 \leq c \leq n$, the proof is completed.   □

Based on Theorem 3, to construct an cheating immune secret sharing scheme, we need a 1-resilient function on V_n satisfying the SAC.

Theorem 4. *Let $n > 0$ be an even integer. Then there exists a secret sharing with its defining function f on V_n such that (i) this secret sharing is cheating immune, (ii) the nonlinearity (see [14]) of f is equal to $2^{n-1} - 2^{\frac{1}{2}n}$.*

Proof. Let h be a bent function [7] on V_{n-2} (n is even). Set $g(x_1, \ldots, x_{n-1}) = (1 \oplus x_{n-1})h(x_1, \ldots, x_{n-2}) \oplus x_{n-1}(1 \oplus h(x_1 \oplus a_1, \ldots, x_{n-2} \oplus a_{n-2}))$ where the Hamming weight of $(a_1, \ldots, a_{n-2})$ is $\frac{1}{2}n - 1$. Set $f(x_1, \ldots, x_n) = (1 \oplus x_n)g(x_1, \ldots, x_{n-1}) \oplus x_n g(x_1 \oplus 1, \ldots, x_{n-1} \oplus 1)$. From the proof of Theorem 17 of the reference [8], f is 1-resilient, satisfies the SAC and has a nonliearty $2^{n-1} - 2^{\frac{1}{2}n}$. Due to Theorem 3, the secret sharing with defining function f is cheating immune. $\square$

4   Conclusions

For given secret sharing, the average cheating probability $\bar{\rho}$ over all cheating and original vectors, satisfies $\bar{\rho} \geq \frac{1}{2}$, and the equality holds $\Longleftrightarrow$ the cheating probability $\rho_{c,\alpha}$ satisfies $\rho_{c,\alpha} = \frac{1}{2}$ for every cheating vector δ_c and every original vector α. In this case the secret sharing is said to be cheating immune. We further have found a relationship between cheating immune secret sharing and cryptographic criteria of boolean functions, and then we have successfully constructed cheating immune secret sharing with a highly nonlinear defining function.

Acknowledgement. The first author was supported by a Queen Elizabeth II Fellowship (227 23 1002).

References

1. E. Biham and A. Shamir. Differential cryptanalysis of DES-like cryptosystems. *Journal of Cryptology*, Vol. 4, No. 1:3–72, 1991.
2. G. R. Blakley. Safeguarding cryptographic keys. In *Proc. AFIPS 1979 National Computer Conference*, pages 313–317. AFIPS, 1979.
3. M. Carpentieri. A perfect threshold secret sharing scheme to identify cheaters. *Designs, Codes and Cryptography*, 5(3):183–187, 1995.
4. M. Carpentieri, A. De Santis, and U. Vaccaro. Size of shares and probability of cheating in threshold schemes. *Advances in Cryptology - EUROCRYPT'93*, LNCS No. 765, pages 118–125. Springer-Verlag, 1993.
5. Y. Desmedt. Society and group oriented cryptography: A new concept. *Advances in Cryptology - CRYPTO'87*, LNCS No. 293 pages 120–127. Springer-Verlag, 1988.
6. T. Rabin and M. Ben-Or. Verifiable secret sharing and multiparty protocols with honest majority. In *Proceedings of 21st ACM Symposium on Theory of Computing*, pages 73–85, 1989.
7. O. S. Rothaus. On "bent" functions. *Journal of Combinatorial Theory (A)*, 20:300–305, 1976.
8. P. Sarkar and S. Maitra. Highly nonlinear balanced boolean functions with important cryptographic properties. *Advances in Cryptology - EUROCRYPT2000*, LNCS No. 1807, pages 485–506. Springer-Verlag, 2000.
9. A. Shamir. How to share a secret. *Communications of the ACM*, 22:612–613, November 1979.

10. D.R. Stinson. *Cryptography: Theory and Practice*. CRC Press, 1995.
11. M. Tompa and H. Woll. How to share a secret with cheaters. *Journal of Cryptology*, 1(2):133–138, 1988.
12. A. F. Webster. Plaintext/ciphertext bit dependencies in cryptographic system. Master's Thesis, Department of Electrical Engineering, Queen's University, Ontario, 1985.
13. A.F. Webster and S.E. Tavares. On the design of S-boxes. *Advances in Cryptology – CRYPTO'85*, pages 523–534. Springer-Verlag, 1986.
14. X. M. Zhang and Y. Zheng. Cryptographically resilient functions. *IEEE Transactions on Information Theory*, 43(5):1740–1747, 1997.

Encryption Sticks (Randomats)

Gideon Samid

Technion – Israel Institute of Technology
Haifa, Israel
samidg@tx.technion.ac.il

Abstract. Recognizing that a trusted, highly random, series of bits is the currency of modern cryptography, one may opt for a physical contraption that houses a supply of random bits, ready for safe and versatile use by individuals and organizations. Usage ranges from a steady supply of random keys to the prevailing symmetric and stream cryptographies, and up to raw one-time-pad protocols. The contraption dubbed encryption stick, e-stick, or Randomat enables one to establish a virtual identity which is highly secure against exposure, and thus empowers people towards candid exchange, anonymous transactions, and wholesale transparency of issues, with potentially broad social implications. The e-stick will be cash purchased in a public shop (anonymity), and this off-Internet item will protect its user from the pervasive data nakedness in cyberspace.

1   Introduction

Two individuals who wish to communicate securely need nothing more than a large enough supply of random bits. Applying the One-Time-Pad encryption (Vernam 1917), they would sit pretty with an unbreakable ciphertext. The only reason for this scenario not to have happened (on a broad basis), is the difficulty in generating the necessary random bits -- ready for use, when needed. This difficulty has two aspects: true randomness, or close enough to it, is a technical challenge, and making such random bits available to the parties -- when they are ready to communicate -- is a distribution challenge.

Owing to these obstacles, the science of cryptography has not been finalized right there in 1917, when Gilbert S. Vernam [1] invented his theoretically secure cipher. Cryptography since then made due with shorter strings of random bits, and later found a way to exchange such strings between strangers -- mounting the distribution challenge. With all that huge body of work that transpired in the last eighty some years, the state of the art is such that the trustworthiness of the supply of random bits is a matter of debate. Random bits used in block ciphers and stream ciphers are first communicated through asymmetric ciphers for which there is no proof of security. In other words, we sport the risk of a cryptographic catastrophe. The original knapsack algorithms have by now been discredited by virtue of effective cryptanalysis. The only viable alternative is RSA and its variants, which rely on the difficulty of factorization, and those methods which rely on the difficulty of computing discrete logarithms. In both cases the difficulty is reduced to matrix inversion. For $n^x n$ size

S. Qing, T. Okamoto, and J. Zhou (Eds.): ICICS 2001, LNCS 2229, pp. 150-154, 2001.

matrices, the old Gaussian methods require n^3 steps. Strassen has reduced it to $n^{log7} = n^{2.807}$, and Coppersmith and Winograd have further reduced it to $n^{2.495}$. [2]. So much is in the public domain. One can not dismiss the possibility that non-public entities have come closer to n^2. All this implies that the mainstay of random bit distribution is of questionable trustworthiness. And since random series may be regarded as the currency of cryptography, such doubts overshadow the whole field of data security.

In light of such apprehension, it was deemed appropriate to revisit the original question of making randomness available to anyone who wishes to communicate in privacy or secrecy.

Cyberspace is intrinsically open. The flow of data is easily intercepted, re-routed, modified, etc. It would seem that since secrecy and privacy depend on the integrity of the underlying randomness, that such precious a resource should originate outside cyberspace. This situation brings to mind what Archimedes long ago said: 'Give me a point outside Earth, and I will move the planet, with a big enough lever'. If we find a way to put randomness in the hands of users -- outside the Internet -- then we will have a way to use the Internet with impunity.

Technology today enables us to cram several megabytes of data in a thumbnail size device, at a low price. This technology, if it were available in 1917, would most likely have sealed the science of cryptology with the invention of Mr. Vernam. Today we may use it either for Vernam or for any of the prevailing cryptographies all based on intractability, and all require a hefty supply of trusted randomness. Moreover, we may distribute these containers of randomness (to be called encryption sticks, e-sticks or Randomats), through distribution channels which handle tangibles like food and clothing. Users would purchase an encryption stick for cash, anonymously, and then use it in cyberspace.

2   The Device

Functionally the e-stick amounts to a container of random bits which are highly protected against unauthorized use. For a rough analogy consider the familiar battery. A "AA" battery will power a wide range of electrical devices. Each device draws power from the battery at its special rate. When the battery is exhausted it is being replaced. It is similar with encryption-sticks. The stick will supply random bits to a large variety of applications. Some will exhaust it faster, some will use the bits sparingly. Much as a radio listener will opt for louder music and pay with a rapid depletion of his batteries, so an e-stick user might empty his stick quickly but gain a higher measure of security. By using One-Time-Pad the bits will disappear very fast, but the user will be compensated with the knowledge that his encryption is theoretically unbreakable. Large keys offer the advent of cryptographic equivocation (not just the customary intractability). As Shannon [3,4] has shown, equivocation is the foundation of theoretical security. Recently, AGS Encryptions Ltd. introduced variable equivocation cryptography where the user balances off security vs. key size.[5]. In mainstay cryptography security increases with the frequency of changing keys. So again, the user will decide how fast to consume the e-stick bits. Technology will continue to offer more bits per dollar and per stick-size, and this will drive down the price of security.

   The authorized use will be: (1) independent, stand-alone, encryption; (2) "Say and Stay" -- bit output ; (3) "Say and Forget" -- bit output. All will be expressed in two physical security modes: (a) no access authentication., (b) access authentication. There will be two versions, one where access will be verified, one without.

   Physical security will be achieved via tamper-resistant construction and the option to authenticate the identity of the user. Tamper proof construction will be based on sensors and indicators that will detect an attempt to pry open the device, and will react by obliterating the data therein.

   The option to authenticate the user will be based on an access code that will be built into the device and only by supplying it will the device respond with the contents of its bits. Such access code may be linked to any of the prevailing access control solutions available at the time.

   The access port will accept: (1) normal authentication code ; (2) silent alarm code; (3) wrong codes.

   The normal authentication code will allow for normal operation. The silent alarm code will trigger an action that would look as if the stick operates properly but in fact, it won't. The wrong code will kill the stick's operation. The silent alarm mode will have several options. The simplest among them is to re-randomize the Randomat's contents. Such re-randomization might occur by XOR-ing fixed size bit strings among themselves.

   In "Stand Alone Encryption" the device will have an input port for the original message, and an output port for the encrypted message. The ports will reverse their input/output role for the respective decryption process. In that mode one could use raw One-Time-Pad. In that case the encryption bits will be erased as they are being used, so that only a duplicate e-stick can decrypt them. In that respect it will be similar to public-key encryption. The encrypting party will not have the means to decrypt its own encryption.

   In another option, using Daniel [5], only parts of the random bits will be erased, and the rest will remain in the device. Yet, in another option, when security demands are not as stringent, the device will be usable again and again, for encryption and decryption (bits at "Say-and-Stay" mode), and security will be hinged on guarding the device itself.

   In "Say-And-Stay" mode the user asks for the value of a particular bit, the device responds with that value, but keeps the value in tact so it can be queried again.

   In the "Say-and-Forget" mode, the device responds to a query by providing the user with the value of a requested bit, but right away destroys that value so it can not be queried again.

   The bits will be organized on the device in one of several configurations: (1) ordered list., (2)n-dimensional array, (3) network. The source of the random bits will be physical: a long term radioactive element (several thousands years half life time). By measuring the actual disintegration of atoms one measures a process which according to quantum mechanics is as purely random as anything conceived. At a given time interval (nanoseconds or smaller), the measured radioactivity may be above its average or below it. The former will be interpreted as one, and the latter as zero. The measured values will be written to the manufactured Randomats.

3   Methodology

E-sticks create options for a large variety of methodologies. They fall into the category of trust management. Encryption in general has a place in human's affairs only because we can not always trust each other. If we could, we had no reason to practice encryption. In particular, the e-stick offers a variety of methods to handle various degree of mutual trust.

This ability to purchase an e-stick without a definite link between the purchaser (and the eventual user), and the particular stick he or she bought is the crucial hub of the retail practice of the e-stick methodology. Such anonymity is not present in any of the prevailing systems in use today, [6]. This aspect may turn out to be the most intriguing one of the e-stick methodology. To insure maximum anonymity a user must be able to purchase an e-stick such that his or her identity is not revealed in the transaction, and then he or she must be able to use it, say, on the Internet without being exposed through the IP address in use. The former may be arranged through cash point of sale in public places, the latter may be arranged via public Internet boutiques where strangers purchase for cash some access time, (or alternatively through libraries). A set of two identical e-sticks will allow two parties to communicate with impunity. Also, two strangers will be able to communicate through a third party who holds a duplicate of each e-stick. Many sources who pry for individual information about people are not necessarily interested in the explicit identity of the individual, but rather interested in his or her conduct and interest profile. Vendors, for instance, would wish to learn much about the taste and lifestyle of an individual, so that they would be able to target him or her for an array of products. It matters to them whether a person would rather buy a philosophy book, or a tennis racket, or perhaps both. Generally people are leery of such vendor's data collection, alas, if that collection will be pinned on a virtual identity of a person (while his real identity remains protected by the e-stick), then the vendors will be satisfied, and so will the individual. That individual will receive targeted offerings, purchase such items, and all the while his or her actual identity is left hidden.

Naturally, an individual could build himself several identities, using several e-sticks. That way an individual would be able to expose one certain virtual identity, and not another. Such may be the   case when an individual would wish to communicate to the police a tip on a crime he or she witnessed. Using a dedicated e-stick, the user would submit the tip, and if it comes to it, he would be able to come forward, claim his reward, and do so without exposing his reading habits, or his very sensitive conversations with an on-line psychologist.

The e-sticks practice will offer another important feature to its users: deniability, [7,8,9]. That is the ability to deny a claim that a specific encrypted message is in fact contained in a captured ciphertext. In practice it means that if someone claims that ciphertext C is an encrypted form of plaintext P, then the writer might (credibly) say, no, C was generated from a different plaintext, say, P'. Since the e-stick is based on 'Say-and-Forget' random bits, there is no way to prove the identity of the bits (assuming the integrity of the device), and thus one may claim any identity to suit a deniability claim. The deniability option is clearly available for One-Time-Pad usage, and similarly for Daniel, and other systems of the kind.

A user of an e-stick will authenticate its ongoing use by continuously employing the e-stick. Since each e-stick has its own unique random series, such continuity will authenticate the user. In case where the e-stick is stolen, the thief will not find in the e-stick any clue to its prior usage, and hence is not likely to know who was contacted using that e-stick, and what was said.

While an e-stick user will be able to hide his actual identity, he will be able to lock himself relative to his virtual identity. And so will others. So that one who used some bits from an e-stick for a purpose will be deemed the one who used other bits thereof.

Encryption sticks might contribute an option to the much discussed digital cash dilemma. Using an e-stick one would approach a virtual banker, provide him with an amount of cash and copy of the stick. The delivery of such can be made anonymously, even through the mail. Subsequently, the depositor will send encrypted orders to the banker as to where, and to whom to pay parts of the deposited cash. The banker will follow such orders for a fee. Even under pressure, the banker will not be in a position to betray the identity of the depositor since he would not know it himself or herself. The depositor will need to express trust in the banker to follow this procedure, since the banker can deny ever receiving the deposit. Alas, such bankers will be soon denounced. The depositor, on his part, will be able to start risking small sums, and when he or she develops confidence in that banker, larger sums can be risked.

4 Conclusion

This paper describes a device and a methodology for broad-based, anonymous distribution of communication-ready random bits. It further outlines various applications and usage of such off-Internet supply of randomness. The underlying premise is the universal reliance on random bits, (shared by all methods of encryption).

References

1. G. Vernam, "The Vernam Cipher" US Patent No 1,310,719.
2. M. Roe "Cryptography and Evidence" Doct. Dissert., Univ of Cambridge, UK, 1997.
3. C. E. Shannon "A Mathematical Theory of Cryptography" Technical Report 45-110-92, Bell Laboratories, 1945.
4. C. E. Shannon "Communication Theory of Secrecy Systems", Bell Systems Tech. Jr. Vol 28, pages 656-715, 1949.
5. G. Samid, "Daniel Encryption: Description and Specifications" AGS Encryptions, Ltd, Tel-Aviv, Israel, 2000.
6. Alfred J. Menezes, Paul C. van Oorschot, and Scott A. Vanstone "Handbook of Applied Cryptography" CRC Press 1997.
7. R. Canetti, R. Gennaro, "Incoercible Multiparty Computation", FOCS'96.
8. D. Beaver: "Plausible Deniability (extended abstract)"; Pragocrypt '96 Proceedings, 1996.
9. Ran Canetti, Cynthia Dwork, Moni Naor, Rafail Ostrovsky "Deniable Encryption" Crypto'97.

Applying NCP Logic to the Analysis of SSL 3.0

Zhimin Song and Sihan Qing

Engineering Research Center for Information Security Technology,
Chinese Academy of Science,
P.O. Box 8718 Beijing 100080, China
zhiminsong69@163.net

Abstract. In this paper we use extended NCP logic to formally analyze SSL 3.0, and show two important weak points of the protocol, which are the server's not assured of the freshness and the origin of the pre-master secret when RSA is used for key exchange. We only give specification and analysis of one authentication mode of SSL 3.0 in detail, but all authentication modes have the two weak points. Especially, the flaw of the freshness of the pre-master secret may result in reuse of the pre-master secret, and we properly remedy it by introducing a nonce.

1 Introduction

SSL protocol [1] is a security protocol that allows client/server applications to communicate over the Internet in a way that is designed to prevent eavesdropping, tampering, or message forgery. TLS 1.0 [2] is a minor modification to SSL 3.0, so here we only discuss SSL 3.0.

Since SSL 3.0 requires the principals' knowledge to both increase and decrease, we need a logic capable of modeling a nonmonotonic protocol. NCP(Nonmonotonic Cryptographic Protocols) [3] is a such kind of logic, which was put forward by Dr. Aviel David Rubin in 1994. In fact, Dr. Sven Dietrich of Adelphi University applied NCP logic to the analysis of SSL 3.0 in his PhD thesis in 1997 [4], but he failed to consider applying the reference rule for asymmetric keys, so resulted in not being able to uncover two important weak points in SSL 3.0, which are server's not being assure of both the freshness and the origin of the pre-master secret when RSA is used for key exchange. In this paper, we mainly describe the way to reveal the two weak points and the way to remedy one of them.

This paper is organized as follows. Section 2 briefly introduces NCP logic. Elements for specifying SSL 3.0 when NCP is used are described in detail in section 3. We then specify one authentication mode in section 4, and analyze the protocol in detail in section 5, uncovering the two weak points. In section 6, solutions to the weak points and possible problems are given. Section 7 concludes by appealing attention to the two weak points.

S. Qing, T. Okamoto, and J. Zhou (Eds.): ICICS 2001, LNCS 2229, pp. 155-166, 2001.
© Springer-Verlag Berlin Heidelberg 2001

2 NCP Logic

NCP logic is the first method proposed for reasoning nonmonotonically about knowledge in cryptographic protocols.

In NCP, there is no idealization step in specifying protocols. One specifies a protocol via local and global sets of the protocol. Global sets contain the principals themselves, the inference rules, the secrets present in the protocol, and possible observers of those secrets. Each principal has an action list and two types of local sets: the possession set for knowledge, and the belief set for beliefs. NCP logic defines actions for dealing with knowledge in a protocol, and inference rules for reasoning about belief.

NCP has defined some actions and inference rules. Actions such as **Forget** and **Forget-secret** are used along with knowledge and belief sets to reason about nonmonotonicity of knowledge in protocols. One can add or extend actions and inference rules to meet his special purpose.

In NCP, the only purpose for a nonce is to link a single challenge to a unique response. A nonce is required to be used only once. When a principal generates a nonce, N_a, the formula $\text{LINK}(N_a)$ is added to his belief set. When a message is received containing N_a, the LINK item is removed from the belief set, and all parts of that message are labeled as being fresh. A reply to the challenge can be accepted only once.

Every message is considered to be broadcast in NCP, and **Update** function is introduced to maintain global knowledge by updating the observers sets of all secrets that have been sent on the network.

The analysis of a protocol begins with the first action in the initiator's action list. If the conditions of an inference rule are satisfied as a result of an action, the rule is applied to the belief set of that principal. Then comes the next action in the same action list. For every **Send** message operation, the observers sets are updated by an **Update** function for any secret sent across the network, and the analysis moves to the first unseen **Receive** action in the action list of the principal specified in the **Send**. As the analysis progresses, possession sets, belief sets, secret sets and observers sets are updated. After the analysis completes, all actions should have been marked as seen. Flaws can be detected at any point in the analysis.

Dr. Rubin also extended NCP for protocols that use asymmetric keys. New actions and inference rules for asymmetric keys are introduced. An important observation is that reasoning about the origin of messages is quite different when dealing with asymmetric key protocols. In addition, Dr. Rubin introduced the notion of binding a key to a principal.

3 Elements for Specifying SSL 3.0

Most of the actions and inference rules we use to analyze SSL 3.0 are chosen from those actions and inference rules in NCP, and we also add some for special use of SSL.

3.1 Actions

We choose 12 actions from NCP's 14 actions [3].except **Check-freshness** and **Bind**.

3.2 Inference Rules

The 6 inference rules we use are as following:

(1) Nonce verification rule

$$(X \in POSS(Q)) \in BEL(P),$$
$$\#(X) \in BEL(P), X \text{ from } Q \in POSS(P)$$
$$\overline{BEL(P) := BEL(P) \bigcup \{Q \text{ believes } \#(X)\}}$$

(1)

(2) Message meaning rule (for symmetric keys)

$$\frac{\{X\}_k \text{ from } Q \in POSS(P), k \in POSS(P)}{BEL(P) := BEL(P) \bigcup \{X \in POSS(Q)\}}$$

(2)

(3) Possible origins rule

$$\frac{X \in POSS(P), X \text{ contains } x_1, R \in Obs(x_1), R \neq P}{x_1 \text{ from } R \in POSS(P)}$$

(3)

(4) Submessage origins rule(1) (for asymmetric keys)

$$\{X\}_{k_p^+} \in POSS(P)$$
$$\frac{X \text{ contains } x_1 \text{ from } Q, X \text{ contains } x_2}{x_2 \text{ from } Q \in POSS(P)}$$

(4)

(5) Submessage origins rule(2) (for asymmetric keys)

$$\frac{\{X\}_{k_q} \in POSS(P), X \text{ contains } x_2}{x_2 \text{ from } Q \in POSS(P)}$$

(5)

(6) Linkage rule(1) (for asymmetric keys)

$$\#(k^-) \in BEL(P), k^- \in POSS(P)$$
$$LINK(N_a) \in BEL(P), X \text{ contains } f(N_a)$$
$$\frac{X \text{ contains } x_1, \{X\}_{k^+} \text{ from } Q \in POSS(P)}{BEL(P) := (BEL(P) - LINK(N_a)) \bigcup \{\#(x_1)\}}$$

(6)

In addition, we slightly modify the **Linkage rule (2)** for asymmetric keys, resulting in the **Signature rule**, which is used to check the freshness of a signature. The **Linkage**

rule for symmetric keys is slightly modified, called **Verify rule**, to check the freshness of the Finished message.

(7) Signature rule (for asymmetric keys)

$$\frac{\#(k^+) \in BEL(P), \; k^+ \in POSS(P)}{\begin{array}{c} LINK(N_a) \in BEL(P), \; X \; contains \; hash(N_a) \\ \{X\}_{k^-} \; from \; Q \in POSS(P) \end{array}}{BEL(P) := (BEL(P) - LINK(N_a)) \cup \{\#(hash(N_a))\}} \tag{7}$$

(8) Verify rule (for symmetric keys)

$$\frac{\#(k) \in BEL(P), \; k \in POSS(P)}{\begin{array}{c} LINK(N_a) \in BEL(P), \; X \; contains \; hash(N_a) \\ \{X\}_k \; from \; Q \in POSS(P) \end{array}}{BEL(P) := (BEL(P) - LINK(N_a)) \cup \{\#(hash(N_a))\}} \tag{8}$$

3.3 Functions

We add 6 functions for special use of SSL 3.0.

(1) Generate-keys($X1$, $X2$, $X3$)

Generates session keys from the master-secret, the client's random and the server's random.

(2) Choose-ciphersuite(X)

Chooses a CipherSuite from the CipherSuite list offered by the client.

(3) Match($X1$,,$X2$)

Checks if the CipherSuite is included in the CipherSuite list.

(4) Finished(P, $X1$, $X2$)

Generates the Finished message by hashing the master -secret and all sent messages.

(5) Ske ($X1$, $X2$, $X3$)

Generates the Server Key Exchange message by hashing the client's random, the server's random and the server's public key.

(6) Cv ($X1$, $X2$)

Generates the Client Certificate Verify message by hashing the master-secret and all sent messages.

4 Specifying SSL 3.0

We have the same assumptions about SSL 3.0 as those made by Dr. Sven Dietrich.

- Anyone who is to be authenticated is in possession of a certificate signed by a CA. The public key of the CA is available to the one who performs authentication.
- Hash functions are secure.
- Supported cryptographic algorithms have not been broken.
- The client and the server can succeed in choosing CipherSuite and an attacker can not manipulate the choosing of CipherSuite.

In addition, we add another assumption that an attacker has no means to obtain the session keys or the private key other than attacking the protocol.

SSL supports three authentication modes: authentication of both the server and the client, server authentication with an unauthenticated client, and total anonymity. Here we only give the specification of the first mode in which both parties are authenticated as an example.

Some assumptions about the first mode:

- We use RSA as an example of key exchange.
- We assume certificates of both the client and the server are issued by a same CA.
- We assume the server's certificate is used only for signing, so the Serve Key Exchange message must be used to carry the server's temporary RSA public key to the client.
- We assume the client's certificate is a RSA or DSS certificate instead of a Diffie-Hellman certificate.

Here are also some notes:

- Some submessages of SSL 3.0 messages are not specified, since they are not useful to the analysis.
- The order of some actions is not explicitly given in the SSL 3.0 Specification. Here we arrange the order of these actions according to NCP logic's requirements without violating the SSL 3.0 Specification.
- In order to comply to NCP work flow, we combine several messages and use one **Send** operation to send them. This has no effect on the analysis of SSL 3.0.

GLOBAL SETS

P = {C, S} /*Principal set. C and S represent the client and the server respectively.*/

R = {RULES, Signature rule, Verify rule} /*Rule set. RULES stands for the first 6 inference rules */

S = {} /* Secret set*/

Observers(S) = {} /* Observers set*/

$$\text{TRUST} = \begin{bmatrix} 1 & 0 \\ 0 & 1 \end{bmatrix} \quad \text{/* Trust matrix */}$$

LOCAL SETS

Principal C

$POSS(C) = \{ k_{CA}^+ ¡ Þ CA, \{k_C^+\}_{k_{CA}^-}, k_C^+ ¡ Þ C, k_C, ciphersuites_C, \text{Finished}(), \text{Generate-keys}(), \text{Match}(), \text{Cv}() \}$ /* ¡Þ indicates a binding of a key*/

$BEL(C) = \{ \#(k_{CA}^+), \#(k_C^-), \#(k_C^+), \#(\{k_C^+\}_{k_{CA}^-}) \}$

$Bindings(C) = \{ k_C^+ ¡ Þ C, k_{CA}^+ ¡ Þ CA \}$ /*Bindings set*/

$BL(C) =$

- Generate-Nonce(N_C)

  Concat(N_C , $ciphersuites_C$)

  Send(S, { N_C , $ciphersuites_C$ })

  Update({ N_C , $ciphersuites_C$ })

  Receive(S, { N_S , $cipher_S$, $\{k_S^+\}_{k_{CA}^-}$, { k_{TS}^+ , $\{Ske(N_C,N_S,k_{TS}^+)\}_{k_S^-}$ }, CertReq, HelloDone})

  Split({ N_S , $cipher_S$, $\{k_S^+\}_{k_{CA}^-}$, { k_{TS}^+ , $\{Ske(N_C,N_S,k_{TS}^+)\}_{k_S^-}$ }, CertReq, HelloDone})

  Apply(Match, { $ciphersuites_C$, $cipher_S$ })

  Apply-asymkey($\{k_S^+\}_{k_{CA}^-}$, k_{CA}^+)

  Apply-asymkey($\{Ske(N_C,N_S,k_{TS}^+)\}_{k_S^-}$, k_S^+)

  Generate-Secret(PMS)

  Apply-asymkey(PMS, k_{TS}^+)

  Generate-Secret(MS)

  Forget-Secret(PMS)

  Apply(Generate-keys, {MS, N_C , N_S })

  Apply(Cv, {MS, SentM})

  Apply-asymkey(Cv({MS, SentM}), k_C^-)

  Apply(Finished, {Client, MS, Sent-Messages})

  Encrypt($Finished_C$, k_{CS})

Send(S, Concat($\{k_C^+\}_{k_{CA}}$, $\{PMS\}_{k_S^+}$, $\{Cv(MS, SentM)\}_{k_C^-}$, ChgCipher, $\{Finished c\}_{k_{CS}}$))

Update($\{$ $\{k_C^+\}_{k_{CA}}$, $\{PMS\}_{k_S^+}$, $\{Cv(MS, SentM)\}_{k_C^-}$, ChgCipher, $\{Finished c\}_{k_{CS}}$ $\}$)

Receive(S, $\{ChgCipher, \{Finished s\}_{k_{SC}}\}$)

Split($\{ChgCipher, \{Finished s\}_{k_{SC}}\}$)

Decrypt($\{Finished s\}_{k_{SC}}$, k_{SC})

Principal S

$POSS(S) = \{ k_{CA}^+ ¡Þ CA$, $\{k_S^+\}_{k_{CA}}$, $k_S^+¡Þ S$, k_S^- , Finished(), Generate-keys(),

Choose-ciphersuite(), Ske()$\}$

$BEL(S) = \{\#(k_{CA}^+), \#(k_S^-), \#(k_S^+), \#(\{k_S^+\}_{k_{CA}})\}$

$Bindings(S) = \{ k_S^+¡Þ S$, $k_{CA}^+¡Þ CA \}$

$BL(S) =$

   Receive(C, $\{ N_C$, $ciphersuites_C \}$)

   Split($\{ N_C , ciphersuites_C \}$)

   Apply(Choose-ciphersuite(), $\{ ciphersuites_C \}$)

   Generate-Nonce(N_S)

   Generate-key-pair(k_{TS}^+ , k_{TS}^-)   /* the server's temporary key pair */

   Apply(Ske, Concat(N_C , N_S , k_{TS}^+))

   Apply-asymkey($Ske(\{ N_C , N_S , k_{TS}^+ \}), k_S^-$)

   Concat(N_S , $cipher_S$, $\{k_S^+\}_{k_{CA}}$, $\{ k_{TS}^+, \{Ske(N_C, N_S, k_{TS}^+)\}_{k_S^-} \}$, CertReq, HelloDone)

   Send(C, $\{ N_S$, $cipher_S$, $\{k_S^+\}_{k_{CA}}$, $\{ k_{TS}^+, \{Ske(N_C, N_S, k_{TS}^+)\}_{k_S^-} \}$, CertReq, HelloDone $\}$)

   Update($\{ N_S$, $cipher_S$, $\{k_S^+\}_{k_{CA}}$, $\{ k_{TS}^+, \{Ske(N_C, N_S, k_{TS}^+)\}_{k_S^-} \}$, CertReq, HelloDone $\}$)

   Receive(C, $\{ \{k_C^+\}_{k_{CA}}$, $\{PMS\}_{k_S^+}$, $\{Cv(MS, SentM)\}_{k_C^-}$, ChgCipher, $\{Finished c\}_{k_{CS}}\}$)

   Split($\{ \{k_C^+\}_{k_{CA}}$, $\{PMS\}_{k_S^+}$, $\{Cv(MS, SentM)\}_{k_C^-}$, ChgCipher, $\{Finished c\}_{k_{CS}}\}$)

   Apply-asymkey($\{k_C^+\}_{k_{CA}}$, k_{CA}^+)

   Apply-asymkey($\{PMS\}_{k_S^+}$, k_S^-)

   Generate-Secret(MS)

Forget-Secret(PMS)

Apply(Generate-keys, $\{MS, N_C, N_S\}$)

Apply-asymkey($\{Cv(MS, SentM)\}_{k_C^-}$, k_C^+)

Decrypt($\{Finished_C\}_{k_{CS}}$, k_{CS})

Apply(Finished, $\{Server, MS, Sent\text{-}Messages\}$)

Encrypt($Finished_S$, k_{SC})

Send(C, $\{ChgCipher, \{Finished_S\}_{k_{SC}}\}$)

Update($\{ChgCipher, \{Finished_S\}_{k_{SC}}\}$)

5   The Analysis of SSL 3.0

When the specification is finished, the analysis begins with the first action in C's behavior list. The first four actions in $BL(C)$ are executed, resulting in new members of the sets $POSS(C)$ and BEL (C). Also, the **Update** action causes $Observers(N_C) = W$ (W represents all the principals). So far, no inference rules can be applied.

$POSS(C) = \{ k_{CA}^+ \dot{\imath} Þ CA$, $\{k_C^+\}_{k_{CA}^-}$, $k_C^+ \dot{\imath} Þ C$, k_C^-, $ciphersuites_C$, N_C, Finished(), Generate-

keys(), Match(), Cv()$\}$

$BEL(C) = \{\#(k_{CA}^+), \#(k_C^-), \#(k_C^+), \#(\{k_C^+\}_{k_{CA}^-}), \text{LINK}(N_C)\}$

$BL(C) =$

- Generate-Nonce(N_C)

- Concat(N_C, $ciphersuites_C$)

- Send(S, $\{N_C$, $ciphersuites_C\}$)

- Update($\{N_C$, $ciphersuites_C\}$)

After the **Update** action, the next action to be executed is in S's behavior list because the **Send** action specifies S.

- Receive(C, $\{N_C$, $ciphersuites_C\}$)

The first ten actions in $BL(S)$ are executed. There are still no relevant inference rules. The new values of S's local sets are:

$POSS(S) = \{ k_{CA}^+ \text{¡Þ} CA,\ \{k_S^+\}_{k_{CA}},\ k_S^- \text{¡Þ} S,\ k_S^-,\ N_C \text{ from } C,\ ciphersuites_c \text{ from } C,\ N_S,$

$k_{TS}^+ \text{¡Þ} S,\ k_{TS}^+,\ Ske(\{ N_C, N_S, k_{TS}^+ \}),\ \{ N_S,\ cipher_s,\ \{k_S^+\}_{k_{CA}},\ \{ k_{TS}^+, \{Ske(N_C,N_S,k_{TS}^+)\}_{k_S^-} \},$

$CertReq, HelloDone\},$ Finished(), Generate-keys(), Choose-ciphersuite(), Ske()\}

$BEL(S) = \{\#(k_{CA}^+),\ \#(k_S^-),\ \#(k_S^+),\ \#(\{k_S^+\}_{k_{CA}}),\ LINK(N_S),\ \#(k_{TS}^-),\ \#(k_{TS}^+),\ \#(Ske(\{ N_C, N_S, k_{TS}^+ \}))\}$

$Bindings(S) = \{ k_S^- \text{¡Þ} S,\ k_{CA}^+ \text{¡Þ} CA,\ k_{TS}^+ \text{¡Þ} S \}$

$BL(S) =$

○ Receive(C, \{ N_C, ciphersuites$_c$ \})

.

.

.

○ Update(\{ N_S, cipher$_s$, $\{k_S^+\}_{k_{CA}}$, \{ k_{TS}^+, $\{Ske(N_C,N_S,k_{TS}^+)\}_{k_S^-}$ \}, CertReq, HelloDone \}\}

The next action is in C's BL.

• Receive(S, \{ N_S, cipher$_s$, $\{k_S^+\}_{k_{CA}}$, \{ k_{TS}^+, $\{Ske(N_C,N_S,k_{TS}^+)\}_{k_S^-}$ \}, CertReq, HelloDone\})

Then the next three actions are executed.

○ Split(\{ N_S, cipher$_s$, $\{k_S^+\}_{k_{CA}}$, \{ k_{TS}^+, $\{Ske(N_C,N_S,k_{TS}^+)\}_{k_S^-}$ \}, CertReq, HelloDone\})

○ Apply(Match, \{ ciphersuites$_C$, cipher$_s$ \})

○ Apply-asymkey($\{k_S^+\}_{k_{CA}}$, k_{CA}^+)

Terms, $\{k_S^+\}_{k_{CA}}$, k_{TS}^+, $\{Ske(N_C,N_S,k_{TS}^+)\}_{k_S^-}$ and k_S^+, are added to $POSS(C)$. $k_S^+ \text{¡Þ} S$ is added to $Bindings(C)$. C trusts S, causing TRUST[1,2] = 1. The next action to be executed is:

• Apply-asymkey($\{Ske(N_C,N_S,k_{TS}^+)\}_{k_S^-}$, k_S^+)

At this point, the conditions for the **Submessage origin rule (2)** for asymmetric keys are satisfied, so $Ske(\{ N_C, N_S, k_{TS}^+ \})$ from S is added to $POSS(C)$. Also, the conditions for the **Signature rule** are satisfied. Once the rule is applied, the freshness of S's signature on its public key, $\#(Ske(\{ N_C, N_S, k_{TS}^+ \}))$, is added to $BEL(C)$, and the LINK(N_C) formula is removed from $BEL(C)$. Then C executes the next three actions:

○ Generate-Secret(PMS)

○ Apply-asymkey(PMS, k_{TS}^+)

○ Generate-Secret(MS)

Terms, *PMS*, *MS* and $\{PMS\}_{k_S^+}$, are added to *POSS(C)*. *PMS* and *MS* are also added to the secret set S. Terms, #(*PMS*) and #(*MS*), are added to *BEL(C)*. The next action is:

- Forget-Secret(*PMS*)

This action will cause *PMS* to be removed from *POSS(C)* and #(*PMS*) to be removed from *BEL(C)*. Then the next seven actions are executed.

○ Apply(Generate-keys, {*MS*, N_C , N_S })

    .

    .

    .

○ Update({ $\{k_C^+\}_{k_{CA}^-}$, $\{PMS\}_{k_S^+}$, $\{Cv(MS,SentM)\}_{k_C^-}$, *ChgCipher*, $\{Finished c\}_{k_{CS}}$ })

Terms, k_{SC}, k_{CS}, $Cv(MS,SentM)$, $\{Cv(MS,SentM)\}_{k_C^-}$, *Finishedc* and $\{Finished c\}_{k_{CS}}$, are added to *POSS(C)*. And k_{SC} and k_{CS} are also added to the secret set S. Terms, #(k_{SC}) and #(k_{CS}), are added to *BEL(C)*. The **Update** action adds S to *Observers(PMS)*. The next action to be executed is in *S*'s behavior list.

- Receive(C, { $\{k_C^+\}_{k_{CA}^-}$, $\{PMS\}_{k_S^+}$, $\{Cv(MS,SentM)\}_{k_C^-}$, *ChgCipher*, $\{Finished c\}_{k_{CS}}$ })

The next two actions are executed.

○ Split({ $\{k_C^+\}_{k_{CA}^-}$, $\{PMS\}_{k_S^+}$, $\{Cv(MS,SentM)\}_{k_C^-}$, *ChgCipher*, $\{Finished c\}_{k_{CS}}$ })
○ Apply-asymkey($\{k_C^+\}_{k_{CA}^-}$, k_{CA}^+)

Terms, $\{k_C^+\}_{k_{CA}^-}$, $\{PMS\}_{k_S^+}$, $\{Cv(MS,SentM)\}_{k_C^-}$, $\{Finished c\}_{k_{CS}}$ and k_C^+, are added to *POSS(S)*. $k_C^+ ¡Þ C$ is added to *Bindings(S)*. S trusts C, causing TRUST[2,1] = 1. The next action to be executed is:

- Apply-asymkey($\{PMS\}_{k_S^+}$, k_S^-)

After this action is executed, *PMS* is added to *POSS(S)*. However, the **Linkage rule (1)** for asymmetric keys does not apply because there is no LINK statement in *BEL(S)*. Thus, S can not conclude that *PMS* is fresh. Also, S cannot conclude that *PMS* comes from the client, since the **Submessage origin rule (1)** for asymmetric keys does not apply because there is no submessage other than *PMS* in $\{PMS\}_{k_S^+}$ coming from the client. *PMS*'s unfreshness will imply the unfreshness of *MS*, k_{CS} and k_{SC}. In fact, when S receives $\{Finished c\}_{k_{CS}}$, it cannot apply the **Verify rule** because the condition is that k_{CS} is fresh. For the remainder of the protocol, S can never conclude that anything received under k_{CS} is fresh.

As for the authentication mode in which only the server is authenticated, the two problems exist as long as RSA is used for key exchange, and the deduction of revealing them is almost the same as the above. The two weak points still exist in the completely anonymous mode with RSA key exchange, but the completely anonymous mode is inherently vulnerable to the man-in-the-middle attack, in which the attacker can impersonate both the client and the server to get the pre-master secret. Thus, comparatively the two weak points are less threatening in this mode.

When Diffie-Hellman is used for key agreement, there will no such two problems. But an anonymous Diffie-Hellman session is also inherently vulnerable to the man-in-the-middle attack.

The problem of the freshness of the pre-master secret may have bad result: compromise of the pre-master secret can cause reuse of it. The attack explored by Dr. Daniel Bleichenbacher [5], which takes advantage of the weakness of RSA PKCS#1 encoding method, can recover the pre-master secret of the attacked session. Then the attacker, taking advantage of the fact that the server cannot be assured of the freshness of the pre-master secret, uses the old $\{PMS\}_{k_S^+}$ to construct the Client Key Exchange message in a new session with the same server, thus resulting in reuse of the old pre-master secret. This weakness in SSL 3.0 is much similar to the one in the Needham and Schroeder Protocol (with shared keys) [6], discovered by Denning and Sacco [7], which is that principal B cannot conclude that the shared key with principal A, K_{ab}, is fresh. The only difference is in that PMS is encrypted by a public key in SSL 3.0 while K_{ab} is encrypted by a symmetric key in the Needham and Schroeder Protocol.

6 Solutions to the Weak Points

It is relatively easier to repair the flaw of the freshness of the pre-master secret. Add a nonce, $N_{S'}$, to the Server Hello Done message. $N_{S'}$ is used in the Client Key Exchange message to assure the server of the freshness of the pre-master secret. The structure of the Client Key Exchange message is now $\{N_{S'}, PMS\}_{k_S^+}$. The length of $N_{S'}$ must be carefully decided, since SSL 3.0 is a protocol of actual implementation.

It is not easy to remedy the flaw of the origin of the pre-master secret without much modification to the basic structure of the protocol. Only a submessage from the client, say $N_{S'}$, can make the server believe that the pre-master secret is really from the client according to NCP's **Submessage origins rule(1)** for asymmetric keys, and this fact has to introduce encryption with the client's public key to ensure that only the client can see the submessage. All these will lead to much modification to the message structures, introduction of new messages and reordering of all messages. Besides, RSA's sharing of the identical structure of the protocol with Diffie-Hellman key exchange must be taken into account.

7 Conclusion

We have applied extended NCP logic to the analysis of SSL 3.0, and shown two weak points of the protocol when RSA is used for key exchange. These two problems exist in any case in which the pre-master secret is transmitted to the server encrypted by the server's RSA public key.

It is from the viewpoint of message structure that SSL 3.0 has these two weak points, which are discovered by applying formal analyzing method to the protocol. The Client Certificate Verify message can only prove the origin of the pre-master-secret and the fact that the client knows the pre-master-secret, but cannot prove the freshness of the pre-master-secret. On the other hand, it is only when the client is authenticated and its certificate is only used for signing that the Client Certificate Verify message is used. Thus, the two weak points are really worthy of attention.

Acknowledgements. I am deeply grateful to Dr. Sven Dietrich for his enlightenment. Paul Kocher kindly provided illuminating discussion and many valuable comments, and I am greatly indebted to him.

References

1. A. Frier, P. Karlton, P. Kocher: The SSL Protocol Version 3.0. Netscape Communications Corp. March 1996. Internet Draft, work in progress.
2. T. Dierks, C. Allen. RFC2246: The TLS Protocol Version 1.0. January 1999.
3. Aviel David Rubin: Nonmonotonic Cryptographic Protocols. PhD thesis, University of Michigan, Ann Arbor. 1994.
4. Sven Dietrich: A Formal Analysis of the Secure Sockets Layer Protocol. PhD thesis, Adelphi University. 1997.
5. Daniel Bleichenbacher: Chosen Ciphertext Attacks Against Protocols Based on the RSA Encryption Standard PKCS#1. Advances in Cryptology--Crypto'98, LNCS vol. 1462, pages 1--12, Springer-Verlag, 1998.
6. Roger M. Needham, M.D. Schroeder: Using Encryption for Authentication in Large Networks. Communication of the ACM, 21(12):993-999, December 1978.
7. Dorothy E. Denning, Giovanni Maria Sacco: Timestamps in Key Distribution Protocols. Communication of the ACM, 24(8):533-536, August 1981.

Performance of WTLS and Its Impact on an M-commerce Transaction

Ian Herwono and Ingo Liebhardt

Communication Networks
Aachen University of Technology
Kopernikusstraße 16, D-52074 Aachen, Germany
Phone: +49/241/80-7248, Fax: +49/241/8888-242
{ian|ilt}@comnets.rwth-aachen.de

Abstract. Transaction security is commonly seen as one of the key factors influencing the success of *Mobile Commerce*. In this paper simulation-based performance measurements of the *Wireless Transport Layer Security (WTLS)* protocol are presented. Its impact on an exemplary m-commerce transaction is discussed.

1 Introduction

Although saturation can be observed in Europe, the market for mobile telephony still faces an overwhelming growth in most of the world's regions. Globally, 240 million[1] people are predicted to use their mobile phones for wireless data exchange by the end of 2004—up from 26 million in 1999. As most of this data exchange is predicted to be business-centred, a considerable amount of users all over the world will be engaged in *Mobile Commerce (M-Commerce)*.

The *Wireless Application Protocol (WAP)* [1] specifies an application framework and network protocols to foster convergence of the Internet and wireless networks like CDPD or GSM/GPRS (Fig. 1). Within the context of m-commerce the *Mobile electronic Transaction (MeT) Initiative* has been formed by the leading mobile manufacturers to define common and consistent usage scenarios, e. g. , mobile payment or ticketing [2]. Rather than developing proprietary solutions to security problems, MeT embraces and extends existing industry standards and technologies—especially WAP. Therefore the performance of the employed WAP security mechanisms—WTLS and WMLScript signText—has a major impact on the overall transaction duration.

In [3] several alternatives for establishing secure channels to mobile devices have been compared whereby the influence of different key lengths and key exchange protocols has not been examined extensively. This work contributes detailed performance measurements of WTLS acquired from our WAP simulation platform.

After giving an overview on WTLS we briefly describe the simulator and present the measurement results. We then discuss the impact WAP's security mechanisms impose on the overall duration of m-commerce transactions by exemplarily investigating a MeT payment using a SET Wallet Server.

---

[1] according to Allied Business Intelligence

S. Qing, T. Okamoto, and J. Zhou (Eds.): ICICS 2001, LNCS 2229, pp. 167–171, 2001.

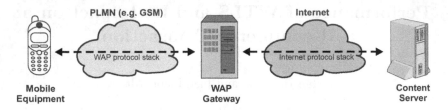

Fig. 1. Typical setup for accessing an Internet server via WAP

2   Wireless Transport Layer Security

The WTLS protocol is based upon the industry-standard Transport Layer Security (TLS) and offers various cryptographic algorithms to provide confidentiality, integrity, and authentication over the air interface. Several symmetric algorithms like DES, 3DES, RC5, or IDEA can be employed for en- and decryption whereas a keyed HMAC hash in combination with MD5 or SHA-1 is used for ensuring message authentication. RSA and ECDH are suggested for anonymous key exchange. In addition RSA-signing and ECDSA can be used for authenticated key exchange. It has to be noted that WTLS is unable to ensure nonrepudiation.

Unlike in RSA handshakes a provision is made for an optimised variant of the ECDH_ECDSA and ECDH handshakes. In this case the amount of data to be transferred across the air interface can be reduced since the server is able to retrieve the client's certificate from a certificate distribution service or from its own sources rather than obtaining it from the client. The flows of messages exchanged within full and optimised handshakes are depicted in Fig. 2. To resume a previous secure session and reuse negotiated security parameters, an abbreviated handshake can be performed. Further details concerning WTLS can be found in [1].

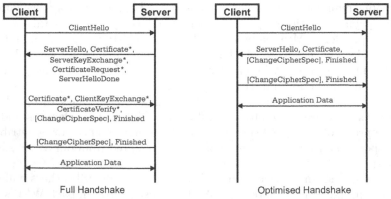

* Indicates optional or situation-dependent messages that are not always sent

Fig. 2. Message flow for WTLS handshakes

3   Performance Evaluation

Our simulation platform is a prototypical, standard-conformant implementation of the relevant protocols WTP, WTLS, WDP, and IP. It is formally specified in SDL[2] and coded using C/C++. Most of the implementations concerning cryptographic computations originate from the free C++ class library Crypto++ 4.1[3]. All following measurements are the results of tests carried out on a SUN Enterprise server equipped with 1664 Mbyte RAM and using one single *dedicated* processor of 400 MHz clock frequency.

3.1   Throughput of WTLS

The WTLS throughput results from the processing times needed for the generation of record IV, the calculation and verification of keyed MAC, and the en- and decryption respectively. Hence the values given in Table 1 do not correspond with the ones resulting from investigations on the pure cipher throughput as—for example—done in [4]. WTLS user data ranging from 256 up to 8192 bytes have been used and the measured throughputs have been averaged. Note that only user data has been taken into account for calculating the throughput whilst the encrypted data additionally includes the MAC and padding. All ciphers operate in CBC mode and a key length of 128 bits has been chosen for AES, Serpent, Twofish, and Mars.

Table 1. Throughput of the WTLS-layer in Mbit/s

keyed MAC	DES	3DES	RC5	IDEA	AES	Serpent	Twofish	Mars
MD5 (enc)	5.81	2.38	9.01	6.52	15.10	3.32	5.63	5.82
MD5 (dec)	5.76	2.37	8.70	5.75	14.76	3.13	5.52	5.69
SHA-1 (enc)	5.14	2.26	7.45	5.61	10.56	2.96	4.78	4.97
SHA-1 (dec)	5.13	2.26	7.40	5.15	11.36	2.92	4.89	5.08

Table 1 shows that AES (Rijndael) in combination with MD5 provides the highest performance. The faster the investigated cipher algorithm, the more weight lies in the selection of the hashing algorithm. However we observe that— contrary to our expectation—the encryption throughput of AES is higher than its decryption throughput when SHA-1 is employed. Even after repeated simulations on different machines and thorough analysis this behaviour remained inexplicable.

---

[2] Specification and Description Language
[3] Please refer to http://www.eskimo.com/~weidai/cryptlib.html for further information.

3.2   Handshake

In contrast to the WTLS throughput, which—even when implemented within a constrained environment—is higher than the underlying network's throughput, attention has to be paid to the duration of a handshake. The overall durations of several handshake procedures have been measured while varying the effective mean throughput of the underlying bearer, which is determined by numerous factors such as available radio resources, network latency and channel quality. The measurement results of four types of full handshakes and one optimised handshake are shown in Fig. 3. The key lengths of RSA and ECDH have been set to 1024 bits and 160 bits respectively. The time needed for the server retrieving a certificate in the optimised variant has been assumed to be 500 ms.

Interestingly, the impact of the various cryptographic methods becomes negligible as the network throughput decreases, and the amount of data[4] transferred during a single handshake (Table 2) gets more important.

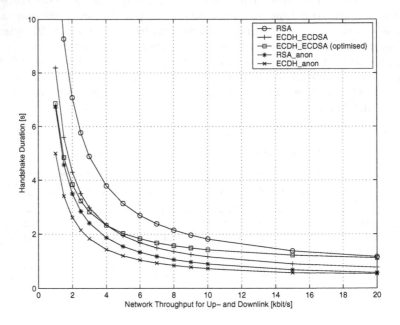

Fig. 3. Duration of examined WTLS handshake procedures

3.3   Impact on an M-commerce Transaction

The *MeT Initiative* has specified a usage scenario for mobile payments using a SET Wallet Server wherein nonrepudiation is granted by application level digital

---

[4] includes WDP- and IP-overhead

Table 2. Size of message groups exchanged during a handshake

	RSA	ECDH_ECDSA	RSA_anon	ECDH_ECDSA(opt)	ECDH_anon
1st msg.	263 bytes	263 bytes	263 bytes	263 bytes	263 bytes
2nd msg.	485 bytes	287 bytes	210 bytes	338 bytes	98 bytes
3rd msg.	780 bytes	310 bytes	221 bytes	154 bytes	115 bytes
4th msg.	116 bytes	116 bytes	116 bytes	–	116 bytes

signatures (WMLScript signText) and SET messages are exchanged between the server and merchants only. Assuming that the WAP gateway and the SET Wallet Server are both hosted by the corresponding credit institute, a secured channel between mobile devices and the server can be established by means of WTLS.

Measurements carried out with ECDSA-signing have resulted in an increase of the transaction duration by 0.11 s if no certificate has been included in the signed string and 0.35 s in case the certificate has been appended. With RSA-signing, the duration increases by 1.73 s and 2.50 s respectively. Given that most of the time is being spent in the SET Wallet Server itself [5], the slight increase is acceptable although these values are not taking a handshake, which eventually is to be performed, into account.

4   Conclusions

According to our performance evaluation it is obvious that, as the WTLS throughput is higher than the expected one of the underlying bearers, the impact of symmetric en- and deciphering becomes negligible. However, costs for the completion of WTLS handshakes have still to be taken into consideration. As exemplarily shown in 3.3, in case a full handshake is to be carried out prior to each transaction, a significant increase in transaction duration is to be expected—depending on the chosen key exchange suite and the available channel quality. Based on this fact, the decision whether to execute a full or an abbreviated handshake should be deliberated.

References

1. WAP Technical Specifications Version 1.2.1, WAP Forum,
   URL: http://www.wapforum.org/
2. "MeT Core Specification" V0.1, MeT, 21-2-2001,
   URL: http://www.mobiletransaction.org/
3. Linder, D., "Transport Security for the next Generation Mobile Terminals", Master's Thesis, Royal Institute of Technology, Stockholm, Sweden, 29-11-2000
4. Schneier, B. et al., "Performance Comparison of the AES Submissions", 3-1-1999
5. Wrona, K. and Zavagli, G., "Adaptation of the SET Protocol to Mobile Networks and to the Wireless Application Protocol", Proc. European Wireless '99, Munich, Germany, October 1999

Enforcing Obligation with Security Monitors

Carlos Ribeiro, André Zúquete, and Paulo Ferreira

IST/INESC R. Alves Redol N°9 1000 Lisboa, Portugal
Carlos.Ribeiro@inesc.pt

Abstract. With the ubiquitous deployment of large scale networks, more and more complex human interactions are supported by computer applications. This poses new challenges on the expressiveness of security policy design systems, often requiring the use of new security paradigms. In this paper we identify a restricted type of obligation which is useful to express new security policies. This type of obligation includes the following general situations: i) when two or more actions oblige each other, i.e. if one action is executed the others must also be executed and reciprocally, and ii) when an action obliges another and the obligatory action is causally dependent on the first action.

1 Introduction

The growing number of Internet users and services raises constantly new challenges for defining and ensuring adequate security policies. Most policies implement solely access control barriers, based on the concepts of permission or prohibition, but the current expansion of electronic business will stress, in a near future, the needs for more sophisticated security policies. In particular, we believe that the concept of obligation will have an increasing importance for the expressiveness of such policies. The need for ensuring obligation has already been recognized by several authors [1,2,3] and is illustrated by the following examples.

Consider that Alice browses through a site where she acquires several goods, when she leaves the site she is *obliged* to pay for the goods she acquired, otherwise the goods are not bought. Usually this policy must be enforced within the site's code, because the security service cannot enforce this kind of policy. Another illustrating example is when Alice registers herself, via a web server, as a student of *Online University*. Once she has done that, she is *obliged* to register herself as a student of, at least, a discipline chosen from a set of available disciplines. On the other hand, Alice could first register herself in a discipline; in this case she is then obliged to register as a student of the *Online University*.

These examples show that there is a clear need for expressing an application-specific obligation in a flexible way; and enforcing obligations with a security monitor has obvious advantages: it is language and application independent, and can be found in a large number of environments (virtual machines, operating systems, etc.).

S. Qing, T. Okamoto, and J. Zhou (Eds.): ICICS 2001, LNCS 2229, pp. 172–176, 2001.

2   Enforceable Obligations

To act upon security policies, a security service must know when someone attempts to violate those policies and what to do when that happens. On most security services, the attempts to violate rules based on permission and prohibition concepts are detected when an event requesting an action occurs and, in that case, the action requested is denied. The difficulty with rules based on obligation is that the time at which a violation attempt occurs and the action to perform when that happens are not so easy to instantiate on a particular instant and action, respectively. First, because a generic obligation does not need to have a deadline and second because there is not a generic action (equal for every situation) to perform in case of violation attempt.

Fortunately, obligation rules are seldom generic. Often what a security manager wants to express is "Conditional Obligations", in which obligations are triggered by pre-condition events: "*U1* must do *O* if *U2* has done *T*". While with the generic type of obligation a system is in an unsafe[1] state until the obligation has been fulfilled, with the conditional obligation a system has two safe states, one before the triggering event (*T*) and one after the obligation (*O*) is fulfilled. Thus, on the impossibility of fulfilling the obligation the system may always return to the safe state before the activating event, i.e. undo *T*. However even conditional obligations cannot be enforced solely by a standard security monitor. Using simple logic[2] it is possible to rewrite the conditional obligation expression into an expression with a dependency on a future event: "*U2* cannot do *T* if *U1* will no do *O*".

Schneider [4] states that with a monitor it is not possible to enforce a security policy in which the acceptability of an event depends on possible future events. Informally, his argument is quite simple: given the executions (sequence of events) τ and τ', in which τ is the prefix of some execution τ', it is not possible to allow τ on the basis that one of its extensions τ' is allowed by the security policy, because the system could stop before τ', and the system would have failed to enforce the policy.

The key issue that differentiates our work from Schneider's is the underlying model of execution. While to Schneider a system evolves through units of execution controlled by the security manager, which are independent from each other, to us those units may be organized in atomic sequences, thus depending on each other. By atomic we mean, in the sense of transactions' ACID properties, either all happens or none happens. Inside these atomic sequences of execution it is possible to define security policies with dependencies on future actions, because it is not possible for a system to stop execution leaving the sequence incomplete.

There are several ways to implement transactions [5], namely by keeping an undo-log with the information needed to reset the system to the initial state in case of failure, or by defining compensating actions for those actions that

---

[1] Unsafe in the sense that the security policy has not been completely enforced until then.

[2] $O \Leftarrow T \equiv \neg T \Leftarrow \neg O$

cannot be undone but can be compensated. However, there are some actions that cannot be undone or compensated, e.g. sending a document to a printer. These actions are called *real actions* on transaction management systems [5] and are already known to require special treatment by those systems in order to achieve atomicity. Implementing security obligations within transactions increases the number of *real actions*, because these must include actions that change human knowledge state (e.g. showing some text on the screen), which are not dealt by most transactional management systems.

3   Implementing Enforceable Obligations

We have implemented the obligation concept within our access control framework. This framework is composed by a security policy language (SPL) and its compiler[6]. SPL is a security language designed to express policies that aim at deciding about the acceptability of events.

An SPL policy is a structure composed of sets and rules, whose purpose is to express simple concepts like "separation of duty", "information flow", or "general access control". Sets contain the entities used by the policies to decide on events acceptability. A rule is a function of events, and may assume three values: "allow", "deny" and "notapply". Its purpose is to decide on the acceptability of the current event. A rule can be simple or composed. A simple rule is a tuple of two logical expressions. The first logical expression decides on the applicability of the rule, and the second decides on the acceptability of the event. Each policy has one special rule called the "query rule", which is identified by a question mark before the name, whose purpose is to define the policy behavior.

A simple policy stating that documents internal to the organization defining the policy cannot be sent to someone outside the organization, can easily be expressed in SPL:

```
policy Private( user set OrganizationUsers ) {
  object set InternalDocs:                  // Policy data
?Private:                                    // Rule name.
  ce.action = "SendEmail" & ce.target IN     // Applicability exp.
  InternalDocs
  :: ce.parameter[1] IN OrganizationUsers    // Acceptability exp.}
```

The rule uses the special variable "ce" to access the current event properties. The applicability expression of the rule states that the policy is defined only for events whose targets are documents internal to the organization and whose action is to send an Email. The acceptability expression states that for those events that satisfy the applicability expression the only events allowed are the ones that send the Email to a user inside the organization.

Given the future-dependent nature of obligation-based policies, they are expressed in SPL by quantifying a variable over the special abstract set FutureEvents, which encompasses all the events they are to be performed after the current event. Figure 1 shows an example of an information flow policy which uses obligation to force applications to register the information flow originated

```
policy InfoFlow () {                         policy HistoryInfoFlow () {
                                             interface ReadFlowActions,
interface ReadFlowActions,                   WriteFlowActions;
interface WriteFlowActions;                  collection ProtObjects;
collection ProtObjects;                      ?InfoFlow:
                                             FORALL te IN PastEvents {        // (1)
?InfoFlow:                                     EXISTS fe IN PastEvents {
  EXISTS fe IN FutureEvents {                    FORALL pe IN PastEvents {
    FORALL pe IN PastEvents {                      FORALL g IN pe.target.groups {
      FORALL g IN pe.target.groups {               ce.action.name = "commit" &   // (2)
        ce.action IN WriteFlowActions &            ce.trans_id = te.trans_id &   // (3)
        ce.task = pe.task &                        te.time < fe.time &           // (4)
        pe.target IN ProtObjects &                 te.time > pe.time &           // (5)
        pe.action IN ReadFlowActions &             te.action IN WriteFlowActions &
        :: ce.target IN g } } }; }                 pe.target IN ProtObjects &
                                                   pe.action IN ReadFlowActions &
                                                   pe.task = te.task
                                                   :: te.target IN g } } } }; }
```

             (a)   (b)

Fig. 1. (a) An information flow policy. (b) The transformation into an history-based policy

by them into SPL rules. This policy is not a strict information flow policy in the sense that it cannot handle implicit flows, as defined in Denning [7]. However, in some situations [8] the information leak resulting from implicit flows does not pose a serious security risk, either because the information on variables determining the sequence of execution is public or because it is not possible to infer the sequence of executions from the results of that sequence. For these situations it is possible to define information flow policies enforceable by event monitors, because the regulation of explicit information flow, from storage to storage, can be performed with just the knowledge on past events properties.

As explained in Sect. 2, the problem of enforcing obligation-based security policies is reduced to allowing or not the event that instructs the transaction monitor to *commit* a transaction, whether or not every obligation was fulfilled at the time of that event. A security policy that allows or denies an event (the commit event) depending on whether or not some events were executed (the obligations) is a history-based policy. In [6], we have shown that history-based policies can be efficiently implemented using special tuned logs for each policy, thus obligation-based can also be implemented efficiently in the same way.

The transformation from the obligation-based policy to the history-based policy can be achieved in two steps. The first step, called "aging", consists of replacing references to events by older references: (i) References to the current event are replaced by references to a past event called "trigger-event" (line (1) of Fig. 1b) ; (ii) References to past events are replaced by references to other past events with an additional constraint specifying their occurrence before the trigger-event (line (5) of Fig. 1b); (iii) References to future events are replaced by references to past events with the additional constraint of occurring after the trigger-event (line (4) of Fig. 1b). The second step consists of inserting in this policy an explicit reference to the event that requests the transaction commit (lines (2) and (3) of Fig. 1b).

Due to space limitations we defer the details on performance of history-based policies to [6]. Nevertheless, the important observation is that, on all tests performed the delay on the commit-event caused by the information flow policy was in the worst case less than $1ms$, which is negligible compared to the actual commit time[3].

4   Conclusion

We have identified a restricted type of obligation which is simultaneously useful to express the security policies of large organizations and can be enforceable by security monitors. This type of obligation includes the following generic situations: i) when the two actions involved in a conditional obligation oblige each other, and ii) when the obligatory action is causally dependent on its trigger action. Our approach consists on using the transaction concept to delay the actual security monitoring until the commit time; thus, avoiding the problem of future dependency inherent to any obligation policy. We have developed a security language and a compiler encompassing the obligation paradigm, and the performance results show that it can be efficiently implemented.

References

1. Jonscher, D.: Extending access control with duties - realized by active mechanisms. Database Security, VI: Status and Prospects. (1992) 91–112
2. Cuppens, F., Saurel, C.: Specifying a security policy: A case study. In: IEEE CS Computer Security Foundations Workshop (CSFW96). (1996) 123–135
3. Marriott, D., Sloman, M.: Implementation of a management agent for interpreting obligation policy. In: IEEE/IFIP 7th Int. W. on Distributed Systems Operations and Management, Italy (1996)
4. Schneider, F.B.: Enforceable security policies. The ACM Transactions on Information and System Security **3** (2000)
5. Gray, J., Reuter, A.: Transaction Processing: concepts and techniques. Data Management Systems. Morgan Kaufmann Publishers, Inc., San Mateo (CA), USA (1993)
6. Ribeiro, C., Zúquete, A., Ferreira, P., Guedes, P.: Spl: An access control language for security policies with complex constraints. In: Network and Distributed System Security Symposium (NDSS'01), San Diego, California (2001)
7. Denning, D.: A lattice model of secure information flow. Comm. of ACM **20** (1977)
8. Edwards, W.K.: Policies and roles in collaborative applications. In: ACM 1996 Conference on Computer Supported Work, New York, ACM Press (1996) 11–20

---

[3] All measurements were taken on a personal computer with a Pentium II at 333MHz running the Sun Java 1.2.2 virtual machine over Windows NT 4.0.

Efficient Software Implementation for Finite Field Multiplication in Normal Basis

Peng Ning[1] and Yiqun Lisa Yin[2]

[1] Department of Computer Science
North Carolina State University, Raleigh, NC 27695, USA
ning@csc.ncsu.edu
[2] NTT Multimedia Communications Laboratories, Inc.
250 Cambridge Avenue, Palo Alto, CA 94306, USA
yiqun@nttmcl.com

Abstract. Finite field arithmetic is becoming increasingly important in today's computer systems, particularly for implementing cryptographic operations. Among various arithmetic operations, finite field multiplication is of particular interest since it is a major building block for elliptic curve cryptosystems. In this paper, we present new techniques for efficient software implementation of binary field multiplication in normal basis. Our techniques are more efficient in terms of both speed and memory compared with alternative approaches.

1 Introduction

Finite field arithmetic is becoming increasingly important in today's computer systems, particularly for implementing cryptographic operations. Among the more common finite fields in cryptography are odd-characteristic finite fields of degree 1 and even-characteristic finite fields of degree greater than 1. The latter is conventionally known as $GF(2^m)$ arithmetic or binary field arithmetic. $GF(2^m)$ arithmetic is further classified according to the choice of basis for representing elements of the finite field; two common choices are polynomial basis and normal basis.

Fast implementation techniques for $GF(2^m)$ arithmetic have been studied intensively in the past twenty years. Among various arithmetic operations, $GF(2^m)$ multiplication has attracted most of the attention since it is a major building block for implementing elliptic curve cryptosystems. Depending on the choice of basis, the mathematical formula for a $GF(2^m)$ multiplication can be quite different, thus making major differences in practical implementation. Currently, it seems that normal basis representation (especially optimal normal basis) offers the best performance in hardware [9,10,11], while in software polynomial basis representation is more efficient [2,3,8].

For interoperability, it is desirable to support both types of basis in software, which can be done either by implementing arithmetic in both bases or by implementing one basis together with basis conversion algorithms. Various

S. Qing, T. Okamoto, and J. Zhou (Eds.): ICICS 2001, LNCS 2229, pp. 177–188, 2001.

basis conversion techniques [4,5,6] have been proposed with performance trade-offs. Because of the overhead of basis conversion, supporting both bases directly seems preferable than basis conversion for certain applications.

There has not been much study related to implementing normal basis multiplication in software, in contrast with the amount of work related to polynomial basis. The main difficulties for fast normal basis multiplication in software are due to the particular computation process: First, when multiplying two elements represented in normal basis according to the standard formula, the coefficients of their product need to be computed one bit at a time. Second, the computation of a given bit involves a series of "partial sums" which need to be computed sequentially in software, while this is easily parallelized in hardware.

In this paper, we present new techniques for efficient software implementation of normal basis multiplication, part of which were originally described in a patent application [13]. At the core of our method are a mathematical transformation and a novel way of doing precomputation, which significantly reduce both time and memory complexity.

To study the effectiveness of our techniques, we compare our approach with the best alternative one[1] developed by Rosing [14]. Our approach is much more efficient than his method in terms of both speed and memory. Speed wise, analysis and experimental results show that there is a significant speed up using our new techniques. Memory wise, the number of bytes stored is only $O(m)$ compared with $O(m^2)$ in [14]. This is especially useful for memory constraint devices – environments that elliptic curve cryptosystems seem more attractive than conventional public key cryptosystems such as RSA. Our techniques for field multiplication can also be combined with elliptic curve arithmetic to provide further speed up.

The rest of the paper is organized as follows. In Section 2, we provide some mathematical background, and in Section 3, we review the related work on normal basis multiplication for both software and hardware. In Section 4, we present our new multiplication techniques, and in Section 5, we summarize experimental results. Some further discussions on related issues are included in Section 6, and concluding remarks are given in Section 7.

2   Mathematical Background

In this section, we first define some basic notations for finite field $GF(2^m)$ and its representation in normal basis. Then, we describe the multiplication formulas for both general normal basis and optimal normal basis.

Since we are considering software implementation, we will use w to denote the word size throughout the paper. For simplicity, we assume that $w|m$.

---

[1] The recent result in [15] has better performance than the Rosing's method for certain choices of m. However, our approach remains the fastest among the known methods. Please see section 3.

2.1   Finite Field $GF(2^m)$ and Normal Basis Representation

The finite field $GF(2^m)$ is the set of all 2^m possible 0-1 strings of length m, with certain rules for field addition and multiplication. The finite field $GF(2^m)$ have various basis representations including normal basis representation.

A binary polynomial is a polynomial with coefficients in $GF(2)$. A binary polynomial is irreducible if it is not the product of two binary polynomials of smaller degrees. For simplicity, we will refer to such a polynomial an irreducible polynomial. Irreducible polynomials exist for every degree m and can be found efficiently.

Let $g(x)$ be an irreducible polynomial of degree m. If β is a root of $g(x)$, then the m distinct roots of $g(x)$ in $GF(2^m)$ is given by $B = (\beta, \beta^2, \beta^{2^2}, ..., \beta^{2^{m-1}})$. If the elements of B are linearly independent, then $g(x)$ is called a normal polynomial and B is called a normal basis for $GF(2^m)$ over $GF(2)$. Normal polynomials exist for every degree m. For certain choices of m, $x^m + x^{m-1} + x^{m-2} + \cdots + x + 1$ is a normal polynomial. Given any element $a \in GF(2^m)$, one can write

$$a = \sum_{i=0}^{m-1} a_i \beta^{2^i}, \text{ where } a_i \in \{0, 1\}.$$

2.2   Multiplication with General Normal Basis

In normal basis, field multiplication is usually carried out using a multiplication matrix, which is an m-by-m matrix M with each entry $M_{ij} \in GF(2)$. Details on how to compute matrix M from $g(x)$ can be found in [4]. The complexity of M, denoted by C_m, is defined to be the number 1's in M. It is well known that $C_m \geq 2m - 1$.

Let $a = (a_0, a_1, ..., a_{m-1})$ and $b = (b_0, b_1, ..., b_{m-1})$ be two elements represented in normal basis, and let $c = (c_0, c_1, ..., c_{m-1})$ be their product. Then each coefficient c_k is computed as follows[2].

$$c_k = (a_k, a_{k+1}, ..., a_{k+m-1}) \ M \ (b_k, b_{k+1}, ..., b_{k+m-1})^T. \tag{1}$$

In a straightforward software implementation of formula (1), a, b, and each column of M are all stored in m/w computer words. A matrix-vector multiplication Mb^T can be carried out with $(m/2)(m/w)$ word operations on average, and hence the total number of word operations for computing c is about $m(m/2)(m/w) = m^3/2w$. Note that the computation time is independent of the complexity C_m.

If we spell out formula (1), we obtain the following equation for c_k.

$$c_k = \bigoplus_{i=0}^{m-1} \left[a_{k+i} \cdot \left(\bigoplus_{j=0}^{m-1} M_{ij} \cdot b_{j+k} \right) \right]. \tag{2}$$

---

[2] Throughout the paper, the additions "+" in the subscripts are understood as additions modulo the degree m, unless otherwise specified.

In formula (2), essentially the same expression is used for each coefficient c_k. More specifically, given the expression for c_k, one can just increase the subscripts of a and b by one (modulo m) to obtain the expression for c_{k+1}. Formula (2) will be useful in later discussions.

2.3 Multiplication with Optimal Normal Basis

An optimal normal basis (ONB) [1,12] is a normal basis which has the lowest complexity. That is, $C_m = 2m - 1$. Optimal normal bases only exist for certain degree m. In the range [150, 600], there are only 101 degrees for which ONB exists.

There are two kinds of normal basis called type I ONB and type II ONB. They differ in the mathematical formulas which define them. The matrix M has the form that the first row has a single non-zero entry, and the rest of each row has exactly two non-zero entries. So the matrix M can be stored more compactly using two tables $t1[i]$ and $t2[i]$, which are the indices of the two non-zero entries in row i of M. Using $t1$ and $t2$, formula (2) can be rewritten as follows.

$$c_k = (a_k \cdot b_{t1[0]+k}) \oplus \left(\bigoplus_{i=1}^{m-1} \left[a_{k+i} \cdot \left(b_{t1[i]+k} \oplus b_{t2[i]+k} \right) \right] \right). \tag{3}$$

3 Related Work

3.1 Hardware

In formula (1), when a new bit c_k needs to be computed, the coefficients of both a and b are rotated to the left by one bit. This fact is useful for efficient hardware implementation of normal basis multiplication [9,10,11], since the same circuit that represents M can be repeatedly used and each coefficient can be computed in one clock cycle.

Even though the sequence of operations for each coefficient is easily parallelized in hardware, it is quite difficult to mimic the same technique in a software implementation since these operations are inherently sequential in software.

3.2 Software

Fast software implementation techniques for normal basis multiplication have been centered around optimal normal basis. In [7], a method for type I optimal normal basis was considered. The idea is to use polynomial-basis-like multiplication and take advantage of the special form of the irreducible polynomials for type I ONB. Their method does not seem to extend to type II ONB or other normal basis.

In [14], Rosing presented an efficient method for ONB multiplication. The main idea is that the partial sum $a_{k+i} \cdot \left(b_{t1[i]+k} \oplus b_{t2[i]+k} \right)$ in formula (3) can be computed simultaneously for different coefficients (different subscript i) using word operations in software. To do this, some preprocessing of b is necessary. At a high level, Rosing's method can be summarized as follows.

- *Precomputation*: compute and store m rotations of b.
- *Main loop*: for each $i = 1, 2, ..., m - 1$, compute the partial sum $a_{k+i} \cdot \left(b_{t1[i]+k} \oplus b_{t2[i]+k} \right)$. As a special case, when $i = 0$, the partial sum $a_k \cdot b_{t1[0]+k}$ is computed.

In the main loop, each partial sum is computed in $O(m/w)$ operations, for a total of $O(m^2/w)$ operation. For the precomputation, the number of operations for computing all rotations of b is also $O(m^2/w)$, and the total number of bytes stored is $m^2/8$. Note that for precomputation, both time and memory grow quadratically as m increases.

Our approach does share a feature similar to Rosing's method: Our approach also computes multiple bits of the (partial) result simultaneously using word operations. However, our approach employs a very different precomputation technique. As we will show in section 5, our technique reduces the time and memory complexity for precomputation from quadratic to linear, yielding a much more efficient algorithm than Rosing's method.

Reyhani-Masoleh et al. recently proposed a series of fast normal basis multiplication algorithms based on some mathematical transformations [15]. According to their timing result [15], our approach is about twice as fast as their most efficient algorithm. For example, the running time for $m = 299$ (ONB) reported in [15] is 114 μs on Pentium III 533 MHz, which can be scaled to 101 μs on Pentium III 600 MHz (our platform). In comparison, our implementation takes 42.36 μs on Pentium III 600 MHz. Note that it is possible to combine our techniques with those in [15]; however, we do not cover this topic here but consider it as possible future work.

4   Our Techniques

In this section, we present our techniques for an efficient software implementation of normal basis multiplication. We begin with a basic method for general normal basis. Then, we present a simple yet effective improvement to the basic method. Finally, we discuss how our approach can be applied to ONB to provide much better performance.

4.1   The Basic Method

At the core of our method is a new way of doing the precomputation, which significantly reduces both time and memory complexity. First, we define the quantities that need to be precomputed. For $i = 0, 1, ..., m - 1$, let

$$A[i] = (a_i, a_{i+1}, ..., a_{i+w-1}),$$
$$B[i] = (b_i, b_{i+1}, ..., b_{i+w-1}),$$
$$C[i] = (c_i, c_{i+1}, ..., c_{i+w-1}).$$

In other words, each $A[i]$ has length w and they are the successive blocks of a in a wrap-around fashion, and similarly for $B[i]$ and $C[i]$. It is easy to see that $c = (C[0], C[w], C[2w], \cdots, C[(\frac{m}{w} - 1)w])$. Now we can rewrite formula (2) using A, B, C as follows:

For t from 0 to $(m/w - 1)$

$$ C[wt] = \bigoplus_{i=0}^{m-1} \left[A[(i+wt) \bmod m] \cdot \left(\bigoplus_{j=0}^{m-1} M[i,j]B[(j+wt) \bmod m] \right) \right]. \quad (4) $$

We can see that the total number of equations in formula (4) is m/w, and one equation in formula (4) corresponds to w consecutive equations in formula (1) or formula (2). In software implementation of formula (4), "$\cdot$" can be computed as a bit-wise AND operation between two words, and "$\bigoplus$" can be computed as a bit-wise Exclusive-OR operation between two words. Therefore, during the computation process, the quantities involved are only $A[i]$'s and $B[i]$'s which have already been precomputed, and the operations involved are only word operations.

The following gives a straightforward implementation of formula (4) in C.

Algorithm 1.
```
precompute arrays A and B;
for (t = 0; t < (m/w); t++) {
    C[w*t] = 0;
    for (i = 0; i < m; i++) {
        temp = 0;
        for (j = 0; j < m; j++)
            if (M[i,j]==1) temp ^= B[(j+w*t)%m];
        C[w*t] ^= A[(i+w*t)%m] & temp;
    }
}
```

The total number of word operations for the main loop is $O(C_m \cdot m/w)$. The number of operations for precomputing the arrays A and B is $O(m)$, and the total number of precomputed bytes is $2 \times m \times (w/8) = w \cdot m/4$, which is $8m$ for typical PC implementation. Note that both time and memory complexity is linear in m for the precomputation phase.

4.2   Further Optimization

We can further speed up the basic method in Section 4.1 by precomputing and storing the arrays A and B in a clever way to avoid all the modulo m computation for indexing in the main loop.

To achieve this, we first extend the definition of array A and B as follows: For $i = 0, ...m - 1$, we define[3]

$$ A[i+m] = A[i] = (a_i, a_{i+1}, ..., a_{i+w-1}), $$
$$ B[i+m] = B[i] = (b_i, b_{i+1}, ..., b_{i+w-1}). $$

---
[3] Here, the addition in $A[i+m]$ and $B[i+m]$ is a real addition without modulo m.

We precompute array A and B, each of which consists of $2m$ elements of length w:

$$A[0], A[1], ..., A[m-1], A[m], A[m+1], ..., A[2m-1],$$
$$B[0], B[1], ..., B[m-1], B[m], B[m+1], ..., B[2m-1].$$

Given A and B, we can improve the C code in Section 4.1:

Algorithm 2.

```
precompute arrays A and B;
for (k = 0; k < m; k += w) {
    C[k] = 0;
    for (i = 0; i < m; i++) {
        temp = 0;
        for (j = 0; j < m; j++)
            if (M[i,j]==1) temp ^= B[j];
        C[k] ^= A[i] & temp;
    }
    A += w; B += w;
}
```

The idea in the above code is the following: When computing $C[0]$, we use word 0 through $m-1$ in array A and B (that is, the first m words). When computing $C[w]$, we use word w through $w+m-1$ in array A and B, which is accomplished by two easy pointer jumping. Similarly, we can compute $C[2w], ..., C[m-w]$.

This way, the arrays A and B are accessed sequentially within the main loop, significantly improving the speed at some cost of the memory. The number of operations for precomputing A and B remains the same, and the total number of precomputed bytes is $w \cdot m/2$, which is $16m$ for typical PC implementation.

4.3 Applying the Techniques to ONB

Algorithm 2 in the preceding section can be simplified using the fact that the inner loop j no longer exists for ONB, since it only involves one or two elements of B. Here we assume the non-zero entry of the first row of M is stored in `t1[0]` and the two non-zero entries of row i $(0 < i < m)$ are stored in `t1[i]` and `t2[i]`, respectively (see section 2.3).

Algorithm 3.

```
precompute arrays A and B;
for (k = 0; k < m; k += w) {
    temp = A[0] & B[t1[0]];
    for (i = 0; i < m; i++)
        temp ^= A[i] & (B[t1[i]] ^ B[t2[i]]);
    C[k] = temp;
    A += w; B += w;
}
```

The implementation for type I ONB can be further improved by taking advantage of the special form of its multiplication matrix. For type I ONB, the non-zero entry of the first row of M is always in column $m/2$, and one of the two non-zero entries of row i is in column $m/2 + i \bmod m$ [14]. Thus, we can compute one non-zero entry row i of M, say t1[i], as $i + m/2 \bmod m$.

This fact can be combined with the precomputation to reduce one table lookup in the inner loop of Algorithm 3. The idea is to further extend the array B by $m/2$ words such that for $i = 2m, 2m+1, \cdots, 2m+m/2-1$, $B[i] = B[i-m]$. Then $B[t1[i]] = B[i+m/2 \bmod m]$ in the inner loop can be replaced by $B[i+m/2]$ (without involving the mod operation), and thus we can use another pointer $D = B + m/2$ and further replace $B[i + m/2]$ with $D[i]$. As a result, the above code can be improved as follows.

Algorithm 4.
```
precompute arrays A and B;
D = B + m/2;
for (k = 0; k < m; k += w) {
    temp = A[0] & D[0];
    for (i = 1; i < m; i ++)
        temp ∧= A[i] & (D[i] ∧ B[t2[i]]);
    C[k] = temp;
    A += w; B += w; D += w;
}
```

5   Performance Results

To evaluate the performance of our methods, we performed a series of experiments for both type I and type II ONB on a Pentium III 600 PC running Windows 2000 Professional. The programs were written in C, and the timing results were computed by averaging the timing for 100,000 multiplications of random field elements. The rest of this section gives the performance data. In particular, our methods are compared with Rosing's method in terms of timings and memory requirements.

In FIPS 186-2 [16], NIST recommenced 10 finite fields: 5 prime fields and 5 binary fields. The lengths of the fields were chosen so that the corresponding elliptic curve cryptographic (ECC) systems would have comparable security to symmetric ciphers of key lengths 80, 112, 128, 192, 256. Since ONB does not exist for every field length m, we choose field lengths that are closest to the NIST recommenced field lengths. Table 1 lists the specific field lengths.

Table 2 shows the timings of type I ONB multiplications for the dimensions in table 1. Compared with Rosing's method, our general method (Algorithm 3) reduces the execution time for type I ONB multiplication by about 70%, while our enhanced method (Algorithm 4) further reduces the time by about 5%. As a result, the execution time of type I ONB multiplication is reduced by about 75%. Table 3 shows the timings of type II ONB multiplications for the dimensions listed in table 1. Though Algorithm 4 cannot be applied to type II ONB,

Table 1. NIST recommenced lengths of binary finite field for ECC.

Symmetric cipher key length	Algorithms	Dimension m of $GF(2^m)$	Type I ONB	Type II ONB
80	Skipjack	163	162	158
112	triple-DES	233	226	233
128	AES-128	283	292	281
192	AES-192	409	418	410
256	AES-256	571	562	575

Table 2. Timings for multiplication with Type I ONB (μs).

Dimension m	Rosing	Algorithm 3	Time Reduced	Algorithm 4	Time Reduced
162	55.48	17.5	68.46%	14.62	73.65%
226	92.74	28.05	69.75%	23.53	74.63%
292	137.39	41.55	69.76%	34.35	75.00%
418	257.57	76.6	70.26%	62.19	75.86%
562	426.21	125.2	70.62%	98.64	76.86%

Table 3. Timings for multiplication with Type II ONB (μs).

Dimension m	Rosing	Algorithm 3	Time Reduced
158	41.26	14.12	66.78%
233	97.44	28.64	70.61%
281	124.68	36.75	70.52%
410	240.05	70.1	70.80%
575	433.42	127.59	70.56%

Algorithm 3 still reduces the execution time by about 70% compared with Rosing's method. It is not difficult to conclude that our methods significantly reduce the time required for multiplication. Figure 1 also shows the overall timings for all three methods, where the dimension m ranges from 150 to 600.

Our methods not only save the execution time of ONB multiplications, but also reduce the memory requirements compared with Rosing's method. To save the precomputed rotations of one operand, Rosing's method requires a temporary array having m entries, each of which keeps one rotation of the operand. Thus, Rosing's method requires $m^2/8$ bytes. In contrast, our general method (Algorithm 3) needs $2m \cdot w/8$ bytes for each operand, and therefore totally requires $m \cdot w/2$ bytes. Our enhanced method for type I ONB (Algorithm 4) needs additional $m \cdot w/16$ bytes, and thus requires $9m \cdot w/16$ bytes in total. As shown in table 4, Algorithm 3 reduces the memory requirement up to 77%, and Algorithm 4 reduces the memory requirement up to 74% for the dimensions in table 1.

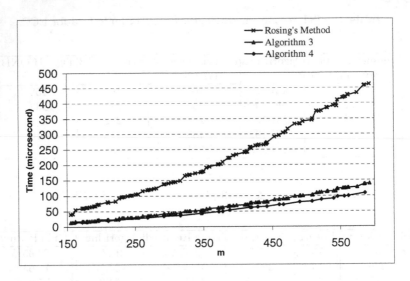

Fig. 1. Timings for all three methods with m ranging from 150 to 600.

Table 4. Memory requirements for precomputation: number of precomputed bytes ($w = 32$).

Dimension m	Rosing's Method ($m^2/8$)	Algorithm 3 ($w \cdot m/2$)	Memory Reduced	Algorithm 4 for Type I ONB ($9w \cdot m/16$)	Memory Reduced
158	3.05K	2.47K	18.99%	-	-
162	3.20K	2.53K	20.99%	2.85K	11.11%
226	6.23K	3.53K	43.36%	3.97K	36.28%
233	6.63K	3.64K	45.06%	-	-
281	9.64K	4.39K	54.45%	-	-
292	10.41K	4.56K	56.16%	5.13K	50.68%
410	20.52K	6.41K	68.78%	-	-
418	21.33K	6.53K	69.38%	7.35K	65.55%
562	38.56K	8.78K	77.22%	9.88K	74.38%
575	40.36K	8.98K	77.74%	-	-

6   Discussions

Normal basis vs. polynomial basis. For interoperability, it is desirable to support both bases in software, which can be done either by implementing both bases directly or by implementing one basis together with basis conversion algorithms.

Various software implementation techniques for polynomial basis have been proposed in recent years. The fastest method is described in [8], and a good survey is given in [3]. Some of the techniques can be very efficient when special irreducible polynomials are used. So the question is whether it is enough to just support polynomial basis in software together with basis conversion.

The general method for basis conversion involves storing a conversion matrix W and computing a matrix-vector multiplication for each conversion [4]. The size of W is $m^2/8$ bytes, which can be quite large for memory constraint devices. For example, when $m = 512$, the memory requirement is over $32K$ bytes (and $64K$ bytes if both W and W^{-1} are stored for efficient conversion in both directions). Methods for storage efficient basis conversion were proposed in [5,6]. Such methods only need to store $O(m)$ bytes and then each conversion takes about $O(m)$ field multiplication. The extra $O(m)$ multiplication can be a slowdown factor for some implementation. We note that all the basis conversion methods assume that both bases are known *before* the communication, and certain quantities related to both bases (e.g., W) are already precomputed and stored. While this is easily done for certain applications, it may not be the case for other applications. In general, computing these quantities on the fly can be time consuming, which adds more complexity to basis conversion. Therefore, due to the overhead of basis conversion, sometimes supporting both bases directly seems preferable than basis conversion.

Using the new techniques in ECC arithmetic. Our techniques for field multiplication can be combined with elliptic curve arithmetic to provide further speed up. Since some field elements are repeatedly used in ECC operations, we do not have to perform precomputation for these elements after the first time they are involved in a multiplication. For example, using projective coordinates, we need 15 finite field multiplication for point addition. Using our method, each multiplication needs to precompute one array for each of the two operands. So we totally need to precompute 30 arrays. By storing some of the precomputed results, the number of precomputed arrays can be reduced to 20. This can be used to further reduce the time for point additions. For example, the precomputation of each operand for $GF(2^{162})$ multiplication takes about 20% of the total multiplication time. Thus, we can save another 13% for each point addition reusing the precomputed results.

7   Conclusions

In this paper, we studied efficient software implementation for $GF(2^m)$ multiplication in normal basis. We presented new techniques for normal basis multiplication. In particular, our methods were optimized for both type I and type II ONB. Our techniques are more efficient in terms of both speed and memory compared with alternative approaches.

References

1. D. Ash, I. Blake, and S.A. Vanstone. *Low Complexity Normal Basis*. Discrete Applied Mathematics, Vol. 25, 1989.
2. E. De Win, A. Bosselaers, S. Vandenberghe, P. De Gersem, and J. Vandewalle. *A fast software implementation for arithmetic operations in $GF(2^n)$*. In Proc. Asiacrypt'96, 1996.
3. D. Hankerson, J.L. Hernandez, and A. Menesez. *Software Implementation of Elliptic Curve Cryptography over Binary Fields*. In Proc. CHES'2000, August 2000.
4. IEEE P1363-2000. *Standard Specifications for Public Key Cryptography*. August 2000.
5. B. Kaliski and M. Liskov. *Efficient Finite Field Basis Conversion Involving a Dual Basis*. In Proc. CHES'99, August 1999.
6. B. Kaliski and Y.L. Yin. *Storage Efficient Finite Field Basis Conversion*. In Proc. SAC'98, August 1998.
7. R.J. Lambert and A. Vadekar. *Method and apparatus for finite field multiplication*. US Patent 6,049,815, April 2000.
8. J. Lopez and R. Dahab. *High-Speed software multiplication in $F(2^m)$*. Technical report, IC-00-09, May 2000. Available at http://www.dcc.unicamp.br/ic-main/publications-e.html.
9. J. L. Massey and J. K. Omura. *Computational method and apparatus for finite field arithmetic*. U.S. Patent 4,587,627, May 1986.
10. R.C. Mullin. *Multiple Bit Multiplier*. U.S. Patent 5,787,028, July 1998.
11. R.C. Mullin, I.M. Onyszchuk, and S.A. Vanstone. *Computational Method and Apparatus for Finite Field Multiplication*. U.S. Patent 4,745,568, May 1988.
12. R.C. Mullin, I.M. Onyszchuk, S.A. Vanstone, and R. Wilson *Optimal Normal Basis in $GF(p^m)$*. Discrete Applied Mathematics, Vol. 22, 1988/1989.
13. P. Ning and Y. L. Yin. *Efficient Software Implementation for Finite Field Multiplication in Normal Basis*. Pending US Patent Application. Provisional patent application filed in December 1997.
14. M. Rosing. *Implementing Elliptic Curve Cryptography*. Manning Publications Co., 1999.
15. A. Reyhani-Masoleh, M. A. Hasan. *Fast Normal Basis Multiplication Using General Purpose Processors*. To appear in the 8th Workshop on Selected Areas in Cryptography (SAC 2001). August 2001.
16. National Institute of Standards and Technology, *Digital Signature Standard*, FIPS Publication 186-2, February 2000.

Playing Lottery on the Internet

Jianying Zhou[1] and Chunfu Tan[2]

[1] Oracle Corporation
500 Oracle Parkway, Redwood Shores, CA 94065
United States
Jianying.Zhou@oracle.com

[2] Kent Ridge Digital Labs
21 Heng Mui Keng Terrace
Singapore 119613
cftan@krdl.org.sg

Abstract. The Internet is used by more and more people for personal and business related communication. This paper presents an integrated scheme for playing lottery on the Internet, which includes purchase of tickets, generation of winning number, and claiming of prize. Fairness between the customer and the service provider is maintained at the stages of purchasing tickets and claiming prize. The customer's identity is kept anonymous to the service provider. The sum of sold tickets and the sum of winning tickets are publicly verifiable. The winning number is generated randomly but verifiably. These features will increase the customer's trust in the Internet lottery service.

1 Introduction

Lottery is one of the most widespread forms of gambling in the world. A typical lottery service operates in the following way.

1. The customer selects the type of lottery service and his lucky number.
2. The customer gets the quotation from the service provider.
3. The customer and the service provider exchange the lottery ticket and the payment physically.
4. The service provider generates and publishes the winning number.
5. The winning customer claims the prize. The service provider will verify the winning ticket before the prize is awarded.

The traditional lottery service has some limitations. Customers need to go to an outlet to buy lottery tickets. They may have to join a long queue in front of the outlet. Obviously, this is less efficient for customers. If customers do not have time to buy lottery tickets personally, they may trouble their friends or relatives to buy tickets for them. Then the customers' anonymity cannot be well protected. These limitations could be removed if customers can play lottery over the Internet.

S. Qing, T. Okamoto, and J. Zhou (Eds.): ICICS 2001, LNCS 2229, pp. 189–201, 2001.
© Springer-Verlag Berlin Heidelberg 2001

In this paper, we present a secure and integrated Internet lottery scheme, which includes purchase of tickets, generation of winning number, and claiming of prize. We identify the desired security requirements for playing lottery on the Internet in Section 2, and review the related work in Section 3. Then, we give an overview of our scheme in Section 4, and propose detailed protocols in Section 5. We conclude the paper in Section 6. The following basic notation is used throughout the paper.

- X, Y: concatenation of two messages X and Y.
- $H(X)$: a one-way hash function of message X.
- $eK(X)$ and $dK(X)$: encryption and decryption of message X with key K.
- $sS_A(X)$: party A's digital signature on message X with key S_A.
- S_A and V_A: party A's private signature key and public verification key.
- P_A and P_A^-: party A's public encryption key and private decryption key.
- $A \rightarrow B : X$: party A sends message X to party B.

2   Security Requirements

When playing lottery on the Internet, the following security requirements should be taken into consideration.

R1. *Fairness on purchase of tickets and claiming of prize*

In the traditional lottery service, when a customer buys a lottery ticket from the service provider, they exchange the money and the ticket face to face, thus fairness is maintained. This is also true when a winner claims the prize from the service provider. In the Internet lottery service, however, the customer and the service provider are distributed over the Internet. After one party receives the other party's item, it may refuse to send its item to the other party, which leaves the other party in an unfair situation. Therefore, a security mechanism is needed to achieve fairness such that either each party gets the other party's item, or no party gets the other party's item at the end of a transaction. Several fair exchange mechanisms are available to satisfy the requirement [1,2,3].

R2. *Anonymity of lottery players*

In the traditional lottery service, when the customer buys a lottery ticket at an outlet, he only needs to pay cash for the ticket. No one knows who the buyer is. If the customer is a winner, he can get the prize by showing the winning ticket. The customer's identity is kept anonymous at the stages of purchasing tickets and claiming prize, thus protecting jackpot winners against blackmail. This requirement is also desirable in the Internet lottery service. An anonymous electronic fund transfer system is needed such that purchase of tickets and claiming of prize will not disclose the customer's identity. The requirement of anonymity has been widely discussed in electronic payment systems [4,5,6,13].

R3. *Verifiable sum of sold and winning tickets*

In the traditional lottery service, the sum of sold tickets is counted by the service provider. As the amount of winning prize is usually related to the sum of sold tickets, the service provider might publish a sum smaller than the actual sum of sold tickets. In addition, the amount of winning prize is usually related to the sum of winning tickets, the service provider might fake winning tickets thus the actual winners will get less of a prize. In the Internet lottery service, it is possible to make the sum of sold tickets and the sum of winning tickets publicly verifiable by the use of cryptographic techniques.

R4. *Random and verifiable generation of winning number*

The winning number should be selected randomly and no ticket is predictably more likely to win than any other tickets. In the traditional lottery service, a random process may be executed or monitored by an outside auditor for the generation of winning number. Unfortunately, as the random process is not repeatable, customers have to trust both the process and the auditing organisation. In the Internet lottery service, it is possible to generate the winning number randomly but publicly verifiable by the use of cryptographic techniques.

3   Previous Work

Some research papers on the lottery service have been published in recent years. Rivest proposed a micropayment scheme based on the use of "electronic lottery tickets" in [10]. In such a scheme, the bank provides an electronic credential to the customer with the micropayment account in good standing. With the credential, the customer can generate lottery tickets and use them to pay for some services provided by the vender. The vender can verify whether a lottery ticket is a winning ticket and claim payment via the bank. The bank pays off winning tickets issued by the customer from the customer's account. This scheme greatly reduces the bank's processing costs since the bank handles only winning tickets instead of each micropayment. Obviously, this scheme is different from the real lottery services, where the roles of buyer and seller are turned around.

Goldschlag and Stubblebine proposed a publicly verifiable lottery scheme based on a delaying function [8]. Each lottery ticket has an equal chance of being selected as a winning ticket. Anyone can calculate the winning number based on the parameters of purchased tickets, and the winning number calculation is repeatable. Since the calculation uses a delaying function, nobody can get the result before the lottery closes.

Syverson presented two versions of a lottery scheme based on the application of the weak protection of secrets [12]. The winning number is determined by the ticket numbers purchased, but no one can control the outcome or determine what it is until after the lottery closes. This is because the outcome is kept secret in a way that is breakable after a predictable amount of time and/or computation.

Sako presented the design and implementation of a lottery server on WWW [11]. The server allows users to define and start a lottery session, participate in that session, and verify its outcome. When a lottery session is initiated, each player submits a random number to the server. The server generates the outcome using a one-way hash function with the concatenation of each player's random number as the input. A rule could be defined to select the winner based on the random and verifiable outcome.

All of these schemes are mainly focused on the mechanisms of winning number generation. There are no integrated mechanisms on fair payment for lottery tickets and claiming of prize. Moreover, the customer's anonymity is not considered either.

4   Overview of a New Scheme

The parties involved in our Internet lottery scheme are the lottery service provider S, the customer C, the bank B, and an *off-line* trusted third party *TTP*. There are several publicly announced dates which are announced well in advance of the running of the lottery service.

- *open of ticket sale*: a time after which customers can purchase lottery tickets.
- *close of ticket sale*: a time after which no new tickets can be purchased.
- *close of winning number generation*: a deadline for customers to be involved in the generation of winning number.

We assume that the lottery is *simple parimutuel*, i.e. the amount of winning prize is solely from the sold tickets, and there is no roll-over of winning prize [12]. We also assume that both the lottery service provider and the customer have an account at their bank.

Purchase of Tickets. A run of Internet lottery starts at the time of *open of ticket sale*. The customer first selects his lucky number N. He also generates two random numbers R_1 and R_2, which will be used in the generation of winning number and claiming of prize (if he is a winner) respectively. Then, the customer submits $(N, H(R_1), H(R_2))$ to the service provider, and gets the quotation from the service provider. After this, the customer requests a cash order from the bank, and exchanges the cash order for the lottery ticket with the service provider. When the service provider deposits the cash order into the bank, the service provider's account will be credited and the customer's account will be debited. The lottery ticket issued by the service provider contains a transaction number, a serial number, the ticket value, and $(N, H(R_1), H(R_2))$.

By the use of a new cryptographic primitive, called the *Certificate of Encrypted Message Being a Signature* (*CEMBS*) [3], the customer and the service provider can fairly exchange the cash order and the lottery ticket. An off-line *TTP* will be involved only if there is something wrong in the exchange. To preserve the customer's anonymity, the customer's identity in the cash order is not disclosed to the service provider, and the ownership of a lottery ticket is not identified by the customer's identity. To make the sum of sold and winning tickets publicly verifiable, the service provider needs to maintain a one-way hash chain. Each sold ticket should be linked into the hash chain. The initial output and the final output of the hash chain, as well as all of the sold tickets should be published at the time of *close of ticket sale*.

Generation of Winning Number. After the ticket-selling session is closed, each customer could be involved in the generation of winning number by submitting his random number R_1 to the service provider. If there is a *denial of service* attack, customers can submit their R_1 to an off-line *TTP*, which are then forwarded to the service provider. The service provider can verify R_1 by checking whether there is a ticket containing $H(R_1)$. Only valid submissions are used in the generation of winning number. The outcome remains random even if most of customers do not submit R_1 for the generation of winning number.

The service provider needs to publish all valid submissions received before the deadline of *close of winning number generation*, thus the process of winning number generation is publicly verifiable, and nobody can predict the outcome before the deadline. As all of the sold tickets are chained and the chain is publicly verifiable, the sum of winning tickets is also publicly verifiable. The service provider cannot forge winning tickets without being detected.

Claiming of Prize. After the winning number is generated, the winning customer claims his prize. The customer first submits his winning ticket to the service provider for verification. If the service provider does not hold R_2 corresponding to $H(R_2)$ in the winning ticket, it means the prize has not been claimed. Then, the service provider requests a cash order from the bank, and exchanges the cash order for R_2 with the customer. When the customer deposits the cash order into the bank, the customer's account will be credited and the service provider's account will be debited.

We use the same techniques as in the ticket-selling session to keep the customer's identity anonymous to the service provider and make the process of prize claim fair to both parties.

Definition of CEMBS. The *CEMBS* technique can be used to prove that an encrypted message is a certain party's signature on a public file without revealing the signature.

Suppose $s = sS_A(m)$ is party A's digital signature on m, and $c = eP_{TTP}(s)$ is the cipher text of s encrypted with the trusted third party's public encryption key. A can generate a *CEMBS*, denoted as *Cert*, to prove that c is indeed the encryption of the signature s without disclosing s. There exists a public verification algorithm **Veri** to check whether $(m, c, Cert)$ is valid.

$$\mathbf{Veri}(m, c, Cert, V_A, P_{TTP}) = yes \text{ or } no$$

If *yes*, the verifier will be convinced that $dP_{TTP}^-(c) = sS_A(m)$.

A *CEMBS* could be constructed on the ElGamal public key encryption scheme [7] and the Guillou-Quisquater signature scheme [9].

5   An Internet Lottery Scheme

The following notation is used in the description of our Internet lottery scheme.

- N: the lucky number selected by C.
- R_1, R_2: the random numbers generated by C.
- \$_C, \$_S: the amount of payment for purchase of ticket and for claiming of prize, respectively.
- *TID*: the transaction ID generated by S.
- *ticket_no*: the serial number of a lottery ticket generated by S.
- $ticket = sS_S(TID, ticket\_no, \$\_C, N, H(R_1), H(R_2))$: a lottery ticket issued by S.
- $salt_1, salt_2$: the random salts generated by C.
- *Account_C, Account_S*: the bank account numbers of C and S, respectively.
- $form\_C = eP_B(Account\_C, salt_1), Account\_S, \$\_C, TID, N, H(R_1), H(R_2)$: the content of an electronic cash order for purchase of ticket.
- $form\_S = Account\_S, eP_B(Account\_C, salt_2), \$\_S, ticket$: the content of an electronic cash order for claiming of prize.
- $cash\_C = sS_B(form\_C)$: an electronic cash order issued to C by B.
- $cash\_S = sS_B(form\_S)$: an electronic cash order issued to S by B.
- $cipher\_cash\_C = eP_{TTP}(cash\_C)$: the cipher text of $cash\_C$ encrypted with the *TTP*'s public encryption key.
- $cipher\_cash\_S = eP_{TTP}(cash\_S)$: the cipher text of $cash\_S$ encrypted with the *TTP*'s public encryption key.
- *Cert_C*: a *CEMBS* generated by C which can be used to verify whether $cipher\_cash\_C$ is the cipher text of B's signature on $form\_C$, i.e.

$$\mathbf{Veri}(form\_C, cipher\_cash\_C, Cert\_C, V_B, P_{TTP}) = yes \text{ or } no$$

- *Cert_S*: a *CEMBS* generated by S which can be used to verify whether $cipher\_cash\_S$ is the cipher text of B's signature on $form\_S$, i.e.

$$\mathbf{Veri}(form\_S, cipher\_cash\_S, Cert\_S, V_B, P_{TTP}) = yes \text{ or } no$$

5.1   Protocol 1: Purchase of Tickets

The protocol for purchase of ticket is as follows.

$$1.\ C \to S : N,\ H(R_1),\ H(R_2)$$
$$2.\ S \to C : TID,\ \$\_C,\ Account\_S$$
$$3.\ C \to B : form\_C,\ sS_C(form\_C)$$
$$4.\ B \to C : eP_C(cash\_C)$$
$$5.\ C \to S : TID,\ eP_B(Account\_C, salt_1),\ cipher\_cash\_C,\ Cert\_C$$
$$6.\ S \to C : TID,\ ticket\_no,\ ticket$$
$$7.\ C \to S : TID,\ cash\_C$$
$$8.\ S \to B : form\_C,\ cash\_C$$

At Step 1, the customer selects his lucky number N, generates two random numbers (R_1, R_2) and calculates their hash values. The customer sends $(N, H(R_1), H(R_2))$ to the service provider, and keeps (R_1, R_2) confidential. Upon receiving the customer's purchase request, the service provider offers the quotation $\$\_C$ at Step 2. TID is used to identify the transaction, and $Account\_S$ is the service provider's bank account number for receiving the customer's payment.

Upon receiving the quotation, the customer requests a cash order from the bank at Step 3. After authenticating the request with the customer's signature and checking the balance of the customer's account, the bank issues the cash order $cash\_C$ at Step 4. The cash order specifies the debiting account ($Account\_C$), the crediting account ($Account\_S$), the amount of payment ($\$\_C$), and the purpose of payment ($TID, N, H(R_1), H(R_2)$). The bank may freeze the amount of payment in the customer's account until $cash\_C$ expires or the recipient claims the payment with $cash\_C$. To preserve the customer's anonymity, $Account\_C$ is encrypted with the bank's public encryption key [1]. To prevent $cash\_C$ from being intercepted by the service provider before issuing the ticket, it is encrypted with the customer's public encryption key in transmission at Step 4.

After receiving the cash order from the bank, the customer generates the cipher cash order ($cipher\_cash\_C$) and a $CEMBS$ certificate ($Cert\_C$), and sends them to the service provider at Step 5. The service provider can verify whether $cipher\_cash\_C$ is indeed the bank's signature on $form\_C$, and whether the crediting account number and the amount of payment are correct. If so, it issues the lottery ticket to the customer at Step 6 [2]. Upon receiving $ticket$, the customer checks $(N, H(R_1), H(R_2))$ to see whether the ticket is what he intends to buy. If so, the customer sends the cash order ($cash\_C$) to the service provider at Step 7. The service provider can get the payment by depositing $cash\_C$ into the bank at Step 8. The bank gets the debiting account number by decrypting $eP_B(Account\_C, salt_1)$, and transfers $\$\_C$ from $Account\_C$ to $Account\_S$.

---

[1] To make the customer's repeat transactions unlinkable by the service provider, a random salt is attached to $Account\_C$ before encryption.

[2] If the service provider aborts after Step 5, the transaction status may not be decided until the time of *close of ticket sale*.

Occasionally, the customer may dislike the lottery ticket he just bought, and wants to abort the transaction by not sending *cash_C* to the service provider at Step 7. Obviously, this is unfair to the service provider where it has issued the ticket to the customer without receiving the payment. With the recovery sub-protocol below, the service provider could force the transaction by sending the lottery ticket and the encrypted cash order to the *TTP* in exchange of the decrypted cash order.

$$7.1 \ S \rightarrow TTP : form\_C, \ cipher\_cash\_C, \ ticket\_no, \ ticket$$
$$7.2 \ TTP \rightarrow S : TID, \ cash\_C$$
$$7.3 \ TTP \rightarrow C : TID, \ ticket\_no, \ ticket$$

The service provider sends out the recovery request at Step 7.1. The *TTP* can get *cash_C* by decrypting *cipher_cash_C*. Then the *TTP* checks whether *cash_C* is the payment for *ticket* by comparing $(\$\_C, N, H(R_1), H(R_2))$ in *cash_C* and *ticket*. The *TTP* also checks whether the time of *close of ticket sale* has not passed yet. If so, the *TTP* sends *cash_C* to the service provider at Step 7.2, and *ticket* to the customer at Step 7.3. If the recovery request arrives after the time of *close of ticket sale* but before the deadline of *close of winning number generation*, the *TTP* only issues a signed revocation notice to both parties, with which the service provider could exclude the ticket as a valid one.

The lottery ticket issued by the service provider need not be kept confidential. Nobody can claim the prize from the service provider even if holding a winning ticket unless R_2 is presented, which is only known to the customer who bought the ticket.

Once a ticket is sold to the customer, the service provider should link the ticket to a one-way hash chain. Suppose the sum of lottery tickets sold by the time of *close of ticket sale* is j. The hash chain could be created as follows.

$$chain_1 = H(ticket_1)$$
$$chain_2 = H(chain_1, ticket_2)$$
$$\vdots$$
$$chain_j = H(chain_{j-1}, ticket_j)$$

The service provider needs to publish $chain_1$ and $chain_j$, as well as $ticket_i$ $(i = 1, 2, \cdots, j)$ at the time of *close of ticket sale*. Then, each customer can check whether his ticket is included in the hash chain, and the total number of sold tickets is publicly verifiable. *ticket_no* could be used to quickly identify the location of a ticket in the hash chain [3].

---

[3] To maintain the scalability, the service provider could create multiple hash chains and allow customers to select which chain their tickets are linked to. The name of the selected hash chain will be added into *ticket* and used with *ticket_no* to identify the ticket location.

The service provider might issue "free" lottery tickets to itself. However, this does not bring profit to the service provider in the *simple parimutuel* lottery. As any valid ticket has to be linked into the hash chain and the total number of sold tickets is publicly verifiable, these "free" tickets will increase the corresponding amount of winning prize. As we will see in Section 5.2 that the generation of winning number is random and out of the service provider's control, these "free" tickets have no higher chance than other tickets to be winning tickets. If they are not selected as winning tickets, the service provider has to pay for them to compensate the actual amount of winning prize.

5.2   Protocol 2: Generation of Winning Number

After the ticket-selling session is closed, each customer could be involved in the generation of winning number by submitting his random number R_1 to the service provider. A signed receipt might be requested by the customer. The protocol for generation of winning number is as follows.

$$1.\ C \rightarrow S : ticket\_no,\ R_1$$
$$2.\ S \rightarrow C : sS_S(ticket\_no, R_1)$$

Of course, if a customer does not want to be involved in the generation of winning number, he can simply give up the right. To make the outcome unpredictable to anybody, we assume there are at least two non-colluding customers who submitted their R_1 to the service provider. The customer's optional involvement improves the scalability compared with the proposal in [11] where the winning number cannot be generated as long as one of the customers does not co-operate.

If there is a denial of service attack when a customer submits his R_1 to the service provider for the generation of winning number, he may invoke the service from an off-line TTP [4].

$$1.\ C \rightarrow TTP : ticket\_no,\ R_1$$
$$2.\ TTP \rightarrow C : sS_{TTP}(ticket\_no, R_1)$$

The TTP passes these submissions received by the deadline of *close of winning number generation* to the service provider. Thus, the service provider cannot influence the outcome by deliberately rejecting some submissions.

Suppose $R_{11}, R_{12}, \cdots, R_{1k}$ are the random numbers received by the deadline of *close of winning number generation*. Without knowing the customer's identity, the service provider can verify R_{1i} $(i = 1, 2, \cdots, k)$ by checking whether there is a ticket containing $H(R_{1i})$. Only valid submissions are used in the generation

---

[4] It mainly protects against the denial of service attack from a dishonest service provider that intends to influence the outcome of winning number generation. Other measures are needed to protect against the distributed denial of service attacks.

of winning number. The service provider needs to publish these submissions. Thus, customers who made valid submissions can check whether their random numbers are used in the generation of winning number. If not, customers can use the signed receipts to prove the service provider's misbehaviour.

Suppose all of the above submissions are valid. The winning number could be generated by the use of a one-way hash function with R_{1i} $(i = 1, 2, \cdots, k)$ as its input. A pre-defined rule could be used to map the winning number to the winning tickets.

$$\text{winning number} = H(R_{11}, R_{12}, \cdots, R_{1k})$$

The number of submissions and each submission received from customers are random, thus nobody (not even the service provider) can predict the outcome before the deadline of *close of winning number generation*. Further, with a one-way hash function, it is computationally infeasible to find the pre-image of a designated winning number.

As the random numbers used in the generation of winning number are published, the process of winning number generation is publicly verifiable. In addition, as the initial output and the final output of the chained tickets have also been published, each winning ticket is publicly verifiable as well. It is computationally hard for the service provider to forge a winning ticket without being detected.

In practice, random numbers submitted to the service provider may not be published instantaneously and the clock may not be well synchronized among all participants. Then, a dishonest service provider may try to fiddle the outcome of winning number generation by adding the favorite random numbers of its valid tickets soon after the deadline of *close of winning number generation*. To prevent such kind of possible cheating, a delaying function [8] could be used in the generation of winning number thus the service provider cannot get the result of winning number until actually publishing all valid random numbers received by the deadline.

5.3   Protocol 3: Claiming of Prize

The protocol for claiming of prize is as follows.

1. $C \rightarrow S$: TID, $ticket\_no$, $\$\_C$, N, $H(R_1)$, $H(R_2)$, $ticket$,
   $eP_B(Account\_C, salt_2)$
2. $S \rightarrow B$: $form\_S$, $sS_S(form\_S)$
3. $B \rightarrow S$: $eP_S(cash\_S)$
4. $S \rightarrow C$: TID, $Account\_S$, $cipher\_cash\_S$, $Cert\_S$
5. $C \rightarrow S$: TID, R_2
6. $S \rightarrow C$: TID, $cash\_S$
7. $C \rightarrow B$: $form\_S$, $cash\_S$

At Step 1, the customer sends the winning ticket to the service provider. The customer's bank account number ($Account\_C$) is also provided for receiving the prize. To keep the customer's identity anonymous, $Account\_C$, to which a random salt is attached, is encrypted with the bank's public encryption key.

Upon receiving the winning ticket from the customer, the service provider checks whether it is indeed a winning ticket by verifying its lucky number N. The service provider further checks whether the prize has been claimed by searching R_2 corresponding to its $H(R_2)$. If N is the winning number and R_2 is not found, the service provider requests a cash order from the bank at Step 2.

After authenticating the request with the service provider's signature and checking the balance of the service provider's account, the bank issues the cash order $cash\_S$ at Step 3. The bank may freeze the amount of payment in the service provider's account until $cash\_S$ expires or the recipient claims the payment with $cash\_S$. To prevent $cash\_S$ from being intercepted by the customer before releasing R_2, it is encrypted with the service provider's public encryption key in transmission at Step 3.

After receiving the cash order from the bank, the service provider generates the cipher cash order ($cipher\_cash\_S$) and a $CEMBS$ certificate ($Cert\_S$), and sends them to the customer at Step 4. The customer can verify whether $cipher\_cash\_S$ is indeed the bank's signature on $form\_S$, and whether the crediting account number and the amount of payment are correct [5]. If so, the customer releases R_2 to the service provider at Step 5. Upon receiving R_2, the service provider checks whether R_2 is the random number matching $H(R_2)$ in the winning ticket. If so, the service provider sends the cash order ($cash\_S$) to the customer at Step 6. The customer can get the payment by depositing $cash\_S$ into the bank at Step 7.

In the above prize claim protocol, a dishonest service provider might use its advantage in the transaction, i.e. holding R_2 at Step 5, to refuse the payment at Step 6 by falsely claiming the prize related to the winning ticket has already been paid. Obviously, this is unfair to the customer where he has released R_2 of his winning ticket to the service provider without receiving the payment. With the recovery sub-protocol below, the customer could get the payment by sending the winning ticket plus R_2 as well as the encrypted cash order to the TTP in exchange of the decrypted cash order.

$$6.1 \ C \rightarrow TTP : form\_S, \ cipher\_cash\_S,$$
$$TID, \ ticket\_no, \ \$\_C, \ N, \ H(R_1), \ H(R_2), \ R_2$$
$$6.2 \ TTP \rightarrow C : TID, \ cash\_S$$
$$6.3 \ TTP \rightarrow S : TID, \ R_2$$

---

[5] Although $Account\_C$ is in cipher text, the customer can verify $Account\_C$ which is encrypted by himself with the bank's public encryption key at Step 1.

The customer sends out the recovery request at Step 6.1 [6]. The TTP can get $cash\_S$ by decrypting $cipher\_cash\_S$. Then the TTP checks whether R_2 matches $H(R_2)$ in $ticket$ which is specified in $cash\_S$ as the winning ticket for receiving the prize. If so, the TTP sends $cash\_S$ to the customer at Step 6.2, and R_2 to the service provider at Step 6.3. Thus, the exchange remains fair.

6   Conclusion

The traditional lottery game may exclude busy people to play because of its inefficient ticket-selling channel. The Internet lottery game can remove the limitation and even provide some new features.

We proposed an integrated Internet lottery scheme covering purchase of tickets, generation of winning number, and claiming of prize. It has the following features.

- The customer and the service provider need not trust each other.
- Both the customer and the service provider are guaranteed not to be cheated when purchasing tickets and claiming prize.
- The customer's identity is not disclosed to the service provider throughout the service.
- The total number of sold tickets and the total number of winning tickets are publicly verifiable. The service provider cannot gain profit by hiding lottery revenue or faking winning tickets.
- The winning number is generated randomly. Nobody, not even the service provider, can predict the outcome.
- Each customer has the freedom to be involved or not in the winning number generation without affecting the randomness of the outcome.
- The process of winning number generation is publicly verifiable.

These features make the Internet lottery service attractive to customers.

Acknowledgements. We thank the anonymous referees for valuable comments. The first author's work was carried out at Kent Ridge Digital Labs. The second author's work was sponsored under the postgraduate scholarship of National University of Singapore.

References

1. N. Asokan, V. Shoup and M. Waidner. *Optimistic fair exchange of digital signatures.* Lecture Notes in Computer Science 1403, Advances in Cryptology: Proceedings of Eurocrypt'98, pages 591–606, Helsinki, Finland, June 1998.
2. G. Ateniese. *Efficient verifiable encryption (and fair exchange) of digital signatures.* Proceedings of 6th ACM Conference on Computer and Communications Security, pages 138–146, Singapore, November 1999.

---

[6] The winning ticket is included in $form\_S$.

3. F. Bao, R. H. Deng and W. Mao. *Efficient and practical fair exchange protocols with off-line TTP.* Proceedings of 1998 IEEE Symposium on Security and Privacy, pages 77–85, Oakland, California, May 1998.
4. M. Bellare, J. Garay, R. Hauser, A. Herzberg, H. Krawczyk, M. Steiner, G. Tsudik, E. Van Herreweghen and M. Waidner. *Design, implementation and deployment of the iKP secure electronic payment system.* IEEE Journal on Selected Areas in Communications, 18(4):611–627, April 2000.
5. J. Camenisch, U. Maurer and M. Stadler. *Digital payment systems with passive anonymity-revoking trustees.* Lecture Notes in Computer Science 1146, Computer Security: Proceedings of 1996 European Symposium on Research in Computer Security, pages 33–43, Rome, September 1996.
6. G. Davida, Y. Frankel, Y. Tsiounis and M. Yung. *Anonymity control in e-cash systems.* Lecture Notes in Computer Science 1318, Proceedings of 1997 Financial Cryptography, pages 1–16, Anguilla BWI, February 1997.
7. T. ElGamal. *A public-key cryptosystem and a signature scheme based on discrete logarithms.* IEEE Transactions on Information Theory, IT-31(4):469–472, July 1985.
8. D. M. Goldschlag and S. G. Stubblebine. *Publicly verifiable lotteries: Applications of delaying functions.* Lecture Notes in Computer Science 1465, Proceedings of 1998 Financial Cryptography, Anguilla BWI, February 1998.
9. L. C. Guillou and J. J. Quisquater. *A paradoxical identity-based signature scheme resulting from zero-knowledge.* Lecture Notes in Computer Science 403, Advances in Cryptology: Proceedings of Crypto'88, pages 216–231, Santa Barbara, California, August 1988.
10. R. Rivest. *Electronic lottery tickets as micropayments.* Lecture Notes in Computer Science 1318, Proceedings of 1997 Financial Cryptography, pages 307–314, Anguilla BWI, February 1997.
11. K. Sako. *Implementation of a digital lottery server on WWW.* Lecture Notes in Computer Science 1740, Proceedings of CQRE'99, pages 101-108, Dusseldorf, Germany, December 1999.
12. P. Syverson. *Weakly secret bit commitment: Applications to lotteries and fair exchange.* Proceedings of 11th IEEE Computer Security Foundations Workshop, Rockport, Massachusetts, June 1998.
13. E. Van Herreweghen. *Secure anonymous signature-based transactions.* Lecture Notes in Computer Science 1895, Computer Security: Proceedings of 2000 European Symposium on Research in Computer Security, pages 55–71, Toulouse, France, October 2000.

Privacy Protection for Transactions of Digital Goods

Feng Bao and Robert Deng

Kent Ridge Digital Labs
21 Heng Mui Keng Terrace, Singapore 119613
{baofeng, deng}@krdl.org.sg

Abstract. In this paper we study the problem of how to protect users' privacy in web transactions of digital goods. In particular, we introduce a system which allows a user to disclose his/her identity information (such as user account or credit card number) to a web site in exchange for a digital item, but privents the web site from learning which specific item the user intends to obtain. The problem concerned here is orthogonal to the problem of anonymous transactions [RSG98, RR98] but commensurate with the general problem of PIR (private information retrieval) [CGK95, CG97]. Most of the existing results in PIR, however, are theoretical in nature and can not be applied in practice due to their large communication and computational overheads. In the present paper, we introduce two practical solutions that satisfy the above two requirements and analyze their security and performance.

1. Introduction

Privacy has been a sensitive issue long before the advent of the Internet. However, the Internet creates many new threats to personal privacy and raises some unique privacy concerns. Such concerns have been magnified in recent years due to the widespread use of world-wide web and the accompanying e-commerce activities. Information sent over the Internet may pass through dozens of different computer systems on the way to its destination. Each of these systems may be capable of monitoring, capturing, and storing online communications. When a user surfs the web, many web sites deposit user's browsing patterns or transaction generated data on the user's hard drive which can be re-used by the web sites when the user returns. Most web browsers invisibly provide web sites with information about user's computer (such as IP address, domain name, screen resolution, available plug-ins) as well as with information about the locations of other web sites a user has visited. The highly connected nature of the Internet makes it easy to automatically collect users' information from many different sources and compile a dossier about an individual – his or her likes and dislikes, shopping patterns, where about and so on. Such data is a potential valuable source of revenue for many businesses -- it is useful to direct marketers as a basis for driving targeted lists of users with similar likes; it can also be the source of abuses that may cause embarrassment for users who have accessed sensitive or controversial materials online.

Not only net users are concerned about privacy when surf the web, organizations are starting to take customers' on-line privacy seriously to build users' confidence on their business. Over the past year, a number of web sites have been caught in high-

S. Qing, T. Okamoto, and J. Zhou (Eds.): ICICS 2001, LNCS 2229, pp. 202-213, 2001.
© Springer-Verlag Berlin Heidelberg 2001

profile blow-ups over how they collect and use user data. After online advertising company DoubleClick revealed its now-abandoned practice to cross reference data about users' offline purchasing behaviour with their online habits, the company's stock dived.

The present paper studies the technical aspect for online privacy protection. A number of systems and tools have been developed to allow web user anonymity while retrieving information on the web. One type of commercial available tools is anonymizer, such as *Anonymizer* from Anonymizer.com [Ano] and *Freedom* from Zero-Knowledge System Inc [ZKSI1]. Anonymizer is a service that submits http requests to web sites on behalf of its users. Because the request is submitted by the anonymizer agent rather than the user, the only IP address revealed to the web site is that of the agent. However, users of this service have to trust the anonymizer to keep their IP addresses and their web activities private since they are not anonymous to the anonymizer itself.

Onion Routing [RSG98] and *Crowds* [RR98] are two anonymity systems that do not require users to trust a single third party to maintain anonymity. *Onion Routing* is a general-purpose infrastructure for anonymous communication over a public network. It operates by dynamically building anonymous connections within a network of real-time Chaum *Mixes* [Cha81]. A *Mix* is a store-and-forward device that accepts a number of fixed-length messages from numerous sources, performs cryptographic transformations on the messages, and then forwards the messages to the next destination in a random order. A single *Mix* makes tracking of a particular message either by specific bit-pattern, size, or ordering with respect to other messages difficult. By routing through numerous *Mixes* in the network, determining who is talking to whom is even more difficult. *Crowds* is a system for protecting users' anonymity on the web. It is named for the notion of "blending into a crowd" and operates by grouping users into a large and geographically diverse group, i.e., crowd, that collectively issues http requests on behalf of its members. In *Crowds*, web servers are unable to trace the source of a request because it is equally likely to have originated from any member of the crowd, and even collaborating crowd members can not distinguish the originator of a request from a member who is merely forwarding the request on behalf of another.

The above anonymous systems are useful for web surfing in which users have no desire or not required to be identified. Therefore, they are mostly useful when users visit free web sites and download free digital goods. However, when users wish to make online purchases using their credit card numbers or membership accounts, they need to provide some identifying or authenticating information. In such situations the issue of privacy protection is not user anonymity, but how to hide users' shopping/surfing patterns as much as possible from web servers. This problem is in essence orthogonal to the anonymity communications problem. The former is concerned with hiding user's surfing activities from the server but the user is required to reveal his/her identification information to the server while the latter is concerned with hiding user's identity but all the user's surfing activities are under the prey eyes of the server.

In this paper we propose a system architecture and the corresponding protocols which protects users' privacy in web transactions of digital goods. It works in conjunction with anonymous systems such as *Anonymizer* [Ano], *Freedom* [ZKSI1],

Crowds and *Onion Routing*. But it serves a very different purpose. Specifically, we introduce a system which allows a user to disclose his/her identity information (such as user account or credit card number) to a web site in exchange for a digital item, but prohibits the web site from learning which specific item the user intends to obtain. Moreover, we require that the system be highly efficient in operations and do not impose unacceptable processing burden in online transactions.

The rest of the paper is organized as follows. In Section 2 we review private information retrieval (PIR) schemes in the literature [CGK95, CG97, KO97, GIKM98 and CMS99]. The original research objective of PIR is to allow users to retrieve information from a database while keeping their query private from the server. So far most of the existing results in PIR are theoretical in nature. We will discuss why they can not be applied in our system. In Section 3 we describe the principle and the architecture of our solution with an emphasis on practicality and feasibility of its implementation. In Section 4 we present our first protocol based on blinding RSA decryption along with its performance and security analysis. In Section 5 we show our second protocol based on commutative symmetric key ciphers. In Section 6 we conclude our paper by discussing some open issues related to privacy protection, such as auditing, royalty payment and compatibility with digital content protection systems.

2. Overview of PIR Schemes

The topic of retrieving information from a database without disclosing what the information is has been studied under the terminology of PIR (private information retrieval). The PIR problem was first formulated and studied in [CGK95], where the solutions assumed multiple databases and aimed at information-theoretical security. However, its assumption that multiple databases would not communicate with one another is considered not realistic in practical applications. Later in [CG97], [KO97], [GIKM98] and [CMS99], PIR schemes with single database were proposed. These solutions were based on computational complexity assumptions, such as the hardness of factoring $n = pq$. Unfortunately, the computational costs of these solutions are very large due to their bit-by-bit processing nature. They require $O(N)$ multiplications modulo a 1024-bit number for retrieval of just one information bit, where N is the total number of bits in the database.

Most PIR schemes based on computational complexity assumption aim at reducing communications cost. The scheme in [CMS99] can achieve a communications cost of poly(log$N$) while those in [CG97], [KO97] and [GIKM98] have communications cost of $O(N^\varepsilon)$ for any $\varepsilon < 1$. Mathematically, these schemes are very beautiful. But from implementation's viewpoint, they are completely impractical since they all have computation complexity at least of $O(N)$ to retrieve just 1 information bit. A practical scheme should process messages file-by-file instead of bit-by-bit.

To give the reader an idea of how PIR schemes work, we present in the following a simplified PIR scheme that was originally from [CG97].

Scenario: A database has many files with a total of N bits. The N bits are arranged into a $\sqrt{N} \times \sqrt{N}$ square table. Let's denote the bit on the ith row and jth line by d_{ij}.

Retrieval: A client desires to obtain a file that spans from the uth bit to the vth bit. He/she retrieves the file 1 bit at a time. To retrieve the bit d_{st}, the client proceeds as follows:

1. The client chooses $n = pq$ for primes p and q, gives n to the database and keeps p and q secret. Hence only the client can judge whether a given number is a quadratic residue or quadratic non-residue mod n.

2. The client randomly chooses $y_1, y_2, \cdots, y_{\sqrt{N}}$ such that all of them except y_t are quadratic residues mod n. y_t is a quadratic non-residue. The client sends all the y_j's to the database.

3. The database computes $z_i = \prod_{j=1}^{\sqrt{N}} y_j^{d_{ij}+1}$, for $i = 1, 2, \ldots, \sqrt{N}$

   and sends all the z_i's to the client.

4. The client checks if z_s is a quadratic residue or not. If yes, d_{st} is 1, otherwise d_{st} is 0.

It is easy to see that the above scheme has a communication complexity of $O(\sqrt{N})$. To achieve $O(N^\varepsilon)$ for any $\varepsilon < 1$, the database arranges the N bits in a matrix with large number of rows and small number of columns, instead of a square matrix. Then the same procedure is applied to the matrix. By recursively applying the procedure, the communication complexity of $O(N^\varepsilon)$ for any $\varepsilon < 1$ can be achieved.

In the more recent papers such as [KO97, GIKM98 and CMS99], database security is treated more carefully, e. g., to guarantee the client to retrieve at most one bit in each execution of the retrieving procedure.

3. The System Architecture

In this section we present our system architecture which protects users' privacy in web transactions of digital goods. Specifically, the proposed system is designed to meet the following four major requirements:

I.   *It allows a user to disclose his/her identity information (such as a user account or credit card number) to a web server in exchange for digital item (i. e., digital product)*

II. *It prevents the web server from learning which specific item the user intends to obtain.*

III. *It prevents the user from obtaining more than what he/she deserves to obtain.*

IV. *It operates efficiently and does not impose unacceptable processing overhead in online transactions.*

There are currently a number of industrial initiatives on digital content distribution and digital right management. One example is EBX [EBX] for secure e-book exchange and the other example is SDMI [SDMI] for secure digital music distribution. Both initiatives adopt the "*Superdistribution*" model [MK90], a general approach to distributing digital content in which the content is made available freely either online or offline and without restriction but is protected from modifications and modes of usage not authorized by its publisher. In *Superdistribution*, a user pays for using the content, not for possessing it. Our system architecture, depicted in Figure 1, is designed to be compatible with the principle of *Superdistribution*.

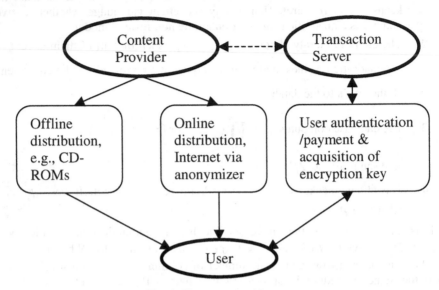

Fig. 1. The system architecture.

The system involves three generic parties as shown in Figure 1. The *content provider* "wraps" a digital item/product in a *secure package* as shown in Figure 2. A secure package contains the encrypted item by an encryption key using a symmetric key cipher, the encrypted encryption key under a master key, and the digital item information (such as summary or a preview of the item, terms of usage and provider information). Since nobody can access the digital item from a secure package without purchasing the encryption key, secure packages can be distributed either online over Internet or offline using CD-ROMs or other physical media. The key purchasing requires a *transaction server* that acts on behalf of the content provider. The transaction server is responsible for recovering of a digital item's encryption key upon user authentication or payment.

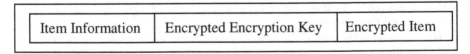

Fig. 2. Secure package.

Specifically, purchasing a digital item is carried out in two steps:
1. There are two cases to consider: a) for online distribution, a user anonymously downloads the secure package of the desired digital item from the content provider via an anonymizer proxy; b) for offline distribution, a

user gets the physical media containing the secure package of the desired item from a physical media such as a CD-ROM.

2. The user obtains the desired digital item's encryption key online from the transaction server using a *key acquisition protocol.*

Without loss of generality and to simplify description, we assume that a user is interested in a single digital item at time. The key acquisition protocol must be designed to have the following properties:

i.   *It allows a user to disclose his/her identity or payment information to the transaction server in exchange for the desired encryption key*

ii. *It prevents the transaction server from learning which specific encryption key the user wants.*

iii. *It prevents the user from obtaining more than one key.*

Note that properties *i* – *iii* correspond to the system requirements *I* – *III* listed at the beginning of this section.

Since secure packages are either distributed offline or accessed online from the content provider through an anonymizer, the content provider can not learn which user has downloaded which secure package. Due to the three properties of the key acquisition protocol to be designed in the following two sections, it is apparent that the system requirements I – III are satisfied. The above reasoning is based on the realistic assumption that many users are engaged in transactions of many digital items so that the content provider and the transaction server can not correlate specific instances of secure package downloading and key purchasing. What is achieved with this model is actually very similar to the unlinkability property of anonymous digital cash [CFN90].

It is easy to see that in our model privacy protection can only be achieved for digital items of the same price or for business models based on user membership subscriptions. For certain e-commerce applications, such as digital libraries and electronic journals, the most likely business model is subscription based where a limit number of goods are provided to a member in a certain period of time. For the situation of digital goods with different prices, we will give it special treatment in the next two sections.

Finally, we would like to emphasize that our privacy protection system requires the transaction server be trusted to the extent that it does not deliberately deny users from receiving the desired digital items. Nothing can prevent a transaction server from denying of service. However, no matter how maliciously a transaction server may perform, the server is never able to learn which item/key a user wants to get. We believe that these privacy protection features do provide business advantage to the merchants. If two merchants sell the same digital goods at the same price while one of them provides privacy protection and the other does not, the former is definitely more attractive to users.

The following two sections will focus on the design and analysis of two key acquisition protocols. In theory, both PIR and oblivious transfer schemes can be adopted in our protocols since they both allow a user to retrieve a message (i. e., encryption key in our context) from a server without the server knowing which message is retrieved. As has been alluded in the last section, available PIR schemes are not efficient due to their bit-oriented processing nature. Moreover, PIR is studied on an abstract model where only two parties are assumed to exist and communicate with each other. Our key acquisition protocols to be presented below are based on two new oblivious transfer schemes which are computationally efficient and require a constant amount of communications between a user and the transaction server regardless of the number of encryption keys stored in the server.

4. Key Acquisition Protocol Based on Blinding RSA Decryption

4.1 Description of the Protocol

Setting up RSA parameters: The content provider setting up the system wide RSA parameters as follows:
1. Pick a 1024-bit RSA module $n = pq$ with primes $p=2p'+1$ and $q = 2q'+1$ where p' and q' are also primes.
2. Choose a random 120-bit number d_p and let $d_q = d_p + 2$.
3. Compute the RSA secret exponent d by the Chinese Remainder Algorithm such that $d = d_p \bmod 2p'$ and $d = d_q \bmod 2q'$.
4. Compute the RSA public exponent e such that $ed = 1 \bmod 2p'q'$. The public key (e, n) is made public and the private key (d, n) is passed securely to the transaction server.

Production of secure packages: Assuming that the content provider has m digital items $M_1, M_2, \ldots M_m$. It constructs a secure package for each item as follows:
1. Randomly choose m 1023-bit numbers $r_1, r_2, \ldots, r_m$.
2. Generate encryption keys by hashing r_i, $K_i = \text{MD5}(r_i)$ for $i = 1, 2, \ldots, m$.
3. Encrypt M_i by key K_i, $C_i = \text{AES}(M_i, K_i)$ for $i = 1, 2, \ldots, m$, where AES stands for Advanced Encryption Standard [AES].
4. Encrypt r_i with the RSA public key, $D_i = (r_i)^e \bmod n$.

The secure package for the ith item M_i is the triplet $<B_i, C_i, D_i>$ where B_i is the digital item information, e. g., a summary of the digital item. All the secure packets are distributed freely.

Assume that a user is interested in the jth item M_j, the user can either anonymously download the secure package $<B_j, C_j, D_j>$ from the content server, or obtains it offline, from, e. g., a CD-ROM. The user then obtains the item's encryption key by running the following protocol with the transaction server.

The key acquisition protocol: The protocol is based on blinding RSA decryption of D_j. Assuming that a user has authenticated himself/herself or has submitted his/her credit card number to the transaction server, the user and the transaction server proceed as follows:
1. The user randomly picks a 1023-bit number R, computes $S = R^e \bmod n$ and $T = 1/R \bmod n$. and sends $U = SD_j \bmod n$ to the transaction server.
2. The transaction server computes $V = U^d \bmod n$ and returns V to the user.
3. The user computes $K_j = \text{MD5}(VT \bmod n)$ to recover the encryption key K_j and then using the key to obtain the digital item $M_j = \text{AES}^{-1}(C_j, K_j)$.

A block diagram representation of the protocol is given in Figure 3.

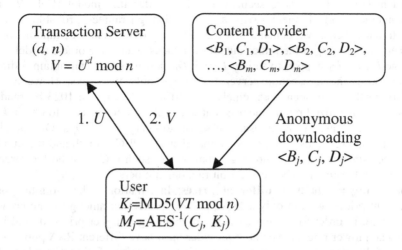

Fig. 3. Key acquisition protocol based on blinding RSA decryption.

4.2 Analysis of the Protocol

Performance analysis: The most heavy computational burden to the transaction server is the decryption operation $V = U^d$ mod n. The encryption operation $D_i = (r_i)^e$ mod n is also expensive, but it is conducted only once for each digital item M_i, while decryption operation is performed per transaction. Hence we want to reduce the cost of $V = U^d$ mod n as much as possible. This is the reason behind the way we choose d. The decryption operation $V = U^d$ mod n can be conducted through first computing U^{d_p} mod p-1 and U^{d_q} mod q-1 and then applying the Chinese Remainder Algorithm. Since d_p and d_q are small 120-bit numbers, the computation is much cheaper than an direct 1024-bit RSA decryption.

Since d is chosen in a special way, the e has negligible probability to be small. The most expensive computation for the user is $S = R^e$ mod n. But this step can be done in advance as a pre-computation, i. e., the selection of R and the computation of S and T can be carried out as soon as the user's machine is power on or during the machine idle time. The only task for the user's machine to do after getting V is computing $K_j =$ MD5(VT mod n) and $M_j =$ AES$^{-1}(C_j, K_j)$. They are very cheap operations.

Security analysis: The problem of speeding up RSA decryption has been studied in cryptography for many years. It has been noticed that choosing small secret exponent d could be dangerous [BD99, Wie90]. So far the best way is to choose small d_p and d_q. The meet-in-the-middle attack with FFT technique provides an algorithm of complexity $O(\sqrt{d_p}(\log_2 \sqrt{d_p})^2)$ to factorize n [Ngu01]. Therefore a 120-bit d_p can provide a security level higher than 2^{72}, which is not much lower than the cost of the best factorization of 1024-bit n. AES provides a security level of 2^{128} that is higher than the factorization of a 1024-bit number and has a better security than DES.

The transaction server conducts blinding RSA decryption like a decryption oracle. Careful attention must be paid here to ensure security. Small or some simply formatted messages may cause security problem under this model [CNS99]. For decryption oracle model, there exists a format that guarantees provable security [BR94]. In our scheme, we demand that the content provider chooses random 1023-bit numbers $r_1, r_2, \ldots, r_m$, which rules out all the attacks against the oracle model.

If some D_i, D_j, D_k happen to satisfy $D_i = D_j D_k \bmod n$, a user can obtain 3 digital items by asking the transaction server to decrypt only two keys. However, the probability for this to happen is extremely small if $r_1, r_2, \ldots, r_m$ are 1023-bit random numbers. The generalized requirement is that a user should not be able to obtain $k+1$ encryption keys by asking the transaction server to decrypt k of D_i's. One possible attack is that the user finds $k+1$ D_i's such that they are all C-smooth and the number of the primes smaller than C is no larger than k. But such a C must be too large to make the attack feasible if D_i's are 1023-bit random numbers.

Accommodating products of different prices: In situations where digital goods have different prices, we can only achieve privacy protection among the goods with the same price. In order to prevent users from obtaining a higher priced digital item but paying at a lower price, the content provider must have different RSA public keys for goods of different prices. Suppose there are 5 categories of digital goods with 5 different prices, the content provider needs to generate 5 different RSA public keys $(n_1, e_1), (n_2, e_2), (n_3, e_3), (n_4, e_4), (n_5, e_5)$ to produce secure packages for the 5 categories of goods, respectively, and attach (n_i, e_i) to the secure packets for goods in the ith category.

5. Key Acquisition Protocol Based on Commutative Symmetric Key Ciphers

The following simple oblivious transfer protocol uses a commutative symmetric key cipher was presented in [Sal90, p.200].

Alice has k secrets $s_1, s_2, \ldots, s_k$. Bob wants to get s_i without Alice knowing what i is.

1. Bob gives Alice k random numbers $y_1, y_2, \ldots, y_k$.
2. Alice returns Bob $z_j = E_A((s_j \mathrm{XOR} y_j))$, $j = 1, 2, \ldots, k$, where E_A is the encryption by Alice's secret key with a commutative symmetric key chiper.
3. Bob sends $x = E_B(z_i)$ to Alice, where E_B is the encryption by Bob's secret key.
4. Alice returns Bob $D_A(x)$, D_A is the decryption by Alice's secret key.
5. Bob computes $s_i = D_B(D_A(x)) \mathrm{XOR} y_i$, D_B is the decryption by Bob's secret key.

However, it was not mentioned in [Sal90] what commutative symmetric key cipher exists. Actually, all the symmetric key ciphers available so far are not commutative except for stream ciphers. Stream ciphers cannot be applied here. When using stream ciphers to encrypt a message, either a random number is required to generate a different key stream or the section of the key stream being used must be specified. That information must be made available in the decryption process, that discloses which message Bob obtains.

In the following protocol, we adopt the exponentiation modulo a prime as our commutative symmetric key cipher. This is the improved version of [BDF00].

5.1 Description of the Protocol

Setting up public parameters: The content provider sets up the system wide public parameter $p = 2p'+1$ where both p and p' are primes and $|p|=1024$.

Production of secure packages: Assuming that the content provider has m digital items $M_1, M_2, ...M_m$. It constructs a secure package for each item as follows:
   1.   Randomly choose m 1023-bit numbers $r_1, r_2, ..., r_m$.
   2.   Generate encryption keys by hashing r_i, $K_i = $ MD5(r_i) for $i = 1, 2,..., m$.
   3.   Encrypt M_i by key K_i, $C_i = $ AES(M_i, K_i) for $i = 1,2,..., m$.
   4.   Randomly pick a 160-bit odd number d and computes $e = 1/d$ mod $2p'$
   5.   Encrypt r_i with e, $D_i=(r_i)^e$ mod p.
The secure package for the ith item M_i is denoted as $<B_i, C_i, D_i>$ where B_i is the item information, i. e., a summary of the item. All the secure packets are distributed freely either online or offline.

The key acquisition protocol: Assuming that a user is in possession of $<B_i, C_i, D_i>$ and wants to get the corresponding encryption key. After the user has authenticated himself/herself or has submitted his/her credit card number to the transaction server, the user and the transaction server engage in the following protocol:
   1.   The user picks a random 160-bit odd number R, computes $S = 1/R$ mod $2p'$ and sends $U = (D_j)^S$ mod p to the transaction server.
   2.   The transaction server computes $V = U^d$ mod p and returns V to the user.
   3.   The user recovers the key as $K_j = $ MD5$(V^R$ mod $p)$ and obtains the jth item from $M_j = $ AES$^{-1}(C_j, K_j)$.

5.2 Analysis of the Scheme

Performance analysis: The encryption operation $D_i = (r_i)^e$ mod p is conducted by the content server only once for each digital item M_i. The transaction server conducts the decryption operation $V = U^d$ mod p once per transaction. Hence we want to reduce the cost the decryption operation as much as possible. This is the reason why we choose d as a 160-bit number. A 160-bit discrete logarithm is safe against all current algorithms for computing discrete logarithm.

Both the computations of $U = (D_j)^S$ mod p and V^R mod p are expensive. We can choose either S or R small. We pick small R because $U = (D_j)^S$ mod p can be computed offline or during the machine idle time.

Security analysis: This protocol achieves information-theoretical security for users since the transaction server has no way to figure out what D_j is from U.

The protocol is fair to the transaction server since no user can get $k +1$ keys through k decryptions. A brute force attack is to find d but it is equivalent to computing discrete logarithm. The other method is to find $k +1$ r_i's by asking the transaction server to decrypt k D_i's. Again, this is infeasible since $r_1, r_2, ...,r_m$ are 1023-bit random numbers.

6. Conclusion and Further Issues

In this paper we have proposed a system architecture for user privacy protection in transactions of digital goods. We also presented two protocols that are secure and highly efficient. Although our system makes use of anonymizers for online distribution of digital goods, they are not absolutely necessary. Some other means can achieve certain degree of user anonymity. For example, using a free proxy can protect user's IP address, domain name and the owner name of the user's host server. By disabling cookies in user's browser, a web site will not be able to correlate the user previous connections to the site.

It is commonly recognized that one of the most important issues for e-commerce of digital goods is content protection and management. This is an on-going effort in a number of industrial initiatives. So far it is still not clear what copyright protection technology will finally be adopted by the industries. There have been extensive research efforts for copyright protection, such as watermarking, fingerprint, tamper-resistant hardware and tamper-resistant software. Although not explicitly stated, tamper-resistant hardware or software are gaining momentum. This is evident from EBX and SDMI technical specifications. In the technical specification of EBX v8.0 [EBX], it is required that all the e-books must be encrypted for any form of distribution and be decrypted within e-book readers, which should be a sort of tamper-resistant system. The proposed system in this paper is in general compatible with EBX and SDMI frameworks. However, additional efforts are required to study detailed integration issues with specific content distribution and protection systems. For example, in EBX v8.0, voucher management plays an important role. Therefore it is necessary to study how to seamlessly integrate our system with EBX's voucher management system.

Another issue is auditing. It is necessary for a transaction server to know the sales figures, such as the number of copies sold for a digital product. Statistic numbers can be gathered from the number of free downloads at the content provider. But such numbers can not precisely reflect the number of sold copies of each digital product, while in practice the numbers are important for royalty payment.

The requirements of privacy protection and collection of royalty statistics look contradictory to each other. This is a subject worth further study. One possible solution is to introduce a trusted party, who provides cryptographic parameters to the content provider for the purpose of digital goods encryption. The parameters many contain some secrets that only the trusted party knows. As a result, the transaction server/content provider cannot learn which product a user obtained, but the trusted party can. Periodically, the transaction server hands all the transaction messages to the trusted party, who then computes how many copies of each product have been sold.

Finally, we world like to point out that an efficient (e. g., without using large number computations) symmetric key cipher with commutative property would greatly increase the efficiency of our second protocol. It may be a challenge to design such a cipher.

References

[AES]   Advanced Encryption Standard, http://csrc.nist.gov/encryption/aes/

[Ano]   Anonymizer.com, http://www.anonymizer.com/
[BDF00]   F. Bao, R. Deng, P. Feng, "An efficient and practical scheme for privacy
            protection in e-commerce of digital goods", Proceedings of The 3rd
            International Conference on Information Security and Cryptology, LNCS 2015,
            Springer-Verlag , pp. 162-170, 2000.
[BR94]   M. Bellare and P. Rogaway, "Optimal asymmetric encryption", Eurocrypt'94,
            LNCS, Springer-Verlag, 1995.
[BD99]   D. Boneh and G. Durfee, "Cryptanalysis of RSA with private key d less than
            $N^{0.292}$", Advances in Cryptology -- Eurocrypt'99, pp. 1-11, Springer-Verlag,
            1999.
[CMS99]   C. Cachin, S. Micali, and M. Stadler, "Computationally private information
            retrieval with polylogrithmic communication", in Proceedings of Eurocrypt'99,
            LNCS, Springer-Verlag, pp. 402-414, 1999.
[Cha81]   D. Chaum, "Ubtraceable electronic mail, return addresses, and digital
            pseudonyms", Communications of the ACM, Vol. 24, No. 2, 1981, pp. 84-88.
[CFN90]   D. Chaum, A. Fiat, and M. Naor, "Untraceable electronic cash", in Proceedings
            of Crypto'88, LNCS, Springer-Verlag, pp. 319-327, 1990.
[CGK95]   B. Chor, O. Goldreich, E. Kushilevita, and M. Sudan, "Private information
            retrieval", Proc. Of 36th FOCS, pp. 41-50, 1995.
[CG97]   B. Chor and N. Gilboa, "Computational private information retrieval", Proc. Of
            29th STOC, pp. 304-313, 1997.
[CNS99]   J. Coron, D. Naccache and J. Stern, "On the security of RSA padding",
            Crypto'99, pp. 1-18, Springer-Verlag, 1999.
[EBX]   Electronic Book Exchange (EBX) Working Group, EBX Specification
            version8.0, http://www.ebxwg.org/
[GIKM98]   Y. Gertner, Y. Ishai, E. Kushilevita and T. Malkin, "Protecting data privacy in
            private information retrieval schemes", Proc. of 30th STOC, 1998.
[KO97]   E. Kushilevita and R. Ostrovsky, "Singal-database computationally private
            information retrieval", Proc. Of 38th FOCS, 1997.
[MK90]   R. Mori and M. Kawahara, "Superdistribution: the concept and the architecture",
            IEICE Transactions, Vol. E.73, No. 7, July 1990
[Ngu01]   P. Q. Nguyen, private communication, 2001.
[RSG98]   M. Reed, P. Syverson, and D. Goldschag, "Anonymous connections and Onion
            Routing", IEEE J. Selected Areas in Commun, Vol. 16, No. 4, pp. 482-494, May
            1998.
[RR98]   M. Reiter and A. Rubin, "Crowds: anonymity for web transactions", ACM
            Transactions on Information System Security, Vol. 1, No. 1, November 1998,
            pp. 66-92.
[Sal91]   A. Salomaa, Public Key Cryptography, EATCS Monographs on Theoretical
            Computer Science Springer-Verlag, 1991.
[SDMI]   SDMI Specification, http://www.sdmi.org/
[Und00]   A. Underwood, "Professional ethics in a security and privacy context - the
            perspective of a national computing society", in Proceedings of ACISP'2000,
            LNCS 1841, Springer-Verlag, pp. 477-486, 2000.
[Wie90]   M. Wiener, "Cryptanalysis of short RSA secret exponents", IEEE Transactions
            on Information Theory, Vol. 36, No. 3, pp. 553-558, 1990.
[ZKSI1]   Zero-Knowledge System Inc., http://www.zeroknowledge.com/
[ZKSI2]   Zero-Knowledge System Inc., http://www.freedom.net/info/diagnostic.html

Equivalent Characterizations and Applications of Multi-output Correlation-Immune Boolean Functions

Jie-lü Xu, Han-liang Xu, Yan Wang, and Shu-Wang Lü

State Key Laboratory of Information Security
Graduate School of CAS, Beijing 100039, PRC
xhlhz@hotmail.com

Abstract. This paper discusses the characterizations of multi-output correlation-immune functions. We first give a decomposition formula of the probability distribution of binary random vectors by using Walsh transform. Then the equivalence of the two different definitions of multi-output correlation-immune functions is proved. Furthermore, we construct a class of keystream generators which can resist the linear and correlation attacks.

1 Introduction

If for any vector $\mathbf{X} = (x_1, x_2, \cdots, x_n)$ in F_2^n, there is a unique vector $\mathbf{Y} = (y_1, y_2, \cdots, y_m)$ corresponding to it, then the correspondence is called a (n, m) logic function, denoted by $\mathbf{Y} = F(x_1, x_2, \cdots, x_n)$, where n and m are called the dimensions of input and output respectively. If $m = 1$, F is called a single-output logic function or simply a logic function. If $m > 1$, F is called a **multi-output logic function.** Let F_2^t be a t-dimensional vector space on F_2. For any $(x_1, x_2, \cdots, x_t) \in F_2^t$, since there is a one-to-one mapping between the vector $(x_1, x_2, \cdots, x_t)$ and its decimal value $x_1 2^{t-1} + x_2 2^{t-2} + \cdots + x_t 2^0$, for the purpose of convenience, we usually use the corresponding decimal value to represent the vector.

Various and extensive applications of multi-output logic functions have been found in the practice of cryptography. For example, in the multi-bit output keystream generator in stream ciphers, the output of every step can be thought as the multi-output logic function value with its corresponding state as independent variables. In block ciphers using 0,1 bits as blocks, the correspondence between plaintext blocks and the corresponding ciphertext blocks can also be seen as multi-output logic functions. The correlation-immunity of logic function is one of the most important factors when measuring the security of a cryptosystem. Note that the order of correlation-immunity correlates closely with the computational complexity of correlation attacks. So if a logic function with weak correlation-immunity is used in a cryptosystem, the system will be vulnerable to correlation attacks. There have been extensive and deep discussions on correlation-immunity of single-output logic functions. In comparison, few deeply discussions

S. Qing, T. Okamoto, and J. Zhou (Eds.): ICICS 2001, LNCS 2229, pp. 214–220, 2001.
© Springer-Verlag Berlin Heidelberg 2001

on correlation-immunity of multi-output logic functions have been published. The concept of multi-output correlation-immune logic functions, which is introduced in [1][2] and is named the multi-output correlation-immune logic function of type I in [3], is a direct extension of the single-output logic function. Also in [3] another concept, named the multi-output correlation-immune logic function of type II, has been put up. It has established a direct connection between the correlation-immunity of multi-output logic functions and that of vector functions. Furthermore, it has been proved that multi-output correlation-immune logic functions of type I form a subset of multi-output correlation-immune logic functions of type II.

In this paper, we will discuss these two characterizations of the correlation-immunity of multi-output logic functions more deeply. Based on the decomposition formula of the probability distribution of binary random vectors which is obtained by using Walsh transform, the equivalence of the two characterizations is proved. Thus a direct connection between the correlation-immunity of multi-output logic functions and that of single-output logic functions can be established. In section 4, using multi-output logic functions, we construct a class of keystream generators which can withstand correlation attacks and best affine approximation (BAA) attacks.

2 Two Definitions of Multi-output Logic Functions

Firstly, we introduce the definition of single-output correlation-immune logic functions.

Definition 1. [1] *Let f be a logic function on F_2^n, $\mathbf{X} = (x_1, x_2, \cdots, x_n)$ are n independent and uniformly distributed random variables. If for any $T = \{j_1, j_2, \cdots, j_t\} \subseteq \{1, 2, \cdots, n\}$ satisfying $|T| = t$ and any $c \in F_2$, random variables $y = f(x_1, x_2, \cdots, x_n)$ and $(x_{j_1}, x_{j_2}, \cdots, x_{j_t})$ are independent mutually, that is, for any $(a_1, a_2, \cdots, a_t) \in F_2^t$ and any $c \in F_2$, the following equation holds:*

$$Prob\{y = c | x_{j_i} = a_i, 1 \le i \le t\} = Prob\{y = c\}$$

Then f is called a $(n, 1, t)$ correlation-immune function or tth-order correlation-immune function on F_2^n.

Lemma 1. [1] *(Xiao-Messay) A logic function $f(\mathbf{X}), \mathbf{X} \in F_2^n$ is a tth-order correlation-immune function $(1 \le t < n)$ $\Leftrightarrow$ For any $\omega \in F_2^n$ with its hamming weight $W(\omega)$ satisfying $1 \le W(\omega) \le t$, $Prob\{f(\mathbf{X}) = \omega \cdot \mathbf{X}\} = 0.5$ holds.*

Next, we introduce the definition of multi-output correlation-immune functions of type I.

Definition 2. [1] *Let F be a function from F_2^n to F_2^m, $x_1, x_2, \cdots, x_n$ are n independent and uniformly distributed random variables. If for any $T = \{j_1, j_2, \cdots, j_t\} \subseteq \{1, 2, \cdots, n\}$ satisfying $|T| = t$ and any $\mathbf{c} \in F_2^n$, random variables $\mathbf{y} = F(x_1, x_2, \cdots, x_n)$ and $(x_{j_1}, x_{j_2}, \cdots, x_{j_t})$ are independent mutually, that is, for any $(a_1, a_2, \cdots, a_t) \in F_2^t$ and any $c \in F_2$, the following equation holds:*

$$Prob\{\mathbf{y} = \mathbf{c}|x_{j_i} = a_i, 1 \le i \le t\} = Prob\{\mathbf{y} = \mathbf{c}\}$$

Then f is called a (n, m, t) correlation-immune multi-output logic function of type I.

Finally, we give the definition of multi-output correlation immune function of type II which is put forward in [3].

Definition 3. [3] Let $\mathbf{F} = (f_1, f_2, \cdots, f_m)$ be a function from F_2^n to F_2^m. If all non-zero linear combinations of its component functions, written as $f(\mathbf{X}) = \bigoplus_{i=1}^{m} c_i f_i(\mathbf{X})$, are $(n, 1, t)$ correlation-immune functions, then $\mathbf{F}$ is called a (n, m, t) multi-output correlation-immune function, where $\mathbf{X} \in F_2^n, c_1, c_2, \cdots, c_m \in F_2$, and $(c_1, c_2, \cdots, c_m) \ne (0, 0, \cdots, 0)$.

3   Equivalence Theorem

A real-valued function with binary variables g is referred to as the following correspondence: For any $\mathbf{X} \in F_2^n$, there is a unique $g(\mathbf{X}) \in R$ corresponding to it, denoted by $g : F_2^n \to R$, where n is the number of independent variables of g, and R is the set of real numbers. Using Walsh function system, any real-valued function with binary variables $g(\mathbf{X})$ can be expanded as :

$$g(\mathbf{X}) = 2^{-n} \sum_{\omega \in F_2^n} S_g(\omega)(-1)^{\omega \cdot \mathbf{X}} \pounds \tag{1}$$

where

$$S_g(\omega) = \sum_{\mathbf{X} \in F_2^n} g(\mathbf{X})(-1)^{\omega \cdot \mathbf{X}} \tag{2}$$

(2) is called Walsh transformation. The corresponding set $\{S_g(\omega) : \omega \in F_2^n\}$ is called Walsh spectrum .

Using Walsh transformation and Walsh spectrum , we can get the following theorem easily.

Lemma 2. *(Lemma of Decomposition) Let* $\xi = (\xi_1, \xi_2, \cdots, \xi_m)$ *be a random vector with dimension* m, $\mathbf{a} \in F_2^m$, *then*

$$Prob\{\xi = \mathbf{a}\} = \frac{1}{2^{m-1}} \sum_{\omega=1}^{2^m - 1} Prob\{\omega \cdot \xi = \omega \cdot \mathbf{a}\} + \frac{1}{2^{m-1}} - 1 \tag{3}$$

Proof. The probability distribution of $\xi = (\xi_1, \xi_2, \cdots, \xi_m)$ denoted by $Prob\{\xi = \mathbf{X}\}$ is a real-valued function with binary variables, written as $g(\mathbf{X}) = Prob\{\xi = \mathbf{X}\}$, whose Walsh transformation is :

$$S_g(\omega) = \sum_{\mathbf{X} \in F_2^n} (-1)^{\omega \cdot \mathbf{X}} Prob\{\xi = \mathbf{X}\}$$

Clearly, in the sense of probability, $S_g(\omega)$ means:

$$S_g(\omega) = Prob\{\omega \cdot \xi = 0\} - Prob\{\omega \cdot \xi = 1\}$$
$$= 2Prob\{\omega \cdot \xi = 0\} - 1$$

From (1), we have

$$Prob\{\xi = \mathbf{a}\} = \frac{1}{2^m} \sum_{\omega=0}^{2^m-1} (-1)^{\omega \cdot \mathbf{a}} S_g(\omega)$$

$$= \frac{1}{2^m} \sum_{\omega=0}^{2^m-1} (-1)^{\omega \cdot \mathbf{a}} (2Prob\{\omega \cdot \xi = 0\} - 1)$$

$$= \frac{1}{2^{m-1}} \sum_{\omega=0}^{2^m-1} (-1)^{\omega \cdot \mathbf{a}} Prob\{\omega \cdot \xi = 0\} - \frac{1}{2^m} \sum_{\omega=0}^{2^m-1} (-1)^{\omega \cdot \mathbf{a}}$$

when $\mathbf{a} = 0$,

$$Prob\{\xi = 0\} = \frac{1}{2^{m-1}} \sum_{\omega=0}^{2^m-1} Prob\{\omega \cdot \xi = 0\} - 1$$

$$= \frac{1}{2^{m-1}} \sum_{\omega=1}^{2^m-1} Prob\{\omega \cdot \xi = 0\} + \frac{1}{2^{m-1}} - 1$$

when $\mathbf{a} \neq 0$, since $\sum_{\omega=0}^{2^m-1} (-1)^{\omega \cdot \mathbf{a}} = 0$ and

$$(-1)^{\omega \cdot \mathbf{a}} Prob\{\omega \cdot \xi = 0\} = Prob\{\omega \cdot \xi = \omega \cdot \mathbf{a}\} - \omega \cdot \mathbf{a}$$

where $\omega \cdot \mathbf{a}$, as real value 0,1, takes part in the operations in the right-hand side of the equation, we have

$$Prob\{\xi = \mathbf{a}\} = \frac{1}{2^{m-1}} \sum_{\omega=0}^{2^m-1} (Prob\{\omega \cdot \xi = \omega \cdot \mathbf{a}\} - \omega \cdot \mathbf{a})$$

$$= \frac{1}{2^{m-1}} \sum_{\omega=0}^{2^m-1} Prob\{\omega \cdot \xi = \omega \cdot \mathbf{a}\} - \frac{1}{2^{m-1}} \sum_{\omega=0}^{2^m-1} \omega \cdot \mathbf{a}$$

$$= \frac{1}{2^{m-1}} \sum_{\omega=0}^{2^m-1} Prob\{\omega \cdot \xi = \omega \cdot \mathbf{a}\} - 1$$

$$= \frac{1}{2^{m-1}} \sum_{\omega=1}^{2^m-1} Prob\{\omega \cdot \xi = \omega \cdot \mathbf{a}\} + \frac{1}{2^{m-1}} - 1$$

Therefore, for any $\mathbf{a} \in F_2^m$, Lemma 2 holds.   □

Lemma 3. *Let $\eta = (\eta_1, \eta_2, \cdots, \eta_t)$ and $\xi = (\xi_1, \xi_2, \cdots, \xi_m)$ be random vectors on F_2 with dimension t and m respectively. Then η and $\xi = (\xi_1, \xi_2, \cdots, \xi_m)$ are independent mutually $\Leftrightarrow \eta$ and every non-zero linear combination of $\xi_1, \xi_2, \cdots, \xi_m$, denoted by $\bigoplus_{i=1}^{m} c_i \xi_i$ are independent, where $c_1, c_2, \cdots, c_m \in F_2$ and $(c_1, c_2, \cdots, c_m) \neq (0, 0, \cdots, 0)$.*

Proof. "⇒" For any $c_1, c_2, \cdots, c_m \in F_2, (c_1, c_2, \cdots, c_m) \neq (0, 0, \cdots, 0)$ and any $c \in F_2$, we write

$$\tau_c(c_1, c_2, \cdots, c_m) = \{\beta | \beta = (\beta_1, \beta_2, \cdots, \beta_m) \in F_2^m, \bigoplus_{i=1}^{m} c_i \beta_i = c\}$$

From the conditions, we have

$$Prob\{\bigoplus_{i=1}^{m} c_i \xi_i = c | \eta = \mathbf{b}\} = \sum_{\beta \in \tau_c(c_1, c_2, \cdots, c_m)} Prob\{\xi = \beta | \eta = \mathbf{b}\}$$
$$= \sum_{\beta \in \tau_c(c_1, c_2, \cdots, c_m)} Prob\{\xi = \beta\}$$
$$= Prob\{\bigoplus_{i=1}^{m} c_i \xi_i = c\}$$

where $\mathbf{b} = (b_1, b_2, \cdots, b_t) \in F_2^t$.

"⇐" By the condition $Prob\{\omega \cdot \xi = \omega \cdot \mathbf{a} | \eta = \mathbf{b}\} = Prob\{\omega \cdot \xi = \omega \cdot \mathbf{a}\}$ and Lemma 2, we can have

$$Prob\{\xi = \mathbf{a} | \eta = \mathbf{b}\} = \frac{1}{2^{m-1}} \sum_{\omega=1}^{2^m-1} Prob\{\omega \cdot \xi = \omega \cdot \mathbf{a} | \eta = \mathbf{b}\} + \frac{1}{2^{m-1}} - 1$$
$$= \frac{1}{2^{m-1}} \sum_{\omega=1}^{2^m-1} Prob\{\omega \cdot \xi = \omega \cdot \mathbf{a}\} + \frac{1}{2^{m-1}} - 1$$
$$= Prob\{\xi = \mathbf{a}\}$$

Therefore, η and ξ are independent.   □

Theorem 1. *(Equivalence Theorem) Let* $\mathbf{F} = (f_1, f_2, \cdots, f_m)$ *be a function from* F_2^n *to* F_2^m. *Suppose that* $x_1, x_2, \cdots, x_n$ *are n independent and uniformly distributed random variables. Then* $\mathbf{F}$ *is a* (n, m, t) *multi-output correlation-immune function of type II if and only if* $\mathbf{F}$ *is a* (n, m, t) *multi-output correlation-immune function of type I.*

Proof. By Lemma 3, Definition 2 and Definition 3, $\mathbf{F}$ is a (n, m, t)multi-output correlation immune function of type I ⇔ For any $\{j_1, j_2, \cdots, j_t\} \subseteq \{1, 2, \cdots, n\}$, random variable $\mathbf{y}$, written as $\mathbf{y} = F(x_1, x_2, \cdots, x_n) = (y_1, y_2, \cdots, y_m)$, and $(x_{j_1}, x_{j_2}, \cdots, x_{j_t})$ are independent ⇔ For any $\{j_1, j_2, \cdots, j_t\} \subseteq \{1, 2, \cdots, n\}$ and any $(c_1, c_2, \cdots, c_m) \in F_2^m$ with $(c_1, c_2, \cdots, c_m) \neq (0, 0, \cdots, 0), (x_{j_1}, x_{j_2}, \cdots, x_{j_t})$ and $\bigoplus_{i=1}^{m} c_i y_i = \bigoplus_{i=1}^{m} c_i f_i(x_1, x_2, \cdots, x_n)$ are independent ⇔ Every nonzero linear combination of component functions of $\mathbf{F}$ denoted by $\bigoplus_{i=1}^{m} c_i f_i(\mathbf{X})$ is a $(n, 1, t)$ correlation-immune function (where $\mathbf{X} \in F_2^n$) ⇔ $\mathbf{F} = (f_1, f_2, \cdots, f_m)$ is a (n, m, t)multi-output correlation-immune function of type II.   □

From the equivalence theorem and the lemma of Xiao-Messay, we can draw the following conclusion: in cryptoanalysis, when investigating the correlation properties of multi-output logic functions, we should consider if there exist correlations between the input and all linear combinations of the output component functions, not considering the correlation properties for some single component function merely.

4   Applications in Designing Keystream Generators

In stream ciphers, the following type of keystream generators (see Fig. 1.) is often used, which is called the nonlinear combination generator,where the output of f function is used as keystream. The initial states of this kind of genera-

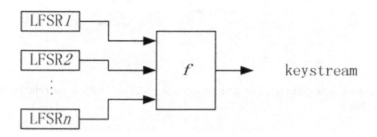

Fig. 1. A nonlinear combination generator. f is a nonlinear combining functinon.

tors are predetermined by the key. If this kind of generator is used to generate keystreams, not only is it easy to implement in engineering, owing to its simple structure, but also the linear complexity of the output sequence is easy to estimate. So, as keystream generators, nonlinear combination generators are quite desirable. Though this type of keystream generators has these advantages, in practical use, we still should choose the logic function f with great carefulness and cautiousness. Otherwise, It'll be easy to restore the key (initial states of the FSRs) through BAA attacks. However, from the spectrum theory of logic function, no matter what kind of logic function f is, there always exists a correlation between certain linear combination of the input sequences and the output keystream, i.e.

$$Prob\{f(x_1, x_2, \cdots, x_n) = \bigoplus_{i=1}^{n} c_i x_i\} > 0.5 \ (or < 0.5)$$

Hence, we can only choose the logic function f as carefully as possible so as to distribute the correlation to different linear combinations of the input variables, but can't eliminate it at all.

This unfortunate situation will be changed by the applications of multi-output correlation-immune logic functions in nonlinear combination keystream generators. which can make it difficult to get the initial states of FSRs in the generator through exploring the output keystream. To illustrate this, we construct one type of keystream generators using multi-output correlation-immune logic functions(see the Fig.2.).

In the Fig. 2, $F(\mathbf{X}) = (f_1, f_2, \cdots, f_n, f_{n+1}, \cdots, f_{n+t})$ is a $(n + t, n + t, n)$ balanced multi-output correlation-immune logic function. $f_1, f_2, \cdots, f_n$ are output of the generator, and they are used directly as the keystream. The one-step delay of $f_{n+1}, f_{n+2}, \cdots, f_{n+t}$ are t input variables of $F(\mathbf{X})$. The rest n input

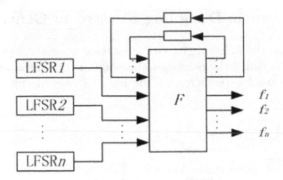

Fig. 2. A nonlinear combination generator using a multi-output correlation-immune logic function **F**.

variables of $F(\mathbf{X})$ are supplied by the output of FSRs of the same step. From the equivalence theory in section 3, we can see that any linear combination of the generator's output $f_1, f_2, \cdots, f_n$, denoted by $\overset{n}{\underset{i=1}{\oplus}} c_i f_i$, and any linear combination of the FSRs' output $x_1, x_2, \cdots, x_n$, denoted by $\overset{n}{\underset{i=1}{\oplus}} c_i x_i$ satisfy:

$$Prob\{\overset{n}{\underset{i=1}{\oplus}} c_i f_i = \overset{n}{\underset{i=1}{\oplus}} c_i x_i\} = 0.5$$

that is, the output $f_1, f_2, \cdots, f_n$ and $x_1, x_2, \cdots, x_n$ are statistically independent. Thus the generator is immune to correlation attacks and linear approximation attacks. Certainly, when this kind of keystream generators is used, the following requirements are important to notice: Firstly, the length of every FSR should be large enough to preclude exhaustive attack; Secondly, the selection of $F(\mathbf{X})$ should make every component function in the output have rather high nonlinearity, and for the third, the output keystream should have large linear complexity.

We won't discuss the constructions of balanced multi-output correlation-immune logic functions here. The reader who is interested it can read [3] for details.

References

[1] Ding Cunsheng, Xiao Guozhen: Stream Ciphers and Applications. Beijing,the publishing company of defence industry, PP.169-173,1994.
[2] K.Gopalakrishnan   and   D.R.Stinson: Three   characterizations   of   non-binary   correlation-immune   and   resilient   functions.   Designs,Codes   and Cryptography,PP.241-251, 5(3),1995.
[3] Chen Lusheng: Cryptographic properties of multi-output Boolean functions. PhD thesis, Nankai University, 2000.

Threshold Undeniable RSA Signature Scheme[*]

Guilin Wang[1], Sihan Qing[1], Mingsheng Wang[1], and Zhanfei Zhou[2]

[1] Engineering Research Center for Information Security Technology;
State Key Laboratory of Information Security, Institute of Software,
Chinese Academy of Sciences, Beijing 100080, P. R. China.
{glwang, qsh, mshwang}@ercist.iscas.ac.cn
http://www.ercist.ac.cn/
[2] Mathematics Department, College of Science and Technology,
Nihon University, Tokyo 101-8308, Japan.
{zhanfei_zhou}@hotmail.com

Abstract. Undeniable signature has been extensively researched after Chaum and Antwerpen first proposed the concept of this special digital signature ten years ago. Up to now, however, almost all the existed schemes are based on discrete logarithm cryptosystems. In this paper, based on an improvement of the practical threshold RSA signature scheme proposed by Shoup at Eurocrypt'2000 and the first undeniable RSA signature scheme proposed by Gennaro, Krawczyk and Rabin at Crypto'97, we present the first, as we know, threshold undeniable RSA signature scheme. Our scheme is secure and robust since all the partial signatures are verifiable by adopting a discrete logarithm equality protocol proposed by Shoup.

1   Introduction

Undeniable signature is a special kind of digital signature with the characteristic that signature cannot be verified without the cooperation of the signer and cannot be denied by the signer if he has signed the signature indeed. (t, n) threshold signature is one kind of group-oriented signature, in which only the subsets with at least t members in a group U can generate a valid signature and any verifier can simply verify an alleged signature if he/she knows U's group public key. However, in a (t, n) threshold undeniable signature scheme, any subset of t members out of n, denoted by U_B, can represent the group U to generate a signature, but without the cooperation of t members, a verifier cannot verify the validity of an alleged signature even if he knows U's group public key. At the same time, any subset of less than t members cannot generate, confirm or disavow a signature even if they cooperate maliciously. Generally speaking, a threshold undeniable signature scheme consists of the following three main sub-protocols.

(1) **Signing Protocol:** t members in subset U_B run this protocol to produce a valid signature for any message, but any attacker I cannot forge a valid

---

[*] Supported by the National Key Basic Research Program of China (No. G1999035810) and the National Natural Science Foundation of China (No. 60083007).

S. Qing, T. Okamoto, and J. Zhou (Eds.): ICICS 2001, LNCS 2229, pp. 221–232, 2001.

signature of group U with non-negligent possibility unless I has corrupted at least t members or U's private signing key has been compromised to I (i.e., *nonforgeability*).

(2) **Confirmation Protocol:** By running this protocol between prover U_B, t members of U, and verifier V, V is convinced that an alleged signature is indeed signed by U. Confirmation protocol should satisfy the following three properties.

- *Completeness*: A signature signed by group U will always be accepted by V if all the members in U_B and V are honest (this means that they properly act as the protocol described).
- *Soundness*: Even a cheating prover U_B cannot convince the verifier V to accept an non-valid signature of U with non-negligent possibility.
- *Zero-knowledge*: On input a message and its valid signature, any possible cheating verifier V interacting with a subset U_B does not learn any information aside from the validity of the signature.

(3) **Denial Protocol:** By running this protocol, prover U_B ensures a verifier V that a signature is not signed by group U. Denial protocol also should satisfy the similar three properties as follows.

- *Completeness*: A signature not signed by U will always pass through the denial protocol such that V believes that it is not U's signature if all the members in U_B and V are honest.
- *Soundness*: Even a cheating prover U_B cannot successfully deny a valid signature of U with non-negligent possibility by running denial protocol.
- *Zero-knowledge*: On input a message and a non-valid signature, any possible cheating verifier V interacting with a subset U_B does not learn any information aside from the the fact that this non-valid signature is in fact not a valid signature of group U.

Besides nonforgeability, a threshold undeniable signature should also be *robust*, meaning that corrupted members should not be able to prevent uncorrupted members from generating signatures.

After Chaum and Antwerpen first proposed the conception of undeniable signature in [6], extensive researches are done to this special kind signature. Chaum [2] presented a zero-knowledge undeniable signature scheme with promising applications in copyright protection of electronic products. By combining the undeniable signature and group-oriented signature [7, 8], Harn and Yang [13] proposed the conception of (t, n) threshold undeniable signature, and presented two concrete schemes in respect of $t = 1$ and $t = n$. But Langford [14] pointed out that their (n, n) threshold undeniable signature scheme only possesses a security of 2-out-of-n, because any two adjacent members can generate a valid threshold signature. Lin etc. presented a general threshold undeniable signature scheme [16], but which is also subjected to Langford's attack [14]. [15] generalized Chaum's zero-knowledge undeniable signature [2] to a (t, n) threshold undeniable signature scheme with a dealer. However, unlike all the above schemes based on discrete logarithm cryptosystems, Gennaro, Krawczyk and Rabin presented the first undeniable RSA signature scheme [12].

In this paper, we will construct the first, as we know, threshold undeniable RSA signature scheme with a dealer. Our Scheme are builded from an improvement to Shoup's threshold signature scheme [20] and Gennaro etc.'s undeniable RSA signature scheme [12]. Our schemes are secure and robust because all the partial signatures are verifiable by adopting a discrete logarithm equality protocol proposed by Shoup [20].

The organization of this paper is as follows. Notations are described in § 2. Shoup's discrete logarithm equality protocol [20] and Gennaro etc.'s undeniable RSA signature scheme are reviewed in § 3 and § 4 respectively. Then, we propose an improvement to Shoup's threshold RSA signature and a newly threshold undeniable RSA signature scheme in § 5 and § 6 respectively. The last two sections are about some discussions and future work.

2   Notations

Our systems consist of a dealer D and a group U with n members $U_i (i = 1, 2, \cdots, n)$. Let t be the threshold value and B denote a subset of size t in the index set $\{1, 2, \cdots, n\}$. The notation $x \in_R X$ means that an element x is selected randomly and uniformly from set X. In this paper, the RSA modulus N is selected as the product of two large secure primes p and q, i.e. there exist two primes p', q' such that $p = 2p' + 1$, $q = 2p' + 1$ and $N = pq$. Let $M = p'q'$, and $L(N)$ denote the bit-length of N.

We denote by Q_N the subgroup of squares in Z_N^*. For any integer x, let $\mathcal{J}(x|N)$ denote the Jacobi symbol symbol of x respect to the base N. In addition, we denote by J_N the subgroup of elements $x \in Z_N^*$ with $\mathcal{J}(x|N) = 1$. Then we know that $Q_N \subset J_N \subset Z_N^*$. Moreover, Q_N is cyclic of order M and J_N is cyclic of order $2M$.

3   Discrete Logarithm Equality Protocol

As a key of modern cryptography, knowledge proving plays an important role in constructing varied protocols and schemes. Among of them, the most extensively used knowledge proving protocols are based on discrete logarithm cryptosystems [3]. In this section, we briefly review a discrete logarithm equality protocol proposed by Shoup [20], which is an improvement to a well-known interactive protocol, due to Chaum and Pedersen [5].

Let g_1, g_2 are two generators of the subgroup Q_N of Z_N^*. Q_N's order is not known. The prover P possesses a secret number $\alpha \in Z_M$ such that $\log_{g_1} h_1 = \log_{g_2} h_2 = \alpha$, i.e. $h_1 = g_1^\alpha$ and $h_2 = g_2^\alpha$. By running the following protocol between the prover P and the verifier V, P convinces V that he indeed possesses the secret α but does not reveals which is it to V. Let $\bar{H}$ be a hash function, whose output is an l_1-bit interger, where l_1 is a second security parameter ($l_1 = 128$, say). For convenience, we will simply denote this protocol as $\mathrm{DLE}(g_1, h_1; g_2, h_2; \alpha)$.

$$\mathbf{DLE}(g_1, h_1; g_2, h_2; \alpha) \ \mathbf{Protocol}$$

(1) P randomly selects $w \in_R [0, \cdots, 2^{L(N)+2l_1} - 1]$, computes $a_1 = g_1^w \bmod N, a_2 = g_2^w \bmod N, c = \bar{H}(g_1 \| g_2 \| h_1 \| h_2 \| a_1 \| a_2)$ and $r = \alpha c + w$. Then, P publishes $Proof_P \overset{\triangle}{=} (r, c)$ as the proof of knowing the secret α.

(2) From the proof (r, c), V first computes $a_1 = g_1^r h_1^{-c} \bmod N$ and $a_2 = g_2^r h_2^{-c} \bmod N$, then determines whether P knows the secret α by checking

$$c \equiv \bar{H}(g_1 \| g_2 \| h_1 \| h_2 \| a_1 \| a_2).$$

4   Gennaro etc.'s Undeniable RSA Signature

In this section, we briefly review the first undeniable RSA signature scheme constructed by Gennaro etc. [12]. In their scheme, the signer publishes the RSA modulus and a sample signature but keeps the usual key pair secretly. The confirmation and denial of a signature are to check whether certain relations between the signature and the sample signature hold.

Stage 1: Setting System Parameters

If user P want to use this system, he first chooses two large secure primes $p = 2p' + 1$ and $q = 2q' + 1$ and let the RSA modulus as $N = pq$. Then he chooses the key pair $e, d \in [1, \varphi(N)-1]$ such that $ed = 1 \bmod \varphi(N)$. In addition, P selects an element $w \in Z_N^*$ of order at least $p'q'$ as the sample message and computes the sample signature $S_w = w^d \bmod N$. At last, P publishes his public key information (N, w, S_w) but keeps his private key information (e, d) secretly. Where, d is used to generate signature and e to verify signature. Furthermore, P chooses a secure parameter l (usually it can be set as 1024).

Stage 2: Generation of Undeniable Signature

As in regular RSA signature scheme, if user P want to sign a message m, he computes $S_m = m^d \bmod N$ and publishes (m, S_m) as his signature on message m.

Stage 3: Confirmation Protocol

A verifier V can not alone verify whether an alleged signature (m, S_m) is signed by P, because V does not know P's verification key e (in fact, P does not publish this information at all). But V and P can run the following confirmation protocol to convince V that (m, S_m) is P's signature on message m.

(3-1) V randomly selects two numbers $c_1, c_2 \in_R [1, N]$, computes the value $C = S_m^{c_1} S_w^{c_2} \bmod N$ and sends it to P.

(3-2) After received C, P computes and sends the value $R = C^e \bmod N$ to V.

(3-3) After received R, V check whether $R \equiv m^{c_1} w^{c_2} \bmod N$ holds. If yes, then V accepts S_m as P's signature on message. Otherwise, V and P has to run the denial protocol to determine whether S_m is indeed not signed by P.

Stage 4: Denial Protocol

V and P can run the following denial protocol to convince V that S_m is not P's signature on message m.

(4-1) V randomly selects two numbers $c_1 \in_R [1, l]$ and $c_2 \in_R [1, N]$, sends $C_1 = m^{c_1} w^{c_2} \bmod N$ and $C_2 = S_m^{c_1} S_w^{c_2} \bmod N$ to P.

(4-2) After received (C_1, C_2), P searches all possible values in $[1, l]$ to find a number r such that $(m/S_m^{e})^r = C_1/C_2^{e} \bmod N$. If such r was found, then P sends it V.

(4-3) V checks whether $r \equiv c_1$. If yes, V convinces that S_m is not signed by P. Otherwise, V believes that P is trying to deny his own signature.

[12] proved two theorems about the completeness, soundness and zero- knowledge of above confirmation protocol and denial protocol. Gennaro etc.'s theorems show that their scheme is secure. In practice, secure parameter l can be selected as a small number, but P and V can run denial protocol several times to guarantee security without loss efficiency. For example, let $l = 1024$ and running the denial protocol for ten times, then $1/2^{100}$ security level can be reached. In other words, the probability of occurring the following event is less than one in a million: V believes that S_m is not signed by P, but in fact S_m is P's signature on message m.

5   Improved Threshold RSA Signature Scheme

In this section, we present an improved threshold RSA signature to Shoup's scheme [20], which has the same security level and is more efficient compared to Shoup's scheme. Furthermore, it seems intractable to directly generalize Shoup's scheme to undeniable environments, but our scheme can be generalized as a threshold undeniable signature if the methods used in [12] are adopted. In the essence, we simplify the signing equation of Shoup's scheme. Now, we first describe our improved threshold signature scheme, then compare the security and efficiency between our scheme and Shoup's.

5.1   Description of Threshold RSA Signature Scheme

The dealer D chooses a RSA modulus N as the product of two large secure primes described in section 2. The dealer D also chooses the RSA public exponent e as a prime such that $n < e < \min\{p', q'\}$, and the secret exponent $d \in Z_M^*$ is the integer which satisfies $de = 1 \bmod M$.

Stage 1. Distribution of Secrets

(1-1) The dealer D randomly selects a polynomial $f(x)$ with order less than $(t-1)$. Let $f(x) = \sum_{j=0}^{t-1} a_j x^j \in Z_M[x]$, where $a_0 = d$ and $a_j \in_R Z_M$ ($j = 1, 2, \cdots, t-1$).

(1-2) Dealer D computes d_i as follows and sends d_i to member U_i secretly:

$$d_i = f(i)(n!)^{-1} \bmod M, \quad i = 1, 2, \cdots, n. \tag{1}$$

For any index subset B with t elements, it is easy to see that these d_i satisfy the following equation according to the Lagrange interpolation formula:

$$d = \sum_{i \in B} d_i \cdot \lambda_{Bi} \bmod M, \quad \text{where } \lambda_{Bi} = \sum_{j \in B \setminus \{i\}} \frac{j \cdot n!}{j - i} \in Z. \quad (2)$$

(1-3) Dealer D randomly selects a generator v of Q_N and computes:

$$v_i = v^{d_i} \bmod N \in Q_N, \quad i = 1, 2, \cdots, n.$$

In addition, D chooses an element $u \in Z_N^*$ such that the Jacobi symbol of u is -1, i.e. $\mathcal{J}(u|N) = -1$.

(1-4) D publishes or broadcasts N, e, n, u, v and all v_i ($i = 1, 2, \cdots, n$).

Stage 2. Generation and Verification of Partial Signatures

If member U_i want to sign an original message m_0, then U_i first computes the digest m as

$$m = \begin{cases} H(m_0), & \text{if } \mathcal{J}(H(m_0)|N) = 1 \\ H(m_0)u, & \text{if } \mathcal{J}(H(m_0)|N) = -1 \end{cases}. \quad (3)$$

This forces that $\mathcal{J}(m|N) = 1$. Now, U_i computes his partial signature as follows:

$$S_i = m^{2d_i} \bmod N. \quad (4)$$

Last, U_i runs the DLE($v, v_i; m^2, S_i; d_i$) protocol (where m^2 is computed under mod N) for constructing the proof $Proof_{U_i}$ to show the validity of partial signature S_i by revealing that $\log_v v_i = \log_{m^2} S_i$ ($= d_i$). U_i publishes or broadcasts ($i, m, S_i, Proof_{U_i}$) as his partial signature message.

Stage 3. Generation and Verification of Threshold Signature

If there is at least t honest members (i.e., they generated valid partial signatures), then by choosing any t honest members U_i ($i \in B$ and $|B| = t$), each member can compute the threshold RSA signature S as follows:

$$S \triangleq \prod_{i \in B} S_i^{2\lambda_{Bi}} \bmod N \ (= m^{4d} \bmod N); \quad (5)$$

A verifier can check the validity of a threshold signature (m_0, S) by the following equality

$$S^e \equiv m^4 \bmod N. \quad (6)$$

Of course, the m in above equality has been processed by the equation (3).

We have accomplished the description of our improvement to Shoup's scheme. The essential improvement is that Shoup's signing equation, displayed by the following equation (7), is modified as equation (5) in our scheme.

$$\bar{S} = S^a m^b \bmod N = m^{4ad+b} \bmod N. \quad (7)$$

Where, a, b are two public integers such that $4a + eb = 1$ since $\gcd(4, e) = 1$, and S is determined by equation (5).

5.2   Discussions of Threshold RSA Signature Scheme

Now, we will briefly discuss the validity, security and efficiency of our scheme.

Theorem 1. (Validity of the Scheme)   *If at least t honest members pro-duced valid partial signatures and correct proofs, then the threshold signature determined by equation (5) satisfies the signature verification equation (6).*

Proof. According to (2), for index subset $B \subseteq \{1, 2, \cdots, n\}$ with t elements we know that there exists an integer k such that $\sum_{i \in B}(\lambda_{Bi} \cdot d_i) = d + kM$. Therefore, from equation (5) and (4), we have

$$S = \prod_{i \in B} S_i^{2\lambda_{Bi}} \bmod N = m^{\sum_{i \in B} 4d_i \lambda_{Bi}} \bmod N$$
$$= m^{4d + 4kM} \bmod N = m^{4d + k\phi(N)} \bmod N = m^{4d} \bmod N. \tag{8}$$

On the other hand, $ed = 1 \bmod M$, so there exists an integer $\bar{k}$ such that $ed = 1 + \bar{k}M$. Hence,

$$S^e = (m^{4d})^e \bmod N = m^{4 + 4\bar{k}M} \bmod N = m^4 \bmod N. \tag{9}$$

So, the signature S on message m satisfies the verification equation (6).   □

Theorem 2. (Unforgeability of the Scheme)   *An attacker I can forge a valid signature to message m in our scheme if and only if he can forge a valid signature to the same message in Shoup's scheme.*

Proof. If attacker I can forge a valid signature S to message m in our scheme such that $S^e = m^4 \bmod N$. Then, by using the public parameters a and b of Shoup's scheme, attacker I can compute a value $\bar{S} = S^a m^b \bmod N$. Following reasonings show that $\bar{S}$ is the valid signature to message m in Shoup's scheme:

$$(\bar{S})^e = (S^a m^b)^e \bmod N = (S^e)^a m^{be} \bmod N$$
$$= m^{4a + eb} \bmod N = m \bmod N.$$

So attacker I has successfully forged the signature on message m in Shoup's scheme.

On the other hand, if attacker I can forge a valid signature $\bar{S}$ to message m in Shoup's scheme such that $\bar{S}^e = m \bmod N$. Then, let $S = \bar{S}^4 \bmod N$. We have

$$S^e = (\bar{S}^4)^e \bmod N = (\bar{S}^e)^4 \bmod N = m^4 \bmod N.$$

Above equalities show that attacker I has successfully forged the signature S on message m in our scheme.   □

Furthermore, as Shoup did in [20], the following theorem holds.

Theorem 3. (Security of the Scheme)   *In the random oracle model for hash function $\bar{H}$, our threshold signature scheme is secure (robust and non-forgeable) assuming the standard RSA scheme is secure.*

In addition, comparing with Shoup's scheme, our threshold signature scheme possesses several advantages as follows.

- **Simple Signing Equation.**   The signing equation in our scheme is $S = m^{4d} \bmod N$, which is simpler than Shoup's signing equation $\bar{S} = S^a m^b \bmod N$. In general, a and b are large integers, and one of them must be negative. Therefore, computing a signature in Shop's scheme is lower than in our scheme.
- **Protecting the Modulus.**   Because one of the two parameters a and b is negative integer in Shoup's scheme, one inverse, $S^{-1} \bmod N$ or $m^{-1} \bmod N$, has to be computed before generating every threshold signature. Once the inverse element cannot be found (of course, this case occurs in a negligent possibility because factoring RSA modulus is difficult.), a factor of N has been found and this RSA cryptosystem is crashed then. Therefore, Shoup's signing equation does a negative effect in protecting the RSA modulus N. But, our scheme is immune to this problem.
- **Scalability.**   Our scheme can be generalized to a threshold undeniable signature scheme (see section 5 of this paper), but Shoup's scheme seems intractable to generalize to this case.
- **Public Exponent.**   In fact, the public exponent e in our scheme can be selected as any element of Z_M^*, not necessarily a prime.

In addition, in order to verify the honesty of the dealer D, verifiable secret sharing [17] or publicly verifiable secret sharing schemes [21, 18] can be introduced. But the discussion about these problems is out the scope of this paper.

6   Threshold Undeniable RSA Signature Scheme

In this section, we propose a threshold undeniable RSA signature scheme with fine properties. As we know, this is the first threshold undeniable signature scheme based on RSA cryptosystem so far. In our scheme, by using Shamir's secret scheme [19], the dealer D distributes the RSA signing and verifying key pair (e, d) to all n members of group U, such that each subgroup of t honest members can generate undeniable RSA signature. At the same time, any t cooperative members can represent group U to confirming or disavowing an alleged signature. In addition, the honesty of each participating member is verifiable in all the three procedures of signature's generation, confirming and denying.

In the essence, this scheme is constructed by combining the Gennaro etc.'s undeniable RSA signature scheme in section 4 and the improved threshold RSA signature scheme in section 5. But to many details, skillful processing are conceived to construct a secure and practical scheme. Now, we describe the scheme in detail.

Stage 1: System Initialization

After selecting a RSA modulus N as the form defined in section 2, the dealer D chooses the signing and verifying key pair as (e, d), such that $ed = 1 \bmod M$ and e is a prime. Supposing n, the number of members in group U, satisfies $n < \min\{p', q'\}$. In addition, let $\bar{e} = e4^{-1} \bmod M$.

Stage 2: Distribution of Secrets

(2-1) The dealer D chooses two random polynomials $f(x), g(x) \in Z_M[x]$, such that $f(0) = d$ and $g(0) = \bar{e}$. Then, D computes the sub-keys as follows.

$$d_i = f(i)(n!)^{-1} \bmod M, \quad \bar{e}_i = g(i) \cdot (n!)^{-1} \bmod M, \quad i = 1, 2, \cdots, n.$$

Hence, to any subset B of size t in $\{1, 2, 3, \cdots, n\}$, sub-keys $d_i, \bar{e}_i$ satisfy the following properties (λ_{Bi} displayed in (2)):

$$d = \sum_{i \in B} d_i \cdot \lambda_{Bi} \bmod M, \quad \bar{e} = \sum_{i \in B} \bar{e}_i \cdot \lambda_{Bi} \bmod M. \tag{10}$$

(2-2) The dealer D selects a random generator w of Q_N and computes:

$$\begin{aligned} S_w &= w^{4d} \bmod N, & T_w &= w^{4\bar{e}} \bmod N. \\ S_{wi} &= w^{2d_i} \bmod N, & T_{wi} &= w^{2\bar{e}_i} \bmod N, \quad i = 1, 2, \cdots, n. \end{aligned} \tag{11}$$

(2-3) The dealer D randomly chooses a fixed element u in Z_N^* such that it's Jacobi value respect to N is -1, i.e.

$$\mathcal{J}(u|N) = -1, \quad u \in_R Z_N^*. \tag{12}$$

(2-4) The dealer D publishes N, n, u, w, S_w, T_w and $S_{wi}, T_{wi}(i = 1, 2, \cdots, n)$, but sends d_i and $\bar{e}_i$ to U_i secretly.

(2-5) U_i verifies the following equations:

$$\begin{aligned} S_{wi} &\equiv w^{2d_i} \bmod N, & T_{wi} &\equiv w^{2\bar{e}_i} \bmod N. \\ S_w &\equiv \prod_{j \in B} S_{wj}{}^{2\lambda_{Bj}} \bmod N, & T_w &\equiv \prod_{j \in B} T_{wj}{}^{2\lambda_{Bj}} \bmod N. \end{aligned} \tag{13}$$

Where, B can be any subset with t elements of $\{1, 2, \cdots, n\}$. If finding any of the above equations does not hold, U_i proclaims this fact, then the dealer D is considered to be failed in distributing the secrets. Otherwise, the dealer is successful.

Stage 3: Generation and Verification of Partial Signature

(3-1) If the member U_i wants to sign the original message m_0, he first computes message digest m of m_0 by using equation (3) such that we always have $\mathcal{J}(m|N) = 1$.

(3-2) U_i computes the partial signature of m as following:

$$S_{mi} = m^{2d_i} \bmod N. \tag{14}$$

Then, U_i runs the DLE($w^2, S_{wi}; m^2, S_{mi}; d_i$) protocol (where, w^2 and m^2 all are computed in mod N) and constructs the proof $Proof_{U_i}$ to indicate that $\log_{w^2} S_{wi} = \log_{m^2} S_{mi} (= d_i)$.

(3-3) Using $Proof_{U_i}$, any member can verify whether the partial signature S_{mi} is signed by U_i.

Stage 4: Generation of Threshold Undeniable Signature

If there are t members $U_i (i \in B$ and $|B| = t)$ who have generated valid partial signatures, then the threshold undeniable signature S_m on message m can be computed by the following equation:

$$S_m = \prod_{i \in B} S_{mi}{}^{2\lambda_{Bi}} \bmod N \ (= m^{4d} \bmod N). \tag{15}$$

Stage 5: Confirmation Protocol

After getting the consent of t members $U_i (i \in B$ and $|B| = t)$, V can run the following confirming protocol with these t members to check whether an alleged signature (m, S_m) is signed by group U.

(5-1) V selects two random numbers $c_1, c_2 \in_R [1, N]$, computes the following challenger C and sends or broadcasts it to every member $U_i (i \in B)$:

$$C = S_m^{c_1} S_w^{c_2} \bmod N. \tag{16}$$

(5-2) After U_i received C, he computes his partial response R_i as:

$$R_i = C^{2\bar{e}_i} \bmod N. \tag{17}$$

Using the protocol $\mathrm{DLE}(w^2, T_{wi}; C^2, R_i; \bar{e}_i)$, U_i produces the proof $Proof_{U_i}$ and broadcasts $(R_i, Proof_{U_i})$. Obtained this information, each member can verify the validity of R_i. If all these t members have produced their correct partial responses R_i, then the response R can be determined by the following equation, and be sent to V:

$$R \overset{\triangle}{=} \prod_{i \in B} R_i^{2\lambda_{Bi}} \bmod N \ (= C^{4\bar{e}} \bmod N). \tag{18}$$

(5-3) V verifies whether the following equality holds after he received R:

$$R \equiv m^{4c_1} w^{4c_2} \bmod N. \tag{19}$$

If yes, then V accepts the signature (m, S_m), i.e. he believes that S_m is U's valid signature on message m. Otherwise, the denial protocol has to be run to determine whether (m, S_m) is not a signature of U.

Stage 6: Denial Protocol

When t members $U_i (i \in B$ and $|B| = t)$ agree to deny an alleged signature (m, S_m), V and $U_i (i \in B)$ run the following denial protocol.

(6-1) V selects two random numbers $c_1 \in_R [1, l], c_2 \in_R [1, N]$, then he computes (C_1, C_2) as follows and sends or broadcasts them to every U_i $(i \in B)$.

$$C_1 = m^{c_1} w^{c_2} \bmod N, \quad C_2 = S_m^{c_1} S_w^{c_2} \bmod N. \tag{20}$$

(6-2) All $U_i (i \in B)$ use their sub-keys $\bar{e}_i$ to compute:

$$S_m{}^{4\bar{e}} = \prod_{i \in B} (S_m{}^{2\bar{e}_i})^{2\lambda_{Bi}} \bmod N, \quad C_2{}^{4\bar{e}} = \prod_{i \in B} (C_2{}^{2\bar{e}_i})^{2\lambda_{Bi}} \bmod N. \quad (21)$$

Then they search all possible values in $[1, l]$ to find a number r such that the following equation holds, and send this r to the verifier V:

$$(m^4/S_m{}^{4\bar{e}})^r = C_1^4/C_2{}^{4\bar{e}} \bmod N. \quad (22)$$

(6-3) V verifies whether $r \equiv c_1$. If yes, then V rejects the signature S_m, i.e. V believes that S_m is not group U's signature on message m. Otherwise, V considers that these members U_i $(i \in B)$ is trying to deny U's threshold signature S_m deliberately.

7   Analysis of the Proposed Scheme

Now, we give a brief discussion about the validity and security of the above threshold undeniable RSA signature scheme. First, it is not difficult to verify the completeness of our scheme according to the descriptions, i.e. if all t members are honest and have produced valid partial signatures, then the determined threshold undeniable signature will pass through the confirmation protocol. Second, Shamir's secret sharing scheme [19] is used to distributing secrets in our scheme, so it can be concluded that an attacker I cannot generate a valid threshold undeniable signature if the number of members controlled by I is less than t. Third, in all the three procedures of generation, confirmation and denial of undeniable signature, all the corrupted members will be identified, because each participating member has to run the DLE protocol for constructing necessary proof to indicate that they have operated properly in these three procedures. Last, from the security of Gennaro etc.'s scheme [12], one can conclude that each sub-key will not be compromised when each member uses it to confirm or deny undeniable signature. Hence, we have successfully proposed a secure, robust and efficient threshold undeniable signature scheme with a dealer.

8   Future Work

In the future research, we will consider to generalize our threshold undeniable RSA signature scheme to the distributing environment where there is no the help of a dealer or a trusted party. Some of relevant works have been done by Frankel, MacKenzie and Yung [11], Damgård and Koprowski [9].

References

1. J. Boyar, D. Chaum, I. Damgård, and T. Pedersen. Convertible Undeniable Signatures. In *Crypto'90, LNCS 537*, pp. 189-205. Springer-Verlag, 1991.

2. D. Chaum. Zero-Knowledge Undeniable Signatures. In: *Eurocrypt'90, LNCS 473*, pp. 458-464. Springer-Verlag, 1991.

3. J. Camenisch, and M. Michels. Proving in Zero-knowledge that a Number Is the Product of Two Safe Primes. In *Eurocrypt'99, LNCS 1592*, pp.107-122. Springer-Verlag, 1999.

4. D. Chaum, and T.P. Pedersen. Transferred Cash Grows in Size. In *Eurocrypt'92, LNCS 658*, pp. 390-407. Springer-Verlag, 1993.

5. D. Chaum, and T.P. Pedersen. Wallet Databases With Observers. In *Crypto'92, LNCS 740*, pp. 89-105. Springer-Verlag, 1993.

6. D. Chaum, and H. Van Antwerpen. Undeniable Signatures. In *Crypto'89, LNCS 435*, pp. 212-216. Springer-Verlag, 1989.

7. Y. Desmedt. Society and Group Oriented Cryptography: A New Concept. In *Crypto'87, LNCS 293*, pp. 120-127. Springer-Verlag, 1988.

8. Y. Desmedt, and Y. Frankel. Threshold Cryptosystems. In *Crypto'89, LNCS 435*, pp. 307-315. Springer-Verlag, 1990.

9. I. Damgård, and M. Koprowski. Practical Threshold RSA Signature Without a Trusted Dealer. In *Eurocrypt 2001* (to appear). Available from http://www.daimi.au.dk/ ivan/papers.html

10. I. Damgård, and T. Pedersen. New Convertible Undeniable Signature Schemes. In *Eurocrypt'96, LNCS 1070*, pp. 372-386. Springer-Verlag, 1996.

11. Y. Frankel, P. D. MacKenzie, and M. Yung. Robust Efficient Distributed RSA-Key Generation. In *30th STOC*, pp. 663-672. ACM, 1998.

12. R. Gennaro, H. Krawczyk, and T. Rabin. RSA-Based Undeniable Signature. In *Crypto'97*, pp. 132-148. Springer-Verlag, 1997.

13. L. Harn, and S. Yang. Group-Oriented Undeniable Signature Schemes without the Assistance of a Mutually Trusted Party. In *Auscrypt'92, LNCS 718*, pp. 133-142. Springer-Verlag, 1993.

14. S.K. Langford. Weakness in Some Threshold Cryptosystems. In *Crypto' 96, LNCS 1109*, pp. 74-82. Springer-Verlag, 1996.

15. N.-Y. Lee, and T. Hwang. Group-Oriented Undeniable Signature Schemes with a Trusted Center. *Computer Communications*, 1999, 22: 730-734.

16. C.-H. Lin, C.-T. Wang, and C.-C. Chang. A Group-Oriented (t, n) Undeniable Signature Scheme without Trusted Center. In: *Information Security and Privacy, ACISP'96, LNCS 1172*, pp. 266-274. Springer-Verlag, 1996.

17. T.P. Pedersen. No-Interactive and Information-Theoretic Secure Verifiable Secret Sharing. In *Crypto'91, LNCS 576*, pp. 129-140. Springer-Verlag, 1992.

18. B. Schoenmakers. A Simple Publicly Verifiable Secret Sharing Scheme and Its Application to Electronic Voting. In *Crypto'99, LNCS 1666*, pp. 148-164. Springer-Verlag, 1999.

19. A. Shamir. How to Share a Secret. *Communications of the ACM*, 1979, 22(11): 612-613.

20. V. Shoup. Practical Threshold Signatures. In *Eurocrypt'2000, LNCS 1807*, pp. 207-220. Springer-Verlag, 2000. Avalaible from http://www.shoup.net/papers/

21. M. Stadler. Publicly Verifiable Secret Sharing. In *Eurocrypt'96, LNCS 1070*, pp. 191-199. Springer-Verlag, 1996.

Two Simple Batch Verifying Multiple Digital Signatures

Min-Shiang Hwang[1], Cheng-Chi Lee[2], and Yuan-Liang Tang[1]

[1] Department of Information Management,
Chaoyang University of Technology,
168 Gifeng E. Rd., Wufeng,
Taichung County, Taiwan 413
{mshwang, yltang}@mail.cyut.edu.tw
http://www.cyut.edu.tw/~mshwang
[2] Department of Computer and Information Science,
National Chiao-Tung University,
1001 Ta Hsueh Road,
Hsinchu 300, Taiwan

Abstract. In this article, we propose two types of multiple digital signatures for batch verification. our schemes not only efficient to reduce computation of verifying these signatures, but also secure to detect forged multiple digital signatures.

1 Introduction

In 1994, Naccache et al. [8] proposed an efficient batch verifying multiple DSA digital signatures. The merit of their scheme is that a signer signed t documents using his/her private key separately and sent the multiple digital signatures to a verifier. The verifier can verify these multiple digital signatures by the signer's public key which need only one verification instead of t verifications. However, this scheme is insecure which is attacked by Lim and Lee [7]. An attacker can easily forge multiple digital signatures to make a false batch verification valid.

Recently, Harn proposed two efficient non-interactive batch verification protocols for DSA-type and RSA-type multiple digital signatures, respectively [2, 3]. For convenience, BV-DSA scheme is short for the DSA-type; and BV-RSA scheme is short for the RSA-type multiple digital signatures in this article. Both BV-DSA and BV-RSA schemes can against Lim and Lee's attack [7]. However, there are some weaknesses in BV-RSA scheme [5].

In this article, we show that there is a weakness in BV-DSA scheme. To overcome the weaknesses in BV-DSA and BV-RSA schemes, we propose two simple and secure improvements of these schemes in this article.

2 The Weaknesses of BV-DSA and BV-RSA Schemes

In the next two subsections, we briefly review the BV-DSA [2] and BV-RSA [3] schemes and some weaknesses in these schemes.

S. Qing, T. Okamoto, and J. Zhou (Eds.): ICICS 2001, LNCS 2229, pp. 233–237, 2001.
© Springer-Verlag Berlin Heidelberg 2001

2.1   The Weakness of BV-DSA Scheme

We briefly review DSA digital signature [4,6] as follows. Let p be a large prime; q be a factor of $(p-1)$; g be a generator with order q in $\mathrm{GF}(p)$; x and y be a signer's private key and public key, respectively. Here, $y = g^x \bmod p$. When a sender wants to send a signed message M to a receiver, he/she must to generate a digital signature (r, s) as follows: $r = (g^k \bmod p) \bmod q$, $s = rk - Mx \bmod q$, and k is a random number which is generated by the sender. Once receiving (M, r, s) from the sender, the receiver can verify the correctness of the signature on the message M by checking the equation $r = (g^{sr^{-1}} y^{Mr^{-1}} \bmod p) \bmod q$. Next, we review Harn's BV-DSA digital signature as follows.

Generating Multiple Digital Signatures:
Assume that a sender, Alice, wants to send t messages $M_1, M_2, \cdots, M_t$ and digital signatures $(r_1, s_1), (r_2, s_2), \cdots, (r_t, s_t)$ to a receiver, Bob, where $r_i = (g^{k_i} \bmod p) \bmod q$; $s_i = r_i k_i - M_i x \bmod q$, $i = 1, 2, \cdots, t$; k_i is a random number; and x is Alice's secret key.

Batch Verifying Multiple Digital Signatures:
After receiving these digital signatures from Alice, Bob verifies the correctness of these multiple digital signatures on messages $M_1, M_2, \cdots, M_t$ using Alice's public key y in the following equation:

$$\prod_{i=1}^{t} r_i = (g^{\sum_{i=1}^{t} s_i r_i^{-1}} y^{\sum_{i=1}^{t} M_i r_i^{-1}} \bmod p) \bmod q. \tag{1}$$

BV-DSA scheme is simple and efficient to verify multiple digital signatures. However, there is a weakness in this scheme. A dishonest signer, Alice, can forge individual signature and make a false batch verification valid. Assume that Alice sends t messages M_i and forged signatures (r_i, s_i'), $i = 1, 2, \cdots, t$, to Bob, where $s_i' = s_i + a_i r_i \bmod q$, $i = 1, 2, \cdots, t$; a_i is an integer such that $\sum_{i=1}^{t} a_i = 0$.

By verifying Equation (1), Bob is convinced that these messages are signed by Alice. However, when a dispute occurs, Alice can deny her digital signatures because $r_i \neq (g^{s_i' r_i^{-1}} y^{M_i r_i^{-1}} \bmod p) \bmod q$, $i = 1, 2, \cdots, t$.

2.2   The Weakness of BV-RSA Scheme

We briefly review the RSA digital signature [1,9] as follows. Let $n = p \times q$, where p and q are two large primes; e and d are a signer's public key and private key, respectively, such that $e \times d \bmod (p-1)(q-1) \equiv 1$. When a signer, Alice, wants to send a signed message M to a receiver, Bob, she must to generate a digital signature S as follows: $S = h(M)^d \bmod n$, where $h(\cdot)$ is a public one-way hash function. Once receiving (M, S) from Alice, Bob can verify the correctness of the signature on the message M by checking the equation $h(M) = S^e \bmod n$. Next, we review BV-RSA digital signature as follows.

Generating Multiple Digital Signatures:
Assume that a signer, Alice, wants to send messages $M_1, M_2, \cdots, M_t$ and signatures $S_1, S_2, \cdots, S_t$ to a receiver, Bob. The multiple signatures $S_1, S_2, \cdots, S_t$ are signed using the Alice's private key d in the following: $S_i = h(M_i)^d \bmod n$, $i = 1, 2, \cdots, t$.

Batch Verifying Multiple Digital Signatures
After receiving these multiple signatures from Alice, Bob verifies the correctness of these multiple digital signatures on messages $M_1, M_2, \cdots, M_t$ using Alice's public key e by checking the following equation:

$$(\prod_{i=1}^{t} S_i)^e = \prod_{i=1}^{t} h(M_i) \bmod n. \tag{2}$$

BV-RSA scheme is simple and efficient to verify multiple RSA digital signatures. However, Hwang et al. shown that there is a weakness in this scheme [5]. A dishonest signer, Alice, can forge individual digital signature and make a false batch verification valid. Hwang et al. [5] also proposed two methods to attack the BV-RSA scheme.

In the first method, a dishonest (Alice) sends messages and the forged digital signatures (M_i, S_i'), $i = 1, 2, \cdots, t$, to a verifier (Bob), where $S_i' = h(M_{f(i)})^d \bmod n$, $i = 1, 2, \cdots, t$; $f(\cdot)$ is a one to one and onto function such that $f(i) = j$, $i = 1, 2, \cdots, t$ and $j = 1, 2, \cdots, t$.

In the second method, a dishonest sends messages and the forged digital signatures (M_i, S_i'), $i = 1, 2, \cdots, t$, to a verifier, where $S_i' = a_i \times S_i \bmod q$, $i = 1, 2, \cdots, t$ and $\prod_{i=1}^{t} a_i = 1$.

By verifying the Equation (2) in the above two methods, Bob is convinced that these messages are signed by Alice. However, when a dispute occurs, Alice can deny her signed messages because of $h(M_i) \neq (S_i')^e \bmod n$.

3   Our Improved Schemes

We have introduced the weaknesses of BV-DSA and BV-RSA schemes in Section 2. A dishonest signer can forge individual digital signatures and make a false batch verification valid.

To remedy these weaknesses of BV-DSA and BV-RSA, we propose two simple and secure improvements of BV-DSA and BV-RSA multiple digital signatures in this section. The key point of our improved schemes is that we make multiple digital signatures in order. The dishonest signer cannot transpose these digital signatures such that a verifier passes the validation of the batch verifying multiple digital signatures.

The Improvement of BV-DSA Scheme:
The difference of BV-DSA and our improved scheme is only in Equation (1). In our improved scheme, Equation (1) is modified as follows.

$$\prod_{i=1}^{t} r_i^{v_i} = (g^{\sum_{i=1}^{t} s_i r_i^{-1} v_i} y^{\sum_{i=1}^{t} M_i r_i^{-1} v_i} \bmod p) \bmod q, \tag{3}$$

where v_i, $i = 1, 2, \cdots, t$, are small random numbers which are randomly chosen by a verifier.

The Improvement of BV-RSA Scheme:
The difference of BV-RSA and our improved scheme is in Equation (2). In our improved scheme, Equation (2) is modified as follows.

$$(\prod_{i=1}^{t} S_i^{v_i})^e = \prod_{i=1}^{t} h(M_i)^{v_i} \bmod n. \tag{4}$$

Next, we analyze the security of our improved schemes as follows. Based on Harn's BV-DSA and BV-RSA schemes, the security of our improved schemes is the same as that of their schemes except that our improved schemes have no those weaknesses of their schemes.

In our improved BV-DSA scheme, a dishonest signer cannot use the same methods in Section 2 to cheat a verifier of passing the batch verifying multiple digital signatures. After receiving some multiple signatures, a verifier randomly chooses some integers and verifies the validation of theses multiple signatures by Equation (3). Once one or more signatures are modified, the verifier fails the validation of the batch verifying signatures. If a dishonest signer wants to make some false multiple digital signatures (r_i, s_i') valid, he/she must to make the following equation holds.

$$\sum_{i=1}^{t} s_i r_i^{-1} v_i = \sum_{i=1}^{t} s_i' r_i^{-1} v_i \pmod{q}. \tag{5}$$

Since the signer did not know the values v_i, he/she is difficult to make the Equation (5) holds.

In our improved BV-RSA scheme, the security analysis is similar to that of our improved BV-DSA scheme. If a dishonest signer wants to make some false multiple digital signatures (S_i') valid, he/she must to make the following equation holds.

$$\prod_{i=1}^{t} S_i^{v_i} = \prod_{i=1}^{t} S_i'^{v_i}. \tag{6}$$

Again, the signer is difficult to make the above equation holds because he/she did not know these random integers v_i.

4   Conclusion

We have shown that there are some weaknesses in BV-DSA and BV-RSA schemes. We also proposed two improvements of BV-DSA and BV-RSA schemes. Our schemes not only simple but also secure to remedy these weaknesses of BV-DSA and BV-RSA schemes.

Acknowledgements. The authors wish to thank many anonymous referees for their suggestions to improve this paper. Part of this research was supported by the National Science Council, Taiwan, under contract no. NSC89-2213-E-324-053.

References

1. C. C. Chang and M. S. Hwang, "Parallel computation of the generating keys for RSA cryptosystems," *IEE Electronics Letters*, vol. 32, no. 15, pp. 1365–1366, 1996.
2. L. Harn, "Batch verifying multiple DSA-type digital signatures," *Electronics Letters*, vol. 34, no. 9, pp. 870–871, 1998.
3. L. Harn, "Batch verifying multiple RSA digital signatures," *Electronics Letters*, vol. 34, no. 12, pp. 1219–1220, 1998.
4. L. Harn and Y. Xu, "Design of generalised ElGamal type digital signature schemes based on discrete logarithm," *Electronics Letters*, vol. 30, no. 24, pp. 2025–2026, 1994.
5. M. S. Hwang, I. C. Lin, and K. F. Hwang, "Cryptanalysis of the batch verifying multiple RSA digital signatures," *Informatica*, vol. 11, no. 1, pp. 15–19, 2000.
6. M. S. Hwang, C. C. Chang, and K. F. Hwang, "An ElGamal-like cryptosystem for enciphering large messages," *accepted and to appear in IEEE Transactions on Knowledge and Data Engineering*.
7. C. H. Lim and P. J. Lee, "Security of interactive DSA batch verification," *Electronics Letters*, vol. 30, no. 19, pp. 1592–1593, 1994.
8. D. Naccache, D. Mraihi, D. Rapheali, and S. Vaudenay, "Can DSA be improved: Complexity trade-offs with the digital signature standard," in *Proceedings of Eurocrypt'94*, pp. 85–94, Lecture Notes in Computer Science, 1994.
9. R. L. Rivest, A. Shamir, and L. Adleman, "A method for obtaining digital signatures and public key cryptosystems," *Communications of the ACM*, vol. 21, pp. 120–126, Feb. 1978.

Square Attack on Reduced Camellia Cipher*

Yeping He and Sihan Qing

Engineering Research Center for Information Security Technology;
State Key Laboratory of Information Security, Institute of Software,
Chinese Academy of Sciences, Beijing 100080, P. R. China.
{yphe, qsh}@ercist.iscas.ac.cn
http://www.ercist.ac.cn/

Abstract. Camellia block cipher, which is 128-bit block size and supports 128-, 192- and 256-bit keys, is one of the NESSIE (New European Schemes for Signatures, Integrity and Encryption) candidates. The Square attack on Camellia is studied in this paper. With the detail analysis of round function in Camellia, Square attack extension to 6 rounds faster than exhaustive key search was found. The result of the paper shows that Square attack is the best attack on Camellia.

1 Introduction

With the development of the computer network, block cipher, as the key technique of security in the network, become more and more important. As AES (advanced encryption standard) draw to its end in USA, Europe starts NESSIE (new European Schemes for Signatures, Integrity and Encryption) project. The main objective of the project is to maintain the strong position of European research while strengthening the position of European industry in cryptography. Same as AES, the NESSIE projective is an open process. There are 17 new block cipher algorithm as the accepted NESSIE submissions and Camellia block cipher [1] is one of them.

Square attack is a dedicated attack on Square cipher that exploits the byte-oriented structure of the cipher and was proposed by the algorithm designer J. Daemen, L. Knudsen and V.Rijmen [2]. The attack is a chosen plaintext attack and independent of the specific choices of S-box and key schedule. Chosen Λ-Set which is a special set of plaintexts, Square attack eliminated some wrong keys based on the balance of ciphertext, and repeated this process with other Λ-Sets until the cipher key can be found. Square attack is also valid for Rijndael [3] and Anubis [6] that are similar in structures to Square. So far the attack is the best attack of AES and become one of the most important method to attack block cipher. H. Gibert and M. Minier [5] extend the attack to 7-round for 196 keybits and 256 keybits version of Rijndael by exploiting the existence of collision

* This project is supported by the National Key Basic Research Program of China under Grant No. G1999035810 and the National Natural Science Foundation of China under Grant No. 60083007.

S. Qing, T. Okamoto, and J. Zhou (Eds.): ICICS 2001, LNCS 2229, pp. 238–245, 2001.

between partial function. With dynamic programming technique N.Ferguson, J. Kelsey and S. Lucks [4] reduced the complexity of Square attack by partial sum.

In this paper, Square attack on Camellia, a Feistel structure cipher, is discussed. with detail analysis of round function, an attack on reduced 6-round of Camellia that requires 13×2^8 chosen plaintext and complexity is 2^{112} cipher executions was found. The result shows that Square attack is valid not only for structure similar to Square but for Feistel structure also. This paper is organized as follows. In section 2 the outline of Camellia is provided. Basic analysis for 4 rounds of Camellia is discussed in section 3. Section 4 describes 5-round attack and extends to 6-round with the detail analysis of round function. In section 5 the complexity of the attack is analyzed and finally concludes the paper.

2   An Outline of Camellia

In this section we briefly described the Camellia algorithm. Camellia is a block cipher supporting 128 bits block size and 128-, 192- and 256 bits keys. The algorithm is composed of encryption and decryption procedure and key schedule. In the following we introduce round structure only for Square attack is independent of the key schedule.

Camellia uses an iterative round function in a Feistel structure with additional input/output whitening and FL-function and FL^{-1}-function inserted every 6 rounds. The round function F[K], that is dependent of round key $K^i \in GF(2^8)^8$ and map a 64 bit block to 64 bit block, is a SPN (Substitution-Permutation Network) structure.

$$F[K]: \quad GF(2^8)^8 \to GF(2^8)^8.$$

The round function is composed of three function, $\sigma[K]$ and P-function as the linear layer and S-function as the non-linear layer, i.e.

$$F[K] = P \circ S \circ \sigma[K]. \tag{1}$$

Where

− S-function uses 4 different S-box S_1, S_2, S_3 and S_4.

$$S: \quad GF(2^8)^8 \to GF(2^8)^8.$$

$$S(x_1, x_2, x_3, x_4, x_5, x_6, x_7, x_8)$$
$$= (S_1(x_1), S_2(x_2), S_3(x_3), S_4(x_4), S_2(x_5), S_3(x_6), S_4(x_7), S_1(x_8)). \tag{2}$$

− P-function is a linear mapping

$$P: \quad GF(2^8)^8 \to GF(2^8)^8;$$
$$P(Z) = Z'.$$

where

$$Z_1' = Z_1 \oplus Z_3 \oplus Z_4 \oplus Z_6 \oplus Z_7 \oplus Z_8$$
$$Z_2' = Z_1 \oplus Z_2 \oplus Z_4 \oplus Z_5 \oplus Z_7 \oplus Z_8$$
$$Z_3' = Z_1 \oplus Z_2 \oplus Z_3 \oplus Z_5 \oplus Z_6 \oplus Z_8$$
$$Z_4' = Z_2 \oplus Z_3 \oplus Z_4 \oplus Z_5 \oplus Z_6 \oplus Z_7$$
$$Z_5' = Z_1 \oplus Z_2 \oplus Z_6 \oplus Z_7 \oplus Z_8 \tag{3}$$
$$Z_6' = Z_2 \oplus Z_3 \oplus Z_5 \oplus Z_7 \oplus Z_8$$
$$Z_7' = Z_3 \oplus Z_4 \oplus Z_5 \oplus Z_6 \oplus Z_8$$
$$Z_8' = Z_1 \oplus Z_4 \oplus Z_5 \oplus Z_6 \oplus Z_7$$

– $\sigma[K]$ is a exclusive-or operation with key

$$\sigma[K](y) = y' \Leftrightarrow y_i' = y_i \oplus k_i, \quad i = 1, 2, \cdots, 8.$$

3 The Basic Result

In this section we shall analyze the balance of the cipher through 4 round considering a special Λ-Set as a chosen plaintext set. This result is a base to attack on Camellia by Square.

3.1 Concept and Notations

First we shall introduce the Λ-Set. A Λ-Set is a 8 bytes vector set of 256 states that are all different in some of the state bytes (active bytes) and all equal in the other states bytes (passive bytes). It's strictly definition is as follows.

Definition 1. *Let Λ be a 8 bytes vector set and λ be the index set of the state bytes. If*

$$\forall x, y \in \Lambda \Rightarrow \begin{cases} x_i \neq y_i & for\ i \in \lambda \\ x_i = y_i & for\ i \notin \lambda \end{cases}$$

was satisfied. the Λ is said to be a Λ-Set and Λ the active bytes index set.

From the definition of Λ-Set and the three basic function described in the previous section, it is easy to see that nonlinear transformation S and key exclusive-or function $\sigma[K]$ convert a Λ-Set into a Λ-Set with identical λ and applying the linear transformation P on a Λ-Set dose not necessarily result in a Λ-Set.

Now we give some notations that will be used in the sequel. We write X^0 for the right half of the 128 bit plaintext and X^1 for the left half. We will use X^i to refer to left input of the i-round, A^i the state at the beginning of the P-function in the i-round and B^i the state at the output of the P-function in the i-round and denote by

$$F[K^i] = P \circ S \circ \sigma[K^i].$$

the round function of the i-round.

3.2   The Basic Result

Consider a Λ-Set as the right half of the 128 bit plaintexts X^0, in which only one byte is active and the left half of the 128 bit plaintexts X^1 being constant. As shown in Figure 1. X^2 is still a Λ-Set with only one active byte for X^1 is constant. The function S and $\sigma[K]$ of the second round transmit the Λ-Set into a Λ-Set to keep λ unchanged. P of the second round convert the Λ-Set into another Λ-Set with more active bytes which will take every value exactly once. This is still the case by S and $\sigma[K]$ of the third round. The Λ-Set is subsequently transformed by P to not necessary a Λ-Set. Since the bytes of A^3 are either constant or ranging over all possible values exactly once, the exclusive -or of each component over the Λ-Set result in 0. Note that each byte of B^3 is linear combination of A^3, for $i = 1, 2, \cdots, 8$, we have

$$\bigoplus_{B^3 = P(A^3), \; A^3 \in \Lambda} B_i^3 = \bigoplus_{A^3 \in \Lambda} \bigoplus_{l=1}^{8} \tau_{li} \bullet A_l^3 = \bigoplus_{l=1}^{8} \tau_{li} \bullet \left(\bigoplus_{A^3 \in \Lambda} A_l^3 \right) = \bigoplus_{l=1}^{8} \tau_{li} \bullet 0 = 0.$$

where $\tau_{li} = 1$ or 0. B_i^3 is said to be balanced.

Theorem 1. *If X^0 is a Λ-Set with only one active byte and X^1 a constant, each byte of X^4 is balanced.*

Proof. According to previous analysis, we know that each byte of B^3 and $X^2$is balanced. Note that Camellia is Feistel structure and $X_i^4 = B_I^3 \oplus X_i^2$, so the result is followed easily.   □

In general this balance is destroyed by S-function of 4-round.

4   Attack on Camellia

In this section we study Square attack on reduced Camellia by balanced result getting from previous section.

4.1   Attack on 5 Rounds

As shown in Figure 1, the 5 rounds of Camellia cipher can be regard as the extension of 4 rounds by adding a round at the end. By means of the basic result in the last section, we shall give an attack on 5 rounds.

First we establish the relationship of X^4, the 4th round input, and X^6, the 5th round output, that is the key for our attack. Note that

$$X^4 = X^6 \oplus B^5.$$

If we know the round key K^5, we can calculate the output of $\sigma[K^5]$and B^5because the output of the 5th round is known. In general we have

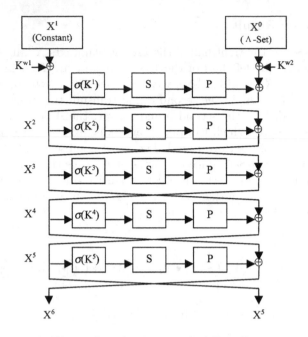

Fig. 1. Attack on 5-round of Camellia

$$X^i = X^{i+2} \oplus P \circ S(K^{i+1} \oplus X^{i+1}), \quad i = 1, 2, 3, 4. \tag{4}$$

This is illustrated in Figure 1.

Consider a Λ-Set as X^0 , in which only one byte is active and the X^1 is constant and record the corresponding ciphertext (X^5, X^6). For any assuming round key K^5, calculate X^4 by equation (4). Do this for all 256 ciphertext in the set and check whether the exor of the 256 X^4 equals zero. If it doesn't, the guessed round key is wrong by theorem 3.1 and is eliminated. A few wrong keys may pass the test, repeating it for several times until the round key can be found. Since by checking a single Λ-Set leaves $1/256$ as candidates and 2^{64} key values must be checked in our attack, the correct key is left only with overwhelming probability with 8 Λ-Sets.

4.2   Extension of 6-Round

In the following a further extension of an attack on 6 rounds, which is faster than exhaustive key search, is studied by improving our 5-round attack.

We shall start our research by a detail analysis of round function. We know that one output byte of $\sigma[K]$ function or S function depends on only one input byte and one output byte of P function depends on only partial input bytes. From the equation (1), it is easy to know that one output byte of round function depends on only partial input bytes also. For example, if 1, 2, 6, 7, 8 bytes of A^5 are known, from equation (3) we can deduce 5th byte of B^5. And hence we have

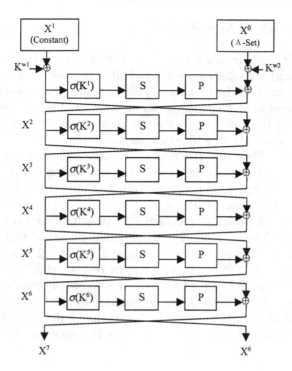

Fig. 2. Extension of 6-round

$$X^4(5) = X^6(5) \oplus B^5(5) = X^6(5) \oplus P(1,2,6,7,8). \tag{5}$$

From this result, an attack on 5 rounds can be improved. As a matter of fact, by assuming only 1, 2, 6, 7, 8 bytes of K^5, we can calculate the corresponding output bytes of function $\sigma[K^5]$ and the function S. And then we get the 5th byte of B^5 from equation (3). By theorem 3.1 and equation (5), if the value of $X^4(5)$ are not balanced over the Λ-Set, the assumed value for the round key bytes $K^5(1,2,6,7,8)$ were wrong.

Based on the improved 5-round attack, now we extend the attack to 6 rounds. Similar to an 5-round attack, take a Λ-Set as X^0 , in which only one byte is active and the X^1 is constant and record 256 corresponding ciphertext (X^6, X^7). By guessing a value for K^6, we calculate X^5 from equation (4). And then assuming the values for 1, 2, 6, 7, 8 bytes of K^5, $X^4(5)$ can be deduced from equation (5).Check whether the exor of all 256 $X^4(5)$ results zero. If it doesn't, the assumed K^6 and 1, 2, 6, 7, 8 bytes of K^5 are wrong. Since by checking a single Λ-Set leaves $1/256$ as candidates and 2^{104} key values must be checked in our attack, the correct key is left only with overwhelming probability with 13 Λ-Set.

5   Complexity of the Attack

The complexity of the attack is discussed in this section. For a 5-round attack, 2^{64} possible round key values must be checked to recover K^5. Since by checking a single Λ-Set of plaintexts leaves about $1/256$ of wrong key as possible candidates, the whole process must be repeated for 8 times of Λ-Sets plaintext. However, after testing with the first Λ-Set of 256 plaintexts, only 2^{56} candidate key values are remained. And only this fraction has to be tested with the second Λ-Set of the plaintexts. Therefore, the first check determines the complexity of the attack. For each given round key value, the calculations of X^4 from equation (4) are not more complex than encryptions and hence the attack complexity is $2^{64} \times 2^8 = 2^{72}$ cipher executions.

For an improved 5-round attack, only 2^{40} possible round key values must be filtered to recover 5 bytes of K^5. The whole process must be repeated for 5 times of Λ-Sets plaintext. The attack complexity is $2^{40} \times 2^8 = 2^{48}$ cipher executions.

In 6-round attack, 2^{104} key values must be test to get K^6 and 5 bytes of K^5, the right key values can be found with overwhelming probability with 13 Λ-Set. The attack complexity, which is also determined by the first test, is $2^{104} \times 2^8 = 2^{112}$ cipher executions. This attack is faster than exhaustive key search. The complexity of Square attack on reduced Camellia cipher are summarized in the table 1.

Table 1. Complexity of the attack

Square attack	Plaintexts	Cipher executions
On 5 rounds	2^{11}	2^{72}
Improved on 5 rounds	5×2^8	2^{48}
On 6 rounds	13×2^8	2^{112}

6   Conclusion

Square attack on Camellia, a Feistel structure cipher, is discussed in this paper. By the detail analysis of round function an attack on reduced 6-round of Camellia that requires 13×2^8 chosen plaintext and complexity is 2^{112} cipher executions was found. This attack is faster than exhaustive key search. The result shows that Square attack works against not only structure similar to that of Square cipher but Feistel structure also.

References

1. K. Aoki, T Ichikawa and M. Kanda. Camellia: A 128-Bit Block Cipher Suitable for Multiple Platforms -Design and Analysis-. 2000, http://www.cryptonessie.org
2. J.Daemen and V. Rijmen. The Block Cipher Square. In Fast Software Encryption'97, Lecture Notes in Computer Science, 1997, Vol.1267, pp.149-165
3. J. Daemen and V. Rijmen. AES proposal: Rijdael, AES submission. http://www.nist.gov/aes
4. N. Ferguson, J. Kelsey and S. Lucks. Improved Cryptanalysis of RIJDAEL. http://www.cs.berkeley.edu/ daw/papers/
5. H. Gilbert and M. Minier. A collision attack on 7 rounds of Rijdael, Third Advanced Encryption Standard Candidate Conference, NIST. April 2000, pp.230-241
6. P. S.L.M. Barreto and V. Rijmen. The ANUBIS Block Cipher, 2000. http://www.cryptonessie.org

Generalization of Elliptic Curve Digital Signature Schemes[*]

Lin You[1,2], Yi Xian Yang[3], and Chun Qi Zhang[3]

[1] Dept. of Math., Hainan Normal University, Haikou 571158, P. R. China
[2] Dept. of Math., Dalian University of Technology, Dalian 116023, P. R. China,
[3] P.O.Box 126, Beijing University of Posts & Telecom., Beijing 100876, P. R. China

Abstract. ECDSA can be viewed as the elliptic curve analogue of DSA. Many variants of (ElGamal) DSA and some general types were proposed in [4]. In this paper, several general types of ECDSA and some new variants of the basic ECDSA are described. From these general types, we can extract the desired, high efficient elliptic curve digital signature schemes. Moreover, their related securities are briefly analyzed.

1 Introduction

The elliptic curve cryptosystems (ECC) was invented by V. Miller [1] in 1985. ECC can be viewed as the analogue of discrete logarithm cryptosystems . The security of ECC is based on the elliptic curve discrete logarithm problem (ECDLP). The elliptic curve digital signature algorithm (ECDSA) is the elliptic curve analogue of the digital signature algorithm (DSA). An original ECDSA was proposed in 1992 by Vanstone [3], and its three variants were given in [6,7]. These signature schemes are basically the analogues of the corresponding ElGamal digital signature schemes. The generalizations of the ElGamal DSA were investigated in [4]. In this paper, we propose several generalizations of ECDSA schemes and also describe some new variants of the basic ECDSA.

2 Elliptic Curve Digital Signature Algorithms

Let $\mathbb{F}_q$ be a finite field with q a prime power , then an elliptic curve E over $\mathbb{F}_q$ is defined as the set of all solutions (x, y) to some Weierstrass equation [2] together with the infinity point $\mathcal{O}$. Let $E(\mathbb{F}_q)$ denote the all $\mathbb{F}_q$-rational point set in E, including $\mathcal{O}$, then $E(\mathbb{F}_q)$ forms an abelian group according to the addition definition [2].

DSA can be regarded as a variant of the ElGamal signature scheme and their security is based on the intractability of the discrete logarithm problems (DLP). The basic ECDSA is the analogue of the (ElGamal) DSA over the elliptic curve. It can be described as follows [5]:

The public parameters for ECDSA include an elliptic curve E over $\mathbb{F}_q$, a base point G of large prime order n in $E(\mathbb{F}_q)$ and a one-way hash function h.

[*] This Project is supported by National 973 High Technology Projects(No. G1999035805) and the NSF of China (No. 60073049, 69882002, 69425001)

S. Qing, T. Okamoto, and J. Zhou (Eds.): ICICS 2001, LNCS 2229, pp. 246–250, 2001.

Basic ECDSA Scheme: To sign a message m, the entity A does the following Step 1–4 :

1. Select $d \in \{1, \cdots, n-1\}$ at random as his private key and computer $P = dG$ over E as his public key .
2. Select $k \in \{1, \cdots, n-1\}$ at random and compute $r \equiv (kG)_x$ mod n, where $(kG)_x$ denotes the x-coordinate of the point $kG \in E(\mathbb{F}_q)$ and is regarded as an integer. If $r = 0$, then go back to step 1.
3. Compute $s \equiv k^{-1}(h(m) + dr)$ mod n. If $s = 0$, then go back to step 1.
4. A's signature for the message m is (r, s).
5. To verify A's signature , the entity B first gets the public parameters and A's public key P, and then checks whether $((s^{-1}h(m))G + (s^{-1}r)P)_x$ mod $n \equiv r$. If it holds, then accept the signature. Otherwise, reject it.

In [6], two shortened schemes of the basic ECDSA, *ECDSS1(ECDSS2)*, are described as: First compute $r_1(r_2) \equiv h(kG, m)$ and $s_1 \equiv k/(r+d)$ ($s_2 \equiv k/(1+rd)$), and then get the signature (r_1, s_1) $((r_2, s_2))$ on m. Finally verify it by checking whether $r_1 \equiv h(s(P+rG), m)$ $(r_2 \equiv h(s(G+rP), m))$.

In [7], another variant, referred to *NR-ECDSA*, was presented as: First compute $r \equiv (kG)_x + h(m)$ and $s \equiv k - dr$, and then get the signature (r, s) on m. Finally verify it by checking whether $h(m) \equiv r - (sG + rP)_x$.

3   Generalizations of ECDSA Schemes

Type 1: Let (α, β, γ) be a permutatiom of $(1, d, k)$. Suppose $r \equiv (kG)_x$ ($r \neq 0$ otherwise select k again). Consider the following equation on the variable s:

$$s\alpha \equiv h(m)\beta + r\gamma \text{ mod } n \tag{1}$$

Solve (1), then we obtain a signature $(r, s) = (r, \alpha^{-1}(h(m)\beta + r\gamma))$ on m if $s \neq 0$, otherwise select k again. To verify the signature, check whether

$$\begin{cases} (s^{-1}(h(m)(\beta G) + r(\gamma G)))_x \equiv r & \text{if } (\beta G, \gamma G) = (G, P) \text{ or } (P, G) \\ (h^{-1}(m)(s(\alpha G) + r(\gamma G)))_x \equiv r & \text{if } (\alpha G, \gamma G) = (G, P) \text{ or } (P, G) \\ (r^{-1}(s(\varphi G) + h(m)(fG)))_x \equiv r & \text{if } (\alpha G, \beta G) = (G, P) \text{ or } (P, G) \end{cases} .$$

No. 1-6 schemes listed in Table 1 are the all possible variants of the basic ECDSA related to the general equation (1).

Type 2: Let (α, β, γ) be a permutatiom of $(1, d, k)$ and $r \equiv (kG)_x + h(m)$. Consider the following equation on variable s:

$$s\alpha \equiv \beta + r\gamma \text{ mod } n \tag{2}$$

Solve (2), then we obtain a signature $(r, s) = (r, \alpha^{-1}(\beta + r\gamma))$ on m if $s \neq 0$, otherwise select k again. Verify it by checking whether

$$r - h(m) \equiv \begin{cases} s^{-1}((\beta G) + r(\gamma G))_x & \text{if } (\beta G, \gamma G) = (G, P) \text{ or } (P, G) \\ s(\alpha G) + r(\gamma G))_x & \text{if } (\alpha G, \gamma G) = (G, P) \text{ or } (P, G) \\ r^{-1}(s(\alpha G) + \beta G)_x & \text{if } (\alpha G, \beta G) = (G, P) \text{ or } (P, G) \end{cases}$$

Then we obtain another six signature schemes No. 7-12 as Table 1 lists.

Table 1. ECC Signature Schemes: Variants of the Basic ECDSA

No.	(α, β, γ)	r	Signature equation	Verification equation
1	$(1, d, k)$		$s \equiv dh(m) + kr$	$(r^{-1}(sG - h(m)P))_x \equiv r$
2	$(1, k, d)$		$s \equiv kh(m) + dr$	$(h(m)^{-1}(sG - rP))_x \equiv r$
3	$(d, 1, k)$	$r \equiv (kG)_x$	$s \equiv d^{-1}(h(m) + kr)$	$(r^{-1}(sP - h(m)G))_x \equiv r$
4	$(d, k, 1)$		$s \equiv d^{-1}(kh(m) + r)$	$(h(m)^{-1}(sP - rG))_x \equiv r$
5	$(k, 1, d)$		$s \equiv k^{-1}(h(m) + dr)$	$(s^{-1}(h(m)G + rP))_x \equiv r$
6	$(k, d, 1)$		$s \equiv k^{-1}(dh(m) + r)$	$(s^{-1}(h(m)P + rG))_x \equiv r$
7	$(1, d, k)$		$s \equiv d + kr$	$(r^{-1}(sG - P))_x + h(m) \equiv r$
8	$(1, k, d)$		$s \equiv k + dr$	$(sG - rP)_x + h(m) \equiv r$
9	$(d, 1, k)$	$r \equiv (kG)_x + h(m)$	$s \equiv d^{-1}(1 + kr)$	$(r^{-1}(sP - G))_x + h(m) \equiv r$
10	$(d, k, 1)$		$s \equiv d^{-1}(k + r)$	$(sP - rG)_x + h(m) \equiv r$
11	$(k, 1, d)$		$s \equiv k^{-1}(1 + dr)$	$(s^{-1}(G + rP))_x + h(m) \equiv r$
12	$(k, d, 1)$		$s \equiv k^{-1}(d + r)$	$(s^{-1}(P + rG))_x - h(m) \equiv r$

4   A More General Type of ECDSA

Suppose $F(x, y, z)$, $U(x, y, z)$, $V(x, y, z)$ and $W(x, y, z)$ are given 3-variable rational functions: $\mathbb{F}_n^3 \longrightarrow \mathbb{F}_n^*$. Construct the following equation set:

$$\begin{cases} F(r, m, kG) \equiv 0 \bmod n \\ kU(r, s, m) + dV(r, s, m) + W(r, s, m) \equiv 0 \bmod n \end{cases} \quad (3)$$

To generate a signature on m, first choose F, U, V and W deliberatively, and then solve r and s from the equation (3). If it has a solution (r, s) with $r \neq 0$ and $s \neq 0$, then we obtain a signature (r, s) on m. Its verification equation is $F(r, m, (-U^{-1}(r, s, m)V(r, s, m))P + (-U^{-1}(r, s, m)W(r, s, m))G) \equiv 0$.

When using (3) to generate a signature, we should notice the followings:

- First F should be chosen so that r can be easily solved and expressed as a rational function of m and kG, or at least a rational function of kG.
- To guarantee both the validity and security of the generated signature (r, s) on m, each of r, s and m(or $h(m)$) has to appear in (3) at least once.
- If $r = 0$ or $s = 0$, then select k or the four functions F, U, V and W again.
- If (3) has more than one solution, then add some redundant bits to specify one determinate signature.
- To lessen the computational cost, F, U, V and W are often chosen to be rational functions with the degree ± 1 or 0 for every variable.

Considering the above conditions, the practical signature schemes generated from (3) can be classified into the following four general types. Suppose f, g and ϕ are 2-variable polynomial functions ($\mathbb{F}_n^2 \longrightarrow \mathbb{F}_n^*$)with the degree 1 or 0 for each variable .

Type 3: Let $(F, U, V, W) = (r - f(kG, m), s, g(r, m), \phi(r, m))$. Then from (3) we obtain the signature $(r, s) \equiv (f(kG, m), k^{-1}(-dg(r, m) - \phi(r, m)))$. Its verification equation is $f((-s^{-1}g(r, m))P + (-s^{-1}\phi(r, m))G, m) \equiv r$. The signature schemes No.5, 6, 11, 12, can be deduced from this general type.

Type 4: Let $(F, U, V, W) = (r - f(kG, m), g(r, m), s, \phi(r, m))$. Then we obtain the signature $(r, s) \equiv (f(kG, m), d^{-1}(-kg(r, m) - \phi(r, m)))$. Its verification equation is $f((-sg^{-1}(r, m))P + (-g(r, m)\phi(r, m))G, m) \equiv r$. The signature schemes No.3, 4, 9, 10, can be deduced from this type.

Type 5: Let $(F, U, V, W) = (r - f(kG, m), g(r, m), \phi(r, m), s)$. Then we obtain the signature $(r, s) \equiv (f(kG, m), -kg(r, m) - d\phi(r, m))$. Its verification equation is $f((-sg^{-1}(r, m))G + (-g(r, m)\phi(r, m))P, m) \equiv r$. The signature schemes No.1, 2, 7, 8 and NR-ECDSA can be deduced from this type.

Type 6: Suppose $F = r - f(kG, m)$ and U does not contain s, while V and W have s only as a factor, then we have the signature $(r, s) \equiv (f(kG, m), k/(dg(r, m) + \phi(r, m))$. Its verification equation is $f((sg(r, m))P + (s\phi(r, m))G, m) \equiv r$.

5   Security Analysis

Generally speaking, the all methods used to solve the DLP can be employed to solve the ECDLP. The known possible attacks on ECDSA or its variants can be classified into four methods : *Solving the ECDLP to get the signer's per-message secret k or private key d, Attacking the employed hash function, Preimage secret attack , Forging the signature.*

The current known algorithms for solving the ECDLP mainly have: *Naive exhaustive search, Pollig-Hellman algorithm , Pollard ρ-algorithm, Parallelized Pollard's algorithm, Semaev-Smart-Satoh-Araki mothod , Weil pairing method* and *Weil descent method.* To avoid these attacks, the basic field $\mathbb{F}_q$ should not be a composite field. The elliptic curve E should not be a supersingular or prime-field-anomalous. The order of the basic point G should be a prime $\geq 2^{160}$.

The attacks on the employed hash function can be avoided when it is chosen to be a both preimage resistant and collision resistant hash function.

Per-message secret attack: If an attacker T knows a per-message secret k, then he can recover A's private key d. Such as for Type 3, $d = g(r, m)^{-1}(-sk - \phi(r, m))$. Suppose k is used to generate two signatures (r_1, s_1) and (r_2, s_2) by Type 4, then $s_1 \equiv d^{-1}(-kg(r_1, m_1) - \phi(r_1, m_1))$ and $s_2 \equiv d^{-1}(-kg(r_2, m_2) - \phi(r_2, m_2))$, and hence $k \equiv (g(r_2, m_2)s_1 - g(r_1, m_1)s_2)^{-1}(\phi(r_1, m_1)s_2 - \phi(r_2, m_2)s_1)$ since $g(r_2, m_2)s_1 - g(r_1, m_1)s_2 \equiv 0$ with negligible probability. It follows that T recovers d.

If the signer A signs two messages m_1 and m_2 with the same d and k in two different signature schemes, say, the basic ECDSA and NR-ECDSA, then T can also recover $k \equiv (s_1 r_2 - r_1)^{-1}(r_2 h(m_1) - r_1 s_2)$ with overwhelming probability. Hence, the per-message secret k should not be used repeatedly .

To avoid T's finding k or d with non-negligible probability by factoring $\gcd(g(r, m), \phi(r, m))$ in Type 3 and Type 4, $g(r, m)$ and $\phi(r, m)$ had better be chosen so that $\gcd(g(r, m), \phi(r, m)) = 1$.

In Type 5, if $g(r, m) \equiv \pm\phi(r, m)$, then T can obtain $k \pm d$ and then recover k or d with non-negligible probability if $k \pm d$ is not large enough.

Forge the signature: To forge a signature on some message m, the forger F first randomly selects $r \in \{1, \cdots, n-1\}$, and then tries to find s through the corresponding verification equation or vice versa. But F has to solve some ECDLP to get s. Such as in Type 5, F has to solve the ECDLP for s: $sG \equiv -g(r,m)G_r - \phi(r,m)P$, where $G_r \in [G]$ (a subgroup generated by G) and is totally determined by r or by both r and m. F can also choose two random values $a, b \in \{1, \cdots, n-1\}$, and then constructs $\bar{r}$, $\bar{s}$ and $\bar{m}$ to satisfy the corresponding verification equation. Such as in Type 4, F computes $\bar{r} \equiv f(aG + b^{-1}P, m)$, and then solve $g(\bar{r}, \bar{m}) + \bar{s}b \equiv 0$ and $g(\bar{r}, \bar{m})a + \phi(\bar{r}, \bar{m}) \equiv 0$ for $\bar{s}$ and $\bar{m}$. If the equations has a solution , then F successfully forges a signature $(\bar{r}, \bar{s})$ on $\bar{m}$. But if the function g or ϕ is chosen to be related to a cryptographic hash function, then the equations has a solution with negligible probability.

6   Conclusion

ECDSA can be viewed as the elliptic curve analogue of DSA. But its security is much stronger than DSA's. Our general types of ECDSA give a lot of choices to generate the desired elliptic curve digital signatures. These general types can be modified to become general schemes of ECDSA with some special properties, such as general blind elliptic curve signature schemes. From these generalized elliptic curve signature schemes we can extract both efficient and secure variants for practical applications.

References

1. Victor Miller. Uses of elliptic curves in cryptography. In *Advances in Cryptology—CRYPTO'85*, LNCS 218, pp. 417–426. Springer-Verlag, 1985.
2. A. Menezes. Elliptic Curve Public Key Cryptosystems. pp. 15–27. Klumer Academic Publishes Group, 1993.
3. S. Vanstone. Responses to NIST's Proposal. *Communications of the ACM*, 35:50–52, 1992.
4. P. Horster, M, Michels and H. Petersen. Meta-ElGamal signature schemes. In *ACM Conference on Computer and Communicatons Security*, May 1994.
5. ANSI X9.62. Public key cryptography for the Financial Services Industry: The elliptic curve digital signature algorithm (ECDSA), 1999.
6. Y. Zhang and H. Imai. How to construct efficient signcryption schemes on elliptic curves. *Information Processing Letters*, 68:227–233, 1998.
7. W.J. Caelli, E.P. Dawson and S.A. Rea. PKI, elliptic curve cryptography, and digital signature. *Computer and Security*, 18:47–66, 1999.

Reasoning about Accountability within Delegation

Bruno Crispo[1] and Giancarlo Ruffo[2]

[1] Cryptomathic S.p.A.
Corso Svizzera, 185 - 10149 Torino, Italy
crispo@cryptomathic.com
[2] Dipartimento di Informatica - Università di Torino
Corso Svizzera, 185 - 10149 Torino, Italy
ruffo@di.unito.it

Abstract. We propose a framework for the analysis of delegation protocols. Our framework allows to analyse how accountability is transferred
(or kept) by delegator when she transfers some of her rights to the delegate. The ability to trace how accountability is distributed among principals of a system is crucial in many transactions that have a legal value,
because accountability is usually a prerequisite to guarantee other well
known security properties (e.g., non repudiation). Our approach starts
from the notion of "provability" to formalise accountability. Then, we
introduce new specifications for the analysis of delegation protocols and
the distribution of credentials necessary to exercise delegated rights.

1 Introduction

In many e-commerce applications, as in the real-life, electronic transactions must
be able to guarantee at least the same degree of accountability provided by
conventional transactions. For example, let us consider the case of a manager
delegating her system administrator to backup her files containing important
documents. In case something goes wrong and the documents will be unrecover-
able, it would be useful for both, the manager and the system administrator, to
have mechanisms that help them to prove to a third party their behaviour and
doing so to determine accountability of facts. From this example it is clear the
importance of the property of accountability that we define as:

*the property whereby the association of a principal with an object, an action
or a right can be proved to a third party.*

This paper provides an original contribution to the problem of the analysis
of protocols that requires accountability. Among all the protocols that require
this property we will focus our attention to delegation protocols. This is motivated by the fact that delegation is usually the general mechanism used to
transfer accountabilities among principals. Besides a lot of work has been done
on the analysis of protocols, but few of these analysis have considered delegation
protocols.

S. Qing, T. Okamoto, and J. Zhou (Eds.): ICICS 2001, LNCS 2229, pp. 251–260, 2001.
© Springer-Verlag Berlin Heidelberg 2001

2   Accountability

For our analysis we start from a framework introduced by Kailar [4] specifically for analysing and describing accountability in order to analyse this property in delegation protocols.

This framework is based on the notion of *provability*, that is the ability of participants in a protocol to *prove* a statement to a third party, that is the basis for accountability. A participant can prove a statement to any other principal if he can convince the latter about the statement. The proof of a statement x is generically defined as the ability starting from known assumptions, to produce a set of statements that can convince any other principal about x. In practice it is enough (and easier) to convince a particular third party (a judge) rather than all the other principals that did not participate to the protocol.

We agree with Kailar that his approach is more suitable to analyse accountability rather than other approaches based on *belief* [1] and its evolution within the protocol, because these approaches focus on what can be proved only by the participants of the protocol, while the point of view of external observers is essential to accountability.

In this section, we provide a short review of the basics of the adopted framework, referring to [4] for a more detailed description.

In section 2.4, we will introduce new postulates that allow to analyse delegation of accountability in communication protocols.

Finally, in section 3, we will analyse two communication protocols with support for delegation: the SPX protocol [7] and the Delegation of Accountability protocol [2]. Our analysis will show the usability of our approach.

2.1   Symbols and Concepts

In a generic communication protocol, we have a group of *principals* $(A, B, ...)$, that exchange *messages* within each other. During the analysis of a protocol, we want to focus on the ability of principals to prove the origin of these messages. The *statement* made by each message is the message interpretation; statements are denoted by lower-case letters $(x, y, ...)$. A *proof* of a statement x is something that convinces another principal of statement x. We are not worrying about the steps of a proof, because they largely depend on the environment where the protocol is designed to work.

Considering our definition of accountability we need to introduce objects, actions and rights into our language. We will denote a *set of rights* with a greek upper-case letter $(\Omega, \Delta, ...)$. Observe that in the rest of the paper, the term *right* is used also to indicate an object (right to *use* a given object) or an action (right to *do* a given action).

To improve the readability of the paper, we will avoid to introduce and use new mathematical symbols. Instead, we will use common phrases like "can prove" or "can exercise" written concatenated (i.e., "CanProve" or "CanExercise"). Moreover, we will introduce only concepts and postulates that are needed to understand the paper and the process of analysing a delegation protocol for proving the accountability property. Informal descriptions of these concepts are given below:

A **CanProve** *x*: Principal *A* can prove the statement *x* to any third party *B*. This implies that *A* is able to perform a sequence of operations that lead to prove statement *x* to a principal *B*, whoever is *B*. This proof does not reveal any secret $y \neq x$.

This is a *Strong proof*, because a principal *A* can prove the given statement to everyone. We talk about *Weak proof* if the ability of the prover permits to prove the given statement only to another principal. In this case, we can write "*A* CanProve *x* to *B*", where *A* and *B* are involved principals. In this paper we will use only strong proof.

K **Authenticates** *A*: The key *K* can be used to authenticate the signature of principal *A*. As a consequence, we can associate *A* to any statement encrypted with K^{-1}. *K* and K^{-1} are public and private counterparts of an asymmetric key pair.

x **in** *m*: *x* is the interpretation of a (group of) field(s) in message *m*. This interpretation is protocol specific.

A **Says** *x*: Principal *A* is responsible of statement *x*. In other words, *A* is accountable of *x*. As a consequence, *A* is accountable for every statement implied by *x*. Moreover, if *A* says any statement composed by two or more parts, she is accountable for each part:

$$\frac{A \text{ Says } (x, y)}{A \text{ Says } x}$$

A **Receives** *m* **SignedWith** K^{-1}: This tells that principal *A* receives a message *m* signed with a private key K^{-1}. If *x* is the message interpretation of *m* (of the interpration of one of the fields of *m*), we can use the following postulate:

$$\frac{A \text{ Receives } m \text{ SignedWith } K^{-1}; x \text{ in } m}{A \text{ Receives } x \text{ SignedWith } K^{-1}}$$

A **isTrustedOn** *x*: Principal *A* is trusted on statement *x*, i.e., *A* has the authority to endorse *x* and is liable for making *x*. If principal *A* is *globally* trusted, then *A* is trusted on *x* by all principals[1].

The following definitions of "CanExercise" appear for the first time in this paper.

A **CanExercise** *Ω*: This denotes the fact that principal *A* can exercise the rights listed in *Ω*. In an access control environment, a principal can exercise a right under some requirements[2]. We use "CanExercise" only to associate principals to rights, in accordance to our definition of accountability.

---

[1] If a principal is trusted on a statement by only another (or a group of) principal(s), we use the notion of *non global trustness*. In this paper we will only talk about global trust, even if more loosely: principal *A* is trusted on *x* by all principals in the intended audience of a proof.

[2] For example, a principal can read/write the files of directory */Doc/Sec* only if she belongs to the *Security* group. We are not concerning on aspects of how this requirements are checked or how this rights are assigned to principals by a system administrator. These aspects are strongly dependent on a given environment.

A **CanExercise** Ω **with** K**:** If we want to specify the authentication key that a principal uses to exercise her rights, we can use this statement. Here, a principal *A* CanExercise the set of rights Ω using K as her authentication key. Of course, the statement "K Authenticates *A*" must be provable.

2.2   Assumptions

Some assumptions related to security constraints must be respected before validating analysis results. The digital signature scheme considered in this framework is public-key encryption paradigm based. *Signature algorithms* are assumed to be strong enough: (1) to be undisputably associated with a single user; (2) to resist against the search of another principal's private key, independently by the available computing power, for a sufficient period of time; (3) to withstand birthday attacks. Moreover, signature algorithms are assumed to provide message origin authentication, message content integrity and message sender non-repudiation. Finally, signature algorithms do not require the consent of the signer.

Another important group of assumptions is related to *Trustness*: principals are trusted not to share their private keys with other principals with whom they do not wish to be accountable, i.e., we trust principals that use caution to share their keys. Moreover, a principal is assumed to trust a statement if she is an authority of the given statement, or if she is convinced on the validity of the statement by a trusted party.

Other important assumptions are about message integrity, availability of services and certificate revocation. It is not possible to fake a signed message or to compute another private key that can be accepted as the authentic signature (*message integrity*); if *A CanProve x*, then we assume that, independently of the availability of the communication service, we can assure that *A* has the ability to send all the messages for proving *x* (*availability of service*); finally, statements proved by revoked public keys are considered valid only if the statements were signed when the related certificates were also valid (*certificate revocation*).

2.3   Postulates

Postulates introduced here are applicable to the analysis of accountability properties in electronic communication protocols. All postulates are given in the form:

$$\frac{P; Q}{R}$$

where P and Q are the premises of the rule: if they hold simultaneously, then the consequence statement R is true.

Conjunction: If *A* can prove that *x* is true and she can also prove that also *y* is true, then *A* can prove that the conjunction $x \wedge y$ is true.

$$\textbf{Conj:} \quad \frac{A \text{ CanProve } x; A \text{ CanProve } y}{A \text{ CanProve } (x \wedge y)}$$

Inference: If A can prove statement x and if x implies y, then A can prove that y is true.

$$\textbf{Inf:} \quad \frac{A \text{ CanProve } x; x \Rightarrow y}{A \text{ CanProve } y}$$

Accountability property of digital signatures: The following postulate can be used to prove that principals are accountable for messages they signed.

$$\textbf{Sign:} \quad \frac{A \text{ Receives } m \text{ SignedWith } K^{-1}; x \text{ in } m;}{A \text{ CanProve } (K \text{ Authenticates } B)}$$

That is, when principal A receives a message m signed with a key K^{-1} and A can prove that this key belongs to B, as a consequence A can prove that B is accountable for any statement x, where x is a message interpretation of m.

Trust relationships: In digital signatures schemas, a proof of a statement x can be given also by showing that x has been endorsed by a trusted authority of x, i.e., A is an authority on x and she says x. As a consequence, A can prove that x is true. This is based on what we said in section 2.2: if A is trusted on a given statement then is able to prove it to another principal. Moreover, if a principal A can prove that another principal is able to prove a statement x, then A can prove x.

Trust postulate is a corollary of the previous considerations:

$$\textbf{Trust:} \quad \frac{\begin{array}{c}A \text{ CanProve } (B \text{ Says } x);\\ A \text{ CanProve } (B \text{ isTrustedOn } x)\end{array}}{A \text{ CanProve } x}$$

2.4   A Specification of the Framework: The *CanExercise* Postulates

This section introduces the formalization of the concept of a principal that can exercise a right (or a set of rights).

A principal can exercise a right if another principal gave her the related permissions. These permissions can be given by a trusted authority (i.e., a system administrator), and can be delegated to another principal, whom, after delegation, can exercise the transferred rights.

In a generic delegation, principal A can delegate another principal B to exercise the set of rights Ω only if A has the ability to exercise them. Moreover, A must be accountable for having delegated B to exercise Ω, and, finally, B must be authenticated when she exercise Ω. The following postulate formalizes these ideas:

$$\textbf{CanExercise1:} \quad \frac{\begin{array}{c}A \text{ CanExercise } \Omega;\\ A \text{ Says (delegation of } \Omega \text{ to } B);\\ (K_{Del} \text{ Authenticates } B);\end{array}}{B \text{ CanExercise } \Omega \text{ with } K_{Del}}$$

That is, principal A can exercise the set of rights Ω and she delegates B to exercise these rights. Key K_{Del} authenticates principal B: when B will exercise Ω, she will be authenticated using K_{Del}.

When we need only to describe the power of a principal to exercise a given set of rights, we can omit the specification of this key. The following postulate relates both ways to use "CanExercise" clause.

$$\textbf{CanExercise2:} \quad \frac{A \text{ CanExercise } \Omega \text{ with } K}{A \text{ CanExercise } \Omega}$$

In our analysis, we want to prove the accountability of a principal on a set of rights that have been delegated by another principal. In other words, the goal of such a proof is to show that:

    delegate CanProve (*delegate* CanExercise Ω with K_{Del})

where K_{Del} is the delegation key of the given protocol.

During analysis of delegation protocols, we will use postulates **CanExercise1** and **CanExercise2** in conjunction with **Inf** postulates, in order to unify "CanProve" and "CanExercise".

Another important goal to verify during analysis of a delegation protocol is the ability for delegator to prove that she is not associated with delegate's actions. When a set of rights Ω has been transferred from A to B and principal B is exercising Ω using delegation key K_{Del}, then principal A is not accountable for this B's activity. This second generic goal can be formalized with the following statement:

    delegator CanProve (K_{Del} Authenticates *delegate*)

3   Analysis of Delegation Protocols

In this section, we show some examples of protocols analysis. In particular, we apply our analysis framework to SPX [7] and to the Delegation of Accountability protocol [2]. In these two analyses it will be possible to show the difference between two different delegation's philosophies: SPX permits grantor to delegate grantee the possibility to act on grantor's behave; in the other approach, grantor transfers the accountability on a set of rights of her own.

3.1   SPX with Support for Delegation

Protocol description. In SPX [7], principals use *authentication tokens* to authenticate each other. The authentication token permits the secure exchange of a session key. A simplified version of SPX is analysed in [4] in order to verify accountability properties. In this section, we summarize the content of the previous analysis and we will show that this protocol doesn't allow accountability on a set of transferred rights.

Involved principals are: a claimant (C), a certificate distribution center (CDC), and a server (S). Moreover, we have also principals TA_1 and TA_2, that, together with CDC, play the role of trusted authorities.

The goal of the protocol is for S to securely receive a delegation key from C. In this delegation context, principal C authorizes another principal (S) to act on her behalf by sharing a set of rights with C for a given period of time. The protocol is not designed for delegation of accountability, because the transferred rights will be still accountable to C.

The protocol description is the following:

1. $C \rightarrow CDC : S$
2. $CDC \rightarrow C : K_{CDC}^{-1}(K_{TA_1}^{-1}(S, K_S, TA_1))$
3. $C \rightarrow S : K_C^{-1}(K_{Del}, T), K_S(K_{des}), K_{des}(K_{Del}^{-1})$
4. $S \rightarrow CDC : C$
5. $CDC \rightarrow S : K_{CDC}^{-1}(K_{TA_2}^{-1}(C, K_C, TA_2))$
6. $S \rightarrow C : Response\ (accept/reject)$

Server S plays the role of the verifier of the claimant's credential. The protocol starts with the request of C for S's public key (message 1). This request is send to the certificate distribution center, that replies (message 2) with a certificate of S, issued by the trusted authority TA_1. This certificate is encrypted with CDC's private key. C sends her delegation public key (K_{Del}) to S (message 3), signing it with her authentication key (K_C^{-1}). K_{Del} is valid for a period of time T. Moreover, C sends to S a symmetric session key (K_{des}) encrypted with S's public key (K_S). C encrypts the private part of the delegation key with the session key K_{des} and she also sends it to S. Finally S asks for C's certificate to CDC (message 4 and 5) and after receiving the certificate, S verifies C's credentials and replies to C the response (message 6).

Reformulating the Protocol. The protocol has been reformulated with the adopted notation by Kailar in [4]. We report here the protocol message interpretation described in the previous analysis. Only messages 2, 3 and 5 were considered relevant to the analysis:

2. C Receives (((K_S Authenticates S)
    SignedWith $K_{TA_1}^{-1}$) SignedWith K_{CDC}^{-1})
3. S Receives (((K_{Del} Authenticates C during T)
    SignedWith K_C^{-1}))
5. S Receives (((K_C Authenticates C)
    SignedWith $K_{TA_2}^{-1}$) SignedWith K_{CDC}^{-1})

Protocol Analysis. As we reminded at the beginning of this section, the delegation goal pointed by the Kailar's analysis was to verify the delegate's ability of proving that the delegation key authenticates delegator. In other words, the goal of the analysis showed by Kailar was:

[Goal] S CanProve (K_{Del} Authenticates C)

Principal C can exercise the transferred set of rights, but S will still be accountable for them, because K_{Del} authenticates her.

As we said in section 2.4, we wish to show that: C CanProve (K_{Del} Authenticates S),

in order to give C the possibility to prove her independency by delegate's actions. If we would be able to show the previous statement, it will be true together with

Goal statement proved by Kailar, meaning that K_{Del} authenticates both delegator and delegate. In this case, we lose accountability property. As a consequence, SPX protocol does not support delegation of accountability.

3.2 The Delegation of Accountability Protocol

Protocol description. The protocol [2] is based on delegation tokens (Gasser et al., Sollins [6], Low et al. [5]).

It allows principals to delegate their own accountability to any other principals. It assumes that each principal can generate public-key pairs and has access to a digital signature service. Moreover, it assumes that each principal can get the public key(s) needed to verify digital signatures that she may receive, included the keys used for authentication purposes. The delegation protocol is specified as follows:

1. $A \rightarrow B$: A, B, m, $K_A^{-1}(m)$
   where m=[A wishes to delegate to B accountability for Ω]
2. $B \rightarrow A$: B, A , m', $K_B^{-1}(m')$
   m'=[B accepts Ω and she will exercise Ω using K_{Del}]
3. $A \rightarrow B$: t = [A, B, m'', $K_A^{-1}(m'')$]
   m''=[Ω, LS, K_A, K_{Del}]

where A is the grantor, B is the grantee, Ω is the set of delegated rights and LS is the time span of delegation token t. (K_A, K_A^{-1}) and (K_B, K_B^{-1}) are respectively the authentication key pairs of grantor and grantee, (K_{Del}, K_{Del}^{-1}) is the delegation key pair that grantee will use to exercise Ω. In message (3), a key rather than a name is used to identify the grantor so if an attacker succeeds to masquerade as the grantor he cannot fraudulently delegate grantor's accountability because he still does not know the key K_A^{-1} necessary to be able to do it.

The grantor is the only one that can enable the grantee to use Ω: the delegation token contains m'', which specifies the characteristics of the present delegation, and also it contains m'' signed by the grantor. When the grantee wishes to use the delegated rghts she must present [t, $K_{Del}^{-1}(t)$] to the end-point, followed by the request of the specific service she wants[3]. The end-point will check the privileges carried in the delegation token against her access control policy. The end-point can be any principal of the system because the token is verifiable by all the components of the system[4]. Thus all the principals can verify the correctness of the delegation token after they get the grantor's and grantee's public key from the authentication service in order to authenticate them in the first two messages of the protocol.

Reformulating the Protocol. The protocol can be reformulated in terms of the described notation:

---

[3] In such a framework, if grantee B is not necessarily honest and step 3 does not take place, she cannot exercise the delegated rights with only delegation key K_{Del} because she misses the delegation token.

[4] We are assuming that an authentication service is available.

1. B Receives ((A wishes to delegate to B accountability for Ω)
                SignedWith K_A^{-1})
2. A Receives ((K_{Del} Authenticates B) SignedWith K_B^{-1})
3. B Receives ((delegation of Ω to B') SignedWith K_A^{-1})

Now we have to list the implicit assumptions and apply the inference rules of the adopted logic to the assumptions and to the messages of the protocol in order to prove our goal: the delegate is accountable to exercise transferred rights.

Goal and Initial State Assumptions. Our primary goal is:

[**Goal1**] B CanProve (B CanExercise Ω with K_{Del})

Let us observe that, if we prove the goal, with the application of **CanExercise2** and **Inf** postulates, we can show the more general fact that:

B CanProve (B CanExercise Ω)

We wish also to show that grantor is able to prove that the delegation key authenticates grantee: if B will exercise Ω using K_{Del}, A cannot be accountable for this. As a consequence, the second goal of our analysis is:

[**Goal2**] A CanProve (K_{Del} Authenticates B)

The initial state assumptions follow here:

[**A1**] A CanProve (K_A Authenticates A);
[**A2**] B CanProve (K_B Authenticates B)
[**A2'**] B CanProve (K_{Del} Authenticates B)
[**A3**] B CanProve (A CanExercise Ω)
[**A4**] A CanProve (B isTrustedOn (K_{Del} Authenticates B)
[**A5**] A CanProve (K_B Authenticates B)
[**A6**] B CanProve (K_A Authenticates A)

Assumptions **A1**, **A2** and **A2'** state that the association between principals and their public keys can be proved.

Of course, we assume that B can prove that A is able to exercise the set of rights Ω (assumption **A3**). A is delegating B to exercise Ω, but B must be convinced that A owns these rights.

We assume also that principal B is trusted when announcing its own delegation key, because she is responsible of the messages signed with this key (assumption **A4**).

Finally, in the protocol we did not specify the part concerned with authentication of principals, because we are focusing on the delegation part. We can assume that the generic goals of a public key distribution protocol are reached before the delegation protocol starts (i.e., using a certificate distribution center, as in the SPX protocol). As a consequence, we can make assumptions **A5** and **A6**.

Analysis. Applying **Sign** postulate on message 3 and **A6**, we obtain:

[**S1**] B CanProve (A Says (delegation of Ω to B))

Using **Conj** postulate on **A3**, **S1** and **A2'**, the following statement is true:

[**S2**] B CanProve (A CanExercise Ω,
                A Says (delegation of Ω to B),
                K_{Del} Authenticates B)

Finally, we obtain **Goal1**, using **Inf** and **CanExercise1** postulates on statement **S2**:

[**Goal1**] B CanProve (B CanExercise Ω with K_{Del})

We can apply **Sign** postulate to message 2 and **A5** assumption to show that:

[**S3**] A CanProve (B Says (K_{Del} Authenticates B))

Finally, **Goal2** is inferred by **Trust** postulate using **S3** and **A4** as premises $\square$.

4   Conclusions

Despite its importance in supporting any commercial and financial transaction, accountability has been usually negletted in the formalisation of protocols. Also, other important security properties (e.g., non-repudiation) rely on accountability and on the possibility to examine unforgeable evidence collected by the party during the execution of a transaction [3]. In this paper, we tried to raise the attention to this issue and in particular we introduced a framework to reason about accountability in the particular case of delegation protocols. Delegation protocols aim to perform the hand-over of rights from delegator to delegate. Our studies however, proved that many of them do not consider the important issue of the accountability associated to those rights. As we said, this lack of specification can vanish or jeopardise the subsequent use of the delegated rights in applications where accountability is required in case of possible disputes (i.e., electronic commerce).

References

1. M. Burrows, M. Abadi, and R.M. Needham. A logic of Authentication. *ACM Transaction on Computer Systems*, 8(1), Febraury 1990.
2. B. Crispo. Delegation protocols for electronic commerce. In *Proceedings of the 6th IEEE Symposium on computers and communications (ISCC01), Hammamet, Tunisia*. IEEE press, 2001.
3. B. Crispo and M. Lomas. A Certification Scheme for Electronic Commerce. In *Security Protocol Workshop*, volume LNCS vol. 1189. Springer-Verlag, 1997.
4. R. Kailar. Reasoning about Accountability in Protocol for Electronic Commerce. In *Proceedings of the IEEE Symposium on Security and Privacy*, 1995.
5. M.R. Low and B. Christianson. Self Authenticating Proxies. *Computer Journal*, 37(5):422–428, October 1994.
6. K.R. Sollins. Cascaded Authentication. In *Proceedings of the IEEE Conference on Security and Privacy*, April 1988.
7. J.J. Tardo and K. Alagappan. SPX: Global Authentication Using Public Key Certificates. In *Proceedings of the IEEE Symposium on Security and Privacy*, 1991.

A Novel Data Hiding Method for Two-Color Images[*]

Gang Pan, Yijun Wu, and Zhaohui Wu

Department of Computer Science and Engineering
Zhejiang University, Hangzhou, 310027, P. R. China
gpan, wzh@cs.zju.edu.cn

Abstract. Binary images have only two colors, which makes the embedding of invisible data difficult. In this paper, we propose a new data hiding method that can hide a moderate amount of data in a host binary image, such as binary cartoon images, scanned texts, signatures, without introducing noticeable artifacts. The proposed method employs subblock pattern classification to maintain visualization effect and mechanics of multilevel supblock to improve the capacity. Extracting of the hidden data does not require the knowledge of the original image. The experiments demonstrate that the proposed method can provide excellent perceptual quality of the marked image. The potential applications include invisible annotation, alteration detection and covert communication.

1 Introduction

With the huge success of the Internet, digitization of various kinds of media is getting wider popularity for the transmission, wide distribution and storage. The advantages of digital media include convenient transmission, effortless access, lossless copy, facile edit and reliable storage. However, they also introduce a new set of challenging problems regarding security, that are not able to be achieved only by encryption. The problems have generated a flurry of recent research activities in the area of digital watermark and data hiding.

The study on digital watermark and data hiding has received great achievements over last several years. Many different methods have been proposed for still image. They can be classified into two categories based on the casting domain: 1) luminance intensity in the spatial domain [1,2], for instance, LSB (Least Significant Bit) approach and Patchwork method, and 2) transform coefficient magnitude in the frequency domain, which modify frequency coefficients after applying a proper transform [3,4,5,6], e.g. DWT, DCT, FFT, etc. The new technique has a variety of potential applications involving digital media, including copyright protection, annotation, covert communication, and alteration detection.

[*] This work supported by Zhejiang Provincial Natural Science Foundation of China under Grant 699035.

However, objectives of most of these methods are color images and grayscale images and will fail to apply to two-color images. As an important class of images, digital binary images are widely used in Internet. There is a significant difference between binary image and other natural images. That is, the binary images are only two colors images without complicated color and texture variation, and change a pixel can be easily detected. This peculiar characteristic makes it more difficult to embed invisible digital information in them. The only solutions known to us dealing with binary image are [7,8]. Wu[7] presented a data hiding scheme for binary images for the first time. It partitions the image into blocks, then tries to embed as many as one data bit in each block via AND operation with a secret key matrix whose size is the same as the blocks. However, the perceived quality is poor because it does not take into account the visualization effect. It introduces many isolated points near the boundaries, which causing noticeable artifacts. An improved method for higher security and capacity proposed by [8], but the visibility of marked image is still a problem, even poorer than [7] in some cases, since it may introduce isolated point in any location of the host image.

This paper addresses to the visibility of marked image. We propose a multi-level supblock based data hiding method that can hide a moderate amount of data in the binary images, e.g. binary cartoon, scanned text, and signatures. The hidden data can be extracted without the original host image. The proposed method greatly outperforms the previous approaches in capability of transparency. The potential applications include invisible annotation, changes detection and covert communication.

The paper is organized as follows. The description of the proposed scheme is presented in Sect. 2. Experimental results and analysis are given in Sect. 3. Finally, concluding remarks are provided in Sect. 4.

2   Description of the Proposed Method

As we mentioned, it is more difficult to embed a piece of critical data in binary images under constraint of the visibility, because there are only two elements in the pixel-value space of in binary images. How to maintain good perceptual quality comes to be the major problem. We have observed that whether a revised pixel is noticeable strongly depends on its neighbors. For instance, if a pixel in homochromous region changes to another color, the difference will be quite noticeable. And it will be hard to detect comparatively if some neighbors of the pixel have the same color as the pixel after modification. Therefore, during embedding, what kinds of pixels to alter should be determined according to conditions of its neighbors.

Our method is motivated by the above observation. Its fundamental thought is summarized below. Firstly it partitions the host image into many blocks, then classify these blocks into different level. The high rank (or level number) represents good visual performance. Given a piece of critical data, our scheme will manage to embed the data in the blocks with highest rank. The "0" and

"1" are respectively represented by a pair of blocks with only difference of the central pixel.

To improve the capacity and insensibility, we introduce the concept of "supblock", which is composed of several base blocks overlaid with each other. Correspondingly, those base blocks with smaller size are called "subblock". With mechanics of supblock, we can examine a local region by means of different combinations of pixels for more subblock patterns.

The block diagram of embedding and extracting is shown in Fig. 1.

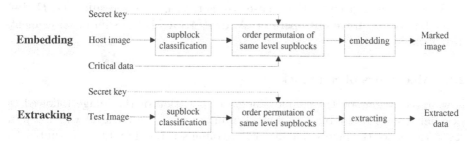

Fig. 1.   The block diagram of embedding and extracting procedures

2.1   Subblock Classification

The objective of subblock classification is to overcome the perceptual quality reduction by pixel modification. In our approach, each subblock is connected with a level number (*rank*) according to its pattern, indicating influence on visibility by assumed change of the central pixel in the subblock. In other words, supposed that the central pixel in a subblock is changed, we consider the variation in connectivity and smoothness and investigate how the visibility effect reduces by such a change, then the rank is determined. The higher rank implies that change of central pixel in subblock reduces visual quality less and should has a higher priority for embedding.

We take the 3-by-3 subblock as a sample, shown in Fig. 2. Whatever is the central pixel in subblocks, change of central pixel of subblock in Fig. 2(b) will obviously got less attention than that in Fig. 2(a). So that pattern of subblock in Fig. 2(b) has higher rank than Fig. 2(a). In this manner, we classify all the patterns into different level. There are 256 (2^8) subblock patterns totally, exclusive of the central pixel. We denote the collection of patterns of rank n by A_n.

There are several approaches for embedding one bit data h in a subblock $\boldsymbol{B}$. We listed two of them below, where the central pixel of the subblock is denoted by c.

a) Let $c = h$.

b) Let $c = (SUM(\boldsymbol{B} \oplus \boldsymbol{K}) + h) \bmod 2$.

(a)   (b)

Fig. 2. Two patterns of 3-by-3 subblock with different rank.

Where K is a given matrix whose size is the same as the subblock B, "$\oplus$" is the bitwise exclusive-OR operator. And $SUM(X)$ is the sum of all elements in matrix X.

2.2   Mechanics of Supblock

If we directly employ the simple scheme of partition of the image followed by examining level of subblock, subblock number of a certain level will be quite restricted, since the pixels of a pattern are often scattered in different subblocks. However, the simple scheme has never taken into account these patterns. To take advantage of the patterns whose pixels are distributed in multi-subblock, it is necessary to mend the simple scheme. In this paper we employ the mechanics of supblock. The supblock is larger than subblock, hence it contains more than one subblock, e.g. a 4-by-4 supblock contains four 3-by-3 subblocks, shown in Fig. 3, and the labeled numbers represent the pixel correspondence between the subblock and the supblock.

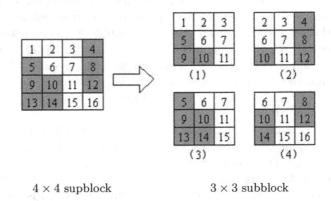

4 × 4 supblock   3 × 3 subblock

Fig. 3. Illustration of supblock mechanics for top level.

Suppose that we have a 4-by-4 supblock S, we denote the ith subblock of the supblock by $B_i(S)$ $(i = 1, 2, 3, 4)$. The *subblock embeddable function* $E_n(S, k)$ of rank n is recursively defined as follows:

i) For $k = 1$,

$$E_n(S, 1) = \begin{cases} 1, & \text{if } B_1(S) \in A_n \\ 0, & \text{else} \end{cases} \tag{1}$$

ii) For $k > 1$,

$$E_n(S, k) = \begin{cases} 1, & \text{if } B_k(S) \in A_n \text{ and } \forall i < k, m \geq n, E_m(S', i) \neq 1 \\ 0, & \text{else} \end{cases} \tag{2}$$

Where S' is the new supblock, supposed that central pixel in $B_k(S)$ is always changed.

The subblock embeddable function $E_n(S, k)$ depicts whether the kth subblock of S is suitable for embedding at rank n. $E_n(S, k)=1$ or 0 respectively means "yes" or "no". The subblock $B_k(S)$ is *n-level-embeddable* if $E_n(S, k) = 1$.

There may be more than one n-level-embeddable subblock in a supblock. For visibility effect, only one of them is picked for embedding. We define the *supblock embeddable indicator function* $\xi(S, n)$ as

$$\xi(S, n) = \begin{cases} \inf\{k | E_n(S, k) = 1\}, & \text{if } \sum_k E_n(S, k) \geq 1 \\ 0 & \text{else} \end{cases} \tag{3}$$

The function $\xi(S, n)$ describes that at rank n, whether the supblock is embeddable, and if so, which subblock is selected for embedding. The supblock S is *n-level-embeddable* if $\xi(S, n) > 0$.

We consider the sample shown in Fig. 3 for top level. In addition, we should define A_N, the pattern set of top level N. Here we let it be the collection of patterns similar to the pattern of Fig. 2(b). For the supblock shown in Fig. 3, we can obtain that $E_N(S, k) = 0$ for $k = 1, 2, 4$ and $E_N(S, 3) = 1$, further, $\xi(S, N) = 3$, meaning the 3rd subblock (Fig. 3(3)) is suggested for embedding.

The efficiency of supblock mechanics will be demonstrated in Sect. 3.

2.3   Embedding and Extracting

During the embedding procedure, the method will try to embed the critical data in the supblocks with high rank. At the same level, all the embeddable supblocks are permuted randomly based on a secret key before the embedding. The permutation has two advantages. First, it avoids selected supblocks cluster. Second, it also improves security. To summarize, the full procedure of embedding is as follows:

1. Partition the binary image into supblocks with the same size, e.g. 4×4.
2. Set *Level*=MAXRANK
3. While *Level* > 0 and NOT finishing all critical data
   a) For each supblock S_i that has not been marked, compute $\xi(S_i, Level)$
   b) Perform the random permutation of the supblocks with $\xi(S_i, Level) > 0$
   c) Embedding the critical data in the permutated supblocks, one supblock for one bit

    d) If finishing the embedding, quit.

    e) *Level* ← *Level* − 1

The embedding of critical data is inverse procedure. It is not difficult to deduce the procedure of extraction. It is ignored here.

3   Experimental Results and Analysis

The experiments summarized below were all conducted with 4-by-4 supblock size and 3-by-3 subblock size, unless otherwise specified. Our experimental results presented are composed of three parts. The first is tests on our method. The comparison with other schemes is performed in the second part. And the last part is a demonstration on application of tampering detection.

3.1   Tests on Our Methods

We have conducted many tests on our method. It really achieves the excellent performance because of the unnoticed changes after embedding. Meanwhile, it has the moderate capacity. Some results are presented in Fig. 4. To embed 200 bits in the host image with size 166×198, 105 pixels are changed, but the marked image differs very little from the original host image. The difference map between Fig. 4(a) and Fig. 4(b) is shown in Fig. 4(c).

    (a)   (b)   (c)

Fig. 4.   Data hiding by our method. (a) the original host image with size 166×198, (b) the marked image after embedding 200 bits, (c) the difference map, indicated by black pixel (totally 105 pixels).

As we mentioned earlier, the supblock mechanics can improves number of subblocks efficiently. We have performed the test on the supblock mechanics using 100 binary images of different sizes and different content. Some of the statistical data are shown in Fig. 5. It indicates that after carrying out the sup-block mechanics, it achieves an increase of number of the embeddable subblocks with 20%–45% percent at different level, compared with using 3-by-3 subblocks directly. Figure 5 shows the comparison of four of the highest ranks.

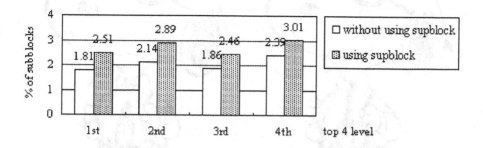

Fig. 5.   Efficiency of supblock mechanics.

3.2   Comparison with Other Methods

To compare with other methods, we have implemented the WU98 scheme [7] and the PAN00 scheme [8]. We use the same blocks size as implementation in our scheme (that is 4-by-4) for WU98 scheme, and use 16×16 of block size for PAN00 scheme since its advantage is exposed only when the block size is large. For fair comparison of images' perceptual quality, size and content of the critical data are same for all of the three methods.

One of the results is shown in Fig. 6. The host image size is 293-by-384 and the amount of the critical data is 480 bits. Obviously, PAN00 scheme introduces image-wide "visual noise", and WU98 also introduces "visual noise" near the boundaries.

In both WU98 scheme and PAN00 scheme, each pixel in a block is changeable. Without considering perceptual loss, they always introduce some isolated pixels, whose neighbors' color is all opposite to its color. It reduces the image quality seriously. Contrarily, our approach achieves the superior performance compared with WU98 and PAN00 schemes.

3.3   Tampering Detection

Because of ease to edit digital images, the authentication of these documents is becoming a great concern during recent years. The proposed scheme can be used for the purpose of tampering detection.

Figure 7 shows a sample of the scanned text for alteration detection. The host image is the first page of the paper by Fabien A. P. Petitcolas etc. After embedding another binary image with 84×125 in the host image, we remove a

(a)   (b)

(c)   (d)

Fig. 6. Comparison with other methods. The amount of hidden data is 480 bits. (a) the original host image with size 293×384, (b) the marked image by PAN00 scheme with block size 16×16, (c) the marked image by WU98 scheme with block size 4×4, (d) the marked image by our method with supblock size 4×4 and subblock size 3×3.

radix point in the marked image. Figure 7(c) is the extracted data after alteration. Obviously, the extracted binary image is significantly different from the original binary image of panda logo.

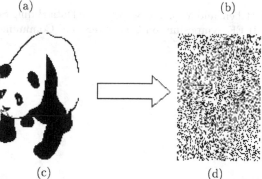

Fig. 7. Alteration detection for scanned text. (a) the marked image with size 1048 × 1380, after embedding 10,500 bits, (b) removing the radix point in the marked image, (c) the critical data (panda logo with size 84 × 125), (d) the extracted critical data after alteration.

4   Conclusion

This paper proposes a new data hiding algorithm for two-color images. The main idea is to use subblock pattern classification and supblock mechanics to select the pixels with least visual quality reduction for embedding. Analysis and experimental results both show that the proposed method can provide the superior performance and greatly outperforms the previous approaches in visibility transparency. It can applied to tampering detection, invisible annotation, and convert communication.

References

1. R.Z. van Schyndel, A.Z. Tirkel, and C.F.Osborne: A Digital Watermark. Proc. IEEE Int. Conf. Image Processing, vol.2, p86–90, 1994
2. W.Bender,N.Morimoto and D.Gruhl: Techniques for DataHiding,IBM System Journal. vol.25, p313–335, 1996
3. I.J.Cox, J.Kilian, T.Leighton, T.Shamoon: Secure spread Spectrum Watermarking for Images,Audio and Video. Proc. IEEE Int. Conf. On Image Processing, Lausanne, Switzerland, Sep. 1996
4. D.Kundur,D.Hatzinakos: Digital Watermarking Based on Multiresolution Wavelet Data Fusion. Proc. IEEE Special Issue on Intelligent Signal Processing,1997
5. C.Podilchuk, W.Zeng: Image Adaptive Watermarking Using Visual Models. IEEE Journal on Selected Areas in Comm., Vol.16, No.4, 1998
6. A.Piva, M.Barni, F.Bartolini, and V.Capellini: DCT-based watermark recovering without resorting to the uncorrupted original image. in Proc. IEEE ICIP'97, Santa Barbara, CA, Oct. 1997, vol.1, pp.520-523.
7. M.Y. Wu, J.H. Lee: A Novel Data Embedding Method for Two-Color Facsimile Images. Proc. Int. Symposium on Multimedia Information Processing, Taiwan, Dec. 1998
8. H.K. Pan, Y.Y. Chen, and Y.C. Tseng: A Secure Data Hiding Scheme for Two-Color Images. Proc. IEEE Symposium on Computers and Communications (ISCC 2000), France, July 3–6 2000, p750–755

An Identification Scheme Provably Secure against Reset Attack

C.-H. Lee[1], X. Deng[1], and H. Zhu[2]

[1] Department of computer science, City university of Hong Kong, Hong Kong
{cschlee, csdeng}@cityu.edu.hk

[2] Department of information and electronics engineering, Zhejiang university,
Hangzhou,310027, PR. China
zhuhf@isee.zju.edu.cn

Abstract. We develop an efficient identification scheme based on Cramer-Shoup test function. The scheme is provably secure against reset attack under post-processing model provided the hardness assumption of the decisional Diffie-Hellman problem as well as the existence of collision free hash functions.

1 Introduction

Smart cards have been used extensively in practice, e.g., in user access control and secure electronic commerce. Since a smart card is no more than some electronic device embedded with a desired chip capable for processing private information, it is vulnerable to the reset attack. We remark that the reset attack is a real security concern since a malicious user can simply disconnect its battery so as to reset its content to the initial state and then re-insert the battery and use it with that state a number of times if the smart card is available to the malicious users, e.g., in the cases that a smart card is lost or is stolen. The above attack has been discussed by Canetti, Goldwasser, Goldreich and Micali in [4]. Based on their simple observations, an interesting question is suggested in [4] that if an adversary is able to run several identification protocols in the role of a verifier with the same prover, each time being able to reset the prover to the same internal statement including the same random tape, can now the adversary learn enough to impersonate the prover later on? The answer is that any identification protocol based on zero-knowledge proof system is not secure under this attack since the knowledge can be extracted by resetting the random tape of the identification protocol polynomial number of times [4,1]. Unfortunately, the extensively used identification protocols, e.g., Fiat-Shamir's identification scheme [7], Schnorr's identification [10] are based on zero-knowledge proof paradigm. Hence the identification protocols mentioned above are insecure under the reset attack. It follows the reset attack is a very dangerous attack if the identification protocol equipped in the stolen smart card is based on zero-knowledge proof paradigm.

S. Qing, T. Okamoto, and J. Zhou (Eds.): ICICS 2001, LNCS 2229, pp. 271–279, 2001.

1.1 Related Works

The pioneer works related to resettable identification protocols are due to Canetti, Goldwasser, Goldreich and Micali [4]. They provide an identification protocol secure against reset attack in the public key model. However this scheme suffers from inefficiency in practice. Later Bellare, Goldwasser and Micali [1], have developed three identification protocols. The first two identification schemes are based on cryptographic primitives (Public key encryption scheme and stateless signature scheme, respectively) while the third protocol is based on the membership in NP languages of [4], which still suffers from inefficiency. It is an interesting problem if we are able to construct efficient identification protocols secure against reset attacks based on the standard intractability assumption such as the decisional Diffie-Hellman assumption rather than cryptographic primitives such as a public key encryption scheme or a digital signature scheme. The adversary's model in [1], allowing the reset attack in concurrent setting, is the strongest model for identification protocols considered to date. Two types of the resettable attacks: concurrent-reset-1 (CR1) and concurrent-reset-2 (CR2), are distinguished in their notable report [1]. In the CR1 setting, the adversary (say Vicky) may concurrently run many identification protocols with the prover (say Alice), resetting Alice to the initial state and interleaving the executions and hoping to learn enough to be able to impersonate Alice in a future time. Later Vicky will try to impersonate Alice. In the CR2 setting, while Vicky trying impersonation Alice, may concurrently run many identification protocols with the honest prover Alice, resetting Alice to the initial state and interleaving the executions. Notice that the CR1 attack is the special case of the CR2 attack, Hence if a identification protocol is secure in the CR2 setting then it is also secure in the CR1 setting. Finally Bellare, Goldwasser and Micali [1] have developed three identification protocols. The first two identification schemes are based on cryptographic primitives (Public key encryption scheme and stateless signature scheme, respectively) while the third protocol is based on the membership in NP languages of [4], which still suffers from inefficiency.

1.2 Our Contributions

We are interested in the construction of efficient identification protocols secure against the reset attack under the standard intractability assumptions. In this report we are able to develop such an efficient identification protocol provided the assumption of the hardness of the decisional Diffie-Hellman problem as well as the existence of collision free hash functions. Our work is not trivial since the identification protocol is NOT based on any security provable cryptographic primitives, e.g., a public key encryption scheme or a digital signature scheme. Hence our method differs from Bellare, Goldwasser and Micali's. Furthermore the identification protocol presented in this report is more efficient than that presented in [1] and [4].

2   Models and Definitions

Our identification protocol is a 3-move protocol. MSG_1 is the first message indicating beginning of the execution of the protocol while MSG_3 is the final message. There are four participants: a trusted third part, a prover, a verifier and an adversary in our identification model. A trusted third part is off-line and it issues a legitimate certificate for a new user instance at initial registration. We adopt Bellare, Goldwasser and Micali's model and distinguish adversary's ability by considering two models of the attacks. In the pre-processing model, the adversary is given access to the prover's oracle before the challenge message MSG_2 is given. However the adversary is permitted to access the prover's oracle in the post-processing model even after the challenge message MSG_2 is given. The differences between the two models are explained in details below.

2.1   Pre-processing Model

The prover sends the first and the last messages. At the end of interaction with the prover, the verifier outputs a decision, which is either *accept* or *reject*. Security definition of the identification protocol under the pre-processing model is similar with the pre-processing (IND-CCA1) setting of Naor and Yung's [8]. In the pre-processing model, an adversary's action is divided into two phases: in the first phase, the adversary interacts with the honest prover instance, not being allowed to interact with the verifier and tries to find the desired help information which will be used in the second phase. In the second phase, the challenge message is given, the access to the prover instance is denied. The adversary tries to to convince the verifier to accept the response message. The adversary, Vicky wins the game if she can make the honest verifier accept the response message. The adversary's advantage is defined by $Adv(Pre-processing)=\Pr[Win = true]$. We say an identification protocol is secure against reset attack in the pre-processing model if $Adv(Pre - processing)$ is negligible.

2.2   Post-processing Model

Security definition under the post-processing model is similar with the definition of post-processing (IND-CCA2) setting of Rackoff and Simon's [9]. The prover, Alice sends $MSG_1=(Cert_A, a)$ indicating the beginning of the protocol, where $Cert_A$ is the certificate of her public key while a is a random string chosen from Z_p^*. Then the honest verifier generates a challenge message known to the adversary. In the post-processing model, the adversary is given access to the prover's oracle even after the challenge message is given. Since the adversary can set Man-In-The-Middle attack between the honest verifier and the honest prover, relaying the message back and forth until the honest verifier accepts, we should carefully define the security of the identification protocol under post-processing model. Fortunately, with the help of the notions called session id suggested by Bellare and Rogaway [3], we can define what the adversary wins the game. We say the adversary wins the game if the honest verifier accepts the response message, which is provided by the adversary and the adversary holds the session id, which is different from that shared between the honest prover and the honest verifier. The advantage of the adversary is defined as Adv(Post-processing) = Pr[Win=true]. An identification protocol is said secure against the reset attack in the post-processing model if Adv(Post-processing) is negligible. By definitions, one knows that an identification protocol is secure against reset attack under post-processing model then it is also secure against reset under pre-processing model.

2.3   Security Assumptions

The aim of this work is to design an efficient identification protocol secure against reset attack under post-processing model. The proof of security is based on the hardness assumption of the decisional Diffie-Hellman as well as the existence of collision free hash functions. We state the assumptions as follows:

Decisional Diffie-Hellman assumption. Let G be a large cyclic group of prime order q. We consider the following two distributions:

- The distribution R^4 of random quadruple $(g_1, g_2, u_1, u_2) \in G^4$, where g_1, g_2, u_1 and u_2 are uniformly distributed in G^4.
- The distribution D^4 of quadruples $(g_1, g_2, u_1, u_2) \in G^4$, where g_1 and g_2 are uniformly distributed in G^2 whilst $u_1 = g_1^r$ and $u_2 = g_2^r$ for an r uniformly distributed in Z_q.

An algorithm that solves the quadruple decisional Diffie-Hellman problem is a statistical test that can efficiently distinguish these two distributions. The decisional Diffie-Hellman assumption means that there is no such a polynomial statistical test. This assumption is believed to be true for many cyclic groups, such as the prime sub-group of the multiplicative group of finite fields.

Computational Diffie-Hellman assumption. Let G be a large cyclic group of prime order q. Let $x, y \in Z_q$ be two random variables. Given (g, g^x, g^y), it is assumed a hard problem to compute g^{xy}.

Collision-free hash function. A hash function is called collision free if it is difficult to find a pair (x, y) so that $H(x) = H(y)$;

Cramer-Shoup encryption scheme[5]: Since the proof of security of the identification scheme is related to the non-malleable property of the Cramer-Shoup encryption scheme, we sketch the Cramer-Shoup encryption scheme as follows:

- Key generation: Let G be a sub-group of prime order q. Random chosen $x_1, x_2, y_1, y_2, z \in Z_q$ and computes $c = g_1^{x_1} g_2^{x_2}$, $d = g_1^{y_1} g_2^{y_2}$ and $h = g_1^z$. The private key is (x_1, x_2, y_1, y_2, z) and the public key is (g_1, g_2, c, d, H), where H is a collision free hash function;

- Encryption: To encrypt a message $m \in G$, it computes $u_1 = g_1^r$, $u_2 = g_2^r$, $e = mh^r$, $\alpha = H(u_1, u_2, e)$, $v = c^r d^{r\alpha}$. The cipher-text is (u_1, u_2, e, v).
- Decryption: Given a putative cipher (u_1, u_2, e, v), it computes $\alpha = H(u_1, u_2, e)$, and tests if $u_1^{x_1 + y_1\alpha} u_2^{x_2 + y_2\alpha} = v$, if this condition does not hold, the decryption algorithm outputs $reject$; Otherwise, it outputs $m = e/u_1^z$.

We call the function $u_1^{x_1 + y_1\alpha} u_2^{x_2 + y_2\alpha} = v$, Cramer-Shoup's test function. The Cramer-Shoup encryption scheme is proved to be secure against adaptive chosen cipher-text attack. That is the scheme is non-malleable under the adaptive chosen cipher-text attack model. In a typical implementation, we choose the group G with large prime order q such that $(p-1) = 2q$. The decryption oracle should test properly encoding of u_1, u_2 and must check that $u_1^q = 1$ and $u_2^q = 1$ so as to ensure that $u_1, u_2 \in G$. This remark also fits for the protocols presented in this report.

3   Identification Scheme Provably Secure under Post-processing Model

The fact that any identification scheme is secure against reset attack under post-processing model implies that the scheme is secure against reset under pre-processing model. Hence it is sufficient for us to develop some efficient identification scheme provably secure against reset attack in the post-processing model.

3.1   Description of Identification Protocol

Key generation: we choose two large primes p and q such that $p = 2q - 1$. Let G(one can regard as Z_q) be a group with prime order q. Let g_1, g_2 be two random generators of G. The private key is (x_1, x_2, y_1, y_2). The public key is $(c = g_1^{x_1} g_2^{x_2}, d = g_1^{y_1} g_2^{y_2})$, and H (a collision free hash function).

- Alice sends $MSG_1 = (Cert_A, a)$ indicating the start of the session, where $Cert_A$ is the certificate of her public key while a is a random string chosen from Z_p^*;
- Bob chooses $r \in Z_q$ and $b \in Z_q$ at random and computes $u_1 := g_1^r$, $u_2 := g_2^r$, $\alpha = H(u_1, u_2, k)$ and $u_3 := H(a, b, c^r d^{\alpha r})$, where $k = ab \bmod p$. Finally he sends the challenge message $MSG_2 := (u_1, u_2, u_3, k)$ to Alice;
- Upon receiving the challenge message $MSG_2 := (u_1, u_2, u_3, k)$, Alice computes $\alpha = H(u_1, u_2, k)$ and $v := u_1^{x_1 + \alpha y_1} u_2^{x_2 + \alpha y_2}$. Finally, she checks whether $H(a, k/a, v) = u_3$. If the challenge message is valid then she sends the response $MSG_3 := H(H(a, v), H(k/a, v), H(k, v))$ to Bob; Otherwise she rejects.
- Bob accepts Alice's response message MSG_3 if and only if $MSG_3 = H(H(a, v), H(b, v), H(k, v))$. The session id of the game is $Sid := (a, b)$.

3.2   Security Analysis

In this section, we want to prove the protocol is secure against reset attack under the post-processing model. We state the attack as follows: given the first message $MSG_1 = (Cert_A, a)$, where $a \in Z_q^*$, and the second challenge message $MSG_2 = (u_1, u_2, u_3, k)$ provided by the honest verifier, the adversary chooses a challenge message MSG_2' different from the target challenge message $MSG_2 = (u_1, u_2, u_3, k)$, then uses the honest prover as the oracle trying to get useful information. Finally the adversary try impersonating Alice as a legal user. We consider the following three cases of the MSG_2' queried by the adversary.

Cramer-Shoup encryption simulator. We add another public key $h(h = g_1^z)$ into the key generation protocol of the identification scheme described above. If the $MSG_2 = (u_1, u_2, u_3, k)$ is a valid challenge message then the prover sends back the response message MSG_3 and outputs the clear-text $m = k/u_1^z$ later. We call this modified identification scheme Cramer-Shoup encryption simulator. Since $k \in G$ is chosen at random, we can view k is a mask of some message m ($k = mh^r$). It is clear that the simulator is equivalent to the actual Cramer-Shoup encryption scheme [5]. Hence the simulator is non-malleable under adaptive chosen cipher-text attack.

Lemma 1. [5] If (g_1, g_2, u_1, u_2) comes from the random quadruple in the Cramer-Shoup simulator, then the probability that the adversary can compute the challenge message $v = u_1^{x_1 + y_1 \alpha} u_2^{x_2 + y_2 \alpha}$ is negligible, where k is a random string and $\alpha = H(u_1, u_2, k)$. In other words, all queries to the prover oracle must come from Diffie-Hellman quadruple.

Lemma 2. [5] There is no information leakage if (g_1, g_2, u_1, u_2) comes from the Diffie-Hellman quadruple in the Cramer-Shoup simulator.

Case 1-Prover Oracle Query

Case 1.1: Given $MSG_2 = (u_1, u_2, u_3, k)$, which is provided by the honest verifier, suppose the adversary provides an input to the prover's oracle with the form $MSG_2' = (u_1, u_2, u_3', k)$. Since H is assumed to be a collision free hash function, it follows the adversary is able to compute $c^r d^{r\alpha}$ with non-negligible probability. That is given u_1, u_2 and $u = cd^\alpha$, the adversary is able to compute $c^r d^{r\alpha}$. However this contradicts the computational Diffie-Hellman problem. Hence the case 1.1 is negligible.

Case 1.2: Given $MSG_2 = (u_1, u_2, u_3, k)$, which is provided by the honest verifier, suppose the adversary provides an input to the prover's oracle with the form $MSG_2' = (u_1, u_2, u_3', k')$, where $k' \neq k$. We want to show that the probability that the adversary can compute u_3' such that $u_3' = H(a, b, c^r d^{r\alpha})$ is negligible. Since H is assumed to be a collision free hash function, it follows the adversary is able to compute $c^r d^{r\alpha'}$ with non-negligible probability. That is the adversary is able to compute a valid mask k' of message m' ($k' = m'h^r$) such that $m/m' = k/k'$ with non-negligible probability. This contradicts the non-malleable property of the Cramer-Shoup encryption scheme [5]. Hence the case1.2 is negligible.

Case 2-Prover Oracle Query

Case 2.1: Given the challenge message $MSG_2 = (u_1, u_2, u_3, k)$ generated by the honest verifier Bob, the adversary tries to query the prover oracle message with the form $MSG'_2 = (u'_1, u'_2, u'_3, k)$. By Lemma 1, we know that (g_1, g_2, u'_1, u'_2) must come from Diffie-Hellman quadruple. Suppose the adversary knows the exact value r' such that $u'_1 = g_1^{r'}$ and $u'_2 = g_2^{r'}$. Then there is no information leaked according to Lemma 2. That is the adversary obtains no useful information from the current conversation.

Case 2.2: We consider the case that the adversary does not know the exact value r' such that $u'_1 = g_1^{r'}$ and $u'_2 = g_2^{r'}$. Since any $r' \in z_q$ can be written as the form $r' = rf_1 + f_2$ (for some $f_1, f_2 \in z_q$), we set $u'_1 = g_1^{r'} = u_1^{f_1} g_1^{f_2} = g_1^{rf_1+f_2}$ and $u'_2 = g_2^{r'} = u_2^{f_1} g_2^{f_2} = g_2^{rf_1+f_2}$, where $f_1, f_2 \in Z_q$ are strings chosen by the adversary. Since H is assumed to be collision free hash function, it follows the adversary is able to compute $c^{r'} d^{r'\alpha'}$ with non-negligible probability by assumption. By the Cramer and Shoup encryption simulator, we can view k the valid mask of the message m such that $k = mh^r$ and also the valid mask of the message m' such that $k = m'h^{r'}$. It follows the adversary can compute the valid cipher-text of message m' with the relationship $k = m'(k/m)^{f_1} h^{f_2}$ with non-negligible probability, where f_1, f_2 are random strings chosen by the adversary. This contradicts the non-malleable property of the Cramer-Shoup encryption simulator. Hence the case 2.2 is negligible.

Case 3-Prover Oracle Query

Case 3.1: Given the challenge message $MSG_2 = (u_1, u_2, u_3, k)$ generated by the honest verifier Bob, the adversary tries to provide the input to the prover oracle with the form $MSG'_2 = (u'_1, u'_2, u'_3, k')$. By Lemma 1, we know that (g_1, g_2, u'_1, u'_2) must come from Diffie-Hellman quadruple. Suppose that the adversary knows the exactly value r' such that $u'_1 = g_1^{r'}$ and $u'_2 = g_2^{r'}$. Then there is no information leaked according to Lemma 2. Hence the case 3.1 is negligible.

Case 3.2: We consider the case that the adversary does not know the exact value r' such that $u'_1 = g_1^{r'}$ and $u'_2 = g_2^{r'}$. In this setting, we set $u'_1 = u_1^{f_1} g_1^{f_2}$ and $u'_2 = u_2^{f_1} g_2^{f_2}$, where $f_1, f_2 \in z_q$ are two strings chosen by the adversary. Since H is assumed to be a collision free hash function, it follows the adversary is able to compute $c^{r'} d^{r'\alpha'}$ with non-negligible probability by the assumption. By the Cramer-Shoup simulator, we can view k as a valid message m such that $k = mh^r$ and k' be a valid mask of m' such that $k' = m'h^{r'}$ respectively. It follows that the adversary is able to compute a valid mask k' of message m' ($k' = m'h^{r'}$) such that $k' = m'(k/m)^{f_1}h^{f_2}$ with non-negligible probability, where $k = mh^r$. This contradicts the non-malleable property of Cramer-Shoup encryption simulator. Hence the case 3.2 is negligible.

The above argument implies that there is no information leaked even in the post-processing model. Hence we have the following statement.

Main result. The protocol described above is secure against reset attack under post-processing model provided the assumption of hardness of decisional Diffie-Hellman problem as well as the collision free hash assumption.

4   Conclusions

We have developed a new identification protocol secure against reset attack under post-processing model. Security proof is based on the hardness assumption of decisional Diffie-Hellman problem as well as the existence of collision free hash assumption. Since there is no random type involved in a prover instance, the reset attack does not work in our protocol. Our work is not trivial since the identification protocol is not based on any cryptographic primitives, e.g., public key encryption scheme, digital signature scheme, which is different from the pioneer works of Bellare, Goldwasser and Micali. And our identification protocol is more efficient than that presented in [1] as well as that presented in [4].

Acknowledgements. The work described in this paper was partially supported by CityU (of Hong Kong) research SRG grant 7001023 and DAG grant 7100133.

References

1. M. Bellare, S. Goldwasser, M. Micali. *Identification protocols secure against reset attacks.* http://wwww-cse.ucsd.edu/users/mihir, 2000.
2. M. Bellare, D. Pointcheval, P. Rogaway. *Authenticated key exchange secure against dictionary attacks.* In Advances in Cryptology - Eurocrypt 2000 Proceedings, In Advances in Cryptology - Proceedings of EUROCRYPT '2000, Brugge, Belgium, Pages 139-155, 2000.
3. M. Bellare, P. Rogaway. *Entity authentication and key distribution.* Extended abstract in Advances in Cryptology - Crypto'93 Proceedings, pages 232-233, Santa Barbara, California, August 1993.
4. R. Canetti, S. Goldwasser, O. Goldreich, S. Micali. *Resettable zero-knowledge.* Proceedings of 32nd Annual Symposium on the theory of Computing, ACM 2000. http://www.research.ibm.com/security/publ.html.
5. R. Cramer, V. Shoup. *A practical public key cryptosystem provably secure against adaptive chosen ciphertext attack.* Advances in Cryptology - Crypto'93 Crypto '98, pages 13-25, Santa Barbara, California, August 1998.

6. W. Diffie, M. E. Hellman. *New directions in cryptography.* IEEE Transactions on Information Theory, IT-22(6):644-654, November 1976.
7. A. Fiat, A. Shamir. *How to prove yourself: practical solutions to identification and signature problems.* Advances in Cryptology: Proceedings of Cryptology-Crypto'86, 1986.
8. M. Naor, M. Yung. *Public key cryptosystem secure against chosen cipher-text attacks.* 22nd Annual ACM Symposium on the theory of computing, pages 427-437, 1990.
9. C. Rackoff, D. Simon. *Non-interactive zero-knowledge proof of knowledge and chosen cipher-text attacks.* Advances in Cryptology: Proceedings of Cryptology-Crypto'91. Pages 433-444, Santa Barbara, California, August 1992.
10. C.P. Schnorr. *Efficient identification and signature for smart card.* Advances in Cryptology: Proceedings of Crypto'89, pages 235-251, Santa Barbara, California, August 1988.

Estimating the Scalability of the Internet Key Exchange

Sanna Kunnari

Oy L M Ericsson Ab, IP Security Competence Center
Tutkijantie 2, 90570 Oulu, Finland
Sanna.Kunnari@ericsson.fi

Abstract. Internet Key Exchange (IKE) is the default automated key management protocol selected for use with Internet Protocol Security protocol. The IKE has been implemented a lot but it has been critized whole the time. The scalability of the IKE is a question to be analyzed more seriously and that is the main issue of this paper. This paper presents estimations on the effort of the IKE negotiation using two different cases. The estimation is done theoretically but there are also concrete packet sizes and transmission times counted. The estimation introduces a scenario where a user needs a secure connection to some application server.

1. Introduction

The default automated key management protocol selected for use with IPSec is the Internet Key Exchange (IKE) under the IPSec Domain of Interpretation (DOI). The major function of the IKE is the establishment and maintenance of Security Associations. A Security Association (SA) is a relationship between two or more entities that describes how the entities will utilize security services to communicate securely [1, 2]. This relationship is represented by a set of information that can be considered a contract between the entities.

This paper aims to discuss the scalability of the Internet Key Exchange (IKE) protocol using the IKE main mode [1]. In this scenario, the main focus is on users, who wish to connect to the services in the Internet. All of these users possess such IKE solutions that support the use of trusted third parties for the key exchange. The three elements of this research are:

- Users,
- Application servers,
- Trusted third parties.

The users require for secured connections and burden the network with dense negotiations. A trusted third party [2] is one type of the service providers in the Internet, because it offers key management and distribution services. The trusted third party can be a certificate authority that provides information of the certificated entities [2] and stores the public keys. Alternatively, the trusted third party can be simply a key distribution center.

Nowadays, the connection to the Internet can be established in many ways. In this research, the users have a connection to the Internet through either a mobile connection or a PC connection.

S. Qing, T. Okamoto, and J. Zhou (Eds.): ICICS 2001, LNCS 2229, pp. 280-291, 2001.

Another important aspect of this research is the application server. A user that requires a secure connection to a server is a topic that is studied and the effort of the corresponding negotiation is estimated. The application servers that are concerned within this research are servers providing WWW-services and email servers.

As the number of the communicating parties raises and the use of the Internet applications becomes more common the traffic jams become evident. The accessibility of the services weakens, which causes communications to delay or break down. Some protocols do not work well in such circumstances, which indicate the lack of scalability. This paper discusses the scalability within IKE protocol framework.

2. The Network

This paper uses a hypothetical communication network that contains N ($N \in Z$, where Z is the set of integers) different users. These users can be gathered under K ($K \in Z$, $1 \leq K \leq N$) different user profiles, which are separated by the security level. The Internet usage can indicate either the use of email services or the use of World Wide Web (WWW) resources. The security level of a user is derived from the encryption level and the properties of the exchanged keys. The key lengths are set within each user profile and they can vary significantly among the different user profiles. The users are denoted by U_i, for $i = 1,..., N$.

2.1. About the Users

The user can be either a mobile user or a PC user, or something completely different. However, only the mobile and PC users are essential in this study. It can be estimated that almost 80 % of the users have a PC connection. Estimated 20 % of the users are mobile users, who possess a normal GSM connection with a speed of 9.6 kbit/s. However, the concrete speed of the GSM communication may be only 6 kbit/s [7]. Correspondingly, the theoretical maximum speed of a GPRS connection is 171,2 kbit/s but the concrete speed currently is only 10-40 kbit/s [7].

2.2. The Resource Allocation

The amount of key exchanges occurring within an hour is essential, because it can provide information of the network resource allocation. An example could be that a web-user initiates 15-30 key exchanges during an hour. Respectively, the email user can initiate 1-3 key exchanges in an hour. The amount of the initiations can be presented on two-dimensional figures using e.g. histogram presentations.

As the transport speed is dependent on the user profile, the different user profiles end up with separate levels for the network resource allocation. The mobile users tend to allocate the resources for longer, because the transport speed is low. For a PC user, the speed of the key exchange is naturally significantly higher.

Another important difference is that the WWW users perform more frequent key exchanges, which causes severe allocation for the network resources. It is a coherent research problem to determine which is the allocation level for each situation.

2.3. Trusted Third Parties

A trusted third party (TTP) is not an unambiguous entity, because the trustworthiness of it is not for sure or solid. The trust placed on the trusted third party varies with the way it is used, and hence motivates the following classification [5].

- A TTP is called *unconditionally trusted* if it is trusted on all matters. For example, it may have access to the secret and private keys of users, as well as be charged with the association of public keys to identifiers.

- A TTP is called *functionally trusted* if the entity is assumed to be honest and fair but it does not have access to the secret or private keys of users.

The basic function of a functionally trusted TTP can be to act as a key distribution center, which delivers the public keys for non-critical communications. A functionally trusted TTP could be used to register or certify users and contents of documents or as a judge [5]. Usually, the functionally trusted third party is guaranteed by some other trusted third party, unconditionally or functionally trusted. This leads to the chain of trust, which is a very useful framework within the authorities.

3. The Protocol Framework

The IKE protocol is the answer from the IPSec group to protocol negotiation and key exchange through the Internet [6]. It provides a way to agree on which protocols, algorithms and keys to use. Secondly, it provides a way to ensure from the beginning of the exchange that you are talking to whom you think you are talking to. Also, it enables to manage the keys after they have been generated and agreed upon. As IKE is a hybrid protocol, it combines parts of Oakley and parts of SKEME with the Internet Security Association and Key Management Protocol (ISAKMP), to negotiate, and derive keying material for Security Associations in a secure and authenticated manner [4].

ISAKMP allows the creation of exchanges for the establishment of Security Associations and keying material. An ISAKMP message consists of an ISAKMP header and some payloads. The appropriate fields and parameters are explained in [2].

In the current specifications, ISAKMP has five default exchange types defined [4]. This research is going to focus on the Identity Protection Exchange, which is the most common exchange mode. The elements of the Identity Protection Exchange are presented in Table 1 below. The notations are defined as follows: I indicates the initiator, R indicates the responder and * indicates payload encryption after the ISAKMP header.

Table 1. The messages in the Identity Protection Exchange.

Identity Protection Exchange	
(1) I → R	SA
(2) R → I	SA
(3) I → R	KE; NONCE
(4) R → I	KE; NONCE
(5)* I → R	ID(I); AUTH
(6)* R → I	ID(R); AUTH

The Identity Protection Exchange is designed to separate the key exchange information from the identity and authentication related information. It provides protection of the communicating identities at the expense of additional messages.

There are two phases in IKE functions. In phase one, two peers establish an IKE SA, which is a secure channel through which the IPSec SA negotiation can take place. In phase two, these two peers negotiate the actual IPSec Security Associations.

Within the Oakley, a basic method to establish an authenticated key exchange is to use Main Mode, which is an instantiation of the Identity Protection Exchange [4]. Both Main Mode and Quick Mode do SA negotiation. The phase one uses Main Mode as the Quick Mode is reserved for the phase two negotiations. During SA negotiation, initiator present offers for potential SAs to responder. Responder must not modify attributes of any offer [4].

The four different authentication methods that are allowed within phase 1 are digital signatures, two forms of authentication with public key encryption, or pre-shared key [4].

3.1. About the Scalability

Public key cryptography is the most flexible, scalable, and efficient way for users to obtain the shared secrets and session keys needed to support the interoperation between the Internet users [8]. Certificates can bind a specific identity of an entity to its public keys and possibly other security-related information. However, the certificates require an infrastructure for generation, verification, revocation, management and distribution. Also, authentication based on digital signatures requires a trusted third party or certificate authority to create, sign and properly distribute certificates.

The IKE framework does not mandate a specific signature algorithm or certificate authority (CA). The framework has two payloads for the certificate purposes. The Certificate payload provides a means to transport certificates or other certificate-related information and can appear in any ISAKMP message. Correspondingly, the Certificate Request payload provides a means to request certificates via ISAKMP and can appear in any message.

The use of pre-shared keys is not scalable within large user groups because it requires external key delivery methods. The expanded use of certificates could increase the scalability of IKE as the public keys could be delivered within the certificate payloads. The need for external delivery messages could be reduced even though the size of the IKE messages would be increased. The certificates require verification mechanisms with the corresponding CAs but that is another issue and outside the scope of this paper. Other ways to increase the scalability could be the use of cross certification between the CAs or the growth of the public key amount and overall availability.

4. Case Studies

Let us consider a situation that user U_i wants to send a secured message to another user U_j, where $1 \le i, j \le N$ and $i \ne j$. The users do not share each other's public keys and it is possible that they have never been communicating before. The user U_i sends a message to the nearest trusted third party and requires the public key of the user U_j. After successful retrieval of the key, the user U_i can begin the IKE negotiation with the user U_j by sending the initiating message. Similarly, the user U_j must contact the trusted third party for the public key of the U_i to be able to respond.

For the IKE SA, both users need to send three separate messages as defined in Table 1 above. The effort of the communication during the phase one is

$$E_{phase\ 1}[U_{ij}] = E_{phase\ 1}[U_i] + E_{phase\ 1}[U_j] = 3 + 3 = 6 \tag{1}$$

messages. In the phase two the initiator U_i sends two messages and the responder U_j replies with one, which can be formulated as $E_{phase\ 2}[U_{ij}] = 3$. The phase two negotiations happen frequently, because the IPSec SA does not have a long lifetime and it must be recreated. The lifetime of the IKE SA is longer; so one single IKE SA can be derived to multiple IPSec SAs. In addition to that, the IPSec SA is unidirectional so the parties usually must accomplish two times the phase two negotiation.

4.1. Case 1: Fixed Application Profile

In the fixed application profile, users and the network are gathered under strict pre-conditions. From the basic elements, this case involves the users and the trusted third parties, since the case considers only users communicating with each other. The users are assumed to be similar by their connection requirements and types.

The most interesting variables here are the number of the users (N) and the link capacity C for each link, where the scale is $0 \le C \le 100$, $M \in Z$ is the number of the TTPs, and the number of the links $\in [0, N+M]$. The maximum value of the link capacity is 100, when the network is working optimally and there are no delays. As the value diminishes, the capacity drops and the effort of the network increase. Therefore, the link capacity is an addition to the effort scenario, which indicates the effect on the network properties and capability.

The discussed IKE negotiations contain the establishment of the IKE SA and also the selection of the IPSec SA in phase 2. In the fixed communication profile, the establishment of a secure channel via IPSec requires 5 specific messages from the initiator and 1 message less from the responder. Anyway, the biggest effort of the IKE negotiation is the local computation of the group parameters for the SAs.

If pre-shared keys and certificate mechanisms are not available, the parties must acquire the public keys of each other from the TTP. In the simplest case, the public key and other relevant information is distributed in one message. The number of messages exchanged between a user U_i and a TTP is denoted by $m_{i,TTP}$, where $1 \leq m_{i,TTP} \leq n$ and $n \in Z_+$. Because it is reasonable to assume that $m_{i,TTP} = m_{TTP}$ for most of the users, the notation m_{TTP} is used in this chapter. In order to create two IPSec SAs, the total amount of messages is

$$L_1 = 2 m_{TTP} + E_{phase\,1}[U_{ij}] + 2 E_{phase\,2}[U_{ij}] = 2 m_{TTP} + 12, \tag{2}$$

where $L_1 \in Z_+$.

4.1.1. The Estimation

The burden that IKE causes to network resources can be derived from the number of the users and the capability of the links between the negotiating parties. If N users are connected to each other as a group, they must create

$$\binom{N}{2} = \frac{N(N-1)}{2} \tag{3}$$

IKE SAs in total. However, if the users are not communicating as a group and there are no parallel communications, the N users need to create only $N/2$ IKE SAs. This research focuses on the assumption that the users form communication groups to the network and may have parallel communications. Therefore, the amount of the messages for N users within the phase 1 exchange is

$$6 * \binom{N}{2} = \frac{6N(N-1)}{2} = 3N(N\text{-}1). \tag{4}$$

Also the potential message exchange with the TTP should be considered in this estimation. If both IPSec SAs are created, the total amount of messages for N users equals

$$L_2 = \binom{N}{2}(2 m_{TTP} + E_{phase\,1}[U_{ij}] + 2 E_{phase\,2}[U_{ij}]) = \frac{N(N-1)}{2}L_1, \tag{5}$$

where $L_2 \in Z_+$. After this message flow, there exists a unidirectional IPSec SA between all users, which simply means that every user can send secured messages to other users.

The link capacity C depends on the link properties and the network interference. The interfering factors can be the amount of the data transmitted over the link or various troubles with the network operability. The link capacity varies between the different network types and areas. As stated before, the link capacity is on a scale $0 \leq C \leq 100$, which makes it possible to compare the effects. If the same link is used by many users, the capacity that can be allocated for each user on the link equals C/l, where $1 \leq l \leq N$ equals the number of the users on the link. The link capacity is a regular variable but the link traffic and the burden caused by it are discrete variables. Therefore, the concrete link capability is a discrete variable that depends on the time and the concurrent network traffic. The value of the link capability can be estimated as

$$D = C * t, \tag{6}$$

where $0 \le D \le 100$ and a time-variant parameter $0 \le t \le 1$. The time-variant parameter indicates the reduction of efficiency that can be caused by the users or by other network operability. The link capability for each user depends on the amount of the users N and the link capacity C.

Now, the effort of the data transfer can be estimated more realistically for the IKE negotiations, because the effect of the capacity has been considered as well. The effort of creating IPSec connections for N users can be formulated as

$$L_3 = D\left(\frac{N}{2}\right)(2\, m_{TTP} + E_{phase\,1}[U_{ij}] + 2\, E_{phase\,2}[U_{ij}]) = D\, L_2, \tag{7}$$

where the capability works as a multiplier to cause the increase of effort.

4.1.2. The Calculation

Let us consider some situations, where 2 users create a secure channel with some typical security levels. The sizes of the exchanged messages are estimated here and the results are presented in the following tables. The connection uses IPv4 and the transport protocol is User Datagram protocol (UDP) [3].

For all the messages, the sizes of the IP and UDP headers are constant. The size of the UDP header is 64 bits, which includes the port numbers and two UDP specific variables. Correspondingly, the size of the IPv4 header is 160 bits, if no options are selected.

The first use-case advantages the revised mode of public key exchange [4], which is presented in Table 2. The group type is 1024-bit MODP, which is considered secured. The field Packet size contains the IP and UDP headers that are inserted to the message.

Table 2. Identity Protection Exchange with more security.

	Message size	Packet size	Explanation
1. message	1856 bits	2080 bits	Only 1 transform payload.
2. message	2464 bits	2688 bits	Nonce length is 1024 bits
3. message	352 bits	576 bits	

As the second case, there is a phase 1 exchange authenticated with signatures, see Table 3. The signature algorithm is RSA with the length of 128 bits. This case has the fourth Oakley group in use, which is the elliptic curve group over the field $GF(2^{185})$. The field Packet size contains the IP and UDP headers that are inserted to the message.

Table 3. Identity Protection Exchange with signatures.

	Message size	Packet size	Explanation
1. message	1472 bits	1696 bits	Only 1 transform payload.
2. message	1376 bits	1600 bits	Nonce length is 1024 bits
3. message	384 bits	608 bits	The RSA size is 128 bits.

The phase two Quick mode progressions for two first examples are gathered into Table 4. The minimal version does not support perfect forward security (PFS) [4] but the more secure version does.

Table 4. Two versions of the Quick Mode.

	Message size	Packet size	Explanation
7. message	960 bits	1184 bits	Initiator sends 1. message, minimal security.
8. message	960 bits	1184 bits	Responder sends 1. message
9. message	384 bits	608 bits	Initiator sends 2. message
7. message	2784 bits	3008 bits	Initiator sends 1. message, more security.
8. message	2784 bits	3008 bits	Responder sends 1. message
9. message	384 bits	608 bits	Initiator sends 2. message

The calculation points out that the amount of the exchanged messages increases rapidly as the number of the users grows. Because the negotiations have to happen quite frequently, the network is swamped by the negotiation efforts. The concrete phase 1 efforts tabulated above suffer the fact that there is only one transform payload suggested, which is not the typical case. Therefore, the message sizes in Tables 2 and 3 must be considered as minimal and the probable sizes are much higher.

Table 5 presents estimations on the transmission time using two typical transmission speeds. Transmission time 1 indicates a normal GSM connection with a speed of 9.6 kbit/s and transmission time 2 indicates a GPRS connection with a concrete speed of 40 kbit/s. The transfer sizes are from the Table 2 (Identity Protection Exchange with more security) and Table 4 (more secure version).

Table 5. Transmission times for mobile communications.

IKE messages	Transfer size (bits)	Transmission time 1 (seconds)	Transmission time 2 (seconds)	Explanation
Phase 1 messages by the Initiator	5344	0,557	0,134	1024-bit MODP and Nonce
Phase 1 messages	10688	1,113	0,267	Responder replies with similar messages.
Phase 2 messages by the Initiator	3616	0,377	0,09	PFS supported, 1024-bit parameters
Phase 2 messages	6624	0,69	0,166	1 message from the Responder.
All messages by the Initiator	8960	0,933	0,224	For one IPSec SA
All messages	17312	1,803	0,433	One IPSec SA created.
All messages with two Phase 2 exchanges	23936	2,493	0,598	IPSec SAs to both directions with alike parameters

The calculated transmission times do not include any resent or echo packets and the transmission speeds are estimated quite optimal. Therefore, the times must be considered as minimal. The calculations show that the effect of IKE is significant in GSM connections. The impacts on GPRS connections depend a lot on the concrete speed but the caused delay is evident anyway. If the connection is always on, the negotiations should not have a severe affect on the transmissions. However, if the connection is not on-line, the negotiations probably cause delay for each application that initiates secure connections.

4.2. Case 2: Variable Profiles for Users

The users have individual requests for their Internet usage. The common and rational way to separate the profiles of the users is to compare the Internet applications in use. The two separate Internet applications studied here are the email and the web-navigation. Additionally, various devices can establish the Internet connection, which causes significant differences in the connection speeds and capabilities. Fundamentally, the case 2 focuses on a scenario, where a user wants a secure connection to an application server. The application server can be either an email or a web server. Figure 1 presents the relationship of the parties that need the secure communications.

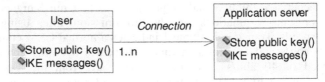

Fig. 1. The communicating parties.

Another difference within the user profiles is the level of the security requirements. The security levels can vary from strictly confidential to public, which causes significant alteration in the security parameters. Other users require fully confidential connections while others suffice with partially or functionally trusted connections. The users possess personal security profiles that define the key lengths, algorithms and protocols in use. The profiles are not constant and they may vary a lot between different users.

If a user and an application server do not know the public keys of each other, a TTP may be needed. The trust relationship between the user and the TTP can be either fully trusted or functionally trusted and the level of trust depends on the cryptographic algorithm in use. It is sufficient to use a functionally trusted TTP for the public key delivery. If the users need symmetric keys, an unconditionally trusted TTP is required [5].

If the user and the application server do already share each other's public keys, the effort of the initiator is only 5 messages. There is no change in the effort of the responder, so now the amount of the messages is the same. If the parties need to ask the public keys from a TTP, it takes at least 2 messages for each query. The number of messages exchanged between a user U_i and a TTP is denoted by $m_{i,TTP}$, where

$1 \leq m_{i,TTP} \leq n$ and $n \in Z_+$. Correspondingly, the number of messages exchanged between a TTP and an application server is denoted by $m_{a,TTP}$, where $1 \leq m_{a,TTP} \leq n$ and $n \in Z_+$.

Figure 2 presents a scenario, where a user asks for a secure access to an application server. In this scenario, the user and the server do not know each other's public keys and they have to contact a TTP to acquire them. The scenario results in an IKE SA, which is stored and used in the creation of the IPSec SAs. Further, the IKE phase 2 message exchanges happen more frequently, because the lifetime of the IPSec SA is typically short and it expires soon. In normal circumstances, there is no more need to contact a TTP.

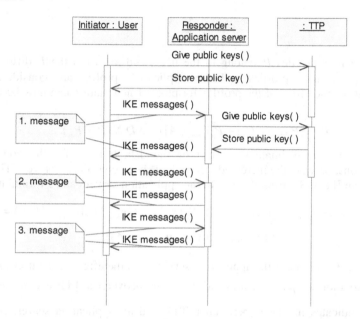

Fig. 2. IKE phase 1 negotiation.

4.2.1. The Estimation

In this scenario the burden that IKE causes to network resources is more difficult to estimate. The various variables include the number of the users, the capability of the links between the negotiating entities, the user profiles and the type of the network usage. If N users, where $N \geq 2$, wish to connect to an application server, they all have to create own bi-directional IKE SA with the server. Therefore, the amount of messages with N users within the phase 1 exchange is

$$N * (E_{phase\,1}[U_i] + E_{phase\,1}[A]) = 6\,N, \tag{8}$$

where user U_i is the initiator and application server A is the responder. The link capacity C (from the previous case) and the number of the users are the key factors, when estimating the value of the link capability. The capability works again as a multiplier to cause the increase of effort. The effort of creating IKE SAs from N users to an application server can now be formulated as

$$D N (E_{phase\ 1}[U_i] + E_{phase\ 1}[A]) = 6\ D\ N. \tag{9}$$

The effect of the user profile is very complex to estimate. The security levels can vary from strictly confidential to public, which causes significant alteration in the security parameters. Because there are K ($K \in Z$, $1 \leq K \leq N$) different user profiles, there is also K different ways to affect the communication effort. The effect of the user profile is denoted by P_i, where $i \in K$ and P_i is on the scale $0 \leq P_i \leq 100$. Also, the effect of an application server, denoted as P_a, is on a scale $0 \leq P_a \leq 100$. For N users, the effect of the user profiles can be estimated by the mean value

$$P = \frac{1}{N} \sum_{j=1}^{N} P_j, \tag{10}$$

where the user profiles P_j belong to the users and are from the K different profile types. If the user profiles and the application profile are considered in the computation, the effect of the profiles for phase 1 negotiation can now be formulated as

$$D N (P\ E_{phase\ 1}[U_i] + P_a E_{phase\ 1}[A]) = 3\ D\ N\ (P + P_a). \tag{11}$$

Now, one can estimate the effort of the data transfer for the complete IKE negotiations, because the increased effects have been considered as well. The effort of creating an IPSec SA from the user to the application server can be formulated as

$$D\ (P_i\ (m_{i,TTP} + E_{phase\ 1}[U_i] + E_{phase\ 2}[U_i]) + P_a\ (m_{a,TTP} + E_{phase\ 1}[U_a] + E_{phase\ 2}[U_a])) = D \tag{12}$$
$$(P_i\ (m_{i,TTP} + 5) + P_a\ (m_{a,TTP} + 4)),$$

where P_a is the effect of the application server, P_i is the effect of the user profile and $i \in K$. Notation $m_{i,TTP}$ indicates the messages between a TTP and U_i and notation $m_{a,TTP}$ indicates messages between a TTP and an application server. As one can imagine, the estimation of the effort for creating IPSec SAs for N users would result in a very long and complicated formula.

In this case, different types of the network usage indicate either a user connecting an email server or a user connecting a web server. There are many other possibilities, where to connect, and they can be compared likewise. There is a big difference between the two usage types as specified in chapter 2.2. Therefore, the network usage type can be thought as an individual factor that has influence to the effort.

5. Conclusions

The IKE has a very important role to play in the creation of the secure virtual private networks. Scalable and secure key determination and distribution mechanisms would be needed but they are not always the present reality. The scalability of the IKE protocol has been discussed in this paper with mathematical estimations and concrete effort calculations. Generally, a possible growth in the effort can cause problems to scalability under any circumstances.

There can be several factors in the networks that affect the communication loads. The interfering factors introduced here are the number of the users, the capability of the networks, the user profiles, the key delivery mechanisms and the type of the network usage. Two use cases were introduced here; users communicating with each other's and a user connecting an application server. The estimations showed that the factors caused interference to the negotiations but the definite amount of the interference depends on the local circumstances. Generally, it was proved that the number of the exchanges increases as the number of the users grows. Also, the number of the messages follows the number of the users linearly.

The role of a trusted third party is essential since the communicating parties usually do not know each other's public keys beforehand. There are different relationships to the trusted third party and one way to classify them is by the trust relationship. Trust is a difficult phenomenon to classify and it has raised interest within the professionals. The trust relationship between the users and the application servers is another thing that is not self-evident and it should be explored more.

The scalability of IKE could grow if the use of certificates would get more common. Certificates can be used to bind a specific identity of an entity to the public keys of it and possibly other security-related information. The advantage is that external methods are not needed for key delivery. However, the current implementations are often based on pre-shared key mechanisms, which is not a scalable solution for large user groups.

References

1. Jäälinoja Sanna: *The Core of the Internet Key Exchange Protocol*, Nordsec'2000 conference 12.-13.10.2000, Reykjavik, pp. 207-221.
2 Jäälinoja Sanna: *Aspects of Cryptography and Internet Security*, M.Sc. thesis, 1999, Oulu.
3. Oppliger Rolf: Internet and Intranet Security, 1998, Artech House, Inc.
4. D. Harkins, D. Carrel: *The Internet Key Exchange (IKE)*, Request for Comments (RFC) 2409, Network Working Group, 1998, Internet: ftp://ftp.isi.edu/in-notes/rfc2409.txt
5. Menezes Alfred J., van Oorschot Paul C., Vanstone Scott A.: *Handbook of Applied Cryptography*, CRC Press, Inc, New York, 1997.
6. Internet Engineering Task Force (IETF), Internet: http://www.ietf.org
7. Mähönen Petri: *Tulevaisuuden mobiilit dataverkot*, 2000, Internet: http://www.tietokone.fi/lukusali/artikkelit/2000tk08/DATAVERKOT.HTM
8. Maughan D., Schertler M., Schneider M., Turner J.: (1998) *Internet Security Association and Key Management Protocol (ISAKMP)*, Request for Comments (RFC) 2408, Network Working Group, 1998, Internet: ftp://ftp.isi.edu/in-notes/rfc2408.txt

An Efficient Information Flow Analysis of Recursive Programs Based on a Lattice Model of Security Classes

Shigeta Kuninobu[1], Yoshiaki Takata[1], Hiroyuki Seki[1], and Katsuro Inoue[2]

[1] Graduate School of Information Science, Nara Institute of Science and Technology
8916-5 Takayama, Ikoma, Nara, 630-1010, Japan
{shige-ku, y-takata, seki}@is.aist-nara.ac.jp
[2] Graduate School of Engineering Science, Osaka University
1-3 Machikaneyama, Toyonaka, Osaka 560-8531, Japan
inoue@ics.es.osaka-u.ac.jp

Abstract. We present an efficient method for analyzing information flow of a recursive program. In our method, security levels of data can be formalized as an arbitrary finite lattice. We prove the correctness of the proposed algorithm and also show that the algorithm can be executed in cubic time in the size of a program. Furthermore, the algorithm is extended so that operations which hide information of their arguments can be appropriately modeled by using a congruence relation. Experimental results by using a protypic system are also presented.

1   Introduction

In a system used by unspecified people, protecting information from undesirable leaking is essential. One of the ways to protect information from undesirable leaking is an access control technique called *Mandatory Access Control* (MAC). MAC requires that data and users (or processes) be assigned certain security levels represented by a label such as top-secret, confidential and unclassified. A label for a data d is called the security class (SC) of d, denoted as $SC(d)$. A label for a user u is called the clearance of u, denoted as $clear(u)$. In MAC, user u can read data d if and only if $clear(u) \geq SC(d)$. However, it is possible that a program with clearance higher than $SC(d)$ reads data d, creates some data d' from d and writes d' to a storage which a user with clearance lower than $SC(d)$ can read. Hence, an undesirable leaking may occur since data d' may contain some information on data d.

One way to prevent these kinds of information leaks is to conduct a program analysis which statically infers the SC of each output of the program when the SC of each input is given. Several program analyses based on a lattice model of SC have been proposed (see **related works** below); however, some of the program analyses can analyze only relatively simple programs which do not specifically contain a recursive procedure. Also, in some cases, the soundness of the analyses have not been proved.

This paper proposes an algorithm which analyzes information flow of a program containing recursive procedures. The algorithm constructs equations from statements in the program. The equation constructed from a statement represents the information flow caused by the execution of the statement. The algorithm computes the least fix-point of these equations. We describe the algorithm as an abstract interpretation and prove the

S. Qing, T. Okamoto, and J. Zhou (Eds.): ICICS 2001, LNCS 2229, pp. 292–303, 2001.
© Springer-Verlag Berlin Heidelberg 2001

soundness of the algorithm. For a given program *Prog*, the algorithm can be executed in $O(klN)$ time where k is the maximum number of arguments of procedures in *Prog*, l is the number of procedures in *Prog* and N is the total size of *Prog*. Based on the proposed method, a prototypic system has been implemented. Experimental results by using the system are also presented.

In the algorithm proposed in this paper and most of all other existing methods, the SC of the result of a built-in operation θ (e.g., addition) is assumed to be the least upper bound of the SCs of all input arguments of θ. This means that information on each argument may flow into the result of the operation. However, this assumption is not appropriate for some operations such as an aggregate operation and an encryption operation. For these operations, it is practically difficult to recover information on input arguments from the result of the operation. Considering the above discussions, the proposed method is extended so that these operations can be appropriately modeled by using a congruence relation.

The rest of the paper is organized as follows. Section 2 defines the syntax and the operational semantics of a program language which will be the target language of the analysis. In section 3, we formally describe the program analysis algorithm, prove the correctness of the algorithm and show the time complexity of the algorithm. A brief example is also presented in section 3. The method is extended in section 4. Experimental results are briefly presented in section 5.

Related Works. [D76] and [DD77] are the pioneering works which proposed a systematic method of analyzing information flow based on a lattice model of security classes. Subsequently, Denning's analysis method has been formalized and extended in a various way by Hoare-style axiomatization [BBM94], by abstract interpretation [O95], and by type theory [VS97,HR98,LR98].

In a type theoretic approach, a type system is defined so that if a given program is well-typed then the program has *noninterference* property such that it does not cause undesirable information flow. [VS97] provides a type system for statically analyzing information flow of a simple procedural program and proves its correctness. The method in [VS97] assumes a program without a recursive procedure while our method can analyze a program which may contain recursive procedures. [HR98] defines a type system for a functional language called Slam calculus to analyze noninterference property. [SV98] showed that their type system in [VS97] is no longer correct in a distributed environment and presented a new type system for a multi-threaded language. How to extend our method to fit a distributed environment is a future study.

A structure of security classes modeled as a finite lattice is usually a simple one such as {top-secret, confidential, unclassified}. [ML98] proposes a finer grained model of security classes called decentralized labels. Based on this model, [M99] proposes a programming language called JFLOW, for which a static type system for information flow analysis as well as a simple but flexible mechanism for dynamically controlling the privileges is provided. However, their type system has not been formally verified.

Recently, control flow analysis of a program which performs dynamic access control such as stack inspection in Java Development kit 1.2 is studied. For example, [JMT99, NTS01] propose methods of deciding for a given program P and a global security property ψ whether every reachable state of P satisfies ψ.

2 Definitions

2.1 Syntax of Program

In this section, we define the syntax and semantics of a programming language which will be the input language to the proposed algorithm. This language is a simple procedural language similar to C.

A program is a finite set of function definitions. A function definition has the following form:

$$f(x_1, \ldots, x_n) \text{ local } y_1, \ldots, y_m \ \{P_f\}$$

where f is a function name ($x_1, \ldots, x_n$ are formal arguments of f, $y_1, \ldots, y_m$ are local variables and P_f is a function body. The syntax of P_f is given below where c is a constant x is a local variable or a formal argument, f is a function name defined in the program and θ is a built-in operator such as addition and multiplication. Any object generated by $cseq$ can be P_f.

$$cseq ::= cmd \mid cmd_1; cseq$$
$$cmd ::= \text{if } exp \text{ then } cseq \text{ else } cseq \text{ fi} \mid \text{return } exp$$
$$cseq_1 ::= cmd_1 \mid cmd_1; cseq_1$$
$$cmd_1 ::= x := exp \mid \text{if } exp \text{ then } cseq_1 \text{ else } cseq_1 \text{ fi} \mid \text{while } exp \text{ do } cseq_1 \text{ od}$$
$$exp ::= c \mid x \mid f(exp, \ldots, exp) \mid \theta(exp, \ldots, exp)$$

Objects derived from exp, cmd or cmd_1, $cseq$ or $cseq_1$ are called an expression, a command, a sequence of commands, respectively. An execution of a program $Prog$ is the evaluation of the function named $main$, which should be defined in $Prog$. Inputs for $Prog$ are actual arguments of $main$ and the output of $Prog$ for these inputs is the return value of $main$.

2.2 Semantics of Program

We assume the following types to define the operational semantics of a program. Let $\times$ denote the cartesian product and $+$ denote the disjoint union.

type val (**values**) We assume for each n-ary built-in operator θ, n-ary operation $\theta_\mathcal{I}$: $val \times \cdots \times val \to val$ is defined. Every value manipulated or created in a program has the same type val.

type $store$ There exist two functions
$$lookup : store \times var \to val$$
$$update : store \times var \times val \to store$$
which satisfies:
$$lookup(update(\sigma, x, v), y) \quad = \quad \text{if } x = y \text{ then } v \text{ else } lookup(\sigma, y).$$
For readability, we use the following abbreviations:
$$\sigma(x) \equiv lookup(\sigma, x), \quad \sigma[x := v] \equiv update(\sigma, x, v).$$
Let $\perp_{store}$ denote the store such that $\perp_{store}(x)$ is undefined for every x.

We define a mapping which provides the semantics of a program. This mapping takes a store and one of an expression, a command and a sequence of commands as arguments and returns a store or a value.

$$\models: (store \rightarrow exp \rightarrow val) + (store \rightarrow cmd \rightarrow (store + val))$$
$$+ (store \rightarrow cseq \rightarrow (store + val))$$

- $\sigma \models M \Rightarrow v$ means that a store σ evaluates an expression M to the value v, that is, if M is evaluated by using σ then v is obtained.
- $\sigma \models C \Rightarrow \sigma'$ means that a store σ becomes σ' if a command C is executed.
- $\sigma \models C \Rightarrow v$ means that if a command C is executed when the store is σ then the value v is returned. This mapping is defined only when C has the form of 'return M' for some expression M.
- Similar for a sequence of commands.

Below we provide axioms and inference rules which define the semantic mapping, where the following meta-variables are used.

$$x, x_1, \dots, y_1, \dots : var \qquad M, M_1, \dots : exp \qquad C : cmd \text{ or } cmd_1$$
$$P, P_1, P_2 : cseq \text{ or } cseq_1 \quad \sigma, \sigma', \sigma'' : store$$

(CONST) $\sigma \models c \Rightarrow c_{\mathcal{I}}$

(VAR) $\sigma \models x \Rightarrow \sigma(x)$

(PRIM) $\dfrac{\sigma \models M_i \Rightarrow v_i \ (1 \le i \le n)}{\sigma \models \theta(M_1, \dots, M_n) \Rightarrow \theta_{\mathcal{I}}(v_1, \dots, v_n)}$

(CALL) $\dfrac{\sigma \models M_i \Rightarrow v_i \ (1 \le i \le n) \quad \sigma' \models P_f \Rightarrow v}{\sigma \models f(M_1, \dots, M_n) \Rightarrow v}$

$\left(\begin{array}{l} f(x_1, \dots, x_n) \text{ local } y_1, \dots, y_m \ \{P_f\} \\ \sigma' = \perp_{store}[x_1 := v_1] \cdots [x_n := v_n] \end{array} \right)$

(ASSIGN) $\dfrac{\sigma \models M \Rightarrow v}{\sigma \models x := M \Rightarrow \sigma[x := v]}$

(IF1) $\dfrac{\sigma \models M \Rightarrow true \quad \sigma \models P_1 \Rightarrow \sigma' \ (rsp. \ v)}{\sigma \models \text{if } M \text{ then } P_1 \text{ else } P_2 \text{ fi} \Rightarrow \sigma' \ (rsp. \ v)}$

(IF2) $\dfrac{\sigma \models M \Rightarrow false \quad \sigma \models P_2 \Rightarrow \sigma' \ (rsp. \ v)}{\sigma \models \text{if } M \text{ then } P_1 \text{ else } P_2 \text{ fi} \Rightarrow \sigma' \ (rsp. \ v)}$

(WHILE1) $\dfrac{\sigma \models M \Rightarrow true \quad \sigma \models P \Rightarrow \sigma' \quad \sigma' \models \text{while } M \text{ do } P \text{ od} \Rightarrow \sigma''}{\sigma \models \text{while } M \text{ do } P \text{ od} \Rightarrow \sigma''}$

(WHILE2) $\dfrac{\sigma \models M \Rightarrow false}{\sigma \models \text{while } M \text{ do } P \text{ od} \Rightarrow \sigma}$

(RETURN) $\dfrac{\sigma \models M \Rightarrow v}{\sigma \models \text{return } M \Rightarrow v}$

(CONCAT) $\dfrac{\sigma \models C \Rightarrow \sigma' \quad \sigma' \models P \Rightarrow \sigma'' \ (rsp. \ v)}{\sigma \models C; P \Rightarrow \sigma'' \ (rsp. \ v)}$

3 The Analysis Algorithm

A security class (abbreviated as SC) represents the security level of a value in a program. Let $SCset$ be a finite set of security classes. Also assume that a partial order $\sqsubseteq$ is defined on $SCset$ and $(SCset, \sqsubseteq)$ forms a lattice; let $\bot$ denote the minimum element of $SCset$ and let $a_1 \sqcup a_2$ denote the least upper bound of a_1 and a_2 for $a_1, a_2 \in SCset$. Intuitively, $\tau_1 \sqsubseteq \tau_2$ means that τ_2 is more secure than τ_1; it is legal that a user with clearance τ_2 can access a value with SC τ_1. A simple example of $SCset$ is:

$$SCset = \{low, high\}, \quad low \sqsubseteq high.$$

The purpose of the analysis is to infer (an upper bound of) the SC of the output value when an SC of each input is given. Precisely, the analysis problem for a given program $Prog$ is to infer an SC of the output value of $Prog$ which satisfies the soundness property defined in section 3.3.

We first describe the analysis algorithm in section 3.1. The soundness of the proposed algorithm is proved in section 3.3.

3.1   The Algorithm

To describe the algorithm, we use the following types.

type sc **(security class)** .
type $store$ **(SC of store)**

$$update : \underline{store} \times var \times sc \rightarrow \underline{store}$$
$$lookup : \underline{store} \times var \rightarrow sc$$

For $\underline{store}$ type, we use the same abbreviations as for $store$ type. If $\underline{\sigma}$ is an element of type $\underline{store}$, then $\underline{\sigma}(x)$ is the SC of variable x inferred by the algorithm. By extending the partial order $\sqsubseteq$ defined on sc to type $\underline{store}$ as shown below, we can provide a lattice structure to $\underline{store}$:

For $\underline{\sigma}$ and $\underline{\sigma}'$ of type $\underline{store}$, $\underline{\sigma} \sqsubseteq \underline{\sigma}' \Leftrightarrow \forall x \in var.\ \underline{\sigma}(x) \sqsubseteq \underline{\sigma}'(x)$.

The minimum element of $\underline{store}$ is $\underline{\sigma}$ satisfying $\forall x \in var.\ \underline{\sigma}(x) = \bot$. We write this minimum element as $\bot_{\underline{store}}$.

type $\underline{fun}$ **(SC of function)** Similarly to type $\underline{store}$, the following functions are defined.

$$lookup : \underline{fun} \times fname \rightarrow (sc \times \cdots \times sc \rightarrow sc)$$
$$update : \underline{fun} \times fname \times (sc \times \cdots \times sc \rightarrow sc) \rightarrow \underline{fun}$$

We use the following abbreviations for $F \in \underline{fun}, f \in fname$ and $\psi : sc \times \cdots \times sc \rightarrow sc$.

$$F[f] \equiv lookup(F, f)$$
$$F[f := \psi] \equiv update(F, f, \psi)$$

For n-ary function f and SCs $\tau_1, \ldots, \tau_n$, $F[f](\tau_1, \ldots, \tau_n)$ is the SC of the returned value of f inferred by the algorithm when the SC of i-th argument is specified as $\tau_i\ (1 \le i \le n)$. Similarly to type $\underline{store}$, we can provide a lattice structure to type $\underline{fun}$. The minimum element of $\underline{fun}$ is denoted as $\bot_{\underline{fun}}$.

type cv-$\underline{fun}$ (covariant $\underline{fun}$) This type consists of every F of type $\underline{fun}$ which satisfies the next condition:

If $\tau_i \sqsubseteq \tau_i'$ for $1 \le i \le n$ then $F[f](\tau_1, \ldots, \tau_n) \sqsubseteq F[f](\tau_1', \ldots, \tau_n')$.

We use the following meta-variables as well as the meta-variables introduced in section 2.2.

$\sigma, \sigma', \sigma'' : \underline{store}$ $F, F_1, F_2 : \underline{fun}$

Below we define a function $\mathcal{A}[\![\cdot]\!]$ which analyzes the information flow. Before defining the analysis function, we explain implicit flow [D76]. Consider the following command.

if $x = 0$ then $y := 0$ else $y := 1$ fi

In this command, the variable x occurs neither in $y := 0$ nor in $y := 1$. However, after executing this command, we can know whether x is 0 or not by checking whether y is 0 or 1. Therefore, we can consider information on the value stored in the variable x flows into the variable y. In general, information may flow from the conditional clause of a "if" command into "then" and "else" clauses and also it may flow from the conditional clause of a "while" command into "do" clause. Such information flow is called *implicit flow*. The function $\mathcal{A}[\![\cdot]\!]$ infers that the SC of implicit flow caused by a command C or a sequence P of commands is the least upper bound of the SCs of the conditional clauses of all the "if" and "while" commands which contain C or P in their scopes. $\mathcal{A}[\![\cdot]\!]$ takes the SC of implicit flow as its fourth argument.

$\mathcal{A} : (exp \times \underline{fun} \times \underline{store} \to sc) + (cmd \times \underline{fun} \times \underline{store} \times sc \to \underline{store})$
$+ (cseq \times \underline{fun} \times \underline{store} \times sc \to \underline{store})$

- $\mathcal{A}[\![M]\!](F, \sigma) = \tau$ means that, for SCs F of functions and an SC σ of a store, the SC of an expression M is analyzed as τ.
- $\mathcal{A}[\![C]\!](F, \sigma, \nu) = \sigma'$ means that, for SCs F of functions, an SC σ of a store and an SC ν of implicit flow, the SC of the store after executing a command C is analyzed as σ'.
- Similar for a sequence of commands.

The definition of $\mathcal{A}$ is as follows:

(CONST) $\mathcal{A}[\![c]\!](F, \sigma) = \bot$
(VAR) $\mathcal{A}[\![x]\!](F, \sigma) = \sigma(x)$
(PRIM) $\mathcal{A}[\![\theta(M_1, \ldots, M_n)]\!](F, \sigma) = \bigsqcup_{1 \le i \le n} \mathcal{A}[\![M_i]\!](F, \sigma)$
(CALL) $\mathcal{A}[\![f(M_1, \ldots, M_n)]\!](F, \sigma) = F[\![f]\!](\mathcal{A}[\![M_1]\!](F, \sigma), \ldots, \mathcal{A}[\![M_n]\!](F, \sigma))$
(ASSIGN) $\mathcal{A}[\![x := M]\!](F, \sigma, \nu) = \sigma[x := \mathcal{A}[\![M]\!](F, \sigma) \sqcup \nu]$
(IF) $\mathcal{A}[\![\text{if } M \text{ then } P_1 \text{ else } P_2 \text{ fi}]\!](F, \sigma, \nu) = \mathcal{A}[\![P_1]\!](F, \sigma, \nu \sqcup \tau) \sqcup \mathcal{A}[\![P_2]\!](F, \sigma, \nu \sqcup \tau)$
where $\tau = \mathcal{A}[\![M]\!](F, \sigma)$
(WHILE) $\mathcal{A}[\![\text{while } M \text{ do } P \text{ od}]\!](F, \sigma, \nu) = \mathcal{A}[\![P]\!](F, \sigma, \nu \sqcup \mathcal{A}[\![M]\!](F, \sigma)) \sqcup \sigma$
(RETURN) Let ret be a fresh variable which contains a return value of a function.
$\mathcal{A}[\![\text{return } M]\!](F, \sigma, \nu) = \sigma[ret := \mathcal{A}[\![M]\!](F, \sigma) \sqcup \nu]$
(CONCAT) $\mathcal{A}[\![C; P]\!](F, \sigma, \nu) = \mathcal{A}[\![P]\!](F, \mathcal{A}[\![C]\!](F, \sigma, \nu), \nu)$

Define the function $\mathcal{A}[\![\cdot]\!] : program \to \underline{fun} \to \underline{fun}$, which performs 'one-step' analysis of information flow for each function $\overline{f}$ defined in a given program as follows:

For $Prog \equiv \{f(x_1, \ldots, x_n) \text{ local } y_1, \ldots, y_m \{P_f\}, \ldots\}$,

$\mathcal{A}[\![Prog]\!](F) =$
$\quad F[f := \lambda \tau_1 \ldots \tau_n.(\mathcal{A}[\![P_f]\!](F, \bot_{\underline{store}}[x_1 := \tau_1] \cdots [x_n := \tau_n], \bot)(ret))$
$\quad \mid f \text{ is an } n\text{-ary function defined in } Prog]$ (1)

For a lattice $(S, \preceq)$ and a function $f : S \rightarrow S$, we write the least fix-point of f as $fix(f)$. For a program $Prog$, the function $\mathcal{A}^*[\![Prog]\!]$ which analyzes information flow of $Prog$ is defined as the least fix-point of $\mathcal{A}[\![Prog]\!]$, that is,

$$\mathcal{A}^*[\![Prog]\!] = fix(\lambda F.\mathcal{A}[\![Prog]\!](F)).$$

As will be shown in lemma 1, $\mathcal{A}[\![Prog]\!]$ is a monotonic function on the finite lattice cv-$\underline{fun}$. Therefore,

$$\mathcal{A}^*[\![Prog]\!] = \bigsqcup_{i \geq 0} \mathcal{A}[\![Prog]\!]^i(\perp_{\underline{fun}}) \tag{2}$$

holds [M96] where $f^0(x) = x$, $f^{i+1}(x) = f(f^i(x))$. Hence, $\mathcal{A}^*[\![Prog]\!]$ can be calculated by starting with $\perp_{\underline{fun}}$ and repeatedly applying $\mathcal{A}[\![Prog]\!]$ to the SCs of functions until the SCs of the functions remains unchanged.

3.2   An Example

In this subsection, we show how our analysis algorithm works. The program which we are going to analyze is written below. In this example, we assume $SCset = \{low, high\}$, $low \sqsubseteq high$.

```
main(x) {                          f(x) {
    while x > 0 do                     if x > 0
        y := x + 1; x := y − 4             then return x * f(x − 1)
    od;                                    else return 0
    return f(x)                        fi
}                                  }
```

In order to analyze this program, we continue updating F using the following relation until F does not change any more.

$$F = F[main := \lambda\tau.(\mathcal{A}[\![P_{main}]\!](F, \perp_{\underline{store}}[x := \tau], \perp)(ret))]$$
$$[f := \lambda\tau.(\mathcal{A}[\![P_f]\!](F, \perp_{\underline{store}}[x := \tau], \perp)(ret))]$$

The table below shows how F changes. The SCs of the i-th column are calculated by using the SCs of the $(i − 1)$th column.

	0	1	2	3
$F[main]$	$\lambda\tau.\perp$	$\lambda\tau.\perp$	$\lambda\tau.\tau$	$\lambda\tau.\tau$
$F[f]$		$\lambda\tau.\perp$	$\lambda\tau.\tau$	$\lambda\tau.\tau$	$\lambda\tau.\tau$

From this table, we can know that $\mathcal{A}^*[\![Prog]\!][main](\tau) = \tau$, that is, the SC of the return value of the main function is low when the SC of the actual argument is low and the SC of the return value of the main function could be $high$ when the SC of the actual argument is $high$.

3.3   Soundness of the Algorithm

As mentioned in section 3.1, the analysis algorithm is a function of the following type:

$$\mathcal{A}^*[\![\cdot]\!] : program \to fname \to (sc \times \cdots \times sc \to sc).$$

$\mathcal{A}^*[\![Prog]\!][f](\tau_1, \ldots, \tau_n) = \tau$ means that for an n-ary function f defined in $Prog$ and for SCs $\tau_1, \ldots, \tau_n$ of arguments of f, $\mathcal{A}^*[\![\cdot]\!]$ infers that the SC of f is τ.

Definition 1. An analysis algorithm $\mathcal{A}^*[\![\cdot]\!]$ is **sound** if the following condition is satisfied.

Assume $Prog$ is a program and $main$ is the main function of $Prog$. If

$$\mathcal{A}^*[\![Prog]\!][main](\tau_1, \ldots, \tau_n) = \tau,$$
$$\perp_{store} \models main(v_1, \ldots, v_n) \Rightarrow v, \quad \perp_{store} \models main(v_1', \ldots, v_n') \Rightarrow v',$$
$$\forall i\, (1 \leq i \leq n) : \tau_i \sqsubseteq \tau.\ v_i = v_i'$$

then $v = v'$ holds.   □

By the above definition, an analysis algorithm is sound if and only if the following condition is satisfied: assume that the analysis algorithm answers "the SC of the returned value of the main function is τ if the SC of the i-th argument is τ_i." If every actual argument with SC equal to or less than τ remain the same then returned values of the main function also remains the same even if an actual argument with SC higher than or incomparable with τ changes. Intuitively, this means that if the analysis algorithm answers "the SC of the main function is τ," then information contained in each actual argument with SC higher than or incomparable with τ does not flow into the return value of the main function.

The following lemma guarantees the validity of the equation (2).

Lemma 1. *(a)* If F is of type cv-$\underline{fun}$ then $\mathcal{A}[\![Prog]\!](F)$ is also of type cv-$\underline{fun}$.
(b) *(monotonicity)* Assume F_1 and $\overline{F_2}$ are of type cv-$\underline{fun}$. If $F_1 \sqsubseteq F_2$ then
$\mathcal{A}[\![Prog]\!](F_1) \sqsubseteq \mathcal{A}[\![Prog]\!](F_2)$.   □

The next two lemmas are used to show that the algorithm presented in section 3.1 is sound in the sense of definition 1.

Lemma 2. *(property of implicit flow)*

(a) If $\mathcal{A}[\![P]\!](F, \underline{\sigma}, \nu) = \underline{\sigma}', \sigma \models P \Rightarrow \sigma'$ and $\nu \not\sqsubseteq \underline{\sigma}'(y)$ then $\sigma(y) = \sigma'(y)$.
(b) If $\mathcal{A}[\![P]\!](F, \underline{\sigma}, \nu) = \underline{\sigma}', \sigma \models$ while M do P od $\Rightarrow \sigma'$ and $\nu \not\sqsubseteq \underline{\sigma}'(y)$ then $\sigma(y) = \sigma'(y)$.   □

Lemma 3. *(noninterference property)* Let $F = \mathcal{A}^*[\![Prog]\!]$.

(a) If $A[\![M]\!](F, \underline{\sigma}) = \tau$, $\sigma_1 \models M \Rightarrow v_1$, $\sigma_2 \models M \Rightarrow v_2$ and $\forall x : \underline{\sigma}(x) \sqsubseteq \tau$. $\sigma_1(x) = \sigma_2(x)$, then $v_1 = v_2$.

(b) If $A[\![P]\!](F, \underline{\sigma}, \nu) = \underline{\sigma}'$, $\sigma_1 \models P \Rightarrow \sigma_1'$, $\sigma_2 \models P \Rightarrow \sigma_2'$, $\underline{\sigma}'(y) = \tau$ and $\forall x : \underline{\sigma}(x) \sqsubseteq \tau$. $\sigma_1(x) = \sigma_2(x)$, then $\sigma_1'(y) = \sigma_2'(y)$.

(c) If $A[\![P]\!](F, \underline{\sigma}, \nu) = \underline{\sigma}'$, $\sigma_1 \models P \Rightarrow v_1$, $\sigma_2 \models P \Rightarrow v_2$ and $\forall x : \underline{\sigma}(x) \sqsubseteq \underline{\sigma}'(ret)$. $\sigma_1(x) = \sigma_2(x)$, then $v_1 = v_2$.

(Proof Sketch) By using Lemmas 1 and 2, the lemma is proved by induction on the application number of inference rules for $A[\![\cdot]\!]$.   □

Theorem 1. The algorithm $A^*[\![\cdot]\!]$ is sound.

(Proof) By lemma 3*(c)*.   □

3.4   Time Complexity

In this subsection, the time complexity of the algorithm $A^*[\![\cdot]\!]$ presented in section 3.1 is examined. Let *Prog* be an input program and let k, l and N be the maximum number of arguments of each function in *Prog*, the number of functions in *Prog* and the total size of *Prog*, respectively. Since the only operations which appear in the algorithm are $\bot$ and $\sqcup$, for each n-ary function f in *Prog*, $A[\![Prog]\!](F)[f]$ can be written as

$$A[\![Prog]\!](F)[f](\tau_1, \ldots, \tau_n) = \tau_{i_1} \sqcup \cdots \sqcup \tau_{i_m}$$

where τ_i $(1 \leq i \leq n)$ is an arbitrary SC and $\{i_1, \ldots, i_m\} \subseteq \{1, \ldots, n\}$. The worst case is that for each execution of $A[\![Prog]\!](F)$, only one τ_j is added to $A[\![Prog]\!](F)[f_1](\tau_1, \ldots, \tau_n)$ for only one function f_1 and $A[\![Prog]\!](F)[f](\tau_1, \ldots, \tau_n)$ remains unchanged for every function f other than f_1. For example, $A[\![Prog]\!](F)[f_1](\tau_1, \tau_2, \tau_3) = \tau_1$ becomes $A[\![Prog]\!](A[\![Prog]\!](F))[f_1](\tau_1, \tau_2, \tau_3) = \tau_1 \sqcup \tau_3$ while $A[\![Prog]\!](A[\![Prog]\!](F))[f](\tau_1, \ldots, \tau_n) = A[\![Prog]\!](F)[f](\tau_1, \ldots, \tau_n)$ for every function f other than f_1. Thus, the maximum number of iterations of $A[\![Prog]\!]$ is kl. On the other hand, it is not difficult to see that one iteration of $A[\![Prog]\!]$ takes $O(N)$ time. Hence, we obtain the following theorem:

Theorem 2. Let *Prog* be a program. The algorithm $A^*[\![Prog]\!]$ can be executed in $O(klN)$ time where k is the maximum number of arguments of each function in *Prog*, l is the number of functions in *Prog* and N is the total size of *Prog*, respectively.   □

4   An Extended Model

The algorithm A in the previous section has been defined for any built-in operator θ as:

(PRIM) $A[\![\theta(M_1, \ldots, M_n)]\!](F, \underline{\sigma}) = \bigsqcup_{1 \leq i \leq n} A[\![M_i]\!](F, \underline{\sigma})$.

This means that we assume information contained in each argument may flow into the result of the operation $\theta_{\mathcal{I}}$. However, this assumption is too conservative for a certain operation. For example, if an operation $\theta_{\mathcal{I}}$ is defined as $\theta_{\mathcal{I}}(x, y) = x$, then it is clear that information in the second argument does not flow into the result of the operation.

Another example is an encryption. Assume that for a plain text d and an encryption key k, the result of the operation $E_{\mathcal{I}}(d, k)$ is the cipher text of d with key k. We may consider that the SC of $E(x, y)$ is *low* even if the SCs of x and y are both *high*.

To express the above mentioned properties of particular built-in operations, we generalize the above definition as:

(PRIM) $\mathcal{A}[\![\theta(M_1, \ldots, M_n)]\!](F, \underline{\sigma}) = \mathcal{B}[\![\theta]\!](\mathcal{A}[\![M_1]\!](F, \underline{\sigma}), \ldots, \mathcal{A}[\![M_n]\!](F, \underline{\sigma})),$

where $\mathcal{B}[\![\theta]\!]$ is an arbitrary monotonic total function on sc:

$$\mathcal{B}[\![\theta]\!] : sc \times \cdots \times sc \rightarrow sc.$$

In particular, $\mathcal{B}[\![\theta]\!](\tau_1, \ldots, \tau_n) = \bigsqcup_{1 \le i \le n} \tau_i$ for the original definition of $\mathcal{A}$.

However, the generalized algorithm is no longer sound in the sense of definition 1. Suppose that we define $\mathcal{B}[\![E]\!](\tau_1, \tau_2) = low$, and consider a program

$$Prog = \{main(x, y) \ \{ \ \text{return } E(x, y) \ \} \ \}.$$

$\mathcal{A}^*[\![Prog]\!][main](high, high) = low$ holds while for distinct plain texts d_1, d_2 and a key k, $E_{\mathcal{I}}(d_1, k) \ne E_{\mathcal{I}}(d_2, k)$. Hence $\mathcal{A}^*[\![\cdot]\!]$ is not sound. Intuitively, the fact that the SC of expression $E(x, y)$ is inferred as *low* means that we cannot recover information contained in the arguments x, y from the result of the encryption. In other words, $E_{\mathcal{I}}(d_1, k)$ and $E_{\mathcal{I}}(d_2, k)$ are indistinguishable with respect to the information in the arguments. To express this indistinguishability, we introduce the following notions.

A relation R on type *val* is called a congruence relation if R is an equivalence relation which satisfies:

for each n-ary built-in operator θ, if $c_i \ R \ c_i'$ for $1 \le i \le n$
then $\theta_{\mathcal{I}}(c_1, \ldots, c_n) \ R \ \theta_{\mathcal{I}}(c_1', \ldots, c_n')$.

In the following, we assume that a particular congruence relation $\sim$ is given. For v, v' of type *val*, if $v \sim v'$ then we say that v and v' are indistinguishable. By the definition, if v_i and v_i' for $1 \le i \le n$ are indistinguishable then for any built-in operator θ, $\theta_{\mathcal{I}}(c_1, \ldots, c_n)$ and $\theta_{\mathcal{I}}(c_1', \ldots, c_n')$ are also indistinguishable. This implies that once v and v' become indistinguishable, we cannot obtain any information to distinguish v and v' through any operations.

Next, we require $\mathcal{B}[\![\cdot]\!]$ to satisfy the following condition.

Condition 4 Assume $\mathcal{B}[\![\theta]\!](\tau_1, \ldots, \tau_n) = \tau$ for an n-ary built-in operator θ. Let c_i, c_i' be of type *val* $(1 \le i \le n)$. If $c_j \sim c_j'$ for each j $(1 \le j \le n)$ such that $\tau_j \sqsubseteq \tau$, then $\theta_{\mathcal{I}}(c_1, \ldots, c_n) \sim \theta_{\mathcal{I}}(c_1', \ldots, c_n')$.   □

The above condition states that:

Let $\mathcal{B}[\![\theta]\!](\tau_1, \ldots, \tau_n) = \tau$. Assume that arguments of θ are changed from $c_1, \ldots, c_n$ to $c_1', \ldots, c_n'$. As long as c_j and c_j' are indistinguishable for each argument position j such that $\tau_j \sqsubseteq \tau$, $\theta_{\mathcal{I}}(c_1, \ldots, c_n)$ and $\theta_{\mathcal{I}}(c_1', \ldots, c_n')$ remain indistinguishable.

Example 1 (nonstrict function). Assume that $\theta_{\mathcal{I}}(x, y) = x$ and $\mathcal{B}[\![\theta]\!](\tau_1, \tau_2) = \tau_1$. For any values c_1, c_1', c_2 and $c_2', c_1 \sim c_1'$ implies $\theta_{\mathcal{I}}(c_1, c_2) = c_1 \sim c_1' = \theta_{\mathcal{I}}(c_1', c_2')$. Hence, condition 4 is met for any congruence relation $\sim$.   □

Example 2 (declassification). Let *mk-rpt* be an operator which takes a patient record and produces a doctor's report. Assume that no information in the argument of *mk-rpt* flows into the result of the operator. In this case, we can define $\mathcal{B}[\![mk\text{-}rpt]\!](high) = low$ with $low \sqsubseteq high$. Condition 4 requires that for any patient records c, c', $mk\text{-}rpt_\mathcal{I}(c) \sim mk\text{-}rpt_\mathcal{I}(c')$. Intuitively, this means that we cannot discover information on a particular patient's record by reading a doctor's report. □

Example 3 (encryption). Let E be an encryption function which takes a plain text and an encryption key as arguments. Assume that no information in the plain text can be discovered by manipulating the encrypted text. In this case, we can define $\mathcal{B}[\![E]\!](high, high) = low$. Condition 4 requires that for any plain texts d, d' and keys k, k', $E_\mathcal{I}(d, k) \sim E_\mathcal{I}(d', k')$. □

Now we can define the soundness by using the notion of indistinguishability as follows:

Definition 2 (generalized soundness). Let $\sim$ be a congruence relation. We say that an algorithm $\mathcal{A}^*[\![\cdot]\!]$ is sound (with respect to $\sim$) if the following condition holds:

> If $\mathcal{A}^*[\![Prog]\!][main](\tau_1, \ldots, \tau_n) = \tau$,
> $\perp_{store} \models main(v_1, \ldots, v_n) \Rightarrow v$, $\perp_{store} \models main(v'_1, \ldots, v'_n) \Rightarrow v'$, and
> $\forall i\,(1 \leq i \leq n) : \tau_i \sqsubseteq \tau.\,v_i \sim v'_i$
> then $v \sim v'$ holds. □

It is not difficult to prove the following theorem in a similar way to the proof of theorem 1.

Theorem 3. If condition 4 is satisfied, then the generalized algorithm $\mathcal{A}^*[\![\cdot]\!]$ is sound in the sense of definition 2. □

5   Conclusion

In this paper, we have proposed an algorithm which can statically analyze the information flow of a procedural program containing recursive definitions. It has been shown that the algorithm is sound and that the algorithm can be executed in polynomial time in the size of an input program. In [Y01], the proposed algorithm is extended to be able to analyze a program which may contain global variables and a prototypic analysis system has been implemented. Table 1 shows the execution time to analyze sample programs by the implemented system. Extending the proposed method so that we can analyze a program which has pointers and/or object-oriented features is a future study.

Acknowledgments. The authors sincerely thank Fumiaki Ohata and Reishi Yokomori of Osaka University for their valuable comments and discussions.

Table 1. Analysis time

Program	Number of lines	Average analysis time (sec)
Ticket reservation system	419	0.050
Sorting algorithm	825	0.130
A program library	2471	2.270

References

[BBM94]   J. Banâtre, C. Bryce and D. Le Métayer: Compile-time detection of information flow in sequential programs, 3rd ESORICS, LNCS 875, 55–73, 1994.

[D76]   D. E. Denning: A lattice model of secure information flow, Communications of the ACM, 19(5), 236–243, 1976.

[DD77]   D. E. Denning and P. J. Denning: Certification of programs for secure information flow, Communications of the ACM, 20(7), 504–513, 1977.

[HR98]   N. Heintze and J. G. Riecke: The SLam calculus: Programming with secrecy and integrity, 25th ACM Symp. on Principles of Programming Languages, 365–377, 1998.

[JMT99]   T. Jensen, D. Le Métayer and T. Thorn: Verification of control flow based security properties, 1999 IEEE Symp. on Security and Privacy, 89–103, 1999.

[LR98]   X. Leroy and F. Rouaix: Security properties of typed applets, 25th ACM Symp. on Principles of Programming Languages, 391–403, 1998.

[M96]   J. Mitchell: *Foundations of Programming Languages*, The MIT Press, 1996.

[M99]   A. C. Myers: JFLOW: Practical mostly-static information flow control, 26th ACM Symp. on Principles of Progmming Languages, 228–241, 1999.

[ML98]   A. C. Myers and B. Liskov: Complete, safe information flow with decentralized labels, 1998 IEEE Symp. on Security and Privacy, 186–197.

[NTS01]   N. Nitta, Y. Takata and H. Seki: Security verification of programs with stack inspection, 6th ACM Symp. on Access Control Models and Technologies, 31–40, 2001.

[O95]   P. Ørbæk: Can you trust your data? TAPSOFT '95, LNCS 915, 575–589.

[SV98]   G. Smith and D. Volpano: Secure information flow in a muti-threaded imperative language, 25th ACM Symp. on Principles of Programming Languages, 355–364, 1998.

[VS97]   D. Volpano and G. Smith: A type-based approach to program security, TAPSOFT '97, LNCS 1214, 607–621.

[Y01]   R. Yokomori: Security analysis algorithm for object-oriented programs, Master's Thesis, Osaka University, 2001.

Defeating Denial-of-Service Attacks on the Internet

Baoqing Ye

Verizon Laboratories, 40 Sylvan Road, LAOMS59, Waltham, MA02451, USA
Baoqing.Ye@verizon.com

Abstract. Network Denial-of-Service (N-DoS) attacks are one of the fastest growing types of attack on the Internet. This paper addresses the vulnerabilities in Internet protocols, as well as deficiencies in flow-control in the Internet, both of which contribute to the loss of resource availability when networks suffer N-DoS attacks. Furthermore, an AFFC (Anti-flooding Flow-Control) model is presented to defend against flooding N-DoS attacks. AFFC policies regulate unresponsive elastic traffic and aggressive best-effort traffic for specific flow classes. Experiments have demonstrated that the deployment of this model can thwart harmful flows and prevent congestion collapse by flooding N-DoS attacks.

1 Introduction

1.1 Network Denial-of-Service Attacks on the Internet

Network Denial-of-Service (N-DoS) attacks corrupt network resource availability to legitimate users. There are growing number of N-DoS attacks in various forms and symptoms on the Internet. The newly emerged N-DoS attacks are Distributed-DoS (DDoS) attacks. Essentially, DDoS attacks bundle classical N-DoS attacks and launch them simultaneously from intermediate machines.

Table 1 contains cases of typical classical N-DoS attacks. Flooding N-DoS attacks deprive legitimate users of network resources such as network bandwidth. Both flooding and non-flooding N-DoS attacks have exploited the vulnerabilities and flaws in Internet protocols' design and implementations.

1.2 Existing Defense Strategies

Most existing defense strategies against N-DoS attacks are based on explicit signature capturing and analysis. For those attacks of which signatures can change in their variants, this type of approach has limitations. For instance, signatures often used in detecting DDoS daemons, such as process commands and communication port numbers, can lose their validity when they are modified in separate attacks. Some researchers have also proposed address-based filtering to shield against malicious sources. This approach, if not infeasible, is difficult and costly to apply on the open Internet where incoming sources are very dynamic.

In order to defend against N-DoS attacks proactively on the Internet effectively, the core vulnerabilities in the TCP/IP protocol suite and Internet infrastructure must be investigated.

S. Qing, T. Okamoto, and J. Zhou (Eds.): ICICS 2001, LNCS 2229, pp. 304–315, 2001.

Table 1. Classical Network Denial-of-Service Attack Examples

	Non-Flooding N-DoS	Flooding N-DoS
TCP-related	Land / Lanierra [HH98]	SYN-Flood [Cert96a]
	TearDrop2	Mstream [Dd00] / ack-flood
UDP-related		UDP-echo-flooding
		Fraggle-attack
IP-related	Tear / TearDrop / NewTear	
	Bonk / Boink [Windows99]	
	Ping-of-Death [Cert96b]	
ICMP-related	ICMP-unreachable	SMURF
		Ping-flood
ARP-related	ARP-redirect / poisoning	

2   Internet Protocols

This section addresses vulnerabilities and flaws in Internet protocols – the TCP/IP suite. Next section analyzes the insufficiencies in network-node flow-control schemes on the Internet.

2.1   Vulnerabilities in Internet Protocols

Application Layer. Security flaws in the Application Layer are often caused by lack of bounds checking. One typical example is buffer-overflow. Flaws need to be patched in a case-by-case basis. Designing and implementing applications with security considerations is crucial.

Transport Layer. There are three features for TCP that make it appealing to N-DoS attackers. First, a limited listening queue within a relatively long time-out period (typically 75 seconds) can help cerate a typical SYN-flood scenario. Second, TCP headers can be manipulated if authentication or integrity is not guarantted, such as the case in the LAND attack.Third, legitimate TCP traffic, which follows congestion control and avoidance algorithms, can unfortunately suffer severe network resources starvation when competing with best-effort traffic under pipe-structured Internet scheduling schemes.
UDP traffic provides best-effort services without congestion control schemes implemented in the protocol. This feature has been taken advantaged by attackers to launch flooding N-DoS attacks to deprive legitimate traffic, especially elastic TCP-friendly traffic.

Network Layer. ICMP, as a help layer for the Network Layer, has the similar non-reponsive features as those in UDP. N-DoS attacks often use ICMP packets to launch flooding attacks. In addition, by manipulating ICMP headers, N-DoS attackers can mute their targets, such as the scenario in the ICMP-unreachable attack.

IP is susceptible to IP-spoofing due to the lack of authentication if without schemes such as IPsec. In addition, IP packets are subject to be fragmented when required. Lack of bounds checking in fragmentation reassembly procedures are vulnerable to various fragmentation attacks such as Ping-of-Death, Tear Attacks, and Bond Attacks.

IPsec provides the authentication and integrity check for IPv4 or IPv6 packets as an option. However, IPsec is not required to use while required to implement. IPsec may not be deployed in all Internet network nodes and hosts other than VPNs. Furthermore, IPsec only protects certain fields of IP-header, which cannot elimination the impacts of all N-DoS attacks. For example, fragmentation attacks can survive the IPsec shield because the fragmentation field is transparent to IPsec.

Link Layer. ARP (Address Resolution Protocol) is used with certain types of network interface (such as Ethernet and token ring) to convert between IP addresses and network interface addresses. A dynamic ARP cache tables often don't prevent crackers from sending packets with forged ARP addresses and trigger ARP cache poisoning attacks, which can be used to mute a victim machine.

2.2 Hardening TCP/IP Suite

There are two aspects in hardening TCP/IP protocol suite. First, design protocols with security considerations, which needs to be fulfilled in many RFC standards. IPsec is an option to provide authentication and integrity check to some extent. One alternative option is to use authentication add-ons. For example, SYN-cookies [ML97] can be used to thwart some TCP-based attacks such as SYN-flood, LAND attacks, and ACK-flood/ mstream-attacks. Second, protocols must be implemented carefully to avoid integrity and security flaws. One example is to reassemble fragments properly with sufficient bounds checking to avoid destructive impacts by fragmentation attacks.

3 Flow-Control in the Internet

Flooding N-DoS attacks work because of the overall weak network flow-control on the Internet.

3.1 Deficient Flow-Control in the Internet

In today's Internet, most network nodes use FIFO (First In First Out) scheduling and Drop-Tail or RED (Random-Early-Detection [FJ93]) buffer management schemes.

Fig. 1 and Fig. 2 demonstrate a scenario that malicious non-responsive flows in a FIFO/RED flow control scheme grab bandwidth from legitimate elastic flows. A NS2 tool [FV00] was used to perform the experiment. A DDoS flooding attack topology is simulated by Fig.1 with seven network nodes and six source nodes. Incoming flow features are described in Table 2. Traffic with mixed legitimate

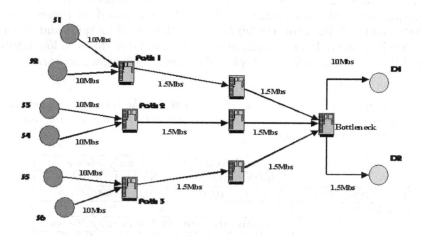

Fig. 1. Simulation Topology

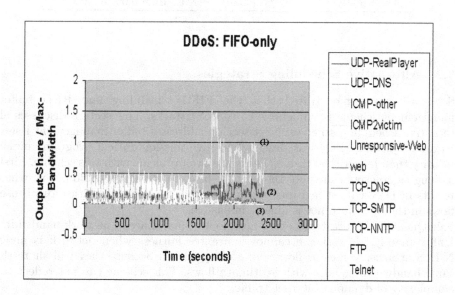

Fig. 2. Flooding N-DoS traffic over FIFO/RED flow-control. *flow(1):ICMP2victim; flow(2):Unresponsive-Web; flow(3): Other legitimate flows*

and malicious flows passes from the network nodes to a bottleneck node and reach the destination D2. Fig. 2 shows the output statistics at the bottleneck node output link, which demonstrates that, as the malicious flows (unresponsive web traffic and ICMP2victim traffic) increases their sending rates and reaches certain level, at about 1600 seconds, most legitimate flows starts to lose output bandwidth shares. This reflects a typical flooding N-DoS attack scenario.

Table 2. Features for incoming flows. *(Packet sizes in the table do not necessarily represent accurate average values for specific protocols. Different sizes are chosen to reflect their influences on outputs)*

	Legitimate TCP-friendly Flows					
	Web	DNS	SMTP	NNTP	FTP	Telnet
Packet Size (Bytes)	600	400	1000	700	1500	500
Window Size (Bytes)	65535					
	Legitimate Non-TCP-Friendly Flows					
	Real Player		UDP-DNS		ICMP	
Packet Size (Bytes)	500		400		300	
Delay (sec/Bytes)	0.08					
	Malicious Flows					
	Unresponsive Web Flow			malicious ICMP Flows		
Packet Size (Bytes)	400			500		
Delay (sec/Bytes)	Gradually decrease from 0.09 to 0.0004					

3.2 Alternative Scheduling Strategies

Sect. 3.1 has demonstrated that the FIFO scheduling and RED buffer-management scheme is vulnerable to N-DoS attacks. This section discusses alternative scheduling schemes. Next section addresses buffer management issue.

Priority Queuing (PQ) was designed to give mission-critical programs higher priority than less critical traffic. There are two problems with this scheme. First, as long as crackers can spoof the priority field, theft-service could occur, which results in DoS against legitimate users. Second, to assign priorities for all user flows in the open Internet is almost infeasible.

Fair Queuing (FQ) restricts every host to an equal share of network bandwidth. Unfortunately, this scheme cannot guarantee fairness when network is under N-DoS attacks. Malicious flows will go unpunished because they will share the same bandwidth equally with legitimate flows. This scheme can not reflect the complexity of dynamic Internet traffic.

Weighted Fair Queuing (WFQ) gives low-volume traffic flows preferential treatment and allows higher-volume traffic flows to obtain equity in the remaining amount of queuing capacity. This scheme itself is susceptible to N-DoS attacks. When attackers generate short flows, which happens often especially spoofed IP addresses are used, WFQ can in fact help N-DoS attackers by giving these low-volume flows preferential treatment.

Class-based-Queuing (CBQ) [FJ95] classifies incoming traffic into appropriate classes and then determine the bandwidth usage for each class. This concept has the flexibility to reflect the dynamic feature of Internet traffic and has the potential to react against flooding N-DoS attacks. CBQ is recommended as the skeleton of the scheduling scheme in the AFFC model proposed in Section 4.

3.3 Existing Congestion Control Schemes in Network Nodes

Congestion control in network nodes is also referred to as buffer management, which is responsible for packet dropping when congestion occurs. Drop-Tail (DT) sets a maximum length for each queue and accepts packets until maximum length is reached. It is known that DT can create a "full-queue" problem. It is vulnerable to N-DoS flooding attacks and is not recommended.

Active Queue Management (AQM) concept manages buffers by setting two minimum and maximum thresholds. One example is the RED, which cannot thwart destructive flooding N-DoS impacts as demonstrated in Sect. 3.1.

3.4 Existing QoS Schemes

There are two major QoS (Quality-of-Service) strategies being proposed– Differentiated Service (Diff-Serv) and Integrated Service (Int-Serv).

Diff-Serv sets bits in an IP header field at network boundaries (autonomous system boundaries, internal administrative boundaries, or hosts). Diff-Serv is essentially a refined priority-scheduling model, which does not solve the flooding N-DoS problem. First, the priority setup is determined by boundaries or end-hosts. Policy setup only reflects a sender's request not network conditions. Second, it is possible that crackers can manipulate the bits in ToS/IPv4 fields or TC/IPv6 fields resulting in theft-of-service, which leads to DoS to legitimate users. Notice in IPsec, these two fields are not included in cryptographic calculations. Indeed, RFC 2475 [Bs98] has specified that a PHB (Per-Hop-Behavior) should include a section detailing the security implications and discussing how the proposed PHB group could be used in DoS attacks as well as detecting such attacks. Current Diff-Serv proposals leave the DoS problem unsolved.

Int-Serv, as a model that predominantly focuses on real-time classes of applications in order to provide guaranteed service for both delay and bandwidth, it does not address the issue on solving N-DoS.

4 Anti-flooding Flow-Control Model in Network Nodes

To defend against N-DoS attacks and guarantee the network resource availability, additional flow-control schemes need to be explored. This section presents an Anti-Flooding Flow-Control (AFFC) model deployed in network nodes to defend against flooding N-DoS attacks. There are four major components in the AFFC model: traffic classifier, dynamic buffer manager, packet scheduler, and early-traffic-regulation. The AFFC procedures target in finding traffic bahavior differences among harmful and normal flows, so as to thwart the destructive impact from flooding N-DoS attacks.

4.1   Traffic Classification

A traffic classifier categories incoming flows into classes based on destination IP addresses (or destination IP address groups) and protocol types. It generates a bandwidth baseline based on arrival-rate pattern for each flow class. The bandwidth baselines are used for scheduling and dynamic buffer management to determine the packet send-rates and drop-rates, which are triggered when potential congestion collapse is detected in bottleneck nodes.

Even though Internet traffic patterns are exceedingly hard to characterize, diurnal patterns in certain focal points do exist [FP99]. Some studies have even demonstrated the existence of diurnal patterns in international backbones [TMW97]. We have performed some experiments and collected statistics locally, which proved the existence of diurnal traffic patterns.

4.2   Dynamic Buffer Management

Buffer management decides when to drop packets and in what dropping rates. In the AFFC model, elastic traffic and best-effort classes are treated separately.

Elastic Traffic. In flooding N-DoS attacks, crackers often use spoofed IP addresses, such as in SYN-flood, ACK-flood / mstream-attacks. Those attacks have one common characteristic – the malicious TCP flows are non-responsive to congestion signals. The harmful traffic if not behaves like constant-bit-rate (CBR) traffic, it will move in aggressive manners with faster arrival-rates, which is distinguishable from the behaviors of legitimate elastic traffic.

In the AFFC model, legitimate elastic flows are reserved based on the following observations. Theoretically, elastic flows follow the TCP-friendly behavior [FF99]:

$$T \leq \frac{1.5\sqrt{2/3} * B}{R * \sqrt{p}} \tag{1}$$

Where T(Bps) is the maximum sending rate for a TCP connection, B(Bytes) is the number of packets sent, R(seconds) is the minimum round trip time using that link, and p(Bps) is traffic drop rate.

Equation (1) shows that, for legitimate TCP-adaptive flows, if the long-term packet drop rate of the connection increases by a factor of x, then the arrival rate from the source should decrease by a factor of roughly $\sqrt{x}$. Notice that when network links are about to be saturated, the round-trip-time R tends to approach constant. The change of R is then negligible.

The dynamic buffer management in AFFC keeps a recyclable pool to record the responsive flows, which decrease-rates of their arrival-rates fall into the range of $(1/a * \sqrt{x}, 1)$. The parameter $a \geq 1$ is added if we consider the impact of possible increase of round-trip-time R in Equation (1), when a network link is increasingly saturated.The flows in the reservoir are permitted to pass when traffic regulation is required and triggered by potential congestion collapse in bottleneck nodes. Other packets are dropped. The permission list is refreshed periodically.

Best-Effort Traffic. For best-effort traffic, which was designed not to respond congestion signals, the AFFC strategy is to regulate sending rate for harmful flow classes in times of potential congestion collapse under N-DoS attacks. Those attacks include UDP flood, ICMP flood, SMURF attacks, Fraggle Attacks, and so forth.

When traffic regulation is needed, problematic flow classes will be singled out based in destination IP address (groups) and protocol types. First, for the harmful flows, packet drop rates will be regulated up to the bandwidth baselines collected from the traffic monitor and classifier. Second, if a potential congestion collapse situation in a bottleneck is not eased and the traffic regulation is still necessary, packet drop rates will be increased in responsive to halving packet sending-rates.

The packet drop-rate regulation can be achieved by adjusting two buffer thresholds $minThresh$ and $maxThresh$.

Let $dropRatio = \frac{currPos - minThresh}{maxThresh - minThresh} * \frac{1}{liinterm}$, $newDropRatio = x * dropRatio$, then

$$newmaxThresh = \frac{(x-1)minThresh + maxThresh}{x} \qquad (2)$$

During the course of traffic regulation, the outgoing bandwidth share λ_{OUT} follows multiplicative decrease for each time interval Δt.

The form of the multiplicative decrease is $\lambda_{OUT}(t) = \frac{\lambda_{OUT}(t - \Delta t)}{k}$. The parameter k is the decrease ratio for the outgoing rate λ_{OUT} in the time frame Δt, used when a given flow's arrival rate is faster than its bandwidth baseline. The k can be set to two to simulate the TCP congestion window algorithm. When the arrival rate is below the baseline while traffic regulation is still required, the factor k will decrease so that the sending rate will reduce at a slower rate.

The output rate bound λ_{OUT} will resume to its original value when traffic regulation signaling stops.

In order to keep balance in the queue Q, the incoming rate $\lambda_{IN}(t)$ needs to be adjusted as $\lambda_{IN}(t) = \lambda_{OUT}(t) = \lambda_0(t) - v(t)$, which yields,

$$v(t) = \lambda_0(t) - \lambda_{IN}(t) \qquad (3)$$

where $\lambda_{IN}(t)$ is the incoming rate, $\lambda_0(t)$ is the raw incoming traffic rate, and $v(t)$ is the drop-rate.

The change factor $x(t)$ of the drop rate $v(t)$ is calculated as

$$x(t) = \frac{v(t)}{v(t - \Delta t)} \qquad (4)$$

Consider the time factor, equation (2) can be represented as

$$newmaxThresh(t) = \frac{[x(t) - 1] * minThresh(t - \Delta t) + maxThresh(t - \Delta t)}{x(t)}$$

$$\qquad (5)$$

Equation (3) to (5) demonstrate an approach to regulate incoming flows in response to flow arrival-rates $\lambda_0(t)$ and outgoing sending rates $\lambda_{out}(t)$.

4.3   Scheduling

The scheduling scheme in AFFC is a CBQ-based multi-queuing approach.
First, classified traffic is put in multiple queues.
Second, when traffic regulation is not required, each class of traffic uses up to the maximum bandwidth available. Flows are not restricted to bandwidth baselines. If potential congestion collapse is detected in a bottleneck node, traffic regulation is required. The dynamic buffer management is activated, as well as scheduling schemes.
Scheduling schemes decide when to send packets and in what rates. In the AFFC model, for elastic traffic, flows in the permit list are forwarded in rates matching their arrival rates, which have already slowed down by sources in responsive to congestion signaling.
For best-effort traffic, sending rates for harmful flows are restricted to their bandwidth baselines, and will decrease by a certain factor $k > 1$ when congestion continues. The following algorithm demonstrates the rate control for harmful best-effort flows. All symbols used match those in Formula (1) to (5).

Proc Rate-Control ($\lambda_{OUT}0$, $\lambda_0 0$, k, ν, minThresh0, maxThresh0) {
$\lambda = \lambda_{OUT}0/k$;
$x = (\lambda_0 0 - \lambda)/\nu$;
maxThresh = ((x-1)*minThresh0 + maxThresh0) / x;
return (maxThresh);
}

4.4   Early Traffic Regulation

Necessity of Early Traffic Regulation. The purpose of Early-Traffic-Regulation (ETR) is to throttle harmful traffic in network nodes prior to bottlenecks in order to avoid flooding N-DoS to cause congestion collapse. Without ETR, legitimate packets discarded in earlier network nodes cannot be saved in later nodes.
In our experiment, with the scenario shown in Fig. 1,if traffic regulation with the dynamic buffer management and scheduling are only applied on the bottleneck, the legitimate traffic outputs start to decline at about 1950 seconds.
In order to effectively control traffic when a network is under flooding N-DoS attacks, AFFC includes a policy to deploy traffic regulation in reverse traffic paths starting from bottleneck nodes.

Back Tracing. Traffic paths need to be determined in order to launch ETR. Using extra ICMP back-tracing messages is promoted in AFFC. Itrace [Bellovin00] is such an example to perform back tracing. There are several advantages to use ICMP-based back tracing approaches. First, they do not require modification of IP headers. Second, they do not require routers to analyze each incoming packets as the Packet Marking and Sampling approach [SWKA00] does. Third, They do not require ISP administrators to interfere or manually perform login processes as the hop-by-hop back-tracing [Cisco] does. Finally, they do not rely on the existence of IPsec as the IPsec-based strategy [CWSW00] does.

Assume a tracing packet needs to pass n routers $R_n- > R_{n-1}- > \cdots- > R_1$ to reach its destination node. Also, assume $P_d[R_i]$ is the packet-drop probability for the network node R_i, and $P_d[R_i] = P_d$. For a network node R_i, an ICMP trace-back message must pass through a number of i other network nodes to reach its destination. The survival probability is: $p_s[i] = (1 - p_d)^i$.

A total of n messages have to successfully arrive the destination in order to rebuild a path. For the n independent routers, the probability of successfully receiving the n messages is:

$$p_s = (1 - p_d)^n * (1 - p_d)^{n-1} * (1 - p_d)^{n-2} * \cdots * (1 - p_d)^{n-(n-1)} = (1 - p_d)^{\frac{n}{2}}$$

Assume it needs k sending times for a back-tracing message to reach the destination. The expectation of the mean sending-times becomes:

$$E[k(p_d, n)] = \frac{1}{p_s} = (1 - p_d)^{-\frac{n}{2}}$$

The number of average sending times $E[k(p_d, n)]$ decreases exponentially as drop-probability p_d decreases for a given hop number n. When $n = 4, P_d = 10$, $E[k(p_d, n)] \approx 1.2$, which survivability is acceptable for back tracing messages and ETR signaling.

4.5   Performance and Cost

Fig. 3 demonstrated AFFC performance with the four steps applied – traffic classification, dynamic buffer management, scheduling, and ETR. In contrast to Fig. 2 where AFFC was not used and the scenario where AFFC was only applied on the bottleneck node, legitimate flows keep having bandwidth availability and their services do not collapse when malicious traffic increase their sending rates. In a bottleneck node, AFFC functions include traffic pattern recognition, buffer

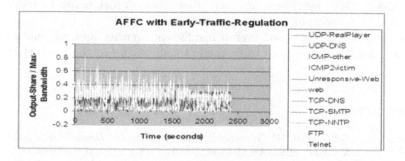

Fig. 3. AFFC performance

management, scheduling, back-tracing path information retrieving from end-users, and ETR signaling to network nodes prior to the bottleneck along traffic paths. The memory requirement is $\theta(7*N*M*K*B)$. N represents the number of diurnal time zones segmented in each day, M represents the number of protocol to be classified, K is the number of continuous weeks to trace and reshape traffic patterns, and B is number of bytes to store each bandwidth baseline. The major computational overhead is from scheduling, which is $O(\lg C)$, where C is the number of classes.

AFFC in network nodes in back-tracing paths performs traffic pattern recognition, active buffer management, scheduling, and ETR signal responding. The overall computational overhead is $O(\lg C)$, where C is the number of classes; and the memory requirement is the same as that of the bottleneck node. For ETR purpose, it is recommended to put a mission critical node behind certain layers of network-node shield, which domain owner has control over wtih.

The cost analysis above assumes all AFFC components are implemented in one piece. In practice, the buffer managment and scheduling in AFFC can either be implemented to replace the FIFO/RED model, or be implemented as a separate filtering module beneath FIFO/RED or any other existing buffer management and scheduling schemes in a network node. The traffic monitoring can be in a passive mode functioning in a separate hardware to alleviate the computational burden on network nodes.

5   Conclusion

The continuous success of N-DoS attacks has exposed the vulnerabilities and flaws in Internet protocol designs and implementations, as well as those in the Internet infrastructure. Those attacks can be categorized based on attack symptoms and protocol types.

The AFFC model presented in this paper is a flow-control-based defense scheme to defend against flooding N-DoS attacks. Experiments have demonstrated the effectiveness of this model to alleviate destructive impacts by harmful flooding N-DoS flows. Computational and memory cost is proportional to the number of flow classes. These overheads can be shifted from network nodes by implementing some AFFC components in separate hardware.

N-DoS attacks have exposed overall insufficient security and reliability on the Internet, defense efforts need to be made by all parties in the Internet community.

References

[Bellovin00]   Bellovin: ICMP Traceback Message, *Internet Draft*, March 2000
[Bs98]   S. Blake, et al: An architecture for Differentiated Services, IETF RFC 2475, December 1998
[Cert96a]   CERT Advisory CA-96.21: TCP-SYN Flooding and IP Spoofing Attacks,
http://info.cert.org/pub/cert_advisories/CA-96.21.tcp_syn_flooding.html, 1996
[Cert96b]   Denial-of-Service Attack via Ping, http://www.cert.org/advisories/CA-96.26.ping.html, 1996

[Cisco]   Characterizing and Tracing Packet Floods Using Cisco Routers,
               http://www.cisco.com/warp/public/707/22.html
[CWSW00]   Ho-Yen Chang, S. Felix Wu, C. Sargor, X.Wu: Towards Tracing Hidden
               Attacks on Untrusted IP Networks, NCSU, June 2000
[Dd00]   Dave Dittrich: Source Code to mstream, a DDoS tool, Bugtraq mailing-
               list, 2000-05-01
[FF99]   Sally Floyd, Kevin Fall: Promoting the Use of End-to-End Congestion
               Control in the Internet, Networking, IEEE/ACM, **Vol., 7**, No.4, August
               1999, P458-472
[FJ93]   Sally Floyed, Van Jacobson: Random Early Detection Gateway for Con-
               gestion Avoidance, IEEE/ACM Transactions on Networking, August,
               1993
[FJ95]   Sally Floyd, Van Jacobson, Link-sharing and Resource Management
               Models for Packet Networks, IEEE/ACM Transactions on Networking,
               Vol. 3, No. 4, August 1995
[FP99]   Sally Floyd, Vern Paxon: Why We Don't Know How To Simulate The
               Internet, http://www.aciri.org/floyd/papers.html, October 1999
[FV00]   Kevin Fall, Kannan Varadhan: ns Notes and Documentation, UCB/
               LBL/USC/ISI/Xerox, http://www-mash.cs.berkeley.edu/ns, Febru-
               ary 25, 2000
[HH98]   Lasse Huovinen, Jani Hursti: Denial of Service Attacks: Teardrop and
               Land, http://www.hut.fi/~lhuovine/hacker/dos.html, March 1998
[ML97]   SYNcookies Mailing List: http://cr.yp.to/syncookies/archive
[SWKA00]   Stefan Savage, David Wetherall, Anna Karlin, Tom Anderson: Practical
               Network Support for IP Traceback,
               http://www.cs.wachington.edu/homes/savage/traceback.hrml,
               February 2000
[TMW97]   Kevin Thomas, Gregory J. Miller, Rick Wiler: Wide-Area Internet Traf-
               fic Patterns and Characteristics, IEEE Network, **Vol11**, No.6, Nov/Dec.
               1997, P10-23
[Windows99]   Windows NT bonk Update,
               http://www.ndsu.nodak.edu/csg/info/bonknt. html, August 1999

A Role-Based Access Control Model and Implementation for Data-Centric Enterprise Applications

Dianlong Zhang, Harald Lukhaub, and Werner Zorn

Department of Computer Science and Engineering
Am Fasanengarten 5, 76131 Karlruhe, Germany
{dzhang, lukhaub, zorn}@ira.uka.de

Abstract. Access control is concerned with limiting the activity of legitimate users in an application. Role-based access control (RBAC) uses role to indirectly describe the access rights. This indirectly mapping is very flexible. However, current RBAC models are not suitable to describe fine-grained access control for data-centric enterprise applications. In this paper, we present a pragmatic role-based access control model for data-centric application. The access control is fine-grained and flexible. An object-oriented implementation is also presented. Users are identified by digital certificates. The proposed model is designed for three-tier enterprise application.

1 Introduction

Access control is concerned with limiting the activity of legitimate users in a system. It is an important technique to achieve both confidentiality and integrity. Traditionally, security takes more concerns about the information flows than access control. However, as more and more distributed objects(components) are deployed in the network, especially Internet, access control has become a very important area of system security. As the architecture and development technologies of distributed information system evolve, how to use and adapt the available access control technologies with the new architecture environments, for example, the three-tier network computing and component-based system, have become one of the main focuses in this area.

Many enterprise applications adopt the three-tier architecture. The clients provide graphical user interfaces to gather user inputs. One or more databases store the application states at the back-end. The application server is stateless. It provides computing services based on the parameters of client requests and the current state of the database. Database-based access control can only control the access to data. Control of complex operations on the data is beyond the ability of the database. Furthermore, database-based control model is not suitable for applications which have a large number of users. Fine-grained access control must be implemented on the application server.

Traditional access control models, such as access control list (ACL), are difficult to maintain, when the user number increases. Since middle last decade, role-based access control model (RBAC) [1] [2] [3] has attracted both researcher and developers. RBAC is very flexible to describe operative permissions and easy to adopt large

S. Qing, T. Okamoto, and J. Zhou (Eds.): ICICS 2001, LNCS 2229, pp. 316-327, 2001.

number of users. However, there is no suitable model to describe fine-grained access control for data-centric enterprise applications, which involve many database operations.

In this paper, we will present an extended RBAC access control model for three-tier enterprise applications. The object-oriented implementation is also presented. The paper is structured as followings. The system architecture, a three-tier model, will be described at first. The problems and requirements will be discussed in section 3. Section 4 gives the system security architecture. The access control model is described in section 5. Section 6 discusses some issues about authorization administration. Section 7 summarizes the model and gives a glance of future work.

2 A Three-Tier Model

We consider distributed systems to be composed of a set of distributed components (objects). The client is thin, since it implements "thin" functionality. It provides user interfaces to users and the necessary modules to access the application server. The application server implements the bulk of business logic and functionality. One or more database servers run at the back-end to store and manage data – the state of the entire application.

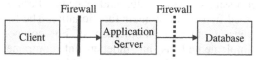

Fig. 1. Typical three-tier system

The architecture of typical three-tier systems is illustrated by Fig. 1. There is usually at least one firewall [8] between client(s) and the application server. These clients access the application server through a middleware, such as Java RMI [10] or CORBA ORB [11]. Clients can not communicate directly with the database, only through the application server. No backward invocation (callback) is allowed. This restriction is very practical. We have experience of a running application which has 2 to 5 firewalls between clients and server. Firewall administrators are usually reluctant to open backward ports.

The application server accesses the database using standard database connectivity, such as ODBC (open database connectivity) or JDBC [12]. Transaction coordination uses standard methods provided by database connectivity. Optionally, there is a firewall between the application server and the database.

The model follows the strict client/server paradigm, i.e. the clients call services provided by the application server. Interaction between clients is not allowed. The application server is stateless. All application states are stored in database. The computing result of every request is calculated depending on the parameter sent with the request and the current state in database. However, the behavior of the application is not deterministic. For example, the same payment may result in a different balance if it is issued at different time.

3 Requirements and Problems

The challenge to develop a suitable access control model comes from two aspects: the structure of enterprise organization and the properties of permissions.

The organizational structure decides the user structure of the system. A user's position in this structure decides his/her access rights in the system. In the Role-Based Access Control Model (RBAC) [1] [2] [3], the role is used as a semantic construct to model what an individual user takes on as a part of the organization, i.e. his job function within the organization that describes the authority and responsibility. Access rights are associated with a role, not directly with a particular user. This indirect mapping makes the RBAC very flexible [1].

In most organizations, roles have a nature hierarchy [1] [4]. The hierarchical role model (RBAC$_1$ in [1]) makes it easy to define a policy and implement access control. The role hierarchy is not always consistent with the organizational hierarchy of the enterprise. An organization may have some strong autonomic sections, which have more rights than the one above them.

The characteristic of permissions depends largely on the system type and its implementation. Permissions can not be treated as simple symbols like that in some general access-control model.

For well modeled objects, their permissions have clear definitions. For example, a Unix file has 3 permissions: read, write, and execute. Permissions of Enterprise Applications are defined first of all by their functionality. The functionality in turn is decided by the business logic to be implemented. For component-based systems, business logic is implemented as an independent component. This means, a component implements a particular business logic, which defines its own permissions. Some components may be developed by different development teams or even by different component vendors. A general permission model is required but difficult.

Let's see the characteristic of components. In this paper, a component is considered as an independent software unit, it has one or more interfaces which can be accessed by other components or programs. Each interface is composed of at least one operation. From this viewpoint, permissions of a component can be defined as a union of interface(s) and/or operation(s).

A component has not only interfaces and operations, it must access data in a database. In three-tier systems, components on the application server access the data in the database in the third tier to perform their business logic. It is the component which accesses the database, not the user! This means a database can only identify which component is accessing it, not which user. Usually, an application server uses a single account (user ID/password) to access a database. Access control mechanism provided by the database can not be applied to the users on client sides. Therefore, the application server is obligated to check whether a user may access a table, a record, and even a column in the database. In other words, access control of data must be carried out in the components running on the application server.

In addition, access control of databases is usually coarse-grained. Permissions of a database are difficult to be defined on record level.

In summary, permissions for enterprise applications can be categorized into two groups: action (operation) and data. Operational permissions are usually easy to be associated with roles. For example, a role 'secretary' can issue payments and check balances. Such operational permissions can be easily modeled in user-neutral way. To model permissions for data access is difficult. For example, a secretary can only issue a payment against a fund/project of his/her institute or research group. Such permissions are directly associated with users.

Another problem for enterprise applications is the continuous evolution of the business logic. Access control or the access control policy are part of the business logic. Access control model must be able to adopt such evolution, i.e. flexible to adopt new business logic or its changing.

The aforementioned problems are addressed from two sides: the system security architecture, and domain concept to model data permissions.

4 System Security Architecture

The system security architecture is given in Fig. 2. Firewalls [8] are used to restrict unwanted network access to the system. Every user must have a digital certificate issued by a certificate authority (CA) [7]. A user usually has only one ID certificate.

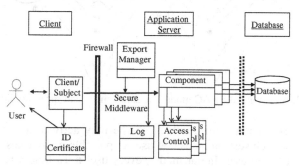

Fig. 2. System security architecture

When a user tries to log on to the system, its ID certificate will be validated. Without a valid ID certificate, a user can not log on to the system.

A Client communicates with a server component through secure middleware. The secure middleware provides three services. The first one is that it provides an object-oriented invocation model. The second is a secure communication channel, data flowing in this channel is encrypted. And finally, the secure middleware provides the ID certificate information to server components, such as who is currently the caller of an operation.

The underlying transport uses the transport layer security protocol (TLS 1.0) [6],which is an extension of the secure socket layer protocol (SSL 3.0) [5].

Every operation is logged in a log file, which is carried out by the ExportManger. Each log item contains the following information: ID of the certificate, user name, referenced component and its operation, the incoming time (and date) and response time. Analyses of the log (auditing) is carried out offline [9].

Besides the entry control by login, every invocation to server components is controlled. Every component has its own access control (a sub-component). In this access control model, a component is the real entity which interprets and carries out the access control polices. The details will be discussed in the next section.

5 Role and Permission Models

5.1 Role and Permissions

The model is illustrated by Fig. 3. As defined in [1] and [2], a role represents a collection of job functions in a commercial and government enterprise. A role describes the authority and responsibility. A role is associated with a number of operations allowed. A user may belong to multiple roles.

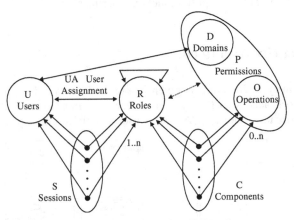

Fig. 3. An extended RBAC model for data-centric enterprise applications

A user establishes sessions during which she/he may activate a subset of the roles she/he belongs to. Each session maps one user to possible many roles. Each session is associated with a single user. In our model, every user must hold a recognized digital certificate. A user is identified by his certificate.

Domain concept is used to model data permission. Data permission is concerned with defining data areas accessible to a particular user. A domain is a set of records and/or tables in a database. Usually, data of enterprise databases are well structured. A domain can be identified by some key attributes. For example, every record in a database is usually labeled by the ID of who has inserted it; this label can be used as key attributed to identify the domain: all records inserted by that user.

A user usually has his accessible domain(s). For example, the chef and the secretary of the distributed computing research group of a computer engineering department should have the right to access financial data of that group. A usual faculty member, can only access the financial data about his research projects. The chef and the secretary have a larger domain, the faculty member has a smaller one. For example, the domain of all projects of the distributed computing research group can be easily identified by two keys: the name of the department (computer engineering) and the name of the research group (distributed computing). The domain for the faculty member is only the project. It can be identified by the name of the department, the name of the research group, and the name of the project (e.g. CCR 9810116).

Operational permissions are used to model actions. In component-based systems, operations are implemented by interfaces. Permissions include interfaces and components itself. A component is considered an executive object. All operations provided by a component are the component itself. This means, if a user or a role is not allowed to access a component, the user can not access any operation of that component.

Permissions are comprised of two independent parts, domains and operations. An empty domain is acceptable. The rationale is that some functions have no domain in the central database, an example is the administrative function of the application server. In practice, some components in the system can be accessed by everyone, who is admitted to the system. Such components are called *no secure* components.

A role is used to reflect the access rights and privileges in a software system. A role is different with an organizational role, such as chef, faculty member, and secretary. Organizational roles may be reflected by access control roles, but are not always coincided with them. For example, an organizational role, at a higher position, does not always imply, that it has more access rights in an information system than another organizational role in a lower position. However, it is very common in practice, that organization roles should be reflected in the enterprise application. Therefore, we will not distinguish both roles in the following discussions.

Each roles has associated domain(s), these domain(s) are accessible by the operations associated with that role.

User assignment (UA) is a relation between user and role, and the relation between user and domain. The role and domain is associated through the relation role-domain.

During a session, a user may activate a subset of the roles he belongs to. Permissions granted to a user are a union of operations associated with the roles. Each role has its own accessible domain. This is the central point of our access control model. Roles are generally defined. Multiple roles can be assigned to a user. Domain is user specific, therefore, it is directly assigned to a user. Domain and role are further associated with each other.

Components are the real entities who interpret and carry out access control policies. A component opens one or more interfaces to a client. These interfaces are comprised of several operations. Therefore, it is very difficult to define a general scheme, with which the security administrator can configure the access control policy of every component from outside. This is especially the case, when considering that the interface of a component is under evolution and may be changed very often.

The access control policy is strongly associated with the structure of a organization, which is usually relative stable. If the structure and organization is changed, the component must also be changed. Therefore, letting the component interpret the access control policies is a reasonable decision.

To carry out the access control policy, a component must do the following checks. First, the component decides whether one (or more) of these roles is acceptable by the invoked operation (interface, component), since every session may have more than one activated role. If none of the roles is acceptable, this session is rejected. For acceptable invocation, the component checks whether the accessing domain of the invocation is in the domain associated with that role. If the accessing domain of the current session is not in that domain, the session is rejected.

Here we come to a very important point. The component checks every permission according to the underline user (user ID) of the invocation. This rule guarantees that the access control is applied to the user, who has initiated the reference, even a component is referenced indirectly.

5.2 Object Representation of Role

It is very common that there are over thousand users in an organization but only a few different roles. The concept of role makes it easy to define an access control policy and then assign access rights to an individual user. When a user is admitted to access the information system, one or some roles are assigned to that user.

Roles may have overlapping responsibilities. In many organizations, there are a number of general operations or functions that can be performed by many members. It is inefficient and administratively cumbersome to specify repeatedly such operations for each role. To improve efficiency, RBAC uses role hierarchy to model such relationship ($RBAC_1$ in [1]). A role hierarchy defines roles that have unique attributes and that may contain other roles. That is, one role may implicitly include the permissions that are associated with another role.

To efficiently implement a role and its hierarchy, we use an object to represent a role. The idea is that each role is represented by an object, or more precisely a class. A domain is also represented by an object. The relationship between role and domain is represented by an association between role and domain.

According to the principle of objects, the sub-class is a extended class of its super-class. The role hierarchy is reflected by the class hierarchy. Therefore, a sub-class has all access rights of the role represented by its super-class.

To illustrate the concept, we will give the role model of an example application For the sake of simplicity, only four roles are illustrated. They are system administrator, signer, evaluator, and booker.

The role evaluator has the right to check the balance and performance of a particular department, division, or project. The role booker has the right to issue a payment. It has also the right of the role evaluator. The role signer is recognized to be able to sign a payment. Only signed payments are valid and can be transferred to the bank.

The role administrator has the right to configure the system profile and do user assignment, i.e. assigning particular role(s) and domain(s) to a user.

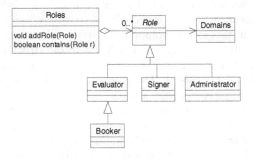

Fig. 4. An example UML model of roles

Fig. 4. illustrates the UML model of these roles. Class *Role* is an abstract class. It is associated with class *Domains*, which is a collection of multiple domains and will be discussed in the next section. Evaluator, Signer, and Administrator are sub-classes of the class *Role*. They represent the roles evaluator, signer, and administrator described above, respectively.

Class Booker represents the role booker, which includes the rights of role evaluator. This hierarchical relationship is reflected by modeling class Booker as a sub-class of class Evaluator.

Class *Roles* is a set of *Role* instances. For example, an instance of *Roles* can be used to represent all possible roles which a user may belong to.

As described in the previous section, each component must check whether an access is allowed. For simplicity, we suppose that a component only accepts one role. The role checking procedure is simplified as following: after receiving an invocation, a component asks the framework who is the user and which roles he/she belongs to. The framework returns an instance of *Roles*. The component then invokes the Roles.contains(acceptableRole) to check whether the user belongs to the acceptableRole. If false, the invocation is rejected, otherwise, the invocation will be proceeded.

This model has greatly simplified the role checking procedure. A Java implementation is given in Fig. 5. This algorithm ensures the maximal rights of the user. For example, if a user has the role booker, the rights of booker are ensured. Using the basic reflection technique, no role name appears in Fig. 5. The checking procedure can be simply extended to accept a list of *Role*. In this case, a component needs only know which roles are acceptable by maintaining a list of *Role* instances. This model is very flexible, especially when a role needs to be changed or a new role is introduced. During compilation, the compiler can easily check whether the acceptable *Role* list of a component is valid. For example, if a role is removed from the system, the developer simply deletes its class file. The compiler will do further works for you.

```
public boolean contains(Role r){
    Iterator iter = roles.iterator();
    Role cr;
    while( iter.hasNext() ){
        cr = (Role)iter.next();
        if( r.getClass().isInstance(cr)) return true;
    }
    return false;
}
```

```
public boolean contains(Domain d){
    Iterator ds = domains.iterator();
    Domain cd;
    while( ds.hasNext() ){
        cd = (Domain)ds.next();
        if( cd.contains(d)) return true;
    }
    return false;
}
```

Fig. 5. Role checking   **Fig. 6.** Checking domain access

In this example, the security manager of the enterprise should be assigned the role administrator. The director of a research group can have the role evaluator. A secretary can play the role booker.

Signer is a special role. The background is the concept of digital signature. A user with role booker can issue a payment, this payment can take into effect only when it is signed. Signer represents the role who has the right to sign a record(payment) in database.

In the above example, the term constraint is already illustrated implicitly. Some roles can not be assigned to one user simultaneously. In Fig. 4., *Roles* is used to represent a group of roles, which is assigned to a user. Some constraints can be validated when a *Role* is added into *Roles*.

Some constraint, such as "a signer can not sign for himself", can only be implemented in the signature component which signs a record in the database. When it receives a signature request, the signature component will validate the signer according to the user id, if the user is the same person who has issued the payment, the request is rejected. It ought to be mentioned that only users who belong to signer can invoke the signature component.

5.3 A Pragmatic Domain Model

Fig. 7. depicts a pragmatic domain model to represent the domain with objects. It gives an example of three key attributes, Department, Division, and Library. Domains can be independent or hierarchical with arbitrary levels.

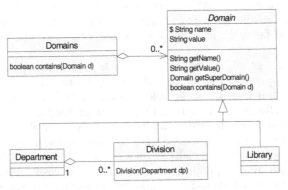

Fig. 7. Domain representation

Class *Domain* in this model is identified by the name and its value of a key attribute in a table of the database. For example, an instance of Department with value "computer engineering" will represent the domain department of computer science; an instance of Library with value "University of Karlsruhe" will represent the central library of the university of Karlsruhe. Since a division is usually in an organization hierarchy, the division of distributed computing can be considered as a domain only when it is placed under a department, e.g. an instance of *Department* with value "computer engineering".

Every key attribute is represented by a class, a static name is used to represent the name of that attribute.

Hierarchical key attributes are modeled in a chain of classes. Fig. 7. depicts a two level hierarchy. The *Department* with name "DEPARTMENT" is above *Division* with name "DIVISION". *Department* has always an empty super-domain, it is at the highest level in our example. *Division* at the lowest level can not exist independently. This is safeguarded by the constructor, which requires an instance of *Department* by construction. *Division* has empty sub-domain, because it is in the lowest level.

An instance of *Domains* can contain multiple *Domain* instances with the same and/or different types. It is a container of *Domain* instances, and is similar to a mathematical set. Two methods, equal and contains, are defined as followings, which are significant for access control.

An instance d1 of a *Domain* is equal to another one d2, if and only if:

$$(d1.name = d2.name) \wedge (d1.value = d2.value).$$

An instance d1 of a *Domain* is said containing another one d2, if:

$$(d1 = d2) \vee (d1 \supset d2).$$

For example, an instance of *Department* with empty sub-domain includes every *Division* instances created under that department. An instance of *Domain* can not include another one if they are not in the same hierarchy. How to decide d1 $\supseteq$ d2 is defined by a particular *Domain*.

Fig. 7. depicts only a hierarchical *Domain* with two levers. However, it should be clear that the model is valid for multi-level hierarchy.

Role is associated with the *Domains*. This *Domains* restricts the data area accessible to the role. However, *Domains* is directly assigned to users not to *Role*.

Control of the domain access is applied to every invocation. For simplicity, we suppose that every invocation referencing to a particular domain, which can be formed as a single instance of *Domain*. The component will build this instance according to the input. The access control model will ask the framework about the user ID and which roles he/she belongs to. The framework returns an instance of *Roles*. The component further retrieves which role is currently valid and its associated *Domains* instance ds. It invokes the ds.contains(referencedDomain) to check whether the user's referencedDomain is accessible. If false, the invocation is rejected, otherwise, the invocation will be proceeded. The implementation of the contains(domain) method is given in   Fig. 6.

As indicated in Fig. 7., every *Domain* must implement the method contains(*Domain* d), since only the *Domain* itself knows its properties, such as the position in the domain hierarchy. The advantage of the design is that it makes the domain access control simple and needs not to be modified to adopt the changes of a particular *Domain*.

5.4 Constraints

There are generally two kinds of constraints: role constraints and user constraints. Constraints are implemented at three different levels: component, class *Roles* (belong to the framework), and authorization administration.

Role constraints: in many applications some roles are considered to be mutually exclusive for purpose of duty which is defined by the business logic. In the example given in the previous section, administrator and booker are mutually exclusive roles. As indicated in the previous section, some components may have embedded access to the control policy, such as that "a signer is not allowed to approve a payment for himself". Such constraints are implemented by the component itself. Not all components implement constraints.

The role container *Roles* plays an important role to implement constraints. It will check acceptableness when a new role is added to it. If the new role is mutually exclusive with any one already in the container, it is rejected.

User constraints take concerns about which users can belong to a particular role. It is an organizational issue and will be handled by authorization administration.

6 Authorization Administration

User assignment is considered two maps: user-role and user-domain. In our model, user assignment is entirely centralized and restricted to being defined by administration officer(s) and executed by a security administrator. The advantage of the centralized approach is the centralization of responsibility. For three-tier systems, it is also the natural requirement that both, user assignment and authorization administration, are centralized on the server side.

There is an authorization database at the back-end. This database stores all information about the users and their assigned role(s) and domain(s). The application server accesses the database through an authority interface, which is provided by the security framework. This authority interface is shown in Fig. 8. User information indicates the user's name, address, e-mail, etc.

```
public interface Authority {
    // returns all roles the given user ID can play.
    public Roles getRoles(String userID);
    // returns user information of the given user ID.
    public UserInfo getUserInfo(String userID);
}
```

Fig. 8. The authority interface

The application server obtains the user ID from the underlying middleware. The middleware, retrieves the user ID from the user's certificate.

There are three important aspects of user assignment. The first is role constraints. The authority administration implements the role constraints described in the previous section to ensure better security.

The second aspect is user constraints. A secretary can not be enrolled as an administrator. This aspect is difficult to guarantee because it is difficult to be formally described. There is no suitable way for the software to identify the organizational position of a user. The security manager and/or administrator must take the responsibility.

The third aspect is concerned with domain assignment. Comparing with role assignment, domain assignment should receive more attention. There are usually a small number of roles. The number of domains may be huge if not uncountable. There are two rules. The first is that most of the domains assigned to a user are mutually exclusive with the domains assigned to a user from another division or department. The second rule is that security administrator should have general understanding on the underlying database. Most enterprise databases are well designed to reflect the enterprise structure. Every key attribute has clear business meaning. They are very easy to grasp if one works within that organization.

User assignment is a part of the entire security administration. There are many other aspects, for example, user management and digital certificate management. Consistency between these is significant for a secure system. It is beyond the scope of this works and will not be discussed in detail.

7 Conclusions

In this paper, we have presented a role-based access control model for three-tier enterprise applications. The basic role-based access control model is extended to meet the requirements of data-centric applications. One of the important features is the novel permission model. The domain concept is introduced to provide fine-grained permissions. Access control can be applied to every row in the database.

The new access control model is implemented on the application server. The application server uses only one or a few database account(s) to access the database. Access control on the application server and the database are separated. This makes the system administration simple and flexible.

Another feature is that both, role and domain, are represented by objects. Object hierarchy is used to reflect the role hierarchy. Role evolution is very simple. The model is simple to be implemented as common facility using object-oriented framework techniques.

The proposed model has been implemented in Java. It has been integrated as part of a component-based framework. The framework has extended the access control to client side. A financial control and management system for state universities in Germany is developed based on this framework. The application has been used by two universities.

Future work will concentrate on two issues. The first is to integrate the digital certificate and user management. Currently, they are managed separately. This has caused some consistency problems in the system. Another issue is to implement constraints. A new constraint model is required to be able to describe complex constraints on role and domain.

References

[1] S. Sandhu, E. J. Coyne: Role-Based Access Control Models, IEEE Computer, February 1996, pp. 38-47.

[2] S. Sandhu, et al.: Role-Based Access Control: A Multi-Dimensional View, Proceedings of Annual Computer Security Applications Conference, 1994.

[3] D. Ferraiolo, J. Barkley, et.al: A Role-Based Access Control Model and Reference Implementation Within a Corporate Intranet, ACM Transactions on Information and System Security, Vol. 2, No. 1, February 1999, pp. 34-64.

[4] J. Park, R. Sandhu: Binding Identities and Attributes Using Digitally Signed Certificates, Proceedings of Annual Computer Security Applications Conference, 2000.

[5] SSL: SSL 3.0 Specification, available at http: //home.netscape.com/eng/ssl3/.

[6] TLS: The TLS Protocol Version 1.0 (RFC 2246), available at http: //www.ietf.org.

[7] J. Feghhi, et al.: Digital Certificates - Applied Internet Security, Addison-Wesley, 1999.

[8] M. Goncalves: Firewalls Complete, McGraw-Hill, 1998.

[9] R. Sandhu: Authentication, Access Control, and Audit, ACM Computing Surveys, Vol. 28, No. 1, March 1996, pp. 241-243.

[10] Java RMI: Java RMI Specification, http://java.sun.com/products/jdk/rmi/.

[11] CORBA: The Common Object Request Broker Architecture: Architecture and Specification 2.0 and 3.0, available at: http://www.omg.org.

[12] JDBC: Java Database Connectivity JDBC™ Specifications.

A Unified Methodology for Verification and Synthesis of Firewall Configurations

Yongyuth Permpoontanalarp and Chaiwat Rujimethabhas

Logic and Security Laboratory
Department of Computer Engineering
King Mongkut's University of Technology Thonburi
91 Suksawasd 48, Ratburana, Bangkok 10140 Thailand
yongyuth@cpe.eng.kmutt.ac.th and s1410008@cc.kmutt.ac.th

Abstract. Firewalls offer a protection for private networks against external attacks. However, configuring firewalls correctly is a difficult task. There are two main reasons. One is that the effects of a firewall configuration cannot be easily seen during the configuration time. Another one is the lack of guidance to help configuring firewalls. In this paper, we propose a general and unified methodology for the verification and the synthesis of firewall configurations. Our verification methodology offers a way to foresee and analyze effects of firewall configurations during the configuration time. Furthermore, our synthesis methodology can generate firewall configurations that satisfies users' requirements. As a result, firewall configurations that are free of many kinds of errors and loopholes can be obtained easily.

1 Introduction

Nowadays, firewalls (e.g.[1,2]) become a widely used mechanism to achieve Internet security. Most, if not all, organizations whose computers have an Internet access are currently using firewalls. Firewalls locate between an internal network and an external network. Firewalls offer a protection for private (and internal) networks against external threats. In particular, firewalls ensure that only authorized information flows between internal networks and the external network are allowed.

Even though firewalls could provide protections against external attacks, configuring firewalls correctly is a difficult task. There are two main reasons. One is that the effects of a firewall configuration cannot be easily seen during the configuration time. Another one is the lack of guidance to help configuring firewalls.

Since the effects of a firewall configuration cannot be seen at the configuration time, many firewall configurations often have errors and loopholes. Most often, such errors and loopholes are discovered only after they actually happen at the execution time. This causes great damage to the system.

Due to the lack of guidance to help configuring firewalls, to configure them requires a great deal of experience which is certainly not available to novice

S. Qing, T. Okamoto, and J. Zhou (Eds.): ICICS 2001, LNCS 2229, pp. 328–339, 2001.

administrators. Moreover, configuring firewalls can be a complex and time- consuming task due to the large number of host computers, required services and firewalls. Furthermore, the networks of computers in any organizations are always changed due to the change of the structure of organizations themselves and the replacement for new equipment. Most often a change of such networks requires a new firewall configuration. Thus, this worsens the situation.

We argue that all these problems occur because of the lack of firewall methodology to analyze the effects of firewall configurations, and to help configuring firewalls. In this paper, we propose a general and unified methodology for verifying and synthesizing firewall configurations.

In [3], we proposed a graph-based model and its methodology to analyze effects of Cisco firewall configurations. In this paper, we extend the model and the methodology there in several aspects. Firstly, we extend the model to be able to deal with both the verification and the synthesis within the same framework. Secondly, we define the notion of correctness of firewall configurations in the context of several kinds of policies whereas [3] deals with one kind of policy only. Those polices are useful not only for the verification but also for the synthesis. Furthermore, we show here that our model is general in that it can be used to analyze effects of Firewall-1 configurations also, not just Cisco firewalls.

Our approach is novel in that it is formal and it combines both verification and synthesis within the same framework. We show that our approach is more general than existing related approaches. Furthermore, we obtain the correctness justification and proof for the verification and the synthesis, respectively.

We discuss the background in section 2, and present our model in section 3. Our verification and synthesis methodology is discussed in section 4 and 5, respectively. The correctness of our methodology is discussed in section 6, related works are discussed in section 7 and conclusion is given in section 8.

2   Background

2.1   Firewall-1 Firewalls

Firewall-1 firewall is a software-based firewall since it is a computer installed software for filtering packets.

Definition 1. *Firewall-1 rules are represented by tuple (SFR, SPR) where SFR stands for a set of filtering rules and SPR stands for a set of firewall property rules.*

Definition 2. *A firewall-1 filtering rule consists of the following : (Source, Destination, Service, Action, Activating FW objects) where*
- Source and Destination stand for senders' IP addresses and receivers' IP addresses, respectively,
- Service consists of a protocol and a port,
- Action stands for whether flow from Source to Destination is allowed or not, i.e.(permit or drop), and
- Activating FW objects stand for names representing firewall objects which perform the filtering of the flow of packets.

Intuitively, a filtering rule defines the permission or prohibition of flows from *Source* to *Destination* via *Activating FW Objects* for *Service*. Note that *any* can be used to specify sources and/or destinations and it means any IP address.

A Firewall-1 property rule defines not only a set of interfaces of a firewall object, but also the direction of the filtering of the flow of packets at all interfaces of the firewall object. Note that the direction is defined for *all interfaces* of a firewall. Moreover, *all interfaces* of a Firewall-1 firewall object enforce the same set of filtering rules.

Definition 3. *A firewall property rule for firewall-1 is defined by (FW object, Interfaces, Direction), where*
- *FW object stands for a name representing a firewall object,*
- *Interfaces stands for a set of all interfaces of FW object, and*
- *Direction stands for the direction of packet filtering, i.e. (in or out).*

3   Our Model

Our model is based on graph theory (e.g. [4]). In particular, network topology can be represented by a graph. Then, we argue that a firewall configuration rule can be understood as a set of paths in the graph. By treating firewall configuration rules as paths, we can reason about the verification and the synthesis of firewall rules intuitively and easily.

First, we propose a general form of firewall rules, called generalized firewall rules as a representation of firewall rules which will be used for the verification and the synthesis. We shall show that Firewall-1 rules can be converted into our generalized firewall rules. The following shows the definition of generalized firewall rules.

Definition 4. *A generalized firewall rule consists of the following: (Source, Destination, Service, Direction, Action, FW Interfaces) where*
- *Source, Destination, Service, Action are identical to those defined for Firewall-1 rules,*
- *Direction means similarly to that in Firewall-1 rule, but it can be inbound, outbound or both (bound), and*
- *FW Interfaces stand for a set of firewall interfaces which perform (or activate) the filtering of the flow.*

Note that the direction *both* means that packet filtering is performed in both directions at specified firewall interfaces. In particular, *both* is defined by both *inbound* and *outbound*. Such a rule with *both* directions is useful for the synthesis of firewall rules in the context of either closed or open policies which will be discussed later.

The conversion from Firewall-1 rules to our generalized firewall rules is straightforward, and is shown by the following definition. The resultant generalized firewall rules preserve the order of filtering rules in firewall-1 rules.

Definition 5. *Given tuple (SFR, SPR) of firewall-1 rules, for each filtering rule FR ∈ SFR and for each firewall property rule PR ∈ SPR of which its FW object appears in Activating FW objects of FR, we can obtain the corresponding generalized firewall rule GR in that*
- Source, Destination, Service and Action in GR are Source, Destination, Service and Action in FR, respectively, and
- Direction and FW Interfaces in GR are Direction and Interfaces in PR, respectively.

The following shows the definition of logical network topology. Our logical network topology can capture the ability of sending packets between two parties in the physical network topology.

Definition 6. *The network topology is a labeled and undirected graph (V,E) where a vertex in V stands for a set of IP addresses, and an edge between two vertices stands for a communication link between two sets of IP addresses.*

Indeed, the set *V* of vertices is defined by the power set of the set of all valid IP addresses. Hence, a vertex is represented by the set of IP addresses that the vertex stands for. An edge between two vertices means that an IP address in the former vertex can send a packet (or information) to another IP address in the latter vertex.

For the internal network, a vertex is represented by a set of a *single* IP address. Such a vertex intuitively stands for an interface to either a computer or a network device. For the external network, there is a special vertex called *all* standing for a set of all valid IP addresses. In particular, *all* = { *x* | *x* is a valid IP address}.

It is required that all firewall interfaces appearing in generalized firewall rules must be present as vertices in the network topology.

Example 1. Physical Network Topology

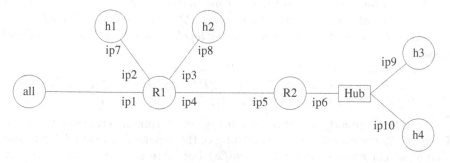

Fig. 1. Network Topology

In figure 1, *R1* and *R2* represent two firewall objects. *h1, h2, h3* and *h4* stand for host computers. *ip1, ip2, ..., ip10* denote IP addresses. In particular, *ip1, ip2, ip3, ip4* are IP addresses of four firewall interfaces of firewall object *R1*. *ip7, ip8, ip9* and *ip10* are IP addresses of interfaces of host computers *h1, h2, h3* and *h4*, respectively. It is easy to represent this topology using our definition of logical network topology. This network topology will be used as examples throughout this paper.

It should be noted that the connections between all firewall interfaces (e.g. *ip1, ip2, ip3* and *ip4*) of firewall object *R1* are determined by a routing table. For convenience here, we assume that such information is present. Any paths passing through those firewall interfaces can be determined, and they visit only necessary firewall interfaces that perform the actual packet filtering.

Since an edge between two vertices represents an ability of sending a packet, the edge is closed under the membership of its vertices. This is expressed by the following definition.

Definition 7. *The logical network topology has the following properties:*
1) $\forall u, v, v1, v2 \in V$ *[$v1 \subset v \wedge v2 \subset v \wedge v1 \cap v2 = \emptyset \wedge v1 \neq \emptyset \wedge v2 \neq \emptyset \rightarrow$*
     $\exists e \in E$ *(f(e) = {u, v})* $\leftrightarrow \exists e1, e2 \in E$ *(f(e1) = {u, v1} $\wedge$ f(e2) = {u, v2})]*
     where f is a function mapping from an edge to its vertices.
2) $\neg \exists e \in E$ *[f(e) = {u, v} and u = v].*

Definition 8. *We use a special name ω to represent all possible non-cyclic paths labeled with all possible services in the network topology. ω is treated as a path itself.*

The following shows properties of ω paths.

Definition 9. *The following are properties of ω.*
1) $P \cup \{P1\} = P \cup \{\omega\}$ *iff [initial(P1) = initial(ω) $\wedge$ terminal(P1) = terminal(ω)]*
     where P and P1 stands for a set of paths and a path, respectively, and initial(P1) and terminal(P1) denote initial and terminal vertex of P1, respectively.
2) $P \cup P' = P \cup \{P1\}$ *if*
     2.1) [initial(P1) = initial(ω) $\wedge$ terminal(P1) = v $\wedge$
          for all paths P2 in T ((terminal(P2) = v) $\leftrightarrow$ (P2 $\in$ P'))]
     where T, v and P' stand for a network topology, a vertex, and a set of paths, respectively.
     2.2) [initial(P1) = v $\wedge$ terminal(P1) = terminal(ω) $\wedge$
          for all paths P2 in T ((initial(P2) = v) $\leftrightarrow$ (P2 $\in$ P'))]
     2.3) [P1 = ω $\wedge$ for all paths P2 (P2 in T $\leftrightarrow$ P2 $\in$ P')]

Note that property *1)* defines the initial and terminal vertices of the ω path. Property *2)* however defines the meaning of the ω path. For example, *2.1)* states that a path of which its initial is *initial(ω)*, but its terminal is an ordinary vertex *v* is equivalent to all paths in the network topology ending at *v*.

We argue that a generalized firewall rule can be considered as a set of (either permitted or prohibited) paths in a network topology, and such paths are defined at a particular interface. Since such a set of paths is defined at a particular interface, it is called a *local* set of paths. The following definition shows the equivalence between a generalized firewall rule and a local set of paths.

Definition 10. *Given a network topology T, a local set of paths which corresponds to a generalized firewall rule $GR_{FWInterfaces}$ defined for interface FW Interfaces is a set of all non-cyclic paths in T which*
a) begin with Source vertex,
b) end at Destination vertex,
c) pass through FW Interfaces vertices in the specified Direction, and
d) are labeled with Service,
where Source, Destination, Service, Direction, FW Interfaces are those stated in $GR_{FWInterfaces}$.

The following defines precisely paths that begin with *Source* vertex, end at *Destination* vertex, and pass through *FW Interfaces* vertices in the specified *Direction*.

Definition 11. *A path that begins with Source (S) vertex, ends at Destination (D) vertex, and passes through FW Interfaces vertices in the specified Direction is the path P that satisfies the following:*
a) S (D) is a specific IP address (ip) iff initial(P) = ip (terminal(P) = ip, resp.).
b) S (D) is a set (gip) of IP addresses iff
initial(P) = sip (terminal(P) = sip, resp.), where $sip \subseteq gip$.
c) S (D) is "any" iff initial(P) = initial(ω) (terminal(P) = terminal(ω), resp.).
d) Direction = inbound iff $\exists F \in FW\_Objects \; \exists i. \; 1 < i \leq n$
[$vertex_i(P) \subseteq FW$ Interfaces $\wedge$ FW Interfaces $\subseteq$ Interfaces-of(F) $\wedge$
$vertex_{(i-1)}(P) \not\subseteq$ Interfaces-of(F)]
where n is the length of path P, and $vertex_i(P1)$ means i-th vertex in path P1.
e) Direction = both iff [initial(P) = initial(ω) $\wedge$ terminal(P) = terminal(ω) $\wedge$
$\exists F \in FW\_Objects$ (FW Interfaces $\subseteq$ Interfaces-of(F))]

Intuitively, a path that satisfies *d)* must be a path that travels to the designated *FW Interfaces* of a firewall from a vertex which is not in *FW Interfaces* of the same firewall. The definition of the *outbound* direction is omitted here due to space limit, but it is similar to that for the *inbound* direction.

As a matter of notations, we use a single IP address to represent the set of the single IP address.

Example 2. The local set of paths that corresponds to rule *(ip15, ip9, ftp, inbound, permit, ip1)* is {*<ip15, ip1, ip4, ip5, ip6, ip9>*}. Note that this path exists due to definition 7. Moreover, the local set of paths that corresponds to rule *({ip9, ip10}, any, http, inbound, permit, ip6)* is {*<ip9, ip6, terminal(ω)>*, *<ip10, ip6, terminal(ω)>*, *<{ip9, ip10}, ip6, terminal(ω)>* }. In addition, the local set of paths that corresponds to rule *(any, any, http, inbound, permit, ip6)* is {*<initial(ω), ip6, terminal(ω)>*}.

Definition 12. *Paths that correspond to a generalized firewall rule obtained from Firewall-1 firewall rules are undirected.*

Note that the *undirected* paths of Firewall-1 mean two-way communications between *Source* and *Destination* parties, initiated by *Source* and responded by *Destination*.

The set operations on paths can be simplified to corresponding set operations on vertices in those paths. Such simplification is useful for the verification of firewall rules.

Definition 13. *Path expressions can be reduced to vertex expressions as follows:*
1) *P1 op P2 = P3 if*
   a) *paths P1, P2 and P3 are of the same length (i.e. n).*
   b) *there is at most one vertex i such that $vertex_i(P1) \neq vertex_i(P2)$ and*
   $\forall j \neq i.\ 1 \leq j \leq n\ [\ vertex_j(P1) = vertex_j(P2)\ ]$
   c) *path P3 is exactly like path P1 (or P2), except that $vertex_i(P3) = vertex_i(P1)$ **op** $vertex_i(P2)$, where **op** is a set operation (e.g. $\cup$ or -).*
2) *$P \cup \{P1\} = P$ if $\exists i\ [vertex_i(P1) = \emptyset\ ]$, where P is a set of paths, and P1 is a path.*

Example 3. Suppose that path $P1 = \{<all,\ ip1,\ ip4,\ ip5,\ ip6,\ ip9>\}$, path $P2 = \{<ip17,\ ip1,\ ip4,\ ip5,\ ip6,\ ip9>\}$ and path $P3 = \{<ip13,\ ip1,\ ip4,\ ip5,\ ip6,\ ip9>\}$. Thus $(P1 \cup P2) - P3 = \{<all - \{ip13\},\ ip1,\ ip4,\ ip5,\ ip6,\ ip9>\ \}$.

Since there may be many rules activating at an interface, we need to process those rules in order to obtain actual effects of those rules at the interface. A set of effective paths at an interface is used to represent the actual effects at the interface, and it is defined as follows.

Definition 14. *A local set of effective and permitted (prohibited) paths at interface fw-i for which an ordered set SGR_{fw-i} of generalized firewall rules is specified, is defined by P_n that satisfies the following two conditions:*
a) *$\forall i.\ 0 \leq i \leq n\ [\ rule\ GR^{n-i}_{fw-i}\ has\ LP_{n-i}\ as\ the\ local\ set\ of\ paths$*
   $\rightarrow (\ P_{i+1} = P_i - LP_{n-i} \leftrightarrow GR^{n-i}_{fw-i}\ is\ a\ drop\ (permit,\ resp.)\ rule\ ) \vee$
   $(\ P_{i+1} = P_i \cup LP_{n-i} \leftrightarrow GR^{n-i}_{fw-i}\ is\ a\ permit\ (drop,\ resp.)\ rule\ )\ ]$
b) *P_n is minimal in that there is no P'_n that satisfies a) and $P'_n \subset P_n$.*
where
- *n is the number of rules in SGR_{fw-i},*
- *GR^j_{fw-i} is the j-th generalized firewall rule in SGR_{fw-i}, defined at fw-i,*
- *P_0 is simply $\emptyset$.*

Note that in condition b), P'_n that satisfies condition a) means that such P'_n is obtained from the same set expressions as P_n, according to condition a).

There might be *several possible sets* of paths that satisfy a) in this definition. By requiring the minimality of the resultant set of effective paths, we can ensure that a set of effective paths must be the one that consists of paths which have been simplified from path expressions to vertex expressions by definition 13 as much as possible. It should be noted that if the subtraction on sets is evaluated correctly, the resultant set would be smaller than that which would have been obtained incorrectly.

Example 4. The followings are examples of local sets of effective paths:
a) Suppose (ordered set) $SGR_{ip6} = \{(ip9,\ any,\ http,\ inbound,\ drop,\ ip6),\ (\{ip9,\ ip10\},\ any,\ http,\ inbound,\ permit,\ ip6)\}$. The local set of effective and permitted

paths at interface *ip6* is $\{<ip10,\ ip6,\ terminal(\omega)>\}$. Note that this set satisfies the minimal requirement in *b)*.

b) Suppose $SGR_{ip6} = \{(ip9,\ any,\ http,\ inbound,\ drop,\ ip6),\ (any,\ any,\ http,\ inbound,\ permit,\ ip6)\}$. The local set of effective and permitted paths is $\{<initial(\omega)\text{-}ip9,\ ip6,\ terminal(\omega)>\}$.

Intuitively, definition 14 can be seen as a transformation from an *ordered* set of firewall rules to *nested* expressions of set operations on paths. The concept that an upper rule takes precedence over a lower rule is still preserved in nested expressions. Further discussion on definition 14 can be found in [3].

The following shows the definition to compute a global set of effective and permitted paths from every local set of effective and permitted paths. Intuitively, a global set of effective paths stands for paths that are effective at all firewall interfaces through which the paths visit.

Definition 15. *The global set of effective and permitted (prohibited) paths is GEP that satisfies the following:*

$$\forall P[P \in GEP \leftrightarrow \bigcap_{i \in fw-interface(P)} LEP_i]$$

where
- LEP_i is a local set of effective and permitted (prohibited, resp.) paths at interface i, and
- fw-interface(P) denotes a set of vertices in path P, which are interfaces to some firewalls.

4   Verification of Firewall Configurations

Before we discuss the verification of firewall configurations, we need to discuss the concept of information flows, first.

Definition 16. *An information flow can be represented by either a path or a triple (source, destination, service).*

The triple represents *end-to-end* information flow which is regardless of paths between the two ends. For simplicity here, we shall focus on the information flow represented by paths, called *path-based* information flows.

4.1   Correctness of Firewall Rules

This kind of reasoning aims to test that effects of a set of firewall rules are those that are intended by a firewall administrator. Initially, a firewall administrator must define a set of intended information flow, and then calculated effects of firewall rules will be compared with the set of intended information flows.

Definition 17. *An intended information flow is tuple (PIF, NIF) where PIF and NIF are two finite sets which represent positive and negative information flows, respectively, for each service.*

Intuitively, positive and negative information flows represent permitted and prohibited information flows, respectively. Moreover, an intended information flow can also be defined for a particular service.

Definition 18. *The intended information flow has the following properties:*
a) PIF $\cup$ NIF $\neq \emptyset$
b) PIF $\cap$ NIF $= \emptyset$

We argue that our definition for intended information flows is adequate for its purpose since it can easily capture the correctness of firewall configurations in the context of many kinds of policies. Intuitively, those kinds of policy offer different ways to characterize the global set of effective and *permitted* paths.

The following shows the definition of the correctness in the context of closed, open, openly neutral and closely neutral policies.

Definition 19. *Given an intended information flow (PIF, NIF), a set of generalized firewall rules is correct in the context of*
a) closed policy iff PIF = GEP
b) open policy iff $\neg \exists F \in NIF$ [$F \in GEP$], and
$$\forall F \in AllFlows(T) \ [\ F \notin NIF \rightarrow F \in GEP \ ]$$
c) openly neutral policy iff (PIF $\subseteq$ GEP) , and $\neg \exists F \in NIF$ [$F \in GEP$]
d) closely neutral policy iff (GEP $\subseteq$ PIF), and $\neg \exists F \in NIF$ [$F \in GEP$]

where GEP is the global set of effective and permitted paths generated from the generalized firewall rules, and AllFlows(T) denotes the set of all possible flows in network topology T.

Intuitively, the closed policy states that *PIF* is exactly the only set of flows globally permitted. On the other hand, the open policy states that what is not in *NIF* is globally permitted. The neutral policies however do not state what globally permitted flows (*GEP*) *exactly* consist of, but it requires that *NIF* must not be globally permitted. In particular, the openly neutral policy states that *GEP* can be any superset of *PIF*. On the other hand, the closely neutral policy states that *GEP* can be just any subset of *PIF*.

4.2   Ineffective Firewall Rules

Our model can reason about rules that produce no effects. We call those rules ineffective.

Definition 20. *Given a set SGR of generalized firewall rules at an interface, rule GR in SGR is ineffective if and only if GEP = GEP′ where GEP and GEP′ are the global sets of effective and permitted paths generated from SGR, and (SGR - GR), respectively.*

Example 5. Rule *(ip9, ip7, http, outbound, permit, ip4)* is ineffective since all the paths from *ip9* to *ip7* visit *ip4* in the *inbound* direction according to the network topology.

5   Synthesis of Firewall Rules

The synthesis methodology takes intended information flows as input, and produces an *ordered* set of generalized firewall rules that satisfies the intended information flows. In other words, such set of generalized firewall rules obtained is correct with respect to those intended information flows.

Before we discuss the synthesis methodology, we need to understand some notations.

Definition 21. *We use LEP_i^+ and LEP_i^- to represent local sets of effective and permitted (and prohibited, respectively) paths at interface i.*

Definition 22. *The local sets of effective and permitted (and prohibited) paths have the following properties:*
a) For any interface i, $LEP_i^+ \cup LEP_i^- = \{\omega\}$.
b) For any interface i, $LEP_i^+ \cap LEP_i^- = \emptyset$.

Proposition 1. *For any interface i, $LEP_i^+ = (\{\omega\} - LEP_i^-)$*

It should be noted that an intended information flow (*PIF, NIF*) can be considered as two *global* sets of effective and permitted (and prohibited, respectively) paths. The following shows the definition for the synthesis of firewall configurations in the context of many policies.

Definition 23. *Given an intended information flow (PIF, NIF) defined for a particular service, the synthesis of a set of generalized firewall rules consists of the following two steps:*
1) Decompose two global sets of effective paths (PIF, NIF) into local sets of effective paths (PIF_i, NIF_i) at firewall interface i, by using definition 15.
2) Generate an ordered set SGR_j of generalized firewall rules defined for firewall interface j from local set (LS) of effective paths, obtained from 1), at the interface j by using definition 14, and the following:
    2.1) For the closed policy, LS is $LEP_j^- = (\{\omega\} - PIF_j)$.
    2.2) For the open policy, LS is $LEP_j^+ = (\{\omega\} - NIF_j)$.
    2.3) For the openly neutral policy,
        If $PIF_j \neq \emptyset$,
            then LS is $LEP_j^+ = (PIF_j \cup PIF_j') - NIF_j$, where $PIF_j' \subseteq \{\omega\}$.
            else LS is $LEP_j^- = \{\omega\} - PIF_j''$, where $PIF_j'' \subseteq \{\omega\} - NIF_j$.
    2.4) For the closely neutral policy,
        If $PIF_j \neq \emptyset$,
            then LS is $LEP_j^+ = PIF_j' - NIF_j$ where $PIF_j' \subseteq PIF_j$ and $PIF_j' \neq \emptyset$
            else LS is $LEP_j^- = \{\omega\}$

Example 6. Suppose that $PIF = \{<ip7, ip2, ip4, ip5, ip6, ip9>\}$, and its service label is *http*. Suppose we want to generate a set of firewall rules that implement the closed policy. Thus, it follows from step 1) that $PIF = PIF_{ip2} = PIF_{ip4} = PIF_{ip5} = PIF_{ip6}$. Let consider only PIF_{ip6}. By 2.1), $LEP_{ip6}^- = \{\omega\} - PIF_{ip6}$.

Since this local set of effective paths is for prohibited paths, it follows from definition 14 that a rule defined for $ip6$ that corresponds to PIF_{ip6} is $(ip7, ip9, http, outbound, permit, ip6)$. As a result, $SGR_{ip6} = \{ (ip7, ip9, http, outbound, permit, ip6), (any, any, http, both, drop, ip6) \}$.

Definition 24. *The following are required desirable properties of a set SGR of generalized firewall rules that is obtained from our synthesis methodology.*
1) Finiteness : SGR must be finite.
2) Effectiveness : SGR must be free of any ineffective rules.
3) Minimal : SGR must be minimal in that there is no other set SGR' of generalized firewall rules such that $GEP = GEP'$ and $|SGR'| < |SGR|$ where GEP and GEP' are global sets of effective paths generated from SGR and SGR', resp.

6   The Correctness of the Verification and Synthesis

The conformance testing technique [5] is employed here to ensure that the model presented in this paper for verification is correct with respect to actual firewall products. Conformance testing is a general technique to ensure that a specification corresponds to an actual implementation.

Similar to the conformance testing done in [3] for Cisco routers, the conformance testing here is carried out by constructing test data and comparing the outputs obtained from our model with those from the actual Firewall-1 firewall. The result obtained shows that the model for verification presented here is correct with respect to the Firewall-1 firewall.

We prove the correctness of the synthesis in the following. Due to space limit, we omit the proof details here.

Theorem 1. *A set SGR of generalized firewall rules that is generated by our synthesis methodology produces the global set GEP of effective paths that satisfies the correctness property for each kind of policy.*

7   Related Works

Firmato [6] offers a synthesis methodology for firewall rules. It offers the use of role-based policy for specifying intended information flows. Such role-based policy is a high-level policy. However, Firmato deals only with the synthesis in the context of *closed policy*. Furthermore, it does not analyze any desirable properties of synthesized firewall rules at all. It would be interesting to incorporate the use of role-based policy to specify intended information flows into our framework.

Filtering postures [7] offers both verification and synthesis of firewall rules. However, the kind of firewall rules that are verified or synthesized is order-insensitive, and thus those rules are very different from actual firewall rules. As a result, it does not offer any understanding on the effect of rule ordering, unlike our approach. Furthermore, the only verification offered by filtering postures is identical to the correctness in the context of *closely neutral policy* in our approach. It does not analyze about properties of synthesized firewall rules.

Fang [8] is a software tool which aims to verify firewall rules. The main verification that Fang offers is the generation of final effects of firewall rules. However, Fang's approach is *ad hoc* in that it simply simulate the final effects of firewall rules without giving any explanation of the effects of ordered rules.

8 Conclusion

We have presented a general and unified methodology for verifying and synthesizing firewall configurations. Our methodology has several benefits in that it can analyze the correctness of firewall configurations and also generate configurations in the context of many kinds of policies.

We have applied our verification methodology to case studies in [9]. We are currently implementing a software prototype of our model. Also, we are applying our synthesis methodology to case studies.

Acknowledgement. The first author would like to acknowledge supports from the Thailand Research Fund, and the National Research Council of Thailand.

References

1. Cheswick W.R. and Bellovin S.M., Firewalls and Internet Security : Repelling the Wily Hacker, Addison- Wesley, 1994.
2. Chapman D.B. and Zwicky E.D., Building Internet Firewall, O' Reilly & Associates, 1995.
3. Permpoontanalarp Y. and Rujimethabhas C., A Graph Theoretic Model for Hardware-based Firewalls, In proceedings of 9th IEEE International Conference on Networks (ICON), Thailand, 2001.
4. Gross J. and Yellen J., Graph Theory and its Applications, CRC Press LLC, 1998
5. Holzmann G.J., Design and Validation of Computer Protocols, Prentice Hall Software Series, 1991.
6. Bartal Y., Mayer A., Nissim K. and Wool A., Firmato : A Novel Firewall Management Toolkit, In proceedings of 20th IEEE Symposium on Security & Privacy, Oakland, CA, 1999.
7. Guttman J.D., Filtering Postures : Local Enforcement for Global Policies, In proceedings of 17th IEEE Symposium on Security & Privacy, Oakland, CA, 1997.
8. Mayer A., Wool A. and Ziskind E., Fang : A Firewall Analysis Engine, In proceedings of 21st IEEE Symposium on Security & Privacy, Oakland, CA, 2000.
9. Rujimethabhas C., A Graph-based Methodology for Hardware-based Firewalls, Master Thesis, Department of Computer Engineering, King Mongkut's University of Technology Thonburi, Bangkok, Thailand, 2001.

Quantifying Network Denial of Service: A Location Service Case Study

Yan Chen, Adam Bargteil, David Bindel, Randy H. Katz, and
John Kubiatowicz

Computer Science Division,
University of California, Berkeley
{yanchen, adamb, dbindel, randy, kubitron}@cs.berkeley.edu

Abstract. Network Denial of Service (DoS) attacks are increasing in
frequency, severity and sophistication, making it desirable to measure
the resilience of systems to DoS attacks. In this paper, we propose a
simulation-based methodology and apply it to attacks on object location
services such as DNS. Our results allow us to contrast the DoS resilience
of three distinct architectures for object location.

1 Introduction

Today's exponential growth in storage, bandwidth, and computational resources
has fundamentally changed the way that applications are constructed. A single
networked computer can now access vast distributed databases, execute programs on remote supercomputers, and communicate with billions of other devices. Opportunities are limited only by the imagination.

Unfortunately, with networking comes the potential for *Denial of Service*
(DoS) attacks, where a DoS attack is any malicious action that reduces the
availability of a resource to one or more users. From 1989-1995 the number of
DoS attacks increased 50% per year [13]. Additionally, a 1999 CSI/FBI survey
reported that 32% of respondents detected DoS attacks directed at their systems [15]. More recently, Yankee Group, an Internet research firm, estimated
that DoS attacks cost $1.2 billion in lost revenues in 2000 [9]. Given the prolif-
eration of DoS attacks, many mission-critical applications claim DoS resilience.
To test these claims, there is a desire for a general methodology to measure the
resilience of a system or service to network DoS attacks.

As the first step towards this ambitious goal, we explore DoS resilience in an
important component of many networked applications: *the object location service* (OLS). Object location services map abstract names to physical locations;
a well-known example is the Domain Name Service (DNS). In addition to administrative convenience, the presence of an object location service permits the
system to create copies of objects close to where they are needed, thereby maximizing locality, availability and reliability. Given its central importance to many
applications, the object location service is a natural target for DoS attacks.

We explore three architectures for object location services: a centralized directory, a replicated directory, and a distributed directory. We subject a realistic
simulation of these services to two classes of denial of service attacks, namely
flooding attacks and *corruption attacks*. We then contrast the DoS resilience of
these architectures and conclude with some thoughts about methodology.

S. Qing, T. Okamoto, and J. Zhou (Eds.): ICICS 2001, LNCS 2229, pp. 340–351, 2001.
© Springer-Verlag Berlin Heidelberg 2001

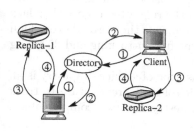

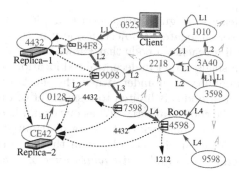

Fig. 1. *A* Centralized Directory Service (CDS): *Clients contact a single directory to discover the location of a close replica. Clients subsequently contact the replica directly. A* Replicated Directory Service (RDS) *provides multiple directories.*

Fig. 2. A Distributed Directory (Tapestry): Nodes connected via links (solid arrows). Nodes route to nodes one digit at a time: e.g. 1010 → 2218 → 9098 → 7598 → 4598. Objects are associated with one particular "root" node (e.g. 4598). Servers publish replicas by sending messages toward root, leaving back-pointers (dotted arrows). Clients route directly to replicas by sending messages toward root until encountering pointer (e.g. 0325 → B4F8 → 4432).

2   Architectures for Object Location

Networked applications are extending their reach to a variety of devices and services over the Internet. Applications expanding to leverage these network resources find that *locating objects* on the wide-area is an important problem. Further, the read-mostly model of shared access, widely popularized by the World-Wide-Web, has led to extensive object replication, compounding the problem of object location. Work on location services has been done in a variety of contexts [8,12,14,27]. These approaches can be roughly categorized into three groups: *Centralized Directory Services (CDS), Replicated Directory Services (RDS),* and *Distributed Directory Services (DDS).*

2.1   Centralized and Replicated Directory Services

A *centralized directory service* (CDS) resides on a single server and provides location information for every object on the network. See Figure 1. Because it resides on a single server, it is extremely vulnerable to DoS attacks. A variant of this is the *replicated directory service* (RDS) which provides multiple directory servers. An RDS provides higher availability, but suffers consistency overhead.

2.2   Distributed Directory Services: The Tapestry Infrastructure

Networking researchers have begun to explore decentralized location services [27, 21,24]. Such services offer a distributed infrastructure for locating objects quickly, with guaranteed success and locality. Rather than depending on a single server to locate an object, a query in this model is passed around the network until it reaches a node that knows the location of the requested object. The lack of a single target in decentralized location services means they provide very high availability even under attack; the effects of successfully attacking and disabling a set of nodes is limited to a small set of objects.

We chose Tapestry [27] as our example of this type of service. Tapestry is an IP overlay network that uses a distributed, fault-tolerant architecture to track the location of every object in the network. Tapestry has two components: a *routing mesh* and a *distributed directory service*.

Tapestry Routing Mesh: Figure 2 shows a portion of Tapestry. Each Tapestry node has a unique hexadecimal address drawn from a random distribution. Tapestry nodes are connected via *neighbor* links of varying levels; these are shown as solid arrows. The level-1 links (L1) from a node connect to the 16 closest, nodes[1] with different values in the lowest digit of the address. Level-2 links (L2) connect to the 16 closest nodes that match in the lowest digit and have different second digits, *etc.*. Such neighbor links provide a route from every node to every other node; the routing process resolves the destination address one digit at a time. This routing scheme is based on the hashed-suffix routing structure originally presented by Plaxton, Rajaraman, and Richa [19].

Tapestry Distributed Directory Service: Tapestry assigns a globally-unique name (GUID) to every object. It then deterministically maps each GUID to a unique *root* node. Storage servers *publish* objects by sending messages toward the roots, depositing *location pointers* at each hop. Figure 2 shows two replicas and the Tapestry root for an object. Location pointers are shown as dotted arrows that point back to replica servers. To locate an object, a client sends a message toward the object's root. When the message encounters a pointer, it routes directly to the object. It is shown in [19] that the average distance traveled in locating an object is *proportional* to the distance from that object.

The root of the tree must know where one or more replicas of the object reside in order to guarantee that replicas can be located. This makes it an obvious target for a DoS attack. We will exploit this vulnerability later[2].

3   Assessing the Risk

DoS attacks are difficult to analyze because they are system-wide phenomena. Viewing components or attackers in isolation often fails to expose interesting behavior. As a consequence, we choose to observe a simulation of a complete system, including realistic network topology, client workloads, server architecture, and attack profiles. Section 4 will describe the simulation environment in detail. Here we wish to understand the *types of attacks* that might be mounted against object location services and how we can *assess their impact*.

---

[1] "Closest" with respect to network latency.

[2] The Tapestry infrastructure in [27] employs multiple roots; we did not simulate this.

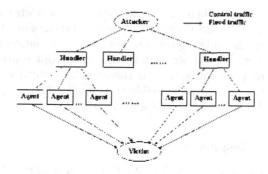

Fig. 3. Structure of a distributed DDoS attacks

3.1 Threat Models

Denial of Service attacks come in many shapes and sizes. In fact, the CERT Coordination Center [6] has proposed the following taxonomy:

- Consumption of network connectivity and/or bandwidth
- Consumption of other resources, *i.e.* CPU cycles or kernel data structures
- Destruction or alteration of configuration information
- Physical destruction or alteration of network components

Specializing this set for object location services, we identify two general classes of attack: *Flooding Attacks* and *Corruption Attacks*:

Flooding Attacks: The most popular network DoS attack is the flooding attack, in which the attacker sends superfluous requests at a high rate. Flooding attacks overload the victim's resources (such as queues and CPU), and also swamp the local routers, gateways and links. These DoS attacks can be classified as *point-to-point* or *distributed*. There are four major point-to-point DoS attacks: TCP SYN flooding, UDP flooding, ICMP flooding and Smurf attacks [10].

Distributed Dos (DDoS) attacks combine point-to-point DoS attacks with distributed and coordinated control. Figure 3 shows the structure of a DDoS attack, with one or more *attackers* controlling *handlers*, with each handler controlling multiple *agents*[3]. Handlers and agents are extra layers introduced to increase the rate of packet traffic as well as hide the attackers from view. Each agent can choose the size and type of packets as well as the duration of flooding. While the victim may be able to identify some agents and have them taken off-line, the attacker can monitor the effects of the attack and create new agents accordingly [10]. In general, attack simulation parameters should be chosen to cover a sufficient spectrum of attack traffic versus legitimate traffic to show interesting results.

---

[3] Compromised hosts responsible for generating packet streams directed at the victim.

Corruption Attacks: When an attacker corrupts or destroys information, we call this a *corruption attack*. There are numerous variants on this type of attack. For instance an attacker might alter configuration information to prevent the use of a client or network. Or, an attacker might corrupt routing tables, causing victim nodes to redirect traffic toward the attacker, which would subsequently drop or deny requests. It is not possible to test all attacks, so typical examples of this category should be simulated and measured.

3.2   Measuring Resilience

DoS attacks reduce resource *availability*. Here, availability refers to a spectrum of service quality, not simply "up" versus "down". Though the choice of Quality of Service (QoS) metrics depends on the system or service being studied, Brown and Patterson have suggested *performance, completeness, accuracy* and *capacity* as starting points [4]. For our particular study, we consider metrics of *response latency, request throughput*, and *time to recover*[4]. We examine the level degradation of a service under attack to assess the *resilience* of that service.

Of course, Denial of Service is *multidimensional* in that system A may be more resilient than system B for one type of attack but less resilient for another. Usually, the particular threat-model under consideration defines a set of dimensions, one for each class of threat. Combining these dimensions to yield a particular *resilience ranking* is a very system-specific task and hard to generalize. Our solution is to be sufficiently specific in the definition of the threat model and only quantify the resilience in that model.

4   Experimental Setup

We built a complete system on top of *ns* [3]. All of our nodes function as both clients and hosts with a subset providing the directory service. Clients send lookup requests to the directory service, which either returns the location of a replica or forwards the request directly to the replica. We selected some nodes to be attackers and measured changes in the availability of system resources.

We used 1000 node network topologies generated by GT-ITM [26] using a transit-stub model. We then extended these topologies with common network bandwidths as recommended in [16]. Our routers use simple drop-tail queuing (we assumed attackers will spoof their IP addresses, defeating any filtering done by more complicated queuing policies). More details are in [5].

4.1   Client Operation

We generated synthetic client workloads using both Zipf's law [1] and hot-cold [20] models. Zipf's law states that if objects are ranked according to their access frequency, then the number of requests of the object with rank i is proportional to $1/i$. In a hot-cold model, a small portion of the objects (10%) receive

---

[4] A corrupted directory service could prevent service entirely, but this is beyond the scope of the current study.

the majority (90%) of the requests. Our network has 500 objects, each with three replicas placed on three randomly chosen nodes. The sizes of objects were chosen randomly from the interval 5kB - 50kB. Nodes request a data object, wait for the data and then request another, such as when a user is following a series of web links.

4.2   Directory Server Operation

We used five different directory services in our simulations:

CDSr. The simplest directory service is the *Centralized Directory Server*(CDS). Here, one non-transit node is chosen to be the directory server. Object requests are made in two stages. First, the directory server is queried and returns the location of a random replica of the object. Second, the requesting node communicates directly with the node hosting the replica and the data is returned.

CDSo. Same as above, except that the directory server returns the location of the replica which is closest to the requesting node.

RDSr. The *Replicated Directory Service*(RDS) is placed on four random, widely-distributed, non-transit nodes. Queries are made as above, except that a node must choose one of the servers to fulfill its request. Here, the choice is made randomly for each request. The replica is also randomly chosen by the directory server as in the CDSr.

RDSo. Same as the RDSr, except that each node sends requests to the nearest directory server. (Replica choice is still random).

DDS. For the DDS, we implemented a simplified version of Tapestry as an extension to *ns*. All messages between nodes are passed by *ns*'s full TCP/IP agent. Messages route through the object's tree to the statistically closest object replica, and the replica responds by sending the data contents directly to the requesting node. Our Tapestry data structures are statically built at the start of the simulation using full knowledge of the topology, and using hop count as the network distance metric. It should also be noted that our implementation is un-optimized and is likely slower than a real implementation would be.

4.3   The Attacks

We modeled two types of attacks in our simulations:

Flooding Attacks. The first attacks we simulated flood some important node(s) and overload their queues to reduce the number of legitimate requests that get through. We randomly designated some nodes "agents"; the agents then stream a constant bit rate at the victim. We varied the number of agents as well as the severity (bit rate) of flooding. The life time of each agent was randomly chosen from 0 - 200 seconds with new agents immediately replacing those taken off-line.

For the CDS and RDS, we attacked the directory server(s). We attacked the closest analogy in Tapestry, the root of a hot object. For comparison with the CDS (RDS), we flood the root of one (four) hot object(s), keeping the number of attacked nodes the same.

Corruption Attacks. As these attacks are system/service-specific, we only simulated two attacks here as examples.

The first attack forces an important node to believe there is a link with negligible latency between the nodes which are actually the farthest apart. We attack the directory server of the CDS, a random directory server of the RDS and the Tapestry root node of a hot object for comparison.

The second attack is specific to Tapestry; a malicious Tapestry node claims to be the root node of all objects. By replying with a negative result to any request it receives, this node can potentially convince clients that requested objects do not exist, denying them access to an existing resource. The question we ask here is "how many nodes are affected?"

5   Results

5.1   Flooding Attacks

We performed simulations of flooding attacks on the CDS, RDS, and Tapestry with hot-cold and Zipf's law workloads. The results were similar for both workloads, so we present only hot-cold results.

Comparison of CDS and Tapestry: First, we compare the performance of CDS with Tapestry. We simulated *one attacker* at a rate of 500 or 2000 bytes every 5 ms or *four attackers* at rates between 500 bytes every 20ms and 500 bytes every 5ms. The results are shown in Figures 4 and 5. These figures reveal that a single attacker does not significantly influence performance, while distributed attackers, each flooding at the same high rate, cause severe denial of service.

While a CDS suffers greatly under severe attacks, Tapestry shows some resistance. This can be explained by the distributed nature of Tapestry. Furthermore, Tapestry satisfies many requests before they reach the root: if we observe the attacked object exclusively, it retains more than 50% of its normal throughput.

One interesting observation, as shown by the two rightmost sets of data in Figures 4 and 5, is that distributed attackers cause more severe DoS than a single attacker, *even when injecting the same amount of flood traffic*. The reason for this is that point-to-point attackers are limited by the bottleneck bandwidth from attacker to the victim.

Figures 6 and 7 show the dynamics of the most severe flooding attacks on CDS and Tapestry. The attack(s) start at 40 seconds and end at 110 seconds. Given our simulation setup, the *time to recover* for CDS with both policies is 40 seconds. As Tapestry is not really affected much, its *time to recover* is negligible.

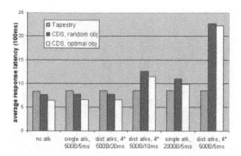

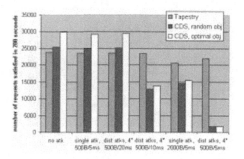

Fig. 4. Average response latency of CDS vs. Tapestry under DoS flooding attacks

Fig. 5. Throughput of CDS vs. Tapestry under DoS flooding attacks

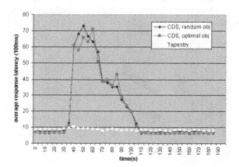

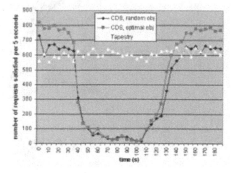

Fig. 6. Dynamics of average response latency of CDS vs. Tapestry under DoS flooding attacks

Fig. 7. Dynamics of throughput of CDS vs. Tapestry under DoS flooding attacks

Comparison of RDS and Tapestry: To explore replicated directory service, we put four servers on widely-distributed, non-transit nodes. We investigated two policies: either the client contacts a random directory server (RDSr) or the closest one (RDSo). We did not simulate consistency traffic between directories.

Again, the single flooding attack has little effect, so we only present results of DDoS attacks in Figure 8 and 9. We randomly selected four non-transit nodes as attackers. Each of these nodes attacks a directory server in a different subnet or the DDS root of a hot object; these attacks have little effect. We also randomly selected sixteen non-transit attack agents in groups of four, each from different subnets. Each group attacked one RDS directory server or the DDS root of a hot object. The attack rate varied from 500 bytes every 10ms to 500 bytes every 1ms, with each agent set to the same rate.

Both forms of RDS and Tapestry are far more resilient to DoS than CDS (observe the difference in flooding rates along the X-axes). Thus, replication and topology-aware locality can significantly increase resilience to DoS attacks. In our simulations, the optimal RDS always performs better than Tapestry. This is because Tapestry may be forced to make traverse bottleneck links multiple

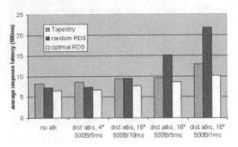
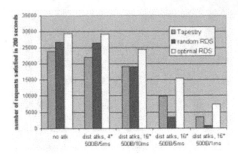

Fig. 8. Average response latency of RDS vs. Tapestry on DDos flooding attacks

Fig. 9. Throughput of RDS vs. Tapestry on DDos flooding attacks

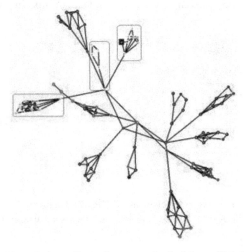

Fig. 10. Nodes accessing each replica of an attacked object. Neighbor table corruption at the black square node renders all nodes enclosed by round-corner rectangles unable to locate the object. Simulation of 100 nodes and 60 objects (15% hot).

times, whereas the clients in the same subnet as an RDS directory server can avoid the bottlenecks entirely. A more interesting observation, however, is that Tapestry comes very close to optimal RDS; as the number of objects and size of network increases, the number of replicated directory servers required to compete with the self-organizing nature of Tapestry is likely to increase, making Tapestry a better overall choice. Meanwhile, Tapestry outperforms the random RDS on severe attacks, lending credence to the locality properties of Tapestry.

5.2   Corruption Attacks

When we compromised routing information at important nodes, the CDS and RDS, which access a random replica, are not affected[5]. The performance of the

---

[5] We assume that the directory server(s) are not routers or gateways.

Table 1. Attempting to rank the five different directory services

Directory services	Flooding attack (80%)	Corruption attack (10%)	Node spoofing attack (10%)	Total score	Rank
CDS, random replica	0.027	N/A	N/A	0.2216	4
CDS, optimal replica	0.023	0.85	N/A	0.2034	5
RDS, random dir server	0.17	N/A	N/A	0.336	3
RDS, optimal dir server	0.48	N/A	N/A	0.584	1
DDS	0.35	0.978	0.76	0.4538	2

CDS which returns the optimal replica was degraded to 85%. The impact to Tapestry is negligible, with overall performance reduced by only 2.2%. We also simulated the Tapestry-specific node spoofing attack. The effects of the attack are displayed in Figure 10. The attack affects 24% of the network.

5.3   Resiliency Ranking

How might we combine the results of previous sections into a single ranking? As suggested in Section 3, we might assign weights to different types of attacks based on perceived severity or frequency. For instance, if we assign 80% weight to flooding attacks and 10% each to two "corruption" attacks, we can roughly rank the directory services as in Table 1. Here we simulate all eight attacks in Figures 4, 5, 8 and 9 for all three types of directory services and report a weighted sum of normalized throughputs. The weights are assigned in proportion to the amounts of flood traffic and the normalization is based on the corresponding directory service performance without attack; this will vary from system to system, but does give an idea how these services differ in terms of DoS resilience.

6   Limitations and Generalizations

While our study is very specific we feel that some of our methodology can be applied in a more general setting. In particular, our approach of simulating a *complete*, well-behaved system and then injecting malicious faults and measuring the consequences should be generally applicable. Of course, we only simulated static clients, servers, and attackers; one future task will be to incorporate more dynamic behavior. We also hope to extend the scope of our simulations to more applications. Note that the specifics, from system setup to the threat model, vary greatly from system to system. We hope to explore techniques for combining results across multiple dimensions, possibly extending the automated approach for weight generation suggested by Bayuk [2]. As more attempts are made to quantify the DoS resilience of different systems, we hope to more completely understand both the nature of DoS attacks and how to measure their impact.

7   Related Work

Early work by Gligor and Yu [11,25] built on the classic notion of a trusted computing base to define a "DoS Protection Base". Yu and Gligor also pointed out that denial of service is in fact an attack on resource availability. Millen believed that DoS is a problem of improper resource allocation [18], while Meadows has characterized the susceptibility of network services to DoS attacks on resources used before remote host authentication [17]. Some attacks rely on protocol weaknesses to consume resources with minimal attacker effort, as in TCP SYN flooding [22]; other attacks depend simply on the ability of an attacker to produce sufficient traffic to overwhelm a victim by brute force [7].

In [22], the authors investigated several approaches to fighting TCP SYN attacks and developed a tool which actively monitored the network for suspicious attack behavior and terminated dangling connections left by the attacker. In [23], the authors describe the use of an end-to-end resource accounting in the Scout operating system to protect against resource-based DoS attacks. Both these works present microbenchmarks testing the effectiveness of the proposed countermeasure. Our approach differs partly in that we investigate attacks on availability of a service, rather than on a particular server.

Brown and Patterson [4] investigate the use of fault injection to benchmark availability and apply their methodology to software RAID systems. Our work is similarly based on injecting faults into a workload and investigating the effect, but our faults are malicious in nature.

8   Conclusions

In this paper, we explored the resilience of several object location services under denial of service attacks. We did this by creating a complete simulation environment, including realistic network topologies, server architectures and client behaviors. We then injected malicious attacks into the system and measured the availability of the attacked services. Not surprisingly, we discovered that distributed organizations are more resilient to DoS attacks than centralized ones. Our simulation framework is a first attempt to quantify the network DoS resilience of arbitrary systems and services.

Acknowledgments. This research is supported by NSF career award #ANI-9985250, DARPA grant #N66001-99-2-8913, and DARPA grant #DABT63-96-C-0056. David Bindel is supported by an NSF Graduate fellowship. We would like to thank David Wagner, Ben Zhao, Adrian Perrig and Lakshminarayanan Subramanian who gave many valuable suggestions.

References

1. V. Almeida, et al. Characterizing reference locality in the WWW. In *Proceeding of the IEEE Conf. on Parallel and Distributed Information Systems*, 1996.
2. J. Bayuk, Measuring Security, *First workshop on information-security-system rating and ranking*, 2001
3. Lee Breslau, et al. Advances in network simulation. *IEEE Computer*, 33(5):59–67, May 2000.
4. A. Brown and D. Patterson, Towards availability benchmarks: A case study of software RAID systems. In *Proceedings of the 2000 USENIX Conference*.

5. Y. Chen, A. Bargteil, R. Katz, and J. Kubiatowicz. Quantifying Network Denial of Service: A Location Service Case Study UCB Tech. Report UCB/CSD-01-1150
6. CERT Coordination Center. Denial of service attacks.
   http://www.cert.org/tech_tips/denial_of_service.html, 1999.
7. Symantec AntiVirus Research Center. W32.dos.trinoo.
   http://www.symantec.com/avcenter/venc/data/w32.dos.trinoo.html, 2000.
8. S. Czerwinski, B. Zhao, T. Hodes, A. Joseph, and R. Katz. An architecture for a secure service discovery service. In *Proceedings of ACM MOBICOM*, August 1999.
9. M. Delio New breed of attack zombies lurk, May 2001.
   http://www.wired.com/news/technology/0,1282,43697,00.html.
10. S. Dietrich, et al. Anaylzing distributed denial of service tools: the Shaft case. In *Proceedings of the 14th Systems Administration Conference*, 2000
11. V. Gligor. A note on the DoS problem. In *Proceedings of the 1983 Symposium on Security and Privacy*, 1983.
12. E. Guttman, C. Perkins, J. Veizades, and M. Day. Service Location Protocol, Version 2. IETF Internet Draft, November 1998. RFC 2165.
13. J. Howard. *An Analysis of Security Incidents on the Internet*. PhD thesis, Carnegie Mellon University, Aug. 1998.
14. T. Howes. The Lightweight Directory Access Protocol: X.500 Lite. Technical Report 95-8, Center for Information Technology Integration, U. Mich., July 1995.
15. Computer Security Institute and Federal Bureau of Investigation. CSI/FBI computer crime and security survey. In *Computer Security Institute publication*, 2000.
16. J. Jannotti, et al. Overcast: Reliable multicasting with an overlay network. In *4th Symposium on Operating Systems Design & Implementation*, Oct. 2000.
17. C. Meadows. A formal framework and evaluation method for network denial of service. In *Proc. of the IEEE Computer Security Foundations Workshop*, 1999.
18. J. Millen. DoS: A perspective. In *Dependable Computing for Critical Applications 4*, 1995.
19. G. Plaxton, et al. Accessing nearby copies of replicated objects in a distributed environment. In *Proceedings of SCP Symposium on Parallel Alg. and Arch.* , 1997.
20. M. Rabinovich, et al. A dynamic object replication and migration protocol for an internet hosting service. In *Proceedings of IEEE ICDCS*, 1999.
21. S. Ratnasamy, P. Francis, M. Handley, R. Karp, and S. Schenker. A scalable content-addressable network. to appear in Proceeding of ACM SIGCOMM, 2001.
22. C. Schuba, I. Krsul, M. Kuhn, and et. al. Analysis of a DoS attack on TCP. In *Proceedings of the 1997 IEEE Symposium on Security and Privacy*, May 1997.
23. O. Spatscheck and L. Peterson. Defending against DoS attacks in Scout. In *Proceedings of SOSP*, 1999.
24. I. Stoica, et al. Chord: A scalable peer-to-peer lookup service for Internet applications. to appear in Proceedings of ACM SIGCOMM, 2001.
25. C. Yu and V. Gligor. Specification and verification method for preventing denial of service. *IEEE Transactions on Software Engineering*, 16(6), June 1990.
26. E. Zegura, K. Calvert, and S. Bhattacharjee. How to model an internetwork. In *Proceedings of IEEE Infocom*, 1996.
27. B. Zhao, J. Kubiatowicz, and A. Joseph. Tapestry: An infrastructure for fault-tolerant wide-area location and routing. UCB Tech. Report UCB/CSD-01-1141.

A Public Key Cryptosystem Based on the Subgroup Membership Problem

Juan Manuel González Nieto, Colin Boyd, and Ed Dawson

Information Security Research Centre
Queensland University of Technology
Brisbane, Australia.
{gonzalez, boyd, dawson}@fit.qut.edu.au

Abstract. We present a novel public key encryption scheme semantically secure in the standard model under the intractability assumption of the subgroup membership problem. We also describe an honest verifier zero knowledge proof of knowledge protocol that can be converted into a signature scheme in the usual way.

1   Introduction

Diffie and Hellman introduced the concept of public key cryptography in their landmark paper in 1976 [6]. They showed how to construct a public key cryptosystem (PKC) using a *trapdoor one-way function*, i.e. a function that is easy to compute but (supposedly) hard to invert without the knowledge of some trapdoor information. In 1978, Rivest, Shamir and Adelman [15] proposed the first concrete example of a PKC, the renowned RSA cryptosystem which has been widely used for the last two decades. Other examples have followed since [14,7, 12,13].

In this paper we present a new PKC that can be proven semantically secure in the standard model under the intractability of the subgroup membership problem [17]. Informally, given a group G, a subgroup H of G and an element $y \in G$, the subgroup membership problem entails deciding whether y is an element of H. In particular, for $p = 2n + 1$, with $n = q_0 q_1$, and p, q_0, q_1 primes, we are interested in the instantiation of the subgroup membership problem to the case with $G = G_n \times G_n$ and $H = G_{q_0} \times G_{q_1}$, where G_n, G_{q_0} and G_{q_1} are subgroups of $\mathbb{Z}_p^*$ of order n, q_0 and q_1 respectively. The "one-wayness" of the scheme is based on the difficulty of finding the projections of an element of the subgroup G_n onto each of the subgroups G_{q_0} and G_{q_1}. With regard to the efficiency of the scheme, both encryption and decryption take two modulo exponentiations, and the encryption has an message expansion factor of 2.

2   Security Notions

Ideally, the security of a PKC is established by finding a reduction of a well known hard problem, such as factoring integers or computing discrete logarithms in a

S. Qing, T. Okamoto, and J. Zhou (Eds.): ICICS 2001, LNCS 2229, pp. 352–363, 2001.

finite group, to breaking the PKC. Firstly, however, a definition of what breaking the cryptosystem means is needed. Different definitions are possible which result in different notions of security. Initially, a PKC was considered secure if given a ciphertext and the public key used in encrypting the corresponding plaintext, an attacker cannot compute the plaintext, i.e. security was equivalent to "one-wayness". Such a definition of security is not sufficient for many situations. It, for example, does not preclude attacks that recover partial information about the plaintext.

In 1984, Goldwasser and Micali [9] proposed a more practical definition of security, *semantic security* (also known as *polynomial indistinguishability*). Informally, under the new definition, a PKC is secure if whatever an attacker can obtain about the plaintext from seeing the ciphertext, she can also obtain without it. In other words, the PKC satisfies semantic security if an attacker does not learn anything about the plaintext from observing encryptions. This definition excludes deterministic schemes such as plain RSA. Bellare and Rogaway [3] proposed OAEP, a scheme to transform any trapdoor one-way permutation such as RSA into a semantically secure PKC. The proof of security relies, however, on the heuristic of substituting hash functions for random oracles. Schemes that are provably semantically secure in the standard model (without assuming random oracles) include the ElGamal cryptosystem [7] based on the decisional Diffie-Hellman problem [4], Paillier's scheme [13] using the composite residuosity assumption, and Okamoto-Uchiyama's cryptosystem [12] based on factoring.

The scheme presented in this paper is proven semantically secure in the standard model on the assumption that a certain number theoretic problem, viz. the subgroup membership problem, is hard. This problem is connected to the integer factorisation problem in that it is certainly not harder. We note that previous cryptosystems relying on the factorisation problem for security seem to either use the random oracle model (such as OAEP) or require a modulus of special form (such as Okamoto-Uchiyama).

3 Preliminaries

Before we describe the new public key cryptosystem (PKC), we review some basic algebraic and number theoretic results that will allow us to discuss its security in section 5.

Firstly, let's consider the multiplicative group $\mathbb{Z}_p^*$ with $p = 2n+1$, $n = q_0 q_1$ and where p, q_0, q_1 are distinct primes. Let $k = |q_0| = |q_1|$, the size of the binary representation of both q_0 and q_1. We denote the subgroups of $\mathbb{Z}_p^*$ of order q_0, q_1 and n by G_{q_0}, G_{q_1} and G_n, respectively. All operations are assumed mod p except where explicitly noted.

Fact 1. *For every element $y \in G_n$ there exist a unique pair $(y_0, y_1) \in G_{q_0} \times G_{q_1}$ such that $y = y_0 y_1 \bmod p$*

Since Fact 1 forms the basis of the new PKC, we will elaborate on it. Firstly, we note that Fact 1 is a direct consequence of $G_{q_0} \cap G_{q_1} = \{1\}$. Thus, a simple counting argument shows that no two elements of $G_{q_0} \times G_{q_1}$ represent the same element in G_n. One can also see the workings of the *Chinese remainder theorem* (CRT) here. If g_0 and g_1 are generators of G_{q_0} and G_{q_1} respectively, then $g = g_0 g_1$ is a generator of G_n, and any element $y \in G_n$ can be expressed as $y = g^x$, where $x \in \mathbb{Z}_n$. Thus, we can write

$$y = g^x = g_0^{x_0} g_1^{x_1},$$

where

$$x \equiv x_0 \pmod{q_0}$$
$$x \equiv x_1 \pmod{q_1}.$$

We know by virtue of the CRT that such a system of equations has a unique solution, namely

$$x = x_0 \alpha_0 + x_1 \alpha_1 \bmod n,$$

where

$$\alpha_0 = q_1(q_1^{-1} \bmod q_0)$$
$$\alpha_1 = q_0(q_0^{-1} \bmod q_1).$$

The following properties will be useful later on:

Fact 2. Properties of α_0 and α_1

1. $\alpha_0 + \alpha_1 \equiv 1 \pmod{n}$.
2. $\alpha_0 \alpha_1 \equiv 0 \pmod{n}$.
3. $\alpha_i{}^k \equiv \alpha_i \pmod{n}$, *for $i = 0, 1$ and for all $k > 0$.*

To see that the third property holds, notice that

$$\begin{aligned}
\alpha_i{}^k \bmod n &= (1 - \alpha_{1-i})^{k-1} \alpha_i \bmod n \\
&= (1 - pol(\alpha_{1-i})\,\alpha_{1-i})\,\alpha_i \bmod n \\
&= \alpha_i,
\end{aligned}$$

where $pol(\cdot)$ is a polynomial of degree $k - 2$.

It is not difficult to see that G_n and $G_{q_0} \times G_{q_1}$ are isomorphic. From Fact 1 the following mapping is a bijection:

$$\begin{aligned}
f : G_{q_0} \times G_{q_1} &\longrightarrow G_n \\
(y_0, y_1) &\longmapsto y_0 y_1 \bmod p.
\end{aligned}$$

Knowledge of the factorisation of $p - 1$ allows us to compute the inverse of $f(\cdot)$, as follows.

$$\begin{aligned}
f^{-1} : G_n &\longrightarrow G_{q_0} \times G_{q_1} \\
y &\longmapsto (f_0(y), f_1(y)),
\end{aligned}$$

where

$$f_i : G_n \longrightarrow G_{q_i}$$
$$y \longmapsto y^{\alpha_i} .$$

In order to help us visualise the above functions, we can identify the subgroup components G_{q_0} and G_{q_1} as "coordinate axes" of G_n, and think of G_n as a Cartesian plane (see Fig. 1). Thus, any element $y \in G_n$ has G_{q_0} and G_{q_1}-coordinates (y_0, y_1) as given by $f^{-1}(\cdot)$. We are unaware of any efficient (i.e. probabilistic poly-

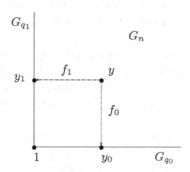

Fig. 1. Projection of $y \in G_n$ onto subgroup components G_{q_0} and G_{q_1}.

nomial time) algorithm that can compute inverses of $f(\cdot)$ without knowledge of the factorisation of $p - 1$, which is thus the trapdoor information. Based on this, we define a new computational problem which we call the *Projection Problem*. Informally, given $y \in G_n$, the projection problem entails finding $(y_0, y_1) \in G_{q_0} \times G_{q_1}$ such that $y = y_0 y_1 \bmod p$. More formally, let k be the security parameter. Let $\mathcal{IG}$ (instance generator) be a probabilistic polynomial time algorithm that on input 1^k outputs a prime $p = 2q_0 q_1 + 1$ with q_0, q_1 two random k-bit primes, and two subgroup generators g_0, g_1 of G_{q_0} and G_{q_1} respectively.

Definition 1 (Projection Problem $\mathcal{PP}$ Assumption). *For every probabilistic polynomial time (in k) algorithm $\mathcal{A}$, for every $\alpha > 0$ and sufficiently large k:*

$$\Pr[\mathcal{A}(p, g_0, g_1, y) = (y_0, y_1)] < 1/k^\alpha,$$

where $y \in G_n$ and $(y_0, y_1) \in G_{q_0} \times G_{q_1}$ such that $y = y_0 y_1 \bmod p$. The probability is taken over the random choice of $(p, g_0, g_1) \leftarrow \mathcal{IG}(1^k)$, the random choice of $y \in G_n$, and the random bits used by $\mathcal{A}$.

As we show below, the complexity of this problem is related to that of the better known *subgroup membership problem*, in that the projection problem is not easier. Informally, given a group G, a subgroup H of G and an element $y \in G$, the subgroup membership problem entails deciding whether y is an element of H.

In our case we are interested in the instantiation of the subgroup membership problem to the case where $G = G_n \times G_n$ and $H = G_{q_0} \times G_{q_1}$. We refer the reader to Yamamura and Saito's paper [17] for a more elaborated treatment of the subgroup membership problem.

Definition 2 (Subgroup Membership Problem $\mathcal{SMP}$ Assumption). *For every probabilistic polynomial time (in k) algorithm $\mathcal{A}$, for every $\alpha > 0$ and sufficiently large k:*

$$|\Pr[\mathcal{A}(p, g_0, g_1, y) = \text{``true''} \,|\, y \in G_{q_0} \times G_{q_1}]$$
$$-\Pr[\mathcal{A}(p, g_0, g_1, y) = \text{``true''} \,|\, y \notin G_{q_0} \times G_{q_1}]| < 1/k^\alpha,$$

where $y \in G_n \times G_n$. The probability is taken over the random choice of $(p, g_0, g_1) \leftarrow \mathcal{IG}(1^k)$, the random choice of $y \in G_n \times G_n$, and the random bits used by $\mathcal{A}$.

As pointed out by Yamamura and Saito [17], popular decisional problems such as the Decisional Diffie-Hellman [4], or the Quadratic Residuosity [9] problems are also examples of the subgroup membership problem.

In order to compare the complexity of computational problems we use the following relation:

Definition 3. *Let $\mathcal{X}$ and $\mathcal{Y}$ be two computational problems. $\mathcal{X} \leq_P \mathcal{Y}$ ($\mathcal{X}$ polytime reduces to $\mathcal{Y}$) if there exists an algorithm that is polynomial time as a function of the input length of $\mathcal{X}$, that solves $\mathcal{X}$ by making use of an oracle that solves $\mathcal{Y}$.*

Lemma 1. $\mathcal{SMP} \leq_P \mathcal{PP}$

Proof. Assume that there exists an efficient algorithm that can find the projections of elements of G_n, i.e. that on input p, g_0, g_1, and $y \in G_n$ outputs $(y_0, y_1) \in G_{q_0} \times G_{q_1}$ such that $y_0 y_1 = y$. Then it is straight forward to construct another efficient algorithm that given $(u_0, u_1) \in G_n \times G_n$ decides if (u_0, u_1) is also in $G_{q_0} \times G_{q_1}$, for in such case the projection of u_0 onto G_{q_1} and of u_1 onto g_{q_0} will be both 1.   □

We can also compare the projection problem with the well known integer factorisation problem and the discrete logarithm problem. Informally, given a positive integer n, the *integer factorisation problem* $\mathcal{IFP}$ entails finding $q_0, q_1, \ldots, q_l$ and $e_0, e_1, \ldots, e_l$ such that $n = \prod_{i=1}^{l} q_i^{e_i}$, where p_i are pairwise distinct primes and each $e_i \geq 1$. The *discrete log problem* $\mathcal{DLP}$ in a finite group is as follows: given two elements g and h of a group G, find x such that $h = g^x \bmod p$.

Lemma 2. *The following relationships hold:*

1. $\mathcal{PP} \leq_P \mathcal{IFP}$
2. $\mathcal{PP} \leq_P \mathcal{DLP}$

Proof. It can be immediately verified that $\mathcal{PP} \leq_P \mathcal{IFP}$. To see that $\mathcal{PP} \leq_P \mathcal{DLP}$, we notice that if one can compute $r = \log_g y$, where $\log_g$ denotes the discrete logarithm in base $g = g_0 g_1$, then the projections of y are simply $y_i = g_i^r$. Furthermore, if one can compute $\alpha_i = \log_g g_i$, then the factorisation of $p - 1$ is obtained as $q_i = \gcd(\alpha_i, p - 1)$, which allows us to obtain the projections of any other element in G_n.   □

4   The Scheme

The PKC consists of three algorithms: key generation, encryption and decryption.

Key Generation. Let k be the security parameter. In order to generate an asymmetric key pair each user does as follows.

1. Choose a random prime p of the form $p = 2n + 1$ where $n = q_0 q_1$ with q_i also prime such that $|q_i| = k$.
2. Select two elements g_i of order q_i. Since the user knows the factorisation of n she can do this easily. g_i is thus a generator of G_{q_i}.
3. Compute $\alpha_i = q_{1-i}(q_{1-i}^{-1} \bmod q_i)$
4. The public key of the user is $PubKey = \{p, g_0, g_1\}$, and the corresponding private key is $PriKey = \{\alpha_0, \alpha_1\}$.

Encryption. The following algorithm encrypts a message $m \in G_n$ using a public key $PubKey = \{p, g_0, g_1\}$ as generated by the key generation algorithm: (see Fig. 2)

1. Choose two random integers $r_i, 1 \le r_i \le n$.
2. Compute $v_i = g_i^{r_i}$. Thus v_i is an element of G_{q_i}
3. Compute $c_i = m v_{1-i}$.
4. The ciphertext is then $c = (c_0, c_1)$.

An implementation of the algorithm would also require an encoding function from the actual message space to G_n. We do not define any such function, for it depends on the application. Cramer and Shoup [5] give suitable examples.

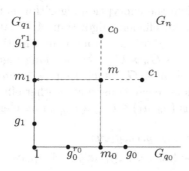

Fig. 2. Encryption of $m \in G_n$.

Decryption. Given a ciphertext c encrypted using $PubKey = \{p, g_0, g_1\}$, the message m can be recovered using the corresponding private key $PriKey = \{\alpha_0, \alpha_1\}$ as follows:

1. Compute $m_i = f_i(c_i) = c_i^{\alpha_i}$.
2. Calculate $m = m_0 m_1$.

We can verify that the above equations actually decrypt to the original message m. From Fact 1, m has a unique representation $(m_0, m_1) \in G_{q_0} \times G_{q_1}$. Hence,

$$c_i = (m_0 m_1) v_{1-i},$$

and since $(m_{1-i} v_{1-i}) \in G_{q_{1-i}}$, it will be "filtered out" by $f_i(\cdot)$, i.e.

$$f_i(cm_i) = (m_0 m_1 v_{1-i})^{\alpha_i} = m_i \ .$$

An interesting property in our scheme is that anyone can transform a ciphertext $c = (c_0, c_1) = (mg_0^{r_0}, mg_1^{r_1})$ into another ciphertext $c' = (c_0 g_0^{r_0'}, c_1 g_1^{r_1'})$, such that both ciphertexts decrypt to the same plaintext m, while keeping the relationship between c and c' concealed. This property is shared with Paillier's and Okamoto and Uchiyama's cryptosystems.

5   Security of the Scheme

In this section we show that the new PKC satisfies the "one-wayness" property under the assumption that the projection problem is hard. We also prove that the scheme is *semantically secure* under the intractability assumption of the subgroup membership problem.

Theorem 1. *The new PKC is one-way if and only if the $\mathcal{PP}$ assumption holds.*

Proof. ($\Rightarrow$) Given the capability to calculate the projections of an element of G_n into G_{q_0} and G_{q_1}, then the encryption algorithm is trivially broken.

($\Leftarrow$) Assume there is an efficient algorithm $\mathcal{A}_C$ that breaks the encryption algorithm without knowledge of the trapdoor information (q_0, q_1). Thus on input p, g_0, g_1 and $(c_0, c_1) \in G_n \times G_n$, the breaking algorithm $\mathcal{A}_C$ outputs the corresponding decryption $m \in G_n$, such that $c_0 = mv_1$ and $c_1 = mv_0$ with $(v_0, v_1) \in G_{q_0} \times G_{q_1}$. Then we can construct another efficient algorithm $\mathcal{A}_P$ that computes the projections $(u_0, u_1) \in G_{q_0} \times G_{q_1}$ of an element $u \in G_n$ as follows:

$$(u_0, u_1) = \mathcal{A}_P(p, g_0, g_1, u)$$
$$= (\mathcal{A}_C(p, g_0, g_1, u, g_0), \mathcal{A}_C(p, g_0, g_1, u, g_1))$$

□

Theorem 2. *The new PKC is semantically secure if and only if the subgroup membership problem assumption holds.*

Proof. ($\Leftarrow$) Assume that the scheme is not semantically secure. This means that there exists an efficient algorithm $\mathcal{A}_D$ such that

$$\mathcal{A}_D(p, g_0, g_1, c_0, c_1, m) = 1$$

if $c = (c_0, c_1)$ is an encryption of m, and 0 otherwise. Then, we can construct another algorithm $\mathcal{A}_S$ that solves $\mathcal{SMP}$, i.e that on input p, g_0, g_1, u outputs 1 if $u = (u_0, u_1)$ is an element of $G_{q_0} \times G_{q_1}$ by simply letting

$$\mathcal{A}_S(p, g_0, g_1, u) = \mathcal{A}_D(p, g_0, g_1, u_0, u_1, 1) \ .$$

($\Rightarrow$) Similarly, it can be easily verified that given $\mathcal{A}_S$, we can construct an algorithm $\mathcal{A}_D$ that contradicts the semantic security of the scheme by defining

$$\mathcal{A}_D(p, g_0, g_1, c_0, c_1, m) = \mathcal{A}_S(p, g_0, g_1, (c_0, c_1)m^{-1}) \ .$$

$\square$

We now analyse the efficiency of our scheme. In accordance to our discussion in Sect. 3, we assume that the best attacks against our scheme entail either factoring $p - 1$ or the ability to take discrete logarithms in G_n. Thus, $p - 1$ should be large enough to make finding its factorisation hard, and therefore the same moduli length recommendations as for RSA apply (see e.g. [10]). That would also ensure that the discrete log problem is hard in both G_{q_0} and G_{q_1}, since $|p| \approx |q_0| + |q_1|$ and $|q_0| = |q_1|$. Encryption requires two exponentiations of fixed bases g_0 and g_1 and two multiplications modulo p. The efficiency of the encryption can be increased by choosing the exponents $r_i \in \{1, \ldots, 2^t\}$ and making $t < k$ but large enough so that computing discrete logs is hard. Decryption requires two exponentiations to fixed exponents and a multiplication. Optimisations that significantly speed up the exponentiations are possible, specially for decryption [11].

Our scheme is thus comparable to the ElGamal cryptosystem, which has the same number of exponentiations for encryption and the same message expansion factor of 2. Decryption in ElGamal requires only 1 exponentiation. However, using simultaneous multiple exponentiation (algorithm 14.88 in [11]), it is possible to speed up the decryption of our scheme to the equivalent of 1.3 ElGamal decryption exponentiations.

6   Identification Scheme

In this section we present a *three-pass honest verifier zero knowledge proof of knowledge protocol* that can be used as an interactive identification protocol. It can also be converted into a signature scheme in the usual way to accompany the new public key cryptosystem.

The protocol is run between two entities: a prover P and a verifier V. Let PK be the set of all public keys $\{p, g_0, g_1\}$ generated by the Key Generation algorithm of Sect. 4. Let $SK(pk)$ be the secret key corresponding to $pk \in PK$. For every

$pk \in PK$ the protocol allows P to prove to V knowledge of the corresponding $SK(pk) = \{\alpha_0, \alpha_1\}$, and hence of the factorisation of $p - 1$. As before, i takes values in $\{0, 1\}$.

Protocol 1.

1. P chooses a random number $r \in \mathbb{Z}_n$, computes $r_i = r \bmod q_i$, $x_i = g_i^{r_i}$ and sends x_i to V.
2. V picks $s_i \in_R \{0, \ldots, 2^t - 1\}$, where $t < k = |q_i|$ is defined to be large enough so that guessing s_i is hard. V then sends s_i to P.
3. P computes $u = r_0 s_0 \alpha_0 + r_1 s_1 \alpha_1 \bmod n$ and sends it to V.
4. V checks that $x_i = g_i^{u s_i^{-1} \bmod n}$ for $i = 0, 1..$

Theorem 3. *Protocol 1 is a proof of knowledge for the relation $R = \{(pk, SK(pk)) : pk \in PK\}$.*

Proof. We use the definition of Bellare and Goldreich [2]. Let P be any prover (not necessarily following the protocol), and $p(pk)$ be the probability that P convinces V to accept the claim that P knows $SK(pk)$. Let $\kappa(pk)$ represent the error probability of V, i.e. the probability that V incorrectly accepts on P's claim on input pk). The above protocol is an interactive proof of knowledge system if the following is satisfied:

1. *Completeness* If P and V follow the protocol, then the probability that V accepts is 1.
2. *Validity* For every $pk \in PK$, there exists an expected polynomial time Turing machine K (*knowledge extractor*) *having oracle access to P, that outputs $SK(pk)$ or a special symbol $\perp$ (for failure), such that if $p(pk) > \kappa(pk)$*

$$Pr[K(pk; P) = SK(pk)] \geq p(pk) - k(pk).$$

The completeness of the protocol is straightforward to verify. In what follows, we construct a *knowledge extractor* K that satisfies the validity requirement as long as the prover will answer correctly to at least two oracle queries. Oracle access means that that K has rewindable black-box access to P. Thus K can query P on any input pk and challenges s_0, s_1 and obtains the corresponding transcripts. Although K has no access to the randomness of P, it can "rewind" any protocol runs and reuse the same randomness. In our case, $\kappa(pk) \geq 2^{-2t}$, i.e. V accepts incorrectly with a probability at least that of guessing s_i.

Knowledge Extractor K

1. Given $pk \in PK$, compute $(x_0, x_1) = x(pk; P)$, where $x(pk; P)$ is the first message output by P on input pk.
2. Choose (s_0, s_1) at random in the same way as V does.
3. Compute $u = u(s_0, s_1, pk; P)$, where $u(s_0, s_1, pk; P)$ is the output of P after receiving the challenge (s_0, s_1).

4. If $x_i = g_i^{us_i^{-1}}$, fix s_i and u and continue to step 5, else output $\perp$ and halt.
5. Rewind P to the state just after step 1. Choose another random pair $(\overline{s}_0, \overline{s}_1)$ in the same way as V does.
6. Compute $\overline{u} = u(\overline{s}_0, \overline{s}_1, pk; P)$.
7. If $x_i = g_i^{\overline{u}\,\overline{s}_i^{-1}}$, then fix $\overline{s}_i$ and $\overline{u}$, and go to step 8, else output $\perp$ and halt.
8. Solve the following equations for $(a_0, a_1) \in \mathbb{Z}_n^2$

$$u \equiv s_0 a_0 + s_1 a_1 \pmod{n}$$
$$\overline{u} \equiv \overline{s}_0 a_0 + \overline{s}_1 a_1 \pmod{n}.$$

If no solution is found repeat from step 5.
9. Calculate $r = a_0 + a_1 \bmod n$. If r has no inverse $\bmod n$, then output $\perp$ and halt.
10. Compute

$$\alpha_0 = r^{-1} a_0 \bmod n$$
$$\alpha_1 = r^{-1} a_1 \bmod n.$$

11. Output $\{\alpha_0, \alpha_1\}$ and halt.

Firstly, let's verify that when u and $\overline{u}$ result in V accepting, then the output corresponds indeed with $SK(pk)$. u and $\overline{u}$ result in V accepting if and only if the following holds:

$$x_i = g_i^{us_i^{-1}} \quad\text{and}\quad x_i = g_i^{\overline{u}\,\overline{s}_i^{-1}},$$

which, in turn, occurs if and only if

$$u = s_0 a_0 + s_1 a_1 \bmod n = s_0 r_0 \alpha_0 + s_1 \alpha_1 \bmod n$$

and

$$\overline{u} = \overline{s}_0 a_0 + \overline{s}_1 a_1 \bmod n = \overline{s}_0 r_0 \alpha_0 + \overline{s}_1 r_1 \alpha_1 \bmod n,$$

where $r_i = \log_{g_i} x_i$. It is not difficult to see from Fact 2 that

$$r^{-1} = (r_0 \alpha_0 + r_1 \alpha_1)^{-1} \bmod n = r_0^{-1} \alpha_0 + r_1^{-1} \alpha_1 \bmod n$$

and that therefore

$$r^{-1} a_i \bmod n = (r_0^{-1} \alpha_0 + r_1^{-1} \alpha_1) r_i \alpha_i \bmod n = \alpha_i .$$

To prove validity, we further have to establish the probability that u and $\overline{u}$ occur such that K outputs $SK(pk)$. Given a fixed u for which V accepts, this probability will be inversely proportional to the acceptance probability of V as long as P gives an accepting response to at least one other query. We can use an identical proof to that used in examples of Bellare and Goldreich [2] for this. Alternatively P only gives an accepting response to one query for this u. In this case the knowledge error function is equal to the acceptance probability of 2^{-2t}.   □

Theorem 4. *Protocol 1 is honest verifier zero-knowledge.*

Proof. To prove Protocol 1 is honest verifier zero-knowledge we show that there exists a simulator S that on input $pk \in PK$ produces conversations that are indistinguishable from real conversations between a prover and verifier following Protocol 1 faithfully on input pk.

Simulator

1. Choose a random number $u \in \mathbb{Z}_n$.
2. Choose random $s_i \in \{0, \ldots, 2^t - 1\}$.
3. Compute $x_i = g_i^{u(s_i^{-1} \bmod n)}$
4. Output $(x_0, x_1; s_0, s_1; u)$

Notice that since $2^t < q_i$, there always exist $s_i^{-1} \bmod n$. It is not difficult to verify that the distribution $< (x_0, x_1; s_0, s_1; u) >$ output by S is identical to the distribution of the conversations between an honest prover and honest verifier following Protocol 1. □

Protocol 1 can be used as an identification protocol in the same way as for example Schnorr's identification scheme [16]. A user P wanting to authenticate to another party V, uses Protocol 1 to convince V that he knows the secret corresponding to a public key $pk \in PK$. The public key needs to be bound to the identity of P using some external procedure, such as certification by a trusted third party. Furthermore, Protocol 1 can be turned into a signature scheme, also in the same way that Schnorr's identification scheme is converted into a signature scheme by substituting the random challenges for $s_i = \mathcal{H}(x_i, m) \in \{0, \ldots, 2^t - 1\}$, for example, where $\mathcal{H}$ is an appropriate one-way hash function (see [16]).

7   Conclusion

We have presented a new public key cryptosystem and associated identification scheme based on the subgroup membership problem. We have proven that the cryptosystem provides semantic security in the standard model while the identification scheme is an honest verifier zero knowledge proof of knowledge. These schemes therefore add to the growing toolkit of provable security primitives that can be used by the protocol designer looking to build complex secure systems with a sound basis.

Further scrutiny of the subgroup membership problem, on which security of the cryptosystem is based, will enable greater confidence in its intractability. At the same time it may be fruitful to explore the possibilities of using the new schemes in various applications.

We have not yet investigated the suitability of the new PKC to achieve the stronger notion of *chosen ciphertext security* (see [1] for example). We note, however, that in the random oracle model we can obtain chosen ciphertext security by applying, for instance, the generic scheme of Fujisaki and Okamoto [8] at practically no computational extra cost.

Acknowledgements. We would like to thank Kapali Viswanathan for his helpful comments and suggestions.

References

[1] M. Bellare, A. Desai, D. Pointcheval, and P. Rogaway. Relations among notions of security for public-key encryption schemes. In *Advances of Cryptology – Crypto '98*, pages 26–45.

[2] M. Bellare and O. Goldreich. On defining proofs of knowledge. In *Advances in Cryptology – CRYPTO '92*, pages 390–420.

[3] M. Bellare and P. Rogaway. Optimal asymmetric encryption – how to encrypt with RSA. In*Advances in Cryptology – EUROCRYPT '94*, pages 92–111.

[4] D. Boneh. The Decision Diffie-Hellman problem. In *Third Algorithmic Number Theory Symposium*, LNCS 1423, pages 48–63.

[5] R. Cramer and V. Shoup. A practical public key cryptosystem provably secure against adaptive chosen ciphertext attack. In *Advances of Cryptology – Crypto '98*, pages 13–25.

[6] W. Diffie and M. Hellman. New directions in cryptography. *IEEE Transactions on Information Theory*, IT-22(6):644–654, November 1976.

[7] T. ElGamal. A public key cryptosystem and a signature scheme based on discrete logarithms. *IEEE Transactions on Information Theory*, IT-31(4):469–472, July 1985.

[8] E. Fujisaki and T. Okamoto. How to enhance the security of public-key encryption at minimum cost. In *PKC '99*, LNCS 1560, pages 53–68.

[9] S. Goldwasser and S. Micali. Probabilistic encryption. *Journal of Computer Security*, 28:270–299, 1984.

[10] A. Lenstra and E. Verheul. Selecting cryptographic key sizes. In *PKC 2000*, LNCS 1751, pages 446–465.

[11] A. Menezes, P. van Oorschot, and S. Vanstone. *Handbook of applied cryptography*. CRC Press series on discrete mathematics and its applications. CRC Press, 1997.

[12] T. Okamoto and S. Uchiyama. A new public key cryptosystem as secure as factoring. In *Advances in Cryptology – EUROCRYPT '98*, pages 308–318.

[13] P. Paillier. Public-key cryptosystems based on composite degree residuosity classes. In *Advances in Cryptology – EUROCRYPT '99*, pages 223–238.

[14] M. Rabin. Digitalized signatures and public key functions as intractable as factoring. Technical Report TR-212, Laboratory of Computer Science LCS, Massachusetts Institute of Technology MIT, January 1979.

[15] R. Rivest, A. Shamir, and L. Adleman. A method for obtaining digital signatures and public-key cryptosystems. *Communications of the ACM*, 21(2):120–126, February 1978.

[16] C. Schnorr. Efficient signature generation by smart cards. *Journal of Cryptology*, 4(3):161–174, 1991.

[17] A. Yamamura and T. Saito. Private information retrieval based on the subgroup membership problem. In *ACISP 2001*, LNCS 2119, pages 206–220.

On a Network Security Model for the Secure Information Flow on Multilevel Secure Network

Ki-Yoong Hong, Ph.D., P.E.[1] and Chul Kim[2]

[1] President of KSIGN and SECUVE, 3F., Cheil Venture Plaza, 728-8, Yeoksam-Dong, Kangnam-Gu, Seoul, 135-080, Korea
[2] Professor, Department of Mathematics, Kwangwoon University, 447-1, Wolgye-Dong, Nowoon-Gu, Seoul, 139-701, Korea

Abstract. We propose a new network security model for secure information flow on multilevel secure network by defining simple security flow concepts. The proposed network security model enables the network to withstand the cascade vulnerability. Therefore, the proposed security model is secure against the potential cascade vulnerability problems.

1 Introduction

Various kinds of network security models have been introduced such as DOD IIS/DNSIX [1], Secure Military Message Systems (SMMS) [2], X.400 MHS Security Model [3][4], Secure Data Network System (SDNS) [5], Secure Unified Message System (SUMS) [6], Secure Communications Service Elements (SCSE) [7], and other approaches [8][9][10][11]. Recently, SNMPv3 requires the user-based security model[12] which defines the elements of procedure for providing SNMP message level security. Therefore there have been many results for network security models based on Mathematical modeling[13].

However, previously developed network security models are unlikely to have a capability to prevent the network system from being violated against the cascading. It seems to be caused by the nature of the security models. Since the security properties of the designed security models are mostly focused on the access control, partly on the information flow, it is insufficient to prevent the illegal information flows on multilevel secure network. This characteristic implies that the information flow can take place as legal without any violation of the access control policy and mechanisms.

In this paper, a new network security model are proposed for secure information flow on multilevel secure network. The proposed network security model enables the network to withstand the cascade vulnerability. Therefore, the proposed security model is secure against the potential cascade vulnerability problems.

S. Qing, T. Okamoto, and J. Zhou (Eds.): ICICS 2001, LNCS 2229, pp. 364–370, 2001.

2   Preliminaries and Assumptions

TCSEC presents the fundamental security policies for the trusted systems. The security policies can be composed of MAC policy, DAC policy, label policy and so on. We introduce a new security policy, so called, a cascade flow control (CFC) policy. The CFC policy states the security requirements for preventing the cascade vulnerability problem. Definition 1 and Definition 2 state the concepts of the*cascade-secure path* and the *cascade-vulnerable path*. Definition 3 describes the CFC informally.

Definition 1. Let the object imply the node or the host on the network. For given objects i and j on a network, let the path (i,j) be *cascade-secure path* if either the object i's TCB(Trusted Computing Base) rating or the object j's TCB rating is greater than or equal to the TCB requirement value for a pair of the object i's maximum sensitivity and the object j's minimum sensitivity.

Statement of Definition 1 can be rewritten formally as follows:

Let S_j's be an elements in the set of data sensitivity level and let C_k's be an elements in the set of user clearance level. Hence $T(S_j, C_k)$ is the table containing the TCB requirements. Let $j \to k$ denote the *cascade-secure path* where

$$r_j \geq T(Max(S_j), Min(C_k))$$

or

$$r_k \geq T(Max(S_j), Min(C_k))$$

holds, where r_i is the TCB rating for each object i.

From the previous definition of the cascading path, the *cascade-vulnerable path* is defined in order to distinguish it from the *cascade-secure path*.

Definition 2. Let $\bar{j} \to \bar{k}$ denote the *cascade-vulnerable path* where

$$T(Max(S_j), Min(C_k)) > r_j$$

and

$$T(Max(S_j), Min(C_k)) > r_k$$

hold.

Definition 3. (CFC Policy) The CFC is a method for information flow control based on the relationship between objects' accreditation ranges for a given path on a network. The CFC policy requires the necessary information flow condition as follows:

An object i can transfer the information, that is sent from a source object j, to an object q only if the paths (j, i) and (j, q) are cascade-secure paths where the object q is the next object for routing.

Let j and k be the source object and the destination object respectively. Let i be the intermediate object to route the information. Let q be the object

i's neighborhood object for routing in the direction of k. From the object i's view point, the object j's information can be transmitted to the object q via the object i if the paths (j,i) and (j,q) are the cascade-secure paths. In this case, it does not matter whether the path (i,q) is the cascade-vulnerable path or the cascade-secure path. The path (j,i) or (j,q) does not seem to be the cascade-vulnerable path even though the path (i,q) is the cascade-vulnerable path. Therefore, two paths (j,i) and (j,q) are sufficient to formulate the CFC policy.

From the view point of the next object q, two paths (j,q) and (j,k) will be checked to verify whether these paths are the cascade-vulnerable paths or not. In this case, the information can be sent from the object j to the object k via the object q if the paths (j,q) and (j,k) are the cascade-secure paths.

3   The Description of a Proposed Network Security Model

In this section, a network security model is formally described such that it has a capability of the secure information flow. Let N denote the given network. Let O_j denote the set of information objects in the j's side. Let's assume that a system state v of a given network N is a 3-tuple $< J, I, \mathcal{Q} >$ where J, I and $\mathcal{Q}$ are the identities to represent the source object, the intermediate object and the next object for routing, respectively.

Definition 4. (The *Cascade Flow* Property) A system state $v =< j, i, q >$ holds the *cascade flow* property **if**

$$j \rightarrow i, j \rightarrow q, o \in O_j, o \notin O_i, \text{ and } o \notin O_q$$

implies

$$O_i = O_i \cup \{o\} \text{ and } O_q = O_q \cup \{o\}$$

Let x, a system request, be a 2-tuple $< OP, \mathcal{Q} >$ where OP is a set of operations and $\mathcal{Q}$ is a next object of a given path. Here OP denotes a set of operation as $OP = \{in, out, route\}$.

1 Let $in(j,i)$ denote the i's receive operation from the direction of j.
2 Let $out(i,q)$ denote the i's transmit operation to the direction of q.
3 Let $route(j, i, q)$ denote the i's route operation from j to the q.

The operation $route(j, i, q)$ implies that $in(j, i)$ and $out(i, q)$.
The following definitions will be used to represent the disallowed operation:

1 Let $\overline{in}(j, i)$ denote the disallowed receive operation. It means that i can not receive the information from j.
2 Let $\overline{out}(i, q)$ denote the disallowed transmit operation. It means that i can not transmit the information to q.
3 Let $\overline{route}(j, i, q)$ denote the disallowed route operation. It means that i can not route the information from j to the q. The $\overline{route}(j, i, q)$ implies the following one of cases:

$\overline{in}(j,\ i)$ and $out(i,\ q)$;
$in(j,\ i)$ and $\overline{out}(i,\ q)$;
$\overline{in}(j,\ i)$ and $\overline{out}(i,\ q)$;

The above three cases should be distinguished to formulate the network security model. These three are called $\overline{route_{in}}(j,\ i,\ q), \overline{route_{out}}(j,\ i,\ q)$, and $\overline{route_{io}}(j,\ i,\ q)$ for each case, respectively. In the following definition, we define the state secure in terms of $route(j,\ i,\ q)$ which denote the i's operation between state j and q

Definition 5. A system state $v\ =\ <j,\ i,\ q>$ is *state-secure* if $\forall j,\ i$ and $q \in N, o \in O_j\ :\ j \to i$ and $j \to q\ \Longleftrightarrow\ out(j,i),\ route(j,\ i,\ q),\ in(i,\ q), O_i = O_i \cup \{o\}$, and $O_q = O_q \cup \{o\}$.

Let's denote a system $\sum$ be a 4-tuple $<X,\ V,\ v_0,\ \phi>$ where X is a set of system requests, V is a set of system states, $v_0 \in V$ is an initial system state, and ϕ is a system transformation, that is a function of the form $X\ \times V\ \to\ V$.

Definition 6. A trace, $\prod$, which is a function of the form $X\ \times V$, of a system $\sum$ is defined as follows:

$\prod(0)$ *means* $<x,\ v_0>$ as an initial trace,
$\prod(1)$ *means* $<x,\ v_1>$ *if* $\phi < x,\ v_0>\ = v_1$,
$\cdots$
$\prod(n-1)$ *means* $<x,\ v_{n-1}>$ *if* $\phi < x,\ v_{n-2}>\ = v_{n-1}$, *and,*
$\prod(n)$ *means* $<x,\ v_n>$ *if* $\phi < x,\ v_{n-1}>\ = v_n$

Definition 7. A transform ϕ is *cascade-secure* **if and only if** it meets the following conditions:

for $\forall x \in X,\ \forall v$ and $v^* \in V$, and $\phi < x,\ v>\ = v^*$,

1 $\overline{j}^* \to \overline{i},\ o^* \notin O_{j^*}$, and $o^* \notin O_{i^*}$ implies $\overline{out}(j^*,\ i^*),\ \overline{in}(j^*,\ i^*),\ o^* \notin O_{i^*}$.
2 $j^* \to i^*,\ j^* \to q^*,\ o^* \in O_{j^*},\ o^* \notin O_{i^*}$, and $o^* \notin O_{q^*}$ implies $out(j^*,\ i^*),\ route(j^*,\ i^*,\ q^*),\ in(i^*,\ q^*),\ O_{i^*} = O_{i^*} \cup \{o^*\}$, and $O_{q^*} = O_{q^*} \cup \{o^*\}$.
3 $j^* \to i^*,\ \overline{j}^* \to \overline{q}^*,\ o^* \in O_{j^*},\ o^* \notin O_{i^*}$, and $o^* \notin O_{q^*}$ implies $out(j^*,\ i^*),\ \overline{route_{out}}(j^*,\ i^*,\ q^*),\ o^* \in O_j,\ o^* \in O_{i^*}$, and $o^* \notin O_{q^*}$

We say a transform ϕ is *transform-secure* **if and only if** it is *cascade-secure* and a trace $\prod$ is *secure* if all its states are *state-secure* and its transformations are *transform-secure*. Also A system $\sum < X, V, v_0, \phi >$ is *secure* if each of its traces is secure.

Since we already define the security of a system in terms of trace, we have to demonstrate the network model is secure against the cascade vulnerability in every states. In the following, a Basic Security Theorem is presented to prove that the proposed network security model is secure against the cascade vulnerability during the information flows. We need the mathematical induction proof on the number of states in the proposed network model to show it is secure in terms of trace as we defined.

Theorem. *Every state of a system $\sum < X, V, \nu_0, \phi >$ is secure if ν_0 is secure and ϕ is transform-secure.*

Proof.
We apply the mathematical induction on n.

1 Let ν_0 be secure. Let $\nu_0 = < j^0, i^0, q^0 >$. From the definition 5, $j^0 \to i^0$ and $j^0 \to q^0$ hold, where $o^0 \in O_{j^0}$. Then,
$out(j^0, i^0)$, $route(j^0, i^0, q^0)$, $in(i^0, q^0)$, $O_{i^0} = O_{i^0} \cup \{ o^0 \}$, and $O_{q^0} = O_{q^0} \cup \{o^0\}$.

2 Let $\nu_1 = < j^1, i^1, q^1 >$ where $\phi(x, \nu_0) = \nu_1$. The following cases are considered :

  1 By the condition 1 of Definition 7:

$$j^1 \to \overline{i}^1, o^1 \in O_{j^1}, \text{ and } o^1 \notin O_{i^1} \Rightarrow \overline{out}(j^1, i^1), \overline{in}(j^1, i^1), \text{ and } o^1 \notin O_{i^1}.$$

This implies ν_1 is secure.

  2 By the condition 2 of Definition 7:

$$j^1 \to i^1, j^1 \to q^1, o^1 \in O_{j^1}, o^1 \notin O_{i^1}, \text{ and } o^1 \notin O_{q^1}$$
$$\Rightarrow out(j^1, i^1), route(j^1, i^1, q^1), in(i^1, q^1), O_{i^1} = O_{i^1} \cup \{o^1\}, \text{ and } O_{q^1} = O_{q^1} \cup \{o^1\}.$$
This implies ν_1 is secure.

  3 By the condition 3 of Definition 7:

$$j^1 \to i^1, \overline{j}^1 \to \overline{q}^1, o^1 \in O_{j^1}, o^1 \notin O_{i^1}, \text{ and } o^1 \notin O_{q^1}$$
$$\Rightarrow out(j^1, i^1), \overline{route_{out}}(j^1, i^1, q^1), o^1 \in O_{j^1}, o^1 \in O_{i^1}, \text{ and } o^1 \notin O_{q^1}.$$
This implies ν_1 is secure.

By 1,2 and 3, ν_1 is secure.

3 Suppose that ν_{n-2} be secure (It is the induction hypothesis).
Then, $\nu_{n-1} = < j^{n-1}, i^{n-1}, q^{n-1} >$ where $\phi(x, \nu_{n-2}) = \nu_{n-1}$. The following cases are considered:

  1 By the condition 1 of Definition 7:

$$\overline{j}^{n-1} \to \overline{i}^{n-1}, o^{n-1} \in O_{j^{n-1}}, \text{ and } o^{n-1} \notin O_{i^{n-1}}$$
$$\Rightarrow \overline{out}(j^{n-1}, i^{n-1}), \overline{in}(j^{n-1}, i^{n-1}), \text{ and } o^{n-1} \notin O_{i^{n-1}}.$$
This implies ν_{n-1} is secure.

2 By the condition 2 of Definition 7:

$$j^{n-1} \to i^{n-1}, j^{n-1} \to q^{n-1}, o^{n-1} \in O_{j^{n-1}}, o^{n-1} \notin O_{i^{n-1}}, \text{ and } o^{n-1} \notin O_{q^{n-1}}$$

$$\Rightarrow out(j^{n-1}, i^{n-1}), route(j^{n-1}, i^{n-1}, q^{n-1}), in(i^{n-1}, q^{n-1}),$$

$$O_{i^{n-1}} = O_{i^{n-1}} \cup \{o^{n-1}\}, \text{ and } O_{q^{n-1}} = O_{q^{n-1}} \cup \{o^{n-1}\}.$$

This implies ν_{n-1} is secure.

3 By the condition 3 of Definition 7:

$$j^{n-1} \to i^{n-1}, \bar{j}^{n-1} \to \bar{q}^{n-1}, o^{n-1} \in O_{j^{n-1}}, o^{n-1} \notin O_{i^{n-1}}, \text{ and } o^{n-1} \notin O_{q^{n-1}}$$

$$\Rightarrow out(j^{n-1}, i^{n-1}), \overline{route_{out}}(j^{n-1}, i^{n-1}, q^{n-1}),$$

$$o^{n-1} \in O_{j^{n-1}}, o^{n-1} \in O_{i^{n-1}}, \text{ and } o^{n-1} \notin O_{q^{n-1}}.$$

This implies ν_{n-1} is secure.

By 1, 2 and 3, ν_{n-1} is secure.

From the results of the above **1,2** and **3**, using mathematical induction hypothesis, every state of a system $\sum < X, Y, \nu_0, \phi >$ is secure.

$\square$

4   Conclusion

In this paper, we propose the network secure model for secure information flow on multilevel secure network. At first, we define cascade-secure path and cascade-vulnerable path to induce a new information flow control policy. Even it is based on the new security policy assumption, called cascade flow control policy, the policy is practical in terms of information flow. It could be cooperative with role-based (access) control policy and applicable to the actual network security management product. And then, we define state secure of a system using trace which is a history of each state according to information flow. Finally we prove that the proposed model is secure by the mathematical induction on the number of states.

The proposed network security model enables the network to withstand the cascade vulnerability. Therefore, the proposed security model is secure against the potential cascade vulnerability problems.

References

1. D. E. Bell, "Security Policy Modeling for the Next-Generation Packet Switch," Proceedings of 1988 IEEE Computer Society Symposium on Research in Security and Privacy, Oakland, CA, pp. 212 - 216, May 1988.
2. J. Landauer, C. Heitmeyer, and J. McLean, "A Security Model for Military Message Systems," ACM Trans. on Computer Systems, Vol. 2, No. 3, pp. 198 - 222, Aug. 1984.
3. CCITT, Data Communication Networks Message Handling Systems, CCITT Recommendations, X.400 - X.420, Nov. 1988.
4. CCITT, Data Communication Networks Directory Recommendations, X.509, Nov. 1988.
5. Charles Dinkel, "SDNS Network, Transport, and Message Security Protocols," NISTIR 90-44250, U.S. DoC NIST, Gaithersburg, MD, Feb. 1990.
6. S. W. Kim and D. K. Kim, "A Message Server Access Control Model Enforcing Multi Security Policies," JW-ISC'95, Japan, Jan. 1995.
7. Nakao Kouji and Kenji Suzukki, "Proposal on a Secure Communications Service Elements (SCSE) in the OSI Application," IEEE Journal on Seleected Areas in Communication, May 1989.
8. J. W. Freeman and R. B. Neel, "An Internet System Security Policy and Formal Model," Proceedings of the 11th National Computer Security Conference, pp. 10 - 19, Oct. 1988.
9. T. D. Graubart, "On the Need for a Third Form of Access Control," Proceedings of the 13th National Computer Security Conference, Baltimore, MD, pp. 296 - 303, Oct. 1993.
10. Ruth Nelson, "SDNS Services and Architecture," Adv. in Cryptology-CRYPTO'89 Proceedings (Lecture Notes in Computer Science 435), G. Doos, J. Hartmanis, and G. Brassard, Editors, Springer-Verlag, pp. 348 - 352, 1989.
11. Vijay Varadharajan, "Network Security Policy Models," Proceedings of Auscript '90, Australia, pp. 74 - 95, 1990.
12. Network Working Group, The Internet Society," RFP 2274 : User-based security model (USM) for SNMPv3, Jan. 1998
13. V. A. Skormin, Leonard J. Popyack(editors), " Int'l Assurance in Computer Networks, " LNCS 2052, May 2001

NIDS Research Based on Artificial Immunology

Wenjian Luo, Xianbin Cao, and Xufa Wang

Department of Computer Science and Technology,
University of Science and Technology of China, HeFei, 230026, China
wjluo@mail.ustc.edu.cn {xbcao, xfwang}@ustc.edu.cn

Abstract. Current network intrusion detection systems are of low intelligence level and have the main deficiency as being unable to detect new intrusive behaviors of unknown signatures.

The protection mechanism of natural immune system has brought us inspirations to design a novel network intrusion detection system. The research on modeling a NIDS with natural immune system just started, including the negative selection algorithm proposed by S. Forrest and the basic system model proposed by J. Kim. Based on their works, this paper proposed a novel system structure including affinity mutation, which was used to improve the performance of anomaly detection, and established an basic system based on artificial immunology. This paper stressed on the novel construction and testing experiments. Result of the experiments proved that the application of the protection mechanism of natural immune system to network intrusion detection system has an exciting perspective.

1   Introduction

The NIDS, a kind of developing system, plays an important role of network security[1, 2]. The protection mechanism of natural immune system is an excellent real paradigm for research on network intrusion detection, especially the mechanism of recognizing non-self pathogens (namely antigen) of the immune recognition, immune evolution, immune regulation mechanism and immune memory mechanism and others. All of them can be extracted and modeled to guide the construction of a novel NIDS. This relative research has just started, D. Dasguptas has a good summarization in his paper[3]. The typical works include: S. Forrest put forward the self/non-self distinguish algorithm based on T-Cell immune response mechanism[4]; S. Hofmeyr analyzed the algorithm offered by S. Forrest and made an experiment about SYN attack[5]; J. Kim analyzed the work of S. Forrest and provided an possible network intrusion detection model[6, 7, 8].

Based on the above works and deep exploration into natural immune system, network intrusion means, network intrusion detection model and system based on artificial immunology, we design and establish a NIDS prototype. With regard at self-learning, based on the work of gene library evolution proposed by J. Kim, we apply affinity mutation to our NIDS, which mainly reflect the evolution

S. Qing, T. Okamoto, and J. Zhou (Eds.): ICICS 2001, LNCS 2229, pp. 371–375, 2001.
© Springer-Verlag Berlin Heidelberg 2001

function of immune system and strongly improve the ability of detecting possible attacks on our NIDS. This paper describes the modules of the system and the corresponding mechanism and offers the result of the experiments.

This paper is organized as follows. Section 2 introduces components of the NIDS based on artificial immunology and corresponding principles; section 3 is the experiment and experimental result; the last section is the conclusion and perspective.

2 The Components of the NIDS Based on Artificial Immunology

2.1 Introduction of Natural Immune Mechanism

The basic function of natural immune system is to distinguish self from non-self, classify the non-self and then eliminate them[9]. Natural immune system consists of immune organs, immune cells and immune molecules. Immune organs consists of central immune organs and peripheral immune organs. Central immune organs are composed of bone marrow and thymus, where lymphocytes and other immune cells generate, differentiate and mutate. While Peripheral immune organs include lymphocytes, spleen, and catarrh tissues, where T-cell and B-cell settle and proliferate, and where immune system responses to antigen's stimulation.

Immune response can be classified into primary immune response and secondary immune response. When the immune system is confronted with an unknown pathogen (namely an antigen), it can selectively generate many antibodies by bone marrow and thymus to recognize and analyze the antigen; and can memorize it after the antigen is recognized. This is the process of primary immune response, which normally needs a long period of time. Secondary immune response, which normally needs a short period of time, means that immune system can give out immune response quickly when the similar antigen intrudes again, activate the corresponding antibody, and eliminate the antigen by complex chemical responses.

During he course of immune response, the activated immune cells undergo affinity mutation to recognize the antigen. Through affinity mutation, the immune system can generate lots of more efficient antibodies to recognize the antigen step by step.

2.2 The Components of the NIDS Based on Artificial Immunology

As the Figure 1 shows, like the model of J. Kim[6, 7, 8], this system is composed of PIDS and SIDS. PIDS produces detector sets and send them to all secondary intrusion detection systems. SIDS detects the network data traffic where it locates, returns the result to PIDS, and drives PIDS to evolve. PIDS and SIDS cooperate with each other in our NIDS and make up of an NIDS, which possesses high self-adaptive ability and can recognize both known and unknown signatures.

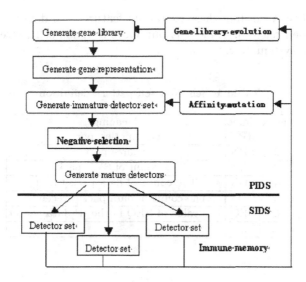

Fig. 1. Structure of NIDS based on artificial immunology

Affinity mutation driven by the feedback from SIDS to PIDS is our best innovation, mainly, by which immature detectors have a good performance. Affinity mutation is the most important evolution approach to improving the self-adaptive ability in natural immune system and our NIDS based on artificial immunology.

2.3 The Feedback Learning Ability

As Figure 1 shows, the affinity mutation and gene library evolution are used to improve the detection probability. For gene library evolution, you can get enough information from reference [6, 7, 8]. Here we explain the affinity mutation.

Firstly activation threshold and non-self threshold are defined. The signature of current network traffic will be regard as non-self if the affinity between the signature and any detector are over, then this signature will be feedback for affinity mutation and gene library evolution. If the affinity between the signature and any detector are over, this signature will be feedback for affinity mutation. By affinity mutation, the system generate lots of similar detectors to justify whether current network traffic is normal or not, just like the generation of the antibody when an antigen intrudes in natural immune system.

3   Experiment

3.1   System Description

By analyzing the TCP/IP protocols and all kinds of attacks, we extract from network data traffic such features that can exactly reflect current network behaviors as the total counts of packets, the total counts of bytes, the total counts of SYN packets. According these extracted features, we define the self-pattern and the non-self pattern. Table 1 is our basic self/non-self pattern adopted in our prototype system now.

Table 1. Self/Non-self pattern definition

Index	Name	Meaning
1	RPN	Destination port
2	SPN	Source port
3	SS	The count of SYN packet
4	SDN	The count of data packet sent
5	RDN	The count of data packet received
6	SEQ	The value of SEQ in the IP data packet
...	...	...

As a NIDS, our system can detect various attacks aiming at the leaks of TCP/IP, and can also detect attacks that have a great effect on network performance, including ports scanning and most Dos attacks.

3.2   Practical Experiment

We build an actual environment to test the ability of AIS-based IDS. On our experimental platform, PIDS is placed on gateway, every SIDS is placed on a terminal of internal network. In our experiment, we use only one SIDS.

Table 2 shows some results of our experiment.

After a lot of experiments, the abilities of this NIDS based on artificial immunology is not bad, especially the ability of recognizing unknown intrusions. It is necessary to note that our IDS dosen't know initially any intrusive signatures, and that the system can learn to detect all attacks by self-signatures and non-self signatures learned before.

It must be noted that SIDS in a terminal can be configured to monitor not only the network behaviors of terminal itself, but also the behaviors of the subnet that it belongs to.

4   Conclusion

Nowadays, network security is an urgent problem. Current network intrusion detection systems can't meet practical requirements. Natural immune system is a real good example to design the defensive mechanism of our open and fragile network, especially IDS.

This paper introduces a feasible structure of NIDS based on artificial immunology and its corresponding basic inspirations from biologic immune system, and put forward a new recognition algorithm and analyzes characteristics

Table 2. Some results of real experiment

Attack type	Attack tools(running system)	AIS(Can or can't)
scanport	Portsacn(win)	Yes
	Haktak(win)	Yes
	Netfox(win)	Yes
	Scan.c(linux)	Yes
	Twwwscan.exe(win)	Yes
Tear Drop	Teardrop.c(linux)	Yes
SYN	Syn.c(linux)	Yes
	Running 2 hours without attacks (heavy network traffic daytime)	There exists false alerts
	Running 8 hours without attacks (light weight network traffic at night)	No false alerts

of the system. Practical experiments prove that the design of detection technologies based on protective mechanism of natural immune system has a promising future.

The ultimate purpose of our artificial immune research is to extract practical models of theories and engineering for network security. It has just started, this work is the first step, and there is much more work to do in the future.

References

1. S. Kumar: Classification and Detection of Computer Intrusions. PH.D thesis, Purdue University (1995)
2. B. Mukherjee, et al.: Network Intrusion Detection. IEEE Network, Vol.8, 3 (1994) 26-41.
3. D. Dasgupta, et al.: Immunity-Based Systems: A Survey. Proceedings of the IEEE International Conference on Systems, Man and Cybernetics, Orlando, Oct.12-15 (1997)
4. S. Forrest, A.S. Perelson, L. Allen, and R. Cherukuri: Self-Nonself Discrimination in a Computer. Proceedings of the 1994 IEEE Symposium on Research in Security and Privacy, Los Alamitos, IEEE Computer Society Press (1994)
5. S. A. Hofmeyr: An Immunological Model of Distributed Detection and its Application to Computer Security. PhD Dissertation, University of New Mexico (1999)
6. J. Kim, et al.: The Human Immune System and Network Intrusion Detection, 7th European Congress on Intelligent Techniques and Soft Computing(EUFIT'99), Achen,Germany, Sep.13-19 (1999)
7. J. Kim and Bentley P.: The Artificial Immune Model for Network Intrusion Detection (1999). Available at http://www.cs.ucl.ac.uk/staff/J.Kim/EUFITaimmune.ps
8. J. Kim and P. J. Bentley: Negative Selection and Niching by an Artificial Immune System for Network Intrusion Detection (1999). Available at http://www.cs.ucl.ac.uk/staff/J.Kim/EUFITaimmune.ps
9. Qi Anshen, Du Chanying. Nonlinear Models in Immunity. Shanghai Scientific and Technological Education Publishing House, Shanghai (1998)

AMBAR Protocol: Access Management Based on Authorization Reduction*

Oscar Cánovas[1] and Antonio F. Gómez[2]

[1] Department of Computer Engineering
[2] Department of Information and Communications Engineering
University of Murcia, Spain
ocanovas@ditec.um.es, skarmeta@dif.um.es

Abstract. In the last years, SPKI, X.509 attribute certificates, or KeyNote has been proposed as mechanisms to create and specify authorization certificates, access control lists, or security policies in distributed environments. In this work we propose a new protocol able to negotiate and use some of these specifications. AMBAR is a multi-layered protocol based on a request/response model. In general, it provides functionality to transmit resource access requests, the authorization information related to those requests (credentials, ACLs), and results obtained from a certificate chain discovery method or compliance checker. It adds security by acting as a separate security layer inserted between the higher protocols and TCP (or another different transport protocol).

1   Introduction

Public key cryptography is widely recognized as being a fundamental technology on which several essential security services can be built. The Internet community is agreeing on the use of systems based on the X.509 standard [10] and the SSL protocol [2] in order to provide basic security services to e-commerce. In recent years, public key cryptography has been also proposed as a tool for solving the problems related to authorization and access control. SPKI/SDSI [8] and KeyNote [4] propose mechanisms for capturing security-relevant information and binding authorization data to public keys. Recently, the PKIX Working Group published a specification [9] defining the X.509 Attribute Certificates (AC) profile. However, most of the current security protocols do not provide any mechanism to negotiate, transmit, or process data related to authorization certificates or security policies.

In this paper, we propose a new access control protocol able to negotiate and to use authorizations based on public key cryptography. AMBAR (Access Control Based on Authorization Reduction) does not depend on a particular type of authorization or identity-based certificate, and it contains a negotiation phase designed to adapt the protocol to access control scenarios with different requirements (anonymity, confidentiality, credential recovery, etc.). In general,

---

* Partially supported by TEL-IFD97-1426 EU FEDER project (PISCIS)

S. Qing, T. Okamoto, and J. Zhou (Eds.): ICICS 2001, LNCS 2229, pp. 376–380, 2001.
© Springer-Verlag Berlin Heidelberg 2001

it provides functionality to transmit resource access requests, the authorization information related to those requests (credentials, ACLs), and results obtained from a certificate chain discovery method or compliance checker.

2   Protocol Requirements

We consider that the access control protocol must accomplish three main goals. First, it must be independent of applications or higher protocols, i.e., it must support any application-specific authorization, policy or request. Second, it must be able to operate with different identity-based infrastructures and authorization systems. Finally, access requests must be managed efficiently with the purpose of obtaining a good response time.

We can find in the literature some access control systems using authorizations [11]. In general, these systems process requests individually, i.e., there is not an implicit concept of protocol session, and therefore every request is transmitted together with the related credentials, ACLs, authorization decisions, etc. This situation is specially problematic when the communication is performed between the same client and server, since most of the exchanged information has been previously transmitted, and some calculations have already been computed. We consider that these protocols should be session-oriented, and they should keep a local cache of the information exchanged in a particular session in order to avoid unnecessary calculations and communications.

Next, we state all the requirements for the protocol. We also include some additional requirements not commented above.

1. The protocol must be able to negotiate which type of identity and authorization certificates will be used.
2. It should offer confidentiality services to protect the transmitted data.
3. The protocol must allow anonymous access to preserve user identity. Additionally, an identified access mode must be implemented too.
4. It must support several credentials distribution methods. In some scenarios, it will be suitable for a client to "push" authorizations to a server, which improves server performance. In other cases, it will be more suitable for a server to request or "pull" the credentials from an issuer or repository.
5. The protocol must provide a method for establishing authorized data streams between clients and servers. Higher level protocols should layer on top this protocol transparently.
6. The design must be modular in order to easily add further functionality.

3   AMBAR Overview

As we will see in this section, we have chosen to create an entirely new protocol layer for authorization. The design has been performed regarding some prudent engineering practices exposed in [1,3].

The AMBAR protocol consists of different components organized, as Figure 1 illustrates, in two layers.

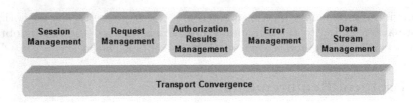

Fig. 1. AMBAR Architecture

- **Session Management module (SM).** This module transmits the client
  and server security preferences, and generates the cryptographic data used
  by the TC layer to protect the subsequent communications (if confidentiality
  was negotiated). Clients and servers negotiate the following parameters:
  - *Symmetric cipher.* Parties select the symmetric cipher and its key length.
  - *Operation mode.* AMBAR supports two operation modes: anonymous
    client mode and fully identified.
  - *Identity-based certificates.* It is possible to select X.509, OpenPGP [5],
    or SDSI certificates.
  - *Authorization-based certificates.* AMBAR supports SPKI certificates,
    PKIX attribute certificates and KeyNote asserts.
  - *Credentials distribution.* Parties can select whether the credentials will
    be provided by the client (push), or will be obtained by the server from
    either a repository or an issuer (pull).
- **Request Management module (RM).** The RM module transmits two
  types of messages: messages related to authorization requests and credentials; and messages related to decisions and ACLs. Contents and the sequence of these messages are determined by the negotiated operation mode
  and the method for distribution of credentials. As we mentioned previously,
  a session-oriented protocol lets the ability to perform some optimizations.
  Therefore, the RM module could be responsible for optimizing access control
  computations.
- **Authorization Results Management module (ARM).** The ARM module generates notifications and transmits the demanded resources. Negative
  notifications are transmitted by the server when the access is denied. If the
  access were granted, there would be two possible response messages: an affir-
  mative notification if the client requested the execution of remote actions; or
  the controlled resource. It also enables (disables) the DSM module when an
  authorization request demanding the establishment (conclusion) of a data
  stream is granted.
- **Error Management module (EM).** Systems use the EM module to signal
  an error or caution condition to the other party in their communication. The
  EM module transmits a severity level and an error description.
- **Data Stream Management module (DSM).** The described re-
  quest/response model is not suitable if we plan to use AMBAR as a transparent layer providing confidentiality, authentication and access control services.

The DSM module, initially disabled, controls the transmission of arbitrary data streams, which are enabled once a request demanding the activation of this module is granted.

- **Transport Convergence module (TC).** The TC module provides a common format to frame SM, RM, ARM, EM, and DSM messages. This module takes the messages to be transmitted, authenticates the contents, then applies the agreed symmetric cipher (always a block-cipher), and encapsulates the results. The cryptographic data used to protect the information is computed by the SM module during the negotiation phase.

4   Some Details of the Protocol

In order to show some details of the messages related to the request/response phase, we will analyze in this section the *push* distribution method using its typical message sequence. Negotiation phase has been omitted due to the lack of space (more information about AMBAR can be found in [6]). Therefore, we will assume that both client and server have already negotiated cryptographic preferences and operation modes. The employed notation is described through the explanation of the messages. We will consider a *transaction* as the different messages related to a specific authorization request, and a *session* as the sequence of different transactions.

In a session based on the *push* method, clients calculate the authorization proof after receiving the ACL controlling the resource from servers.

1	**Request**	$C \Rightarrow S \; \{T_{ID}, T_{Step}, SFlag, Request, [Asserts]^{0..N}\}_{k_{SYMM_s}}^{k_{MAC}}$
2	**ACL**	$S \Rightarrow C \; \{T_{ID}, T_{Step}, ACL\}_{k_{SYMM_c}}^{k_{MAC}}$
3	**Calculation**	$C \Rightarrow S \; \{T_{ID}, T_{Step}, Calculation\}_{k_{SYMM_s}}^{k_{MAC}}$
4	**Neg_Notification**	$S \Rightarrow C \; \{T_{ID}, T_{Step}, Notification\}_{k_{SYMM_c}}^{k_{MAC}}$
4	**Aff_Notification**	$S \Rightarrow C \; \{T_{ID}, Notification\}_{k_{SYMM_c}}^{k_{MAC}}$
4	**Resource**	$S \Rightarrow C \; \{T_{ID}, Resource\}_{k_{SYMM_c}}^{k_{MAC}}$

The *Request* message, generated by the RM module, represents the authorization request formulated by the client. It contains an identifier of transaction T_{ID}, a transaction step identifier T_{Step}, a flag indicating whether this is a request for a data stream ($SFlag$), a set of asserts or authorizations related to the request, and the authorization request. Data are ciphered using K_{SYMM_S}, and are authenticated with K_{MAC} (derived during the SM phase). All messages analyzed in this section will be protected in the same way.

The server response, generated by the RM module, is the *ACL* message. It contains the ACL protecting the resource, the same T_{ID} included in the request, and an incremented transaction step identifier T_{Step}.

Once the client receives the ACL, it creates a certificate chain from its public key to the ACL entry related to the resource. That chain may be composed by authorization and ID certificates, and it is the output of the certificate chain discovery method (or trust management engine). The client-side RM module sends that result to the server in the *Calculation* message.

The final step is the server response to the calculation. If the calculation were wrong, the server would send a *Neg_Notification* message. That message includes the error description (*Notification*), an incremented transaction step T_{Step}, and the T_{ID} identifier (included in all the ARM messages). On the other hand, when the server validates the request, it returns the *Resource* message (when the requested resource is a file, document, etc.) or an *Aff_Notification* message (if the request is for a remote action).

5   Conclusions

We have introduced AMBAR as a new protocol able to negotiate and to use some of the proposed specifications for distributed authorization architectures. It proposes a message format for transmitting authorization information, and it has been designed session-oriented in order to optimize the way the authorization decisions are made (saving unnecessary calculations and transmissions). AMBAR does not depend on a particular type of authorization or identity-based certificate, and it can be easily extended to support future proposals. Currently, AMBAR has been implemented in C++ and it is being tested using authorization certificates based on SPKI [7].

References

1. M. Abadi and R. Needham. Prudent engineering practice for cryptographic protocols. *IEEE Transactions on Software Engineering*, 1(22):6–15, January 1996.
2. A. O. Alan, P. Freier, and P. C. Kocher. *The SSL Protocol Version 3.0*, 1996. Internet Draft.
3. R. Anderson and R. Needham. Robustness principles for public key protocols. Number 963 in Lecture Notes in Computer Science. Springer, 1995.
4. M. Blaze, J. Feigenbaum, J. Ioannidis, and A. Keromytis. *The KeyNote Trust Management System Version 2*, September 1999. Request For Comments (RFC) 2704.
5. J. Callas, L. Donnerhacke, H. Finney, and R.Thayer. *OpenPGP Message Format*, 1998. Request For Comments (RFC) 2440.
6. O. Canovas and A. F. Gomez. AMBAR Protocol: Access Management Based on Authorization Reduction. Technical report, University of Murcia, May 2001. UM-DITEC-2001-7.
7. Intel Corporation. *Common Data Security Architecture (CDSA)*. World Wide Web, http://developer.intel.com/ial/security, 2001.
8. C. Ellison, B. Frantz, B. Lampson, R. Rivest, B. Thomas, and T. Ylonen. *SPKI certificate theory*, September 1999. Request For Comments (RFC) 2693.
9. S. Farrel and R. Housley. *An Internet Attribute Certificate Profile for Authorization*. Internet Engineering Task Force, 2001. draft-ietf-pkix-ac509prof-06.
10. R. Housley, W. Ford, and D. Solo. *Internet Public Key Infrastructure, Part I: X.509 Certificate and CRL Profile*, January 1999. Request for Comments (RFC) 2459.
11. A. Maywah. An implementation of a secure web client using SPKI/SDSI certificates. Master's thesis, M.I.T., May 2000.

Chinese Remainder Theorem Based Hierarchical Access Control for Secure Group Communication

Xukai Zou[1], Byrav Ramamurthy[1], and Spyros S. Magliveras[2]

[1] University of Nebraska-Lincoln, Lincoln NE 68588, USA,
xkzou@cse.unl.edu, byrav@cse.unl.edu
[2] Florida Atlantic University, Boca Raton, Florida 33431, USA,
spyros@fau.edu

Abstract. Secure group communication with hierarchical access control refers to a scenario where a group of members is divided into a number of subgroups located at different privilege levels and a high-level subgroup can receive and decrypt messages within any of its descendant lower-level subgroups; but the converse is not allowed. In this paper, we propose a new scheme CRTHACS, which is based on the Chinese Remainder Theorem. The scheme not only enables secure hierarchical control but also provides the following properties: hiding of hierarchy and receivers, authentication of both senders and messages, and a mechanism for the receiver to directly derive the key of a message.

1 Introduction

Secure group communication (SGC) with hierarchical access control (HAC) refers to a scenario where a group of members is divided into a number of subgroups located at different privilege levels and a high-level subgroup can receive and decrypt messages within any of its descendant lower-level subgroups; but the converse is not allowed. HAC is generally enforced using cryptography based techniques [2] i.e., cryptographic keys play a primary role in the control of access rights. If the members in a higher level subgroup possess or can derive the key of a lower level subgroup, the members have the right to access the messages within the lower level subgroup. Cryptography based techniques for SGC with HAC can be divided into two main types: *dependent key schemes* [1],[3],[6],[8], in which any subgroup key is directly derived from its parent's key; thus indirectly from any of its ancestors' keys, and *independent key schemes* [5], in which all subgroup keys are independent and however, there are some precomputed parameters from which, an ancestor can compute the keys of all its descendants.

In this paper we propose a new scheme which belongs to the second category, viz., an independent key scheme. The scheme is based on the Chinese Remainder Theorem (CRT) [10]. In the scheme, every subgroup can select and change its own key independently, which is an important security factor [5]. In addition, the scheme also provides the following properties: (1) hiding the hierarchy and receivers, (2) authentication of both senders and messages, and (3) a receiver

S. Qing, T. Okamoto, and J. Zhou (Eds.): ICICS 2001, LNCS 2229, pp. 381–385, 2001.

can directly derive the key of the message sender regardless of how far down the hierarchy the sender is from the receiver. Hiding the hierarchy is a good feature in the sense that the less hierarchical information subgroups know, the more secure the system will be, and the easier it is to insert or delete a subgroup. Moreover, there is no overhead cost in storing the hierarchy information. Hiding receivers is useful in situations when outsiders (i.e., non-group members) are not allowed to know who the receivers are, when the sender is not allowed to know who the receivers are, or when it is difficult for a sender to know who the receivers are. We call the scheme Chinese Remainder Theorem Based Hierarchical Access Control Scheme (CRTHACS) and present the scheme in the next section.

2   Chinese Remainder Theorem Based Hierarchical Access Control Scheme for Secure Group Communication

2.1   CRTHACS Components and Initialization

There is a Group Controller (GC) in CRTHACS. The entire group is divided into subgroups and the subgroups are located at different nodes of a hierarchy (the most general case is a Directed Acyclic Graph, i.e. DAG [2]). Every subgroup has a subgroup controller which is responsible for managing all members in its subgroup and communicating with the GC. We do not consider here how subgroup controllers manage their subgroups, however we remark that any group key management protocol such as the key tree scheme [7],[11] can be used. We denote subgroups by $G_1, G_2, \cdots, G_m$. For simplicity, we also use $G_1, G_2, \cdots, G_m$ to denote the subgroup controllers. We also denote the ancestors of G_i by $G_{i_1}, \ldots, G_{i_k}$.

The GC has a pair of public and private keys (P_{GC}, S_{GC}) with P_{GC} being made public. The GC performs the following tasks. It maintains the entire structure of the group; generates a random set of pairwise relatively prime numbers $N_0, N_1, N_2, \cdots, N_m$; publicizes N_0 and sends N_i to G_i securely, i.e., N_i is encrypted by G_i's public key P_i; computes COM_CRT_i (see equation (1)) using the CRT algorithm and sends COM_CRT_i back to G_i securely.

Every subgroup G_i is associated with the following six elements $(P_i, S_i, K_i, N_i, COM\_CRT_i, \mathcal{N}_i)$ where P_i, S_i and K_i are generated by subgroup controller G_i whereas N_i, COM_CRT_i and $\mathcal{N}_i$ are generated by the GC. P_i is the public key of G_i and is made public. However all other five elements are kept secret. S_i is the private key of G_i corresponding to P_i. P_i and S_i are used to encrypt and decrypt the other four elements. K_i is the data key of G_i and is used to encrypt data messages. N_i is the positive integer received from the GC and will be used in CRT computation. COM_CRT_i, a positive integer, is called a CRT key and is computed from K_i using the CRT algorithm by the GC (see equation (1)). All ancestral subgroups of G_i can use COM_CRT_i to compute key K_i using the CRT algorithm too. $\mathcal{N}_i$ is also a positive integer (see equation (2)) and will be used in another type (i.e., data message) of CRT computation (see equation (3)).

Every participant j has its own public key and private key (p_j, s_j) and p_j is made public. Participant j in a subgroup G_i also knows its subgroup's six elements, of which j receives P_i, S_i, K_i from the G_i and $N_i, COM\_CRT_i, \mathcal{N}_i$ from the GC.

The GC and subgroup controllers collaborate to compute the CRT keys as follows. Every subgroup G_i selects its own subgroup data key K_i. After sign-ing and encrypting the key,[1] G_i sends $E_{P_{GC}}(E_{S_i}(K_i))$ to the GC where E is a public-key encryption algorithm or a signature algorithm.[2] The GC decrypts the key K_i, determines all the ancestors $G_{i_1}, G_{i_2}, \ldots, G_{i_k}$ of G_i and figures out all the public keys P_{i_j} and CRT numbers N_{i_j} of these ancestors. Let these param-eters be $P_{i_1}, P_{i_2}, \cdots, P_{i_k}$ and $N_{i_1}, N_{i_2}, \cdots, N_{i_k}$. The GC establishes the system of congruences (1) and then computes COM_CRT_i using the CRT algorithm.

$$
\begin{aligned}
COM\_CRT_i &\equiv E_{P_{i_1}}(K_i) \bmod N_{i_1}, \\
COM\_CRT_i &\equiv E_{P_{i_2}}(K_i) \bmod N_{i_2} \\
&\vdots \\
COM\_CRT_i &\equiv E_{P_{i_k}}(K_i) \bmod N_{i_k}
\end{aligned}
\tag{1}
$$

The GC also computes $\mathcal{N}_i$ (see equation (2)). Then the GC signs and encrypts $(N_i, COM\_CRT_i, \mathcal{N}_i)$, and sends the result (i.e., $E_{P_i}(E_{S_{GC}}(N_i, COM\_CRT_i, \mathcal{N}_i)))$ to G_i. The subgroup controller G_i and all participants in subgroup G_i decrypt the result to get N_i, COM_CRT_i and $\mathcal{N}_i$.

$$
\mathcal{N}_i = N_{i_1} \cdot N_{i_2} \cdots N_{i_k}
\tag{2}
$$

Remarks: The COM_CRT_i contains the information of P_{i_j} and N_{i_j} of all the ancestral subgroups of G_i. However G_i does not know who its ancestors are. Moreover, even though $\mathcal{N}_i$ contains the N_j of its ancestral subgroups, G_i cannot obtain these N_j from $\mathcal{N}_i$ because of the difficulty of partitioning the product into the specific factors and in the specific order (this problem is NP-complete). As a result, the hierarchy is totally hidden.

2.2   Data Communication

Whenever a participant j with identity ID_j in G_i sends a message M, it does: (1) encrypts M using K_i, i.e., $\{M\}_{K_i}$ where $\{x\}_k$ means encrypting x with k using some symmetric encryption function [10]; (2) computes a keyed MAC of $\{M\}_{K_i}$ under K_i, i.e. $MAC_{K_i}(\{M\}_{K_i})$ where the MAC could be any of the known *Message Authentication Codes*, such as MD5 [9]; (3) establishes the system of congruences:[3]

$$
\begin{aligned}
CRT_i &\equiv COM\_CRT_i \bmod \mathcal{N}_i \\
CRT_i &\equiv E_{s_j}(MAC_{K_i}(\{M\}_{K_i})) \bmod N_0
\end{aligned}
\tag{3}
$$

(4) computes CRT_i by the CRT algorithm. This CRT_i contains all the infor-mation about its ancestral subgroup keys, the MAC, and the signature of the sender itself; (5) broadcasts (or multicasts) the tuple $(ID_j, CRT_i, \{M\}_{K_i})$.

---

[1] In order to verify the signature, the verification information should be included in this message. We omit it for simplicity.

[2] For simplicity, when E is used on a private key, the result represents a signature.

[3] The second congruence includes the sender's signature in the CRT value.

When a receiver receives $(ID_j, CRT_i, \{M\}_{K_i})$, it does: (1) computes $x = CRT_i \bmod N_0$; (2) decrypts x using j's public key to get $MAC_{K_i}(\{M\}_{K_i}) = E^{-1}_{p_j}(x)$, where E^{-1} stands for the decryption algorithm corresponding to E; (3) If the receiver is in G_i, then it computes $MAC_{K_i}(\{M\}_{K_i})$ using its own K_i. If it is in any G_{i_j} of G_i's ancestor subgroups, it first computes $CRT_{i_j} = CRT_i \bmod N_{i_j}$ and decrypts CRT_{i_j} to get $K_i = E^{-1}_{S_{i_j}}(CRT_{i_j})$, then computes $MAC_{K_i}(\{M\}_{K_i})$ under K_i. Otherwise, the receiver ignores the message; (4) compares the above two MACs. If the two MACs are equal, then both the sender and the message are authenticated. The receiver decrypts the message using K_i. Otherwise, the message is not intended for this receiver or the message was modified during transmission. Therefore the receiver discards the message.

2.3   Dynamic Key Management

In SGC with HAC, there are two levels of dynamics: low level dynamics by which we mean that a member may join/leave a subgroup and which is operated by subgroup controllers and is dependent on the subgroup key management protocol, and high level dynamics which include the following operations: adding/inserting a new subgroup, removing an existing subgroup, merge two subgroups, split a subgroup and modifying an existing subgroup key, all of which are easily done in CRTHACS. For example, when a new subgroup G_i is added into the hierarchy, the GC computes G_i's COM_CRT_i by equation (1) and sends COM_CRT_i, $\mathcal{N}_i$ and N_i to G_i. If G_i has descendant subgroups (i.e., G_i is inserted into the hierarchy), the GC also needs to recompute the COM_CRT values for all descendent subgroups of G_i so that these COM_CRT include the information of G_i's public key P_i and the corresponding N_i. All other subgroups are not affected.

2.4   Security and Performance Analysis

The CRTHACS scheme is secure because of the independence of subgroup data keys and the difficulty of partitioning the product into the specific factors and in the specific order along with the security of underlying cryptosystems.

As for the performance of the CRTHACS scheme, there are three complexities to be considered: space, time, and communication complexity, by which we mean the size of key-related materials, including the CRT parameters, communicated between the GC and the subgroups (subgroup controllers and participants) or between subgroup controllers and subgroup members. There are three classes of entities: Group Controller (GC), Subgroup Controllers (G_i) and participants (p_j). The complexities are summarized in the following table.

	Space*	Time**	Communication***
GC	$O(mHL)$	$O(mM(HL)log(H)) + O(mHM(L)log(L))$	$O(HL)$ (GC and G_i/p_j)
G_i	$O(HL)$	Independent of m and H	
p_j	$O(HL)$	$O(M(2L)) + O(2M(L)log(L))$	

Note: H: the maximum number of ancestors a subgroup may have; L: the length of a large integer in bits; m: the number of subgroups; $M(n)$: the time to multiply two n-bit integers in bit operations; $O(n)$ is measured in bits, not in bytes.

* counts the space for representing P_i, S_i, K_i, N_i, COM_CRT_i and $\mathcal{N}_i$, which require large integers, possibly 1024-bit numbers but ignores the space for representing the access control structure or membership, which need small integers.
** counts the complexity of the CRT algorithm, i.e.,
$O(M(kL)log(k)) + O(kM(L)log(L))$ [4],[10], where k is the number of moduli but ignores the time consumed on key generation, encryption and decryption, which will depend on the special algorithms selected.
*** the key materials between subgroup controllers and subgroup members depend on the subgroup key management protocol selected and are ignored here.

3   Conclusion

In this paper, we have proposed a new scheme for group communication with hierarchical access control. The scheme has highly desirable properties including scalability, the ability to deal with the dynamical problems related to insertion and deletion of subgroups, and the property of hidding the hierarchy and receivers.

Acknowledgments. We thank Dr. G. Noubir and Dr. J.C. Birget for useful discussions on this work.

References

1. S. G. Akl and P. D. Taylor. Cryptographic solution to a problem of access control in a hierarchy. *ACM Transactions on Computer Systems*, 1(3):239–247, 1983.
2. J.-C. Birget, X. Zou, G. Noubir, and B. Ramamurthy. Hierarchy-based access control in distributed environments. *To appear in the Proceedings of the ICC2001 Conference, June 11-14*, 2001.
3. G. C. Chick and S. E. Tavares. Flexible access control with master keys. *Advances in Cryptology: CRYPTO '89 LNCS*, 435:316–322, 1990.
4. G. H. Chiou and W.T.Chen. Secure broadcasting using the secure lock. *IEEE Transaction on Software Engineering*, 15(8):929–934, 1989.
5. C. H. Lin. Dynamic key management schemes for access control in a hierarchy. *Computer Communications*, 20:1381–1385, 1997.
6. S. T. Mackinnon, P. D. Taylor, H. Meijer, and S. G. Akl. An optimal algorithm for assigning cryptographic keys to control access in a hierarchy. *IEEE Transactions on Computers*, 34(9):797–802, September 1985.
7. G. Noubir. Multicast security. *European Space Agency, Project: Performance Optimisation of Interner Protocol Via Satellite*, April 1998.
8. R. S. Sandhu. Cryptographic implementation of a tree hierarchy for access control. *Information Processing Letters*, 27:95–98, 1988.
9. B. Schneier. *Applied Cryptography: Protocols, Algorithms, and Source Code in C, 2nd Edition*. Addsion-Wesley, Reading, MA, 1995.
10. D. R. Stinson. *Cryptography: Theory and Practice*. CRC Press, Inc., Boca Raton, Florida, 1995.
11. C. K. Wong, M. Gouda, and S. S. Lam. Secure group communications using key groups. *SIGCOMM '98, Also University of Texas at Austin, Computer Science Technical report TR 97-23*, December 1998.

Dispatching Mobile Agents with Secure Routes in Parallel

Yan Wang and Kian-Lee Tan

Department of Computer Science
National University of Singapore
3 Science Drive 2, Singapore 117543
{ywang, tankl}@comp.nus.edu.sg

Abstract. In a distributed environment like the Internet, mobile agents can be employed to perform autonomous tasks such as searching and negotiating. However, for mobile agents to be widely accepted, performance and security issues on their use have to be addressed. In this paper, we propose a parallel dispatch model with secure route structures for protecting the dispatch routes of agents. This model facilitates efficient dispatching of agents in a hierarchical manner, and ensures route security by exposing minimal route information to hosts. To further enhance route robustness, we also propose a mechanism with substitute routes that can bypass temporarily unreachable hosts, using substitute hosts for deploying right dispatch branches and make later attempts to these failed hosts.

1 Introduction

In recent years, there have been increasing interests in deploying mobile agents carrying both code and data for distributed processing in an environment such as the Internet. For example, in electronic commerce (EC), a pool of mobile agents can be dispatched from a host to related e-shops to gather information, such as price, stock status, warranty and delivery service etc., for goods specified by a customer [1], [2], [3], [4]. Clearly, an efficient strategy is to dispatch a large number of agents to work in parallel [5], [6]. This will also provide customers with the possibility to find the "best" e-shop to make his/her purchases.

However, for mobile agent technologies to be accepted, performance and security issues on their use have to be addressed. First, to deploy a large number of agents require significant overhead to dispatch the agents. Novel methods for dispatching agents are desirable. Second, when a mobile agent arrives at a host for execution, the code and data will be exposed to the host and the resources at the host may also be exposed to the mobile agent. Thus, security mechanisms should be set up to protect mobile agents from malicious hosts as well as to protect hosts from malicious agents. Some works have been done to protect the hosts, e.g., the access privilege protocol [7], [8] and the role based mechanism [9] restrict an agent's access to resources of a host. Protecting the agent is also a difficult task. In particular, in EC environment, since e-shops are competitive, it is important to protect the routes of a mobile agent if it should visit a list of hosts (e-shops) or if it should dispatch other mobile agents to other hosts. If a malicious host knows the route information, it may tamper with it so

S. Qing, T. Okamoto, and J. Zhou (Eds.): ICICS 2001, LNCS 2229, pp. 386–397, 2001.

that its competitors that may offer better prices or services will not be visited. This calls for novel methods to be designed.

In this paper, we focus on the issues of efficiently dispatching mobile agents while protecting their routes. We first present a hierarchical dispatch model, which can efficiently dispatch a large number of mobile agents in parallel and is robust in the sense that an agent can be dispatched to any of the embedded hosts by delaying the trials to temporarily unreachable hosts. However, this comes at the cost of exposing all the addresses of descendent agents to hosts and hence it is not secure in the context of protecting mobile agents from malicious hosts. Based on this model, we present a security enhanced parallel dispatch model, which will not expose the information of all descendent agents except the children agents. Thus, we preserve the efficiency of the hierarchical model while ensuring routes security. In addition, we also give a solution to facilitate robustness without sacrificing on security and efficiency.

In this paper, we employ well-known cryptography technologies such as the asymmetric encryption algorithm, signature generating algorithm and X.509 authentication framework [10], [11]. In the following, we assume that there exists a secure environment including the generation, certification and distribution of public keys and each host can know the authentic public key of other hosts.

2 A Basic Security Enhanced Model for Parallel Dispatch

2.1 Binary Dispatch Model

In this paper, we assume an infrastructure where a set of marketplaces is connected to the Internet. Requests by users go through the agent A_{MSMA} running at the Master Server for Mobile Agents (MSMA), which is an execution environment for mobile agents. In MSMA, a customer agent can be created or dispatched. We call an agent a Worker Agent (WA) if its sole responsibility is to perform the tasks assigned to it, e.g., accessing data. If an agent also dispatches other agent besides performing the task of accessing data, it is called a Primary Worker Agent (PWA).

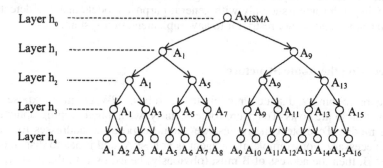

Fig. 1. Dispatch tree with 16 WAs

In this section, we introduce the proposed parallel dispatch model. For simplicity, we restrict our discussion to a *binary* dispatch model where an agent can dispatch two other agents resulting in a binary tree structure. Clearly, the model can be easily generalized to dispatch multiple (more than 2) agents. As shown in Figure 1, A_{MSMA} is responsible for dispatching PWAs and distributing tasks to them. Suppose A_{MSMA} has to dispatch 16 agents to different hosts. Now, they can be divided into 2 groups led by two PWAs, say A_1 and A_9. When agents A_1 and A_9 are dispatched, each of them has 8 members including itself. For A_1, it will dispatch A_5 and distribute 4 members to it. Then A_1 will transit to the same layer (i.e., h_2) as A_5, which is called a virtual dispatch. But now A_1 has 4 members only. Following the same process, A_1 will dispatch A_3 and A_2. At last, after all dispatch tasks have been completed, A_1 will become a WA and start its data-accessing task. In this model, in certain layer, a PWA can choose any of its members except itself to be the right child agent. In this way, any right branches can be surely deployed and any unreachable hosts can be bypassed to a later attempt. As a whole, since all PWAs are dispatched to different hosts, the dispatch process can be preformed in parallel. When there are $n=2^h$ mobile agents and Δt is the average time for dispatching a mobile agent, $(h+1)\Delta t$ will be the time for dispatching n mobile agents in the binary way. So, the dispatch complexity will be $O(logn)$. Thus, the proposed model is both robust and efficient.

There are three alternative implementations for a PWA to create and dispatch a child agent in the IBM Aglet system [12]. The first approach is that the MSMA passes the child agent to the PWA who creates the child agent and encapsulates arguments such as the route and tasks and then dispatches it. This method is expected to be inefficient in a WAN environment. The second is to compress the framework of child agents to a .jar file and attach it to the PWA when it is dispatched. The child agent is created from the compressed file for being dispatched. The third one is to adopt the clone-like strategy. If some mobile agents have the same type of tasks, they can be put to the same group where a PWA can easily create a child agent by locally making a copy and modifying the static data. After encapsulating the route to the copy, the PWA can dispatch it to a remote host. A secure clone environment that provides security mechanisms to detect illegally forged agents is also an important issue that is out of the scope of this paper. The common feature for three alternatives is that arguments can be encapsulated to an agent when it is created. Here we address the secure dispatch route issue only with general-purpose models that can detect illegally forged agents, and do not restrict it to any implementation system.

2.2 Securing the Route Structure

In the basic binary dispatch model, to be robust, PWAs must expose all route information to the hosts. To ensure route security, we applied cryptographic technique to the model. To protect the routes, we should expose the addresses to a host only when necessary. For example, if an agent is at host A, and it has to dispatch an agent to host B, then the address of B must (obviously) be exposed to the host A; however, no other addresses should be exposed.

For the binary dispatch model, it is more complicated than traditional serial migration model since a PWA has different dispatch tasks in different layers. Only the operations for a WA are simple. For the binary dispatch model, a basic definition of route structure, is as follows:

(1)   For a PWA at CH, $r(CH) = P_{CH}[PWA, ip(RH), r_L, r_R,$
$S_{MSMA}(PWA, ip(PH), ip(CH), ip(RH), r_L, r_R, t)]$

(2)   For a WA at CH, $r(CH) = P_{CH}[WA, ip(MSMA),$
$S_{MSMA}(WA, ip(PH), ip(CH), ip(MSMA), t)]$

$\qquad\qquad\qquad\qquad\qquad\qquad\qquad\qquad\qquad\qquad\qquad$ **(1)**

Where $r(CH)$ denotes the route structure at the current host, CH, where the agent should go; $ip(H)$ denotes the IP address of host H; RH and PH denote the right child's host and the parent host respectively; r_L and r_R denote the encrypted route for the left and right children respectively; $P_{CH}[M]$ denotes the message M is encrypted by the public key of the current host CH; and $S_{MSMA}(D)$ denotes the signature signed on document D by host MSMA using its secret key S_{MSMA} and t is the timestamp at which the signature is generated. t is unique for all routes within a dispatch tree. The addresses of PH and CH only appear in the signature for verification.

Starting the binary dispatch process with secure routes, the agent A_{MSMA} dispatches two PWAs to different hosts, each being encapsulated with an encrypted route for future dispatch task. We call them the first left PWA (PWA_{1L}) and the first right PWA (PWA_{1R}). When an agent has successfully arrived at the current host CH, the carried route $r(CH)$ can be decrypted with the secret key of CH so that the agent can know:

− it is a PWA or a WA. This is used to determine the next task of the agent;
− the signature signed at host MSMA $S_{MSMA}(PWA, ip(PH), ip(CH), ip(RH), r_L, r_R, t)$ for a PWA, or $S_{MSMA}(WA, ip(PH), ip(CH), ip(MSMA), t)]$ for a WA.
    If it is a PWA, it will also know
− the address $ip(RH)$ of the right child host RH;
− the encrypted route r_R for the right child agent, which can only be decrypted by the right child host;
− the encrypted route r_L for the left dispatch.
    If it is a WA, it will know the address of MSMA, $ip(MSMA)$, the home host where A_{MSMA} is residing. With this address, the WA can send its result to A_{MSMS}.

Clearly, under this model, at any layer, only the address of the right child agent is exposed to the current host so that the right dispatch can be completed. For a PWA, if it has $m = 2^k$ members, only k addresses of its members are exposed to the host.

2.3 Algorithm for Agent Dispatch with Secure Routes

The algorithm for dispatching agents is described as follows:

Algorithm 1: Binary dispatch with secure routes

Step 1: when an agent A is successfully dispatched to host CH, it will use the secret key of CH, S_{CH}, to decrypt the carried route $r(CH)$.

$$r = S_{CH}[r(CH)]$$

Step 2: if A is a WA, go to step 6, otherwise, A is a PWA, it will dispatch another agent to $ip(RH)$, encapsulating the route r_R to it.

Step 3: if the dispatch is successful, host RH will send a message including its signature to CH.

$$msg1 = S_{RH}(Entity_{RS}, ip(RH), t)$$

where Entity$_{RS}$ is the full entity of the dispatched agent including its code, state and data. t is the timestamp when the agent is received successfully.

Once getting such a message, host CH will keep S_{RH}(Entity$_{RS}$, ip(RH), t) in its database as a successful dispatch record.

Step 4: Now A should try to complete its left dispatch. Let r=$S_{CH}[r_L]$

Step 5: if A is still a PWA, go to step 2, otherwise go to step 6

Step 6: A starts its task for data accessing

Step 7: when the data-accessing task is completed, A will dispose after successfully sending a message to agent A$_{MSMA}$.

$$msg2=P_{MSMA}[ip(PH), ip(CH), Result_{CH},$$
$$S_{MSMA}(WA, ip(PH), ip(CH), ip(MSMA), t_1),$$
$$S_{CH}(ip(PH), ip(CH), Result_{CH}, t_2)]$$

where S_{MSMA}(WA, ip(PH), ip(CH), ip(MSMA), t$_1$) is the signature from MSMA, which is included in the decrypted route of the agent. Here it is used for showing the identification of the agent. S_{CH}(ip(RH), ip(CH), Result$_{CH}$, t$_2$)] is the signature generated by current host CH. Result$_{CH}$ is the result obtained at CH. PH is the parent host of CH and t$_2$>t$_1$.

3 Resolving Security Threats

In this section, we will examine several security issues that will be encountered when dispatching mobile agents and show how our model resolves them.

3.1 Preventing a PWA from Dispatching a Child Agent

During the period of dispatching a child agent, a malicious host may peek the code of the agent and make it skip the dispatch process in certain layer after the route is decrypted. Note that skipping a host would mean skipping all other addresses that may be triggered by that host. In the worst case, assuming host H$_1$ is the malicious one, as shown in Figure 1, if the dispatch of A$_5$ from H$_1$ is not in fact performed, those agents in the group including A$_5$ to A$_8$ will not be activated. This means the successful interception to the dispatch of a PWA will affect all members included in the aborted PWA. However this attack can be detected in this model.

Taking the case in Figure 1 as an example, if H$_1$ makes A$_1$ skip the process of dispatching agent A$_5$, agent A$_{MSMA}$ cannot receive any messages from each agent of A$_5$, A$_6$, A$_7$ or A$_8$. If this happens, since the four agents belong to the same group led by agent A$_5$, A$_{MSMA}$ will suspect first that A$_5$ may have not been dispatched. A$_{MSMA}$ will ask hosts H$_1$ and H$_5$ to show whether the predefined dispatch has been performed. Apparently, if the dispatch has been carried out, H$_1$ will receive the confirmation message with the signature S_{H5}(Entity$_{A5}$, ip(H$_5$), t) from H$_5$. H$_1$ cannot forge this signature without H$_5$'s secret key. So, no matter what H$_1$ claims, the attack can be detected.

If the skipped dispatch is for a WA, such as A$_7$ doesn't dispatch A$_8$, it can also be detected since H$_7$ cannot show a correct signature from H$_8$ to show the dispatch is successful.

3.2 Route Skip Attack

There is yet another case that can be handled in this model. Consider a partial dispatch route: PWA A_i at host H_i dispatches A_j to H_j and A_j dispatches A_k to H_k, or there are more PWAs between A_j and A_k. In this model, the encrypted route encapsulated to a PWA includes the encrypted route for its right child agent, which can only be decrypted at the child's host in the dispatch route. That means when a PWA is dispatching an agent, it does not know what the agent is, a PWA or a WA, and how many members the agent has. So the case described above that A_i directly dispatches A_k is not likely to take place without the involvement of A_j. That is why the encrypted route is in a nested structure. In the worst case, even if H_i can successfully predict that H_k is its descendent in the dispatch route and makes A_i dispatch a forged agent to H_k, the attack will not be successful either.

Suppose A_k is a WA, the forged route for A_k should be
$$r(H_k)'=P_{Hk}[WA, ip(H_i), S_{MSMA}(WA, ip(H_i), ip(H_k), t)],$$
while the genuine route should be
$$r(H_k)=P_{Hk}[WA, ip(H_j), S_{MSMA}(WA, ip(H_j), ip(H_k), t)]$$
The genuine $r(H_k)$ can only be obtained at H_j when A_j arrives there and decrypts its route. So if A_i want to forge A_j, it must be able to forge $S_{MSMA}(WA, ip(H_j), ip(H_k), t)$. Otherwise, the attack will be detected if the address of parent host in the signature is not $ip(H_j)$. Furthermore, the signature is also required to be included in the returned result for the verification by A_{MSMA}. So since forging the signature is impossible, this kind of attack cannot success.

3.3 Tampering a PWA to Dispatch an Agent to a Wrong Host

Since the hosts are in a competitive situation, if a malicious host knows a host where an agent will be dispatched from it, and the remote host may probably offer a better service than itself, it may tamper the address so that the agent can be dispatched to another host which is known not to be able to provide a competitive offer. The tamper can be done just after the encrypted route is decrypted. However, when an agent is dispatched to a wrong host, its encrypted route will not be correctly decrypted there. Without the correct route, the verification process cannot be undertaken. Even if the destination host can get the correctly decrypted route, the route will show that is a wrong destination since the address of the destination host is included in the signature in the route generated by MSMA that cannot be tampered with. Thus, in both situations, the attack can be detected by the destination host and the agent will be returned to the sender. Meanwhile, this error will be recorded by the destination host for future investigation.

3.4 Sending the Result of a WA to A_{MSMA} Directly or Not

In this model, when a WA has fulfilled its data-accessing task, it will send a message to A_{MSMA} directly by encrypting the result, the signature by the host as well as the signature by the MSMA originally included in the agent's route. The structure is shown as message (2) in section 2.3. The whole message is encrypted with the public key of MSMA so that it can only be decrypted by agent A_{MSMA}. We choose this way in this model with regard to both security and performance issues. An alternative is that a PWA should be responsible for dispatching agents and collecting data from them. If PWA A_i dispatched PWA A_j which dispatched WA A_k and A_k encrypted its result with the public key of MSMA and sent it to A_j where H_j cannot decrypt. To send the whole result set to A_i, A_j should encrypt its own result together with the encrypted result from A_k. If they are put as two separate encrypted results, deletion or tamper attacks may easily occur in the returning path especially when a large number of results are sent to a PWA. Meanwhile, this will increase the burden of a PWA and the performance will definitely become worse.

A possible solution preventing the results from being tampered or deleted that may take place at any host where a PWA resides is for the receiving side to send a reply to the sending side, just like the process for dispatching. The reply should be a signature generated on the received message by the secret key of the receiving side. In this way, deletion and tampering can be detected by the verification among the MSMA, sending side and receiving side. However, the performance will become inferior.

In comparison, in our model, since a WA only visit one host, the host would not delete the result or prevent its offer from being returned once the agent has been successfully dispatched there. In case the attack occurs, based on the detection of successful dispatch, the problem should be with the side of the host where the agent has arrived. In terms of performance, since each WA has different starting time and ending time for the data-accessing task and each offer will be in small size, the returned results can hardly cause the A_{MSMA} to become a bottleneck.

3.5 Replay Attack

In a malicious host, the replay attack may occur. Consider the following scenario, that a malicious H_i who has a PWA residing in it and it dispatched agent A_j to host H_j. After the normal process has been completed, H_i may replay the dispatch with a forged agent so that on one hand it can get the offer information from H_j constantly and periodically if H_i tampers the agent so that it sends the result to H_i, and on the other hand, excessive agents may jam H_j. However, when an agent is dispatched from H_i to H_j as a replay attack, the timestamp included in the signature from MSMA cannot be tampered with. By verifying the signature, H_j can easily detect the replay attack and H_i will face the risk to be reported.

Similarly, another type of replay attack is for a host, which a WA had earlier resided, to repeatedly counterfeit the WA and send messages to the agent A_{MSMA}. Since the A_{MSMA} is the root agent, it will be disposed of once all WAs have completed their tasks successfully. In addition, if A_{MSMA} repeatedly receives offers from the same host, it will close the communication channel and start an investigation.

3.6 Collusion Attack

If in a normal sequence, host H_a should dispatch an agent to H_b. Assuming H_a and H_c are in a collusion tie, the agent is dispatched to H_c. In this way H_a and H_c make an attempt to skip the visit to H_b who is their competitor and send their own offers instead. However H_c can hardly forge the signature by H_b that should be included in the message returned to A_{MSMA}. In such a case, the counterfeited message can be detected when it is returned and this will cause the investigation against H_c and H_a. Since H_b will report that no such agent has ever been dispatched to it and H_a cannot show the correct dispatch record which should include the signature by H_b, the attack can be identified. The attack can be successful only when H_a, H_b and H_c make a collusion attack sending a result from H_b encapsulating the price from H_c. However, in a healthy competitive environment, the probability is fairly low. Even if it can take place, the future negotiation or buying agents will visit H_b not H_c and if H_b cannot offer the goods with the provided price, it will result in a commercial cheating, which is the same as a merchant's giving a nominal price and causing the abortion of the purchase. This will cause the deduction of the merchant's credit standing and little agents will be dispatched later to such merchants.

4 Robustness Enhanced Extension

So far we have presented a security enhanced dispatch model for mobile agents. However, like Westhoff's model [13], each PWA only knows the RH to which its right child agent should be dispatched at a certain stage and should the host where the right child agent should go be unavailable, the right dispatch branch cannot be deployed and all the members grouped in this agent will thereby not be activated.

As mentioned in the section 2.1, the binary dispatch model is robust in that a PWA can know all the destination addresses of its children agents. It can choose any of them to be the right child PWA. However, its robustness is built on the basis that all these addresses are exposed to the host. Therefore, its robustness is not feasible with regard to the security. Anyway, it is clear that a PWA should have an alternative for dispatching its right child agent so that if the predefined right child agent cannot be successfully dispatched due to some reasons from the destination host, the PWA can have another route for the right dispatch.

Li proposed a robust model in [14] for serial migration of agents and the route robustness is enhanced by dividing a route, say $\{ip(H_1), ip(H_2), ..., ip(H_n)\}$, into two parts, say $\{ip(H_1), , ..., ip(H_i)\}$ and $\{ip(H_{i+1}), ..., ip(H_n)\}$, which are distributed to two agents A_1 and A_2 respectively. A_1 and A_2 are in partner relationship. Each agent residing at any host knows the addresses of the next destination and an alternative host. The latter is encrypted by the public key of its partner agent. In case the migration cannot be performed, the encrypted address will be sent to the partner agent for decrypting. With its assistance, the agent can continue its migration.

The problem for Li's model is that since A_1 and A_2 are two agents that should dynamically migrate, when one needs the other's assistance, locating each other will be costly for both time and system resources though some mechanisms have been proposed by [15], [16]. Meanwhile, the model is a serial one so it is not efficient. Additionally, using the secret key of a dynamically migrating agent is not secure. But the idea of using the mutual assistance of the two agents to enhance the robustness is good and can be easily used in our model, where the two first PWAs in the left and right branches can do it better. Since they don't need to migrate, sending messages to them is fairly simple and fast. Encrypting and decrypting the route using the keys of the host where the first PWA resides is more secure.

For robustness, the route structure in equation (1) can be extended as follows:

(1) For a PWA at CH, r(CH)=P [PWA, ip(RH), r , r , r ', S   (PWA, ip(PH), ip(CH), ip(RH), r_L, r_R, r_R', t)], where r_R'=P_{APWA}[ip(SH), r(SH), S   (ip(SH), r(SH), t)] is the substitute route for the right branch of host CH, SH is the new substitute host.

(2) For a WA at CH, r(CH)=P [WA, ip(PH), ip(MSMA), S   (WA, ip(PH), ip(CH), ip(MSMA), t)]
                                                                                        (2)

In route structure (2), r_R' is encrypted by the public key of the first PWA in another branch of the whole dispatch tree, which here is termed as Assistant PWA (APWA).

Suppose A_1 is the first PWA in the left dispatch sub-tree. A_m is the right one. If current host CH is the descendent of A_1, then r_R' is encrypted by the public key of A_m, P_{Am}. Otherwise, if CH is in the right dispatch sub-tree from the root node, r_R' is encrypted by P_{A1}.

If the dispatch failure occurred when A_i is dispatching A_j, and A_i is in the left dispatch sub-tee, A_i should report it to A_m attaching the substitute route r_R'

$$msg1=P_{Hm}[ip(H_j), ip(H_i), r_R', S_{Hi}(ip(H_j), ip(H_i), r_R', t)]$$

When A_m gets such a message, it will

Step 1: Detect whether H_j has got down. If it is true, then go to step 2, otherwise go to step 3

Step 2: Am will decrypt r_R', r=S_{Hm}[r_R'], and send it to A_i through a message

$$msg2=P_{Hi}[ip(SH), r(SH), S_{MSMA}(ip(SH), r(SH), t_1),$$
$$S_{Hm}(ip(SH), r(SH), S_{MSMA}(ip(SH), r(SH), t_1), t_2)]$$

    Stop.

Step 3: If A_j is in the correct state, A_m will tell A_i about it and record the request in a database.

There are two reasons for A_i to send a request to A_m. One is that H_j has a temporary failure when A_i is trying to dispatch an agent there. Another reason is that host H_i is malicious and attempts to know more addresses by sending a cheating request. However, the failure report will be confirmed by A_m before replying any decrypted routes. And the request is saved by A_m for future investigation.

In this way by route structure (2), a PWA will have a substitute route for the dispatch of its right child agent. Once the original dispatch is not successful, with the assistance of its APWA, it can have another destination to dispatch.

What we should address is that the substitute host is originally included in the members for the right dispatch branch. Taking the dispatch tree in Figure 1 as an example, if the dispatch failure occurred when A_1 is dispatching A_5, A_1 can get an substitute route with the assistance of A_9. Suppose the substitute host is H_6, A_1 will dispatch an agent A_6 to H_6 and A_6 will deploy the right dispatch branch. To be more fault-tolerant, the address of H_5 will still be included in this branch. But it is put to be a leaf node so that A_5 will become a WA only for another attempt to dispatch it. Suppose the new sequence is A_6, A_7, A_8 and A_5, in which A_8 will make another attempt to dispatch A_5. If the dispatch problem with A_5 is temporary, a later attempt will be successful so that in such a case, all hosts will be visited as usual. If the dispatch failure occurred again, the reply from A_9 will show that A_5 is a WA and no more substitute route will be provided.

5 Discussions and Conclusion

In the proposed model, we aim to expose only the necessary addresses to hosts. If a PWA A_i has 2^k agents in its whole branch, only k addresses are exposed to host H_i since these agents should be dispatched directly by A_i in different layers. As a matter of fact, a PWA does not know what the dispatched agent is, how many members it has and with the security mechanisms attacks can be detected. Since this model adopts parallel dispatch, the dispatch efficiency is high.

As Westhoff's model [13] adopted a fully serial migration, the migration complexity is $O(n)$ if there are n hosts to be visited and it provides secure route structure without any robustness mechanism. Li's model [14] ensures both security and robustness. As the addresses of n hosts are distributed to two agents, the whole migration time can be theoretically half of that of the first model. However the time complexity is $O(n)$. In comparison, in our model the efficiency is greatly improved while both the security and robustness are ensured. Either the fully binary dispatch model or the model with 1 substitute route, the dispatch complexity is $O(logn)$.

With regard to the complexity for generating routes, three models have different performances. As pointed by [13], when the route adopts the nested structure, it will help to prevent route tampering or deleting attacks and detect them as early as possible. The nested route structure is also adopted by Li's model and our model. Based on this condition, taking the time for encrypting a route as a constant for simplifying, the complexity for generating routes can be estimated as follows.

For Westhoff's model, the route with n addresses can be generated after the route with $n-1$ addresses has been generated. So, the complexity $T(n)$ can be calculated as $T(n)=O(n)$ from the following,

$$\begin{cases} T(n)=T(n-1)+C \\ T(1)=C, \ C \ is \ a \ constant \end{cases}$$

For Li's model, suppose the hosts in the predefined sequence are $\{H_i, H_{i-1}, H_{i-2}, H_{i-3}, ..., H_2, H_1\}$, if host H_{i-1} is not reachable, H_{i-2} will become next destination from H_i and H_{i-1} will never be visited for this journey. So the generated normal route with $i-3$ addresses will be used for generating the substitute route with $i-2$ addresses. The route generating complexity with 1 substitute route is

$$\begin{cases} T(n)=T(n-1)+2C \\ T(1)=C \end{cases}$$

And $T(n)$ is $O(n)$.

In our model, the complexity for generating routes without substitute routes is $T(n)=O(n)$, where T(n) is

$$\begin{cases} T(n)=2T(n/2) \quad (n=2^k) \\ T(i)=2T(i/2)+C \quad (2 \leq i \leq 2^{k-1}) \\ T(1)=C \end{cases}$$

When generating the first substitute route for a branch, only a few steps should be taken in the left sub-branch of this branch. The number of the steps is up to the height h of the sub-branch. The complexity for the our model generating 1 substitute route is

$$\begin{cases} T(n)=2T(n/2)+C & (n=2^k) \\ T(i) \leq 2T(i/2)+hC & (h \leq k-1,\ 2 \leq i \leq 2^{k-1}) \\ T(1)=C \end{cases}$$

And hereby $T(n)$ is $O(nlogn)$.

In our model, a failed host will be tried for a second time while Li's model skips it. Otherwise the complexity of Li's model for generating routes will become extremely worse since the sequence of hosts in the substitute route has been changed and the route should be generated again. When a route includes 1 substitute route, the complexity will be $T(n)=T(n-1)+T(n-2)+2C$, $T(1)=C$ and $T(n)$ is $O(2^n)$.

For future work, we will work toward a global e-commerce framework with security mechanisms that is suitable for parallel processing by mobile agents. Some improvements should be done to current model to provide more substitute route with less loss of time complexity and the evaluation model on both security and commercial credit is also needed since in our model the hosts where APWAs reside are the most important to global dispatch. Based on this environment, activities on merchant assessment, information gathering and negotiation can be deployed by mobile agents automatically and safely.

Acknowledgement. This work is partially supported by the research grant of Strategic Program on Computer Security from NSTB of Singapore.

References

1. Sohn, S. and Yoo, K. J.: An Architecture of Electronic Market Applying Mobile Agent technology. Proceeding of 3rd IEEE Symposium on Computers and Communications (ISCC '98), Athens, Greece, (1998) 359-364
2. Corradi, A., Montanari R., and Stefanelli C.: Mobile Agents in E-commerce Applications. Proceedings of 19th IEEE International Conference on Distributed Computing Systems, Workshops on Electronic Commerce and Web-based Applications, Austin, Texas, USA, (1999) 59-64
3. Chrysanthis, P., Znati, T., Banerjee, S., and Chang, S.K.: Establishing Virtual Enterprises by means of Mobile Agents. Proceeding of Ninth International Workshop on Research Issues on Data Engineering: Information Technology for Virtual Enterprises (RIDE-VE '99), Sydney, Australia, (1999) 116-123
4. Rodrigo, T. D. and Stanski, A.: The Evolving Future of Agent-based Electronic Commerce. In Rahman S. M. and Raisinghani M. S.Electronic (eds.): Commerce: Opportunity and Challenges, Idea Group Publishing, Hershey, USA, (2000) 337-351
5. Silva, L., Batista, M., Martins V., and Soares, G.: Using Mobile Agents for Parallel Processing. Proceeding of International Symposium on Distributed Objects and Applications (DOA'99), Edinburgh, Scotland, (1999) 34-42
6. Papastavrou, S., Samaras G., and Pitoura, E.: Mobile agents for World Wide Web distributed database access. IEEE Transactions on Knowledge and Data Engineering, Vol. 12, Issue 5 , (2000) 802 –820
7. Karjoth, G., Lange D.B., and Oshima, M.: A Security Model for Aglets. IEEE Internet Computing, July-August (1997) 68-77
8. Varadharajan, V.: Security enhanced mobile agents. Proceedings of the 7th ACM conference on Computer and communications security, Athens, Greece, (2000) 200 – 209
9. Ubayashi, N., Tamai, T.: RoleEP: role based evolutionary programming for cooperative mobile agent applications. Proceedings of International Symposium on Principles of Software Evolution, (2000) 232 –240

10. Wayner, P.: Digital Copyright Protection. SP Professional, Boston, USA, (1997)
11. CCITT Recommendation X. 509-1989: The Directory-Authentication Framework. Consultation Committee, International Telephone and Telegraph, International Telecommunication Union, Geneva (1989)
12. Lange, D., and Oshima, M.: Programming and Deploying Java Mobile Agents with Aglets. Addison-Wesley Press, Massachusetts, USA (1998)
13. Westhoff, D., Schneider, M., Unger, C. and Kenderali, F.: Methods for Protecting a Mobile Agent's Route. Proceedings of the Second International Information Security Workshop (ISW'99), Lecture Notes in Computer Science, LNCS 1729, Springer-Verlag, Berlin Heidelberg New York, (1999) 57-71
14. Li, T., Seng, C.K. and Lam, K.Y.: A Secure Route Structure for Information Gathering. Proceedings of 2000 Pacific Rim International Conference on AI, Melbourne, Australia, (2000)
15. Belle, W.V., Verelst, K. and D'Hondt, T.: Location transparent routing in mobile agent systems merging name lookups with routing. Proceedings of 7th IEEE Workshop on Future Trends of Distributed Computing Systems, (1999) 207 –212
16. Maass, H.: Location-aware Mobile Applications Based Directory Services. Mobile Networks and Applications, Baltzer Science Publishers BV, (1998)

TH-SMS: Security Management System in Advanced Computational Infrastructure

Yu Chen, Qian Fang, Zhihui Du, Zhenchun Huang, and Sanli Li

Department of Computer Science, Tsinghua University, Bei Jing,
P.R. China
chenyu@tirc.cs.tsinghua.edu.cn

Abstract. Proposed by Ministry of Education P.R.C, Advanced Computational Infrastructure (ACI) aims at sharing geographically distributed high-performance computing and huge-capacity data resource among the universities of China. With the fast development of large-scale applications in ACI, the security requirements become more urgent. After analyzing the background of ACI, the paper describes the special security needs in ACI, and then presents TH-SMS, a security management system based on ACI. According to its three level structure, the implantations of TH-SMS are discussed. Especially for task security management, several new security techniques KCKPT, DP-VPN are introduced in the paper. Finally, compared with other security systems TH-SMS proves to be more effective and flexible.

1 Introduction

With the fast development of high-performance applications, a lot of large-scale applications exceed the competence of only one supercomputer. Being connected by high-performance networks, geographically distributed supercomputers are enabling large-scale applications, such as scientific simulation, collaborative engineering, etc., which is also called as grid computing environment. Currently many effective research works have been done on grid computing environment all around the worlds, and some important advanced computational infrastructures, including National Partnership of Advanced Computational Infrastructure--NPACI [1] and National Computational Science Alliance-NCSA [2], got successful harvest in USA. Ministry of Education P.R.C also proposed a grid computing project--Advanced Computational Infrastructure (ACI) [3], which aims at sharing high-performance computing and huge-capacity data resource among the universities of China.

However, widespread usage of such applications in ACI crucially depends on the availability of appropriate security mechanisms. Because of using large numbers of geographically distributed dynamic resources, the ACI applications are different from traditional client-server applications. The resources in the large-scale environment are connected across Internet, and they could join and leave the computing environment dynamically. To ensure security, the resources require authentication mechanisms to prevent malicious users, and users also require authentication of resources to protect important data and to prevent the counterfeit owners of resources. As the important data between users and owners of resources flow are exposed in unsecured Internet,

S. Qing, T. Okamoto, and J. Zhou (Eds.): ICICS 2001, LNCS 2229, pp. 398–407, 2001.

the requirements for the integrity and confidentiality of data become more and more urgent. However, most of ACI users pay more attentions on performance of the parallel distributed applications instead of their security.

Aimed at resolving complex security problems and guaranteeing high performance of applications in ACI, a three-level security management system TH-SMS is presented in the paper and two new security techniques are provided: KCKPT [4] and DP-VPN along with the mature security techniques.

The paper is organized as follows: the background of ACI is described in section 2; the structure of security management system TH-SMS is figured out in section 3; according to its three level structure, the implementations of TH-SMS and the new security techniques KCKPT, DP-VPN are discussed in section 4; related works are analyzed in section 5. And finally in section 6, we make some conclusions and address our future work.

2   The ACI Background

In order to effectively utilize high-performance computing and data resource, improve native computing technologies, and cultivate experienced experts across different subjects, Ministry of Education P.R.C proposed ACI project in 2000. In ACI project, the high-performance computers and other advanced instruments are connected through high-speed network, which could be shared by the universities in China to collaborate across different research subjects. The first step of ACI project is to develop an ACI testbed, which connects high-performance parallel computers TH-NPSC in Beijing and SU-NPSC in Shanghai with convenient Web user interface. Our research group realized an ACI testbed [5] in 2001. Therefore, the researchers no matter in Beijing or Shanghai could use geographically distributed high-performance computers, networks and information in ACI testbed conveniently. The final goal of ACI is to connect high-performance parallel computers and data centers in most universities of China and build a huge virtual laboratory, which facilitates the researchers to develop and utilize high-performance computing and data information. The structure of grid computing node in ACI testbed is shown in figure 1.

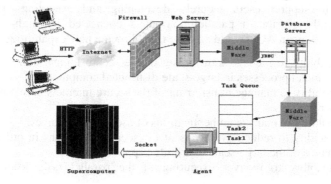

Fig. 1. Grid computing node in ACI testbed

Most of high-performance parallel computers are composed of high performance SMP PCs with Linux operating systems. Based on the distributed database and network techniques, the software architecture of our ACI system includes security system, parallel development tools, performance analysis tools, parallel applications, application-level checkpoint system, user management system, task management system, and resource management system. The ACI architecture has the following characteristics:

1. The integral interfaces in ACI are based on Web technology, so it is easily interacted and independent of computer hardware and operating systems.
2. The main program language for developing is Java. Hence, migration of ACI software system to other operation systems or hardware is easy to implement. C program language is also adopted in some performance sensitive aspects.
3. Information store and management are based on database. With complex index structures and high-performance search operations, database provides faster access than file systems.
4. All computing nodes in ACI adopt Linux as their operating systems, because of its open source and rich software support. Hence, our security mechanisms could be inserted into Linux kernel leading to high security rank in ACI.

As an Internet infrastructure, ACI testbed must satisfy the security requirements of resource users. According to these requirements, ACI testbed should own the abilities to defense illegal attacks and destroys and to recover systems after disasters. Apparently, enhancing security capabilities in ACI testbed would affect performance of the large-scale distributed applications. Hence, in order to ensure high performance of the applications, several dynamic parallel security technologies should be introduced to reduce security overheads. In a word, the security problems and technologies in ACI testbed are more complex and comprehensive than those in common Internet conditions.

3   Security Management System

In order to support users securely developing and executing applications on geographically distributed parallel computers connected by high-speed network, security solutions in ACI should provide the following new capabilities:

1. The capability to manage transferring of the secure logical communication links among parallel processes in large-scale distributed computations.
2. The capability to manage transferring of the secure interacts between the users and Web user interfaces.
3. The capability to manage authentications of users and resources.
4. The capability to reduce overheads of the security solutions in order to guarantee performance of the large-scale distributed applications.
5. The capability to recover executing of the parallel tasks after unexpectable disasters.
6. The capability to ensure integrity of operating system.

In order to satisfy the requirements of security, high-performance and convenience at the same time, new security policies and methods should be introduced. To meet with user's demands we present a security management system TH-SMS with three-level structure, based on which we could apply different security policies and tools to protect different levels of ACI infrastructure. Hence, user could access resources in a more painless and seamless way. The abstract structure of TH-SMS in ACI is shown in figure 2.

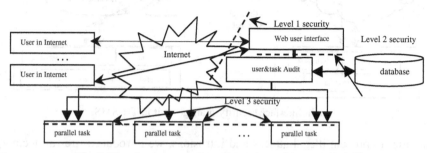

Fig. 2. The abstract structure of security architecture in ACI

The first level of security structure is interface security management between Internet users and Web user interfaces, and its duties are to avoid information between users and interfaces to be leaked or counterfeited, and to defense illegal attacks and intrusions.

The second level of security structure is user security management. It stores the security ranks and resource limits of users into a database. When user accesses resources in ACI, it prevents illegal accesses and restricts different users with different access privileges.

The third level of security structure is task security management. To ensure tasks' security, its duties are to monitor states of the running parallel tasks, encrypt communication data between parallel tasks and disable hostile tasks. In order to recover tasks from unexpected disasters, it checkpoints middle executive images of the parallel tasks to prepare for later recoveries. It also ensures the integrity of operating system. Furthermore, in order to guarantee the performance of tasks, it adopts dynamic parallel security technologies to reduce security overheads.

4   Implementation

4.1   Interface Security Management

In ACI testbed, the interface security management system concerns two aspects:

1. Prevention of illegal attacks and intrusions from Internet.
2. Prevention of illegal information leak and counterfeit.

Generally speaking, the security problems above are also concerned in common Internet WWW services, and the solutions are comparatively steady now. Hence, we adopt two mature security techniques in our management system to realize the security capabilities above. The structure of interface security management in TH-SMS is show in figure 3.

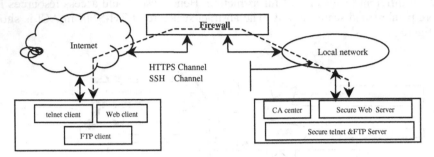

Fig. 3. Interface security management in TH-SMS

In order to prevent illegal attacks and intrusions, we introduced firewall technique into TH-SMS to isolate network of high-performance computers from Internet. The valid services for high-performance computers are permitted to go through firewall, and other invalid services are disabled by firewall. Firewall was realized in Linux OS kernel without hardware support in TH-SMS, and the computer locating firewall has two network interface cards. One is connected to Internet, and the other is connected to local high-speed network. Special security policies are developed in Linux kernel for firewall to strictly check every packet from Internet. As the results, only valid packets from Internet could go through the firewall, and illegal attacks and intrusions are prevented effectively and stably.

In order to prevent illegal information and counterfeit, we adopt Security Sockets Layer (SSL)[6] and Secure SHell(SSH) techniques[7] in TH-SMS. The interact protocols between Internet users and ACI software systems are HTTP, Telnet and FTP protocol, so their communication channels should be encrypted to guarantee their security.

To ensure HTTP channels' security, we adopt SSL and HTTPS protocols, and use OpenSSL, Apache and mod-SSL software to build security Web server. We also build a Certifying Authority (CA) to sign the Certificate Signing Requests, and the result is a real Certificate, which can be used for our secure Apache web server.

To ensure channels' security for protocols of Telnet and FTP, we adopt OpenSSH software to encrypt all information in Telnet and FTP sessions. OpenSSH is a free version of SSH suite of network connectivity tools, which increasing numbers of people in Internet are coming to rely on. Many users of telnet, rlogin, ftp, and other such programs might not realize that their password is transmitted across the Internet unencrypted, but it is. OpenSSH encrypts all traffic (including passwords) to effectively eliminate eavesdropping, connection hijacking, and other network-level attacks.

4.2 User Security Management

In TH-SMS, user security management is used to protect valid rights of the valid users, and to prevent the illegal users and illegal resource accesses from the valid users.

The process of accessing resource of ACI testbed in our TH-SMS system is as follows: if a user wants to access ACI testbed, first he should apply a valid account to enter ACI system; after user security management system checks the information of the user, it would send security account and certification information to the user through security HTTPS or secured email with PGP sign; moreover, the information of the user such as the security rank, the right to access resources in ACI is recorded in a database behind firewall.

When user submits a task to ACI testbed, user security management system in TH-SMS will check the security information of the user stored in database. If the user has the right to access the resource acquired by the user's task, TH-SMS would permit ACI testbed to execute this task; otherwise, this requirement to submit task will be refused. The submitting process is shown is figure 4.

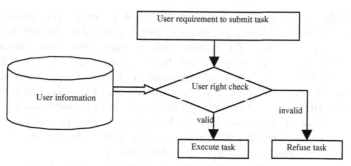

Fig. 4. User security management inTH-SMS

4.3   Task Security Management

The missions of task security management system in ACI testbed include three concerns:

1. To checkpoint middle executive images of tasks.
2. To parallel encrypt communication data among high-performance computers connected by Internet.
3. To prevent executions of hostile tasks.
4. To monitor SUID programs and to protect software integrity of computers.

4.3.1 KCKPT and TH-MPI

Composed of large number of PCs, long-lived distributed computations in ACI have high risks of failure and unexpected disasters. To overcome the drawbacks, we provide application level checkpoint techniques in TH-SMS to store the intermediate executive images of tasks in ACI testbed. Therefore, when meeting with unexpected disasters, the executive image of task could be recovered and continue to execute after recovery.

Currently more and more parallel applications are based on MPI, since the MPI standard has proven effective and sufficient for most of high-performance applications. In order to reduce checkpoint overheads, we developed a OS kernel supported checkpoint technique - KCKPT [4], and designed an OS Kernel integrated Fault Tolerant MPI -- TH-MPI [4]. With supports of fault detecting and fault tolerance from KCKPT in OS level, TH-MPI is implemented in a more transparent, effective and extensive way. With dynamic kernel module and diskless checkpointing technologies, checkpointing overheads are effectively reduced in TH-MPI. Furthermore, TH-MPI supports programs with shared dynamic library, whereas other fault tolerant systems couldn't support them. Through testing in our prototype environment, the initial performance results of TH-MPI are stirring. With the techniques above, we could effectively store the intermediate executive images of parallel tasks and recover from an unexpected crash.

4.3.2 DP-VPN

In ACI testbed, it is the most possible that user's task executes simultaneously on the nodes in both Beijing and Shanghai, so information required by the task is commonly exchanged across Internet. To ensure task security, the communication data transmitted between Beijing and Shanghai should be encrypted. However, leaving the task itself to do data encryption would increase implementation difficulties and lead to unnecessary developing overheads. The common way to resolve the problem is to utilize VPN (Virtual Private Network) [8] technique, but the overheads of encrypting large amount of communication data for high-performance parallel computers are relatively heavy. Sequentially, the routers among geographically distributed high-performance parallel computers will become bottlenecks.

To solve the overhead problem above, we develop a new security technique -- Dynamic Parallel Virtual Private Network (DP-VPN) in TH-SMS. DP-VPN, which is realized in IP layer, provides high-performance secure point-to-point connections. Therefore, the data transported among high-performance parallel computers, could be parallel encrypted in the IP layer of Linux kernel. Supposing there are M computing nodes and N routers in a parallel computer, and N<<M, the main processing steps of DP-VPN are shown below:

1. Developing a dynamic route table for each computing node in the parallel computer. When initializing the route table for each computing node, we set the default router of node $i(0<i<M+1)$ as router j $(0<j<N+1)$, and j=i mod N. When adding or deleting routers, we calculate and reset the route table for each computing node in the parallel computer and send the message to local resource manager.
2. Collecting network information in time. We use SNMP protocol to collect network information among geographically distributed parallel computers, and send the information to local resource manager. All resource managers synchronize the network information, and save the best network route information in time for geographically distributed parallel computers.
3. Developing dynamic route table between routers in geographically distributed parallel computers. To construct the route table, we get the best network route information from local resource managers.

Among the security protocols for VPN, we adopt IPSec [9] as our basic VPN security protocol. We also enhance FreeSWAN [10] to support DP-VPN and set up the route and security policies to meet with our special purposes in ACI testbed. Each high-performance computer has N VPN routers to connect with other high-performance computers. Therefore, the applications need not to concern security problems when communicating with others across Internet. However, the overheads of encryptions and decryptions in one router could not be ignored. If we adopt TRI-DES [11], a widespread encrypting algorithm, the performance of VPN router would decrease at least about 25%. Whereas, when adopting our DP-VPN technique, changing the route policies in local network and adding more VPN routers, the potential bottlenecks would be eliminated.

The structure of VPN is shown in figure 5.

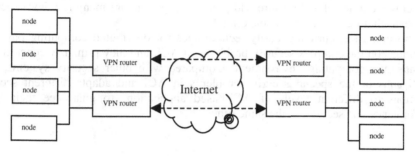

Fig. 5. The structure of VPN based on IPSec

Many hacker techniques are based on SUID and stack-flow. In order to prevent executions of hostile tasks, monitor SUID programs and protect software integrity of computers, we utilize sXid [12] to monitor the changed states of SUID programs and use Tripwire [13] to protect integrity of the whole software on computers. We also add a security patch in Linux kernel to support the unexecuteable stack in kernel. Conclusively, after adopting the security techniques mentioned above, ACI testbed is much more secured, stable and recoverable.

5   Related Work

For its increasing importance, many research works have been done on security spanning from theories to practices, especially in distributed systems. However, there are still few security solutions and techniques aiming at ACI systems. On the other hand, being a geographically distributed, dynamic, and high-performance parallel computing environment, ACI should acquire more attentions on its security problems.

Kerberos [14] has been widely used from the 1980s, but its current version from MIT still relied on conventional cryptography and AS/TGS combination. Although optional Kerberos extensions, such as PKINIT, PKTAPP, PKCROSS etc., have been proposed to support usage of public key cryptography, Kerberos still remains a fairly heavyweight solution suited for intra-domain security.

DCE is a mature distributed computing platform developed by Open Group. It is based on conventional shard-key cryptography with trusted third parties, and it also aims at the intra-domain security solutions.

Furthermore, the security solutions in Kerberos and DCE are based on traditional client/server computing mode and concern little of dynamic resources and high-performance parallel computing, which are the primary characteristics of ACI systems. Hence, they are not adaptable to the security problems of ACI-based applications.

The goals of Legion project [15] based on Globus [16] are similar to those of ACI systems. Based on object-oriented software technology, Legion implements an object-based architecture for applications and provides much flexibility in particular security mechanisms. Every object in Legion contains hooks allowing security services to be added or deleted freely. However, not all the applications adopt the object-oriented architecture that Legion defined. Moreover, Legion only defines a high-level security model without actual architecture and protocols, so there are many low-level security problems that Legion does not concern left.

To summarize, current security technologies for distributed computing pay little attentions on the complex security problems in ACI, and they primarily concern with client/server computing environment. Compared with other security systems, TH-SMS aims at the special security problems in ACI and adapts different security solutions to different levels of ACI-based applications to guarantee their high-performance and security at the same time.

6   Conclusion

ACI testbed is an advanced distributed system which facility users to use the geographically distributed high-performance computers and databases. To insure its security, we designed and realized TH-SMS, a security management system with three-level structure: interface security management, user security management and task security management. According to different levels of ACI infrastructure, we implement different security policies and techniques to ensure security comprehensively. Furthermore, to reduce security overheads, KCKPT and DP-VPN are introduced into task security management in TH-SMS. Conclusively, based on these security solutions in TH-SMS, ACI testbed could present safer and securer services for users in an effective and stable way. In the future, we will develop TH-SMS to support more heterogeneous architectures and operating systems connected in dynamic networks.

References

1.   http://www.npaci.edu
2.   http://www.ncsa.edu
3.   Li SanLi, Huang ZhenChun, He Chuan, SUTH-A Testbed of Advanced Computational Infrastructure. Technology Report, Tsinghua University, 2001
4.   Yu Chen, Zhihui Du and Sanli Li, TH-MPI: OS Kernel integrated Fault Tolerant MPI. Euro PVM/MPI 2001, Greece, submitted, 2001
5.   Wu Jianfeng, The design and realization of High Performance Communication in Cluster and Advanced Computational Infrastructure, Doctoral dissertation, Tsinghua University, P.R. China, 2001
6.   K. Hickman and T. Elgamal. The SSL protocol. Internet draft, Netscape Communications Corp., June 1995.

7. T. Ylonen, T. Kivinen, and M. Saarinen. SSH protocol architecture. Internet draft, November 1997.
8. http://www.vpnc.org
9. R. Atkinson,RFC 1826: IP Authentication Header, August 1995
10. P. Karn et al. The ESP Triple DES Transform, RFC 1851, September 1995
11. http://www.tripwire.org/
12. ftp://marcus.seva.net/pub/sxid/
13. http://www.freeswan.org/
14. J. Kohl and C. Neuman. The Kerberos network authentication service (v5). Internet RFC 1510, 1993.
15. A. Crimshaw, A. Ferrari, F. Knabe and M. Humphrey, Legion: An Operating System for Wide-Area Computing. Technical Report, University of Virginia, 1999
16. I. Foster and C. Kesselman. The Globus project: A progress report. In Heterogeneous Computing Workshop, March 1998.

Cryptography and Middleware Security

Ulrich Lang[1], Dieter Gollmann[2], and Rudolf Schreiner[3]

[1] University of Cambridge Computer Laboratory, Cambridge, United Kingdom
ulrich.lang@cl.cam.ac.uk
[2] Microsoft Research, Cambridge, United Kingdom
diego@microsoft.com
[3] ObjectSecurity Ltd., Cambridge, United Kingdom
rudolf@objectsecurity.com

Abstract. Middleware gives applications an abstract view of the underlying technology. Access control policies define the authorisations of principals. When no suitable representation of principals is available on the middleware layer, policies resort to using verifiable identifiers of underlying cryptographic mechanisms. However, this approach collides with the aim of hiding mechanism-specific details, which include the underlying cryptographic mechanisms. This paper analyses the difficulties of fitting cryptographic mechanisms into a middleware security architecture without breaking either security or the original middleware design goals.

1 Introduction

To hide from applications the inherent complexities of object invocation in distributed systems, a middleware layer is interposed between the application and the underlying technology, acting as a client-side proxy for target objects. To facilitate portability, flexibility, and technology independence, middleware architectures specify a set of standardized interfaces between the application layer, the middleware layer, and the underlying technology. Interoperability and platform independence is achieved through a standardized object interface definition language and standardized communications protocols.

As this paper will illustrate, middleware architectures may not represent the participants in the system in a way suitable for expressing security policies. As a result, policies need to use cryptographic identifiers from the underlying security technology, which breaks most of the middleware abstraction goals. We will discuss the problems, potential solutions, and the additional problems these solutions may introduce. Although the Common Object Request Broker Architecture (CORBA), a widely used middleware architecture, is used as a basis for our discussion, our analysis applies to middleware in general.

Section 2 briefly introduces middleware, the CORBA architecture and design goals, and the terminology used. We will also describe the basic steps involved in an object invocation. Section 3 outlines the security requirements for middleware and summarizes the main features of the CORBA Security Services specification. Section 4 covers the role and architectural position of cryptography in middleware security and examines the different choices of identifiers used

S. Qing, T. Okamoto, and J. Zhou (Eds.): ICICS 2001, LNCS 2229, pp. 408–418, 2001.

in security policies. Section 5 compares potential solutions for integrating cryptography into a middleware security architecture and the problems they would introduce, pointing to MICOSec as a proof-of-concept implementation of the CORBA Security Services.

2   Middleware

Object-oriented middleware enables software objects to transparently call other objects across networks. This is achieved by mediating all remote method invocations through an Object Request Broker (ORB). On a conceptual level the ORB is often referred to as a "software bus", analogous to a hardware bus that provides hardware devices with an abstract interface to the communications mechanism. This conceptual entity is implemented by the ORB libraries on each node and by the underlying technology, which includes all mechanisms that reside below the middleware layer, e.g. virtual machine, operating system, network, transaction monitors, security mechanisms. It is the goal of middleware to hide as much details of the underlying technology as possible from the applications.

2.1   CORBA

The Common Object Request Broker Architecture (CORBA) [CO98] standardizes interfaces for such an ORB. CORBA object interfaces are specified in a standardized Interface Definition Language (IDL), and objects can be located with Interoperable Object References (IORs). CORBA specifies a number of additional object services such as naming, events, persistence, time, and security. The following general design goals are postulated:

Abstraction & Transparency: CORBA hides many of the inherent difficulties of distributed object computing from the application programmer. All object calls appear to be local invocations, i.e. the application programmer does not even need to know where an object is located on the network at the point the invocation is carried out (location transparency), as illustrated in section 2.2.

Technology Independence & Flexibility: Object interfaces are described in IDL, which can be compiled into a variety of target programming languages and platforms. Thus, interfaces are independent of the programming language used to implement the client and server objects. CORBA also has its own communications protocols, which run on top of a variety of conventional network protocols. The most commonly used CORBA protocol is the Internet-Inter-ORB-Protocol (IIOP) specifying how CORBA messages are transported via TCP/IP.

Scalability: CORBA was designed to support systems with a potentially large number of objects and users and does not pose any restrictions on these number, and does without unique persistent identifiers for objects.

Interoperability: Interoperability between objects running on compliant CORBA products from different vendors is facilitated by standardised communications protocols and an interface definition language. However, CORBA cannot always provide interoperability if the underlying technology does not match. For example, if different security service implementations use different cryptographic algorithms then CORBA will not be able to abstract from these inherent incompatibilities – how should the recipient know how to decrypt a message encrypted with an unknown or unsupported algorithm?

Portability & Reusability: Porting of objects between ORB products and re-use of objects in new applications is possible as CORBA standardises the interfaces visible from the application layer. So-called 'CORBA wrappers' can provide IDL interfaces to legacy systems.

This paper will show that some of these design goals cannot be achieved when security is put in place. In particular, security clashes with transparency, scalability, and technology independence, and thus with interoperability and portability.

2.2   Middleware Abstraction: Object Invocation

This section will illustrate how the middleware architecture provides the abstraction from details of the underlying network and object location. The application uses opaque object references that point to the target objects. We will go through the basic steps involved in an object invocation to give an understanding of how network abstraction is achieved (Figure 1).

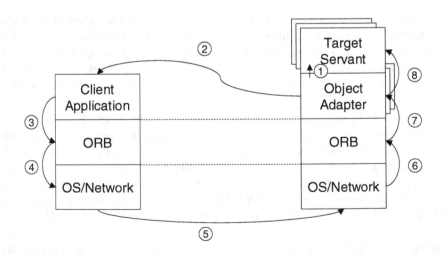

Fig. 1. CORBA Invocation

A so-called object adapter separates a CORBA object from the servant[1] implementation. Object adapters are created by their underlying ORB and are responsible for the mapping between an object and the corresponding servant, and for object and servant lifecycles. There can be several object adapters per ORB, typically arranged hierarchically, and several objects per object adapter.

Before an object can be invoked, it has to be registered with its object adapter. Depending on the particular implementation, the object adapter can then create the servant instance (1), or, to save resources, decide to instantiate the object only once it gets invoked.

During object registration, an Interoperable Object Reference (IOR) is created, which encapsulates details specific to the underlying technology[2]. The application can use this reference without understanding any of the content – it is always used in the same way by the client (similar to the usage of a pointer in object-oriented programming), no matter where the target object resides, which type of network is used, etc. As far as the application is concerned, all details of the underlying network can be ignored. The object reference is thus often called opaque or transparent. Internally, the object reference contains mechanism specific details used by the ORB and the underlying technology, such as addressing information about the target, including hostname, port number, object adapter identifier, and object identifier. For scalability reasons, CORBA does not provide unique persistent identifiers for object adapters and objects.

This IOR is then transferred to the client (2), either through a naming service or by other out-of-band means. When the client tries to invoke the target, it supplies the IOR to its ORB (3), which uses the addressing information to establish a network connection to the target (4). Then the client ORB can package the invocation parameters into a standardized CORBA request format and send them across the network (5) to the target[3].

On the target side, the ORB receives the incoming request (6) and passes it up to the object adapter that matches the addressing information (7). The object adapter then passes the operation parameters up to the object implementation (i.e. the servant), which executes and, optionally, sends a reply back over the existing network connection[4].

---

[1] CORBA divides target applications into servers, which are used to launch the ORB and the object implementations, and servants, which contain the actual object implementations behind the IDL interface.

[2] Only transient object references should point to object instances. If an instance is destroyed and re-instantiated, the old object reference should not automatically point to the new object as the state or the context with the object may have been lost. CORBA also has persistent references, which can only be used in special cases.

[3] More precisely, the application inputs the arguments into so-called stubs, which represent the target interface on the client-side.

[4] CORBA also supports asynchronous messages called call-backs, but they are not relevant here.

3   Middleware Security

Having illustrated how middleware can abstract the underlying network for applications, we now turn to the basic security concepts required in middleware systems and discuss why it is difficult to achieve a similarly elegant solution with respect to middleware security. The central security component is the reference monitor controlling which clients can access which target objects (or, more fine-grained, which target operations) under which circumstances. Hence, it is clear that there need to be a representation of all participants in the access control policy. We will call this representation identifiers.

In middleware, message identifiers are generally not directly relevant to security enforcement[5]. Messages are just a way of conveying an invocation from the caller to the target and back, and thus include the identifier of client or target, so that a policy can be enforced based on these identifiers.

To give these identifiers a meaning, they need to be linked to the principal they represent. A principal in a middleware system can either be a human user who initiates an invocation, or an object instance[6] which (re-)acts without human intervention. The link can be established by the middleware through *principal authentication*, which often involves checking whether the principal possesses a secret, such as a password or a private key.

To avoid the need for principal authentication every time an object gets invoked, the authenticated identifier is stored in a credentials token. It can then be re-used for *request authentication*[7] whenever an object is invoked within the security context represented by the credentials tokens on both sides. *Security context establishment* securely transfers authenticated identifiers to the remote side, where it can be used for local security enforcement.

3.1   CORBA Security Services

The CORBA Security Services specification (CORBASec) [CS99] specifies the security functionality components authentication, message protection, authorization, audit, and optionally non-repudiation [ISO1]. Instead of implementing all the security functionality itself, CORBASec acts to some extent[8] like an API which calls underlying security mechanisms such as Kerberos [KN93], SESAME

---

[5] Of course, messages do have identifiers which allow the ORBs to associate replies with requests, but they are not unique, are chosen at random for each message, and are not persistent.

[6] More precisely, a principal should be linked to the information inside an object and not to the object instance. After all, it would be possible to re-instantiate an object if it crashes, and it should still have the same principal identifier.

[7] In CORBA, this is done transparently by the underlying security technology (e.g. SSL) whenever an object invocation occurs.

[8] Some services are implemented on the ORB layer using so-called interceptors, e.g. access control and audit. However, they rely strongly on the services provided by the underlying security technology, such as authentication and message protection.

[PP95], and SPKM, through an interface modelled after GSS-API [LJ97]. Therefore the functionality offered by CORBASec is always limited by the functionality offered by the underlying security mechanisms.

CORBASec was first published in 1995 and consequently went through several updates to mitigate a number of discovered architectural problems, in particular regarding interoperability and portability. In version 1.5, SSLIOP, the SSL-Inter-ORB-Protocol was added to the specification to meet industry demand. The current draft version 1.8 comprises around 450 pages. There exist a number of additional security-related documents, most notably the Security Domain Management Membership Service revised submission [DM00], and a final submission for Common Secure Interoperability v2 (CSIv2), which is supposed to enhance the interoperability between different CORBASec implementations, and between CORBASec and Enterprise Java Beans.

Although SSL is widely used as a basic security mechanism for CORBA security, it does not integrate well into the CORBA security architecture. SSL works as a secure transport mechanisms establishing a network connection as part of the security context establishment. Therefore SSL has to be integrated as an alternative transport mechanism into the ORB. This way, the security context is set up automatically when the ORB opens a new network connection.

4   Cryptography and Middleware Abstraction

Cryptographic mechanisms are used to guarantee the authenticity and sometimes the confidentiality of claimed identifiers. Authentication protocols generally check that a particular cryptographic key was used when a message was formed. The key can be the principal's key or the key of a certification authority that guarantees that a particular key belongs to a particular principal. Public-key cryptography is often used together with identity certificates, which primarily bind a principal's identifier to its public key. Alternatively, a symmetric key can belong to an authentication server, e.g. in Kerberos systems, which guarantees the identity of the principal. Access control relies on a guaranteed semantic link between the keys and the corresponding principals. Cryptography does not as such guarantee this link and one usually relies on the assumption that only the principal and no-one else has access to its private key.

Once both communicating parties have checked that the expected party is on the remote end, cryptographic mechanisms are used for message protection. This can be done automatically by the network, e.g. when SSL is used.

Cryptography also plays a role in non-repudiation. Effective non-repudiation can only be achieved on the application layer, because principals have to consciously agree to an action to make them directly responsible for it. Automatic evidence generation on lower system layers would remove that responsibility from the principal and is therefore not recommended. Because non-repudiation has to be provided at the application layer, it is not directly related to middleware security, and will thus not be discussed any further in this paper.

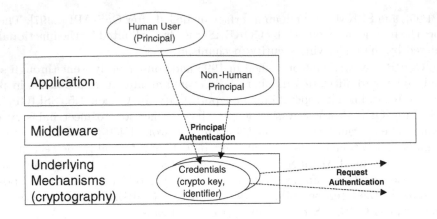

Fig. 2. Principal Authentication, Credentials, Request Authentication

4.1   Architectural Position of Cryptography

To meet the design goals of transparency, abstraction, interoperability, and portability, all information should have a technology independent representation on the middleware layer. In other words, all used technology (e.g. network, operating system, name service) should be hidden underneath the middleware layer. This also applies to cryptographic algorithms and protocols, in some cases even to keys and certificates.

Principals reside above the middleware layer, as they are either parts of the client or target application or human users who conceptually reside "above" the application layer. During principal authentication, the ORB associates the principal's security information, such as its key and identifier (e.g. its private key and its X.509 certificate), with the application from which invocations will be made. Hence, although credentials objects reside on the middleware layer, they contain information specific to the underlying security mechanisms (e.g. keys).

After principal authentication, the middleware or the underlying security mechanisms have access to the credentials information associated with the principal on whose behalf they act. Whenever the application invokes a target object, the credentials are used to authenticate the remote principal and to protect the message. In this way, many invocations can be carried out using the principal's key material without the need for repeated principal authentication. Figure 2 illustrates (exemplary for the client side) where principal authentication, credentials, and request authentication reside in the middleware architecture and how they are related:

In summary, the cryptographic mechanisms are located below the middleware, whereas the principals represented by the cryptographic identifiers reside above the middleware layer. The reference monitor, which resides on the middleware layer, enforces its access control policy based on these cryptographic identifiers.

4.2   Identifiers for Middleware Security Policies

For access control on the middleware layer, all principals and target objects need to have a representation in the policy. To comply with the CORBA design goals, this policy information needs to be technology unspecific, i.e. abstracted from the underlying security mechanisms. Architecturally, it would be preferable to represent the principals with information available at the middleware layer, but we will illustrate in the following why this is not possible. Also we will show why it is useful to have an unchanging name for target objects.

Principal Identifiers. A client in object-oriented middleware systems such as CORBA does not have its own object interface and thus is by definition not an object. A CORBA client is only defined by the fact that it uses an object reference to invoke a target through matching stubs, which represent the target interface on the client-side. The only way to name clients effectively is by using the cryptographic identifiers of its associated principal, which conflicts with the aforementioned abstraction requirement that cryptographic material should reside below the middleware layer. Target-side principals could be described by cryptographic identifiers in the same way, but we will show below why this introduces additional problems on the target side.

Target Object Identifiers. Target-side access control needs a representation of the target object to be able to link a policy to its corresponding object. The target object[9] could be represented by its interface, by its instance, or by its cryptographic identifier. Note that both the object reference and the target interface do not appear on the middleware layer, they are logically situated on the layer above. Object location and authenticated identities of the caller and target are concepts of the layers below. Moreover, CORBA does not provide unique naming of object instances as this is not scalable.

The interface type is not a useful identifier for the target because, due to interface inheritance in object-oriented systems, the link to the actual implementation running behind an interface may be tenuous. In fact, it is normally not possible to find the most derived interface of an object implementation. Although CORBA provides an interface repository that contains the interface descriptions and most derived interfaces of the objects, such repositories are not used for security purposes for performance and assurance reasons. In addition, the interface type describes the target at the wrong granularity. In most cases there will be a large number of objects with the same interface (e.g. bank accounts), but policies often refer to particular object instances.

---

[9] By object, we do not mean the interface or the instance of an object. For example, we would like to represent a particular category of bank account objects (e.g. Alice's bank account), regardless of their particular object instances (and associated object references). Also there might be other bank account objects of the same interface type, so we do not mean the interface either. We rather mean the particular information associated with an object.

The target object instance is represented by its object reference, which in CORBA contains the hostname, the port number, the object adapter identifier, and the object identifier. The identifiers for object and object adapter are not unique, and in most cases chosen randomly by the underlying object adapter or ORB, respectively. Hence the object reference will change if an object instance gets destroyed and re-instantiated and so it is not a useful representation of the target object in the policy. After all, the same policy should apply to an object, regardless if it has been destroyed and re-instantiated or not. This shows that the target identifier should represent the information inside an object, and not the instance or interface. In example of bank accounts, the policy should be linked to a particular client bank account, regardless of the object instance, but it should not apply to all account objects with the same interface.

The target could also be represented by its cryptographic identifier, with the same implications as for the client-side. However, there is often the additional problem that the granularity of the underlying security mechanism does not match the granularity required on the middleware layer. For example, if SSL is used, then all principals behind a particular port will have the same cryptographic identifier, which can be undesirable.

5   Towards a Solution

Cryptographic identifiers for principals should remain hidden below the middleware to enable interoperability, portability, and abstraction. As observed there is no notion for clients on the middleware layer, and although there is a notion for the target, this target representation can change dynamically for the same object[10]. We will now outline how cryptographic identifiers and other target identifiers could be mapped onto static, mechanism-independent, interoperable identifiers, and which potential problems this introduces. In this way, both principals and targets can be expressed in target-side access control (or audit) policies. Also, target identifiers are necessary for associating policy enforcement rules with their respective target objects. Client-side access control policies are possible, but rare in practice and will therefore not be discussed in this paper.

5.1   Cryptographic Identifier Abstraction

Assume that principals are represented in the access control policy with simple name strings, such as "Alice" and "Bob". During request authentication, the underlying security protocol needs access to the corresponding cryptographic identifier to check who is invoking the target. The mapping between the name string and the associated key can be either achieved through a local mapping table or by distributing identity certificates (e.g. X.509). However, there are potential semantic problems if the granularity of the underlying authentication mechanism is not fine enough to guarantee an unambiguous mapping. For example, in the case of SSL, if several principals with different names reside behind

---

[10] More precisely, for the information inside the object, not the object instance as such.

the same socket, they all share the same cryptographic identity. This shows that although this mapping is technically easy to achieve, it is often not advisable to abstract away the nature of the underlying security mechanism. Although it preserves interoperability, abstraction, and portability, it also introduces the risk of semantic mismatches when the underlying security mechanism changes.

5.2 Target Identifier Abstraction

Although the information in the object reference is transient (as explained in Section 2.2) it can be semi-automatically mapped onto a static domain name by the object adapter at the time the object reference is created (see [DM00]). The domain name could be provided by the administrator together with the request to register a new object. The object adapter then puts the mapping between the domain name and its own name with the randomly chosen object identifier into a local mapping table.

This way, a particular user's bank account object could always have the same name in the local mapping table. Whenever an invocation arrives, the middleware can use the information from the request (which originally came from the object reference) to map back to the target name. The associated policy can then be located by using the domain name. With this level of indirection, the policy need not be modified each time an object is re-instantiated, and thus abstracts the dynamicity caused by the scalability requirement.

5.3 MICOSec: Proof of Concept

As a proof of concept, ObjectSecurity has developed MICOSec [OS00], an Open-Source CORBA security services implementation. MICOSec is based on the MICO ORB [MU00], a C++ implementation of the CORBA specifications. MICO was chosen for its transparent structure and its high degree of conformance to the CORBA standard.

In its current version, MICOSec uses MICO's built-in SSL[11] support for its authentication and message protection services. Both client-side user identities and target-side identities are based on X.509 certificates, which are managed by a public key infrastructure. In addition to the basic security functionality, domain name based access control and audit services have been implemented.

6   Conclusion

It is difficult to fit cryptographic security mechanisms into a middleware security architecture without breaking the middleware design goals such as abstraction, transparency, interoperability, scalability, and portability. Middleware security policies need to express the participants in the system, but no suitable representation of such participants is available on the middleware layer. There is no

---

[11] SSL is built around the concept of secure connections (sessions), which are conceptually equivalent to security associations on the middleware layer.

notion of "principals", client applications do not have an identifier, and target identifiers such as the object reference or the interface type are not suitable. As a result, security policies have to draw on the verifiable identifiers of the underlying cryptographic mechanisms.

The reference monitor implemented on the middleware layer thus relies on the guaranteed identifiers of the underlying cryptographic mechanisms the middleware tries to hide[12]. As a result, the whole concept of ORB level separation from the underlying security technology breaks: introducing the middleware layer not only separates the application from the underlying network, it also separates the security problem from the security solution.

We have presented some potential workarounds, which involve the mapping of cryptographic identifiers onto a suitable representation on the middleware layer. Unfortunately, this approach can introduce a new set of problems related to the semantics and granularity of identifiers.

Acknowledgements. The first author was supported by DERA.

References

[CO98]   Object Management Group, *CORBA Architecture and Specification*, 1998

[CS99]   Object Management Group, *CORBA Security Services Specification*, v1.7 (draft), 1999

[DM00]   Object Management Group, *Security Domain Membership Management Service*, Revised Submission, 2/2000

[HP99]   Humenn, P., *Summary of MDI discussions*, OMG SecSIG Mailinglist, 9.3.1999

[ISO1]   ISO 7498-2, *Information processing systems – Open Systems Interconnection – Basic Reference Model – Part 2: Security Architecture*, 1989

[KN93]   Kohl, J. and Neumann, C., *The Kerberos Network Authentication Service V5*, RFC 1510, 1993

[LJ97]   Linn, J., *Generic Security Service Application Program Interface, Version 2*, RFC 2078, 1997

[LS00]   Lang, U., and Schreiner, R., *Flexibility and Interoperability in CORBA Security*, Electronic Notes in Theoretical Computer Science, Volume 32, Elsevier, 2000,
         www.elsevier.nl/gej-ng/31/29/23/show/Products/notes/index.htt

[MU00]   MICO Group, *MICO User's Guide*, 2000

[OS00]   ObjectSecurity, *MICOSec User's Guide*, 2000

[PP95]   Parker, T. and Pinkas, D., *SESAME V4 – Overview*, 1995

---

[12] It is feasible, but difficult, to use cryptographic mechanisms on the application layer, but this would break most of the middleware design goals.

Cryptanalysis of the Hwang-Rao Secret Error-Correcting Code Schemes

Kencheng Zeng[1], Chung-Huang Yang[2], and T.R.N. Rao[3]

[1] SKLOIS, Graduate School of Chinese Academia Sinica, P.O.Box 3908, Beijing 100039, Peoples Republic of China
[2] National Kaohsiung First University of Science and Technology, 1 University Road, Yenchao, Kaohsiung 824, Taiwan, chyang@computer.org
[3] Center for Advanced Computer Studies, University of Louisiana, Lafayette, Louisiana 70504-4330, U.S.A., trao@cacs.louisiana.edu

Abstract. In this paper, the cryptanalytic strength of two Hwang-Rao Secret Error-Correcting Code (SECC) schemes is examined under a known-plaintext attack. In particular, we found the existence of key information redundancy in all SECCs used in the electronic codebook (ECB) mode. Also, our investigations indicate the existence of *synergism* in the SECC schemes, that is, the security of SECC (containing three transformations, Ψ and $\mathbf{E}$ and $\mathbf{P}$) is much stronger than the individual strength of either Ψ or $\mathbf{E}$ or $\mathbf{P}$.

1 Introduction

Using error-correcting codes as cryptosystems was introduced by McEliece [1, 2,3,4]. McEliece's proposal was to use a Goppa code as the underlying basis of an ingenious public-key scheme. Rao and Nam [5,6,7] subsequently introduced a new approach to the private-key algebraic-coded cryptosystems requiring simple error-correcting codes (distance ≥ 6 codes). Hwang and Rao [8] then devised a class of private key cryptosystems, called the Secret Error-Correcting Codes (SECCs).

A SECC provides both data security and data reliability while retaining the full error-correcting capability of the introduced code for possible channel errors. Also in a SECC scheme, any unauthorized user would find it hard to correct channel errors without the decoding keys and the presence of channel errors introduces additional level of security to the system. In this research, we will examine the cryptographic strength of SECCs used in the electronic codebook (ECB) mode. Figure 1 illustrates the three transformations, Ψ and $\mathbf{E}$ and $\mathbf{P}$, involved in the SECC scheme operating in ECB mode.

The ciphertext C is given by

$$C = \mathbf{E}(\Psi(M)) \cdot \mathbf{P}$$

S. Qing, T. Okamoto, and J. Zhou (Eds.): ICICS 2001, LNCS 2229, pp. 419–428, 2001.

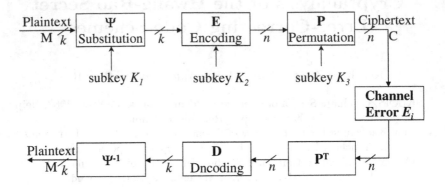

Fig. 1. Hwang-Rao Secret Error-Correcting Code (SECC)

where Ψ is a cryptographic transformation selected by the subkey K_1, $\mathbf{E}$ is the encoding of an (n , k) nonlinear code selected by the subkey K_2, and $\mathbf{P}$ is a random $n \times n$ permutation matrix selected by the subkey K_3. The cryptographic transformation Ψ is installed with the purpose of withstanding chosen plaintext attacks like those done in [6] and the Preparata code [9] was mentioned as the underlying basis of $\mathbf{E}$.

Preparata codes [9] are a family of $(n = 2^r - 1, k = 2^r - 2r, 5)$ optimal double error-correcting codes, for even $r \geq 4$. The representation of Preparata codes in terms of polynomials over $GF(2)$ modulo $\left(x^{2^{r-1}-1} + 1 \right)$ is as follows. Let α denote a primitive element of $GF(2^{r-1})$; $g(x)$ the minimum polynomial for the α; $g_3(x)$ the minimum polynomial for the α^3; $\{r(x)\}$ a $\{2^{r-1}-1, 2^{r-1}-r, 3\}$ Hamming code generated by $g(x)$; $\{s(x)\}$ a $[2^{r-1} - 1, 2^{r-1} - 2r, 6]$ BCH code generated by $(1 + x)g(x)g_3(x)$; $f(x)$ the nonzero code polynomial of the dual code of $\{m(x)\}$ such that $f^2(x) = f(x)$; $u(x) = 1 + x + x^2 + ... + x^{2^{r-1}-2}$; $q(x) \in \{0, 1, x, x^2, ..., x^{2^{r-1}-2}\}$; $b \in \{0,1\}$. Then the 3-block binary vectors of the form $w = [m(x) + q(x), b , m(x) + (m(1) + b)u(x) + q(x) \cdot f(x) + s(x)]$ are the codewords of the Preparata codes.

We will examine the security of SECC using Preparata code in the presence of a random error vector of weight ≤ 1, as shown in Fig. 2, we called it SECC Scheme I in this research.

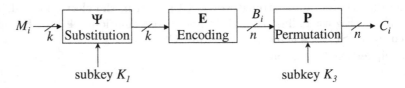

Fig. 2. Hwang-Rao SECC Scheme I

In all that follows, we assume that the Preparata code of interest is fixed and known to the cryptanalyst, for the number of possible Preparata codes of a given code length $n = 2^r - 1$ is $\frac{\Phi(2^{r-1}-1)}{r-1}$, which is very small (less or equal to 48 for code length $n \leq 1023$). In order to increase the error-correcting capability of SECC using Preparata codes, Hwang and Rao also suggest to use the $|\,u\,|\,u + v\,|$ code construction method [10, p. 76]. This scheme, shown in Figure 3, will be called SECC Scheme II.

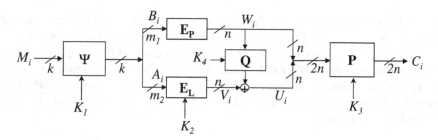

Fig. 3. SECC Scheme II

For the SECC Scheme II, the ciphertext C_i is given by

$$C_i = (W_i \,,\, U_i) \cdot \mathbf{P}$$
$$= (W_i \,,\, W_i \cdot \mathbf{Q} \,+\, V_i) \cdot \mathbf{P} \,,$$

where $W_i = \mathbf{E_P}\,(B_i)$, $V_i = \mathbf{E_L}\,(A_i)$, $(B_i \,,\, A_i) = \mathbf{\Psi}\,_{K_1}(M_i)$, $\mathbf{E_P}$ denote the encoding a $(n \,,\, m_1)$ Preparata code; $\mathbf{E_L}$ is the generator matrix of a $(n \,,\, m_2)$ linear code selected by the subkey K_2; $k = m_1 + m_2$; $\mathbf{P}$ is a $2n \times 2n$ permutation matrix, $\mathbf{Q}$ is an $n \times n$ permutation matrix, both randomly selected by the subkeys K_3, K_4 respectively. [1].

In the following sections, the cryptanalytic strength of above two SECC schemes is examined under a known-plaintext attack. In particular, we found the existence of key information redundancy in all SECCs used in the electronic codebook (ECB) mode. That is, we could perform exhaustive searching applied to the subkey K_1. and recover other subkeys. Since exhaustive searching has been applied, the conclusions obtained do not mean that the schemes considered here are cryptographically insecure, rather they show that under a known-plaintext attack all the additional functions introduced into the schemes do not contribute substantially to their cryptographic strength. To counterattack, key expansion might be used, where a short key is stretched into a long one [11].

2   A Known-Plaintext Attack to the SECC Scheme I

Suppose we have s plaintext-ciphertext pairs, denoted by (M_1, C_1), (M_2, C_2), ..., (M_s, C_s), then our attack can be described as the following two steps.

---

[1]   We also use the symbol $\mathbf{E_L}$ to denote the linear code selected by K_2

2.1   Determining the Subkey K_1 by Exhaustive Searching

First, we will try to find the unknown subkey K_1 by a brute-force approach. Let $\overline{K_1}$ denote the subkey in trial, then for each given given plaintexts M_i, $1 \leq i \leq s$, compute $\overline{B_i} = \mathbf{E_P}\left(\mathbf{\Psi}\left(M_i\right)\right)$ under the control of the trial key $\overline{K_1}$. It is clear that the permutation $\mathbf{P}$ is a (Hamming) weight preserving transformation. Therefore, we can use the condition.

$$weight\left(\overline{B_i}\right) \; = \; weight\left(C_i\right), \qquad 1 \leq i \leq s$$

to search for the correct subkey K_1. Let p_i denote the probability for a randomly chosen codeword of the Preparata code to have weight i, then we have $p_i < \frac{1}{2}$ for any $4 \leq i \leq n-4$, as can be seen from the symmetry of the weight enumerator of the Preparata codes [10, p.473]. Thus, the probability p for a false $\overline{K_1}$ to pass the test on s plaintext-ciphertext pairs is $p < \frac{1}{2^s}$. The correct subkey K_1, in general, will be uniquely determined if we have $s > |K_1|$ (length of the subkey K_1 in bits) such pairs.

2.2   Determining the Permutation P

Once the subkey K_1 has been found, we note that

$$\mathbf{B} \cdot \mathbf{P} \; = \; \mathbf{C} \, ,$$

where $\mathbf{B}$ is the $s \times n$ matrix

$$\mathbf{B} = \begin{bmatrix} B_1 \\ B_2 \\ \cdots \\ \cdots \\ B_s \end{bmatrix}$$

and $\mathbf{C}$ is the $s \times n$ matrix

$$\mathbf{C} = \begin{bmatrix} C_1 \\ C_2 \\ \cdots \\ \cdots \\ C_s \end{bmatrix}$$

Now the permutation $\mathbf{P}$ can be determined by comparing the n columns in the matrix $\mathbf{B}$ with the n columns in the matrix $\mathbf{C}$.

3   A Known Plaintext Attack to the SECC Scheme II

Our attack is based on utilizing the linearity of $\mathbf{E_L}$, $\mathbf{Q}$, and $\mathbf{P}$ and we will again assume that s plaintext-ciphertext pairs, (M_1, C_1), (M_2, C_2), ..., (M_s, C_s), are given.

3.1   Determining the Subkey K_1

Let $\overline{K_1}$ denote the subkey in trial and $(\overline{B}_i, \overline{A}_i) = \mathbf{\Psi}_{\overline{K_1}}(M_i)$. We begin by finding a maximal set of linearly independent solutions $\lambda^{(1)}, \lambda^{(2)}, ..., \lambda^{(N)}$ of the system of homogeneous linear algebraic equations

$$\lambda \overline{\mathbf{A}} = \mathbf{0},$$

where $\overline{\mathbf{A}}$ is the $s \times n$ matrix with $\overline{A}_j, 1 \leq j \leq s$ as rows and

$$\lambda = (\lambda_1, \lambda_2, ..., \lambda_s)$$

denotes the s-dimensional vector of unknowns. We know from a well-known theorem in linear algebra (see, for example, [12, p. 76]) that $N \geq s - m_2$, and it follows from the linearity of the (linear) code $\mathbf{E_L}$ that

$$\sum_{j=1}^{s} \lambda_j^{(i)} \mathbf{E_L}(\overline{A}_j) = \mathbf{E_L}\left(\sum_{j=1}^{s} \lambda_j^{(i)} \overline{A}_j\right) = \mathbf{0}, \quad i = 1, 2, ..., N.$$

Therefore, if $\overline{K_1}$ is the right choice, then

$$\sum_{j=1}^{s} \lambda_j^{(i)} C_j = \left(\sum_{j=1}^{s} \lambda_j^{(i)} \mathbf{E_P}(\overline{B}_j), \sum_{j=1}^{s} \lambda_j^{(i)} \left(\mathbf{E_L}(\overline{A}_j) + \mathbf{E_P}(\overline{B}_j) \cdot \mathbf{Q}\right)\right) \cdot \mathbf{P}$$

$$= \left(\sum_{j=1}^{s} \lambda_j^{(i)} \mathbf{E_P}(\overline{B}_j), \sum_{j=1}^{s} \lambda_j^{(i)} \mathbf{E_P}(\overline{B}_j) \cdot \mathbf{Q}\right) \cdot \mathbf{P}$$

and hence we shall have

$$2\,weight\left(\sum_{j=1}^{s} \lambda_j^{(i)} \mathbf{E_P}(\overline{B}_j)\right) = weight\left(\sum_{j=1}^{s} \lambda_j^{(i)} C_j\right), \quad 1 \leq i \leq N. \quad (1)$$

We then determine the unknown K_1 by exhaustive searching and use (Eq. 1) as our key identification criterion. This is a good criterion, for we know that under some general conditions the probability that a pair of randomly generated l-vectors will have the same (Hamming)weight is

$$p = \frac{1}{2^{2l}} \sum_{r=0}^{l} (C_l^r)^2 = \frac{1}{2^{2l}} C_{2l}^l < \frac{1}{4},$$

so one can expect to determine K_1 uniquely if $s > m_2 + \frac{|K_1|}{2}$. We emphasize that the basic idea in designing the key identification criterion (Eq. 1) is to eliminate the influence of the subkeys K_2, K_3, K_4 in trying to determine the subkey K_1.

3.2   Determining the Image Set $\mathbf{T} = \mathbf{P}(i) \mid n < i \leq 2n$

Once K_1 has been found, we will determine the image set $\mathbf{T}$ of the half interval $[n + 1, 2n]$ under the permutation $\mathbf{P}$. We start with finding a maximal set of linearly independent solution vectors

$$\mu^{(1)},\ \mu^{(2)},\ ...,\ \mu^{(L)},\quad L \geq s - m_1,$$

of the system of homogeneous linear algebraic equations

$$\mu\,\mathbf{W} = 0,$$

where $\mathbf{W}$ is the $s \times n$ matrix with $W_j, 1 \leq j \leq s$, as rows and

$$\mu = (\mu_1,\ \mu_2,\ ...,\ \mu_s)$$

is the s-vector of unknowns. Then we shall have for each $1 \leq i \leq L$,

$$\Phi^{(i)} = \sum_{i=1}^{s}\mu_j^{(i)}C_j = \left(\mathbf{0}^{(n)},\ D^{(i)}\right) \cdot \mathbf{P},$$

where

$$D^{(i)} = \sum_{j=1}^{s}\mu_j^{(i)}\mathbf{E_L}(A_j),\quad 1 \leq i \leq L,$$

are codewords in $\mathbf{E_L}$. Since the dimension of the linear code $\mathbf{E_L}$ is m_2, the probability that there exists among these codewords a linear basis for $\mathbf{E_L}$ will be [13]

$$p = \prod_{L-m_2+1}^{L} \left(1 - \frac{1}{2^i}\right),$$

which is nearly equal to 1 when s is sufficiently large, say, $s \geq m_1 + m_2 + 4$. Now suppose such a basis does exist, then we can determine $\mathbf{T}$ according to the rule:

$$k \in \mathbf{T} \iff k - th\ component\ of\ \Phi^{(i)}\ is\ 1\ for\ some\ i \in [1, L].$$

This criterion for determining $\mathbf{T}$ is based on the simple observation that if we fix a certain linear basis of the code $\mathbf{E_L}$, then for any $1 \leq k \leq n$ there is a codeword belonging to that basis such that its k-th component will be 1. For otherwise it would mean that the k-th location is redundant for the code $\mathbf{E_L}$.

3.3   Decrypting Ciphertexts without Knowning K_2, K_3, K_4

Once the subkey K_1 is determined from the given s plaintext-ciphertext pairs, we could decrypt any other ciphertexts without knowing K_2, K_3, K_4. To recover the plaintexts, we arrange the numbers of the two sets $\mathbf{T}$ and $\mathbf{S} = \mathbf{I}^{(2n)} - \mathbf{T}$ in some fixed, say increasing, order as

$$\mathbf{S} = \{s_1, s_2, ..., s_n\}, \quad \mathbf{T} = \{t_1, t_2, ..., t_n\}$$

and for any $2n$-vector

$$C = (c_1, c_2, ..., c_{2n})$$

write

$$C(\mathbf{S}) = (c_{s_1}, c_{s_2}, ..., c_{s_n}), \quad C(\mathbf{T}) = (c_{t_1}, c_{t_2}, ..., c_{t_n}) .$$

Since $\mathbf{\Psi}(M) = (B , A)$, we will first find B and A from the received error-free ciphertext C, then recover the plaintext M.

To find B, let r be the dimension of the linear closure $< \mathbf{E} >$ of the Preparata code and find from among the codewords W_i, $1 \leq i \leq s$, a linear basis

$$W_{\alpha_1} , W_{\alpha_2} , ..., W_{\alpha_r}$$

for $< \mathbf{E} >$. As given in the above discussion, the success probability of doing this is nearly 1. Then we shall have

$$C(\mathbf{S}) = \sum_{k=1}^{r} \xi_k C_{\alpha_k}(\mathbf{S})$$

and after having computed the coefficients ξ_k by solving the corresponding system of non-homogeneous linear algebraic equations, we shall have

$$W = \sum_{k=1}^{r} \xi_k W_{\alpha_k}$$

and

$$B = \mathbf{E}_P^{-1} (W).$$

To find A, we replace $C(\mathbf{T})$ by

$$C^*(\mathbf{T}) = C(\mathbf{T}) + \sum_{k=1}^{r} \xi_k C_{\alpha_k}(\mathbf{T}) ,$$

and find from among the vectors $\Phi^{(i)}(\mathbf{T})$, $1 \leq i \leq L$, a set of m_2 linearly independent ones

$$\Phi^{(\beta_1)}(\mathbf{T}), \; \Phi^{(\beta_2)}(\mathbf{T}), \; ..., \; \Phi^{(\beta_{m_2})}(\mathbf{T}) .$$

Once such a set has been found, $C^*(\mathbf{T})$ can also be expressed as a linear combination of them:

$$C^*(\mathbf{T}) = \sum_{k=1}^{m_2} \eta_k \Phi^{(\beta_k)}(\mathbf{T}) .$$

The combination coefficients η_k can be computed by solving the corresponding system of n equations in m_2 unknowns and it follows from the linearity of $\mathbf{E_L}$ that

$$A = \sum_{k=1}^{m_2} \eta_k \sum_{j=1}^{s} \mu_j^{(\beta_k)} A_j + \sum_{k=1}^{r} \xi_k A_{\alpha_k} .$$

Plaintext M can then be obtained by

$$M = \mathbf{\Psi}^{-1}(A , B) .$$

3.4   Determining the Subkeys K_2, K_3, K_4

We shall illustrate how to determining the subkeys K_2, K_3, K_4 by considering the case where $\mathbf{E_L}$ is an (n , m_2) cyclic code generated by a polynomial

$$g(x) = x^d + g_{d-1}x^{d-1} + \dots + g_0, \quad d = n - m_2$$

with coefficients $g_i, 0 \le i \le d-1$ to be specified by the subkey K_2.

First, consider the generator matrix

$$\mathbf{G} = \begin{pmatrix} 0 & 0 & \cdots & 0 & 1 & g_{d-1} & \cdots & g_1 & g_0 \\ 0 & 0 & \cdots & 1 & g_{d-1} & g_{d-2} & \cdots & g_0 & 0 \\ \cdots & \cdots & \cdots & \cdots & \cdots & \cdots & \cdots \cdots \cdots \\ 1 & g_{d-1} & \cdots & g_2 & g_1 & g_0 & \cdots & 0 & 0 \end{pmatrix} \quad (2)$$

together with the $m_2 \times m_2$ non-singular matrix

$$\mathbf{Y} = \begin{bmatrix} Y^{\beta_1} \\ Y^{\beta_2} \\ \cdots \\ Y^{\beta_{m_2}} \end{bmatrix}$$

with rows

$$Y^{\beta_k} = \sum_{j=1}^{s} \mu_j^{(\beta_k)} A_j$$

and the $m_2 \times n$ matrix

$$\mathbf{\Phi} = \begin{bmatrix} \Phi^{(\beta_1)}(\mathbf{T}) \\ \Phi^{(\beta_2)}(\mathbf{T}) \\ \cdots \\ \Phi^{(\beta_{m_2})}(\mathbf{T}) \end{bmatrix} .$$

Both $\mathbf{Y}$ and $\mathbf{\Phi}$ can be computed from the known plaintext-ciphertext pairs and we have

$$\mathbf{G} = \mathbf{Y}^{-1} \mathbf{\Phi} \mathbf{R} ,$$

where $\mathbf{R}$ is an $n \times n$ permutation matrix. This means the matrix $\mathbf{G}$, i.e., the subkey K_2 can be determined by reducing the product $\mathbf{Y}^{-1} \cdot \mathbf{\Phi}$ to the canonical form (Eq. 2) through column permutation.

Once $\mathbf{E_L}$ has been found, we can determine the value of $\mathbf{P}(n + i) \in \mathbf{T}$, $1 \le i \le n$, by comparing the columns of the matrices

$$\begin{bmatrix} D^{(1)} \\ D^{(2)} \\ \cdots \\ D^{(N)} \end{bmatrix}, \quad \begin{bmatrix} \varPhi^{(1)}(\mathbf{T}) \\ \varPhi^{(2)}(\mathbf{T}) \\ \cdots \\ \varPhi^{(N)}(\mathbf{T}) \end{bmatrix}$$

and determine the values $\mathbf{P}(i) \in \mathbf{S}$ by comparing the columns of

$$\begin{bmatrix} W_1 \\ W_2 \\ \cdots \\ W_s \end{bmatrix}, \quad \begin{bmatrix} C_1(\mathbf{S}) \\ C_2(\mathbf{S}) \\ \cdots \\ C_s(\mathbf{S}) \end{bmatrix}.$$

Finally, by comparing the first n columns with the last n columns in the matrix with the rows

$$R_i = C_i \cdot \mathbf{P}^{-1} + (\mathbf{0}^{(n)}, \mathbf{E_L}(A_i)), \quad 1 \le i \le s,$$

we can easily determine the permutation $\mathbf{Q}$.

4   Conclusions

We have shown that, in the presence of sufficient plaintext-ciphertext pairs, both the SECC Scheme I and Scheme II can be attacked by exhaustive searching applied to the subkey K_1. Since exhaustive searching has been applied, the conclusions obtained do not mean that the SECC schemes considered here are cryptographically insecure, rather they show that under a known-plaintext attack all the additional devices introduced into the schemes do not contribute substantially to their cryptographic strength. To counterattack, key expansion might be used, where a short key is stretched into a long one.

The above investigations also indicate the existence of *synergism* in the SECC schemes, that is, the security of SECC using nonlinear codes (containing three transformations, $\mathbf{\Psi}$ and $\mathbf{E}$ and $\mathbf{P}$) is much stronger than the individual strength of either $\mathbf{\Psi}$ or $\mathbf{E}$ or $\mathbf{P}$.

References

1. R.J. McEliece, "A Public-Key Cryptosystem Based on Algebraic Coding Theory," *DSN Progress Report*, Jet Propulsion Laboratory, Calif., Jan. & Feb. 1978, pp. 114-116.
2. A. Canteaut and N. Sendrier, "Cryptoanalysis of the Original McEleice Cryptosytems," *Proc. Asiacrypt'98*, 1998, pp. 187-199.
3. P. Louidreau, "Strengthening McEliece Cryptosystem," *Proc. Asiacrypt'2000*, 2000, pp. 585-598.

4. P. Loidreau and N. Sendrier, "Weak keys in the McEliece public-key cryptosystem," *IEEE Transactions on Information Theory*, Vol. 47, No. 3 , March 2001, pp.1207 -1211.

5. T.R.N. Rao and K.H. Nam, "A Private-Key Algebraic-Coded Cryptosystem," *Proc. Crypto'86*, 1986, pp. 35-48.

6. R. Struik and J. van Tilburg, "The Rao-Nam Scheme is Insecure Against a Chosen-Plaintext Attack," *Proc. Crypto'87*, 1987, pp. 445-457.

7. T.R.N. Rao and K.H. Nam, "Private-Key Algebraic-Code Encryptions," *IEEE Trans. Info. Theory*, 1989, pp. 829-833.

8. T. Hwang and T.R.N. Rao, "Secret Error-Correcting Codes (SECC)," *Proc. Crypto'88*, 1988, pp. 540-563.

9. F. P. Preparata, "A Class of Optimum Nonlinear Double-Error-Correcting Codes," *Information and Control* , Vol. 13, 1968, pp. 378-400.

10. F.J. MacWilliams and J.J.A. Sloane, *The Theory of Error-Correcting Codes*, North-Holland, Amsterdam, 1977.

11. C.P. Schnorr, "On the construction of random number generators and random function generators," *Proc. Eurocrypt'88*, 1988, pp. 225-232.

12. A. Adrian Albert, *Fundamental Concepts of Higher Algebra*, University of Chicago Press, 1956.

13. K.C. Zeng, C.H. Yang and T.R.N. Rao, "On the Linear Consistency Test (LCT) in Cryptanalysis with Applications," *Proc. Crypto'89*, 1989, pp. 164-174.

A Role-Based Model for Access Control in Database Federations

Eric Disson, Danielle Boulanger, Gilles Dubois

MODEME Team, UMR CNRS 5055,
Université Jean Moulin Lyon 3,
15, quai Claude Bernard 69007 Lyon, France
{disson, db, dubois}@univ-lyon3.fr

Abstract. Data access security in federated information systems with loose coupling among local data sources is hard to achieve mainly for two reasons: local data information source heterogeneity (data models, access security models, semantics...), local autonomy which do not allow to create a global integrated consistent security schema. To solve some of such problems we propose a role-based object model to describe the local data access security schemas (discretionary and non-discretionary models). Interoperability among the various local data sources is achieved by a rich descriptive layer at the federated level. The global security policy allows to define the choices concerning information flow control both for importation (from the federation to a local system) and exportation (from a local system to the federation).

1 Introduction

In the field of information system cooperation, various approaches range from tight integration based on global schema construction to interoperability involving dynamic mediation processes. Global integration leads to a consistent global data schema but do not respect local autonomy and is not realistic when numerous information sources are willing to cooperate. On the other hand, loose coupling provides a good framework for scalable federative systems but requires knowledge-intensive processes to dynamically accommodate different data models and contexts [1]. In such approaches the main issues are related to data models discrepancies, semantic heterogeneity and security models inconsistencies.

Security in federated databases is very complex because a large set of diverse users is expected to use a pool of component databases containing data of varying sensitivities with different security requirements.

Two main assumptions are taken in federated databases: *autonomy* and *heterogeneity* [2]. The first refers to the ability of the local database system to retain a most large degree of control over the aspects of the federated system. The highest heterogeneity level is the semantic heterogeneity between local entities of the federation. Another heterogeneity problem is the difference between local organizational security methods (different schemes of user types and objects).

S. Qing, T. Okamoto, and J. Zhou (Eds.): ICICS 2001, LNCS 2229, pp. 429–440, 2001.

Federated security systems must support both open and / or closed security axioms and logical access modes.

In database federation security plays an increased role. As the need to share information securely and the need to maintain the autonomy of local databases joining a federation often present conflicting requirements, some of the aspects of autonomy have to be sacrified in order to achieve an actual federation. However, local database administrators would only offer their local data to the federation, if secrecy and integrity were still guaranteed. So, the federation security system has to be at least as secure as each of the local systems and on the other hand as transparent as possible to users.

To deal with both semantic heterogeneity and security in a federated context, we conciliate an object oriented model as a canonical descriptive model and a role based access model as a canonical security model. Since local information systems actually cooperate, a loose coupling among them exists.

In section 2 and 3 we discuss some related works and present our approach. In section 4 we expose the canonical model; in section 5, local security model is shown. Section 6 presents the federated flow control policy.

2   Related Works

Several approaches are used to define federated security models:
-    using views and granting authorizations on the views to allow or prevent a global user to access information within a federation. In Goyal's [3] approach access rules are used to authorize or deny the access to a global view.
-    extending an existing access control model (such as DAC or MAC) to deal with the problems of autonomy and heterogeneity.

The CHASSIS (Configurable, Heterogeneous, And Safe, Secure Information Systems) project [4] is a tight coupled system with discretionary access control and a right granting system. In tightly coupled systems, a federation authority exists and the federated database system has its proper access model. In case of conflicts, prohibitions override permissions. Access rights can be granted to individual users and to roles. Multiple role activation is controlled by an *activation conflict relation*. Several rules exist to infer implicit rights according to the data model. In this approach the global schema has more importance than local ones. Some other propositions [5] use a multi-level access control but in a relatively compatible and homogeneous database system. Several propositions [6] and [7] use a role-based access control model for DAC and MAC simulation in non federated systems but their approaches of access model heterogeneity are relevant for database federation security. The *AMAC* model uses both MAC and DAC models at the federated level [8]. It supports an automated labeling object system to compute large data queries in a federated system. These approaches have two limitations: the federated manager has a bad local security visibility and the sub-transaction (part of the global query) to a local system could be aborted later affecting the performance of the federated system; the lack of logical secured architecture do not permit how the federated security can be enforced.

One of the issues in the Distributed Object Kernel (DOK) [9] is the development of a federated access control and a secured logical architecture. It allows the DOK system to enforce federated security policies in the context of autonomous, distributed and heterogeneous databases. The authors consider DAC and MAC access control. The federated level of the DOK system supports a bottom-up approach for access control: the Global Access Control (GAC) is derived from all the local security policies and ensures that no violation or overriding of local policies is possible. The DOK system is an open system: the federated access list for an aggregate is explicited as a union of the different security information defined in the local databases. If only one database allows the reading of the aggregate, according to global policies, the user has 'read access' to the required information.

Some propositions focus on security object similarity evaluation like [10]; the authors propose similarity criteria and associated metrics to compare security specifications of different applications. They consider security specifications according to a role-based model providing powerful authorization mechanisms suitable for similarity analysis. They use a set of basic criteria called *affinity criteria* (like synonymy, genericity...), some dictionaries of terms and roles, and a global similarity coefficient to compute the authorization affinity between two roles. They deal with the highest level of data semantic heterogeneity and not with the access model heterogeneity level.

Security in federated information systems is a critical issue. When a high security level is defined it often implies a tight coupling among local databases. Similarly a loose coupling leads to local information sources autonomy and consequently to a poor global security level.

3   Our Approach

We propose a global framework dedicated to autonomous preexisting data sources cooperation provided with an acceptable security level based on a rich descriptive object oriented layer.

To constitute the descriptive layer we define metadata insuring an homogeneous representation of each local available information source [11], [12]. The layer supports global queries treatment through Data Descriptive Objects (DDO) and Semantic Links (SemL). DDO and SemL are dedicated to the abstract description of the local data entities structure and the semantic links among them. For a given data model (relational, object, rule-based...) a set of DDO classes is defined to allow a description of the model as precise as required at the federated level. Thus for each local data entity a DDO is instantiated in the descriptive layer. To improve the expressiveness of the description, a set of SemL classes is also created (notice that SemL are not data model dependent) to express semantic links among the data. It allows to implement inner links at the local level as well as inter-database links: semantic links like synonymy, hyperonymy and hyponymy describe syntactic and conceptual equivalencies among the data entities. The resulting semantic network constitutes a knowledge base used for global imprecise queries processing.

We use a Role-Based Access Model [13] to describe each local security policy at the global cooperation level. This model is enriched by specific metadata describing data manipulation rights. We do not use data definition rights and rights administration concepts in global system with the loosely cooperation hypothesis. Such access rights are administrated only by local data owners or "security officers". RBAC models are efficient for simulating other access policies [14], [15] and respect the loosely coupled cooperation hypothesis. The local security items are modeled with two concepts: the security object (passive data entity) and the security subject (active entity like user) are described with Security Descriptive Objects (SDO) which are instantiated from SDO classes (Data, User...). The Application SDO class describes the general security strategy of the local system. The local security authorization units like groups (DAC policies), roles (RBAC policies) or MAC "containers" (result of Cartesian product between MAC category and MAC classification hierarchy of the local model) are described by Access Policy Descriptive Objects (APDO). Each SDO references related semantic descriptive objects (DDO). The overall security accommodation process of the local information sources is as follow: 1- lexical and data semantic description, 2- description of each local security exported schema with the corresponding security descriptive classes, 3- distribution in security domains at the global level. The security domains are sub-graphs extracted from the object security descriptive layer providing a secured functional frame. We now present security metadata insuring a global secured framework for the cooperation structure.

4   The Federated Canonical Model

The figure 1 highlights our data and security canonical model. Successively we specify local access policy descriptive classes, local access schema descriptive classes and link classes.

Our objectives are:
- to represent local access schemas respecting different access policies (DAC, MAC, RBAC).
- to establish access equivalence between described schemas.
- to control the federated information flow with:
  - the respect of local user profiles.
  - the respect of local exportation policies (information flow from a local system to the federation).

4.1   Local Access Policy Descriptive Classes

Access Policy Descriptive Object (APDO):
An Access Policy Descriptive Object is defined by the tuple < FID; LD; LAP; LAMT; LMT; {role} >. FID is the Federated Identifier of the local system; LD is the Local Designation. LAP is the Local Access Policy which can be chosen in the set { DAC; RBAC; MAC^S; MAC^L } with DAC for Discretionary Access Control [16], RBAC for Role-Based Access Control, MAC^S and MAC^L for respectively mandatory model with strict ✩-property and mandatory model with liberal ✩-property [17].

LAMT is the Local Access Mode Table and defines the correspondences between the local access modes and the federated access modes. The Local Mandatory Table (LMT) defines the correspondences between the local secrecy hierarchy level of a mandatory system and the federated secrecy level hierarchy. LMT attribute is null-valued in case of DAC or RBAC system description. {role} is a set of Roles which describe discretionary user group, role and mandatory category.

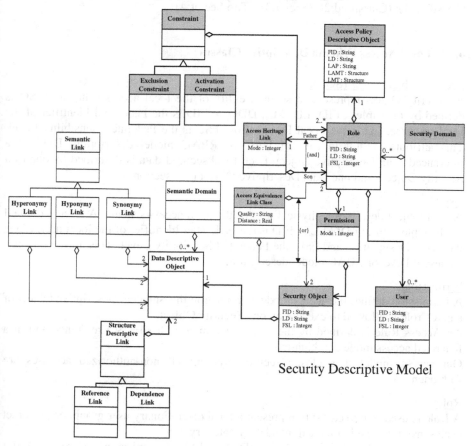

Data Descriptive Model

Security Descriptive Model

Fig. 1. UML [18] representation of Data and Security Descriptive Model.

Local Access Mode Table (LAMT):

At the federated level we use five logical access modes: read-only (r), execute (x), append (a), upgrade (u) and delete (d) with $r \perp x \perp a \perp u \perp d$. Each local access mode is described by a federated access mode combination. For example, in Unix system the "write" access mode is described by the federated access mode combination a + u + d. All the local access mode descriptions are defined in the Local Access Mode Table.

Local Mandatory Table (LMT):
The Local Mandatory Table defines a local secrecy hierarchy in a mandatory system. Each sensibility level is associated with its index in the hierarchy. The dominate level is always the first. The LMT references all the local sensibility couples. For example, a local system with the hierarchy of sensibility Non-Classified < Classified < Secret < Top Secret is described by the LMT {(Non-Classified,1); (Classified;2); (Secret;3); (Top Secret;4)}.

4.2   Local Access Schema Descriptive Classes

Security Object Class (SOC):
A Security Object represents a secured entity of the local access schema. A SO is defined by the tuple < FID; LD; ML; DDO >. FID is the Federated Identifier of the local resource. LD is the Local Designation. FSL is the Federated Sensibility Level. This attribute is null in case of DAC or RBAC model description. DDO is a referenced Data Descriptive Object. Each local secured data is described by one to n Security Objects and one Data Descriptive Object (see section 5).

User:
A User Object describes a physical user of the local access schema. A User is defined by the tuple < FID; LD; FSL >. FID is the Federated Identifier of the local user. LD is the Local Designation and FSL, the Federated Sensibility Level. This attribute is null in case of DAC or RBAC model description.

Permission:
A Permission defines the access mode combination the Subjects Descriptive Object of a given role is allowed to execute on one Security Object.
An Access Rule is defined by the tuple < so; m > with so a SO reference and m a federated access mode combination.
Our access model is a closed security system: all non-authorized accesses are forbidden.

Role:
A Role is used in two cases: to represent a local discretionary user group, or to extract each sensibility level of a local mandatory category.
A Role is described by the tuple < FID; LD; FSL; {Permission}; {User}; {AHL} {CLO}; {AELO} >. FID is the Federated Identifier of the described element. LD is the Local Designation of the described element. FSL is the Federated Sensibility Level. This attribute is null in case of DAC or RBAC model description. {Permission} is the set of Permissions which defines access modes to Security Object that are allowed for the Subject Descriptive Object. {AHL} is the set of Access Heritage Links. {CLO} is the set of Constraint Link Objects, and {AELO}, the set of Access Equivalent Link Objects (see the section 5).

4.3   Link Classes

Access Heritage Link (AHL):
An Access Heritage Link defines an access mode combination from a "father" role to a "son" role with the tuple < "father"; "son"; Mode > where "father" is the "father" role reference, "son" is the "son" role reference and Mode is a federated access mode combination that Subject Descriptive Objects of the "father" role are allowed to execute on all the Security Objects of the "son" role. A null Mode means that all SDO of the "father" role may execute Access Rules of the "son" role (complete access).

Constraint Link Class (CLC):
Two types of Constraints are used in our system:
An Exclusion Constraint Link Object (ECLO) references two or more roles. A User can be referenced in only one role in a set of roles which references the same ECLO.
An Activation Constraint Link Object (ACLO) references two or more roles. For a given user session a User is active in only one role even if it is referenced in other role of the same ACLO.

5   Local Access Policy Description

The security canonical model is used to describe Discretionary Access Policy (group model and role model) and Mandatory Access Policy (with mono or multi level or polyinstantiation).

5.1   Discretionary Model Description

Discretionary security models govern the users' accesses to information on the basis of the users' identities and of rules. These rules specify, for each user and secured resource in the system, the type of access the user is allowed to apply on the resource. We consider the discretionary model in the federation descriptive system with the following concepts: user, secured resource, access mode, positive access rule (authorization), negative access rule (interdiction) and user group (with inclusion relations between user groups).
A local discretionary access system is described with the three entity types presented above. Five steps are required:
-    Access Model Descriptive Role instantiation: The Local Access Mode Table is created and contains the federated access mode combinations (equivalent to each local access mode).
-    For each local user and local secured resource, are created respectively one User and one Security Object. Each Security Object is connected to its Data Descriptive Object.
-    For each Security Object, are created as much Roles as there is different local access rules (i.e. different combinations of access modes) in the Access Control List of the local secured resource. A Permission (with the proper combination

mode) binds each Role and the related Security Object. The Users are referenced in the Role so called Direct Access Role.

- For each local user group, a Role is created. The corresponding Users are referenced in the role. To provide an access to the group resources several permissions are instantiated and define users group rights on each resource: each permission references the Security Object and is referenced in the role.
- For each inclusion relation between two local user groups, an Access Heritage Link Object is created and links the two corresponding roles. The AHL mode is not specified: a user of the "father" group can access to the Security Object of the "son" group.

5.2   Mandatory Model Description

Mandatory security models govern the access to information on the basis of the classification of subjects and objects in the system [17]. Objects are passive entities storing information. Subjects are active entities accessing the objects. Generally, a subject is considered to be an active process operating on user's behalf. Mandatory access classes are associated with every object and subject in the system. A secrecy level hierarchy (with the relation "dominate") is used to qualify each object and subject (mandatory clearance).

Two axioms define access rules of a subject to an object (referenced in the same category):

- Read axiom: A subject with a mandatory clearance c can read all the objects with a secrecy level dominated by c.
- Write or ☆-property: A subject with a mandatory clearance c can write on all objects with a secrecy level strictly equal to c (strict ☆-property) on all objects with a secrecy level dominating c (liberal ☆-property).

Mandatory models can belong to three categories relatively to the security object granularity. In single-level mandatory models, the components of Security Objects (i.e. attributes in an object class or in a relational table) have the same secrecy level [19], [20]. In our proposition, each mandatory object is described by one single SO (security description) referencing one DDO (data description). An attribute must have the same Mandatory Level as its class level. In multi-level mandatory models, attributes in an object class or in a relational table are mandatory objects. Their levels of sensibility can dominate or be equal to the level of sensibility of their classes / relational tables [21], [22]. Each mandatory object is described by one single SO (security description) referencing one DDO (data description) but in this case, Mandatory Levels of Attribute and classes / relational tables are not necessarily equal. In poly-instantiated multi-level mandatory models. Instance attribute can be multi-valued. The attribute value captures the secrecy level equal to subject's clearance level [23]. Each attribute is described by one DDO and n SO (SO have different Mandatory Levels); n is the secrecy level number in the local mandatory hierarchy of sensibility.

A local mandatory access system is proposed in six steps:

- A Local Model Descriptive Object describes the local access security policy. First the Local Access Mode Table is created and contains the federated access mode combinations which is equivalent to each local access mode (mainly read-only and write-only local access modes). Then the Local Mandatory Table is created to translate the local secrecy level hierarchy.

- For each local subject with a given clearance level *cl*, is created a User with secrecy levels. Ex: Mr. Smith has a clearance level "Secret" in a mandatory system with the LMT {(Non-Classified,1);(Classified;2);(Secret;3);(Top Secret;4)}. Mr. Smith subject is described by three UDO with the Mandatory Clearance 3.

- Security objects describing the local mandatory objects:
  Single level objects with a given secrecy level sl: is created one SO with a Mandatory Level equals to sl. The SO points to its related DDO.
  Poly-instantiated objects in a lattice-based access model: are created as much SO as there is secrecy levels in the local sensibility hierarchy. Each SO has a different Mandatory Level. All the SO reference a single DDO.

- For each local mandatory category is created as much roles as there is secrecy levels in the local sensibility hierarchy. The User (subject of the local mandatory category) having a Mandatory Clearance n is referenced in the role with a Mandatory Level n.

- Mandatory security axioms:
  Read axiom and strict ☆-property:
    For each role with a Mandatory Level n are created two permissions (with mode = a+u+d ≈ write and with mode = r for read) per SO referenced in the role.
    In a described local mandatory category, Access Heritage Links (with mode = r) bind each role of a given level n (dominant) with the role of the level n-1 (dominated) providing a descending read access heritage.

  Read axiom and liberal ☆-property:
    For each role with a Mandatory Level n is created two permissions (with mode = a+u+d ≈ write and with mode = r for read) per SO referenced in the role.
    In a described local mandatory category, Access Heritage Links (with mode = r) bind each AMDR of a given level n (dominant) with the AMDR of the level n-1 (dominated) providing a descending read-only access heritage.
    In a described local mandatory category, Access Heritage Links (with mode = a+u+d) bind each AMDR of a given level n (dominated) with the AMDR of the level n+1 (dominant) providing an ascending write-only access heritage.

The Figure 2 illustrates such a local mandatory model description. The local mandatory model is composed of:

- A local single-level mandatory policy with a liberal ☆-property (EX2 IS:APDO).
  The following Local Access Mode Table: Read (r) and Write (a+u+d).
  The local hierarchy of sensibility is Non-Classified (NC), Classified (C), Secret (S) and Top Secret (TP) with the dominate relation ">": TS > S > C > NC. The Local Mandatory Table is: 1. Non-Classified, 2. Classified, 3. Secret and 4. Top Secret.

- A mandatory category: Finance.

-   The following Objects of the category Finance: Sales Result (NC), Salary (C), Account 105 (S), Financial Plan (TS)
    The subject Smith with "Secret" clearance level belonging to the category Finance.

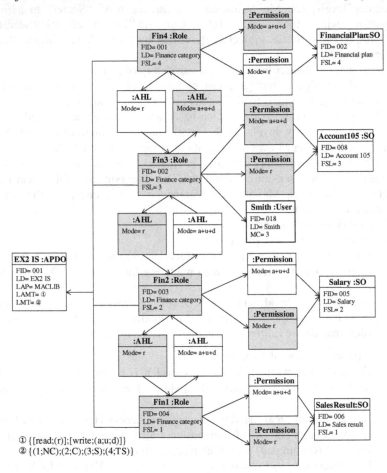

Fig. 2. An example of mandatory model description with liberal ☆-property.

The User 018 is created with Mandatory Clearance 3. The User is referenced in the right role.

-   The "read" axiom is implemented by a descending access heritage (AHL with Mode = r). The liberal ☆-property is implemented by an ascending access heritage (AHL with mode = a +u +d). This heritage does not exist in a mandatory model with strict ☆-property.
-   An Activation Constraint Link Object is referenced by the fourth role and forbids the simultaneous activation of Smith's User.

This MAC schema description respects the MAC information flow acyclicity (see the grayed sensibility hierarchy of Mr. Smith's session).

6   Federated Flow Control Policy

In each local information system the security manager must define the flow control policies adapted to the exchanges between the system and the federation. The import policy (input flow of the local system) is defined to be strict. Each local system must respect it. The export policy (output flow of the local system) is either strict or liberal.

- Strict import policy: in our proposal, all the local systems adopt the same import access policy. At any time the following security axiom has to be valid: "for a given local user, the access to a global data must be equivalent to the access to a local data belonging to the user's local profile. A user profile is defined as a set of access rights to local objects. In our proposal the set of access rights is stored in the (one or more) Roles which reference the proper User at the descriptive layer of the framework.

- Strict or liberal export policy: the export policy in a local system defines the way local data can be "son" from the federated level. In the case of a liberal export policy, the access requests from the federated level are automatically performed on local Security Objects. Access equivalencies defined among the DDO referenced in the User and the actual local data are used to verify the user's rights on the concerned data. Access rules on the Security Objects related to the federated user predominate access rules defined at the local level.

In the case of a strict export policy, a first mapping allows to detect which Role of the local system corresponds to Roles related to the global user. Then a second mapping is performed to verify the correspondence of access rights related to the Security Objects referenced in the Role.

7   Conclusion

We described a global proposal providing a secured framework for information systems cooperation. It is obvious that security in federated systems is a complex issue when local autonomy is respected, due to the dynamic evolution of local systems and the complex mappings required to yield various security models and policy interoperability. Our proposal tries to give an appropriate answer to such problems by combining a dynamic description of local information sources and a global security policy derived from local ones. However many questions are still in research phase. In particular further work is required to evaluate the impact of nested transactions during the query resolution process to the provided security framework. A validation phase for our description model is also necessary to be sure it can describe almost any local security policy at the local level.

A prototype is under current development in C++ language to implement the proposed security level on top of an existing cooperative information system (with IBM Universal DB2 7 and MS SQL Server 2000 DBMS) in a multi-agent environment. All the objects are implemented with C++ persistent classes using the POET™ Object Database Management System [24].

References

1. Dubois G., Boulanger D.: Semantic Cooperation of Legacy Information Systems: an Object-Oriented Framework. Workshop on Database and Expert Systems Applications (DEXA'97), Toulouse, France, 1-2 Septembre (1997).
2. Shet A.P., Larson J.A.: Federated Database Systems for Managing Distributed Heterogeneous and Autonomous Databases. ACM Computing Surveys vol.22 n°3, 1990.
3. Goyal M.L., Singh G.V.: Access Control In Heterogeneous Database Management Systems. Computers and Security, 10(7), North-Holland, 1991.
4. Jonscher D., Dittrich K.R.: An Approach for Building Secure Database Federations. Int.'l Conf. On Very Large Databases, Santiago, 1994.
5. Olivier M.S.: A Multilevel Secure Federated Database. Database Security VII, North-Holland, 1994.
6. Sandhu R. S.: Role Hierarchies and Constraints for Lattice-based Access Controls. Fourth European Symposium on Research in Computer Security, Rome, Italy, 1996.
7. Sandhu R. S., Munawer Q.: How to do Discretionary Access Control Using Roles. ACM Role-Based Access Control Workshop, 1998.
8. Pernul G.: Canonical Security Modelling for Federated Databases. Interoperable Database Systems, North-Holland, 1993.
9. Tari Z., Fernandez G.: Security Enforcement in the DOK Federated Database System. Database Security X, 1997.
10. Castano S., Martella G. and Samarati P.: Analysis, comparison and design of role-based security specifications. Data & Knowledge Engineering 21, 1997.
11. Boulanger D., Dubois G.: An Object Approach for Information System Cooperation. Information Systems vol. 23, n°6, 1998.
12. Boulanger D., Disson E., Dubois G.: Object-Oriented Metadata for Secured Cooperation of Legacy Information Systems. International Workshop on Model engineering IWME'00, Sophia-Antipolis and Cannes, France, 12-16th June 2000.
13. Disson E.: A Role-based Access Model for Federated Databases Security. Poster session ESORICS 2000, Toulouse, 4-6th October 2000.
14. Nyanchama M., Osborn S.: Modeling mandatory access control in role-based security systems. Database Security VIII: Status and Prospects. Chapman-Hall, 1996.
15. Sandhu R.S., Coyne E.J., Feinstein H.L., Youman C.E.: Role-Based Access Control Model. IEEE Computer, Vol 29, n°2, 1996.
16. Lampson B.W.: Protection. Princeton Symposium of Information Science and Systems. 1971.
17. Bell D.E., LaPadula L.J.: Secure Computer System: Unified Exposition and Multics Interpretation. Technical Report MTR-2997, MITRE Corp., Bedford, Mass, 1976.
18. OMG, Unified Modeling Language Specification, version 1.3, March 2000.
19. Jajodia S., Kogan B.: Integrating an object-oriented data model with multi-level security. IEE Symposium on Security and Privacy, 1990.
20. Millen J.K., Lunt T.F.: Security for Object-Oriented Database Systems. IEEE Symposium on Research in Security and Privacy, 1992.
21. Keefe T., Tsai W.: Prototyping the SODA Security Model. Database Security III: Status and Prospects, North-Holland, 1990.
22. Lunt T.F.: Multilevel Security for Object-Oriented Database Systems. Database Security III: Status and Prospects, North-Holland, 1990.
23. Denning D.E.: Secure distributed data views: the Sea View formal security model. Technical Report A003 SRI International, 1987.
24. www.poet.com

A Useful Intrusion Detection System Prototype to Monitor Multi-processes Based on System Calls

Hongpei Li, Lianli Chang, and Xinmei Wang

National Key Laboratory on Integrated Services Networks,
Xidian University
Xi'an 710071, P.R.China
hplee@263.net, xmwang@ns2.xidian.edu.cn

Abstract. Based on studying of process behaviors classification, a practical intrusion detection system prototype is discussed. As one of the key elements, the system behaviors classifier (Naive Bayesian Classifier) can identify malicious system behaviors effectively by classifying the sequences of system calls as normal or abnormal. However, an extended intrusion detection mechanism by monitoring multiple processes to detect intrusions that can modify the behaviors of system programs (such as: Trojan Horses, Buffer overflow attacks, and viruses.) is proposed.

1 Introduction

Intrusion detection systems rely on a variety of observable data to distinguish between legitimate and illegitimate activities. In 1996, Forrest and others introduced a simple intrusion detection method based on monitoring the system calls that used by active, privileged process [1]. Their work shows that a program's normal behavior can be characterized by local patterns in its traces. The process trace is an ordered list of system calls used by process from the beginning of its execution. Deviations from patterns can identify security violations of executing process [1-3]. From then on, many research groups use the sequence of system calls into the kernel of operating system as the observable sample to distinguish normal and intrusive behavior. Several methods have been used to generate more accurate and more compact models of the system-call data. Several papers about these experiments on alternative models applied to system calls are available [4-6]. In general, there is more than one security-critical program (system program or application program) executing in system, and an executing program may consist of one or more processes. As a program is a passive entity, to monitor a program means to monitor the executions of the program. So how to monitor multi-processes executing in parallel is one of the most important problems to design the intrusion detection system based on system call sequences. However, existing studies only discuss the condition of one executing process.

In this paper, we give out an abnormal detector that based on Naive Bayesian Classifier to identify a process trail is normal or abnormal at first. Then discuss how to use this abnormal detector to construct a process-monitor that can monitor multi-processes that running in parallel.

S. Qing, T. Okamoto, and J. Zhou (Eds.): ICICS 2001, LNCS 2229, pp. 441-450, 2001.
© Springer-Verlag Berlin Heidelberg 2001

2   System Behaviors Classifier

The goal of the intrusion detection system is to distinguish the illegitimate behavior (non-self) from the legitimate behavior (self)[7]. Therefore an intrusion detection system can be defined as a classification system to analyze system behaviors or security-events and identify the malicious behaviors from all the system behaviors [6]. In this section, a classification model and a classifier that can be used to monitor system program executing is discussed at first.

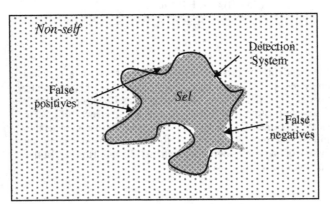

The universe set of system behavior patterns U

Fig. 1. The definition of the Intrusion Detection System Classification Model based on the sets of system behavior patterns

2.1   Classification Model

This model can be defined over the universe set of system behavior patterns (U), where U is a finite set of finite system behavior patterns. U can be partitioned into two sets, S and N, called self and non-self respectively, such that $S \cup N = U$ and $S \cap N = \phi$. Self-patterns represent acceptable or legitimate system behaviors (or security-events), and non-self patterns represent unacceptable or illegitimate system behaviors (or security-events). In the figure 1,each point in the plane represents a pattern. If the point lies within the shaded area, it is self. Otherwise it is non-self. A detection system attempts to encode the boundary between the two sets by classifying patterns as either normal or anomalous [7].

As the analysis above, an intrusion detection system (D) can be defined as: $D = (f, P)$, where f is a binary classification function, and P is a set of patterns drawn from U representing the knowledge of the detection system, $P \subset U$. The classification function f will map the pattern set P and a given pattern $p \in U$ to a binary classification of normal or anomalous, that is, , $f : U* \times U \rightarrow \{normal, anomalous\}$, where $U*$ is the power set of U. Apparently, a given system behavior pattern $p \in U$ is normal if it is in the detection system patterns set P, and is anomalous otherwise, that is:

$$f(P,p) = \begin{cases} normal & if \quad p \in P \\ anomalous & otherwise \end{cases}.$$

In practice, we might not acquire enough knowledge to describe the normal behavior of system accurately. This will lead the classification function give out error result. If the detection system fails to classify self patterns as normal, false positive errors are generated. And if non-self patterns are not classified as anomalous, false negatives are generated.

2.2   Naive Bayesian Classifier

Along with decision trees, neural networks, and nearest nbr, the Naive Bayesian Classifier provides one of the most practical learning methods based on Bayes Theorem. If the training set is moderate or large enough, or the attributes that describe instances can give conditionally independent classification, the Naive Bayesian Classifier can be used successfully.

2.2.1.   Naive Bayesian Classifier

Assume target function $f : X \rightarrow V$, where each instance $x \in X$ described by attributes $\langle a_1, a_2, \cdots a_n \rangle$. V is the instance class set, each instance class $v_i \in V (i = 1 \cdots N)$, Most probable value of $f(x)$ is the class (in most probable) of instance x:

$$f(x) = v_{MAP} = \arg \max_{v_j \in V} P(v_j | a_1, a_2, \cdots, a_n)$$

$$= \arg \max_{v_j \in V} \frac{P(a_1, a_2, \cdots, a_n | v_j) P(v_j)}{P(a_1, a_2, \cdots, a_n)} \qquad (2\text{-}1)$$

$$= \arg \max_{v_j \in V} P(a_1, a_2, \cdots, a_n | v_j) P(v_j)$$

Naive Bayes assumption:

$$P(a_1, a_2, \cdots, a_n | v_j) = \prod_{i=1}^{n} P(a_i | v_j). \qquad (2\text{-}2)$$

The Naive Bayesian Classifier can be defined as bellow:

$$v_{NB} = \arg \max_{v_j \in V} P(v_j) \prod_{i=1}^{n} P(a_i | v_j). \qquad (2\text{-}3)$$

2.2.2   Naive Bayes Classifier Learning Algorithm
NBCLA(X){

For (each target value $v_j \in V$){

$$\hat{P}(v_j) \leftarrow estimate \quad P(v_j);$$

For each attribute value $attr_k$ of each attribute $Attr_i$

$$\hat{P}_i(attr_k | v_j) \leftarrow estimate \quad P_i(attr_k | v_j);$$

}

}

After the classifier having been trained by Naive Bayes Classifier Learning Algorithm, we can use it to classify new instance.

2.2.3.   The Classification Procedure of Naive Bayes Classifier
Classify_New_Instance(x){

$$v_{NB} = \arg\max_{v_j \in V} \hat{P}(v_j) \prod_{i=1}^{n} \hat{P}_i(a_i | v_j)$$

}

2.2.4   Discussion

1. Conditional independence assumption ($P(a_1, a_2, \cdots, a_n | v_j) = \prod_{i=1}^{n} P(a_i | v_j)$) is

   often violated, but it works surprising well any way. Note that it does not need to estimate posteriors $\hat{P}(v_j | x)$ correctly. The value needed is only that [8]:

   $$\arg\max_{v_j \in V} \hat{P}(v_j) \prod_{i=1}^{n} \hat{P}_i(a_i | v_j) = \arg\max_{v_j \in V} P(a_1, a_2, \cdots, a_n | v_j) P(v_j).$$

   $$(2\text{-}4)$$

2. If none of the training instances with target value v_j have the attribute value a

   ($Attr_i = a$), then we will get:

   $$\hat{P}_i(a | v_j) = 0, \text{ and } \hat{P}(v_j) \prod_{i=1}^{n} \hat{P}_i(a_i | v_j) = 0 \qquad (2\text{-}5)$$

   In this case, we cannot classify the new instance (the value of attribute $Attr_i$ is

   a) correctly. Typical solution is Bayes estimate for $\hat{P}_i(a | v_j)$:

   $$\hat{P}_i(a | v_j) = \frac{n_c + mp}{n + m} \qquad (2\text{-}6)$$

Where:

- n is number of training examples for which $v = v_j$.

- n_c is number of examples for which $v = v_j$ and $Attr_i = a$.

- p is prior estimate for $\overset{\wedge}{P_i}(a|v_j)$.

- m is weight given to prior(i.e., number of "virtual" examples).

2.3   System Behaviors Classification

Forrest organized system call traces into sequence windows to provide context. She also showed that a database of known good sequence windows can be developed from a reasonably sized set of non-intrusive *sendmail* executions and the intrusive behavior can be determined by finding the percentage of system call sequences that do not match any of the known good sequences [2].

As an intrusion detection system is used to identify the malicious behaviors from a lot of system behavior [6], we can use classifier to distinguish between legitimate and illegitimate activities. First, we collect enough traces of system calls executed by a program (for example, lpr, include all executing-conditions: normal and abnormal). Then organize the system call trace data into short sequence of length k (in our experiments [6], it assigned 7). For training purpose, each short sequence is assigned a classified label of "normal" (if it can be obtained from proper operations of the program monitored) or "abnormal". An example of the system call short sequence and its label is shown in Table 1. In the table, the statistic of each system call sequence's frequency in the train data is also provided. These statistics can be used by the Naive Bayesian Classifier's learning algorithm.

Table 1. System call short sequence classification and statistics

System Call Sequences (Len=7)	Class Label	Frequency in the train data sets
5 3 67 67 5 139 67	normal	2025
67 6 5 3 67 67 6	normal	3995
106 105 105 107 106 105 105	normal	19865
... ...	......	
107 10 10 10 10 6 4	abnormal	999
4 4 4 4 33 51 59	abnormal	999
4 33 38 5 3 6 54	abnormal	1
... ...	... ...	

Using Naive Bayes Classifier to identify the program's behavior, it does not need to estimate the posteriors $\hat{P}(v_j|x)$ correctly. Consequently, the program behaviors classification can be made much easier. And we can use the forecast ability of classifier to identify some unknown abnormal program behaviors also. All these make us believe that our classification technique based on Naive Bayes Classifier can improve Forrest's technique, for it does not depend on a threshold percentage of abnormal sequences.

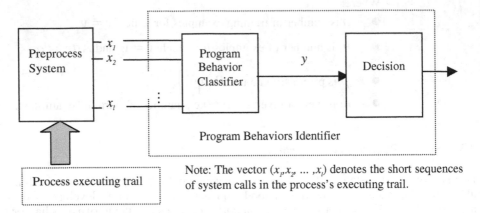

Fig. 2. Program Behaviors Identifier based on the classifier of short sequences of system calls

3   Intrusion Detection System Prototype Based on System Behaviors Classifier

Based on the above discussion, we now do more work on how to apply the program behavior classifier to monitor the running of security-critical programs.

3.1   Program Behaviors Identifier

In Fig.2, a program behaviors identifier framework is given. It is based on the idea that intrusions can be detected by observing the behavior of individual-program. Anomalous behaviors of a program indicate that the program is subverting for intrusive purpose. Obviously, the program behaviors classifier (Naive Bayesian Classifier) is the key element of the program behaviors identifier. However, it can only classify a single system call sequence (system behavior) as anomalous or normal, not classify the process (execution of program) as anomalous or normal. Furthermore, some occasional anomalous behaviors, which are expected during normal system operation, may not indicate one program is being misused. So a decision module is introduced into our program behavior identifier. It is also important to capture the temporal locality of anomalous events in order to recognize intrusive behavior. As a result, we desire an algorithm that provides some memory of recent event. The leaky bucket algorithm fits this purpose well. It keeps a memory of recent events by incrementing a counter of the classifier's output y, while slowly leaking its value. Thus, as the process many anomalies, the leaky bucket algorithm [6] will quickly accumulate a large value in its counter. Similarly, as the classifier give a normal output, the bucket will "leak" away its anomaly counter back to zero.

During program execution, the program behavior classifier outputs the system call sequence's classification and puts the result into a leaky bucket. During each time-step, the level of the bucket is decreased by a fixed amount. If the level in the bucket rises above some threshold at any point during execution of the program, the program is flagged as anomalous.

The advantage of using a leaky bucket algorithm is that it allows occasional anomalous behavior, which is to be expected during normal system operation, but it is quite sensitive to large numbers of temporally co-located anomalies, which would be expected if a program were really being misused. In conclusion, the leaky bucket emphasizes anomalies that are closely temporally co-located and diminishes the values of those that are sparsely located. So the temporal locality of anomalous sequences characteristic of programs under attack can be used to distinguish intrusive behavior from simple anomalous noise, thus, to avoid a large number of false positives.

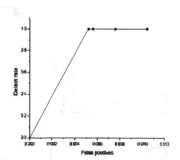

Fig. 3. The performance curve of Program Behaviors Identifier based on Naïve Bayes Classifier

Our experiment's result (Fig.3) shows that the Program Behaviors Identifier (based on Naïve Bayes Classifier) can be used to identify the abnormal executing of monitor-program with high performance (high detect rate with very low false positive) [6].

3.2   Process Behavior Identifier

The Program Behaviors Identifier only identify one specifically program's execution is being misused or not. Apparently, it is not enough. As there usually multiple programs execute concurrently in a real system, we must monitor all of them and identify which program's executing is the monitor process. In order to solve this problem, a process behavior identifier is presented (Fig.4).

In the process behavior identifier, there are some (at least one) program behaviors identifiers, each one corresponding a specifically program's execution[1]. The input data, short sequence of system calls of one process outputted by the preprocess sub-system, will be processed by each program behaviors identifier in parallel. If one program behaviors identifier$_i$'s output y_i is "abnormal", the input data is not the executing trace of program represented by program behaviors identifier$_i$. So if all of the program behaviors identifiers output "abnormal", the process behavior identifier will output "abnormal". According to the input data, if the process is not in the set of executing traces of monitored programs, it means an intrusion is occurring. As each program can be distinguished from others [1] obviously, when process

---

[1] Each program behaviors identifier must be trained by its corresponding program's execution traces.

behavior identifier output "normal", only one program behaviors identifier of the process behavior identifier can output "normal".

So the process behavior identifier given here can classify one process as anomalous or normal and identify which program's executing is the monitor process.

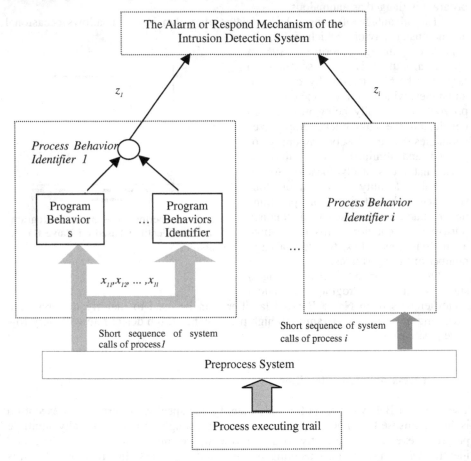

The vector $(x_{i1}, x_{i2} \dots , x_{il})$ denotes the short sequences of system calls in the i process's executing trail

Fig. 4. A Practical Intrusion Detection System Prototype based on the process behaviors classification

3.3 A Practical Intrusion Detection System Prototype

There are always many programs executing concurrently in a real system, and the audit system should record the traces of all monitoring programs[2]. However, the

---

[2] The audit system must be configured only to record the executing traces of programs defined by those program-behavior identifiers in process behavior identifier.

process behavior identifier defined above can only monitor one process. Our intention is to classify entire sessions (which are usually composed of multiple programs' executions) as anomalous or normal. As a result, one Practical Intrusion Detection System Prototype based on the process behavior classification is presented (Fig.4).

According to the prototype defined, the output data of preprocess system consists of time series to be analyzed. It is expected to be a series of pairs of positive integers, one pair per line, where the first integer identifies the data stream and the second is the element of the data stream. In our work, the stream identifier is the process identification number (PID), and the element of the data stream is system call numbers. So we can identify each process trace from the audit trail (processes executing trail) by the process identification number. When preprocess system deal with the audit trail, if it encounter a new PID different from those processes that are being monitored, it will fork a new process behavior identifier to monitor the process with this PID. If the monitored process executes to end (end of the data stream or encounter a process exit identification), the corresponding process behavior identifier will be killed. Then the IDS based on this prototype can monitor multi-processes in parallel.

The Alarm or Respond Mechanism of the Intrusion Detection System will collect the results of all the process behavior identifiers, make a high-level decision, and give alarm and respond policy. If a session contains a single anomalous execution of a program, it is flagged as anomalous.

4   Conclusion

In this paper, the classification model of system behaviors for intrusion detection is discussed at first. Then, one practical intrusion detection system prototype based on the classification of process behaviors is presented. Using the system behaviors classifier (Naive Bayesian Classifier) as the key element, the prototype can identify the malicious system behaviors by classifying the system calls sequences as normal or abnormal. Apparently, the Naive Bayes Classifier's forecast capability can improve the ability of IDS to detect the variations of known attacks. As result, an extended intrusion detection mechanism by monitoring multiple processes to detect intrusions that can modify the behaviors of system programs (such as: Trojan Horses, Buffer overflow attacks, and viruses.) is proposed.

References

1. S. Forrest, S. A. Hofmeyr, and T. A. Longstaff. A Sense of Self for Unix Processes. In IEEE Computer Society Press, Editor, 1996 IEEE Symposium on Security and Privacy, Los Alamitos, CA, 1996: 120-128.
2. S. A. Hofmeyr, S. Forrest, and A. Somayaji, Intrusion Detection Using Sequences of System Calls, Journal of Computer Security, 1998, 6:151-180.
3. P. Kosoresow and Steven A. Hofmeyr. Intrusion Detection via System Call Traces. IEEE Software, Sept./Oct., 1997: 35-42.

4. C. Warrender, S. Forrest, and B. Pearlmutter, Detecting Intrusion Using System Calls: Alternative Data Models, 1999 IEEE Symposium on Security and Privacy, (USA), 9-12, May, 1999:133-145.
5. W. Lee, S. J. Stolfo, and P. K. Chan. Learning patterns from UNIX process execution traces for intrusion detection. In AAAI Workshop on AI Approaches to Fraud Detection and Risk Management, pages 50-56. AAAI Press, July 1997.
6. Hongpei Li, Some Key Problems Research in Intrusion Detection, Ph.D. dissertation, Xidian University, Xi'an China, 2001.
7. S. A. Hofmeyr, An Immunological Model of Distributed Detection and Its Application to Computer security, Ph.D. dissertation, University of New Mexico,1999.
8. Tom Mitchell, Machine Learning, McGraw-Hill, 1997.

A Digital Nominative Proxy Signature Scheme for Mobile Communication

Hee-Un Park and Im-Yeong Lee

Division of Information Technology Engineering Soonchunhyang University, KOREA
heeun@cse.sch.ac.kr   imylee@sch.ac.kr

Abstract. Based on the development of mobile communication, the future mobile communication systems are expected to provide higher quality of multimedia services for users than today's systems. Therefore, many technical factors are needed in this systems. Especially the secrecy and the safety would be obtained through the introduction of the security for mobile communication. In this paper, we presents a digital nominative proxy signature scheme that processes a user's digital signature and encryption using the proxy-agent who has more computational power than origins in mobile communication.

1 Introduction

With the rapid expansion of computer applications and digital communication networks, information community realms are common tendency and a new culture's paradigm that "Information society" has been came over. In this environment, each person's digital information has been exchanged using digital communication networks profitably and swiftly. And also various applications connected with computer and network have been studied. Among them, wireless has become a widely discussed researching topic.

With the inclusion of mobile data and voice services in the future, users will be provided with higher quality of personal multimedia mobile communication services than today's systems.[1]~[5]

But, in wireless communication, signal transmission is done through radio channels on air. So it is vulnerable to attacks from wiretappers or intruders. Attackers usually carry out the attempt to gain access to personal information and the use of the systems without paying.

Moreover, security features that user authentication, non-repudiation and so on are negotiated importantly in mobile communication. Therefore to get the confidentiality, safety and user authentication from illegal actors except true users, nominative signature scheme is proposed.[7] This scheme achieve these objectives : only a verifier can confirm the signer's signature and if necessary, only verifier can prove to the third party that the signature is issued to him(her) and is valid. However this is not efficient, because it needs more computational power such that modular exponential in personal mobile devices that have less capability than general PC to compute them.

S. Qing, T. Okamoto, and J. Zhou (Eds.): ICICS 2001, LNCS 2229, pp. 451–455, 2001.

So in this paper, we present the required security properties for supporting authentication and safety to entities in mobile communication. Based on those proposed properties, we consider conventional digital signature schemes.[7][8][9][10] Also to provide safety and process efficient digital signature on personal mobile device, we propose the new digital signature paradigm that nominative proxy signature in public key cryptography. The proposed scheme provides the safety to proxy agent from the illegal actors on mobile communication additionally.

2 Security Features

In this section, we descript the required properties and characteristics to take the trustability and efficiency on a application based on mobile communications as follow.[11]

- *User confidentiality* : In case that the origin sending a message to receiver, the message is sent to receiver safely and correctly to make only him confirmed the origin's identity from a attacker's wiretapping. So user confidentiality is need on open network, some methods can be applied it.
- *Authentication* : It should be possible for the receiver of a message to ascertain origin; an intruder should not be able to masquerade as someone else and to verify that it has not been modified in transit; an intruder should not be able to substitute a false message for a legitimate one.
- *Non-repudiation* : A sender should not be able to falsely deny later that he sent a message.
- *Efficiency* : On mobile communication, the computational cost and time is smaller than that required by the general PC to reduce the charge of personal mobile device.
- *Safety* : On mobile communication, however true-entity he is, he must can not forgery or change the message excepted a origin.

3 Proposing the Nominative Proxy Signature

To satisfy the security features in mobile communication, we propose the new solution that nominative proxy signature. In the proposed scheme, we introduce a proxy agent to get the efficiency on mobile communication. Also to satisfy the security features that confidentiality and authentication in section 2, a proxy signature message is encrypted with a verifier's public key and sent by a proxy agent.[7][8][9] Additionally because proxy agent generates the signature information with a agent's secret information and origin's signature request information, this scheme provides the non-repudiation and safety.

3.1 System Parameter

For the convenience of describing our work, we first define the following set of symbols:

· p, q : A large prime number $p \geq 512$ bit, $q \mid p\text{-}1$
· g : g is a generator for Zp^*
· X_A, X_B, X_G : Signer A, Verifier B and Proxy agent's secret information
· $Y_A \equiv g^{XA} \bmod p$: A's common information
· $Y_B \equiv g^{XB} \bmod p$: B's common information
· $Y_G \equiv g^{-XG} \bmod p$: Proxy agents common information
· s_i : Signers one-time secret information for a signature($i \in_R Z$)
· T_i, M : i'th Time-stamp and Message
· $H()$: Secure 128bit one-way hash function

3.2 Implementing Nominative Proxy Signature

(1) Proxy generation : A origin A generates a signature request information as follows;

$$a_i \in_R Z^p \ (i \in_R Z)$$
$$d_i \equiv H(M \| T_i)$$
$$l \equiv g^{ai} \bmod p$$
$$s_i \equiv (X_A \cdot d_i + a_i \cdot l) \bmod p \tag{1}$$

A holds in check the generating the illegal signature by proxy agent, when s_i is generated by himself using the one time random number a_i and d_i.

(2) Proxy delivery : A origin A gives (s_i, l, M, T_i) to a proxy agent, G, in a secure manner.

(3) Proxy verification : G checks

$$g^{si} \equiv (Y_A^{H(M \| Ti)} \cdot l^l) \bmod p \tag{2}$$

If the computed value is correct, the origin and received message are consider with trust.

(4) Nominative proxy signing by the proxy agent : G chooses a random number r and R. And then generates K to prevent a origin's illegal acts.

$$r, R \in_R Z_p$$
$$K \equiv g^{R \cdot r \cdot XG} \bmod p \tag{3}$$

G generates D, Z and e, and the he process a nominative proxy signature $Sa(Z)$.

$$D \equiv Y_B^R \bmod p$$
$$Z = (Y_B \| K \| D \| M)$$
$$e = h(Z)$$
$$S_a(Z) \equiv (X_G \cdot r - R \cdot s_i \cdot e) \bmod q \tag{4}$$

When D and e is generated by G, the G's public key is used to confirm the signature only by a verifier. In this phase, the confidentiality is supported between G and a verifier.

(5) Nominative proxy signature delivery : Proxy agent G sends $(M \| T_i \| l \| K \| D \| R \| S_a(Z))$ to a verifier.

(6) Verification of the nominative proxy signature : A verifier B generates e and b to check the received signature.

$$h(Y_B \| K \| D \| M) \equiv e \tag{5}$$
$$b \equiv (Y_A^{H(M \| Ti)} \cdot l^l) \bmod p \tag{6}$$

B verifies the nominative proxy signature with the generated information e, b and so on.

$$(g^{Sa(Z)}b^{R \cdot e}K)^{XB} \bmod p \equiv D \tag{7}$$

The verifying signature is processed in this way;

$$
\begin{aligned}
(g^{Sa(Z)}b^{R \cdot e}K)^{XB} \bmod p &\equiv (g^{r \cdot XG - R \cdot si \cdot e}\ (Y_A^{H(M\|Ti)} \cdot l^l)^{R \cdot e}\ g^{R - r \cdot XG})^{XB} \bmod p \\
&\equiv (g^{r \cdot XG - R \cdot si \cdot e}\ (g^{XA \cdot H(M\|Ti)} \cdot g^{ai \cdot l})^{R \cdot e}\ g^{R - r \cdot XG})^{XB} \bmod p \\
&\equiv (g^{r \cdot XG - R \cdot si \cdot e}\ (g^{ai \cdot l + XA \cdot H(M\|Ti)})^{R \cdot e}\ g^{R - r \cdot XG})^{XB} \bmod p \\
&\equiv (g^{r \cdot XG - R \cdot si \cdot e}\ g^{si \cdot R \cdot e}\ g^{R - r \cdot XG})^{XB} \bmod p \\
&\equiv (g^{R})^{XB} \bmod p \\
&\equiv Y_B^{R} \bmod p \\
&\equiv D
\end{aligned}
$$

3.3 Analysing the Proposed Scheme

When the above all schemes are applied to mobile communication, the nominative proxy signature scheme offers the attractive properties.

• *Satisfying user confidentiality* : The proposed scheme has the nominative signature's user confidentiality. So the proposed nominative proxy signature protects the origin's identity from a illegal third part.

• *Providing authentication* : The proposed scheme has some basic properties that supported from general digital signatures. Specially to get the authentication on mobile e-commerce, in this scheme, a proxy agent process the nominative proxy signature.

• *Non-repudiation* : During the generating signature, a proxy agent input the his secret information for signature. Therefore this scheme supports the non-repudiation of the fact that origin requests nominative proxy signature to a proxy agent.

• *Efficiency* : When a origin will generate the signature, he use a proxy agent who has more computational power than him. So even if a origin has personal mobile device, this scheme would support the efficiency.

• *Providing safety* : When a signature request information is sent to proxy agent, a origin gives one time secret signature information. Also when the signature is generated by proxy agent, he input his secret information to the signature. Because a origin and proxy agent dose not can generate a illegal signature, this scheme provides the safety.

Table 1 shows the comparisons of the several schemes mentioned, based on a security features.

Table 1. Comparison of each scheme

feature \ scheme	User confidentiality	Authentication	Non-repudiation	Efficiency	Safety
Nominative signature	O	O	O	X	X
Proxy signature	X	O	X	O	X
C. Gamage scheme	O	O	X	O	X
Proposed scheme	O	O	O	O	O

4 Conclusion

With the rapid expansion of computer and digital networks, in a new culture's paradigm that Information society, the more various applications including e-commerce will have been supported. In this environment, to get the confidentiality and authentication on mobile communication, a digital signature is one of the most important research topics of modern cryptography.

The nominative signature satisfies the confidentiality using the secure channel between a signer and verifier on mobile communication. But, this scheme doesn't support the efficient, because the exponential modulo computation is executed in a signer's personal mobile device during on signing process. In case the proxy signature, the efficiency is provided by a proxy agent, but the confidentiality and user non-repudiation could not be supported. C. Gamage's proxy signcryption scheme satisfies the confidentiality, authentication and efficiency, but the non-repudiation and safety is not supported, because a origin and proxy agent can make a illegal signature.

So in this paper, we present a new nominative proxy signature scheme to solve the conventional schemes. The proposed scheme satisfies all required security properties for supporting authentication, safety, efficiency, confidentiality and non-repudiation in mobile communication.

References

1. ETSI ETS GSM 02.09, "European Digital Cellular Telecommunications System (Phase 2); Security Aspects," Version 4.2.4, September 1994.
2. ETSI ETS 3000175-7, "DECT Common Interface, Part 7: Security Features," October 1992.
3. UMTS Forum, "A regulatory framework for UMTS," Report no. 1, 1997.
4. ETSI ETR 33.20, "Security Principles for UMTS," Draft 1, 1997.
5. ITU, "Security Principles for Future Public Land Mobile Telecommunication Systems," Rec. ITU-R M. 1998.
6. Y. Zheng, "Signcryption and Its Applications in Efficient Public Key Solutions," Proc. ISW'97, LNCS 1397, pp.291-312, 1998.
7. S. J. Kim, S. J. Park and D. H. Won, "Nominative Signatures," Proc. ICEIC' 95, pp.II-68-II-71, 1995.
8. M. Mambo, K. Usuda and E. Okamoto, "Proxy Signatures," Proceedings of SCIS 95, pp.B1.1.1-17, 4-27 Jan, 1995.
9. M. Mambo, K. Usuda and E. Okamoto, "Proxy signatures for delegating signing operation," Proc. Third ACM Conference on Computer and Communications Security, pp.48-57, 1996.
10. C. Gamage, J. Leiwo and Y. Zheng, "An Efficient Scheme for Secure Message Transmission using Proxy-Signcryption," Proceeding of the Twenty Second Australasian Computer Science Conference, 18-21 Jan, 1999.
11. H. U. Park and I, Y. Lee, "A 2-pass key agreement and authentication for mobile communication," Proceedings of ICEIC 2000, pp.115-118, 2000.

Hierarchical Simulation Model with Animation for Large Network Security

Mi Ra Yi and Tae Ho Cho

School of Elec. & Com. Eng Modeling & Simulation Lab., Sungkyunkwan University
Suwon, 440-746, South Korea
{miracle,taecho}@ece.skku.ac.kr

Abstract. Trying to display all the graphic objects representing the dynamics of the models being simulated causes the distraction of focus. Especially, keeping the focus is needed when the model is large and complex like a security simulation model, which includes the dynamics of attacks that become more sophisticated as the network is wide spread. This paper presents a simulation modeling environment for animation in which the users can have better focus on the dynamics of security systems by selectively choosing the hierarchical level and components with in a level of the hierarchically structured model.

1 Introduction

Recently, many organizations use Internet TCP/IP protocols to build intranets to share and disseminate internal information. A large scale (and complex) attack on the networks can cripple important world-wide Internet operations [1]. The cooperative attacks are not convinced by each security system, but judged by relations among them.

In the field of intrusion detection, early systems were designed to detect attacks upon a single host [1,2,3]. Although they could collect reports on a single local area network, these systems did not aggregate information on a wider scale [1]. As intrusions become more sophisticated, it becomes beyond the scope of one intrusion detection system to deal with them. The need arises for systems to cooperate with one another, to manage diverse attacks across networks and time [4]. In practice, later security systems consider the role of networks, especially for the large size networks. For example, Cooperating Security Managers (CSMs) [5] are designed to be used in large and heavily interconnected network. The AAFID (Autonomous Agents For Intrusion Detection) [6] is composed with agents, transceivers, monitor, and user interface to detect attacks on large network. The GrIDS (Graph-based IDS) [1] project at UC Davis analyzes network activity by using a hierarchical aggregation scheme in order to scale to large network.

Security simulation evaluates the performance (the efficiency and vulnerability) of security systems in a network and predicts dynamics of the security systems, when security policy is changed. The security simulation is needed to consider the sophisticated attacks. When the target network is large and complex, however, the users have difficulty in analyzing dynamics and results of the security models. When a user desire

S. Qing, T. Okamoto, and J. Zhou (Eds.): ICICS 2001, LNCS 2229, pp. 456-460, 2001.
© Springer-Verlag Berlin Heidelberg 2001

to observe the dynamics of the security models on a large scale network (topology), trying to display all the graphic objects representing the dynamics of the models being simulated causes the distraction of focus. The redundant graphic objects also increase the computer computation overhead.

This paper presents a simulation modeling environment for animation in which the users can have better focus on the dynamics of security systems by selectively choosing the hierarchical level and components with in a level of the hierarchically structured model. Our approach for the hierarchical modeling environment is based on the DEVS (Discrete EVent system Specification) formalism [7], which is theoretically well grounded means of expressing modular and hierarchical models.

2 DEVS Formalism

DEVS(Discrete EVent system Specification) formalism is a modeling methodology to simulate the discrete event system on continuous time. The DEVS modeling approach supports hierarchical, modular construction of both DEVS models and the counterpart systems they represent. The hierarchical animation environment is designed based on the hierarchical and modular property of DEVS. A DEVS model can be either an atomic model(M) or a coupled model(DN) [7] as follows.

$$M = < X, S, Y, \delta_{int}, \delta_{ext}, \lambda, t_a >$$
$$DN = < D, \{M_i\}, \{I_i\}, \{Z_{i,j}\}, select >$$

In Fig. 1, the left half part of the diagram shows the model structure and the abstract simulator. The behavior is specified in the model structure and the abstract simulator generates the behavior specified in the model.

3 Hierarchical Simulation Animation Environment

The hierarchical animation environment represents an environment which allows users to observe desired levels and components within the levels of hierarchically structured models. The core component of the hierarchical animation environment is an animation execution module called an abstract hierarchical animator [8]. The hierarchical animation environment is composed of four components, the *model* that specifies behavior of a target system, the *simulator* that generates the behavior specified in the model, schedules simulation events, the *animator* that schedules animations which reflects the simulation results, and the *animation* that animates images on the screen.

In the hierarchical animation each model is paired up with an animator to control the animation object assigned to the model, whereas in the general animation environment an animator controls all the animation objects of the models. Therefore, the structure of the animator is identical to that of the simulator in the hierarchical animation. An abstract animator (or hierarchical animator) consists of root-co-animator, co-animator and animator like the abstract simulator consists of root-coordinator, coordinator and simulator. There are three reasons for the structuring of the animator in hierarchical fashion. *First,* it ensures ease in the synchronization between simulation and animation, *second,* it ensures ease in the hierarchical specification of models with the animation information, *third,* it provides increased reusability.

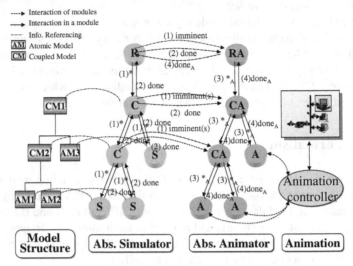

Fig. 1. Model structure, abstract simulator and abstract animator

The animators keep the variables (t_{LA}, t_{NA}, L, AL, $done_A$-list, to-be-done$_A$-list) for the synchronization between simulation and animation, and these variables are updated and delivered by control messages with several types (Imminent, done, $*_A$, $done_A$, $pause_A$, $ask-done_A$). The abbreviations of simulators and animators are R (root-co-ordinator), C (co-ordinator), S (simulator), RA (root-co-Animator), CA (Co-Animator), A (animator). For example a CA's t_{LA}, the latest time of an animation completion, is updated when it receives the $done_A$-message, which reports the completion of an animation.

There are four phases of operations in a simulation cycle. Fig. 1 shows all the control messages passed between the abstract simulator and the abstract animator for the hierarchically structured model. The number in the head of the message means the phase. In 1st phase the *-message indicates that a specified event is starting. In 2nd phase the done-message reports the event scheduling is done. In 3rd phase the $*_A$-message indicates that an animation is starting. In 4th phase the $done_A$-message reports the animation is done. Then, the operations for the next event are started again in the 1st phase.

4   Implementation & Testing

We have implemented a sample network with security systems in Fig. 2. Components in each level are: Level 1(Network), Level 2(Subnet0, subnet64, Subnet128, subnet192), Level 3(DNS_1, DNS_Server, DNS_1, DNS_2, …), Level 4(A1, A2, …). Fig. 3 shows the simulation animation of the sample system on each observation level.

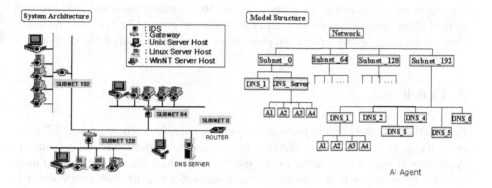

Fig. 2. Architecture and model structure of the sample security systems

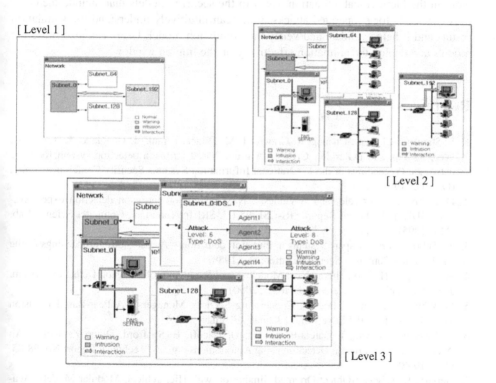

Fig. 3. Hierarchical simulation in each level

The accuracy of animation for displaying simulation results can be evaluated by how to utilize the event scheduling times of models. Since the time elapsing of displaying the graphic images depends on the computing power of the subsystem, the ratio of the animation time to the simulation time is not guaranteed to be one. Hence, the proper animation algorithm is important for the animation accuracy. The algorithm of the hierarchical animator guarantees the animation error to be restricted within one event to the next, i.e., the error in graphics is not accumulated out of this interval.

5 Conclusion

Despite the various efforts to perform the valid simulation, there are many difficulties in verifying the model code, validating the model and understanding the simulation. Animation is one of the popular output methods to reduce the difficulties. In this paper, we have designed and implemented a hierarchical animation environment for simulation, and showed its usefulness. The developers and the security specialists can selectively observe the level and components of the security systems of a large network in the hierarchical animation. Even in the security models that include the complex dynamics for cooperated attacks, users can intuitively understand the simulation results and it helps validate and verify the simulation model. Users can also reuse the models and deploy the animation effectively on the limited window.

References

1. S. Stainford-Chen, S. Cheung, R. Crawford, M. Dilger, J. rank, J. Hoagland, K. Levitt, C. Wee, R. Yip, and D.Zerkle : GrIDS - A graph based intrusion detection system for large networks. Proceedings of the 19th National Information Systems Security Conference, Vol.1. (Octorber 1996)
2. D.Anderson, T. Frivold, and A.Valdes. : Next generation intrusion detection expert system(NIDES). Technical Report SRI-CSL-95-07, SRI International, Computer Science Lab. (May 1995)
3. M. Sebring *et al.* : Expert Systems in intrusion detection – A case study. Proceedings of the 11th National Computer Security Conference (1988)
4. H. J. Kim, T. H. Cho : Hierarchical Modeling and Simulation of Intrusion Detection System. JSST International Conference (October, 2000)
5. G. White, E. Fisch, U. Pooch : Cooperating Security Managers - A Peer-Based Intrusion Detection System. IEEE Network. (January/February 1996)
6. J. Balasubramaniyan, J. Garcia-Fernandez, D. Isacoff, E. Spafford, Diego Zamboni : An Architecture for Intrusion Detection using Autonomous Agents. Technical Report No. 98-05, (June 1998)
7. Bernard P. Zeigler : Object-Oriented Simulation with Hierarchical, Modular Models. Academic Press. (1990)
8. Cho, T. H. : A Hierarchical, Modular Simulation Environment for Flexible Manufacturing System Modeling". Ph. D. dissertation, Univ. Of Arizona, Tucson. (1993)

Fair Electronic Cash Based on a Group Signature Scheme*

Greg Maitland and Colin Boyd

Information Security Research Centre
Queensland University of Technology
Brisbane, Australia.
{g.maitland,c.boyd}@qut.edu.au

Abstract. Several new group signature schemes have been proposed in recent years. In addition, several applications for group signatures (including electronic cash) have been suggested.

A new cash scheme based on a recent group signature by Ateniese, Camenisch, Joye and Tsudik is presented. Its construction uses a general framework suitable for a number of group signature schemes. We also identify the challenges faced by such schemes.

1   Introduction

Unlike ordinary signatures, group signatures allow a group member to create anonymous (and unlinkable) signatures. Upon verifying a signature, the verifier does not learn the identity of the group member that created the signature. However, should the need arise, a group signature can be 'opened' by a trusted party and the identity of the member who created the signature will be revealed.

Several proposals [3,6,4] have introduced group signatures into electronic cash schemes. The anonymity and unlinkability afforded by group signatures suggests that they may have a role to play in anonymous electronic cash scheme design. The existing proposals have utilised group signatures in different roles, where the group has been formed from the banks that issue the electronic coins [3], the customers that spend the electronic coins [3,6] and indeed the coins themselves [4].

A general structure for using group signatures to form a 'group of customers' has been developed but, due to the limited amount of space available, this framework will not be described here. Instead, a new cash scheme based on a recently proposed group signature scheme is described in order to illustrate the construction. The main benefits of the new cash scheme compared to [6] relate to the underlying group signature scheme's improved efficiency and provable security.

---

* This research is part of an ARC SPIRT project undertaken jointly by Queensland University of Technology and Telstra

S. Qing, T. Okamoto, and J. Zhou (Eds.): ICICS 2001, LNCS 2229, pp. 461–465, 2001.

Main Contribution: We focus on the 'group of customers' model for apply-ing group signatures to electronic cash scheme design and illustrate a general construction for these schemes. A new scheme is presented and the properties of the scheme are analysed with a view to identifying key unresolved issues. In particular, withdrawal protocol diversion and additional-overspending framing are discussed.

2   A New Offline Fair Cash Scheme

This section presents a new offline fair cash scheme based on the group signa-ture scheme proposed by Ateniese, Camenisch, Joye and Tsudik [1]. This group signature scheme is provably coalition-resistant and quite efficient.

Setup: Let $\epsilon > 1$, k, and ℓ_p be security parameters. Let λ_1, λ_2, γ_1, and γ_2 denote lengths satisfying $\lambda_1 > \epsilon(\lambda_2 + k) + 2$, $\lambda_2 > 4\ell_p$, $\gamma_1 > \epsilon(\gamma_2 + k) + 2$, $\gamma_2 > \lambda_1 + 2$. Define the integral ranges $\Lambda =]2^{\lambda_1} - 2^{\lambda_2}, 2^{\lambda_1} + 2^{\lambda_2}[$ and $\Gamma =]2^{\gamma_1} - 2^{\gamma_2}, 2^{\gamma_1} + 2^{\gamma_2}[$. Finally, let $\mathcal{H}$ be a collision-resistant hash function $\mathcal{H} : \{0,1\}^* \to \{0,1\}^k$. (The parameter ϵ controls the tightness of the statistical zero-knowledgeness and the parameter ℓ_p sets the size of the modulus to use.)

The Group Manager: The initial phase involves the group manager (GM) setting the group public and his secret keys, $\mathcal{Y}$ and $\mathcal{S}$, as follows:

- Select random secret ℓ_p-bit primes p', q' such that $p = 2p' + 1$ and $q = 2q' + 1$ are prime. Set the modulus $n = pq$.
- Choose random elements $a, a_0, g, h \in_R Q_n$ where Q_n is the group of quadratic residues in $\mathbb{Z}_n^*$ and is of order $p'q'$.
- The group public key is: $\mathcal{Y} = (n, a, a_0, g, h)$.
- The corresponding secret key (known only to GM) is: $\mathcal{S} = (p', q')$.

The Revocation Manager: The revocation manager (RM) chooses a random secret element $x \in_R \mathbb{Z}_{p'q'}^*$ and publishes $y = g^x \bmod n$.

The Bank: The bank selects an appropriate set of parameters to support the chosen blind signature scheme for issuing authorities.

The Customer: Each customer $\mathcal{C}_i$ who wishes to join the customer group inter-acts with the group manager in order to acquire:

- A private key x_i known only to the user such that $x_i \in \Lambda$. The associated public key is $C_2 = a^{x_i} \bmod n$ with $C_2 \in Q_n$.
- A membership certificate $[A_i, e_i]$ where e_i is a random prime chosen by GM such that $e_i \in_R \Gamma$ and A_i has been computed by the GM as $A_i := (C_2 a_0)^{1/e_i} \bmod n$.
- GM creates a new entry in the membership table for $[A_i, e_i]$.

Withdrawal: The withdrawal process involves the customer and bank completing the following tasks.

- The customer completes the commitment phase of the signing process.
    - Generate a random value $w \in_R \{0,1\}^{2\ell_p}$.
    - Compute: $T_1 = A_i y^w \bmod n$; $T_2 = g^w \bmod n$; $T_3 = g^{e_i} h^w \bmod n$.
    - Randomly choose:
    $$r_1 \in_R \pm\{0,1\}^{\epsilon(\gamma_2+k)} \quad , \quad r_2 \in_R \pm\{0,1\}^{\epsilon(\lambda_2+k)},$$
    $$r_3 \in_R \pm\{0,1\}^{\epsilon(\gamma_1+\ell_p+k+1)} \quad , \quad r_4 \in_R \pm\{0,1\}^{\epsilon(2\ell_p+k)}.$$
    - Compute:
    $$d_1 = T_1^{r_1}/(a^{r_2} y^{r_3}) \bmod n; \quad d_2 = T_2^{r_1}/d^{r_3} \bmod n;$$
    $$d_3 = g^{r_4} \qquad\qquad \bmod n; \quad d_4 = g^{r_1} h^{r_4} \quad \bmod n.$$
    The result is the commitment values $\{T_1, T_2, T_3, d_1, d_2, d_3, d_4\}$.
- The customer obtains an authority $Auth\,(T_1, T_2, T_3, d_1, d_2, d_3, d_4)$ from the bank via a blind signature protocol. The message which is signed is a predetermined set of values chosen from the set $\{T_1, T_2, T_3, d_1, d_2, d_3, d_4\}$. For instance, the authority could be a signature on the message $(T_1 \parallel T_2)$. In this way, the customer's identity is bound to the authority because (T_1, T_2) is a modified ElGamal encryption of the customer's membership certificate and uniquely identifies the customer.

Payment: During the payment process, the payment transcript msg is signed using the group member's signing keys.

- The customer retrieves the previously calculated values T_1, T_2, T_3, d_1, d_2, d_3 and d_4 along with the previously obtained authority $Auth$.
- The customer uses the values T_1, T_2, T_3, d_1, d_2, d_3, d_4 and the message msg to complete the challenge and response phases of the signing process.
    - *Challenge Phase:* Calculate
    $$c = \mathcal{H}\,(g \parallel h \parallel y \parallel a_0 \parallel a \parallel T_1 \parallel T_2 \parallel T_3 \parallel d_1 \parallel d_2 \parallel d_3 \parallel d_4 \parallel msg)$$
    - *Response Phase:* Compute
    $$s_1 = r_1 - c(e_i - 2^{\gamma_1}) , \quad s_2 = r_2 - c(x_i - 2^{\lambda_1}) ,$$
    $$s_3 = r_3 - ce_i w \qquad , \quad s_4 = r_4 - cw. \text{ (all in } \mathbb{Z} \text{)}$$
    The resulting group signature is $(c, s_1, s_2, s_3, s_4, T_1, T_2, T_3)$.
- The customer sends the merchant the group signature signature on the payment transcript msg plus the corresponding authority $Auth$.
- The merchant verifies the group signature $(c, s_1, s_2, s_3, s_4, T_1, T_2, T_3)$ of the payment transcript msg as follows:
    1. Compute:
    $$d_1' = a_0{}^c T_1^{s_1 - c2^{\gamma_1}}/(a^{s_2 - c2^{\lambda_1}} y^{s_3}) \bmod n,$$
    $$d_2' = T_2^{s_1 - c2^{\gamma_1}}/g^{s_3} \bmod n,$$
    $$d_3' = T_2^c g^{s_4} \bmod n,$$
    $$d_4' = T_3^c g^{s_1 - c2^{\gamma_1}} h^{s_4} \bmod n.$$
    $$c' = \mathcal{H}(g \parallel h \parallel y \parallel a_0 \parallel a \parallel T_1 \parallel T_2 \parallel T_3 \parallel d_1' \parallel d_2' \parallel d_3' \parallel d_4' \parallel msg)$$

2. Accept the group signature if and only if $c = c'$ and

$$s_1 \in \pm\{0,1\}^{\epsilon(\gamma_2+k)+1}$$
$$s_2 \in \pm\{0,1\}^{\epsilon(\lambda_2+k)+1}$$
$$s_3 \in \pm\{0,1\}^{\epsilon(\gamma_1+2\ell_p+k+1)+1}$$
$$s_4 \in \pm\{0,1\}^{\epsilon(2\ell_p+k)+1}$$

- The merchant confirms that the attached authority $Auth$ is correct with respect to the pre-determined set of values from $\{T_1, T_2, T_3, d_1', d_2', d_3', d_4'\}$.

Deposit: The deposit process proceeds as follows:

- The merchant sends to the bank the group signature on the payment transcript msg plus the authority i.e. $[msg, (c, s_1, s_2, s_3, s_4, T_1, T_2, T_3), Auth]$.
- The bank verifies the group signature and the authority using the same operations as the merchant. If this is successful, the bank checks for double-spending by searching its list of previously used authorities. If the authority is not found, the authority is added to the list and the payment is accepted as valid. If the authority has been previously used, the bank sends both transcripts to the revocation manager RM and requests that the identity of the customer be revoked.

Identity Revocation: To open a signature and reveal the identity of the actual customer who created a given signature, RM executes the following procedure:

1. Check the signature's validity as per the merchant's verification procedure.
2. Recover A_i (and thus the identity of C_i) as $A_i = T_1/T_2^x \bmod n$.
3. Generate a proof that $log_g y = log_{T_2}(T_1/A_i \bmod n)$

3   Observations

The 'group of customers' offline model was first proposed by Lysyanskaya and Ramzan [3] and subsequently expanded upon by Traoré [6]. The structure of the new scheme follows that of Traoré [6] and hence it has the same general security properties. The weaknesses described previously by Traoré [6] have their origins in the level of coin transfer-resistance that is achieved.

The group signature signing process binds a customer's identity to the signature during the commitment phase by encrypting the customer's identity under T_1 and T_2. Therefore, it is not possible for any other customer to spend the 'coin'. In this sense, the 'coin' is bound to the identity of a particular customer. Whether or not this customer is the withdrawing customer depends on the blind signature used to create the authority. In Brands' cash [2], the restrictive blind signature used to create the authority achieves tight binding and prevents the withdrawal protocol from being diverted. As a result, the signing keys of customer withdrawing the 'coin' must be known in order to spend the 'coin'.

The exact details of the commitments used in creating an authority have not been specified. Different choices can provide different properties. If all the values in the set $\{T_1, T_2, T_3, d_1, d_2, d_3, d_4\}$ are signed when forming an authority, the knowledge extraction process for the group signature scheme will reveal the customer's private key and group membership certificate in the event that the customer overspends. As has been previously noted by Nyang and Song [5] in connection with Brands' cash scheme [2], the bank can then falsely accuse the customer of additional overspending.

If the values T_1, T_2, d_3 are used in forming the authority, the customer's A_i can be extracted if double-spending occurs. This allows the bank to independently identify the customer but the bank can not create false payment transcripts. If the values T_1, T_2 are used, the bank can still detect the double-spending event. The revocation manager can open the offending transcripts and identify the overspending customer – the reason for using group signatures to begin with.

4   Conclusions and Further Work

We have presented a new offline cash scheme based on an efficient and provably coalition-resistant group signature scheme. The group signature properties are used to deliver anonymity, unlinkability and revocation services. A blindly signed authority from the bank is used to detect double-spending. The exact nature of this authority has been left as flexible.

The scheme discussed in this paper is susceptible to diversion and this can lead to perfect crimes [7] such as blackmailing and money laundering. Designing an authority mechanism which is resistant to diversion is an open problem with respect to the underlying group signature scheme used in this paper.

References

1. Giuseppe Ateniese, Jan Camenisch, Marc Joye, and Gene Tsudik. A practical and provably secure coalition-resistant group signature scheme. In *Advances in Cryptology—CRYPTO 2000*, LNCS 1880, pages 255–270. Springer-Verlag, 2000.
2. Stefan Brands. Untraceable off-line cash in wallets with observers. In *Advances in Cryptology—CRYPTO '93*, LNCS 773, pages 302–318. Springer-Verlag, 1993.
3. A. Lysyanskaya and Z. Ramzan. Group blind digital signatures: A scalable solution to electronic cash. In *Financial Cryptography: Second International Conference, FC '98*, LNCS 1465, pages 184–197. Springer-Verlag, 1998.
4. Toru Nakanishi, Nobuaki Haruna, and Yuji Sugiyama. Unlinkable electronic coupon protocol with anonymity control. In *International Workshop on Information Security (ISW'99)*, LNCS 1729, pages 37–46, 1999.
5. DaeHun Nyang and JooSeok Song. Preventing double-spent coins from revealing user's whole secret. In *Second International Conference on Information Security and Cryptology (ICISC'99)*, LNCS 1787, pages 13–20. Springer-Verlag, 1999.
6. Jacques Traoré. Group signatures and their relevance to privacy-protecting off-line electronic cash systems. In *Australasian Conference on Information Security and Privacy (ACISP'99)*, LNCS 1587, pages 228–243. Springer-Verlag, 1999.
7. S. von Solms and D. Naccache. Blind signatures and perfect crimes. *Computers and Security*, 11:581–583, 1992.

Fair Exchange of Digital Signatures with Offline Trusted Third Party

Chuan-Kun Wu[1] and Vijay Varadharajan[2]

[1] Department of Computer Science, Australian National University
Canberra, ACT 0200, AUSTRALIA. chuan@cs.anu.edu.au
[2] Department of Computing, Macquarie University
North Ryde, NSW 2109, AUSTRALIA. vijay@ics.mq.edu.au

Abstract. In this paper we show how fair exchange of digital signatures can be made possible without a separate verifiable encryption. This means that the fair exchange protocol can be established based on an existing signature algorithm without modification, except that the users need to get a ticket from an off-line trusted third party to enable the fair exchange. The trusted third party is needed to make a judgment only when there is a dispute. Explicit protocols based on different digital signature algorithms are proposed.

Keywords: Digital signature; Fair exchange; Electronic commerce

1 Introduction

Fair exchange is a protocol by which two entities, A and B, can exchange data (e.g. signed document, electronic cash/check, electronic product, commitment of providing goods and/or services, etc.) in such a way that, the entity who provides the data last, cannot take advantage over the other, even when time is sensitive. It is reasonable to assume that there is a trusted third party (TTP) who acts as a judge when possible disputes occur.

Fair exchange protocols apply only to messages with known properties, e.g. digital signatures and digital cash. Fair exchange of signatures can be made in two steps: verifiable signature commitment and signature verifiable encryption. Verifiability is essential as otherwise the verifier cannot be convinced whether a message is useful or simply garbage. The idea of designing verifiable signature commitment is different from that of verifiable signature sharing [6] [13], because in the former case the whole signature is wrapped while in the latter case the signature is split into pieces and distributed to different proxies. However, the idea for designing verifiable encryption protocols can be very similar.

A common application of fair exchange of signatures occurs in contract signing. In this case the signature of both parties can be exchanged in a bit-by-bit fashion (e.g. in [2] [9] [11]), by means of bit commitment. If one party stops the bit-by-bit exchange, neither of them has the other party's signature. It is effectively a fair exchange protocol, though there may exist one bit unfairness. However, this is not practical for long signatures, as the computational complexity can become very high.

S. Qing, T. Okamoto, and J. Zhou (Eds.): ICICS 2001, LNCS 2229, pp. 466–470, 2001.

In some other protocols (e.g. [7] [14] [15]), a trusted third party (TTP) is required to be on-line. Fair exchange is essentially done by the TTP. This is still not efficient. For instance, in a real world situation, judgment from a court is needed only when disputes occur; otherwise the judge is unaware of what is happening (except when he intentionally monitors the situation). Therefore it is desirable to design fair exchange protocols where a trusted authority stays off-line.

In [1,3] fair exchange protocols are proposed where the TTP has not to be on-line. This property enables the TTP to serve a large number of users where we assume that the majority of users is honest. So the TTP is needed only when there is a dispute. The protocols proposed in [1] make use of general verifiable encryption protocols which normally need a zero-knowledge proof. This is inefficient as the complexity for the zero-knowledge proof is normally high. Recently a RSA based fair payment protocol was proposed in [3] which modifies the undeniable signature protocols presented in [8] to formulate a confirmation protocol. Although verification encryption is not employed in [3], interactive proof is needed for signature confirmation.

2   Fair Exchange of Discrete Logarithm Based Signatures

In this paper we only consider discrete logarithm based signatures as they have similar assumptions to set up. There have been a number of signature algorithm proposals based on discrete logarithm problem over a primitive field (e.g. [12] [4] [5]). Except for a minor difference in further requirement on the properties (e.g. [10]) or a less requirement on q [4], the most common assumption made is as follows: Let p, q be large primes such that $q|(p-1)$, g be a generator for the subgroup of Z_p^* of order q, where Z_p^* is the largest multiplicative group in $Z_p = \{0, 1, ..., p-1\}$. All the numbers p, q and g are known to the public. It is also assumed that there is a publicly known hash function $H(x)$ mapping from arbitrary numbers in Z to fixed length numbers in Z_q.

To set up a key, user $\mathcal{X}$ chooses a random number $x \in Z_q$ as his private key, and computes $h = g^x \bmod p$ as his public key[1].

2.1   Fair Exchanges for DSS-Based Signatures

As a typical example, the Digital Signature Standard (DSS [5]) is based on discrete logarithm problem with the same assumption for the primes p and q as above. we here briefly describe how fair exchange protocols can be established based on DSS.

The setup assumption and key generation in DSS are very much similar to other discrete logarithm based digital signature schemes, i.e. each user chooses a secret x, and computes a public key $y = g^x \bmod p$, where g and p are public

---

[1] In practice the public key needs to be authorized, and a certificate containing the public key, the identity of the user, validity period of the public key, etc., is issued. This certificate is kept by the user and is sent to the receiver, or published somewhere which is publicly accessible.

parameters. Apart from this, every user who wants to execute the fair exchange protocol must register from the TTP as follows: user $\mathcal{X}$ and the TTP mutually agree on a random number $v \in Z_q$. These cannot be chosen by the user only.

Signature generation. Choose $k \in Z_q^*$ at random, let $r = (g^k \bmod p) \bmod q$, and $s = k^{-1}(H(m)+xr) \bmod q$, where $H()$ is a publicly known hash function as is assumed in Schnorr signature scheme. The signature is the pair (r, s).

Signature verification. Let $u_1 = H(m)s^{-1} \bmod q$ and $u_2 = rs^{-1} \bmod q$. Verify whether equation $r == (g^{u_1}h^{u_2} \bmod p) \bmod q$ holds.

In [1] a DSS based signature commitment protocol is proposed which is proved to be secure against any forgeries. Here we modify it so that verifiable encryption is not required but still achieve the same purpose, namely the confirmation on the convertibility of the signature commitment into a normal signature by the TTP. In order to do this, we assume that in the registration, the user has the public information $\gamma = g^v \bmod p$, $\gamma' = g^{v^{-1}} \bmod p$, $\tau = g^w \bmod p$ and $\lambda = \gamma'^{w\gamma} \bmod p$ authorised and issued by the TTP, where the TTP has recorded v and w (v and w are also known to the user) associated with the user's identity.

DSS Signature Commitment
In the following discussion we will use $\alpha\|\beta$ to denote the concatenation of α and β. Now we can give the following protocol.

Producing a Signature Commitment
- Produce a reference signature using private information v and w which are shared by the user and the TTP:

$$v' = v^{-1}(H(m) + w\gamma) \bmod q.$$

- Let $\alpha = g^{u_1} \bmod p$, $\beta = h^{u_2} \bmod p$, $\delta = h^{v'} \bmod p$.
- Let $r = (\alpha\beta \bmod p) \bmod q$, $c = r^{-1}H(m) \bmod q$, $e = H(\alpha\|\beta\|\delta\|c)$, and $z = (v' + eu_1) \bmod q$.
- Commitment: the tuple $(\alpha, \beta, \delta, z)$.

Verification of Signature Commitment
- Compute $r = (\alpha\beta \bmod p) \bmod q$, $c = r^{-1}H(m) \bmod q$, $e = H(\alpha\|\beta\|\delta\|c)$, and $\alpha' = g^{v'} \bmod p = \gamma'^{H(m)}\lambda \bmod p$.
- Check whether $g^z \equiv \alpha'\alpha^e \pmod{p}$ and $h^z \equiv \delta\beta^{ce} \pmod{p}$?

Theorem 1. *The DSS signature commitment protocol described above has the following properties:*

Completeness: *An honest prover will always be successful in convincing the verifier that a valid signature commitment is produced, i.e., it succeeds in the signature commitment verification.*

Privacy: *The verifier will learn nothing about the signature from the signature commitment except being able to check the validity of the signature commitment.*

Soundness: *To forge a signature commitment is no easier than forging a normal signature which is assumed to be computationally infeasible.*

Convertibility: *Given parameter v, the signature commitment can be converted into normal signature which is publicly verifiable. This can be done by the TTP as the TTP has recorded the value of v and w.*

Fair Signature Exchange and Dispute Resolution

Protocols for fair exchange and for dispute resolution can be made possible. For *fair exchange* of signature commitment and consequently the full signature, the idea is to use a timestamp to constrain the time for signature commitment exchange, and when final signature exchange is not complete after some pre-set time, an *abortion* protocol is executed to force the exchange to be aborted. This is requested by one party and executed by an off-line TTP after verifying the validity of the request. No party will take any liability on further exchange of signatures after the abortion protocol being executed. If the protocol has gone to enough detail, a *dispute resolution protocol* is used to solve disputes by forcing the exchange to be complete. This is also requested by a party with sufficient information regarding the other party's signature commitment and is executed by the off-line TTP. The trick for the TTP being able to recover the signature given information of a signature commitment is that the TTP has a common key with every user, where the shared key plays important role in signature commitment generation. The detail of these sub-protocols are omitted here.

Properties

Compared with the signature commitment protocol based on DSS proposed in [1], the DSS signature commitment protocol described above has the following properties:

- Only one hash function is required which is available from the DSS algorithm. In [1] another random hash function $H'()$ is used in generating signature commitments, we do not see its necessity.
- Computational complexity in producing a signature commitment is simpler than that in [1], as we only use three modular exponentiations rather than four as in the case of [1].
- Computational complexity in verifying the signature commitment is higher than that in [1], as α' has to be computed in the verification. This actually transfers the load on signature commitment creation as the case in [1] to the verification in this scheme. One more modular exponentiation is involved for the purpose of signature convertibility verification.
- Validity of v' can be verified which ensures the signature convertibility, but the verifier learns nothing about the value of v'. This validity verification is done by only one additional modular exponentiation with the help of some authorized information by the TTP.
- The protocol above is explicitly proved to be at least as secure as forging normal signatures.

3   Conclusion

In this paper we have proposed a fair exchange protocol of digital signatures with off-line trusted third party. The prerequisite is an existing signature algorithm which does not need to be re-established. In this paper, there is no need for verifiable encryption protocols which are normally executed via an interactive zero-knowledge proof. This protocol has been shown to have good properties.

References

1. N.Asokan, V.Shoup, M.Waidner, "Optimistic fair exchange of digital signatures (extended abstract)", *Advances in Cryptology — Eurocrypt'98*, K. Nyberg (Ed.), LNCS 1403, Springer-Verlag, 1998, pp.591-606.
2. I.B. Damgard, "Practical and provably secure release of a secret and exchange of signatures", *Advances in Cryptology — Eurocrypt'93*, T.Helleseth (ed.), LNCS 765, Springer-Verlag, 1994, pp.200-217.
3. C. Boyd and E. Foo, "Off-line fair payment protocol using convertible signatures", *Advances in Cryptology — Asiacrypt'98*, LNCS 1514, Springer-Verlag, 1998.
4. T.ElGamal, "A public key cryptosystem and a signature scheme based on discrete logarithms", *IEEE Transactions on Information Theory*, Vol. **IT**-31, No.4, 1985, pp.469-472.
5. FIPS PUB 186, "Digital signature standard", available on-line at `http://bilbo.isu.edu/security/isl/fips186.html`.
6. M.K. Franklin and M.K. Reiter, "Verifiable signature sharing", *Advances in Cryptology — Eurocrypt'95*, L.C. Guillou, J.J. Quisquater (eds.), LNCS 921, Springer-Verlag, 1995, pp.50-63.
7. M.K. Franklin and M.K. Reiter, "Fair exchange with a semi-trusted third party", in *Proceedings of the 4th ACM Conference on Computer and Communication Security*, April 1997, pp.1-5.
8. R.Gennaro, H.Krawczyk, and T.Rabin, "RSA-based undeniable signatures", *Advances in Cryptology — Crypto'97*, B.S. Kaliski Jr. (Ed.), LNCS 1294, Springer-Verlag, 1997, pp.132-149.
9. W.Mao, "Publicly verifiable partial key escrow", *Information and Communications Security, Proceedings*, Y.Han, T.Okamoto, S.Qing (Eds.), LNCS 1334, Springer-Verlag 1997, pp.409-413.
10. W.Mao, "Verifiable escrowed signature", *Information Security and Privacy*, LNCS 1270, Springer-Verlag, 1997, pp.240-248.
11. T. Okamoto and K. Ohta, "How to simultaneously exchange secrets by general assumption", in *Proceedings of the 2nd ACM Conference on Computer and Communications Security*, 1994, pp.184-192.
12. C.P. Schnorr, "Efficient signature generation for smart cards", *Journal of Cryptology*, Vol.4, No.3, 1991, pp.161-174.
13. M.Stadler, "Publicly verifiable secret sharing", *Advances in Cryptology — Eurocrypt'96*, U.Maurer (ed.), LNCS 1070, Springer-Verlag, 1996, pp.190-199.
14. M.Stadler, *Cryptographic Protocols for Revocable Privacy*, Ph.D. thesis, Swiss Federal Institute of Technology, Zürich 1996.
15. J. Zhou and D. Gollman, "A fair non-repudiation protocol", in *Proceedings of the 1996 IEEE Symposium on Security and Privacy*, Oakland, CA, 1996, IEEE Computer Press, pp.55-61.

SECUSIM: A Tool for the Cyber-Attack Simulation

Jong Sou Park, Jang-Se Lee, Hwan Kuk Kim,
Jeong-Rye Jeong, Dong-Bok Yeom, and Sung-Do Chi

Department of Computer Engineering
Hangkong University, Seoul, KOREA
{jspark, jslee2, rinyfeel, harusali, dbyeom,
sdchi}@mail.hangkong.ac.kr

Abstract. The cyber attack simulation tool, SECUSIM, is presented for specifying attack mechanisms, verifying defense mechanisms, and evaluating their consequences. The tool has been successfully developed by employing the advanced modeling and simulation concepts such as SES/MB (System Entity Structure / Model Base) framework, DEVS (Discrete Event System Specification) formalism, and experimental frame. SECUSIM is currently implemented on the basis of Visual C++ and enables a simulation of twenty attack scenarios against hundreds network components.

1 Introduction

As we increasingly rely on information infrastructures to support critical operations in defense, banking, telecommunication, transportation, electric power and many other systems, cyber attacks have become a significant threat to our society with potentially severe consequences [1]. A computer and network system must be protected to assure security goals such as availability, confidentiality and integrity. That is, the deep understanding of system operation and attack mechanisms is the foundation of designing and integrating information protection activities [2]. Therefore, the advanced modeling and simulation methodology is essential for classifying threats, specifying attack mechanisms, verifying protective mechanisms, and evaluating their consequences. That means, we need to establish the advanced simulation system for analyzing vulnerabilities of given infrastructure as well as the expected consequences of successful attacks and the effect of the defense policy [3].

Cohen [3], who was a pioneer in the field of network security modeling and simulation, interestingly suggested a simple network security model. However, cyber attack and defense representation that is based on cause-effect model [3] is so simple that practical difficulty in application comes about. Amoroso suggested that the intrusion model [4] should be represented by sequence of actions, however, the computer simulation approach was not considered clearly. Wadlow [5] suggested an intrusion model, but it failed to go beyond the conceptual modeling level. Finally, Nong Ye [2] noticeably proposed a layer-based approach to complex security system, but failed to provide a practical modeling and simulation techniques of the relevant layers.

S. Qing, T. Okamoto, and J. Zhou (Eds.): ICICS 2001, LNCS 2229, pp. 471-475, 2001.

In order to deal with those restrictions and limitations, we have been successfully developed the network security simulation tool, SECUSIM, that is able to specify attack mechanisms, verify defense mechanisms, and evaluate their consequences. To achieve this, we first have defined the node and link vulnerability metrics for providing the proper mechanisms for evaluating the given information infrastructure. Then behaviors of the cyber-attack, defense, and consequences are coherently characterized within the state transition diagram of discrete event model. We also proposed the functional level of modeling complexity so that we can make it not too complex but meaningful enough. Such a functional level has been successfully developed using the hierarchical and modular discrete event simulation environment underlying DEVS formalism [6,7,8].

2 Simulation Methodology

Fig.1 shows the overall methodology using the SES/MB [6]. Phase I represents the conceptual specification stage, in which the decomposition, taxonomies, coupling specification and constraints of given information network system can be specified by SES (System Entity Structure) [6]. In Phase II, the network component models as well as the attacker models, and analyzer models can be built through DEVS (Discrete Event System Specification) formalism [6,7] and saved into MB (Model Base). Especially, based on this basic behavior model for network component, command-level modeling using pre/post-condition can be accomplished by grouping and characterizing of commands that are used in various services. In phase III, the simulation model may be constructed by integrating the dynamic models in MB along with the network structure of the SES so that the cyber attack simulation can be performed. Finally, the simulation result can be analyzed in Phase IV so that the security characteristics and policies of each network component may be evaluated [8].

3 Main Features of SECUSIM

SECUSIM is currently implemented on the basis of Visual C++ and enables a simulation of twenty attack patterns against hundreds network components. The software architecture of SECUSIM (Fig. 2) consists of the following five modules;

- **GUI**: It basically has the functionality for initialization and modification of network components attributes based on the simulation condition and result. It also supports the packet level graphic animation during simulation.
- **Network Configurator**: It provides graphic editing capabilities for constructing the network structure.
- **Simulation Engine**: It proceeds the simulation by executing the network component models based on the given attack scenario. It also produces the simulation results for the GUI.

- **Component Model Base**: It is a model base that contains behavior characteristics represented by DEVS formalism. It basically consists of various servers, routers, gateways, firewalls, links, etc.
- **Attack Scenario Database**: It is a database that contains command-level cyber attack scenarios in order to inject the cyber attack commands to the given network via simulation.

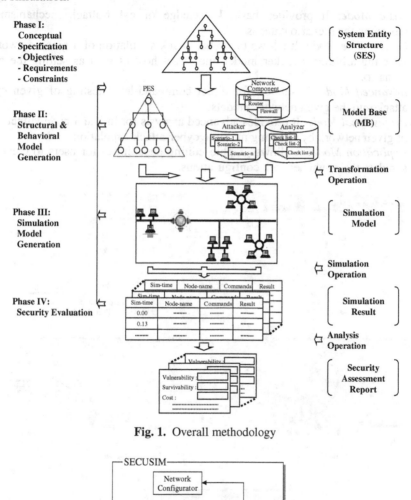

Fig. 1. Overall methodology

Fig. 2. The software architecture of SECUSIM

SECUSIM supports five modes of usages for allowing the step-by-step analysis (see Fig.3) as follows;

(1) *Basic Mode*: It provides basic knowledge of cyber-attack mechanisms by retrieving the scenario database.
(2) *Intermediate Mode*: It allows the cyber attack simulation of a given network by selecting arbitrary attacker model and target host as well as setting the attack scenario.
(3) *Advanced Mode*: It support for direct command-level testing of given cyber-attack into the given network models.
(4) *Professional Mode*: It provides advanced analysis for link and node vulnerability of given network by allowing multiple cyber-attack simulation.
(5) *Application Mode*: It allows graphic editing capabilities for users to create and simulate their own network configurations.

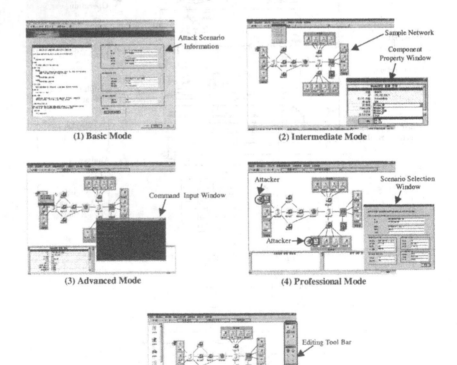

Fig. 3. Screen copies of 'SECUSIM'

4 Conclusions

We have successfully developed the cyber attack simulation tool, SECUSIM, that is able to specify attack mechanisms, verify defense mechanisms, and evaluate their consequences. The tool takes advantage of a hierarchical and modular modeling and simulation environment so that it efficiently supports to construct the security model as well as to analyze node and link vulnerabilities of given network model through simulation. SECUSIM is currently implemented on the basis of Visual C++ and enables a simulation of twenty attack patterns against hundreds network components. We leave here future further studies for automated model generation and also identification of unknown cyber-attacks through the simulation.

Acknowledgements. This work is in part of "Support Project of University Information Technology Research Center" supported by the Ministry of Information & Communication of Korea (supervised by IITA) and in part of "Internet Information Retrieval" Regional Research Center Program supported by the Korea Science and Engineering Foundation.

References

1. T. A. Longstaff, Clyde Chittister, Rich Pethia, Yacov Y. Haimes, "Are We Forgetting the Risks of Information Technology", IEEE Computer, pp 43-51, December, 2000.
2. N. Ye, C. Hosmer, J. Giordano, J. Feldman, "Critical Information Infrastructure Protection through Process Modeling and Model-based Information Fusion", Proceedings of the Information Survivability Workshop, 1998.
3. F. Cohen "Simulating Cyber Attacks, Defenses, and Consequences", IEEE Symposium on Security and Privacy Special 20th Anniversary Program, Berkeley, CA, May, 1999.
4. E. Amoroso, Intrusion Detection, AT&T Laboratory, Intrusion Net Books, January, 1999.
5. T. A. Wadlow, The Process of Network Security, Addison-Wesley, 2000.
6. B. P. Zeigler, Object-oriented Simulation with Hierarchical, Modular Models: Intelligent Agents and Endomorphic systems, Academic Press, 1990.
7. B.P. Zeigler, Multifacetted Modeling and Discrete Event Simulation, Academic Press, 1984.
8. S. D. Chi, J. S. Park, K. C. Jung, J. S. Lee, "Network Security Modeling and Cyber-attack Simulation Methodology", Lecture Notes on Computer Science series, 6th Australian Conf. On Information Security and Privacy, Sydney, July, 2001.

A New Semantics of Authentication Logic

Yifa Li

The Information Security Institute of the University of Information Engineering,
Zhengzhou, 450002, `alphalee@371.net`

Abstract. This paper discusses the semantics of authentication protocol, and then proposes a new formal logic system of authentication. It is useful and effective, not only in analyzing key establish protocols, but in analyzing identification authentication protocols, electronic commerce protocols and non-repudiation protocols. And my logic needn't the protocol idealization that has caused many problems in other BAN-like logic systems.

1 Introduction

Michael Burrows, Martin Abadi and Roger Needham published a famous paper "*A Logic of Authentication*" in 1989. This paper proposed a new method for authentication protocol analysis. It's useful in finding the leakage of some authentication protocols, and is named as BAN logic.

Of course the BAN logic is helpful to analysis the security of some protocols, but just like some researchers have indicated that sometimes the analytic result is not accurate, so it's not a perfect method. In 1990, Li Gong et al improved the BAN logic and proposed a new logic named as GNY logic. In 1994, P. Syverson et al proposed another logic method named as SVO logic. After that many other logic methods appeared. It's known that all of these logic methods are named as BAN-like logic.

Mr. Wenbo Mao and Sihan Qing etc discussed the limitations of BAN logic, and other researchers found the limitations of GNY and SVO logic in the last few years. They concluded that idealization process is vital in causing many inaccurate results.

I think that the basic cause is the semantics and the postulates, not the idealization process. I find that the idealization is unnecessary if the semantics and the postulates are well defined. This paper first defines the semantics, then gives the axioms. Limit to the length, examples will be given in other papers.

2 The Semantics

2.1 Some Basic Notations

In our paper, we use the following notations:

Let S denote the center name or the server's identifier, and Ω' denote the set of all center names; we use A, B, C denote the user name or user's identifier, and the Ω'' denote the set of all user names. Let $\Omega=\Omega'\cup\Omega''$, called host name set.

Let $\Im$ denote the set of all time-stamps, $\aleph$ denote the set of all nonce; $\Re'$ denote the set of attributed symmetric keys, $\Re''$ the set of session keys. $\Re=\Re'\cup\Re''$ is the set of all

S. Qing, T. Okamoto, and J. Zhou (Eds.): ICICS 2001, LNCS 2229, pp. 476–482, 2001.

symmetric keys. Let $\wp'$ denote the set of all public keys, $\wp''$ the set of all private keys, $\wp = \wp' \cup \wp''$ the set of all asymmetric keys.

Also, we use P, Q, R denote an arbitrary host or host name, in other words, P, Q, R are the host name variables. Similarly, let X, Y, Z denote an arbitrary bit string, Σ'' denote the set of all bit string; Γ, Φ denote an arbitrary set.

Definition 1 We call a bit string Y is a term including X, if X is a bit string, and Y is composed of X concatenated with other bit strings. We denote it as $Y = \rho(X)$. Also, we call Y concludes X, or X is concluded in Y.

Definition 2 Let X be a bit string, CF, CF′ be cryptographic functions, a term implying X is defined as follows:

(1) $CF(\rho(X))$ is a term implying X;

(2)   If Y is a term implying X, then $CF'(\rho(Y))$ is also a term implying X;

(3)   The set of all terms implying X is generated as in (1) and (2).

We denote a term implying X as $Y = \tau(X)$, and call Y implies X, or X is implied in Y.

Note: A cryptographic function is referred to an encryption function, or a decryption function, or a signature function, or a hash function.

When we use key K to encipher message X, we can obtain a cipher-text $Y = CF(X, K)$, where CF is the encipher function. Generally, it is denoted as $Y = \{X\}_K$, and here we denote it as $Y = [X]K$ for the convenience. A hash function is denoted by $H(X)$.

Examples: $[X]K$ is a term implying X, $[Y, H(X)]K$ and $[Y, [X, Z]K]K'$ are also terms implying X.

Definition 3 Let $\tau(X)$ be a term implying X, if we can obtain X from $\tau(X)$ by some algorithm and some especially message, then we say that X is retrievable from $\tau(X)$, and denote it as $X \cong \tau(X)$. For instance, $\tau(X) = [X]K$, then X can be retrieved from $[X]K$ provided K^{-1} is known; but no one can retrieve X from $H(X)$, so $H(X)$ is irretrievable.

Definition 4 We say that a bit string is fresh if it is generated in recent time, and denote it as $\#(X)$.

2.2 The Messages

Definition 5 A message is defined as follows:

(1)   The element of set $\Omega \cup \Im \cup \wp \cup \Re'$ is a message;

(2)   If X, Y are messages, then(X,Y), the bit string of X concatenated with Y, is a message;

(3)   If $X_1, \dots, X_N$ are messages, then $F(X_1, \dots, X_N)$ is a message, where F is an arbitrary function. Especially that $H(X)$ and $[X]K$ are messages if X is a message.

(4)   The set of all Messages is generated as above.

We denote the set of all messages as Σ.

Definition 6 If a bit string X is not a message, we say that X is a confusion code.

Definition 7 We say that a bit string X is a truthful message or message X is truthful if we can conclude that X is really a message.

Note: A nonce or a cipher-text is just like a confusion code. So it's necessary to give above definition. Many BAN-like logic systems give the definition "recognizable".

Surely a recognizable bit string is indeed a message, but we argue that a message is not always recognizable. For example, when a host transmits an enciphered message, he can believe that it is message, but he can't recognize it.

2.3 The Formula

Definition 8 Let Σ'' be the set of all bit strings; $\Gamma \subseteq \Sigma''$ be a set; X, Y$\in \Sigma''$ be bit string variables; P, Q$\in \Omega$ be hosts. We say that the symbol string X$\in \Gamma$, X=Y, X$\in \Sigma$, #(X), X$\cong \tau$(X), P$\ni$X, P$\lhd$X, X$\succ$P, P$\Rightarrow$Q and &(P) are atomic formulas. We interpret some atomic formulas as follows:

(1)   P$\ni$X: P generates X;
(2)   P$\lhd$X: P sees X;
(3)   X$\succ$P: X is given to P, or P is the receiver of X;
(4)   P$\Rightarrow$Q: Q is P's communicative object, or P's communicative object is Q;
(5)   &(P):   P is taken parting a protocol communication.

Definition 9 A formula is defined as follows:

(1)   An atomic formula is a formula;
(2)   If E is a formula, P$\in \Omega$, then (P$\models E$), ($\neg E$), ($\forall$x)E is also formulas;
(3)   If E and F are formulas, then ($E \rightarrow F$) is also formulas;
(4)   All formulas are generated as above.

Here, (P$\models E$) represents that P believes that formula E is correct; ($\neg E$) represents that the negation of E; ($E \rightarrow F$) represents that if E, then F; ($\forall$X)E represents that, E holds for all X.

Note: The symbols $\in$, =, #, &, $\ni$, $\lhd$, $\succ$, $\Rightarrow$, $\cong$ are first order predicates, the symbol $\models$ is a second order predicate, $\forall$ is a quantifier, $\neg$(negation), $\rightarrow$(conditional) are connectives.

Definition 10 For the convenience, we define some new formula symbols with the defined formula as follows:

(1)   ($E \wedge F$) is the abbreviation of formula $\neg(E \rightarrow (\neg F))$, that is E and F;
(2)   ($E \vee F$) is the abbreviation of formula ($\neg E \rightarrow F$), that is E or F;
(3)   ($E \leftrightarrow F$) is the abbreviation of formula ($E \rightarrow F$)$\wedge$($F \rightarrow E$) , that is , E if and only if F;
(4)   X$\neq$Y, (X$\notin \Gamma$) is the abbreviation of formula $\neg$(X=Y), $\neg$(X$\in \Gamma$);
(5)   ($\Gamma \lhd X$) is the abbreviation of formula ($\forall$R)((R$\in \Gamma$)$\rightarrow$(R$\lhd$X)), where X $\in \Sigma''$£$\neg \Gamma \subseteq \Omega$;
(6)   ($\Gamma \trianglelefteq X$) is the abbreviation of formula ($\forall$R)((R$\lhd$X)$\rightarrow$(R$\in \Gamma$));
(7)   ($\Gamma| \trianglelefteq X$) is the abbreviation of formula (($\Gamma \lhd X$)$\wedge$($\Gamma \trianglelefteq X$));
(8)   (P$\lhd \Gamma$) is the abbreviation of formula ($\forall$X)((X$\in \Gamma$)$\rightarrow$(P$\lhd$X));
(9) $\Gamma \models E$ is the abbreviation of formula ($\forall$R)(R$\in \Gamma \rightarrow$R$\models E$), where $\Gamma \subseteq \Omega$;
(10)   P$\xleftrightarrow{K}$Q is the abbreviation of formula (K$\in \Re$)$\wedge${P,Q}$\models$ (K$\in \Sigma \wedge$ {P,Q}$| \trianglelefteq$ K);
(11)   (K$\mapsto$P) is the abbreviation of formula (K$\in \wp'$)$\wedge$(P$\lhd$K^{-1})$\wedge$(P$\models$K$^{-1}\in \wp''$);

(12) $(X \succ \Gamma)$ is the abbreviation of formula $(\forall R)((X \succ R) \rightarrow (R \in \Gamma))$;

(13) $Q| \sim X$ is the abbreviation of formula $(\exists K)(K \in \Re \cup \wp'' \wedge Q \ni [\rho(X)]K)$;

(14) $P| \approx X$ is the abbreviation of formula $(P| \sim X) \wedge \#(X)$;

(15) $\Diamond\ (X,P)$ is the abbreviation of formula $((\exists Q)((Q| \sim X)) \wedge (X \succ P))$;

(16) $P|\equiv \Diamond\ (X)$ is the abbreviation of formula $P|\equiv \Diamond\ (X,P)$;

Note: Although we defined some new formulas, the set of all formulas is not expanded.

3 Axioms

Now we give some axioms. In the following axioms, we always assume that W, X, Y, $Z \in \Sigma''$ is an arbitrary bit string; P, Q, $R \in \Omega$ is an arbitrary host; $K \in \Re \cup \wp$ is a key; $\rho(X)$ is a term including X; $\tau(X)$ is a term implying X; F is a function; H is hash function; [X]K is encryption function with key K, or a decryption function with key K, or a signature function with key K; $\Sigma_1 = \Omega \cup \Im \cup \wp \cup \Re'$ is the known message set; Σ' is the set of all bit strings transmitted in a given protocol.

Axiom about General Functions, abbreviated to AGF:

AGF: $(P \lhd \{X_1,\ldots,X_n\}) \rightarrow (P \lhd F(X_1,\ldots,X_n))$;(Function F is public)

Axiom about Cryptographic Function, abbreviated to ACF:

ACF: $\{X,Y\} \subseteq \Sigma \rightarrow ((F(X)=[X]K \vee F(X)=H(X)) \rightarrow (F(X)=F(Y) \leftrightarrow X=Y))$;

Axiom about Truthful Message, abbreviated to ATM:

ATM: $(P|\equiv X \in \Sigma) \leftrightarrow (P \lhd X \wedge ((X \in \Omega \cup \Im \vee P|\equiv X \in \wp \vee P|\equiv X \in \Re \vee (X=\rho(Y) \wedge P|\equiv Y \in \Sigma) \vee (X=H(Y) \wedge P|\equiv Y \in \Sigma) \vee (X=\tau(Y) \wedge P|\equiv Y?\tau(Y) \wedge P|\equiv Y \in \Sigma) \vee P \ni X))$;

Axiom about Determining Some Basic Set, Such as Ω, $\Im$ and $\aleph$, abbreviated to ADS:

ADS: $X \in \Gamma \rightarrow (P|\equiv X \in \Gamma \leftrightarrow (P \lhd X \wedge P|\equiv X \in \Sigma))$;($\Gamma$ is Ω', Ω'', $\Im$, $\aleph$, $\Re$ or Π)

Axiom about Key's Basic Properties, abbreviated to AKP:

AKP1: $((K^{-1})^{-1}=K)$;

AKP2: $(P \lhd K^{-1}) \rightarrow (P \lhd [X]K \rightarrow P \lhd X)$;

Axiom about Symmetric Key, abbreviated to ASK:

ASK: $K \in \Re \rightarrow (P \lhd K \rightarrow P \lhd K^{-1})$;

Axiom about Asymmetric Key, abbreviated to AAK:

AAK1: $K^{-1} \in \wp'' \leftrightarrow K \in \wp'$;

AAK2: $P|\equiv K \in \wp' \rightarrow ((P \lhd K) \wedge P|\equiv (Q \lhd K^{-1} \rightarrow Q| \lhd K^{-1}))$;

Axiom about Believing Theorems, abbreviated to ABT:

ABT: $E \leftrightarrow (\forall P)(P|\equiv E)$;(where E is an arbitrary theorem of arithmetic system or an arbitrary axioms of this system)

Axiom about Interchanging Belief Predicate with Quantifier, abbreviated to IBQ:

IBQ: $(\forall X)P|\equiv E(X) \leftrightarrow P|\equiv (\forall X)E(X)$;(where $X \neq P$, and $E(X)$ is a formula which X is free occurred in E)

Axiom about Interchanging Belief Predicate with Negation, abbreviated to IBN:

IBN: $(P|\equiv \neg E) \leftrightarrow \neg(P|\equiv E)$;

Belief Modus Ponens, abbreviated to BMP:

BMP: $(P|\equiv(E{\rightarrow}F))\leftrightarrow(P|\equiv E{\rightarrow}P|\equiv F)$;

Axiom about Belief Absorption, abbreviated to ABA:

ABA: $(P|\equiv(P|\equiv E))\leftrightarrow(P|\equiv E)$;($E$ is an arbitrary formula)

Axiom about See Predicate, abbreviated to ASP:

ASP1: $((P \lhd X){\rightarrow}(P\ni X\vee X\in \Sigma_1\cup\Sigma'\vee(P \lhd \tau(X)\wedge P|\equiv X \cong \tau(X)))$;

ASP2: $(P \lhd \rho(X){\rightarrow}P \lhd X)$;

ASP3: $(P \lhd X\leftrightarrow P|\equiv P \lhd X)$;

Axiom about Message Generation, abbreviated to AMG:

AMG1: $P\ni X{\rightarrow}(P \lhd X\wedge P|\equiv \lozenge\ (X))$;

AMG2: $X\in \Im\cup\aleph\cup\Re{\rightarrow}(P\ni X{\rightarrow}P|\equiv\#(X))$;

AMG3: $X\in \aleph\cup\Re{\rightarrow}(P\ni X{\rightarrow}P|\equiv(\forall R)(R\ni X{\rightarrow}R{=}P))$;

AMG4: $\tau(X)\in \Sigma\leftrightarrow(\exists Q)(Q\ni\tau(X))$;

AMG5: $P\ni F(X){\rightarrow}P \lhd X$;

AMG6: $P\ni X\leftrightarrow P|\equiv P\ni X$;

Axiom about Naming the Participator, abbreviated to ANP:

ANP1: $P\in \Omega'{\rightarrow}(P| \approx Q{\rightarrow}P|\equiv\&(Q))$;

ANP2: $(P\in \Omega''\wedge P{\neq}Q){\rightarrow}(P|{\sim}Q{\rightarrow}P{\Rightarrow}Q)$;

ANP3: $P\in \Omega'{\rightarrow}((P|{\sim}Q \succ R\wedge Q{\neq}R){\rightarrow}P|\equiv Q{\Rightarrow}R)$;

ANP4: $P|\equiv Q| \approx X{\rightarrow}P|\equiv\&(Q)$;

ANP5: $(P|{\sim}X \succ Q){\rightarrow}P{\Rightarrow}Q$;

(Note: ANP4 and ANP5 do not name the host directly, but they name the host name implicitly)

ANP6: $X\in \wp'{\rightarrow}R|\equiv((P\in \Omega'\wedge P{\neq}Q){\rightarrow}(P|{\sim}(Q,X){\rightarrow}X{\mapsto}Q))$;(This axiom is about the public key certificate, we assume that in a public key certificate the owner's name (host name) is always ahead of the key)

Axiom about Message Retrieving, abbreviated to RET:

RET: $(P|\equiv X \cong\ [\rho(X)]K\leftrightarrow P \lhd K^{-1})$;

Axiom about Message Receipt, abbreviated to REC:

REC1: $(P{\neq}Q\wedge P|\equiv Q\ni H(X)){\rightarrow}P|\equiv X \succ P$;

REC2: $(P\xleftrightarrow{K} Q\wedge P|\equiv Q\ni[X]K){\rightarrow}P|\equiv X \succ P$;

REC3: $K\in \Re{\rightarrow}((P|\equiv \lozenge\ (K)\wedge P \lhd\ [X]K){\rightarrow}P|\equiv X \succ P)$;

REC4: $(P \lhd\ [X]K\wedge K{\mapsto}P){\rightarrow}(P|\equiv X\in \Sigma{\rightarrow}P|\equiv X \succ P)$;

REC5: $(P \lhd\ [X]K^{-1}\wedge X{=}\rho(P)\wedge P|\equiv K{\mapsto}Q){\rightarrow}(P|\equiv X\in \Sigma{\rightarrow}P|\equiv X \succ P)$;

REC6: $(\rho(X)\ \succ P{\rightarrow}X \succ P)$;

Axiom about Fresh Message, abbreviated to AFM:

AFM1: $(X\in \Im){\rightarrow}(P|\equiv Q|{\sim}\rho(X){\rightarrow}P|\equiv\#(\rho(X)))$;

AFM2: $X\notin \Omega{\rightarrow}(\#(X)\leftrightarrow\#\rho(X))$;

AFM3: $\#(X){\rightarrow}\#H(X)$;

AFM4: $(\#(X)\vee\#(K)){\rightarrow}\#([X]K)$;

Thus we totally have forty axioms as above, which are divided to eighteen classes.

4 Rules and Theorems

We have two inductive rules: MP(Modus Ponens) and GN(Generalization), just like the predicative formal system. The rule MP is referred that if we have formula E and $(E \to F)$, then we can obtain F. The rule GN is referred that if we have formula E, then we can get $(\forall X)E$.

Note: Now we have defined a second order system, and denote it by $\mathcal{L}'$. We call it LEE logic for the convenience.

It's obviously that our system $\mathcal{L}'$ is an expansion of the arithmetic axiom system. Hence, all of the arithmetic theorems also held in $\mathcal{L}'$.

In our system, there exists such formula: $(\forall E)(P|\equiv(E \to E))$, but we do not discuss it because it's unnecessary for authentication protocol analysis.

Definition 11 Let $E_1, E_2, ..., E_N$ be a formula sequence, if each E_i is either an axiom or induced by rules from the formulas ahead of E_i, then we call E_N is a theorem. Sometimes, we denote a theorem E by $\vdash E$.

Definition 12 Let Γ be a set of some formulas, $E_1, E_2, ..., E_N$ be a formula sequence, if each E_i is either an axiom or a member of Γ, or is induced by rules from the formulas ahead of E_i, then we call E_N is derived from Γ, or Γ generates E_N, and denote it by $\Gamma \vdash E_N$.

There are lots of theorems in our logic system, such as:

$\{P \xleftrightarrow{K} Q, P \lhd [X]K\} \vdash P \lhd X$;

$\{P \lhd [X]K, K \mapsto P\} \vdash P \lhd X$;

$\{P \lhd [X]K^{-1}, P|\equiv K \mapsto Q, P|\equiv X \in \Sigma\} \vdash P|\equiv Q|\sim X$;

We can prove a lot of such useful theorems. We'll publish some of them in other papers.

5 Conclusions

Our logic has many advantages. We list some of them as follows:

Firstly, our logic is useful and effective, not only in analyzing key establish protocols, but in analyzing identification authentication protocols, electronic commerce protocols and non-repudiation protocols.

Secondly, we can express the goals of a protocol accurately with well-defined formulas.

Thirdly, we needn't the protocol idealization which has caused many problems in BAN-like logic.

Fourthly, we can define "secure protocol" accurately towards different kind of protocols.

We have already analyzed many protocols. We'll publish them in other papers.

References

1. M. Burrows, M. Abadi, R. Needham. A logic of authentication, ACM trans. on Computer Systems, 1990, 8(1): 18-36.
2. Li Gong, R. Needham, R. Yahalom, Reasoning About Belief in Cryptographic Protocols, Proc. 1990 IEEE Symp. Security and Privacy, 1990, 234-248.
3. P. Syverson, P. Van Oorshot. On Unifying Some Cryptographic Protocol Logics, Proc. IEEE Symp. Security and Privacy. 1994, 14-28.
4. Li Gong, Cryptographic Protocols for Distributed Systems, Ph. D. Thesis, 1990.
5. C. Boyd, W. Mao, Limitations of Logical Analysis of Cryptographic Protocols, Eurocrypt'93.
6. Sihan Qing, Notes on Logic Analysis of Cryptographic Protocols, Chinacrypt'96, 214-219.
7. T. Y. C. Woo and S. S. Lam. Authentication for Distributed Systems. Computer Vol. 25, No. 1, January 1992, 39-52.
8. Yifa Li, A New Semantics of BAN Logic. PhD Thesis.

Robust and Fragile Watermarking Techniques for Documents Using Bi-directional Diagonal Profiles

Ji Hwan Park[1], Sook Ee Jeong[2], and Chang Soo Kim[1]

[1] Div. of Elec. Computer and Telecommnu. Eng., Pukyong Nat'l Univ.
599-1, Daeyon3-dong, Nam-gu, Busan, 608-737, Korea
jpark@pknu.ac.kr
cskim@dolphin.pknu.ac.kr
[2] Dept. of Computer Science, Pukyong Nat'l Univ.
599-1, Daeyon3-dong, Nam-gu, Busan, 608-737, Korea
waterpur@unicorn.pknu.ac.kr

Abstract. A number of techniques have been recently proposed to prevent unauthorized user from illegal copying or redistribution of multimedia contents. One approach for copy protection is robust watermarking technique that purposes to resist several attacks such as signal processing, geometric distortion, etc. On the country to robust watermarking, the other approach is fragile watermarking that purposes to detect slight changes to the watermarked contents. In this paper we find out the problems of a marking and identification scheme for document images using one directional diagonal profile that we proposed. And then we suggest robust watermarking technique to resolve these problems using bi-direction diagonal profiles; left-directional diagonal profile and right-directional diagonal profile. According to this robust watermarking technique, it can reduce the side information, which needs in watermark extraction procedure and find the pixel position on document image with only the indexes of bi-directional diagonal profiles. Finally, in addition to robust watermarking scheme, we suggest fragile watermarking technique that can locate or characterize the forged region using the feature of bi-directional diagonal profiles and reverse process.

1. Introduction

As the growth of high technology, it is possible to access the multimedia contents such as document, audio, video by unauthorized users, these illegal accessed contents, furthermore, can be copied or redistributed to the third parties. To protect these multimedia contents, copy protection technique has been introduced and this can be classified into two categories. One is robust watermarking that purposes to resist attacks that attempt to remove or destroy the watermark. The other is fragile watermarking that mainly purposes to detect even slight changes to the watermarked contents. The main application of fragile watermarks is in content authentication, it, therefore, can be used to prove that object has not been modified and might be useful if digital contents are used as evidence in court.

Specially, we mention on digital watermarking for the text document images in this paper. This technique has applications wherever copyrighted electronic documents are

S. Qing, T. Okamoto, and J. Zhou (Eds.): ICICS 2001, LNCS 2229, pp. 483-494, 2001.

distributed. One of the examples is virtual digital library where users may download copies of documents, for example, books, but are not allowed to further distribute them or to store them longer than for a certain predefined period. In this type of application, a requested document is watermarked with a requester specific watermark before releasing it for download. If later on illegal copies are discovered, the embedded watermark can be used to determine the original ones.

In section 2 we briefly review several watermarking techniques for document image. And then we mention the problems of watermarking technique[12] using one directional diagonal profile. In section 3 we propose robust watermarking scheme using bi-directional diagonal profiles and also propose fragile watermarking technique that can extract the forged region using reverse process. Then we present experimental results, conclusions in section 4 and 5.

2. Watermarking Techniques for Text Documents

Digital watermarking techniques for text document image are mainly classified two categories; spatial domain technique and frequency domain technique.

Spatial domain technique by Brassil *et al.*[3][4][8] and Low *et al.*[2][6][7] slightly moves the location of words or lines; this is perceptually invisible even after embedding the watermark. According to this, embedded watermark can be detected using feature detection, correlation detection, centroid detection even though it has been corrupted by copying, scanning, fax transmission. Feature detection is most directly applicable for detecting line shifting, it has an advantage that does not require any information on the original unmarked document, but also has a disadvantage of relatively poor performance on documents that have suffered significant distortions. Although centroid detection can be applied to detect both line and word spacing, its performance in the presence of noise is satisfactory only for line spacing. It is more reliable but requires centroid of original unmarked document profile. Correlation detection performs much better than centroid detection on word spacing, but its performance is sensitive to how accurately can be compensated for the translation of the profile. This method requires the profile of original unmarked document.

Frequency domain digital watermarking technique by Lui *et al.*[9] uses the original Cox *et al.* algorithm[5] as a representative frequency domain technique. This technique marks the watermark using word or line shifting algorithm by Brassil *et al.* and Low *et al.*   mentioned above, then measures similarity in Cox *et al.* algorithm between original watermarked document image and possibly corrupted watermarked document image to detect watermark. This technique has an advantage of robustness against noise.

We had proposed a watermarking algorithm[12] using one directional diagonal profile. It can easily detect the attempt to change the marked document by comparing the entire profile between original marked document and possibly changed document, because if the marked document has changed, it has influence on the entire profile of document. In other words, someone who intends to attack has changed several lines or words on document, line and word shifting technique only results in changing the profile of corresponding lines or words. But, in the previous scheme, it results in changing the entire profile of document, not some particular region because of the feature of diagonal profile.

And we had introduced two different decoding models in this scheme[12]. In decoding model I, we could just detect the watermark on noisy diagonal profile, while we could extract the watermark after removing the noise in decoding model II. Model I, furthermore, needs small amount of side information in decoding procedure, while it also has a disadvantage of ambiguity in watermark extraction procedure since it could not exactly separate between the watermark and the noise on the diagonal profile. On the other hand, model II resolve ambiguity in watermark extraction, while it has a disadvantage that needs original unmarked document to decode the watermark.

The other problem of the proposed method using one directional diagonal profile cannot find the original pixel position of watermark with only the indexes of profile of marked document. We have to memorize the actual position on marked document. We, therefore, propose a new technique using bi-directional diagonal profiles; left directional diagonal profile and right directional diagonal profile in section 3 to progress the problems in decoding model I, II. The technique for the bi-directional diagonal profiles does not need the original unmarked document to extract the watermark. The watermark can be extracted using the information about the indexes of two diagonal profiles only, such that we can reduce the side information in watermark extraction procedure. It, furthermore, makes possible to implement fragile watermarking technique using the feature of the bi-directional diagonal profiles and reverse process.

3. Watermarking Using Bi-directional Diagonal Profiles

3.1 Bi-direction Diagonal Profiles

In general, one directional diagonal profile(i.e. right directional diagonal profile) of the document images is a projection of two-dimensional array. To making the diagonal profile is to compute an index for the histogram bucket for the current row and column. Let the row and column be noted by i and j, respectively. Suppose that the dimensions of the image are n row and m columns, so i and j range from 0 to n-1 and 0 to m-1, respectively, and assume that the index k for the diagonal can be computed by an affine transformation of the row and column. The index k can be described as (1). And the diagonal profile will require $n+m$-1 buckets.

$$k = i - j + m - 1, \qquad 0 \le k \le n + m - 2 \tag{1}$$

The bi-directional diagonal profile is to expand one directional diagonal profile. Figure 1 is an example of left and right directional diagonal profiles. For right directional diagonal profile, the upper right pixel is mapped into the first position of the right directional diagonal profile, and then the lower left pixel is mapped into the last position of one. While, for left right directional diagonal profile, the lower right pixel is mapped into the first position of the left directional diagonal profile, and then upper left pixel is mapped into the last position of one.

In this example, $n = 18$, $m = 18$, therefore, each diagonal profile consists of 35 buckets. A dotted black pixel on original document image is corresponded to a dotted pixel on each directional diagonal profile using Eqn (2) and (3) in below.

$$D_L(k) = n + m - i - j - 2 \tag{2}$$

$$D_R(k) = i - j + m - 1 \tag{3}$$

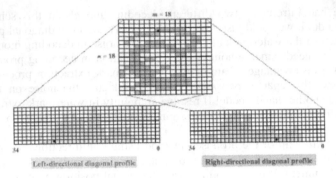

Fig. 1. An example of bi-directional diagonal profiles

3.2 Watermark Embedding Procedure

Before mentioning the embedding procedure, we predefine the each document image. At first, we assume that the page is represented as follows. Figure 2 is an example of document image.

$$f(i, j) \in \{0,1\}, \quad i \in [0, n-1], \quad j \in [0, m-1] \tag{4}$$

where, n and m, whose values depend on the scanning resolution, are the height and width of the page, respectively. The image of text line is simply the function restricted to the region of the text line

$$f(i, j) \in \{0,1\}, \quad i \in [t, b], \quad j \in [0, m-1] \tag{5}$$

where, t and b are the top and bottom boundaries of the text line, respectively. And the image of a word can be represented as follows.

$$f(i, j) \in \{0,1\}, \quad i \in [t, b], \quad j \in [s, e] \tag{6}$$

where, s and e are the start and end of the word in text line.

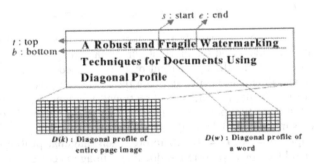

Fig. 2. Illustration of document image

In this method, the embedding algorithm of watermark to generate copyright information for original owner of document images is described as follows. Figure 3 is the watermark embedding process.

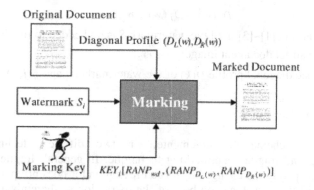

Fig. 3. Watermark embedding process

[Step1] Randomly choose a word to embed $S_i \in \{0,1\}$, generate diagonal profile $D_R(w)$ and $D_L(w)$ of the chosen word $f(i, j)$.

$$D_L(w) = \begin{cases} D_L(w)+1, & if \ f(i,j)=1 \\ D_L(w), & otherwise \end{cases} \qquad (7)$$

where, $w = p + q - x - y - 2 \ (0 \le w \le p + q - 1), t \le i \le b, s \le j \le e, 0 \le x \le p - 1, 0 \le y \le q - 1, p = b - t + 1, q = e - s + 1$

$$D_R(w) = \begin{cases} D_R(w)+1, & if \ f(i,j)=1 \\ D_R(w), & otherwise \end{cases} \qquad (8)$$

where, $w = x - y + p - 1 \ (0 \le w \le p + q - 1), t \le i \le b, s \le j \le e, 0 \le x \le p - 1, 0 \le y \le q - 1, p = b - t + 1, q = e - s + 1$

[Step2] Embed S_i on selected $D_R(w)$ as following conditions.

$$D_R(w) = x - y + p - 1 \qquad (9)$$

$$\hat{D}_R(w) = D_R(w) + W(S_i) \qquad (10)$$

- Divide $D_R(w)$ into two blocks b_l, b_r.
  S_i = '0' (white pixel value) : embed one pixel on randomly chosen position of b_l
  S_i = '1' (black pixel value) : embed one pixel on randomly chosen position of b_r
- Randomly selected position is a pixel that is adjacent to the black pixel value that it has the same bucket index on text document image.
- Maintain the corresponding embedded position of the word on a table to prevent from reselecting of embedded position.
- Avoid the word that does not have plenty of width because the embedded watermark should not be visible under normal observation.

[Step3] Embed the watermark on $D_L(W)$ by calculating the corresponding diagonal index of $D_L(W)$ which is the same with the embedded watermark on $D_R(W)$.

$$D_L(w) = p + q - x - y - 2 \tag{11}$$

$$\hat{D}_L(w) = D_L(w) + W(S_i) \tag{12}$$

[Step4] Repeat Step[1]~[3] until the watermark S_i is embedded to finish.

[Step5] Reconstruct document image $\hat{f}(i, j)$.

[Step6] Produce diagonal profile $\hat{D}(k)$ of the watermarked page $\hat{f}(i, j)$.

3.3 Decoding Procedures

Our decoding scheme is implemented in two different techniques; robust watermarking and fragile watermarking technique. In general, fragile watermarking technique can specify the changed or forged region and it does not purpose to extract the watermark. We, but, focus on both of the extraction of the embedded watermark and characterization of the forged region. Figure 4 is shown these two processes.

3.3.1 Robust Watermark Scheme to Extract the Watermark

Now, let's look into the watermark extraction procedure. Before mentioning the extraction of the watermark, our method can be detected in two ways. If you only want to detect the change of the watermarked document, you can easily detect whether the document has been changed or not by comparing the number of vertical strip between the diagonal profile $\hat{D}(k)$ of watermarked document $\hat{f}(i, j)$ and the diagonal profile of $D^*(k)$ of possibly corrupted or changed document $f^*(i, j)$.

[Step1] Generate digitalized document $f^*(i, j)$ which is possibly corrupted.

[Step2] Generate $D^*(k)$ of $f^*(i, j)$.

[Step3] Extract watermark S_i on $f^*(i, j)$ using

$KEY_i[RANP_{wd}, (RANP_{D_L}(w), RANP_{D_R}(w))]$. Eqn(13), (14) are the same with Eqn(9),(11), but we mention again for Eqn(15).

$$D_R(w) = x - y + p - 1 \tag{13}$$

$$D_L(w) = p + q - x - y - 2 \tag{14}$$

$$i = |x|, \quad j = |y| \tag{15}$$

where, $RANP_{wd}$ shows randomly chosen position of the word and $(RANP_{D_L}(w), RANP_{D_R}(w))$ are the randomly chosen position on each directional diagonal profile to embed the watermark.

[Step4] Repeat Step[3] until the watermark S_i is finished to extract.

3.3.2 Fragile Watermarking Scheme to Extract Forged Region

In this decoding process, we can exactly find the forged region using reverse processing. We first find the information of all pixel value $POS_i[PIXP_{D_L}(w), PIXP_{D_R}(w)]$ which consist of the indexes of each directional diagonal profile from $\hat{f}(i, j)$, and then determine whether a pixel on $f^*(i, j)$ is forged or not as Eqn (16).

$$f_{forged\_regions}(i, j) = \begin{cases} f_{forged\_regions}(i, j) = 0, & if \ f^*(i, j) = POS_i \\ f_{forged\_regions}(i, j) = 1, & otherwise \end{cases} \qquad (16)$$

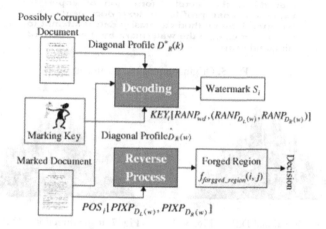

Fig. 4. Watermark decoding process

4. Experimental Results

To test how well marked documents could be extracted and characterized the forged region, and we performed the following experiments. The original and the marked document were printed on HP Laser Jet 6P. The original image size with 901×622 scanned 300dpi on HP5200C. And we also use the binary image size with 50×33 which consists of initial of author for the watermark. We sequentially read the secret information, and then randomly embedded on the document image using two diagonal profiles. The original document has been made 10pt Times New Roman font, the entire page of document consists of 13 lines and 87 words. To be satisfied the condition of perceptual transparency, we embedded the watermark on the word that is composed over 60 pixels of width. Figure 5 and 8 are original unmarked image and watermarked image. Figure 6 and 7 are left and right directional diagonal profile of Figure 5. Figure 10 and 11 are left and right directional diagonal profile of Figure 8. Figure 9 is extracted watermark from Figure 8. We produced a noisy document image to test fragile watermarking technique by copying one time from original marked document image on Zerox 330. For Figure 12, we could only get noise that is produced by copying through the reverse processing. Finally, we experiment on the cropping of the word "*watermarking*" in Figure 13, and then we could get cropped words as the forged regions in Figure 14 through the reverse process. And we changed the meaning of word "*document*" to "*image*" and also changed "*feature of diagonal profile*" to "*diagonal profile's feature*" as Figure 15. Figure 16 is the extracted forged region in Figure 15. Specially, Figure 16 is presented with Figure 15 to compare original document and forged regions.

In these days, open computer network, so called internet, makes possible to use intellectual properties without any degradation of multimedia data such as audio, image, video and text document. In this paper, we introduce a new watermarking scheme to prevent from discourage illicit copy or distribution of text document. We propose the watermarking and extraction by embedding the secret information of copyright using diagonal profile to text document. This watermarking method can easily detect attempt to remove or change the watermark by the feature of diagonal profile.

Fig. 5. Original unmarked document

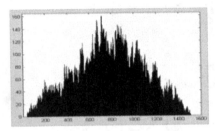

Fig. 6. Left directional D.P. of Fig. 5   **Fig. 7.** Right directional D.P. of Fig. 5

In these days, open computer network, so called internet, makes possible to use intellectual properties without any degradation of multimedia data such as audio, image, video and text document. In this paper, we introduce a new watermarking scheme to prevent from discourage illicit copy or distribution of text document. We propose the watermarking and extraction by embedding the secret information of copyright using diagonal profile to text document. This watermarking method can easily detect attempt to remove or change the watermark by the feature of diagonal profile.

Fig. 8. Watermarked document   **Fig. 9.** Watermark

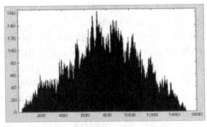   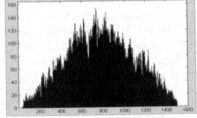

Fig. 10. Left directional D.P. of Fig. 8   **Fig. 11.** Right directional D.P. of Fig. 8

Fig. 12. Forged region by copying one time

In these days, open computer network, so called internet, makes possible to use intellectual properties without any degradation of multimedia data such as audio, image, video and text document. In this paper, we introduce a new   scheme to prevent from discourage illicit copy or distribution of text document. We propose the   and extraction by embedding the secret information of copyright using diagonal profile to text document. This   method can easily detect attempt to remove or change the watermark by the feature of diagonal profile.

Fig. 13. Cropped document("watermarking")

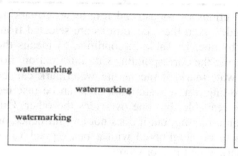

watermarking

watermarking

watermarking

Fig. 14. Extracted forged region of Fig. 13

In these days, open computer network, so called internet, makes possible to use intellectual properties without any degradation of multimedia data such as audio, image, video and text image.   In this paper, we introduce a new watermarking scheme to prevent from discourage illicit copy or distribution of text image.   We propose the watermarking and extraction by embedding the secret information of copyright using diagonal profile to text image.   This watermarking method can easily detect attempt to remove or change the watermark by the diagonal profile's feature.

Fig. 15. Changed meaning of word

In these days, open computer network, so called internet, makes possible to use intellectual properties without any degradation of multimedia data such as audio, image, video and text uocument. In this paper, we introduce a new watermarking scheme to prevent from discourage illicit copy or distribution of text uocument. We propose the watermarking and extraction by embedding the secret information of copyright using diagonal profile to text uooument. This watermarking method can easily detect attempt to remove or change the watermark by the diagonal of diagonal profile.

Fig. 16. Extracted the forged region from Fig. 15

From these results, we could extract the watermark from the watermarked document without the original marked document, could find the forged region from changed document images. The extraction procedure only needs randomly selected position of words and the indexes of two directional diagonal profiles to corresponding embedded watermark position. It, therefore, results in reducing the side information in decoding. Table 1 more specifically shows the side information, which needs in decoding procedure when we use one directional diagonal profile and bi-directional diagonal profiles.

Table 1. Comparison of the side information

One Directional Diagonal Profile		Bi-directional Diagonal Profiles	
Model I	Model II	Robust watermarking	Fragile watermarking
Marked Document	Original Document	Key Information	Pixel Positions of Marked Document
Key Information	Key Information		
	Marked Document		

To find out how well satisfy the conditions of robust and fragile watermarking technique, we present these in Table 2 and 3. And these conditions are selected from [10][11] for document watermarking technique. In Table 2, condition 6) means the watermark should be extracted by only using the corresponding side information. For condition of modification and multiple watermark, it means the watermark can be removable the first watermark and the adding a new watermark and can be inserted the second watermark such that both are readable, but one overrides the other. Our technique, furthermore, does not robust on cropping, but it does not any influence on skewing because the watermark embeds to be neighbored with a black pixel value such that the skewing occurs along the marked text line or words.

Table 2. Satisfying conditions for robust watermarking technique

Conditions for Robust Watermarking	
1) Perceptual Transparency	✓
2) Large Marking Key Space	✓
3) Robustness against skewing	✓
4) Modification and Multiple Watermarks	✓
5) Difficult to deduce from the detection side information	✓
6) Watermark should be orthogonal during watermark detection	✓
7) Computational Cost	✓

As one of the important conditions for fragile wtaermarking, this technique does not have to use original unmarked document. It is really important condition in fragile watermarking system. And our technique can detect the forged region and locate the alternation region.

Table 3. Satisfying conditions for fragile watermarking technique

Conditions for Fragile Watermarking	
1) Detect tampering	✓
2) Locate the alteration made to a marked document image	✓
3) No need original image	✓
4) Perceptual Transparency	✓

5. Conclusions

Document delivery by computer network offers information providers the opportunity to reach a large audience more quickly and cheaply than does media-based distribution. To facilitate the transition to network distribution, we proposed a robust watermarking technique and a fragile watermarking technique using bi-directional diagonal profiles. We could get each unique position of original or watermarked document image by the feature of bi-directional diagonal profiles without original one. According to this reason, this robust watermarking technique reduces the side information in decoding. If the watermarked document images have been changed in line or word shifting technique, it just results in changing profile of corresponding changed region. On the contrary to this technique, when the changes against even small regions have been occurred in our technique, it has an influence on entire diagonal profile. Furthermore, if the watermarked image has been changed or deleted on arbitrary position of text document by and attacker, the original owner of document can easily detect the difference of its document by comparing the number of vertical strip between the diagonal profile of original document and a diagonal profile of possibly changed one. And we show how to extract the watermark, how well locate or characterize the forged region from several changed document images. In the experiment, we could extract any kind of forgery against document images using reverse processing scheme in decoding procedure.

Acknowledgment. This paper was accomplished with research fund provided by Korean Council for University Education, support for 2000 Domestic Faculty Exchange.

References

1. R. Jain, R. Kasturi, B. G. Schunck, "Machine Vision", MaGraw-Hill, 1995.
2. S. H. Low, N. F. Maxemchuk, J. T. Brassil, and L. O'Gorman, "Document Marking and Identification Using Both Line and Word Shifting", *in Proc. Infocom '95*, pp. 853-860, April, 1995.
3. J. T. Brassil, S. H. Low, N. F. Maxemchuk, and L. O'Gorman, "Hiding Information in Document Images", *in Proc. 1995 Conf. Information Sciences and Systems*, pp.482-489, March 1995.

4.   J. T. Brassil, S. H. Low, N. F. Maxemchuk, L. O'Gorman, "Electronic Marking and Identification Techniques to Discourage Document Copying", *in IEEE J. Selected Area Commun.* Vol. 13, pp. 1495-1504, Oct. 1995.

5.   I. Cox, J. Killian, T. Leighton and T. Shamoon, "Secure Spread Spectrum Watermarking for Multimedia", *in Proc. of First Int. Workshop of Information Hiding,* pp 183-206, May. 1996.

6   S. H. Low, N. F. Maxemchuk and A. M. Lapone, "Document Identification for Copyright Protection Using Centroid Detection", *in IEEE Trans. Commun.* Vol. 46, pp. 372-383, March 1998

7.   S. H. Low, A. M. Lapone, N. F. Mexemchuk, "Performance Comparison of Two Text Marking and Detection Methods", *in IEEE J. Selected Areas Communication,* Vol. 16, No. 14, May 1998.

8.   J. T. Brassil, S. H. Low, N. F. Maxemchuk, "Copyright Protection for the Electronic Distribution of Text Documents", *in Proc. of the IEEE,* Vol. 87, No. 7, July 1999.

9.   Y. Lui, J. Mant, E.Wong, S. H. Low, "Marking and Detection of Text Documents Using Transform-domain Techniques", *in SPIE* Vol.3657, Jan. 1999.

10. E. T. Lin, E. J. Delp, "A Review of Fragile Image Watermarks", *in Proc. of Multimedia & Security Workshop (ACM Multimedia '99), Multimedia Contents,* pp. 25-29, 1999

11. L. Miller, I. J. Cox, J. M. Linartz, T. Kalker, "A Review of Watermarking Principles and Properties", *in Digital Signal Processing Multimedia System,* pp. 461-485, 1999.

12. J. H. Park, S. E. Jeong, Y. Huh "A New Digital Watermarking for Text Document Images Using Diagonal Profile", *to appear in IEEE Pacific-Rim Conf. on Multimedia,* Oct., 2001

Redundancy, Obscurity, Self-Containment & Independence

Seenil Gram

Seenilgram@my-deja.com

Abstract. Positive impact of redundancy is an aspect not much explored. This paper presents a new look at redundancy, particularly as related to public-key cryptography, pointing to a new way of building security.

Keywords. Public key, encryption, security, noise, redundancy

1 Introduction

While largely viewed as undesirable, redundancy and message expansion resulted from encryption are hardly by choice. However, the room provided by redundancy may facilitate some cryptographic techniques employed to obscure the encryption key and/or the ciphertext. The McEliece system[1], with the introduction of randomization, may serve as a good example.

Intuitively, when redundancy is closely related to, or purely determined by, the structure of the cryptographic keys and transformations, two issues become prominent. First, although random, the noise can still be of 'structure'. One normally can not just throw in random bits verbatim as noise but has to, instead, work within the allowance of the keys. NTRU[2] is an example in this respect. The other issue is that the amount of noise to introduce is limited. Unless noise is totally independent of the keys, the requirement of unique decipher may put a ceiling, generally a quite 'tight' ceiling, on the amount of noise that can be incorporated.

This paper suggests a new approach to the introduction of redundancy that neither depends upon the key structure nor affects the encryption operation.

2 A Different Approach

Given an encryption key, we would desire to be able to introduce into it any noise, and any sufficient amount of noise, unrestricted by any structure the key may have. At the same time, the effective decryption operation must be able to uniquely and

S. Qing, T. Okamoto, and J. Zhou (Eds.): ICICS 2001, LNCS 2229, pp. 495-501, 2001.

unambiguously recover the original data. Noise of such characteristics is referred to as *independent noise*.

We would like, for any (plaintext) message **m**, to have a pair of transformations t and T satisfying:

$$t(<o, k>) = <O, K>, \text{ and}$$
$$T(<O, K>(\mathbf{m})) = <o, k>(\mathbf{m})$$

where o is an operation (the equivalent of the encryption operation); O is one other such operation; k (K) is an encryption key without (with) independent noise; and $<o, k>$ ($<O, K>$) is a pair indicating operation by o (O) with key k (K).

One concrete realization of the concept is to adopt the notion of *self-containment*, the property of a sub-unit of a computational unit (analogously a digit of an integer) being independent of the values of any other sub-units with regard to certain computational operations.

Let $f_1, f_2, ..., f_n$ be arbitrary and/or random functions mapping from $[0, 2^h)$ to $[0, 2^h+\delta)$, for suitable integers δ and h. E.g. $h = 32$ and $-3\times2^{h-1} \leq \delta \leq 3\times2^h$. (These functions can be dynamic and sessional). Let all other parameters defined and used here be consisted entirely of arbitrary and/or random bits.

Let $X = \{x_1, x_2, ..., x_n\}$ and $W = \{w_1, w_2, ..., w_n\}$ be sets of positive integers satisfying:

$$x_i > \beta_{i-1}x_{i-1} + \beta_{i-2}x_{i-2} + ... + \beta_1x_1 + \beta_0x_0 + \gamma_iw_i + \gamma_{i-1}w_{i-1} + ... + \gamma_1w_1$$

for $1\leq i\leq n$ (e.g. $n = 32$), where $\gamma_i = f_i(\beta_i)$ and $\beta_i \in [0, 2^h)$ and x_0, for convenience, is defined to be 0. We call the increasing property of x_i with respect to its index superincreasing.

Let $<Y, U> = <\{y_1, y_2, ..., y_n\}, \{u_1, u_2, ..., u_n\}> = I^r(I^{r-1}(...(I^1(<\pi(X), \pi(W)>))...))$, where π is a permutation (with π^{-1} as the inverse permutation) and I^j, for $1\leq j\leq r$, is an iteration defined to be:

$$I^j(<A, B>) = I^j(<\{a_1, a_2, ..., a_n\}, \{b_1, b_2, ..., b_n\}>)$$
$$= <\{\underline{a} \mid (a\times e_j) \bmod m_j, a\in A\}, \{\{\underline{b} \mid (b\times e_j) \bmod m_j, b\in B\}>$$

where $m_j > \beta_1a_1 + \beta_2a_2 + ... + \beta_na_n + \gamma_1b_1 + \gamma_2b_2 + ... + \gamma_nb_n$, and e_j and m_j are relatively prime (with e_j^{-1} being the multiplicative inverse of e_j modulo m_j)

Let $Z = \{z_1, z_2, ..., z_n\}$ be the transformed version of Y and $V = \{v_1, v_2, ..., v_n\}$ be the transformed version of U satisfying the following:

a. $p_0, p_1, ..., p_{t-1}$ are pairwise co-prime
b. $z_i = (z_{i,0}, z_{i,1}, ..., z_{i,qt-1})$ for $1\leq i\leq n$ and $q \geq 1$, i.e. z_i are in vector form
c. $J = \{j_0, j_1, ..., j_{k-1}\}$ is an arbitrarily and/or randomly chosen set of indices
   where $0\leq j_0, j_1, ..., j_{k-1}<t$.

d. $S = \{s_0, s_1, ..., s_{k-1}\}$ is an arbitrary and/or random set of indices satisfying:

    $1 \le s_0, s_1, ..., s_{k-1} < qt$ and $J = S \bmod t = \{s_0 \bmod t, s_1 \bmod t, ..., s_{k-1} \bmod t\}$

e. $\prod \mathbf{p}_{j \in J} > \beta_1 y_1 + \beta_2 y_2 + ... + \beta_n y_n + \gamma_1 u_1 + \gamma_2 u_2 + ... + \gamma_n u_n$

f. $z_{i, s \in S} = y_i \bmod \mathbf{p}_{(s \bmod t)}$

g. $z_{i, s \notin S}$ are random numbers modulo $\mathbf{p}_{(s \bmod t)}$ for $0 \le s < qt$

h. $v_i = (v_{i,0}, v_{i,1}, ..., v_{i,qt-1})$ for $1 \le i \le n$

i. $v_{i, s \in S} = w_i \bmod \mathbf{p}_{(s \bmod t)}$

j. $v_{i, s \notin S}$ are random numbers modulo $\mathbf{p}_{(s \bmod t)}$ for $0 \le s < qt$

Secret Key: X, W, S, π^{-1}, $m_1, m_2, ..., m_r$, and $e_1^{-1}, e_2^{-1}, ..., e_r^{-1}$.
Public Key: Z, V, $f_1, f_2, ..., f_n$, and $\mathbf{p}_0, \mathbf{p}_1, ..., \mathbf{p}_{t-1}$.

Encryption: The input data stream is taken **n** blocks, $d_1, d_2, ..., d_n$, at a time. Each of these **n** blocks is of **h** bits. The blocks are encrypted to $c_0, c_1, ..., c_{qt-1}$ in the following way:

$$c_s = ((d_1 \times z_{1,s} + d_2 \times z_{2,s} + ... + d_n \times z_{n,s}) +$$
$$(f_1(d_1) \times v_{1,s} + f_2(d_2) \times v_{2,s} + ... + f_n(d_n) \times v_{n,s})) \bmod \mathbf{p}_{(s \bmod t)}$$

Decryption: The decryptor, with knowledge of **S**, simply discards the c_s where $s \notin S$. The remaining c_s are then converted back from the residue system by the $\mathbf{p}_j$ using the Chinese Remainder Theorem (CRT), to arrived at a subset sum ρ (of **Y** and **U**) in the normal positional number system representation. Next, the inverse iteration(s) can be applied to convert ρ to the corresponding subset sum of **X** and **W**:

    for **i** from **r** down to 1 do
       $\rho = \rho \times e_j^{-1} \bmod m_i$
    end for loop

Finally, the normal decomposition of a superincreasing subset sum can be used to recover the data bits $d_1, d_2, ..., d_n$:

    for **i** from **n** down to 1 do
       $\underline{d}_i = \lfloor \rho / x_i -$
       $\rho = \rho - \underline{d}_i \times x_i - f_i(\underline{d}_i) \times w_i$
    end for loop
    $\{d_1, d_2, ..., d_n\} = \pi^{-1}(\{\underline{d}_1, \underline{d}_2, ..., \underline{d}_n\})$

3   Security Considerations

In this section, analysis of security is presented. For convenience, we shorthand "normal positional representation" to NPR and refer to the example cryptosystem given in the previous section of this paper as SYS.

First, we formally specify and define the major notations to be used.

We will adopt the notations used for SYS and view the encryption key as a matrix (formed by the row vectors v_i and z_i), and we refer to $p_{0 \leq j \leq t-1}$ as *final moduli* and to $m_{1 \leq i \leq r}$ as *iteration moduli*.

Definition: *Residue* and *Representative*
In the notation used for SYS, we refer to $v_{i,j}$ and $z_{i,j}$ (for $1 \leq i \leq n$ and $0 \leq j < qt$) as residues. We further refer to $v_{i,j}$ and $z_{i,j}$, for $j \in S$, as real residues and to others as fake residues.
Let A be a number in NPR and $B = \{b_1, b_2, ..., b_n\}$ be a set of residues in CRT reduced from A by a set of pairwise co-prime numbers P. We refer to B as the representative (of A) if B is a set of real residues and the product of all members of P is greater than A.

Definition: *Polynomially Distinguishable & Polynomially Indistinguishable*
We say that A and B are polynomially distinguishable if the identification of either A or B, with non-negligible success rate, is of polynomial complexity. Otherwise, we say A and B are polynomially indistinguishable.

Definition: *Binary Set*, *Compact Set* and *Density*
Let $A = \{a_1, a_2, ..., a_n\}$ be a set used in forming subset sum in the following way:

$$\sum_{i=1}^{n} a_i x_i .$$

We call A a binary set if x_i takes on only two distinct values, and a trinary set if it takes on only three distinct values; else we call A a compact set. Denoting a as the largest element in A, the density of A, with $x_i \in [0, 2^h)$ for some positive integer h, is defined to be:

$$\frac{nh}{\lg_2(a)} .$$

Observation: *Verifiability*
Let the largest number in $Y \cup U$ be θ. We observe that, to avoid overflow during encryption, the construct of SYS has k real residues in any row vector (i.e. v_i or z_i) represent an NPR number no larger than θ, yet any k residues with at least one fake residue will, with high probability, represent an NPR number greater than θ. Therefore, if a set of k residues are tested to represent an NPR number no larger than θ, with high probability they are real residues. In fact, once a set of residues in a row vector whose corresponding (final) moduli have a product greater than θ. are tested to represent an NPR number no larger than θ, with high probability, they are a representative.

Observation: *Complexity Upperbound*

Let l denote the size of the smallest representative in $\mathbf{v_i}$ and $\mathbf{z_i}$. We observe that the value of l depends on the value of $\mathbf{k}$ and the sizes of $\mathbf{p_j}$ but is smaller than $\mathbf{k}$ by only a small constant. Even though the value of neither $\mathbf{k}$ nor l nor θ is made publicly known, for our security analysis, we may conservatively assume that they all are or they all can be pretty accurately estimated. According to *Verifiability Observation*, once l or more indices are chosen where the corresponding indexed residues in $\mathbf{v_i}$ and $\mathbf{z_i}$ are tested to represent NPR numbers no larger than θ, the indices are almost always those of real residues comprising representatives. One can obviously bruteforce all possible combinations of l or more residues, and the complexity is upperbounded approximately by:

$$\prod_{i=1}^{l} \frac{q(t-l+i)}{i}.$$

Theorem: *Existence*

There exists an asymmetric encryption key that is polynomially indistinguishable from random bits.

We will not prove *Existence Theorem* directly. Instead, we establish a security aspect of SYS by restating the *Existence Theorem* as the following lemma that we prove. It should be obvious that the establishment of the following lemma would automatically have established *Existence Theorem*.

Lemma: *Indistinguishability*

The real residues (and the fake residues) are polynomially indistinguishable. And thus the encryption key is polynomially indistinguishable from random bits.

Proof of *Indistinguishability Lemma*

First, we develop an informal argument. We observe that any real residue is just an element in $\mathbf{U}$ or $\mathbf{Y}$ reduced by a final modulus. (If the reduction is multiplicative modular reduction with some random multiplier, this observation still applies.) Since all of $\mathbf{X}$ and $\mathbf{W}$, by the very construction as specified for SYS, are random, and the iteration moduli and modular multipliers for the transformation of $\mathbf{X}$ and $\mathbf{W}$ are random as well, the whole process in producing the real residues is random. We further observe that due to the nature of the process, there are two and only two properties associated with the encryption key, namely the superincreasing property and the property revealed in *Verifiability Observation*.

By CRT and the theorem of Szabó (1961)[3], the identificaion of representatives is required for the exploitation of the properties. Therefore, without knowing the indices of the real residues comprising representatives, we are not able to distinguish real and fake residues.

Let the exploitation function $\mathbf{O}$ be an oracle that we call upon to distinguish any real residue, and let $\mathbf{D}$ be a distinguisher for distinguishing real residues. To exploit the properties, $\mathbf{D}$ has to make calls to the oracle, supplying the indices of real residues comprising representatives. But those are what **D** is looking for and can not get without the use of the oracle.

Formally, we define **D** and **O** as follows:

$$\mathbf{D}(\phi) = \Phi \text{ and } \mathbf{O}(\phi) = \Phi'$$

where ϕ, Φ and Φ' are each a three-tuple (**V**, **Z**, A) with A being a list of sets of indices for residues. If **D** identifies any real residues or if **O** verifies any real residues through either of the two properties, it will output their indices as a set in A, else it will output an empty set in A. Without loss of generality, we assume the sets are output in the list in a certain order, e.g. the row order of the matrix of **V** and **Z** defined for SYS.

Let us assume that the two properties can be exploited without us knowing any indices of real residues comprising representatives.

We have four and only four basic configurations to consider:

1. $\mathbf{O}(\phi)$ is called after a call to $\mathbf{D}(\phi)$ which is called first
2. $\mathbf{D}(\phi)$ is called after a call to $\mathbf{O}(\phi)$ which is called first
3. $\mathbf{O}(\phi)$ is called within a call to $\mathbf{D}(\phi)$ which is called first
4. $\mathbf{D}(\phi)$ is called within a call to $\mathbf{O}(\phi)$ which is called first

If **D** can not distinguish any real residue, it will not be able to at any point during its execution. **O**, on the other hand, can not exploit the two properties unless indices of real residues comprising representatives are supplied as input in A. Considering that we do not have the indices for the top level calls to either **D** or **O** as assumed, each of the configurations can be easily verified as unable to distinquish any real or fake residue. Using induction, any nested levels of calls between **D** and **O** in any of the combinations of the four basic configurations can be easily shown to fail as well. The two properties of the encryption key are not exploitable. We have reached a contradiction.

Therefore, **D** is a function that identifies real residues without relying on the properties of the real residues. In other words, **D** is a distinguisher applying no criteria for its selection (of indices) and is no better than bruteforcing the possible combinations of the residues, which according to *Complexity Upperbound Observation* is of at least exponential complexity.

In conclusion, it requires at least exponential complexity to distinguish the real residues and, as a direct consequence, the encryption key itself can only be distinguished from random bits with at least exponential complexity.

Since **S** is not obtainable with less than exponential complexity, the following lemma follows.

Lemma: *Key Security*
Obtaining a corresponding decryption key from an encryption key of SYS is of at least exponential complexity.

The strength of the ciphertext produced by SYS is analyzed next.

Since it requires at least exponential complexity to distinguish the decryption key of SYS from random bits, the ciphertext by SYS is effectively the subset sum of a random set. Since the subset sum problem of random sets is **NP-complete**, the ciphertext by SYS is of exponential complexity (at least in the worst case scenario) under the assumption of **NP $\supseteq$ EXP**, which can be seen as a simple, direct result from *Indistinguishability Lemma*.

We observe that the encryption key set can be of high density (e.g. take **n=h=32**, **t=100**, and the 100 largest primes smaller than 2^{16} as the final moduli, the density is at least 1.28). The average number (2^c) of solutions to a random subset sum problem is related to the density of the set in the following manner:

$$ \mathbf{d} - 1 = \frac{\lg_2(2\mathbf{n}) + \mathbf{h} + \mathbf{c}}{\lg_2(a)} . $$

where **d** is the density, **2n** is the number of elements in the set, 2^h-1 is the maximum number of times an element can be added to the subset sum, a is the largest element in the set, and **c** is the exponent associated with the average number of solutions to a random subset sum.

We now consider the general strength of the ciphertext by SYS, particularly in terms of lattice basis reduction (LBR) which has been the most general and successful in attacking knapsack type cryptosystems. We first observe that LBR (with its various improvements) is ineffective or inefficient dealing with compact sets. However, if a compact set can be easily converted to a binary set, LBR can be a threat, especially when the set is of low density. High density compact sets may still be vulnerable. An example is the cryptographic scheme proposed by Orton[4]. The problem with such sets is that the 'extra' elements that make the sets dense are highly linear with other elements in the sets. In SYS, the functions f_i are non-linear as there is no restriction on what f_i should be, and f_i are not restricted by, or related to, any other key parameters in any fashion. The non-linearity leaves out the chance for an equivalent binary set to facilitate attacks like LBR.

Therefore, by the non-linearity of f_i and the density of the set(s), the easy instances of subset sum problems, where it is only required to find any one solution, are removed. The problem posed by SYS requires the finding of a specific subset (or vector), uniquely determined by f_i, from an exponential number of subset sum solutions.

References

[1] R. McEliece, JPL DSN Progress Report, pp. 42-44, January-February 1978, pp. 114-116

[2] J. Hoffstein, J. Pipher and J. Silverman, *NTRU, A Ring-Based Public Key Cryptosystem*, *Algorithmic Number Theory*, (ANTS III), Portland, OR, June 1998, J.P. Buhler (ed.), Lecture Notes in Computer Science 1423, Springer-Verlag, Berlin, 1998, pp. 267-288.

[3] D. Knuth, *The Art of Computer Programming*, Vol. 2, 3rd Ed., Addison Wesley, 1998, p. 291

[4] G. Orton, *A Multiple-Iterated Trapdoor for Dense Compact Knapsacks*, Advances in Cryptology EUROCRYPTO '94 Proceedings, Berlin: Springer-Verlag, 1995, pp. 112-130

Author Index

Lecture Notes in Computer Science

For information about Vols. 1–2144
please contact your bookseller or Springer-Verlag

Vol. 2184: M. Tucci (Ed.), Multimedia Databases and Image Communication. Proceedings, 2001. X, 225 pages. 2001.

Vol. 2185: M. Gogolla, C. Kobryn (Eds.), «UML» 2001 – The Unified Modeling Language. Proceedings, 2001. XIV, 510 pages. 2001.

Vol. 2186: J. Bosch (Ed.), Generative and Component-Based Software Engineering. Proceedings, 2001. VIII, 177 pages. 2001.

Vol. 2187: U. Voges (Ed.), Computer Safety, Reliability and Security. Proceedings, 2001. XVI, 249 pages. 2001.

Vol. 2188: F. Bomarius, S. Komi-Sirviö (Eds.), Product Focused Software Process Improvement. Proceedings, 2001. XI, 382 pages. 2001.

Vol. 2189: F. Hoffmann, D.J. Hand, N. Adams, D. Fisher, G. Guimaraes (Eds.), Advances in Intelligent Data Analysis. Proceedings, 2001. XII, 384 pages. 2001.

Vol. 2190: A. de Antonio, R. Aylett, D. Ballin (Eds.), Intelligent Virtual Agents. Proceedings, 2001. VIII, 245 pages. 2001. (Subseries LNAI).

Vol. 2191: B. Radig, S. Florczyk (Eds.), Pattern Recognition. Proceedings, 2001. XVI, 452 pages. 2001.

Vol. 2192: A. Yonezawa, S. Matsuoka (Eds.), Metalevel Architectures and Separation of Crosscutting Concerns. Proceedings, 2001. XI, 283 pages. 2001.

Vol. 2193: F. Casati, D. Georgakopoulos, M.-C. Shan (Eds.), Technologies for E-Services. Proceedings, 2001. X, 213 pages. 2001.

Vol. 2194: A.K. Datta, T. Herman (Eds.), Self-Stabilizing Systems. Proceedings, 2001. VII, 229 pages. 2001.

Vol. 2195: H.-Y. Shum, M. Liao, S.-F. Chang (Eds.), Advances in Multimedia Information Processing – PCM 2001. Proceedings, 2001. XX, 1149 pages. 2001.

Vol. 2196: W. Taha (Ed.), Semantics, Applications, and Implementation of Program Generation. Proceedings, 2001. X, 219 pages. 2001.

Vol. 2197: O. Balet, G. Subsol, P. Torguet (Eds.), Virtual Storytelling. Proceedings, 2001. XI, 213 pages. 2001.

Vol. 2198: N. Zhong, Y. Yao, J. Liu, S. Ohsuga (Eds.), Web Intelligence: Research and Development. Proceedings, 2001. XVI, 615 pages. 2001. (Subseries LNAI).

Vol. 2199: J. Crespo, V. Maojo, F. Martin (Eds.), Medical Data Analysis. Proceedings, 2001. X, 311 pages. 2001.

Vol. 2200: G.I. Davida, Y. Frankel (Eds.), Information Security. Proceedings, 2001. XIII, 554 pages. 2001.

Vol. 2201: G.D. Abowd, B. Brumitt, S. Shafer (Eds.), Ubicomp 2001: Ubiquitous Computing. Proceedings, 2001. XIII, 372 pages. 2001.

Vol. 2202: A. Restivo, S. Ronchi Della Rocca, L. Roversi (Eds.), Theoretical Computer Science. Proceedings, 2001. XI, 440 pages. 2001.

Vol. 2204: A. Brandstädt, V.B. Le (Eds.), Graph-Theoretic Concepts in Computer Science. Proceedings, 2001. X, 329 pages. 2001.

Vol. 2205: D.R. Montello (Ed.), Spatial Information Theory. Proceedings, 2001. XIV, 503 pages. 2001.

Vol. 2206: B. Reusch (Ed.), Computational Intelligence. Proceedings, 2001. XVII, 1003 pages. 2001.

Vol. 2207: I.W. Marshall, S. Nettles, N. Wakamiya (Eds.), Active Networks. Proceedings, 2001. IX, 165 pages. 2001.

Vol. 2208: W.J. Niessen, M.A. Viergever (Eds.), Medical Image Computing and Computer-Assisted Intervention – MICCAI 2001. Proceedings, 2001. XXXV, 1446 pages. 2001.

Vol. 2209: W. Jonker (Ed.), Databases in Telecommunications II. Proceedings, 2001. VII, 179 pages. 2001.

Vol. 2210: Y. Liu, K. Tanaka, M. Iwata, T. Higuchi, M. Yasunaga (Eds.), Evolvable Systems: From Biology to Hardware. Proceedings, 2001. XI, 341 pages. 2001.

Vol. 2211: T.A. Henzinger, C.M. Kirsch (Eds.), Embedded Software. Proceedings, 2001. IX, 504 pages. 2001.

Vol. 2212: W. Lee, L. Mé, A. Wespi (Eds.), Recent Advances in Intrusion Detection. Proceedings, 2001. X, 205 pages. 2001.

Vol. 2213: M.J. van Sinderen, L.J.M. Nieuwenhuis (Eds.), Protocols for Multimedia Systems. Proceedings, 2001. XII, 239 pages. 2001.

Vol. 2214: O. Boldt, H. Jürgensen (Eds.), Automata Implementation. Proceedings, 1999. VIII, 183 pages. 2001.

Vol. 2215: N. Kobayashi, B.C. Pierce (Eds.), Theoretical Aspects of Computer Software. Proceedings, 2001. XV, 561 pages. 2001.

Vol. 2216: E.S. Al-Shaer, G. Pacifici (Eds.), Management of Multimedia on the Internet. Proceedings, 2001. XIV, 373 pages. 2001.

Vol. 2217: T. Gomi (Ed.), Evolutionary Robotics. Proceedings, 2001. XI, 139 pages. 2001.

Vol. 2218: R. Guerraoui (Ed.), Middleware 2001. Proceedings, 2001. XIII, 395 pages. 2001.

Vol. 2220: C. Johnson (Ed.), Interactive Systems. Proceedings, 2001. XII, 219 pages. 2001.

Vol. 2221: D.G. Feitelson, L. Rudolph (Eds.), Job Scheduling Strategies for Parallel Processing. Proceedings 2001. VII, 207 pages. 2001.

Vol. 2224: H.S. Kunii, S. Jajodia, A. Sølvberg (Eds.), Conceptual Modeling – ER 2001. Proceedings, 2001. XIX, 614 pages. 2001.

Vol. 2225: N. Abe, R. Khardon, T. Zeugmann (Eds.), Algorithmic Learning Theory. Proceedings, 2001. XI, 375 pages. 2001. (Subseries LNAI).

Vol. 2229: S. Qing, T. Okamoto, J. Zhou (Eds.), Information and Communications Security. Proceedings, 2001. XIV, 504 pages. 2001.

Vol. 2230: T. Katila, I.E. Magnin, P. Clarysse, J. Montagnat, J. Nenonen (Eds.), Functional Imaging and Modeling of the Heart. Proceedings, 2001. XI, 158 pages. 2001.

Vol. 2232: L. Fiege, G. Mühl, U. Wilhelm (Eds.), Electronic Commerce. Proceedings, 2001. X, 233 pages. 2001.

Vol. 2233: J. Crowcroft, M. Hofmann (Eds.), Networked Group Communication. Proceedings, 2001. X, 205 pages. 2001.

Vol. 2239: T. Walsh (Ed.), Principles and Practice of Constraint Programming – CP 2001. Proceedings, 2001. XIV, 788 pages. 2001.

Vol. 2241: M. Jünger, D. Naddef (Eds.), Computational Combinatorial Optimization. IX, 305 pages. 2001.